RETRIBUTION

DEDICATION
For David (Klaus) Shore

RETRIBUTION

THE
SOVIET RECONQUEST
OF CENTRAL UKRAINE,
1943

PRIT BUTTAR

OSPREY PUBLISHING
Bloomsbury Publishing Plc

Kemp House, Chawley Park, Cumnor Hill, Oxford OX2 9PH, UK
29 Earlsfort Terrace, Dublin 2, Ireland
1385 Broadway, 5th Floor, New York, NY 10018, USA
Email: info@ospreypublishing.com
www.ospreypublishing.com

OSPREY is a trademark of Osprey Publishing Ltd

First published in Great Britain in 2019

© Prit Buttar, 2019

A catalogue record for this book is available from the British Library.

Hardback ISBN: 978 1 4728 3532 1
Paperback: 978 1 4728 3535 2
ePub: 978 1 4728 3533 8
ePDF: 978 1 4728 3531 4
XML: 978 1 4728 3534 5

Index by Fionbar Lyons
Typeset by Deanta Global Publishing Services, Chennai, India
Printed and bound in Great Britain by CPI (Group) UK Ltd,
Croydon CR0 4YY

MIX
Paper | Supporting
responsible forestry
FSC
www.fsc.org   FSC® C013604

24 25 26 27 28   10 9 8 7 6 5 4 3

Image acknowledgement
Front cover: Tanks and troops from 3rd Ukrainian Front advance. (TopFoto)

The Woodland Trust
Osprey Publishing supports the Woodland Trust, the UK's leading woodland
conservation charity.

www.ospreypublishing.com
To find out more about our authors and books visit our website. Here you will
find extracts, author interviews, details of forthcoming events and the option to
sign-up for our newsletter.

CONTENTS

LIST OF MAPS

AUTHOR'S NOTE

The naming of places in a region like the Ukraine is fraught with difficulty, as so many names have changed since the end of the Soviet Union. Wherever possible, I have attempted to use the names that were current in 1943. I have avoided referring to the enemies of Germany as 'Russians', and have instead tried to describe these units as 'Soviet', as large numbers of the soldiers in their ranks came from non-Russian parts of the Soviet Union.

I am hugely grateful for the generous help I received from a great many people, in particular the members of the Facebook Eastern Front Research Forum, who showed huge generosity and enthusiasm. Without your help, guys, this would have been a far lesser book.

DRAMATIS PERSONAE

GERMANY

Balck, Hermann – commander XLVIII Panzer Corps
Brandenberger, Erich – commander XXIX Corps
Breith, Hermann – commander III Panzer Corps
Busse, Theodor – chief of staff, Army Group South
Chevallerie, Kurt von der – commander LIX Corps
Choltitz, Dietrich von – acting commander XLVIII Panzer Corps
Crisolli, Wilhelm – commander 6th Panzer Division
Dostler, Anton – commander XLII Corps, later commander VII Corps
Edelsheim, Maximilian Reichsfreiherr von – commander 24th Panzer Division
Frölich, Gottfried – commander 8th Panzer Division
Gille, Herbert – commander *SS-Wiking*
Hauffe, Arthur – commander XIII Corps
Hausser, Paul – commander II SS Panzer Corps
Hax, Georg – NCO in *SS-Totenkopf*
Henrici, Sigfrid – commander XL Panzer Corps
Heyden, Hans-Wilhelm von – battlegroup commander, 24th Panzer Division
Hollidt, Karl-Adolf – commander Sixth Army
Hörnlein, Walter – commander Grossdeutschland
Hoth, Hermann – commander Fourth Panzer Army
Källner, Hans – commander 19th Panzer Division
Kempf, Werner – commander eponymous Armee Abteilung, later renamed Eighth Army
Kirchner, Friedrich – commander LVII Panzer Corps
Kleist, Ewald von – commander Army Group A
Kluge, Günther von – commander Army Group Centre

Knobelsforff, Otto von – commander XLVIII Panzer Corps
Koch, Erich – Gauleiter of East Prussia and Ukraine
Krüger, Walter – commander *SS-Das Reich*
Krüger, Walter – commander 1st Panzer Division
Küchler, Georg von – commander Army Group North
Mackensen, Eberhardt von – commander First Panzer Army
Manstein, Erich von – commander Army Group South
Manteuffel, Hasso von – commander 7th Panzer Division
Mattenklott, Franz – commander LVII Corps
Mellenthin, Friedrich von – chief of staff, XLVIII Panzer Corps
Mieth, Friedrich – commander IV Corps
Mitzlaff, Berndt von – battlegroup commander, 8th Panzer Division
Moser, Eduard – German soldier in 16th Panzergrenadier Division
Müller-Hillebrand, Burkhart – battlegroup commander, 24th Panzer Division
Nehring, Walther – commander XXIV Panzer Corps
Nostitz-Wallwitz, Gustav-Adolf von – battlegroup commander, 24th Panzer Division
Ott, Eugen – commander LII Corps
Palm, Walter – battlegroup commander, 24th Panzer Division
Radowitz, Joseph von – battlegroup commander, 8th Panzer Division
Raus, Erhard – commander XI Corps, later commander Fourth Panzer Army
Rosenberg, Alfred – head of Ostministerium
Scheele, Hans-Karl von – commander LII Corps
Schell, Adolf von – commander 25th Panzer Division
Schörner, Ferdinand – commander XL Panzer Corps (replaced Henrici)
Schulz, Johannes – acting commander 9th Panzer Division
Schwerin, Gerhard Graf von – commander 16th Panzergrenadier Division
Sieberg, Friedrich – commander 14th Panzer Division
Simon, Max – commander *SS-Totenkopf*
Sommer, Peter – acting commander *SS-Das Reich*
Stadler, Sylvester – panzergrenadier regiment commander, *SS-Das Reich*
Unrein, Martin – commander 14th Panzer Division after the death of Sieberg
Vogelsang, Fritz – artillery officer, 16th Panzergrenadier Division
Vormann, Nikolaus von – commander 23rd Panzer Division
Wietersheim, Wend von – commander 11th Panzer Division
Wöhler, Otto – commander Eighth Army
Zeitzler, Kurt – chief of general staff at *OKH*

SOVIET UNION

Abdullin, Mansoor – Red Army infantryman

Antonov, Alexei Innokentyevich – first deputy chief of the general staff

Biryuzov, Sergei Semenovich – chief of staff, Southern Front, later renamed 4th Ukrainian Front

Budyonny, Semyon Mikhailovich – inspector of cavalry

Cherniakhovsky, Ivan Danilovich – commander Sixtieth Army

Chibisov, Nikandr Evlampievich – commander Thirty-Eighth Army

Chistiakov, Ivan Mikhailovich – commander Sixth Guards Army

Chuikov, Vasily Ivanovich – commander Eighth Guards (formerly Sixty-Second) Army

Danilov, Alexei Ilyich – commander Twelfth Army

Degen, Ion Lazarevich – tank commander, Third Tank Army

Ehrenburg, Ilya Grigoryevich – Soviet journalist and writer

Fadin, Alexander Mikhailovich – tank commander, V Guards Tank Corps

Gagen, Nikolai Alexandrovich – commander Fifty-Seventh Army

Getman, Andrei Levrentovich – commander VI Tank Corps

Glagolev, Vasily Vasilyevich – commander Forty-Sixth Army

Katukov, Mikhail Efimovich – commander First Tank Army

Khomenko, Vasily Afanasevich – commander Forty-Fourth Army

Khoroshunova, Irina – resident of Kiev

Kirichenko, Ivan Fedorovich – commander XXIX Tank Corps

Kobylyanskiy, Isaak – junior Red Army artillery officer

Konev, Ivan Stepanovich – commander Steppe Front, later renamed 2nd Ukrainian Front

Kovalenko, Vasily Ivanovich – tank commander, Fifty-Seventh Army

Kravchenko, Andrei Gregorovich – commander V Guards Tank Corps

Krivoshein, Semen Moiseevich – commander III Mechanised Corps

Krivov, Georgi Nikolayevich – tank commander, Fifth Guards Tank Army

Lelyushenko, Dmitry Danilovich – commander Third Guards Army

Likhterman, Matvey Tsodikovich – paratrooper, 3rd Guards Airborne Brigade

Malinovsky, Rodion Yakovlevich – commander Southern Front

Managarov, Ivan Mefodevich – commander Fifty-Third Army

Molotov, Vyacheslav Mikhailovich – foreign minister

Moskalenko, Kirill Semenovich – commander Fortieth Army, later commander Thirty-Eighth Army

Otroschenkov, Sergey Andreyevich – tank commander, Fifth Guards Tank Army

Poluboyarev, Pavel Pavlovich – commander IV Guards Tank Corps

Rodimtsev, Alexander Ilyich – commander XXXII Guards Rifle Corps

Rotmistrov, Pavel Alexeyevich – commander Fifth Guards Tank Army

Rybalko, Pavel Semenovich – commander Third Tank Army

Sharokhin, Mikhail Nikolayevich – commander Thirty-Seventh Army

Shtemenko, Sergei Matveyevich – head of Operations Directorate, Stavka

Shumilov, Mikhail Stepanovich – commander Seventh Guards Army

Sidorchuk, Pyotor Michailovich – commander 5th Guards Airborne Brigade

Solomatin, Mikhail Dmitrievich – commander I Mechanised Corps

Tolbukhin, Fedor Ivanovich – commander Southern Front, later renamed 4th Ukrainian Front

Trofimenko, Sergei Georgievich – commander Twenty-Seventh Army

Trufanov, Kuzma Grigorevich – commander XVIII Tank Corps

Usyk, Mikhail – resident of Kharkov

Vasilevsky, Alexander Mikhailovich – chief of general staff

Vasiliev, Ivan Dmitrievich – commander XIX Tank Corps

Vatutin, Nikolai Fyodorovich – commander Voronezh Front, later renamed 1st Ukrainian Front

Zatevakhin, Ivan Ivanovich – deputy commander Soviet airborne forces, commander II Airborne Corps

Zhadov, Alexei Semenovich – commander Fifth Guards Army

Zhukov, Georgi Konstantinovich – deputy commander-in-chief, Soviet Armed Forces

INTRODUCTION

The fighting on the Eastern Front between 1941 and 1945 dwarfed conflicts elsewhere in the Second World War. In terms of numbers of men, tanks, guns and aircraft, the casualties suffered by all sides, and the huge numbers of civilians who were killed or displaced – by both sides – means that there is a considerable case for arguing that the outcome of the war was decided in the struggle between the Wehrmacht and the Red Army. Whilst the Pacific and Atlantic theatres may have been physically larger, they do not compare in terms of the scale of the fighting. Furthermore, although the battlefield stretched from the Arctic Circle to the Caucasus, one of the critical areas of contention – arguably, the region deemed by both sides as the most vital for the outcome of the entire campaign – was the Ukraine.

The war between Germany and the Soviet Union started in June 1941 when the Wehrmacht crossed the frontier in strength, supported by the armies of Finland, Romania and Hungary, followed not long after by troops from Italy and Spain. Regardless of suggestions that Stalin was preparing for an invasion of Germany, the reality was that Nazi Germany launched itself upon a war of conquest, intending to destroy and dismember the Soviet Union, but the roots of the conflict can in many respects be traced back to a previous era, when the Russian Empire was still under the rule of the tsars.

The concept of *Mitteleuropa* ('Middle Europe') as a political entity arose from growing interest in the first half of the 19th century for some form of closer union between the Russian Empire and the European Powers; the first use of the word *Mitteleuropa* in any clear proposals was in 1848, when the Austrian statesman Karl Ludwig von Bruck collaborated with the German economist Lorenz von Stein to describe a series of interlocking confederations that would cooperate in a variety of fields.[1] Whilst Austrian diplomats were the initial enthusiasts for such a development, there was little interest amongst the German states, and the defeat of Austria in the Austro-Prussian War of 1866 led to the rising dominance of first Prussia and then Germany in Central Europe. In an era dominated by concepts of social Darwinism, the original broad-brush proposals of economic cooperation were gradually replaced by concepts of dominance and annexation.

Like other European nations, Germany strove to establish a colonial empire and rapidly acquired territory in Africa, centred primarily around German East Africa, Cameroon and German Southwest Africa. The former was assigned to British control at the end of the First World War, forming first Tanganyika and then Tanzania; the latter ultimately became Namibia in 1990. German colonial rule differed considerably from that of Britain or France, with the overt intention of creating through settlement a large white German population, with indigenous people reduced to little more than helots. This harsh policy led to uprisings against the Germans, and although the suppression of such revolts in German East Africa ultimately led to an efficient, enlightened administration, the situation in Southwest Africa was very different. The revolt of the Herero and Namaqua people was brutally suppressed with widespread mass killings; it is estimated that half the Namaqua and 80 per cent of the Herero were slaughtered either during the revolt or in mass executions after German control was restored.[2] Inevitably, when the concept of *Mitteleuropa* was adopted by German thinkers in terms of creating a land empire mainly from territory controlled by Russia, the intention was to replace much or even all of the population with ethnic German settlers. Unlike the British and French colonial empires, the goal was to create an empire that was German in every sense of the word.

In late 1914, when it seemed that Germany might achieve the dreamed-of rapid defeat of France and then turn east in strength, there were belated attempts in Berlin to draw up a list of demands to be submitted to a future peace conference. The *Septemberprogramm* was the creation of Kurt Riezler, the private secretary of Chancellor Theobald von Bethmann-Hollweg, and in addition to securing massive financial reparations and further territory from France, together with annexation of Luxembourg and the reduction of Belgium to a vassal state of Germany, the programme called for the creation of a number of new states from territory in European Russia, which would all remain under firm German control.[3] Whilst the programme was never formally adopted – and the French victory on the Marne made any immediate prospect of its implementation impossible – other Germans continued to dream of an empire in Eastern Europe, and in 1915 Friedrich Naumann, a German politician, wrote a book entitled *Mitteleuropa*, further developing the concept of settling new eastern territories with ethnic Germans, though he acknowledged the need for a flexible approach to non-Germans in order to ensure harmonious rule.[4]

When the Russian Revolutions of 1917 swept away the tsars and left the Russian Army unable to continue the war, it seemed as if the moment for the realisation of *Mitteleuropa* had come, and the Treaty of Brest-Litovsk went a considerable way towards achieving the German dream; the Baltic States were to be settled by Germans who would 'reinforce' the existing Baltic German aristocracy, and the newly independent Ukraine would be firmly under German hegemony. The collapse of Germany in late 1918 led to Bolshevik Russia repudiating the treaty, and there followed a series of conflicts as the Baltic States attempted to assert their independence both from Bolshevik and German control. Many German veterans of the First World War fought against the Bolsheviks in these wars as part of the *Freikorps*, and in many cases believed that they had been promised generous grants of land in the Baltic States in return for their service. When they were forced to return to Germany empty-handed, this added to a growing sense of resentment that major German gains in the east had been snatched from their hands.

There were many in Germany after the First World War who felt that the Treaty of Versailles was unfairly harsh upon their country, and in several respects these opinions helped fuel the rise of the National Socialists, who in the turbulent landscape of German politics in the late 1920s seemed to offer the strongest hope of restoring German prestige, status and pride. Writing in 1925, Hitler made clear his intentions to fight a war of conquest against Russia in order to seize sufficient territory for colonial settlement and to safeguard Germany forever.[5] Whilst Germany – both before and after Hitler's accession to power – cooperated closely with the Soviet Union in economic and military fields, there remained an underlying hostility towards Germany's eastern neighbour and there seemed a widespread belief on both sides that, ultimately, this would lead to war. Josef Stalin ignored frequent warnings from a variety of sources about German intentions and preparations, believing that while Britain remained undefeated in the west, Germany was unlikely to attack the Soviet Union, and in any event the Red Army was sufficiently strong to act as a powerful deterrent to any attack and to defeat such an invasion should it occur. Even when German deserters attempted to warn the Soviet troops along the border in the summer of 1941 that an attack was imminent, most were treated as potential spies and shot.[6]

Whilst there can be little doubt that Stalin intended to attack Germany at a moment of his choosing, the precise details of his plans remain the subject of controversy. Writing in 1987 under a pseudonym, the Soviet defector Vladimir Bogdanovich Rezun – who had worked for many years as an officer in both the Soviet Army and military intelligence – suggested that a Soviet attack on Nazi

Germany was planned to commence just a few days after Hitler's invasion started, and gave a range of evidence: the Soviet forces along the frontier had been issued with maps that covered German territory but had few or no maps that would be of use in fighting a defensive war against German invasion; German-language phrase books that were given to the troops included how to ask for the locations of Nazi party offices, something that would be of no use if fighting on Soviet territory; and Stalin had altered the call-up age for universal military service from 21 to 18, allowing the Red Army to increase in size from less than 1.9 million men in 1939 to about 5 million by the spring of 1941.[7] Other writers have been deeply critical of Rezun's allegations, in particular the lack of any firm evidence in the form of strategic or operational orders, and have suggested that any Soviet planning about a potential attack on Germany represented little more than sensible operational contingencies.[8] However, it is beyond dispute that Stalin had as little faith as Hitler in the longevity of the non-aggression pact that Molotov, the Soviet foreign minister, agreed with his German counterpart Joachim von Ribbentrop in 1939. Even while the pact was being negotiated, Hitler was telling his generals:

> Everything I undertake is directed against Russia; if the West is too stupid and blind to understand this, I will be forced to come to terms with the Russians, to strike at the West, and then after subduing it to turn against the Soviet Union with my massed forces.[9]

Just a few days later, Stalin told his confidants:

> Of course, it's all a game to see who can fool whom. I know what Hitler's up to. He thinks he's outsmarted me but actually it's I who have tricked him.[10]

The Germans attempted to portray their attack on the Soviet Union in 1941 as a necessary preventive measure to pre-empt an attack by the Red Army, but at the same time Hitler's rhetoric left little doubt that this was a war intended to seize the European territories of the Soviet Union in order to turn the long-standing German dreams of an eastern empire into reality. Many within German circles doubted that it would be possible to achieve either military success or convert any military gains into economic benefits for Germany, at least in the short term; in the last months of 1940, as it became clear that there would be no invasion of Britain and as planning for an attack on the Soviet Union began to gather pace, several leading German figures produced a document warning that attempts to exploit the Baltic States, Belarus and the Ukraine would place a considerable strain upon German resources and would have a negative effect on the overall economy for a considerable period of time.[11] In a manner that would be repeated on many occasions in the years that followed, Hitler refused to listen to experts whose opinions differed from his own and he ordered Hermann Göring, his nominated heir and a man with a multitude of responsibilities, including oversight of German industry, to prepare plans for the ruthless exploitation of the territories that the Germans would swiftly capture.

Starting in March 1941, Göring and his officials drew up documents under the overall codename *Oldenburg*, and ultimately these documents formed the 'Green Folder' that was presented as evidence at the Nuremberg Trials after the war. Aware that the availability of oil in particular was a considerable problem for Germany, Göring placed a high priority on the early capture of Soviet oil wells in the Caucasus. Access to the iron and coal mines of the eastern parts of the Ukraine was also considered important, as was the capture of the agricultural plains of southern Russia and the Ukraine – these would solve all of Germany's food problems and avoid the risk of food shortages destabilising the home front, as had occurred during the 'Turnip Winter' in the First World War.

A separate German committee under the control of Hubert Backe, who had been born to German parents who had emigrated to the Caucasus in the 19th century, looked at the matter of food supplies in more detail. Backe was born in Tbilisi and he and his family were interned during the First World War as potential enemies. He witnessed the Bolshevik Revolution and moved to Germany during the Russian Civil War, bringing with him a hatred of communism and deep-seated resentment for the manner in which he and his family had been treated. In May 1941, he and his committee drew up what became known as the 'Hunger Plan', describing how it would be necessary to feed the Wehrmacht using food seized in occupied parts of the Soviet Union and how this, combined with shipments of food back to the German Reich, would inevitably create mass starvation. Since the end of the First World War, the urban population of the Soviet Union had increased by about 25 million people, and cities and towns were dependent upon the plentiful agricultural produce of the Ukraine. The language used in German plans left no room for ambiguity:

> Many tens of millions of peoples ... will become superfluous and will die or must emigrate to Siberia. Attempts to rescue the population from death through starvation by obtaining surpluses from the black earth zone [the Ukraine] can only come at the expense of the provisioning of Europe. They prevent the

possibility of Germany holding out until the end of the war, they prevent Germany and Europe from resisting the [British] blockade. With regard to this, absolute clarity must reign.[12]

If this resulted in cities becoming depopulated with the subsequent loss of industrial production, the Germans accepted that this was a necessary price that would have to be paid, and would help transform the newly industrialised parts of European Russia back into forests and farmland; with access to the natural resources of the newly acquired territories, German industry would easily be able to expand and produce whatever material goods were required. For the planners in Germany, the equation was simple: there was sufficient produce from the Ukraine to feed Germany and the rest of Europe, or to feed the Soviet population, but not both. The death through starvation of much of the Soviet population was seen as both a consequence of food requisition and a step towards creating space for future German settlement.[13]

Further plans for managing the new territories that would be gained in the east were drawn up under the overall heading of *Generalplan Ost*.[14] The former Soviet Union would be dismembered and each part used to create a *Reichskommissariat* ('Reich Commissariat'), and in early 1941 development of these new administrations was a task assigned to the new *Reichsministerium für die Besetzten Ostgebiete* ('Reich Ministry for the Occupied Eastern Territories' or *Ostministerium*) under Alfred Rosenberg. An early adherent to Nazi ideology, Rosenberg wrote extensively about 'Jewish Bolshevism' and the threat that it represented to Germany, but many within the Nazi Party regarded him as an intellectual whose views had little relevance in day-to-day affairs; his best-selling book, *Der Mythus des 20. Jahrhunderts* ('The Myth of the 20th Century'), which dealt at length with racial issues, particularly the 'Jewish question', was dismissed by Hitler as 'stuff that nobody can understand'.[15] As the new ministry developed and needed to start recruiting the personnel it would require to run the new territories, other parts of the government decided to take advantage of this:

[They regarded the transfer of staff to the *Ostministerium* as] a welcome opportunity to rid themselves of personal enemies, obnoxious meddlers and incompetent chair-warmers ... [resulting in] a colourful and accidental conglomeration of Gauleiters, Kreisleiters, Labour Front officials, and a great number of SA [*Sturmabteilung* or 'Storm Detachment', the early paramilitary wing of the Nazi Party] leaders of all ranks, who assumed high positions in the civil administration after listening to a few introductory lectures delivered by Rosenberg's staff.[16]

Many of these officials who were transferred to his *Ostministerium* remained loyal to their previous masters, most of whom were engaged in an internal struggle to create or maintain their personal empires. In any event, Rosenberg's personal views on how the territories should be run were in stark contrast to the views of Hitler and others; Rosenberg stated as early as 1940 that Germany should seek to build on the aspirations for independence in many parts of the western Soviet Union to create a series of friendly buffer states. The view of Hitler and others, that the conquered regions should be exploited ruthlessly and their populations replaced by German settlers, prevailed.

The Ukraine was a clear target for the German invasion. Its huge agricultural produce had featured in German demands to separate the region from the rest of Russia during the Brest-Litovsk negotiations with the Bolsheviks in 1917 and 1918, with the intention of creating a state that would be entirely under German control, and such thoughts played a large part in German thinking as planning for a war with the Soviet Union developed. In addition to the agricultural yield of the region, the eastern Ukraine, in particular the Donbas area, was seen as an industrial region of huge importance to the Soviet Union – seizing it would, it was believed, strike a fatal blow at the ability of the Soviet Union to continue fighting, and would at the same time provide valuable resources for Germany. And ultimately, the Reich's requirement to secure control of the oilfields of the Caucasus would depend upon first seizing the Ukraine as a vital stepping-stone. Speaking in October 1941, when many in the German hierarchy believed that the final defeat of the Soviet Union was imminent, Hitler made clear what lay in store for the Ukraine and its current inhabitants:

> In 20 years the Ukraine will already be a home for 20 million inhabitants besides the natives. In 300 years the country will be one of the loveliest gardens in the world. As for the natives, we will have to screen them carefully. The Jew – that destroyer – we shall drive out. Our colonising penetration must be constantly progressive until it reaches the stage that our own colonists far outnumber the local inhabitants.[17]

In the complex racial pyramid adopted by the Nazis, the Ukrainians held a relatively lowly position. They were regarded as superior to Russian Slavs and the undesirable Jews and Gypsies, but inferior to Baltic Slavs, many of whom had ancestry that included German settlers from the Middle Ages. It was believed that some of the Ukrainian population might be regarded as sufficiently Germanic to form part of the future population of the region, but the rest were expected to wither away and disappear. When discussing the future shape of the Ukraine and other eastern regions, Hitler repeatedly drew on examples from European history. Imperial colonies fell broadly into two categories – those that were exploited for their resources, such as India and much of Africa, and those that were extensively settled by the colonial powers and the local inhabitants driven out, such as Australia, South Africa and North America. Hitler intended that the new German colonies in the east would involve both trends, with the region being both exploited and settled. To a large extent, this attitude was certain to cause problems, as any policy of displacing the local population would inevitably disrupt both agricultural and industrial production, but such matters were ignored. As for the fate of native Ukrainians, Hitler often reminded his entourage about the native Americans – a hundred years after the white man arrived in their lands, he often said, nobody remembered them or what had happened to them. The same would be the case in the Ukraine.

The territory that would become *Reichskommisariat Ukraine* or *RKU* was a rich area, and in the heated and byzantine world of Nazi intrigues and empire building, control of the region became an important area of contention. One of the main protagonists in this manoeuvring was Erich Koch, the Gauleiter of East Prussia. After a period of unspectacular service on the Eastern Front in the First World War – largely in rear area units – he worked as a railwayman before being dismissed for political agitation. He became a rising figure in the Nazi Party and by the time that the invasion of the Soviet Union began, he had already expanded his area of control from East Prussia into adjacent parts of Poland. Much to Rosenberg's dismay, Hitler appointed Koch to be Gauleiter of *Reichskommissariat Ukraine*, creating a complex and ultimately unworkable tangle of responsibilities. Although Rosenberg's *Ostministerium* had nominal authority over the territories that would be occupied, Göring – due to his responsibilities for the Four Year Plan for German industry – would control the manner in which industrial and mineral resources were exploited, and Heinrich Himmler, head of the SS, would be responsible for all police matters. Koch was widely seen as one of Hitler's favourite gauleiters and had already established a reputation for brutality during the time that he controlled parts of Poland; he would now oversee the seizure of grain and other agricultural produce for the Reich, as well as general civilian matters.[18] Rosenberg's ministry was increasingly losing out in the regime's internal bids for power.

Stalin's policies of collectivisation of farming across the Soviet Union in the late 1920s were not popular in the Ukraine, leading to widespread protests and even local peasant revolts. A combination of events – lack of cooperation by Ukrainian farmers, the imposition of new crops such as sugar beet and cotton, failures to harvest and store grain efficiently – led to a cycle of worsening food shortages, and in an attempt to prevent famine in Soviet urban areas there were forced requisitions, creating a terrible famine in the countryside during 1932 and 1933. Millions of Ukrainians died; the precise figure remains a subject of controversy, and for many years the Soviet Union officially denied that there had been a famine, but it is generally agreed that perhaps six million people perished in what was largely a man-made disaster.[19] At first, the famine was caused largely through mismanagement, but there can be little doubt that Stalin and his officials understood perfectly well that forcible requisitions of food to alleviate shortages in urban areas would result in commensurate shortages in the countryside. When members of the Ukrainian Politburo informed Moscow that the rural areas were in desperate need of help, Stalin blamed them for the problems and dismissed many of the reports as fiction, deriding one official:

> They tell us ... that you're a good orator, but it transpires that you're a good story-teller. Fabricating such a fairy-tale about famine! ... Wouldn't it be better for you to leave [your government post] and join the Writers' Union: you'll concoct fables, and fools will read them.[20]

The truth was that Stalin and other senior figures were well aware of what was happening. Semyon Mikhailovich Budyonny, a cavalry commander and comrade of Stalin from the days of the Russian Civil War, wrote to the Soviet leader from Sochi and described seeing tired, emaciated people and horses from the windows of his train.[21] The chairman of the Ukraine's Central Executive Committee told a visiting American:

> We know millions are dying. That is unfortunate but the glorious future of the Soviet Union will justify it.[22]

The legacy was huge resentment of the Communist regime, which was often seen in the Ukrainian countryside as an imposition upon the Ukraine by Russian Bolsheviks. Consequently, when the Wehrmacht invaded in June 1941, many Ukrainians welcomed the Germans as liberators and soldiers often entered villages and small towns where they were greeted by cheering peasants who offered them bread and salt, a traditional Ukrainian gift for honoured visitors.[23] However, there were variations in the attitude of the local population towards both the Germans and the Soviet authorities. Older Ukrainians, who had memories of a time before communist rule, were more likely to welcome the

Germans as liberators; younger adults who had grown up during the Soviet era were by contrast more likely to be in favour of Soviet rule. Many of these younger Ukrainians were drafted into the Red Army when the conflict with Germany began, and were therefore not in the region when the Wehrmacht advanced in 1941, with the result that the pro-German sentiment of the older generation tended to prevail in many areas, particularly in the countryside. In the cities with their industrial districts, there was far less support for the Germans.

The German plans called for conquered territory to be handed over to the relevant *Reichskommissariat* as soon as the front line had moved to the east – the army was to retain control of only a limited area extending to a depth of no more than 120 miles or 200km behind the front – but even in these early days of German occupation, there were clear signs of what lay ahead. Perhaps in response to the disquiet in some military circles about the behaviour of German troops during the invasion of Poland, Hitler issued orders that German troops would be exempt from the laws of conduct that usually applied in war zones. It is sometimes difficult for modern readers to appreciate the degree to which both German and Soviet populations were indoctrinated by their governments; the Nazis had been in power since 1933, Stalin and his colleagues for longer, and the consequence was that most of the populations of both nations had been subjected to an almost unopposed stream of conditioning and propaganda. For the German soldiers who entered the Soviet Union in 1941, this meant that they generally believed that theirs was a superior nation and that others were inferior and could therefore be treated as inferiors.

There were substantial numbers of Ukrainian exiles who hoped that the Germans would help them establish an independent state, and the German authorities actively encouraged this belief, working closely with organisations such as the *Orhanizatsiya Ukrayins'kykh Natsionalistiv* ('Organisation of Ukrainian Nationalists' or *OUN*) prior to the invasion. This group was first formed in Vienna in 1929 and rapidly incorporated other right-wing nationalist Ukrainian movements, but in 1940 it broke into two wings, the more moderate *OUN-M* ('*Melnykivtsi*' or 'Melnykites') under Andriy Atanasovich Melnyk and the more radical *OUN-B* ('*Banderivtsi*' or 'Banderites') led by Stepan Andrijowycz Bandera. Moving into the rural areas of the Ukraine in the wake of the advancing Wehrmacht, the *OUN* attempted to set up local cells to identify fellow nationalists and to make preparations for Ukrainian independence; such steps were tolerated by the Germans for only a limited time and the *OUN* activists rapidly realised that they would receive little help from Germany to achieve their aspirations.

From the outset, a prime target for mistreatment was the Jewish population of the Soviet Union. As a consequence of laws in force during the 19th century, Jews had been forbidden from settling anywhere other than the western parts of what became the Soviet Union and even by 1941 most Russian Jews still lived in this region. Their numbers had been increased by Jews fleeing the German conquest of Poland, and the initial swift advance of German troops led to large Jewish communities rapidly coming under German control. The region had a long history of anti-Semitism and violent pogroms and the Germans swiftly made use of Ukrainians to carry out attacks against the Jews. Despite the attempts of many Germans after the war to lay the blame for all atrocities at the door of the SS and to portray the troops of the Wehrmacht as simple soldiers who were unaware of what was happening in the hinterland, there can be no doubt that from the outset the Wehrmacht was extensively involved in atrocities. Nor was it simply a question of army personnel joining in once the killings began; extensive orders and proclamations were issued before the invasion to make clear to the troops that they were expected to behave with unprecedented harshness. Some senior officers like Manstein later claimed that they had not passed on instructions such as the infamous 'Commissar Order', which required the execution of all captured Red Army personnel suspected of being political commissars, but there is abundant evidence that most of these denials are untrue. Indeed, many commanders added their own instructions to those from Berlin. General Erich Hoepner, commander of Fourth Panzer Group (later Fourth Panzer Army) in the northern sector of the Eastern Front, made a speech to senior officers in his command in May 1941:

> The war against Russia is an important chapter in the struggle for existence of the German nation. It is the old battle of Germanic against Slav peoples, of the defence of European culture against Muscovite-Asiatic inundation, and the repulse of Jewish-Bolshevism. The objective of this battle must be the destruction of present-day Russia and it must therefore be conducted with unprecedented severity. Every military action must be guided in planning and execution by an iron will to exterminate the enemy mercilessly and totally. In particular, no adherents of the present Russian-Bolshevik system are to be spared.[24]

The city now known as Lviv was one of the first urban centres to experience the reality of German occupation. It had previously been known as Lemberg, one of the leading urban centres of the Austro-Hungarian Empire, and became the Polish Lvov after the end of the First World War. As was the case with many parts of what now became eastern Poland, it had a very mixed population with large communities of ethnic Poles, Russians, Ukrainians and Jews. In 1939 it was part of the territory assigned to Soviet control as part of the Molotov-Ribbentrop Pact. Immediately, as was the case in other cities and towns seized by Stalin, the NKVD (*Narodnyi Komissariat Vnutrennikh Del* or 'People's Comissariat for Internal Affairs') started a wave of arrests of any who were deemed to be enemies, either active or potential, of the Soviet Union. As German troops approached Lviv just a week after the beginning of the invasion, NKVD troops started to execute thousands of prisoners; an uprising by Ukrainians briefly drove the NKVD personnel from Lviv before they returned to continue the killings, many of them in Brygidki, a former nunnery. It seems that the proportion of Jews in the ranks of the NKVD in the region was higher than average, but whilst both Ukrainian nationalists and Germans attempted to use this as a justification for what followed, they ignored the fact that a large proportion of those executed by the NKVD were also Jews, many of whom had been arrested as intelligentsia who might form the focus of anti-Soviet activity, as soon as the Red Army occupied the area in 1939.

The first German troops to reach the city were the men of 1st Gebirgs ('Mountain') Division. Formed a year before the start of the Second World War, the division was made up largely of Bavarian and Austrian troops and prided itself as an elite formation, but from the outset its record was blemished by involvement in war crimes. When German troops reached the city of Przemyśl in southeast Poland in 1939, the division took part in rounding up Jews in the city. In 1941, when German troops invaded Yugoslavia before the beginning of hostilities with the Soviet Union, 1st Mountain Division was again involved in criminal activities. There were numerous cases of civilians being executed out of hand, and the division's reports after the end of the fighting in Yugoslavia dispassionately recorded that out of 498 prisoners taken by the division, 411 were executed.[25] On 30 June, just eight days after crossing the frontier into the Soviet Union, the division secured control of Lviv, swiftly driving off the retreating Red Army and the last of the NKVD personnel. In the First World War, the Jewish communities of both Lemberg and Przemyśl had suffered greatly when the Russians occupied the area, and had greeted the arrival of German and Austro-Hungarian troops with enthusiasm. Now, they waited in dread.

Within a few hours of the arrival of German troops, local Ukrainian militias had formed and immediately attacked the Jewish population of the city, regardless of whether they had any connection with the NKVD. The German *RSHA* (*Reichssicherheitshauptamt* or 'Reich Main Security Office', part of the SS) produced a report in mid-July, praising the actions of the Ukrainians:

During the first hours after the departure of the Bolsheviks, the Ukrainian population took praiseworthy action against the Jews ... About 7,000 Jews were seized and shot by the [Ukrainian] police in retribution for inhuman acts of cruelty.[26]

As soon as German troops occupied Lviv, the *OUN-B* published a Proclamation of Ukrainian Independence, stating unequivocally that any form of union with Germany was only possible if the latter recognised Ukrainian independence.[27] The proclamation came as a complete surprise to the Germans, who immediately demanded that the new Ukrainian government be disbanded. When the *OUN-B* refused, Bandera and Yaroslav Stetsko, who had been declared prime minister of the Ukraine, were arrested and detained in the Sachsenhausen concentration camp. Thereafter, the Ukrainian nationalists had no illusions – if they were to achieve independence, they would have to fight both the Germans and the Soviets.

In order to control the new colonies to be created in the east, the Germans would need help on the ground, and the intention was to identify ethnic Germans, the descendants of settlers who had moved from German lands to the Ukraine in the preceding centuries. Invited into the Russian Empire by Peter the Great and Catherine the Great, these settlers had at least to some extent retained their German identity, and a special *Sonderkommando Russland* ('Special Command Russia') was created by the SS to identify them and use them to establish civilian administrations. By the end of August 1941, the local sections of this SS unit, under the command of Klaus Siebert, had identified about 130,000 ethnic Germans in the occupied parts of the Ukraine. A few had the requisite skills to become administrators, but many did not; nevertheless, they rapidly formed *Selbstschutz* ('self-defence') groups, which were armed by the Germans and used as auxiliaries in the killing of Jews and others.[28]

The people of the Soviet Union had been prepared for war. Soviet publications repeatedly warned the population about the threat from German spies and a series of films appeared in the late 1930s portraying an attack by Germany, in which the brave communists always triumphed. Despite this, there was still a considerable sense of shock when the war actually began. Kiev was bombed on the first day, but the raids – largely directed at railway and road bridges – did little damage; there appeared to be more danger from the city's defences, as Irina Khoroshunova, a graphic designer who was 28 years old in 1941, wrote in her diary:

Children scream and cry during air raids, and then play with the shrapnel of anti-aircraft shells afterwards. Mothers cry and the younger children tremble during the attacks. The men have all become very serious. Everyone's mood is alarmed, even fearful, because although the sky is blue and clear, bombs fall from it and there seems to be no escape from them.

Today [26 June] was the worst morning. Anti-aircraft guns and machine-guns were firing from all sides. Shrapnel fell like rain. The windows rattled and the house shook like during an earthquake … [The raid] was in the morning and the fear and horror still hasn't gone. Fear rises when a plane approaches. And it seems that the next bomb will be the one that will kill you.[29]

As is often the case, people rapidly became accustomed to the new circumstances and life soon settled down. The heavily censored news reports of the war mentioned the loss of some cities, but this was widely interpreted as a series of tactical withdrawals and Khoroshunova and others waited impatiently for the beginning of the great counteroffensive that had featured so strongly in pre-war films. But even at this early stage, there were ominous signs that things weren't going well – refugees arrived from the western parts of the Soviet Union in large numbers, and whilst it was difficult for ordinary people to get permission to travel, the NKVD evacuated their own families and personal possessions. There were exhortations to be alert for German spies, leading to widespread suspicion of anyone who was a stranger. The construction of defences around Kiev began in early July, despite assurances that the front line was still far to the west, and Khoroshunova and her family moved to the suburbs on the east bank of the Dnepr; within days, when there were no new developments, they returned to their home. By late July, some residents of Kiev claimed to have heard artillery fire somewhere to the west and fortifications began to appear on the city streets. There were shortages of food and scuffles amongst those queuing for what little was available. News of the fall of Smolensk in mid-August caused considerable disquiet – the optimists believed that it was part of a grand strategic manoeuvre, while others became fearful that the Germans were winning the war. Despite the construction of fortifications, there were rumours that Kiev would be abandoned without a fight, resulting in a mixed reaction: on the one hand, many citizens wanted their city to be defended, but on the other hand, they feared the destruction that might result. In mid-September, the steady stream of reports that towns and cities elsewhere were being captured by the Germans once more caused alarm, with many guessing – accurately – that there was a growing threat that Kiev would be encircled. On 16 September, German forces attacking from north and south met at Lokhovitsa, some 120 miles (200km) east of Kiev. Despite bitter resistance by the encircled Red Army units, Kiev was occupied three days later. Khoroshunova saw the Germans for the first time:

> The Germans are completely different from us. [They have] huge vehicles, all fitted out with strange equipment. There are whole columns of the most diverse machines. They have a clean, well-fed appearance. Everything about this army distinguishes it from our troops, our people.
>
> The sight of these well-fed, well-nourished conquerors increased still further the feeling of deep bitterness amongst the people, because our soldiers had to walk for hundreds of kilometres on broken roads with blistered feet, often barefoot or wearing inadequate shoes. And they have few vehicles. All they have is a sense of duty, an oath to the Motherland, which they honour with resignation.[30]

Almost immediately, proclamations appeared in both German and Ukrainian, and a Ukrainian-language newspaper was published, though it did not give the names of its editorial staff:

> The newspaper made a big impression. There were no insulting statements or libels. But the manner in which it glorified the Germans, calling them 'fair-haired knights and liberators' and the use of the slogan 'the destruction of Bolshevism and the Jews' had a depressing effect. There was a long article in the newspaper describing the stages of the Ukraine's struggle for independence.[31]

The occupying authorities moved quickly to establish a new order. Germans, Czechoslovaks and Ukrainians would, they assured the population, be entitled to full rights. Russians, Poles and Jews would be treated very differently. Rumours that had circulated through the population of Kiev before the arrival of the Germans were now replaced by equally alarming reports:

> [The rumours] said that the Soviet Union had perished, and that there was a split in the [Communist] Party. Stalin and Kaganovich were isolated, with Molotov, Voroshilov and others against them. Then they said that Stalin had shot himself, then that he had been shot by Voroshilov, then that he had fled to Washington … Just like a foul smell that spread quickly, the poisonous rumours proliferated through the people … Three days ago there was nothing to suggest the collapse of the Soviet system, and these rumours must be German propaganda. Yet you need a lot of self-control to disbelieve them … we learned that as well as Kiev, the

Germans have taken Poltava, and that four Soviet armies were destroyed near Kiev. I don't know about Poltava, whether it's true or not. But we already knew for certain that something terrible happened to our troops near Kiev. It's painful, hard to accept, and humiliating. Our troops left Kiev on 18 September. Many Party officials, women and officials such as those from the telegraph and telephone exchanges left with them. They say that our people managed to break through the ring of encirclement. The Germans cunningly killed our people, opening a passage through the encirclement in order to destroy our troops elsewhere ... In confused fighting, squeezed from all sides by their foes, our armies numbering 600,000 had no room to manoeuvre. There was nowhere to hide, no means of defending themselves. And the Germans bombarded this mass of people with heavy shelling and bombing and mortars, and machine-gunned them from the air ...

The figures are 220,000 killed and wounded, 380,000 taken prisoner.

Such are the dry figures of this terrible tragedy that took place near Kiev. Why did it happen? Who is to blame for the death of so many of our people? It isn't for me to answer this question. Perhaps the future will give answers to those who live to see it. But now there is just the terrible spectre of this defeat, so monstrous that it cannot be comprehended. The hospitals are overcrowded with the wounded. Hundreds, thousands of women are searching through the lists for their sons, husbands, fathers.[32]

The attacks on Jews in Lviv at the end of June 1941 were merely part of the first wave of killings. The advancing Wehrmacht was accompanied by SS units known as *Einsatzgruppen* ('task groups') that enforced Hitler's racial policies to the full. Jews and other 'undesirable' elements of the population, including anyone suspected of being a communist, were rounded up and either imprisoned or executed immediately. In order to aid the *Einsatzgruppen* in their task, Field Marshal Walther von Brauchitsch, commander-in-chief of the army until December 1941, ordered all field commanders to ensure that all Jews in occupied areas were identified and registered, and the details passed to the *Einsatzgruppen*. Wehrmacht units were specifically ordered to cooperate fully with the *Einsatzgruppen*; although some army officers refused to do so – notably Field Marshal Ewald von Kleist in the Caucasus – most cooperated, some with considerable enthusiasm.[33] *Einsatzgruppe C*, under the command of Gruppenführer Otto Rasch, accompanied the German Army Group South into the Ukraine and was soon extensively involved in atrocities. Romanian troops captured Odessa on 16 October after protracted fighting and a few days later, an explosion destroyed the headquarters of the Romanian forces in the city, killing

67 people including the local Romanian commander. The bomb had been left behind by the retreating Red Army with a delayed-action fuse, but Jews and communists – the terms were often used almost interchangeably by the Germans – were immediately blamed. Within two days, over 5,000 civilians, mainly Jews, had been killed. A further 19,000 were killed in shootings or burned alive in warehouses in the port district on 23 October, and a column of over 20,000 was force-marched from Odessa to the town of Dalnik. Here, many were tied together and thrown into a deep ditch, where they were shot. Deciding that killing all of them in such a manner would take too long, the Romanian commander – Lieutenant Colonel Nikolai Deleanu – ordered the rest to be put into four warehouses. Loopholes were created in the walls and machine-guns then fired through the loopholes, while other soldiers shot anyone trying to escape through windows. Three of the warehouses were then set ablaze; the fourth was shelled the following day.[34] It should be noted that whilst this atrocity was carried out mainly by Romanian troops, German soldiers also took part. Similarly, there were several explosions in Kiev caused by devices left by the NKVD and Red Army, but inevitably the Germans blamed the Jews and killings began. Jews and suspected communists were driven through the streets of Kiev to the Jewish cemetery in Lukyanovka and to a ravine near Babi Yar, to the northwest of Kiev. Over two days at the end of September 1941, personnel of *Einsatzgruppe C* and Ukrainian police troops slaughtered nearly 34,000 Jews.[35] Khorosunova and other citizens of Kiev could only watch events with mounting horror:

> Some say that the Jews are being machine-gunned, all of them shot. Others say that 16 columns were assembled and they are being sent elsewhere. But where? Nobody can answer. One thing is known: they [the Germans] take all their documents and possessions. Then they are driven to Babi Yar and there – I do not know what's there. All I know is that something terrible happens, something monstrous, something unimaginable, which can neither be understood nor explained.
>
> … Already everyone is saying that the Jews have been killed … indiscriminately, old people, women, children … a Russian girl went with her friend to the cemetery and crossed the fence to the other side. She saw how naked people were led to Babi Yar and could hear a machine-gun firing.
>
> These rumours are spreading. The horror of them is too much to comprehend. But we are forced to believe, since it is a fact that the Jews have been executed. It's driving us mad. It's impossible to live with the awareness of this …

I write and my hair stands on end. I write but these words are meaningless. I write because it is necessary that the people of the world know about this monstrous crime and avenge it. I write and in Babi Yar the massacre of the defenceless, of innocent children, women, and old people continues, and it is said that many are buried half-dead, because the Germans are economical and do not like to spend extra bullets ...

Was there ever anything like this in the history of mankind? Nobody could have imagined something like this. I cannot write any more. I can't write, I can't try to comprehend, because comprehending what is happening will drive us insane. Nobody gains from this. Prisoners are driven endlessly through the city. The Jews are driven naked. If they ask for water or bread they are killed on the spot.[36]

Many Ukrainians hoped that they would be given independence by the Germans, and the widely resented policies of collectivised farming would be reversed. But despite the *OUN* cooperating with the Wehrmacht during the fighting in the Red Army, the Germans showed no inclination to recognise a new Ukrainian regime. The few concessions that the Germans made to the Ukrainians were those that would have little material impact upon the occupation. One such was the return of Orthodox Christianity, something that Khoroshunova's generation regarded as completely alien:

The discrepancy between religious morality and reality is now more cynical than ever. During the reign of religion in the past, the preaching of love for one's neighbour at least tried somehow to mask violence of every kind, but now the bloody ghost of Babi Yar rises above the churches in which Ukrainians in European suits sing hymns and bless the murderers, who they call 'fair-haired knights'.

In Babi Yar, hundreds, thousands, no – tens of thousands of half-living people were buried with the dead. We know for certain that blood flowed from Babi Yar for several kilometres. And beatings continue even now. Every day they lead the newly condemned to the Lukyanovka cemetery, they led them there yesterday, the day before yesterday, today too.[37]

As the Wehrmacht moved east, territory was assigned to Koch's *RKU* on 1 September, and any lingering hopes that German occupation would be better than Soviet rule rapidly disappeared. Koch chose not to be present himself, instead sending his deputy, Paul Dargel, who had overseen negotiations with the army about the handover. Dargel was every bit as committed to Hitler's racial policies as Koch, but was a better administrator. He set up the headquarters of *RKU* in Rivne, which was to be the new capital of the region. The lives of some 17 million inhabitants were in his hands, and he wasted no time in creating six *Generalkommissariate*, with a host of regional and town commissars working under their control. As with many aspects of Nazi rule, the takeover of the Ukraine was a somewhat chaotic affair. The trains carrying Dargel's subordinates to their new posts were repeatedly held up by bad weather. To make matters worse, despite attempts by Dargel and others to create a regime that would be light on bureaucracy – only the minimum office equipment was provided for each subdivision of *RKU* – Rosenberg's *Ostministerium* continued to produce voluminous instructions on how the territories should be managed. These resulted in confusing and often contradictory divisions of responsibility between the new civil administration and other bodies, such as the SS.[38]

The tone of the occupation was set in an early document from Koch to his subordinates:

If these people [the Ukrainians] work for ten hours a day, eight of those must be for us. All sentimental considerations must be put aside. These people must be ruled with iron force as this will help us to win the war. We have not liberated the Ukraine for their pleasure, but to secure the essential *Lebensraum* and food supply for Germany.[39]

This message was reiterated many times, even in 1943 when the tide had clearly changed in favour of the Soviet Union:

We did not come here to dispense Manna from heaven, we came here to create the preconditions of victory … We are the master race and must bear in mind that the most insignificant German worker is racially and biologically a thousand times as valuable as the local population.[40]

In pursuance of such policies, one of the first steps undertaken by *RKU* was to close all schools and other centres of education; Koch declared that there was no need for Ukrainian children to attend schools, as they would be told all they needed to know by their German masters.[41] Conditions for the population deteriorated rapidly as food supplies were requisitioned and fuel – oil, wood and electricity – was diverted for the needs either of the military or the German homeland. Enforcement of curfews and forced labour was brutal, with execution replacing imprisonment as the punishment for most crimes. Tens of thousands of Ukrainians – not just the Jews and suspected communists – died in the first winter of German occupation. In August 1941, Hitler gave orders that Kiev was to be utterly destroyed, but the order would have been almost impossible to implement even if the Wehrmacht hadn't had its hands full fighting the Red Army. Instead, starvation was expected to achieve the same outcome.

In the First World War, the Germans anticipated making considerable gains from territories they occupied in the east, and the results were disappointing for several reasons. Firstly, implementation of the policies was poorly managed, with many inefficiencies. Secondly, there was no consideration given to future years – inadequate amounts of grain were left in the area to sow for the next crop, and local people were given little or no incentive to cooperate. Thirdly, the expectations of what could be achieved were hugely over-optimistic. Similar mistakes were made throughout the occupied parts of the Soviet Union in the Second World War, particularly in the Ukraine. Koch's *Zentralhandelsorganisation Ost* ('Central Trading Organisation East') proved to be clumsy and clashed repeatedly with the attempts of other agencies to carve out their own empires. The expectation had been that some four million tons of grain would be extracted from the Ukraine by the end of 1942; the true figure was less than half that, and the disruption caused by the war meant that, far from being the bread-basket that Hitler had expected, the Ukraine produced far less food than it had before the war – in 1942, for example, fields under cultivation fell to less than two thirds of pre-war levels, and these fields produced less than 40 per cent of the yields achieved before the German invasion.[42] In an attempt to protect his own reputation from any damage, Koch ordered 'Ukrainian trains' loaded with food to be sent to major German cities as a visible symbol of the successes of *RKU*.

The result of German food requisitions was mass starvation across the Ukraine, worsened by a harsh and prolonged winter in 1941–42. Together with the shipment of tens of thousands of Ukrainian civilians to be used as forced labour in the occupied territories and in Germany, shortages of fuel and farming equipment and no consideration for the need to leave sufficient grain for future crops to be sown ensured that matters would only get worse. At first, civilians like Khoroshunova exchanged what few possessions they had for food, but soon they had nothing left to sell. Faced with a choice between starvation and working for the Germans, many felt they had no choice but to take whatever work was offered. Khoroshunova made an ominous entry in her diary in mid-1942: the city's cats and dogs had gradually disappeared.

In expectation of a swift victory, little or no attempt was made in the early months of occupation to get Ukrainian industry working again, not least because the retreating Red Army had taken with it as much factory machinery as it could, and had tried to destroy what was immovable. There was also a critical shortage of skilled workers. When it became clear that the war was likely to drag on for many years, attempts were made to improve the living conditions of Ukrainians and to get the factories working again, but the Ukrainian population – which would almost certainly have supported the Germans if Rosenberg's proposals of creating pro-German satellite states had been followed – was in little mood to cooperate. In Kiev and elsewhere, large numbers of civilians were held as hostages and were then executed as punishment for acts of sabotage. On a few carefully hidden radio sets, people in the larger cities tuned in to hear crackly broadcasts by Radio Moscow and learned of the defeat of the Wehrmacht outside Moscow, and that Leningrad continued to hold out. Slowly, partisan activity began to increase. This in turn led to further repression, and those suspected of being partisans or aiding them were hanged from city lampposts:

Yesterday three people were hanged.

On Shevchenko Boulevard, two children asked me where the hanged people were. I thought they were asking about those who had been hanged earlier and said that they were no longer there. But when I came to the end of the boulevard I saw a terrible new spectacle. Thin ragged ropes were hanging from lampposts, and there were three corpses on the ground in the mud and snow.

The blood from their broken heads flowed along with the water over the pavement ... Their heads were disfigured and bloodied. Two of them, apparently, were Jews. One was wearing a German overcoat. People stood around silently. A policeman was walking around. He did not let us get closer. I couldn't see if it was possible to recognise the dead. Who were they? What did they do? Did they do something for our people, or did they die for nothing? Their blood was still fresh and bright red. All three corpses lay in the same way, all faces turned in the same direction.[43]

Whilst some may have been intimidated by such acts, others reacted by doing whatever they could to undermine German control, but the requirements of survival were such that any work offered by the occupying forces attracted dozens of volunteers:

There was a large crowd of people at the [stock] exchange. In the rooms where women with specialist skills could register, there was a huge gathering. These unemployed women of all ages were looking for any kind of work ... At the table was an energetic manager surrounded by a crowd of people, praying and begging, waving their blue cards [identity cards for the unemployed were blue, while those who were employed had pink cards, entitling them to slightly better rations].

Then several red-faced, well-groomed German women with their hair loose, wearing military clothes, appeared. They chatted with the manager and gazed at the miserable, hungry crowd with disinterest. They were well-fed and self-satisfied. Our tragedy didn't touch them.

One of them wanted 15 women to work in the commissariat as clerks. The hungry crowd all rushed forward with cries. Women trampled each other and begged the manager and the German women, stretching out their blue cards.[44]

Red Army soldiers who had been unable to retreat, Jews fleeing the near-certainty of death, and ordinary Ukrainians took up arms against the invaders, though in fewer numbers than elsewhere on the Eastern Front. One estimate suggests that in early May 1942, there were fewer than 2,000 partisans active in the area – by contrast, the partisan movement in Belarus at this time numbered more than 150,000.[45] Nevertheless, the Ukrainian partisans were a substantial irritation to the Germans, often knocking out railway lines and bridges, though they mainly targeted their attacks on the police forces and other Ukrainians who collaborated with the occupiers. And despite the starvation, mass killings, and forced labour, many Ukrainians did collaborate. Members of the *OUN* and other nationalist Ukrainian bodies helped the Germans organise police and paramilitary units that were used widely, both in the Ukraine and in other German-occupied areas like Poland, often in the execution of civilians. Other Ukrainians were used as guards in prison camps and concentration camps. Some researchers have pointed out that Ukrainians who had worked closely with communist authorities before the German invasion were often the first to volunteer to serve the new masters.[46] Inevitably, many of those who collaborated with the Germans, particularly in police and paramilitary roles, found themselves clashing with pro-communist partisans.

The German plans for the attack on the Soviet Union, and its subsequent dismemberment, were based upon an expectation of a quick victory. Many factors fed into this belief. In the First World War, German forces had consistently defeated the Russians; although Russian soldiers fought as bravely as those of every other army, the quality of their leadership, the tardiness of the Russians to field sufficient artillery with enough ammunition, and the demoralisation and disintegration that followed the February and October Revolutions in 1917 undermined every attempt of the Tsar and his generals to deliver the crushing blow upon the Central Powers that Russia and its allies had expected. In the opening campaigns of the new war, the Wehrmacht overwhelmed the Poles with apparent ease before turning west and crushing the British, French and Belgian forces. It seemed as if a similar campaign, albeit on a larger scale, would lead to the rapid destruction of the Soviet Union. Finally, Stalin's purges of the Red Army in the 1930s had stripped it of much of its leadership, and its poor performance in the Winter War against Finland in 1939 suggested that the new commanders who had replaced the thousands who were imprisoned or executed were ill-equipped to conduct a modern war. However, such beliefs were misplaced. The Red Army was not the antiquated colossus with which Russia entered the First World War in 1914. Indeed, Soviet military thinkers had spent the years between the wars writing extensively about future conflicts, though many of their ideas – like those of their contemporaries in other countries – would prove to be wrong. In terms of equipment, the numbers of tanks and guns deployed by the Red Army were immense; however, shortages of spare parts and a lack of radios in the huge tank fleet meant that the forces available could not be used as efficiently as the German units opposing them. Perhaps the worst area of over-confidence that led to the German predictions of rapid victory was the inaccurate assessment of the successes of the early campaigns, as there had been little consideration of the setbacks experienced by the Wehrmacht during these battles. German tanks had proved to be under-armed and under-armoured in comparison to their opponents, particularly in the west; Germany's constant fuel shortages meant that there was insufficient fuel for anything more than a brief campaign; reliance on horses in infantry units had resulted in armoured columns rapidly out-distancing the slower-moving infantry divisions, a problem that was certain to get worse on the vast battlefields of the Soviet Union; and German industry was simply unprepared for warfare on such a scale. A telling sign of this is that the Luftwaffe fielded fewer aircraft for the invasion of the Soviet Union than it had deployed for the invasion of Poland two years before.

By the end of 1941, the dream of rapid conquest was in tatters as the German advance stalled before Moscow. Huge damage had been inflicted upon the Red Army, but the sheer size of the Soviet forces had been badly underestimated by Hitler and others. Expectations that the Soviet Union would prove to be a rotten structure, likely to collapse at the first serious challenge, proved to be groundless. Instead, it was the Wehrmacht that came perilously close to destruction, strewn across the snow-covered landscape as its offensive burned out and the Red Army unleashed its counterattack. Any final hope of a swift victory over the Soviet Union died in Stalingrad, and even the dreams of success over a longer timescale were gone when the German armoured forces failed at Kursk in the summer of 1943. Everywhere, the Wehrmacht faced strong Soviet attacks, nowhere more so than in the Ukraine.

The deteriorating position of Germany was also apparent to the Ukrainians living in the occupied towns and cities. Khoroshunova noted that by the summer of 1942, the allies of the Germans did not appear to be particularly enthusiastic about the war:

> There are a lot of Italians in the city. They are swarthy with black hair, small cheerful men. But those who have seen them from closer say that their cheerfulness disappears and is replaced by gloomy silence when they are loaded into vehicles and sent to the front.[47]

By mid-1943, information about the catastrophic German defeat at Stalingrad was spreading through the Ukraine. Increasingly, there were air raids by Soviet planes and the partisan movement continued to grow. Interactions between German troops and Ukrainian civilians changed, with many Germans now speaking openly that that they were not in favour of the war:

> Many Germans are beginning to understand the monstrous venture into which Hitler thrust them, filling their heads with *Blitzkriegs* and convincing them they were God's governors on earth. But we see how these Fritzes, Hanses and Erichs generally curse the war and their Führer for being sent to die in our land. And more and more often we hear bitter words from ordinary German soldiers: 'Why did we come here? Why are we at war with you?'[48]

The German forces, which had entered the Soviet Union to create a new empire from European Russia, now found themselves struggling to survive. From the summer of 1943 until the end of the war, only the most credulous officers continued to believe that the miraculous appearance of new weapons or other magical solutions would change things in their favour. The Red Army was stronger in every field – manpower, tanks, guns, and aircraft – and the quality of its leadership continued to improve, with each campaign subject to rapid and careful scrutiny to ensure that any mistakes that had been made would not be repeated. By contrast, the German high command – with Hitler at its summit –

increasingly retreated into a fantasy world where the Führer's will was sufficient to overcome all material disadvantages. Officers who failed to carry out impossible orders were dismissed and replaced by those believed to be more willing to adhere to Hitler's instructions. In any case, the pool of experienced and skilled manpower available to the Germans was declining rapidly. Many senior commanders had fallen out of favour, though as the conflict continued some of them were grudgingly given new appointments; the battle-hardened junior officers and NCOs (non-commissioned officers) who had given the Wehrmacht such an advantage in much of the war were disappearing as a result of the constantly increasing casualty lists; and despite the major increases in armaments production achieved by Albert Speer, who had been appointed armaments minister early in 1942, the new weapons were frequently misused to create new formations rather than bringing battered units back to something approaching their establishment strength. As it advanced across territories that had been held by the Germans since the dazzling advances of 1941, the Red Army found increasing evidence of the brutality of Hitler's occupation policies, and a grim mood of revenge spread throughout the Soviet forces, with the additional desire to deal with those who were seen to have collaborated with the hated fascists. Doomed to fight a losing war, the Germans could do little more than struggle to hold back the tide of inevitable retribution.

CHAPTER 1

SUMMER 1943: THE DECISIVE SHIFT

Many battles have been suggested as the turning point of the Second World War. The earliest possible moment of decision is perhaps the Battle of Britain in 1940, which ended – at least temporarily – any prospect of Germany being able to knock Britain out of the war before turning east against the Soviet Union. The next is the Battle of Moscow at the end of 1941, though this is perhaps more controversial. Undoubtedly, the Wehrmacht came close to capturing the Soviet capital, but it is questionable whether, after the casualties it had suffered in the long drive from the frontier, it still had the strength to hold onto the city after completing its capture. Perhaps the best summary would be that the defeat of the Germans before Moscow ended any remaining prospect of a swift victory over the Soviet Union and thence a rapid realisation of all the dreams of new territories for exploitation.

By the summer of 1942, it seemed as if the Wehrmacht had recovered its strength and was once more unstoppable. Although much of the Eastern Front settled down to positional warfare, heavy fighting continued at several key locations. In the north, the Red Army repeatedly attempted to break the ring of encirclement around Leningrad; in the centre, repeated Soviet attacks on the Rzhev Salient to the west of Moscow led to huge casualties, particularly for the Red Army, with little gain; and in the south, Hitler's armies defeated the last of the Soviet counteroffensives that had continued through the winter and spring and pushed east, securing the remaining parts of the Ukraine and reaching the Volga at Stalingrad. At the same time, large formations pushed into the Caucasus, seemingly poised to secure the vital oilfields that had long been a priority for the German invasion forces.

The German defeats of the winter seemed like a fading dream, but the reality was that they had left their scars. Most infantry formations of the Wehrmacht did not recover their numerical strength after the losses of 1941, and the quality of the replacement drafts was far from the highly trained and battle-hardened troops who had entered the Soviet Union in June 1941. For the panzer divisions, the situation was in some respects worse. In order to give the armies unleashed in the drive to Stalingrad and the Caucasus any chance of success, panzer divisions elsewhere on the Eastern Front were required to reduce their strength, often to as little as a single battalion of tanks. Newer tanks were being built in Germany – the latest version of the Pz.III, *Ausführung L* ('Version L'), had started to appear in late 1941 and its improved armour and particularly its long-barrelled 50mm gun were greatly welcomed by tank crews who were increasingly coming up against the Soviet T-34s, against which earlier German tank guns were relatively ineffective. But even this 50mm gun could only penetrate the armour of its opponents at ranges of significantly less than 1,000m. Further variants of the Pz.III were produced through 1942, but the size of the chassis prevented the use of a larger gun and it became increasingly clear that the combat value of this workhorse of the Wehrmacht was approaching its end. In early 1943, the commander of 6th Panzer Division's panzer regiment wrote in a report:

> The Pz.III is in no way suited to the requirements of fighting in the east. Its armour is too thin, and the calibre of its gun is inadequate. By contrast, the assault guns have provided outstanding service in the fighting on the steppe, even though they do not have a rotating turret and must face the enemy to aim. The reason for [their good performance] is their substantially stronger armour and their large guns.[1]

By this stage of the war, production of Pz.III tanks had almost ceased, with its chassis being used to produce increasing numbers of *Sturmgeschütz III* assault guns; by dispensing with a turret and mounting the gun on a fixed superstructure with only limited lateral traverse, it was possible to increase both the thickness of the armour and the calibre of the gun, giving the 'F' variant of the vehicle, equipped with a long-barrelled 75mm gun, the ability to engage Soviet tanks at long range with every chance of success.

Whilst the Pz.III formed the backbone of the panzer divisions in 1942, there were also increasing numbers of the slightly larger Pz.IV. Despite Hitler's instructions for later versions to be armed with a long-barrelled 75mm gun, many of the Pz.IVs in service in 1942 still had short-barrelled 75mm guns, which were very effective at short range but of little value outside built-up areas. As the year continued, increasing numbers of later versions of the 'F' variant and its successor, the 'G' variant, began to appear in the 'heavy companies' of panzer battalions. Whilst the armour and armament of these tanks was comparable with the Soviet T-34s, the better radios and optical sights of the German tanks ensured that, vehicle for vehicle, the long-barrelled Pz.IV was more than a match for its Soviet opponents.

The new equipment was a major improvement on the large fleet of Pz.II and Pz.35(T) vehicles with which much of the panzer force was equipped in 1941, but the numbers produced fell far short of what was needed both to replace the losses that had been suffered and to allow for further expansion. Despite this, 1942 saw several new panzer divisions created; some, like the rearmed SS divisions, were lavishly equipped and armed, at the expense of experienced Wehrmacht units. Three new panzer divisions – 25th, 26th and 27th – were created in the Wehrmacht and struggled to get sufficient equipment to reach establishment strength. The official 'establishment strength' of panzer divisions was changed in 1942 in an attempt to improve the flexibility of the formations and to recognise the realities of what could be supplied, with each division now consisting of a panzer regiment of two panzer battalions, supported by two motorised infantry regiments each with two battalions, an artillery regiment, and anti-tank, anti-aircraft, reconnaissance and combat engineer units. During 1942, the motorised infantry regiments were renamed panzergrenadiers, but in most divisions only a single regiment – in many cases, just one battalion of one regiment – was mounted in armoured half-tracks. The rest of the infantry relied on trucks for transport, limiting their mobility. It became common practice for panzer divisions to organise the bulk of their panzer regiments, their half-track-mounted infantry, and those elements of their anti-tank and artillery formations that had armoured vehicles into a primary or armoured battlegroup; the rest of the division was then used to support this primary group.

Regardless of the quality of the new tanks being produced in 1942, the soldiers of the Wehrmacht complained constantly that their equipment wasn't sufficiently numerous, and was taking too long to develop. Whilst such complaints are found in the annals of almost every army in history, there was considerable justification in the case of Germany. Design, development and production of weaponry was badly organised and productivity was poor compared to the war industries of countries like Britain, not least because of the factional infighting within the Nazi hierarchy. On 8 February 1942, armaments minister Fritz Todt was flying aboard a military plane after his personal aircraft had been grounded by mechanical problems, and was killed when the plane exploded near the airport in Königsberg shortly after take-off. The local Luftwaffe command eventually investigated the circumstances of the crash, and its report included a description of what happened:

> [A short distance] from the airport and the end of the runway the pilot apparently throttled down, then opened the throttle again two or three seconds later. At that moment a long flame shot up vertically from the front of the plane, apparently caused by an explosion. The aircraft fell at once from an altitude of approximately 20m … It caught fire at once and a series of explosions demolished it.[2]

Whilst the military plane – a converted Heinkel bomber – was likely to have been carrying demolition charges to be used in the event of crashing in enemy territory, the manner in which it apparently exploded was never determined, but the Luftwaffe enquiry concluded nevertheless that sabotage could be ruled out, and therefore no further investigation into the cause was necessary. It is possible to speculate that the crash was not accidental; the German setbacks in the Soviet Union during the winter of 1941–42 had a profound impression on Todt, leaving him convinced that Germany could not win the war. Perhaps fearing for his life, Todt had very recently placed a substantial sum of money in his personal safe, marked as a gift for his personal secretary in the event of anything happening to him. Regardless of the cause of the crash, Göring appeared at Hitler's headquarters in Rastenburg very shortly after it, the timings suggesting that he must have left his hunting lodge in East Prussia as soon as the crash was announced in the early morning. As minister with responsibility for the Reich's Four Year Plan, Göring suggested to Hitler that he should take over armaments production too, but was dismayed to discover that Hitler had already given the role to the 36-year-old architect Albert Speer, who was staying in Rastenburg having chosen not to travel with Todt that day.[3] Speer had no knowledge whatever of industrial production, but used his experience of managing large-scale building projects to address many of the organisational problems that constrained armaments production. Wider standardisation, the increasing use of production lines rather than teams of craftsmen who would see to the complete assembly of an item from start to finish, and a more rational system for ensuring longer production runs led to dramatic improvements in armaments production. In just six months his efforts led to a 25 per cent increase in the production of tanks, a 27 per cent increase in the production of guns, and a remarkable 98 per cent increase in the production of munitions.[4] With little regard for Nazi racial ideology, Speer deliberately copied the principles laid down by Walther Rathenau, a Jewish industrialist who, as head of the German war ministry's *Kriegsrohstoffabteilung* ('War Raw Materials Department' or *KRA*), had outlined similar changes to existing practices in order to improve the productivity of German war industry during the First World War.

The Red Army also spent much of 1942 replacing out-of-date equipment and altering the structure of its armoured forces. The light T-60, manned by a crew of two, was originally developed in the late 1930s to replace several obsolete vehicles and was equipped with just a 12.7mm machine-gun. By the time it entered production, this had been upgraded to a 20mm gun, but whilst this was adequate to deal with the German Pz.II and Pz.35(T), it was too small to threaten the better-protected Pz.III and Pz.IV. The tank's armour was also too thin, and although this was increased in 1942 the additional weight made the tank slow and less capable on soft ground. Upgrading the gun to a larger weapon proved impossible due to the small size of the turret, and despite being produced in large numbers, the tank proved to be of very little combat value. Amongst soldiers in the Red Army, it became known as *Bratskaya Mogila na Dovoikh* – 'a grave for two brothers'.[5]

By 1942, the unpopular T-60 was scheduled for replacement by the T-70. It went into production in March 1942 with an odd arrangement of two engines, one for each track. Its 45mm gun was a definite improvement on the poor armament of its predecessors, but the usefulness of the tank was severely restricted by the one-man turret – the occupant of the turret could attempt to command the tank and coordinate with other units, or he could operate the gun, but simply didn't have time to perform both roles. By the end of the year, it was clear that light tanks of this sort were of very limited value, and they were increasingly replaced by T-34s or armoured cars.

The famous T-34, probably the best tank of the war, had been available to the Red Army at the start of the conflict but in very limited numbers, and many of these were crippled due to the shortage of spare parts. It was born from a project in the late 1930s to replace the Red Army's fleet of light cavalry tanks and slower infantry support tanks with a single vehicle. All tanks are ultimately a compromise between three factors – mobility, armour and firepower – and the T-34 outclassed its early contemporaries in all three. Its 76mm gun could deal with any tank even at long range, and its wide tracks and powerful diesel engine gave it excellent cross-country performance. Whilst the thickness of its armour – 45mm – was modest by the standards of tanks from the later years of the war, it was at least as thick as any other tank in service in 1941, and the innovative use of sloping armour effectively increased the thickness, making it very difficult for German tanks and anti-tank guns to engage it effectively. In one action in 1941, the crew of a 37mm anti-tank gun reported that they fired 23 rounds at a single T-34, hitting it repeatedly and succeeding only in jamming its turret ring with a round that became lodged between the turret and the hull.[6] Production of the T-34 was badly affected during 1941 as tank factories were moved from threatened areas to the Urals; the combined facility created in Chelyabinsk by factory machinery from both Kharkov and Leningrad became known as 'Tankograd', and once it started operating at full capacity, it became one of the most productive armaments factories anywhere in the world during the Second World War. Only the tractor factory in Stalingrad continued to produce T-34s until the evacuated factories resumed production. Like all Soviet tanks, the efficacy of the T-34 was limited in the first year of the conflict with Germany due to radio shortages, but by mid-1942 this had been remedied, and further improvements included the addition of handles on the exterior of the tank that could be used by 'tank rider' infantry.

There were further problems with the T-34 that reduced its effectiveness. It was prone to mechanical breakdowns, with poor quality track pins being particularly likely to break under modest strain. The original turret design was also poor, accommodating only two men and thus leading to a poor firing rate compared to German tanks. The optical equipment of the tank was inferior to German equipment, but the main problem for Soviet armoured units remained poor training and operational use, and as 1942 unfolded, both of these factors came under increasing scrutiny. The heavy tanks of the Red Army – the KV-1 and KV-2 – also had problems. They were almost immune to German anti-tank weaponry in the early stages of the war, but like the T-34 they were limited in their efficacy by too few radios and in many cases by poor design; the gearbox of the KV tanks was notoriously difficult for drivers to use effectively, with many keeping a hammer handy in order to be able to free the gear lever, which would often become stuck.

After the mayhem and chaos of the German invasion in 1941, improving tank production and the appearance of increasing numbers of troops allowed the Red Army to create its first tank armies, consisting of three tank corps and sometimes a separate tank brigade, one or two rifle divisions, and various support formations. The motorisation of the infantry and support elements was poor and the tank armies were often used in a front-line role, holding a section of front line alongside regular armies. As a result, they were often badly degraded in fighting before they found themselves in a position to exploit enemy weakness, and any rapid advance by the tank elements rapidly outstripped the supporting infantry and artillery units. The tank corps, with a paper establishment of 100 tanks, was perhaps the equivalent of a weak panzer division in firepower, though most panzer divisions were capable of outfighting a Red Army tank corps in 1942 due to better training, better operational and tactical skill, better gunsights, and the advantages of coordination that came from all tanks being equipped with radios.

There were several important differences between the Wehrmacht and the Red Army in the manner in which they evolved, one of the most important being that the latter proved better at analysing its performance and improving upon it. A policy of such analysis originated in the First World War, where it worked in an imperfect manner, often merely reinforcing the existing point of view of senior army officers; for example, after the disastrous Russian attacks on the German lines at Lake Naroch in the spring of 1916, the official investigation somewhat predictably concluded that far more artillery ammunition would be required for future attacks, an obsession that had persisted since the opening battles of the war.[7] More recently, the poor performance of the Red Army during the 1939 fighting against Finland led to a rather more measured report, and many of its recommendations were still being implemented when war with Germany broke out in 1941. The fighting of the first few months was again the subject of detailed study; Alexander Mikhailovich Vasilevsky, chief of staff at *Stavka* (the Red Army's high command), described the conclusions that were drawn from the battles that stopped the Wehrmacht outside Moscow:

> A number of big shortcomings in troop control and military action came to the fore during the counteroffensive around Moscow ... True, a deep carpet of snow hampered the advance, but the main factor was the lack of tanks, aircraft and ammunition where they were most needed. Formations, units and elements assumed a two-line battle order and attacked after a brief, insufficiently strong artillery bombardment; the artillery cover of the attacking infantry and tanks deep in the enemy defences was not efficient enough and sometimes was not employed at all. The tank units were usually employed as direct support for the infantry and rarely received independent missions. Gradually, however, the Soviet troops gained experience and began to act more successfully.[8]

Similarly, when the new tank armies first went into action against the German forces advancing on the Don and Volga in 1942, their performance left much to be desired and this was considered at every level, from the manner in which tanks were deployed on the battlefield, through the equipment that was used, and the operational doctrine that had been followed. Pavel Alexeyevich Rotmistrov, who held the rank of colonel at the time and was chief of staff of a mechanised corps, submitted his personal findings:

> The difficulty is that while there isn't much difference in speed between the light (T-60) tank and the medium (T-34) tank on the roads, when moving across country the light tanks are quickly left behind. The heavy (KV) tank is already behind and often crushes bridges, which cuts off units behind it. Under battlefield conditions, this has meant that too often the T-34 alone arrived; the light tanks had difficulty fighting the German tanks anyway, and the KVs were delayed in the rear. It was also difficult to command these companies because occasionally they were equipped with different types of radios or none at all.[9]

The Red Army then attempted to learn from the conclusions of the reports. Lieutenant General Iakov Nikolayevich Fedorenko, deputy defence minister and head of the tank and mechanised troops directorate, was instrumental in far-reaching changes that transformed the Soviet tank forces. The Red Army was constantly reminded of the skilful manner that German units cooperated effectively in combat, allowing them to outmanoeuvre superior forces; training of Soviet tank crews was altered to try to emulate this, and to improve coordination with accompanying infantry, artillery and anti-tank teams. This in turn required all tanks to be equipped with radios, and the slow KV-1 tanks were removed from the establishment of tank brigades. Instead, the new brigades fielded a larger number of T-34s and T-70s, increasing the strength of the tank corps to 180 tanks, allowing it to engage a panzer division with rough parity. Increases in artillery were also initiated, though the plans ran ahead of production and most units fielded fewer guns than intended. Nevertheless, the fighting power of Soviet armoured forces improved steadily through the year. By contrast, the heavy hand of Hitler at the head of the German hierarchy resulted in little or no attempt to learn from setbacks; instead, Hitler simply blamed the officers involved, increasingly replacing them with men that he regarded as more likely to obey his instructions to the letter. The highly flexible doctrine of *Auftragstaktik* – 'mission-based' tactics that allowed subordinates considerable freedom to improvise in order to achieve the objectives of their superiors – became increasingly restricted in a stifling environment in which Hitler would query the redeployment of individual divisions and even smaller units.

While the Red Army continued to refine the composition and use of its armoured forces in 1942, the Wehrmacht drove on across eastern Ukraine to reach the Don along much of its length before crossing the river in two directions. One powerful force, consisting of Sixth Army and Fourth Panzer Army, marched on Stalingrad on the lower Volga; another, primarily formed from First Panzer Army, burst over the lower Don and advanced towards the Caucasus. Instead of making determined but ultimately doomed attempts to stop the German advance, Soviet commanders pulled back and tried to keep their forces intact; Hitler and others interpreted the comparative lack of prisoners as a sign that the Red Army was effectively at the end of its strength, and succumbed to strategic greed. The long, exposed flank that was created along the middle Don was left largely in the hands of Germany's allies – the Hungarians, Italians and Romanians, who had little armoured support and few anti-tank guns – while German resources were concentrated on the two thrusts across the Don. Even assigning the Don flank to allied armies did not release sufficient resources for the Germans to carry out both advances as Soviet resistance began to stiffen. Increasingly, Hitler's obsession with capturing Stalingrad resulted in fuel, ammunition and air support being directed towards the ruined city on the Volga, leaving Kleist's First Panzer Army spread out across the Caucasus; although the city of Maikop fell to the Germans, Göring's plans for rapid exploitation of its oil assets failed in the face of demolitions carried out by the retreating Red Army.

After further adjustments in the organisation of its tank armies, *Stavka* unleashed a series of attacks in September 1942, intended to break through the German lines immediately north of Stalingrad in order to bring succour to the hard-pressed troops of General Vasily Ivanovich Chuikov's Sixty-Second Army in Stalingrad. The attacks failed, though the German defenders were hard-pressed on many occasions. Veteran Wehrmacht officers were shocked to see the manner in which new drafts of reinforcements from Germany wilted and suffered catastrophic casualties before they could learn the tough art of survival on the Eastern Front, and as the repeated German attempts to destroy the last strongholds of the Soviet Sixty-Second Army failed to achieve their objectives, many senior officers questioned the wisdom of leaving so many troops on the Volga with their flanks exposed.[10] Almost all of those senior officers were sacked and replaced by Hitler. Meanwhile, the Red Army continued to analyse its setbacks and the failure of the armoured forces to break through the German defences. One of the formations that had been thrown into the fight was VII Tank Corps, which suffered heavy losses from Luftwaffe attacks – it went into action without the support of an organised anti-aircraft regiment, as Rotmistrov, who was now commanding the tank corps, later recalled:

We suffered heavy losses, particularly of T-60 and T-70 tanks, which had light armour. We estimated that during just a single day, the enemy air force carried out up to 2,000 sorties against us using the full force of its *Luftflotte IV*. Moreover, well aware of what the Soviet forces were attempting, the German fascist command withdrew some of its armoured and motorised formations from Stalingrad and threw them at us. The Germans dug in their tanks and assault guns on most of the high ground, organised formidable strongpoints, and made lavish use of anti-tank guns.

In extremely fierce battles over the next seven days, particularly at the Kotluban state farm, parts of our corps advanced a mere 4km [2.4 miles], but this ground was gained only through major sacrifices. We lost 156 of the 191 tanks with which we started combat operations near Stalingrad.[11]

The enquiry that followed found several reasons for the failure of Rotmistrov's forces. The distance they had to cover was substantially greater than had been anticipated, and Rotmistrov was heavily criticised for failing to show better leadership. Just how much difference he could have made, given the poor armour of his light tanks and the lack of protection against German air attack, or indeed how he might have handled matters differently, was never made clear, and no disciplinary action was taken against Rotmistrov.

The Red Army's counterattacks in the Battle of Moscow in late 1941 ended any hope of a swift German victory over the Soviet Union; the counteroffensive that encircled the German Sixth Army in Stalingrad in November 1942 effectively ended any hope of victory in either the short or long term. The manner in which the Red Army burst through the flanks of the German defences, deliberately targeting the sectors held by weak Romanian units and staggering the timing of the attacks to maximise confusion, became recurrent themes in the fighting that followed as the entire German position in the southern sector of the Eastern Front collapsed. Within a few short weeks, the situation changed entirely: from apparently being on the verge of completing its capture of Stalingrad, the Wehrmacht found itself facing the real threat of complete destruction.

Just as Hitler had become convinced in mid-1942 that the hard work of defeating the Red Army had been accomplished and all that remained was to exploit victory, Stalin and *Stavka* became over-optimistic about what they could achieve. There were several objectives apparently within reach, which would leave the German position untenable: the capture of the Don crossings at Rostov would isolate the German forces in the Caucasus, as would a thrust to the Sea of Azov; and a thrust to the crossings over the lower Dnepr might result in the envelopment of all the German forces that were struggling to restore the situation in the eastern Ukraine. With so many German formations trapped in Stalingrad and the relief effort that was mounted by Fourth Panzer Army defeated, and with the Romanian, Italian and Hungarian troops that were deployed along the Don flank apparently unable to halt determined Soviet attacks, it seemed as if it was only a matter of time before the decisive collapse of the German lines occurred. Had the Red Army concentrated on just one objective, it might well have succeeded at least in compounding the destruction of the German Sixth Army in Stalingrad with another major encirclement further to the west, but the simultaneous pursuit of multiple objectives with formations that were increasingly worn down by the high tempo of operations gave the Wehrmacht a slender window of opportunity to recover the situation. Aided greatly by the arrival of fresh troops from other sectors of the Eastern Front and particularly from garrison duties in Western Europe, Field Marshal Erich von Manstein, commander of the German Army Group Don, fought a campaign of great skill and masterful timing to smash the Soviet armoured groups that were approaching the Sea of Azov and the Dnepr. As the spring thaw of 1943 turned the landscape into a sea of mud and enforced a much-needed halt in operations, the two sides were almost back to the lines they had held a year before. In terms of territory, the Red Army had only a large bulge around Kursk to show for their efforts, but the tide had turned against Germany. The destruction of such large German forces in Stalingrad, followed shortly after by the surrender of similar numbers of men in North Africa, left the Wehrmacht badly weakened, whereas the Red Army – despite losing more men in the winter fighting than the Wehrmacht – was full of confidence and better armed than ever before. It might have failed to strike a mortal blow during the winter fighting, but nonetheless it could look forward to the summer campaign with confidence.

As the battles in the Ukraine subsided in the spring of 1943, Manstein's victories lifted the gloom and pessimism that had been hanging over Hitler and the entire German high command ever since the encirclement of Sixth Army at Stalingrad. Thoughts turned to the next phase of fighting, and immediately clear differences arose between Hitler and his entourage and the men in the front line. For Manstein and his subordinates, it seemed almost inconceivable that there could be any consideration of a new strategic offensive; the best that could be expected was a series of operational successes that would wear down the Red Army and force Stalin to discuss peace terms. Whilst such a viewpoint may have been justified from a purely military perspective, it highlights the lack of political awareness of the German military. In their meeting in Casablanca in January

1943, the major powers allied against Nazi Germany issued a declaration that they would continue the war until the unconditional defeat of Germany. It seems that President Franklin D. Roosevelt was the most enthusiastic proponent for this declaration, believing that it would make it almost impossible for Stalin to consider the sort of peace that Manstein and other German senior military figures believed might be achieved. In a clarification on the declaration, Roosevelt stated:

> We mean no harm to the common people of the Axis nations. But we do mean to impose punishment and retribution upon their guilty, barbaric leaders.[12]

This statement gave a clue to a possible way out for Germany: the intention of the Allies was to defeat and punish Germany's leadership. Allen Dulles, who was head of the Office of Strategic Studies (OSS, the wartime predecessor of the CIA), had no doubt that had Germany actually sued for peace, the Casablanca Declaration would not have been an insurmountable barrier:

> [It was] merely a piece of paper to be scrapped without further ado if Germany would sue for peace. Hitler had to go.[13]

If the German military had been prepared to unseat Hitler, it might have been possible to negotiate some form of peace with the Allied Powers, even without first grinding down the Red Army in a series of strategically defensive battles as Manstein proposed; but the unwillingness of the army's leadership to break the oath of loyalty that they had given to Hitler made such considerations irrelevant.

In the spring of 1943, Manstein and his staff at Army Group South made a careful assessment of the capabilities of both friendly and enemy forces, together with the likely intentions of the enemy. Despite the defeats inflicted upon the Red Army that resulted in the swift recapture of Kharkov and the restoration of a defensive line along the valley of the Donets, the fundamental weakness of the German position in the Ukraine was unaltered. Due to the manner in which the front line ran from the Sea of Azov roughly towards the north-west, there was a constant threat of a Soviet drive to the lower Dnepr or the Sea of Azov, and Manstein had little doubt that further Soviet attacks would follow in the summer:

> The bulge in the German front, which ran down the Donets and Mius from a point below Kharkov, embracing the valuable coal-mining and industrial region south of that city, was just begging to be sliced off. Should the enemy succeed in

breaking through around Kharkov or even across the Middle Donets, he could still achieve his aim of the previous winter and destroy the German southern wing on the Black Sea coast ... By the same stroke he would regain possession of the precious Donets area and the granaries of the Ukraine, in addition to opening the way to the Balkans and Romanian oilfields ... In no other sector of the Eastern Front was the Soviet Union offered such immense opportunities in the military, economic or political fields.[14]

In light of this likelihood, Manstein suggested that there were two options for the Wehrmacht. The first was to wait for the Red Army to launch attacks, which would progress broadly towards the southwest and the lower Dnepr; German forces would concede ground, with mobile formations held in reserve behind the Dnepr and then unleashed in a counterattack into the flank and rear of the Soviet forces in what became known as the 'backhand blow'. The alternative was to seize the initiative and strike the Red Army before it could launch its offensive, an option labelled 'the forehand blow'. Manstein and his staff preferred the first option, which they had already described as early as February 1943, but this would necessitate the abandonment – albeit temporary – of the entire Ukraine east of the Dnepr. Hitler objected to the plan on precisely these terms, stressing repeatedly the value of the resources of the Ukraine and the impact that their loss, even for a short time, might have on Turkey and Romania. The value of Ukrainian sources was almost certainly overstated, as the grain harvest was far lower than in previous years and little or no attempt had been made to restore captured industrial areas, and political considerations about a temporary withdrawal behind the Dnepr had to be offset against the positive impact of a successful backhand counter-blow. However, there was the possibility that Manstein's plan might misfire, and the Red Army might succeed not only in reaching the Dnepr, but then defeating the German counterattack. In any event, as Manstein later reflected, Hitler was increasingly inflexible on the matter of conceding territory. Whenever the issue was raised, he would point out that the generals had wanted to pull back in front of Moscow, but Hitler had insisted on standing firm, a decision that probably saved the Wehrmacht from being scattered and destroyed. Whilst such a policy was probably correct in late 1941, its blanket application to all other circumstances left no room for flexibility.

With the 'backhand blow' turned down by Hitler, Manstein had no choice but to consider the 'forehand' option, i.e. a German pre-emptive attack. The obvious target was the large salient that the Red Army had captured around Kursk, from where they could attack into the flanks of either Army Group South or Army Group Centre. If the Wehrmacht attacked before the Red Army had recovered from its mauling in early 1943, it might be possible to cut off the salient and destroy the substantial Soviet forces that it contained. In order to deny the Red Army sufficient time to rebuild its armoured forces, the offensive – codenamed *Zitadelle* ('Citadel') – would be launched by Army Group South and Army Group Centre in early May, as soon as the terrain was dry and firm enough to support the deployment of large numbers of tanks.

Albert Speer's reorganisation of Germany's war industry was beginning to bear fruit, with increasing numbers of tanks and guns being manufactured. Furthermore, new types of armoured vehicles were beginning to arrive. During 1942, the first of these – the Pz.VI or Tiger tank – had been rushed into service, and despite numerous teething problems and an inauspicious debut when it was used on unsuitable boggy terrain near Leningrad, it proved itself during the winter fighting as Manstein struggled to recover from the disaster at Stalingrad. Its armour was almost impervious to most Soviet guns and its lethal 88mm gun could kill enemy tanks at long range. However, it was expensive to produce and would only be available in modest numbers; instead of being used to equip panzer divisions, it was deployed in *Schwere Panzer Abteilungen* ('heavy tank battalions'), though the SS divisions were given Tiger tanks for their heavy tank companies, and the *Grossdeutschland* division of the Wehrmacht had its own integral Tiger formation. The Tiger wasn't the only vehicle entering service armed with a powerful 88mm gun; in addition, a longer-barrelled gun was mounted on a different turretless chassis to create a heavyweight *Sturmgeschütz*; weighing 65 tons, it was nearly three times the weight of the highly successful *Sturmgeschütz III*, and Hitler ordered that 90 of the new monsters – known either as 'Ferdinands' in honour of their designer, Ferdinand Porsche, or 'Elefants' – should be deployed in time for the coming offensive against Kursk. Whilst the Ferdinands boasted massive armour that made them immune to enemy guns and had a lethal gun, they had a critical design flaw: as originally built, they had no secondary armament of machine-guns. If they became isolated from their own infantry support, they would be very vulnerable to attack by enemy infantry. Their bulk also limited their usefulness, especially in the Ukraine where most smaller bridges would be unable to bear their weight.

The third vehicle entering service in the Wehrmacht at this time was the Pz.V, or Panther tank. This had been designed specifically as a response to the Soviet T-34 and featured sloping armour and a powerful long-barrelled 75mm gun. The final design was selected as early as May 1942, but for a variety of reasons it was not possible to commence large-scale production until the end of the year.

A small number of Panthers reached front-line units and training establishments in February, and it became clear that the new vehicle had many teething issues. In particular, its engine and transmission were prone to breakdowns. The carburettor and fuel pump had a worrying tendency to develop leaks, resulting in several tanks bursting into flames while being driven, and although repeated attempts were made to fix this issue, Panther crews complained about the smell of gasoline to the very end of the war.

Hitler had hoped that significant numbers of all three new combat vehicles would be available for the onset of *Zitadelle* and that they would make a decisive difference in the battle. Slow production and other delays resulted in only a trickle of Panthers reaching the front line, where they were used to equip two independent tank battalions in readiness for the new offensive. Crew and driver training was inadequate, and at one point the entire fleet of Panthers had to be recalled for remedial work.[15] The consequence was that as the planned start date for *Zitadelle* approached, the number of new tanks in the front line was disappointingly low. There was also growing evidence of Soviet defensive preparations in the Kursk salient, and General Walther Model, whose Ninth Army would deliver the northern thrust into the salient, met Hitler on 27 April to express his reservations about the prospects for success.[16] He suggested that the longer the preparation phase continued, the lower the likelihood of success, and Manstein repeated his suggestion of a 'backhand blow' that would have the benefit of being fought in open ground rather than across terrain that the Red Army was carefully fortifying. Instead, Hitler postponed the operation to allow for more tanks to be delivered to the front line. This delay of course also meant that the Red Army would benefit from the delivery of new tanks – and given that Soviet tank production far outstripped German production, further delay would harm the chances of success in *Zitadelle* rather than improve them. Additional delays followed, and despite calls from almost everyone – the officers of both army groups, the senior officers around Hitler, and industrialists like Speer – for the operation to be abandoned entirely, it commenced on 5 July.

Model and Manstein were right to be concerned that delay would be of greater benefit to the Red Army than to the Wehrmacht. In addition to enjoying far better tank production and not having to deal with troubleshooting new equipment, the Red Army's formations rapidly regained their fighting strength. Even if Manstein had been allowed to commence *Zitadelle* immediately after the spring thaw, it is likely that it would have failed in the face of strengthened Soviet formations. The constant analysis of both successes and failures continued, though not always with complete accuracy. The over-optimism with which

Stavka urged its armies forward in pursuit of the apparently beaten Wehrmacht in January and February 1942 was blamed largely on reports from front-line officers, even though many of them had repeatedly highlighted the problems caused by such a high tempo of operations. Much of the blame was placed at the door of General Nikolai Fyodorovich Vatutin, who commanded Southwest Front during the winter campaign. Sergei Matveyevich Shtemenko, who was appointed head of the *Stavka* Operations Directorate in the weeks before the beginning of *Zitadelle*, later wrote about the winter fighting:

> The command of Southwest Front knew that it might run into strong enemy reserves, and even warned its subordinate staffs about this, but it put its own interpretation on the latest information about increasing enemy resistance ... The command of the front explained all this away with its favourite argument about the headlong retreat of the Nazi forces ...
>
> To this day it remains a riddle how Vatutin, who certainly had considerable powers of circumspection and always paid due attention to reconnaissance, should on this occasion have been so long in appreciating the danger that had arisen in the path of his front. The only explanation seems to have been his utter conviction that the enemy was no longer capable of marshalling his forces for decisive battle.[17]

Marshal Alexander Mikhailovich Vasilevsky, the chief of the Soviet General Staff, broadly agreed with this assessment, though accepted that over-optimism influenced decisions at every level:

> The commanders of Southwest and Voronezh Fronts incorrectly assessed the strategic situation that had taken shape by mid-February ... They looked upon the regrouping of enemy forces that had begun on about 10 February ... as the beginning of an enemy withdrawal of his Donbas grouping beyond the Dnepr. Basing himself on this wrong evaluation, Vatutin ... asked permission of *Stavka* to use all the forces of his front to make a sudden offensive so as to destroy the enemy completely between the Donets and the Dnepr and to reach the latter before the spring thaw set in.
>
> ... On 17 February, after the liberation of Kharkov, Stalin personally informed Vatutin by telephone that the new plan of operation ... had been confirmed ... Thus both *Stavka* and the General Staff had made the same mistake as the commanders of Southwest and Voronezh Fronts: they did not expect the enemy offensive operations because they thought him already beaten.[18]

General Filipp Ivanovich Golikov, commander of Voronezh Front, was dismissed, though unlike failed German generals he was not left to languish in disgrace; instead, Stalin appointed him deputy defence minister. Vatutin was moved from Southwest Front to replace Golikov at Voronezh Front – it seems that his energy and enthusiasm for offensive operations had caught Stalin's eye and protected him from any fallout. It is also possible that despite his criticism of Vatutin, Stalin knew that almost everyone in the Soviet chain of command had become over-optimistic.

Despite the setbacks in March 1943, the Red Army had good reason to look forward with greater confidence than its opponent, fielding more men, tanks, guns and planes than ever before. Nor had Manstein's counteroffensive had any lasting effect on morale; confidence remained high that the Germans could be driven out of Soviet territory. Consideration now moved to how best to achieve this. Whilst it was possible for the Red Army to prepare for another offensive operation to commence immediately after the spring thaw, Vasilevsky and other senior figures soon became aware of German plans for the attack on Kursk. This information came from a variety of sources: reconnaissance; partisan reports; deserters; and the 'Lucy' spy network, which was run by Rudolf Rössler, a German who had fled to Switzerland when Hitler came to power and who became a conduit for information from anti-Hitler plotters in the upper echelons of the German military. As early as the end of March, Stalin was aware of the German plans for an attack and he and the ever-aggressive Vatutin considered a pre-emptive attack.[19] Others were more cautious, and on 8 April Marshal Georgi Konstantinovich Zhukov, the deputy supreme commander, submitted a memorandum to Stalin after discussing matters with Vasilevsky, in which he concluded:

> I consider it inexpedient for our troops to take the offensive in the coming days with the aim of pre-empting the enemy. It will be better if we exhaust the enemy on our defenses, destroying his tanks and then, by introducing fresh reserves and transitioning to a general offensive we will finally achieve the destruction of the enemy's main grouping.[20]

Stalin remained doubtful that the Red Army would be able to stop a powerful attack by the concentrated firepower of the Wehrmacht, backed by the panzer formations of the SS, but his generals persuaded him that the policy proposed by Zhukov and Vasilevsky offered a greater likelihood of success than a pre-emptive strike, not least because the latter option had a high likelihood of creating the sort of fluid situation in which the Germans had repeatedly excelled. The troops defending the Kursk salient therefore began the construction of defences in greater depth and density than ever before. Even if Army Groups Centre and South managed to batter their way through the opposing Soviet forces over some 80 miles (133km) of fortifications, they would then face a further defensive line across the base of the salient manned by Steppe Front with a similar depth.[21]

Most of the defence of the Kursk Salient would be the task of the conventional armies, with the tank armies held in reserve both to launch counterattacks against German tank concentrations and to be ready for Zhukov's transition to offensive operations. Learning from the experiences of the winter fighting, tank armies underwent further reform. A decree had already been issued at the end of January 1943, and with minor modifications this formed the basis for the future structure of tank armies, which would henceforth consist of two tank corps and a mechanised infantry corps. They would also have a motorcycle regiment, an anti-aircraft artillery battalion, an anti-tank artillery regiment, a regiment of howitzers, another of rocket launchers, and extensive support units. These would include two tank recovery and repair battalions, to try to ensure that the large numbers of tanks that broke down or suffered battle damage short of complete destruction could be restored to action as fast as possible. Each tank corps would have three tank brigades and a motorised infantry brigade with supporting artillery, signals and combat engineer units, with a total strength of 168 tanks and 56 artillery pieces, including those for engaging tanks and aircraft. By comparison, a panzer division – if at full strength – would have 200 tanks and over 180 artillery pieces of all descriptions.[22] However, the additional support provided to each tank corps by the other elements of the tank army would ensure that the two formations were likely to engage on the battlefield in terms of near parity numerically.

Whilst the fighting in the two winters of the war on the Eastern Front – 1941–42 outside Moscow, and 1942–43 in Stalingrad and the eastern Ukraine – brought an end to any real possibility of Germany defeating the Soviet Union, the Battle of Kursk in July 1943 effectively extinguished any prospect of the Wehrmacht being able to grind down the Red Army and force a negotiated peace through exhaustion. The delays in starting the offensive eliminated all the reasons that Manstein had used in suggesting the operation in the first place – any element of surprise disappeared, and instead of being able to force the Soviet armoured forces, still recovering from their mauling in the winter, into a battle in which they would suffer further losses, the German panzer divisions that had been rebuilt and rearmed so painstakingly found themselves opposing a force that was also rearmed and ready for battle.

On 5 July, the northern part of the German offensive, mounted by Model from Army Group Centre, battered its way into the Soviet defences using its infantry with support from assault guns and *Schwere Panzer Abteilung 505*, equipped with 45 Tiger tanks; the panzer divisions were to be held in reserve until a breakthrough had been achieved. When a potential weakness in the Russian defences was detected, the Tigers were regrouped and sent forward to force a breach and ran into a counterattack by about 90 T-34s. In the fighting that followed, the heavy German tanks lived up to expectations, knocking out about half the Soviet tanks for the loss of just seven Tigers. Of these, five were merely disabled and would be able to return to combat quickly.[23] Nevertheless, the tank engagement bought sufficient time for the Red Army to deploy further reserves to cover the German advance. Model's forces were also supported by 45 Ferdinands, but by the end of the day almost all of these had been disabled when they ran into minefields. Repair of the Ferdinands was complicated by the fact that the vehicles were far heavier than the towing capacity of the vehicles used by German engineer units, delaying their speedy return to service.[24]

The following day the Red Army counterattacked, but its attempt was poorly coordinated and the Germans were able to beat off the attackers with comparative ease. However, their attempts to penetrate deeper into the Soviet defences foundered in bitter fighting in and around the towns of Olkhovatka and Ponyri. For three days the opposing sides engaged in attacks and counterattacks, suffering heavy losses for no significant gain, and when they met on 9 July Model and Field Marshal Günther von Kluge, commander of Army Group Centre, agreed that Model's Ninth Army lacked the strength to force a breakthrough as originally planned. Both German commanders were aware of Soviet preparations for an offensive further to the northeast, which would strike into the rear of the forces attempting to drive into the Kursk salient from the north, and when this offensive – codenamed *Kutuzov* by *Stavka* – began on 12 July, Kluge had no choice but to pull most of the panzer divisions that had waited in vain for a breakthrough out of line and send them to stop the Soviet advance. By the time that fighting died down in mid-August, the Germans had been driven from Orel and the surrounding area and forced back to the west, suffering over 86,000 casualties. Red Army losses, with 430,000 killed or wounded, represented a huge price for comparatively modest gains in terms of territory.[25] Zhukov was critical about the manner in which troops were thrown against the strong German defences instead of being moved to strike at weaker areas, but this would have resulted in a delay in the transition to offensive operations, and all those involved, from Stalin to the front-line commanders, were anxious to force a result as soon as possible.[26] Nevertheless, the northern threat to the Kursk salient was eliminated.

On the southern flank of the salient, German operations made greater progress. Generaloberst Hermann Hoth, commander of Fourth Panzer Army, deployed much of his armour in the initial attack, organised into a series of arrowheads with the heavyweight Tiger tanks at the tip and Pz.IIIs and Pz.IVs to either side, in an attempt to prevent Soviet anti-tank guns from inflicting heavy losses on the lighter tanks and half-tracks. Whilst the central element of Army Group South's attack – II SS Panzer Corps – made good progress, the divisions of XLVIII Panzer Corps on its western flank fared less well. The corps included the Panzergrenadier Division *Grossdeutschland*, which was the largest division in the Wehrmacht and more powerful than a conventional panzer division; in addition, *Grossdeutschland* was assigned the Panther tanks of 10th Panzer Brigade to help its infantry break through the Russian lines. Almost immediately, the hopes and expectations that Hitler had placed in the new tanks were dashed as the brigade suffered heavy losses in a minefield. To make matters worse, the broken-down tanks clogged the main line of advance, resulting in further delays and congestion; throughout the first day, Soviet artillery and aircraft attempted to make the most of this with repeated attacks.[27] To the east of Fourth Panzer Army was General Werner Kempf's eponymous *Armee Abteilung* with III Panzer Corps; it made even less progress than XLVIII Panzer Corps, barely managing to secure a foothold in the Soviet defences.

In intense summer heat, punctuated by sudden thunderstorms that briefly turned roads into rivers of mud, the German troops struggled forward against tenacious resistance over ground that greatly favoured the defenders. Despite the modest success of II SS Panzer Corps, the offensive was badly behind schedule by the end of the first day. On 6 July, Vatutin's Voronezh Front had intended to deliver a counterattack using General Mikhail Efimovich Katukov's First Tank Army at first light, but the Germans attacked first. In any event, Katukov and his staff felt that the moment was not right for a counterattack:

> We could advance against the Germans ... but what of it? After all, their tank forces not only outnumbered us, but they also had a significant advantage in armament. This was incontrovertible. The enemy Tigers could use their 88mm guns against our vehicles at a distance of up to 2km, a range at which the 76.2mm cannons of our T-34s were ineffective. In short, the Hitlerites would be able to conduct a successful firefight with us at long range. What purpose was served by giving them such an advantage? Was it not better to postpone the counterstrike in these conditions, to continue to bet on our carefully prepared deep defence?

Let the fascists climb ahead in the hope that they would soon be able to break through and achieve operational freedom. Let the Hitlerites get bogged down and perish in our defences. We would in the meantime be grinding down the enemy's equipment and troops. And when we had drained their strength and smashed the fascists' armoured fist, then an advantageous moment would arise for a powerful counterattack. But such a moment had not yet arrived.[28]

The leading brigade of Katukov's army was already in action against the German tanks and reported rapidly escalating losses, confirming Katukov's fears. To his relief, the counterattack was abandoned.

Losses mounted on both sides as the German forces fought their way into the depths of the Soviet defences, penetrating about 20 miles (34km) over three days. On 10 July, the divisions of Obergruppenführer Paul Hausser's II SS Panzer Corps were within striking range of the town of Prokhorovka. Progress had been delayed by the need to switch elements of the corps to help XLVIII Panzer Corps to the west, and Kempf's troops to the east were also struggling to keep up. The tactics recommended by Katukov and others had yielded good results, depleting the German armour, but Soviet losses had been far higher and a consequence of the continuing (albeit slow) German advance was that many disabled and lightly damaged German tanks were returned to service almost immediately by the tireless repair teams that were integral to panzer and panzergrenadier divisions. Now, with his divisions gathered together, Hausser believed he was finally close to achieving a breakthrough. In his path lay the Soviet Fifth Guards Tank Army, commanded by Rotmistrov, preparing to launch an attack of its own.

The five-day battle that followed at Prokhorovka rapidly became almost legendary. The official Soviet version of events described the fighting to the southwest of the town as the largest tank battle of all time. Rotmistrov's summary in his memoirs was typical of this viewpoint:

Here on 12 July 1943 occurred an armoured encounter battle unparalleled in its magnitude in military history, generally known as the 'bloodbath of Prokhorovka'. More than 1,500 tanks and large numbers of artillery and aircraft on both sides engaged in fighting in a small area of ground.[29]

The official Soviet history of the war was unequivocal about the battle:

In the engagement, the complete superiority of Soviet military hardware and the Soviet military art over the military skill of the German-Fascist army was demonstrated ... [the Fifth Guards Tank Army's attack's] success to a significant extent depended on the correct selection of the time to start it, and its purposeful and thorough preparation.[30]

Other accounts describe the German forces as deploying large numbers of Panther and Tiger tanks and Ferdinand assault guns; in reality, the Ferdinands were all deployed with Army Group Centre against the northern side of the Kursk salient, and Army Group South's Panthers were operating further to the west in support of XLVIII Panzer Corps. For many years, an accurate appraisal of both the numbers of vehicles involved and the battle itself was rendered almost impossible by the inaccessibility of official Red Army records, but recent changes have led to more accurate assessments of the fighting at Prokhorovka. It is likely that Rotmistrov's Fifth Guards Tank Army used about 672 tanks and self-propelled guns in combat on its entire front. II SS Panzer Corps had started the offensive with 494 tanks and assault guns, and still had 294 in service when it encountered Rotmistrov's tanks. Of these, the number of Tiger tanks was probably less than 20. On its southwest flank, III Panzer Corps from *Armee Abteilung Kempf* contributed a further 120 vehicles. The clash of armour immediately southwest of Prokhorovka is likely to have involved perhaps 500 vehicles in all, perhaps a third of the number given in Soviet accounts. It is only by including other fighting in the general area that the numbers approach 1,500.[31]

The reality about the timing of Rotmistrov's counterattack was also rather different from the official version of events. Katukov was right to fear an engagement with the advancing German armour in open terrain, where the superior firepower of the German tanks would put them at a decisive advantage. The first planned counterattack was therefore rightly cancelled, but the planned attack by Rotmistrov's army at Prokhorovka was based upon the assumption that the German divisions had been adequately ground down and were near the end of their strength. Soviet intelligence estimates had advised Vatutin on 9 July that the opposing German forces had lost 2,460 tanks and assault guns since starting their advance, a figure that was nearly twice the total number of vehicles deployed by Army Group South; even allowing for the efforts of German repair teams, it was an estimate that was far in excess of reality. Vatutin's natural instinct to conduct an active defence rather than wait passively for the enemy to batter himself to exhaustion upon the Soviet defences played a major part in throwing the Red Army's reserves into the battle. When Rotmistrov's attack was launched, artillery coordination was poor and there was little attempt to coordinate air support with ground forces.

The outcome of the great clash of armour was effectively a stalemate. Despite a numerical superiority of a little over 2:1, Rotmistrov's attack failed to drive back the Germans, and II SS Panzer Corps was even able to gain ground on 12 July.

However, the losses suffered by both sides were considerable. Rotmistrov claimed that his formations destroyed 400 German tanks, including 70 Tigers; this is far in excess of the entire armoured strength of the forces opposing him.[32] The records of II SS Panzer Corps state that, by 13 July, the number of tanks and assault guns available had fallen from the previous day's figure of 294 to 131 – some 163 were destroyed or disabled.[33] Rotmistrov's units are estimated to have lost 359 vehicles; as the Germans controlled the battlefield at the end of the day, they were able to recover many of their damaged tanks and destroy Soviet tanks that had only been disabled.[34] The overall casualties suffered in the Battle of Kursk are estimated at 54,000 for the Wehrmacht and 178,000 for the Red Army.[35]

The battle for Prokhorovka was portrayed by the Soviet Union as the decisive moment of the Kursk campaign, when the fighting power of the German panzer arm was dealt an irreparable blow, but the raw figures for losses make clear that this is a misrepresentation. It is more accurate to say that, from a German point of view, the turning point had already passed with the repeated delays in starting the offensive making it almost impossible for Manstein's original intentions – to force Soviet armoured forces that had not recovered from their winter losses to give battle on unfavourable terms – to be achieved. The inability of Army Group Centre's Ninth Army to penetrate the northern defences of the Kursk salient made any major victory almost impossible, regardless of what Army Group South might achieve, but it was events far from the Eastern Front that effectively brought the campaign to an end. On 10 July the Western Allies launched Operation *Husky*, the invasion of Sicily. At the end of the first day's fighting at Prokhorovka, fearing further landings on the Italian mainland and possibly even in southern France, Hitler ordered the cessation of the Kursk offensive and the transfer of forces to the west, and informed Kluge and Manstein of his decision, as the latter later described:

> The commander of Army Group Centre, Field Marshal von Kluge, reported that Ninth Army was making no further headway and that he was having to deprive it of all its mobile forces to check the enemy's deep incursions into the Orel salient. There could be no question of continuing with *Zitadelle* or resuming the operation at a later date.
>
> Speaking for my own army group, I pointed out that the battle was now at its culminating point, and that to break it off at this moment would be tantamount to throwing a victory away. On no account should we let go of the enemy until the mobile reserves he had committed were completely beaten.[36]

Whilst the losses suffered by the German armoured forces to date were not catastrophic and there remained a good possibility of defeating Rotmistrov's Fifth Guards Tank Army, Manstein's assessment ignored the fact that even if II SS Panzer Corps, aided by III Panzer Corps, had succeeded in crushing the opposing Soviet armoured forces, there would still have been no prospect of a breakthrough – the full 80-mile depth of the Steppe Front's defences across the base of the Kursk salient would block any penetration to the east, while an attempt to push on to the north would leave the eastern flank of the advancing German forces exposed. Manstein was overruled and forced to release at least one of the divisions of II SS Panzer Corps.

The Red Army's strategy for the campaign had been to allow the Germans to weaken themselves against the prepared defences of the Kursk salient before launching its own offensive. Stalin had repeatedly expressed concerns that these defences would not be able to stop the Germans, but for the first time in the war the concentrated striking power of Germany's panzer divisions failed to break through. The Soviet success in defeating *Zitadelle* was undoubtedly significant, as Vasilevsky later wrote:

> We were unable then [immediately after the battle] to analyse thoroughly the results of the Battle of the Kursk Bulge. Yet one thing was clear: we had not only won a great battle. We had matured in it. Our propositions in working out the plan of a summer campaign had been justified; we had learned how to assess the enemy's intentions better than we had done in the past. We had had enough willpower, character, sheer stamina and nerve to avoid a miscalculation, a premature battle engagement or presenting the enemy with a chance to retrieve the situation. Elaboration of the operational and strategic assignments had been done successfully. Troop control had grown in skill at all levels. In a word, our leadership qualities had displayed both a creative skill and a superiority over the military skill of the Nazi command.[37]

It is perhaps an exaggeration to say that operational and strategic missions had all been fulfilled successfully; the detailed study that followed – and indeed, some of the comments of senior officers at the time – revealed avoidable errors. But the ability of the Red Army to learn from both success and failure stands out in sharp contrast to the manner in which the Wehrmacht now functioned. Soviet officers who made mistakes were frequently given the opportunity to learn from them, whereas Hitler was prone to sacking and even arresting those who he judged had failed him. Despite the formidable professionalism of the German officer corps,

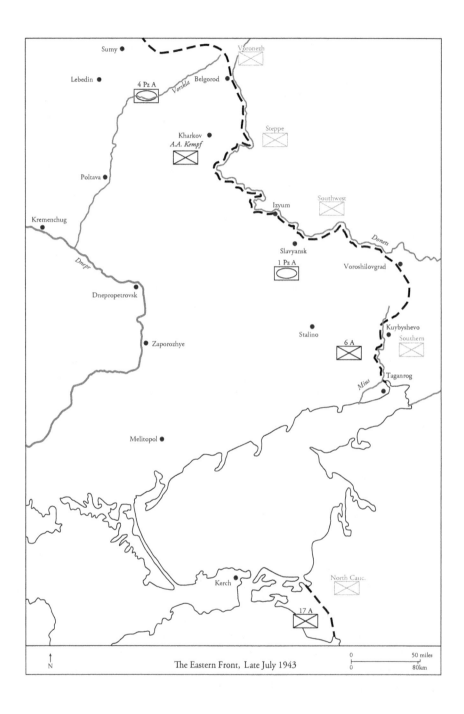

The Eastern Front, Late July 1943

N

0   50 miles
0   80km

the manner in which their amateur commander-in-chief constantly interfered increasingly nullified their ability to demonstrate their expertise, whereas the Red Army grew in confidence and skill almost with every battle.

Many accounts have attempted to portray *Zitadelle* as a battle in which the strength of the Wehrmacht's panzer arm was definitively broken, but this is surely an exaggeration. Whilst German losses were heavy, they were not catastrophic and in any case were far lower than those suffered by the Red Army. The real importance of the German failure was that the initiative now passed to the Red Army. Henceforth, the Wehrmacht would be fighting a reactive war in the east, with Stalin and his generals free to choose where and when they struck.

The cost to the Red Army was huge, but so were its resources. The Kursk offensive was effectively over less than two weeks after it commenced, and there was still plenty of excellent campaigning weather for the Red Army to strike. Manstein had long feared a determined Soviet attack towards the Dnepr and it now seemed only a matter of time before the attack would fall upon his troops. Army Group South faced an indefinite period of having to fend off its foe wherever it chose to attack.

CHAPTER 2

THE MIUS

It was only with considerable reluctance that Stalin was persuaded to wait for the German offensive at Kursk behind carefully prepared defences. For a variety of reasons, his instinct was to resume offensive operations as soon as possible after the spring thaw, and even when he conceded that it would perhaps be better to wait until the Wehrmacht had exhausted itself in a failed offensive, he insisted that preparations for offensive operations continued. The blow launched to recapture Orel from the German Army Group Centre has already been described, and detailed planning for this operation developed through much of the year; consequently, it was launched without delay when the moment was judged to be ripe. By contrast, planning for Soviet offensive operations south of the Kursk salient took place even as *Zitadelle* was unfolding, and evolved to take account of developments in the battle.[1]

The circumstances of the front line had not changed sufficiently as a result of the limited German advance of July to alter the likely direction of any renewed Soviet assault. The previous winter had seen the cities of Belgorod and Kharkov come under Soviet control for a short period and Manstein correctly judged that they would be early targets of the Red Army. To the southwest, the Dnepr crossings remained vulnerable, and a Soviet drive to the river, either as part of the same operation to recapture Belgorod and Kharkov, or as a follow-on operation, would have the same consequences that such a drive had threatened in the first weeks of 1943 – German forces operating to the east of the river would be threatened with isolation and destruction. But whilst Manstein's assessment of Soviet intentions was accurate, he was wrong in assuming that the losses suffered by the Red Army in stopping the German advance towards Kursk would be sufficient to result in a lengthy delay. The reality was that Red Army resources and advanced planning were sufficient to ensure that the operation could be launched in early August, just over a week after Fourth Panzer Army abandoned its attempts to break the Soviet defences on the southern side of the Kursk salient.

In 1916, the Russian Army had successfully launched a number of attacks on the forces of the Central Powers, achieving considerable successes against the armies of the Austro-Hungarian Empire. One characteristic of these attacks was the manner in which attacks were made over several days at different points of the front line, resulting in the few defensive reserves spending much of the battle marching to intercept Russian advances, only to find that new attacks then developed in the areas they had vacated. This policy was a recurring feature of Soviet operational thinking in the Second World War, and achieved similar results – the two attacks that encircled Stalingrad in November 1942 commenced on consecutive days, with the consequence that all available German reserves were already scrambling to intercept the northern thrust when the southern attack broke through. Now, the Red Army repeated the same ploy, with largely similar results. Although the units that had been so heavily engaged stopping the German advance on Kursk would recover their strength far faster than the Germans expected, it would still take time for them to prepare and deploy for an offensive. Meanwhile, the Soviet forces facing the rest of Manstein's Army Group South along the line of the Donets and Mius were fresh and ready to attack, and on 17 July, while fighting continued in the Kursk salient, the Soviet Southwest and South Fronts attacked at several points.

On the southern end of the long German battle-line were the divisions of the recently re-created Sixth Army of General Karl-Adolf Hollidt. In the aftermath of the encirclement of the original Sixth Army in Stalingrad, Hollidt took command of a rag-tag force of improved battlegroups, newly arrived reinforcements, and the more combat-worthy remnants of Romanian units, rapidly welding them into *Armee Abteilung Hollidt*, which doggedly fought its way back towards the line of the Mius through the winter. This force was then renamed Sixth Army during the spring pause in fighting, and it now found itself in the path of the Red Army's advance. In order to maximise the chances of success during *Zitadelle*, much of the Eastern Front had been stripped of resources that were then thrown at the salient, but the Red Army faced the prospect of attacking infantry in positions that they had occupied for several months. Nevertheless, by the end of the first day of the Soviet attack Hollidt's infantry divisions were already giving way. Whilst the units committed in *Zitadelle* had been brought up to full establishment strength for the operation, this had been at the expense of other sectors, and Hollidt's four infantry divisions were no match for the full-strength units of General Rodion Yakovlevich Malinovsky's Southern Front.

Isaak Kobylyanskiy was an artilleryman in one of the divisions deployed by the Red Army to attack across the Mius. His unit was in the second wave, a short distance behind the front line, and he described an attack by the Luftwaffe:

Just as the day began to break, the hum of approaching German Stuka dive-bombers was audible. In a minute, a squadron of nine bombers formed 'the snake' (a single line), then, while diving one after another, made a steep turn (the well-known German 'carousel') and dropped their howling deadly bomb load on our position (because of their dive sirens we called these bombers 'musicians'). The first element attacked, followed by the second and third elements, and then the first squadron of bombers flew away. But at the same time another squadron initiated the same manoeuvres and conducted another triple bombardment. Without a pause, the third squadron came and [then] the fourth. It seemed that there was no end to this hell. We had no anti-aircraft guns, our fighters were nowhere to be seen, and the 'musicians' had no reason to fear our rifle and sidearm fire. Unfortunately, the sky was absolutely cloudless, and the relentless bombardment continued with undiminished fury.

The bombers didn't strike our front line – it was too close to the German positions. Therefore, our division was exposed to the full brunt of their attacks. By noon the bright sky had darkened with dust and propellant gases, and it remained that way until dusk.

Deafened by the roar of aircraft engines, the howl of falling bombs, and the thunder of explosions, we lay in a state of constant tension. Only during the few short seconds of silence were we able to look round.[2]

Whilst Kobylyanskiy – and other soldiers on both sides of the front line – lamented the lack of friendly air power, the pilots of the Soviet fighter squadrons were doing their utmost. Nikolai Fedorovich Isayenko, who would finish the war as a colonel, was in a unit on the Mius front that started to receive Yakovlev Yak-1 fighters in place of their Lavochkin-Gorbunov-Gudkov LaGG-3 planes in mid-July. The two were fairly similar, but the LaGG-3 was unpopular – pilots regarded it as too heavy and underpowered, and its hardened timber frame frequently burst apart when hit by heavy shells from enemy aircraft, earning it the nickname of *Lakirovanny Garantirovanny Grab* or 'lacquered guaranteed grave'. The two aircraft had the same engine and radio, and the squadron was switched from one plane to the other without a period of training and sent straight into action, though the number of missions was reduced to give the pilots time to get used to their new machines. The timing of the transfer was therefore unfortunate and reduced fighter cover just as Southern Front needed air support, and coincided with an increase in the activity of the Luftwaffe:

Initially, enemy fighter opposition was minimal but increased dramatically from 21 July. Instead of sending pairs of 'Messers' [the Soviet nickname for Messerschmitts and often used to describe all German single-engined fighters], the Nazis began to use groups of six or even ten Me-109s and FW-190s and these planes turned out to belong to the 'special' Fascist squadrons we had already encountered in the Kuban from the 'Udet' [*Jagdgeschwader 3*] and 'Molders' [*Jagdgeschwader 74*] groups ... We were compelled to continue to send out only four Yaks on combat missions.

... In just 16 days in July, the pilots of 611th Fighter Regiment flew 630 missions and shot down 13 Fascist fighters. But despite the courage of the pilots, the regiment suffered losses. Senior Lieutenant Tretyakov [who had been credited with shooting down at least four German planes in this period] did not return from a reconnaissance mission over the enemy airfields near Amyrosievka, and the pilots Kostyukhin, Avyamukov, Veselov, and Tribul died bravely.

There were losses in the other regiments. Trying to investigate the reasons for our losses, Major Shchirov and I repeatedly flew with groups of Yaks on combat missions. The shortcomings in the training of young pilots became increasingly obvious and the division commander did everything possible to eliminate these shortcomings. But it was not possible to remedy such shortcomings when operating two different aircraft, and it was impossible to get training [i.e. two-seater] aircraft. Therefore, we hurried to transfer all our pilots ... to the Yaks as soon as possible.[3]

Assessing the number of aircraft destroyed in combat has always been a difficult issue, with pilots understandably claiming 'kills' when they had just disabled an enemy plane, or two pilots claiming 'kills' when they simultaneously attacked the same aircraft. In an account of an attack on a German bomber group in August, Isayenko describes how he personally shot down two Ju-88s and helped destroy several German fighters in an unlikely action in which he seemed to have an unrealistic amount of ammunition available.[4] No side in the Second World War was immune to this; indeed, the impact of air operations on ground targets was similarly prone to exaggerated claims. Nevertheless, soldiers struggling on the ground constantly lamented the failure of their aerial colleagues to support them adequately.

The only armoured reserves available to Hollidt consisted of 16th Panzergrenadier Division and 13th Panzer Division. The latter had been part of the German forces that penetrated into the Caucasus in 1942, where it was briefly encircled by counterattacking Soviet forces in November. At several stages, it had been designated for withdrawal to a rear area where it was to be replenished and brought back to strength, but the rolling crises of the winter resulted in it almost constantly moving from one sector to another. The Crimea and surrounding region was, like the Donbas region of the eastern Ukraine,

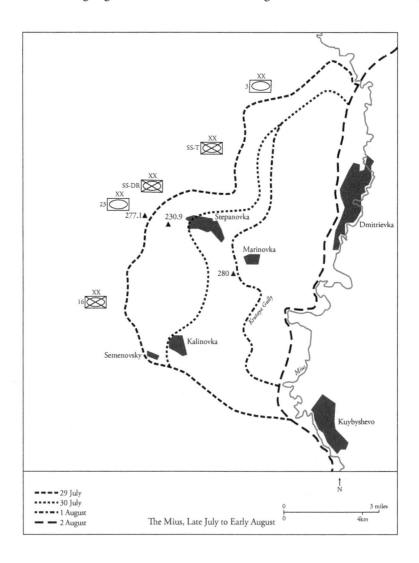

The Mius, Late July to Early August

29 July
30 July
1 August
2 August

0   3 miles
0   4km

regarded by Hitler as an area that had to be held at all costs; if it were to come under Soviet control, the Romanian oilfields would be within bombing range, and the entire region was regarded by many senior Nazis as an area of great racial importance, as it was believed by them to be the ancestral homeland of the Gothic tribes and hence of many of the people who settled between the Rhine and Elbe in the closing decades of the Roman Empire. After it was finally pulled out of the front line, 13th Panzer Division was deployed in the *Gotenstellung* ('Gothic Positions') defending the German bridgehead around Kuban in the Taman Peninsula, to the east of the Crimea. It had little rest here, in constant contact with Soviet forces, and just a couple of days before Malinovsky's attack it was pulled back into the Crimea, from where it was now rushed to reinforce the collapsing infantry divisions of Sixth Army. Subordinated to General Erich Brandenberger's XXIX Corps, the division – with little more than half the strength of a fully equipped and manned panzer division – was thrown into action immediately. Generalleutnant Hellmut von der Chevallerie had commanded 13th Panzer Division since late 1942, and the long winter had left the division's personnel deeply familiar with the role in which they now found themselves.

The German 16th Panzergrenadier Division, commanded by General Gerhard Graf von Schwerin, had previously been designated 16th Motorised Infantry Division. It spent much of the winter of 1942–43 covering the vast space between the southern approaches of Stalingrad and the nearest elements of First Panzer Army in the Caucasus; its reconnaissance battalion carried out a deep sweep towards Astrakhan and achieved the status of being the Wehrmacht unit to travel furthest to the east. It suffered substantial losses in the fighting in the Mius sector as the German line was pulled back in the face of the repeated Soviet offensives of the winter and spent much of 1943 on the shores of the Sea of Azov being brought back to strength. When the Red Army attacked on 17 July, elements of the division were rapidly dispatched to strengthen the front line; as was often the case, the division's reconnaissance battalion found itself being used as an improvised battlegroup, relying on its mobility to intervene repeatedly as the day progressed:

> The division moved forward and the reconnaissance battalion was thrust into action at the centre of the penetration. A slaughter of Russian tanks! My reconnaissance troop pulled out of the front and we spent the day pushing into the front line at various points and were able to offer help everywhere. Towards the evening, we broke through to the encircled *Kampfgruppe Fischer* [part of the division's 156th Panzergrenadier Regiment, commanded by Oberstleutnant Otto Fischer] and enabled it to withdraw without losses.[5]

A battery of the division's 146th Artillery Regiment commanded by Major Fritz Vogelsang was operating in support of the reconnaissance battalion, in terrain where even modest high ground assumed commanding importance:

> We crossed the grey steppe and the dry, yellow *balkas* [narrow gorges, often dry durng the summer] at speed until we reached Hill 277.1, a pyramid-shaped elongated height crowned by an ancient Hun burial mound, with light bushland to the south and west, otherwise completely bare and encrusted with rocks. It dominated the entire area for 15–20km [9–12 miles], hence our mission to halt the Russian attack here at all costs while, after brief preparation, the division itself would roll up the Russian penetration from the south.[6]

It took most of the day for 16th Panzergrenadier Division's main forces to assemble, delayed in their approach by constant harassment by Soviet aircraft. By the end of 17 July, the Soviet units had penetrated about two miles into the German defences on a front of about eight miles (13km), and Hollidt wanted to use 16th Panzergrenadier Division in a thrust from the south to restore the original line along the Mius. The terrain was generally swampy with numerous streams running across the path of the German division, and when the attack began the following day the Red Army put up determined resistance whilst launching further heavy attacks of its own, as a member of the division's combat engineers later recalled:

> [There were] enemy attacks at about 0830, and the enemy rolled up our position, [there was] dreadful chaos and all guns were turned towards the Russians. After running a few hundred metres, we came across Major Muschner who drove us to make a counterattack with his machine-pistol at his hip. Despite the 88mm gun to our rear, which worked assiduously, we only managed to recover a small segment of our position, namely a small hillock ... In the midst of this hillock lay Leutnant de Bra with his head completely bandaged, until he was hit by a final bullet an hour later. Six other comrades lay near him and when the handful of men who were still with us pulled back late in the afternoon when T-34s attacked, we learned that a further 24 comrades from our company were dead and 27 were missing.[7]

Vogelsang's artillery was impeded at first by mist, which soon dispersed as the summer sun rose higher:

By 0900 it was clearer. The fighting resumed at full intensity. I quickly jumped in my vehicle to drive further forward. There was one air attack after another and a bomb exploded right next to our command post. The air was teeming with Red ground attack planes.

The Russians gathered their forces and suddenly pushed forward towards Stepanovka and Marinovka. As if emerging from the earth, 45 heavy tanks rolled in. Several heavy and light batteries and countless mortars opened up supported by the gurgling howl of Stalin organs and made the ground tremble. The roar of the engines of ground attack aircraft making low passes eliminated any chance of understanding anything said to one another. Clouds of smoke mushroomed up around our foxholes. The undergrowth behind us was under constant drumfire. It was only after our 12 guns intervened in location after location that the situation stabilised a little. A pause for breath!

To our right, the division advanced with 156th Grenadier Regiment and the panzer battalion. There was at least a hope of some relief! It was still to be seen what lay in front of the units we had deployed. Only small groups were still moving across the landscape.

What a day!

During the afternoon there were constant air attacks on us by between six and 30 ground attack planes with bombs, fixed weapons and rockets with pauses of about 15 minutes between. There were 20 air attacks just around our observation post on Hill 277.1 reducing it to a mess of shells, shrapnel and stones. Added to this was round after round from the numerous enemy guns on the ground. Fortunately, despite my fears we had just two wounded, while around us there were heavy casualties.

Stepanovka and Marinkovka were lost. A counterattack by the armoured reconnaissance battalion made only slow progress and was then brought to a halt by overwhelming enemy defensive fire. Two heavy dive-bomber attacks by our planes on the two villages brought no palpable relief …

Finally at 1900 I had a moment to reach the command post at the bottom of the hill. What a blessing! I had barely got there when a sudden hammering by all manner of weapons began … Tank shells, artillery shells exploded, machine-guns rattled constantly. There were loud cries that tanks had broken through! Under heavy fire we ran up the slope to see and immediately brought down blocking fire from all our batteries. After a few minutes shells flew overhead towards Stepanovka. Through the combined fire of all our weapons in our position we succeeded in stopping the Russian surprise attack on Hill 230.9, a low, broad mound covered with wheat and sunflowers, and thus shot up two out of seven attacking tanks.[8]

The planned elimination of the Soviet penetration failed completely, and by the end of the day the Russians had actually extended their positions. Hollidt ordered a further attack for 19 July; modest reinforcements had arrived in the shape of 23rd Panzer Division, which had been serving further north with First Panzer Army for much of the month, and it was ordered to attack from the north, with XVII Corps, commanded by General Willi Schneckenburger, in overall control. Despite its name, 23rd Panzer Division was weak in tanks as a result of losses suffered in earlier fighting and its attack rapidly stalled. On the southern side of the Soviet positions, Vogelsang's unit found itself caught up in a sudden attack:

Suddenly ... just before our own attack was to commence, the Russians appeared with 11 heavy tanks and infantry on Hill 230.9 at first light. We came under heavy fire at the same moment. All contact with our batteries was lost in an instant. The observation post of 8th Battery was overrun, the command of 7th Battery was shot up, and there was no sign of 9th Battery. There was wild chaos on Hill 230.9 with friend and foe intermingled. In the midst of the red tanks one could see our own people emerging from foxholes and firing, and to the south the black [German] tank hunters and scouts were probing forward. The [Soviet] tanks drove in zigzags and tried to overwhelm the foxholes and their occupants who were firing wildly.

But the moment of surprise passed – our Westphalian and Austrian armoured reconnaissance troops weren't so easily upset! Quickly, they organised the units not already engaged with the enemy. Soon we could see black and grey figures crouching and moving forward energetically against the Russians through the sunflowers from the south ...

Soon mortar shells were landing just a few metres from the tanks which at first continued to try to evade them by driving in zigzags, but were then so heavily bombarded that their crews pulled back hastily. Now contact was restored with 7th Battery and its guns roared with clear, hard impacts. The shells passed a hairsbreadth above our heads, barely able to clear our hill and still strike their target.

The *Panzerjägers* and riflemen took advantage of the immediate confusion amongst the Russians. They swarmed forward cunningly and after a few moments none of the ten [Soviet] tanks were still running. Their accompanying infantry was thrown back into Stepanovka, followed by our shells and the fire of the heavy infantry weapons of the reconnaissance battalion. A solitary tank accompanied by 40–60 men broke through our position and drove on to Saur Mogilsky, where it was disabled at midday.

At the same time as this attack on us, the Russians made a rapid thrust with strong infantry and tank forces against the high ground south of Stepanovka, thus overrunning 9th Battery's observation post.

It was only at 1300 that we managed to get a clear report of the fate of our observation posts. The commander of 8th Battery with a few of his men came back from Hill 230.9, blackened and battered. He had taken cover in a foxhole amongst the [Soviet] tanks and had been forced to endure the fire of both the enemy's and our guns. He was deeply impressed by the precision and power of our guns whose shelling he was able to observe from such close proximity! His missing men appeared later, some of them wounded, having taken part in the fighting as infantry.

A little later, the commander of 9th Battery reached our command post, which had moved forward to just south of Stepanovka. He had been surprised when the firing had barely started before heavy mortar fire severed all communications. At the same moment, tanks appeared amongst the foxholes and all vehicles and radio equipment were crushed. With difficulty, they carried back Leutnant Pfaff, who had been badly wounded by a mortar explosion. In small groups, he and his personnel, mixed in with the riflemen, pursued by red tanks, moved slowly from cover to cover taking their wounded with them and broke through to us.[9]

The Soviet attack had been stopped but German losses were heavy, particularly in the reconnaissance battalion of 16th Panzergrenadier Division, and the division's attempts to carry out the ordered attack into the southern flank of the Russian bridgehead made little impression:

Oberleutnant Teufel had taken command of the tank platoon and was determined to carry out this attack. Given the overall situation, it was a sure-fire suicide mission. Before Teufel climbed aboard his tank, I exchanged a few words with him and urged him to show the utmost caution. But Teufel was a daredevil and wanted to be in action. Soon the tanks disappeared from our view and we waited anxiously for radio reports. After a short while Teufel reached the village [the immediate objective of the attack] and drove into it. Then radio contact was lost – and despite constant attempts to restore communication, we received no reply. We could only hope.

When the infantry managed to penetrate into the village a few days later we found out the truth about the fate of the platoon. All the tanks were shot up, their turrets turned to the rear, which meant that they must have come under fire from behind, and it was soon all over. The crews couldn't be located at first and we hoped that they had been taken prisoner. Then we found an elderly civilian nearby who had not left his village; this man led us to a well. We found our comrades trussed up and hanged upside down and drowned. There were clear signs of maltreatment. The sight was unbearable. I drove back to the battalion with this barbarous act in my mind. Later I learned from other comrades that some of the tank crew who had been taken prisoner were found in some shot-up houses, nailed to a table through their tongues. Before they died, they had been mutilated in an unimaginable manner.[10]

As the Red Army advanced west, its personnel came across increasing evidence of the often-arbitrary brutality of German occupation policies and frequently took revenge on any German soldiers who they had captured. However, it is also possible that these men of 16th Panzergrenadier Division were victims of mistaken identity. During the 1930s, the elderly August von Mackensen – father of Eberhard von Mackensen, who was the commander of First Panzer Army in 1943 – frequently appeared at military functions wearing the traditional dress of the Prussian 2nd Life Hussars Regiment. During the time of Frederick the Great, the Prussian Hussars had adopted a black uniform with the *Totenkopf* insignia of skull and crossbones, and in emulation of Mackensen, widely seen as the elder statesman of the German Army, the new panzer arm adopted a black uniform, complete with *Totenkopf* badges. Unfortunately for the *Panzertruppen*, Julius Schreck, who led the *Stabswache* – an early SS unit that would ultimately grow into the *LSSAH* division – also chose the Prussian hussar uniform as a model for his personnel, and many Red Army personnel simply identified all Germans wearing black uniforms with *Totenkopf* symbols as being members of the hated SS. Some used a simple means of distinguishing between the two groups – SS personnel wore the German eagle badge on their sleeve, while Wehrmacht personnel wore it on their chest – but others were either not aware of the distinction or chose to ignore it.

Far from being able to reduce the Soviet penetration, 16th Panzergrenadier Division was forced to pull back from its starting positions. The commander of one of the panzergrenadier battalions was killed in action along with dozens of other men, and it was clear that it would not be a simple task to restore the front line along the Mius. However, the Soviet attempts to advance had also largely been halted and a day of comparative calm followed. On 21 July, after bringing forward reinforcements and supplies, the Red Army attacked again and it was only at the cost of considerable losses – the reconnaissance battalion was reduced to barely 100 men and an attached battalion of infantry to 150 men – that the line was held. The Soviet II and IV Guards Mechanised Corps made a final attempt to break through into open space the following day and 16th Panzergrenadier Division, now operating as part of XXIV Panzer Corps, was once more in the thick of the action. Commanded by General Walther Nehring, XXIV Panzer Corps had been rebuilt after being almost completely destroyed in the winter fighting of 1942–43, when it lost several commanders in the course of a few chaotic days as it disintegrated under repeated Soviet attacks. Originally, the corps had been intended as reinforcements for the southern part of *Zitadelle*, but was now pressed into action to shore up the front line. To Hollidt's relief, the advancing Soviet columns were finally halted, with intermittent, less severe attacks continuing over the next few days, as Vogelsang wrote in his diary:

> The Russian tank attacks have stopped. Instead they have been replaced by a new tactic. In small groups [the enemy] infiltrates forward through the overgrown fields and can be properly engaged only with great difficulty. In continuous small isolated attacks he tries to break up the front a small piece at a time and to wear down the defenders. So far, these insignificant attacks have been repulsed along the entire front.
>
> Despite reports from deserters about a planned attack by about 1,000 men, the night passes uneventfully in our sector. From the afternoon it starts to rain. In place of the heat, smoke and burning steppe there is dirt and mud – both equally unpleasant![11]

The Red Army was left in control of a deep penetration extending up to ten miles into the German positions. Whilst it had been a bulwark of the defence against the Soviet attack, 16th Panzergrenadier Division had paid a heavy price – as the fighting died down, it reported that the combined strength of its two panzergrenadier regiments amounted to perhaps 550 men, barely the strength of a single battalion. From bitter experience, the Germans knew that the Soviet bridgehead would rapidly be developed into the start point for further attacks, and its speedy elimination was therefore essential. This would not be possible unless further reinforcements arrived.

In the bridgehead that they had secured, the Red Army units now began to redeploy to defend their gains. Kobylyanskiy moved the single surviving field gun in his platoon into a new position, where he had the misfortune of experiencing friendly fire, a curse of armies throughout the ages:

Partway up the slope of the hill, about 500m from the battalion's [main] positions, we unexpectedly came under 'friendly' fire from a salvo of a Soviet multiple rocket launcher, the famous 'Katyusha'. It was a terrible minute: 16 large-calibre rockets exploded around us one after another. It took a minute or two to regain our senses and our breath. After this terrifying ordeal, I fully believed our newspaper reports that some German soldiers, caught in a barrage from 'Stalin's organs' (the German soldiers' nickname for the 'Katyusha') went crazy from the experience.

At last we reached the battalion command post atop the hill. The officers there were indignant at the stupid scoundrel whose error resulted in the 'Katyusha' rockets landing a half kilometre short of the enemy trenches.[12]

Further north, an attack by the Soviet Southwest Front against the German First Panzer Army crossed the Donets to the southeast of Izyum and achieved a similar penetration. This advance too was brought to a halt, but only by the commitment of effectively the last German reserves in the entire sector. For the moment, the line stabilised, but as was the case in Sixth Army's sector on the Mius, the result was a substantial Soviet bridgehead, and if the Wehrmacht was to sustain its line along the Donets and Mius valleys, both bridgeheads demanded urgent attention.

Manstein had long argued for the abandonment of the Donbas region and a withdrawal to the line of the Dnepr, on the grounds that maintaining a presence so far east positively invited Soviet attempts to isolate and destroy the German forces involved. On every occasion that the matter was raised, Hitler rejected such requests on the grounds that the industrial and mineral resources of the region were vital to the German war effort, and the loss of the region would have serious political consequences in the Balkans and Turkey. Manstein was now ordered to use some of the armoured forces that had been involved in *Zitadelle* to restore the defensive line further south.

Since he appointed himself as commander-in-chief at the end of 1941, Hitler had repeatedly interfered with the functioning of army groups, armies, corps and even divisions, often issuing orders from his distant headquarters regarding the deployment of individual regiments. Manstein's preference was to concentrate the armour released from *Zitadelle* in an attack against the Soviet bridgehead near Izyum before continuing further south to restore Sixth Army's lines on the Mius, largely because the limited railway capacity available to him would delay the rate at which the armoured forces could be redeployed and it would be easier to create an adequate concentration of forces in the Izyum sector than on the Mius. To his immense irritation, Hitler intervened on the eve of the attack and forbade the use of any of the released divisions in First Panzer Army's sector. Instead, the reduction of the Mius bridgehead was to take priority. Manstein had repeatedly protested about such interference during the desperate days of the winter campaign, and he now submitted a further complaint to General Kurt Zeitzler, chief of staff at *OKH* (*Oberkommando des Heeres* or 'Army High Command'):

> If my misgivings about coming developments are disregarded, and if my intentions as a commander, which aim merely at removing difficulties for which I am not responsible, continue to be frustrated, I shall have no choice but to assume that the Führer has not the necessary confidence in this headquarters. I am far from believing myself infallible. Everyone makes mistakes – even great captains like Frederick and Napoleon. At the same time I would point out that Eleventh Army [Manstein's command in the first half of 1942] won the Crimean campaign under very difficult conditions and that when faced with an almost hopeless situation at the end of last year, Army Group South still mastered it.
>
> If the Führer thinks he can find any army group commander or headquarters staff with better nerves than we had during the past winter, with more initiative than we showed in the Crimea, on the Donets or at Kharkov, with greater powers of improvisation than were displayed by us in the Crimean or winter campaign, or with the ability to foresee the inevitable more clearly than we have done, I am fully prepared to hand over to them!
>
> As long as I remain at this post, however, I must have the chance to use my own head.[13]

It was a carefully weighted and calculated protest. During the previous winter, when Manstein was desperately juggling his forces to try to prevent the complete collapse of the Eastern Front, Hitler had surprised him by accepting full personal responsibility for the disaster at Stalingrad; in other words, he had admitted his fallibility at a time when Manstein was demonstrating a level of skill and judgement that had to be almost perfect if the Wehrmacht was to survive. Despite this admission, Hitler interfered repeatedly in the campaign, particularly with his demands that Kharkov was to be held at all costs (instead, his so-called ultra-loyal SS Panzer Corps abandoned the city rather than risk being encircled) and then recaptured as a top priority (a demand ignored by Manstein, who correctly judged that counterattacks against Soviet forces further south were far more important; if they succeeded, Kharkov would be recaptured as a matter of course, whereas if they failed, any attempt to retake Kharkov would be irrelevant). In short, any analysis of the winter fighting demonstrated the truth of Manstein's points: Hitler had made a catastrophic strategic blunder at Stalingrad, and his constant interference in the fighting that followed was almost always detrimental, whereas Manstein's command – first Army Group B, then renamed Army Group South – had fought a campaign of astonishing virtuosity in the most adverse conditions imaginable. The carefully worded complaint made these facts abundantly clear to Zeitzler, and therefore Hitler.

Zeitzler had spent the previous winter fielding such complaints from Manstein, and was very sympathetic to the views of the commander of Army Group South. Using far more diplomatic language, he had made the same points repeatedly to Hitler, though rarely with any success. On this occasion, it isn't known whether he even showed Manstein's signal to Hitler, and had he done so it would have achieved nothing. Hitler's interference was based upon continuing uncertainty about which forces should be sent west to shore up Italy and to deter landings on the European mainland following the invasion of Sicily. At first, he issued instructions that all of II SS Panzer Corps – consisting of the panzergrenadier divisions *SS-Das Reich*, *SS-Totenkopf*, and *Leibstandarte SS Adolf Hitler* (usually abbreviated to *LSSAH*), which despite their designation were actually far more powerful than a Wehrmacht panzer division – was to be dispatched to Italy, but almost immediately changed his mind. Only *LSSAH* would travel west, and the other divisions were to remain in the Ukraine to deal with the expected Soviet attacks. But with decisions about major formations being made in Hitler's distant headquarters, the army group and army commanders in the field were left struggling to make plans that would still be valid just a day or two later.

For Manstein, Zeitzler and other professional officers, steeped in the culture of the German general staff and its systems of methodical analysis and assessment, the situation was essentially one of a mismatch between the strategic desires of Hitler – to hold onto all the territory currently controlled by Germany – and the resources available. The failure of *Zitadelle* ended any lingering prospect of the Wehrmacht securing a strategic victory large enough to allow it to dictate events on the Eastern Front, and all that remained was to deal with each crisis as it arose. Hitler's arguments about the economic and industrial importance of the Donbas region were at the heart of the matter, but for precisely the opposite reasons that Hitler believed. If control of these resources was so critical, then the war could no longer be won, as it was militarily impossible to retain control of the region in anything but the short term.

In the view of Manstein – who, as he concisely pointed out in his complaint, had proved to be Germany's finest operational thinker in the most testing circumstances conceivable – the very best that could now be achieved was a war in which the Red Army might be ground down in a series of strategically defensive battles. Ultimately, he argued, military failure would force the Soviet Union to discuss peace terms. This was a viewpoint that he had articulated during the preceding winter:

> To hold the Don-Donets salient for any length of time was not possible, even in a purely defensive context … In the event of the Supreme Command's having to remain on the defensive in 1943 on account of the loss of Sixth Army and its 20 divisions, an all-out attempt to defend the entire Donets basin would mean committing all the forces there that could possibly be made available. That, however, would give the enemy a free hand to take the offensive with far superior forces at any point he cared to pick on the remainder of the front …
>
> The only means of achieving an offensive solution – always assuming that this were in the least feasible – consisted in the first place of drawing the enemy westwards towards the lower Dnepr on our southern wing. Having once achieved this, we had to launch a powerful attack from the Kharkov area and smash the Russian front [and then] turn south and surround the enemy on the Sea of Azov.[14]

This 'backhand blow' had been Manstein's preference for the year's campaign from the outset, but as he acknowledged, there was no possibility of Hitler accepting it:

> Hitler … had already been told by Zeitzler himself – so the latter informed me – that the only question now [in February 1943] was whether to abandon the Donets area by itself or lose the army group [Manstein's command] along with it. Hitler's answer had been that although his chief of staff was probably right from the operational point of view, the surrender of the Donets area was impossible for economic reasons.[15]

This was a nonsensical argument. If it was operationally impossible to retain the Donets, all considerations of economic need were irrelevant and amounted to nothing more than wishful thinking. However, the desire of Manstein to fight a war intended to exhaust the Red Army and create the conditions in which a negotiated peace might be possible was just as fanciful as Hitler's economic argument. The Allied Powers had made clear at the Casablanca conference that there could be no peace until and unless Hitler and the Nazis were removed from power. Manstein must have known that there was no possibility of Hitler voluntarily relinquishing his grip on power, and he had shunned the tentative approaches of some of the anti-Hitler conspirators. In almost any other circumstances, logic would have dictated to the German leadership that as it was no longer possible to achieve a victorious outcome on the battlefield, it was essential to explore diplomatic routes out of the conflict. But Hitler showed not the slightest interest in pursuing such a path, at least partly because he knew that the Allied Powers would never negotiate with him. The consequence was therefore that the Wehrmacht had no choice but to continue a hopeless struggle and stave off final defeat for as long as it could.

The overriding problem was Hitler himself, for several reasons. He was seen by the Allied Powers as someone who could not possibly be trusted, and while he remained Germany's political leader there would never be any possibility of a diplomatic solution. From a German perspective, his dominance of almost every aspect of German leadership – political, diplomatic, military, even economic – raised frequent difficulties for those who had the necessary knowledge and skills in each of those fields. In his memoirs, Albert Speer offered a useful insight:

> Amateurishness was one of Hitler's dominant traits. He had never learned a profession and basically had always remained an outsider in all fields of endeavour. Like many self-taught people, he had no idea what real specialised knowledge meant. Without any sense of the complexities of any great task, he boldly assumed one function after another. Unburdened by standard ideas, his quick intelligence sometimes conceived unusual measures which a specialist would not have hit on at all. The victories of the early years of the war can literally be attributed to Hitler's ignorance of the rules of the game and his layman's delight in decision making. Since the opposing side was trained to apply rules which Hitler's self-taught, autocratic mind did not know and did not use, he achieved surprises. These audacities, coupled with military superiority, were the basis of his early successes. But as soon as setbacks occurred he suffered shipwreck, like most untrained people. Then his ignorance of the rules of the game was revealed as another kind of incompetence: then his defects were no longer strengths. The greater the failures became, the more obstinately his incurable amateurishness came to the fore. The tendency to wild decision had long been his forte; now it speeded his downfall.[16]

Speer had already achieved an extraordinary increase in productivity in Germany's war industries by the summer of 1943, and despite constant British and American air attacks he continued to make improvements. However, he was under no illusions that this could be sustained in the long term. Even by making changes to the alloys used in the production of steel for armoured vehicles, for example, he knew that Germany would soon start to run out of vital raw materials. Tungsten for armour-piercing ammunition and even brass for shell and bullet cartridges would soon become rate-limiting factors in production, which might have strengthened Hitler's economic arguments. In reality, the rapidly diminishing stocks of such resources – or their consumption at a rate that comfortably exceeded the ability of mines under German control to replenish them – merely reinforced the opposite argument. If areas like the Donbas could not be held for sound operational reasons, there would inevitably come a time when however well it fought, the Wehrmacht would simply run out of essential supplies. Even the extraordinary increases in production that had been achieved might easily be lost if the Western Allies' bombing raids continued to devastate German cities. In late July, Hamburg was attacked repeatedly, creating huge firestorms that left tens of thousands dead and large areas of the city in ruins. In a meeting of his Central Planning Committee, Speer stated:

> If the air raids continue on their present scale, within three months we shall be relieved of a number of questions we are at present discussing. We shall simply be coasting downhill, smoothly and relatively swiftly.[17]

A short while later, there was a further demonstration of the fragility of the German war effort. Bombers of the USAAF struck at Schweinfurt, where much of the ball-bearing production of German industry was based. As a consequence, production fell immediately by a third, and the continued manufacture of a wide range of military equipment was only possible by raiding stockpiles that had been intended as spare parts; this in turn created a shortage of spares. A second raid a few weeks later resulted in further disruption and the loss of two thirds of ball-bearing production. Fortunately for the Germans, the US bomber formations had suffered heavy losses and the Allied commanders erroneously concluded that the raids were having little effect. Had they been continued, the consequence for Germany would have been catastrophic.

It was vital to find a way out of the war before resources were completely exhausted. But whilst Hitler continued to search for a military solution, his background continued to hinder matters, as Speer recorded:

> Hitler's technical horizon … was limited by the First World War. His technical interests were narrowly restricted to the traditional weapons of the army and the navy. In these areas he had continued to learn and steadily increase his knowledge, so that he frequently proposed convincing and usable innovations. But he had

little feeling for such new developments as, for example, radar, the construction of an atom bomb, jet fighters, and rockets. On his rare flights in the newly developed Condor he showed concern that the mechanism which let down the retracted landing gear might not function. Warily, he declared that he preferred the old Junkers 52 with its rigid landing gear.[18]

On the battlefield, the immediate matter was the timely elimination of the Soviet bridgeheads across the Donets and Mius. It was usual practice for troops moving any significant distance to be transported by rail in order to avoid wear and tear on motor vehicles, especially on the poor roads of the Soviet Union, but the rail network rarely had sufficient capacity for all the tasks required of it. The movement of supplies and military equipment alone would have taxed it to the limit, but the additional requirements of the occupation authorities for movement of agricultural produce and forced labour created an almost impossible burden, not least because there was little coordination between the competing bodies – they tended to dispatch their own traffic with little regard to what was already running on the rails, often resulting in lengthy delays. An additional strain was placed upon the system by Hitler's insistence on trying to exploit the coalfields of the Donbas region. The coal – which Hitler had repeatedly told Manstein and others was essential for Germany, and by preventing Soviet access to it the Germans had an important advantage – was actually too poor to be used to power locomotives. It had to be transported back to Germany so that it could be used for other purposes, with the coal for the transport locomotives having to be shipped all the way from Germany. The net benefit of the coal from the Donbas to the German war effort was therefore minimal, and Manstein and others repeatedly commented that there was no evidence that deprivation of this coal had resulted in any impairment in the Soviet war effort. In an attempt to win the argument with Hitler about Ukrainian coal, Zeitzler contacted Albert Speer and asked him about the consequences of abandoning the Donbas coalfields. Speer replied that there would be no impact upon German industrial production, largely because he had never taken into account any coal from that region; far from conceding the point, Hitler angrily forbade Zeitzler from contacting Speer without express permission. Finally, railway lines and bridges were easy targets for partisan attacks; it became normal practice for trains to have troops constantly on the look-out for such attacks, and units being transported to new locations were often required to detrain in order to deal with partisan groups.

Given the limitations of the rail network, Army Group South ordered *SS-Totenkopf* and *SS-Das Reich* to move from their preparation areas near Izyum to their new area of operations largely by road, while many of the supply and support services would travel by train. The distance that would have to be covered was over 110 miles (180km) and this placed a heavy strain on vehicle engines that had already been worked hard during the fighting in the Kursk salient in July. Along poor quality roads, the armoured vehicles and trucks of *SS-Das Reich* trundled south, raising huge clouds of dust that would have been easily visible to Soviet reconnaissance flights. *SS-Totenkopf* was forced to use the same roads due to the paucity of roads heading in the right direction; degradation of the roads by the passage of the vehicles of *SS-Das Reich* resulted in additional delays.

The German strike force for the restoration of the Mius position consisted of III Panzer Corps with 3rd Panzer Division, II SS Panzer Corps with *SS-Totenkopf* and *SS-Das Reich*, and XXIV Panzer Corps with 23rd Panzer Division and 16th Panzergrenadier Division, though the allocation of the divisions to their parent corps headquarters would change once they arrived in their new operational area. Like all the German forces being gathered, 3rd Panzer Division had suffered losses during *Zitadelle* and its workshops were full of damaged vehicles; repairs were further delayed by the need for the division to redeploy to the south, but at least its equipment and personnel were able to travel by rail. However, this was not without consequence. When the trains carrying the division were moving through Charzyzk, between Stalino (now Donetsk) and Voroshilovgrad (now Luhansk), a Soviet air raid struck an ammunition train that was in the station and the blast inflicted further losses.[19] The loss of the ammunition train would also result in shortages of artillery ammunition in the coming days.

The panzer and panzergrenadier divisions took advantage of two or three days after arriving at their new locations to position their artillery and to make other preparations. One of the most important results of this pause was that it gave the division workshops time to repair damaged vehicles and thus increase the strike power of the divisions. When *LSSAH* was withdrawn and sent to the west, it was ordered to leave behind its tanks, providing *SS-Das Reich* with a welcome boost. Despite this, the division remained far below its establishment strength, reporting on 28 August that it had 33 Pz.IIIs, 17 Pz.IVs, two Tigers, 28 assault guns, and two captured T-34s available. It had captured far larger numbers of Soviet tanks, but as there was no provision of spare parts for these, they were abandoned when they broke down.[20] Along the roads running to the Mius sector from further north, workshop teams struggled to repair the vehicles that had broken down on the long approach march.

The assault would be carried out with 3rd Panzer Division on the northern flank, *SS-Totenkopf* to its south, then *SS-Das Reich* and 23rd Panzer Division, and finally 16th Panzergrenadier Division and 23rd Panzer Division on the southern flank. When the Germans attacked on 30 July, there were mixed results at first. In some areas, they advanced swiftly, but in other areas – for example, where 3rd Panzer Division's armoured battlegroup found itself in a dense minefield – progress was far slower. The advance by 16th Panzergrenadier Division began later than the attacks by other units and was also held up by minefields around Semenovsky, but the day's objectives were largely reached. A member of the panzergrenadier division recorded in his diary:

> 1340: Today's objectives have been reached. Many prisoners were taken, and they all look very grubby. They weren't so badly dressed a year ago. We can see that the Russians haven't much left. They no longer have any leather gear, and we no longer see them wearing boots. Instead they have tattered shoes with gaiters. By 1400 it is quiet around us, no more enemy visible. Also no shelling for some time! Our troops are already far ahead and we can no longer see them.[21]

The scale of the fighting on the Eastern Front was such that it was impossible even for the immense resources of the Soviet Union to ensure that all units received adequate quantities of uniforms, boots etc., and for much of the year the priority had been firstly to ensure that the armies facing the Germans around Kursk were in the best possible shape, and secondly to prepare the armies on either flank that would be used in the counteroffensives that followed immediately after. Despite its huge losses in the war to date, the Red Army was far from reaching the end of its strength.

On the second day, 23rd Panzer Division succeeded in making a breach in the Soviet defences and, with the two SS divisions continuing to struggle to make headway in the face of determined resistance, it was decided at the end of the day to shift the point of main effort to the south. *SS-Totenkopf* experienced tough fighting, with some ground being gained on 31 July, followed by repeated Soviet counterattacks during the night. Throughout the second day of the attack, *SS-Das Reich* fended off repeated Soviet counterattacks, claiming the destruction of 26 tanks and the capture of 1,400 prisoners. By the end of 31 July, the division had secured the village of Stepanovka but the lack of progress by *SS-Totenkopf* to the north hindered further advances; additional disruption was caused by a sudden cloudburst that resulted in a flash flood in the gully where the division headquarters of *SS-Das Reich* was operating, resulting in the loss of several vehicles. On 1 August, as the Soviet units appeared to be withdrawing in 23rd Panzer Division's sector, all the German armoured formations received an order from the chief of staff of Sixth Army, Generalmajor Max Bork, to push forward rapidly 'without regard to securing flanks'.[22] During the afternoon, *SS-Totenkopf* made another attack, struggling forward across ground it had contested the day before, through a heavy curtain of Soviet artillery fire, as Rottenführer Georg Hax – a junior NCO in the division's reconnaissance battalion – wrote in his diary:

> And we were to advance through that?! 'Spread out but keep contact' was the word. Whoever heard the command followed. We ran forward a further 200m but then we were covered by Russian shells. A shower of hand grenades forced us to ground. Heinze was hit. The enemy batteries swiftly and frequently changed their targets. At one point they plastered the ground behind us and cut us off from any reinforcements, and then they directed their murderous fire once more upon our tanks. Despite this we gained ground in stages. Untersturmführer Radde was wounded but tried to keep up. Another 300m separated us from the Russian positions. As we sprang forward, we could see the Red Army troops with their heads and shoulders sticking up out of the brown earth. There were more Russians in a foxhole. To our left, we lost contact with our 1st Company. Nor was there any movement on the right with Hugo Lechner's platoon …
>
> Schubert was wounded. Erich Wolf bandaged his leg. Untersturmführer Radde needed to go back. But there was no contact to the rear. Otto Schubert decided it was best to wait and shouted to us, 'Dig in!' But that was almost impossible. The sun had baked the loamy soil almost rock-hard.[23]

Another soldier in the same company was on one flank of the attempted advance:

> I had contact with an Unterscharführer from the [neighbouring] 3rd Company. Things looked dreadful for us. Trenches and foxholes were strewn over the landscape. Shot-up, burned out tanks were all around. Casualties, friend and foe, lay amongst them, some on top of them. Under the burning sun, some had started to decompose. Their corpses gave off a dreadful smell. Shots flew everywhere. It seemed impossible to take cover.[24]

During the afternoon, the Luftwaffe attacked the artillery that had caused heavy casualties amongst the advancing panzergrenadiers, and the Soviet positions were finally reached. Supported by their own artillery, the men of *SS-Totenkopf* continued their painful advance, and the arrival of a small group of the division's tanks swung matters in their favour:

The tanks rolled up and then onwards. Now we too were mobile again. It was hard to run with all the things we had to carry – machine-gun tripods, ammunition boxes, etc. We couldn't keep up with the tanks. Bullak was able to clamber onto one of the tanks that had stopped right next to him. Soon he was lying next to the turret, his gun blazing. That was the last time I saw him. About 30 tanks had rolled past us. Otto Schubert and I ran like mad through the shell-bursts and tanks. An unflappable motorcycle messenger drove up to the lead tank. 'Man, what are your nerves made of?' I thought to myself. The group of tanks drew away to the right and was soon 300–400m from us. Their turrets turned to the left. Their guns fired constantly …

When the tanks moved off, the enemy artillery fire on us ceased. Now our own artillery gave fire support for our attack, which resumed. Apparently our forward observers were not 'right on target' as our shells as well as those of the Russians fell amongst our tanks. One Pz.III was already ablaze, hit by one of our shells. The crew baled out in their shirtsleeves and put the flames out with an extinguisher, climbed back in and rolled on towards the enemy. All this unfolded in just seconds.[25]

By the end of the day, the hard-fought battle had swung firmly in favour of *SS-Totenkopf*, and elsewhere too the Germans were gaining ground, albeit at a pace that was disappointing. On the other side of the front line, the Soviet artillery officer Kobylyanskiy was alarmed by the clear presence of German troops on both of his flanks. Short of ammunition – he had no high explosive rounds left – he monitored the telephone exchanges of his battalion in the hope of learning more, and was not reassured by the declaration of the unit's political deputy commissar that the situation had been completely restored during the night. The following morning, his concerns proved to be well-founded:

I was awakened by a push on my shoulder and Nazarenko's angry cry, 'Junior Lieutenant! Germans!' I leaped up. It was now completely light. Nazarenko silently pointed at the hollow to the right of us, where three Germans were walking calmly. The distance was about 150m. We quickly turned the gun and fired an armour-piercing shell [as they had no other ammunition available], but the Germans quickly took cover behind a thick bush. We saw them, however, and our next three shots were on target.

It was strangely quiet in front of us, and our telephone was deathly silent. I sent Nazarenko to find the break in the line and to ascertain what was going on in the battalion's trenches. He came back in a minute. 'There's not a living soul there!' It meant that the battalion's riflemen had abandoned their positions during the night without saying a word. The situation was now extremely serious.[26]

Worse news arrived a few minutes later when a man sent to summon the field gun limber returned to report that the limber and its personnel had vanished. After disabling their gun, Kobylyanskiy and his men withdrew to the regimental command post. They found it under attack by German tanks and infantry and took cover in a cluster of bushes. From here, they had to try to escape by running between the tanks:

> There was another 'island' of dense shrubs some 70m ahead, but the tanks were between our current position and that sanctuary. Nevertheless, someone rushed into the gap between the armoured monsters. Another followed him, and a third. Tarasov took off at a rush, and in a few seconds I started my own dash. I was running in a slight crouch; my heart pounding with nervousness and fear. Suddenly, when I had reached a point just between the tanks, a tremendous blow knocked me down.
>
> I simultaneously felt intense pain in my right hip joint and caught the smell of burning cloth and flesh. Pressing the wound with my hand, I lay without stirring, being absolutely horror-struck – there was no way to avoid capture with such an injury. Tarasov lay three metres in front of me, groaning in a low voice, 'Brothers, don't desert me!'. Gradually I began to consider the situation: the tank shell obviously hadn't landed right next to me; otherwise I'd have been smashed completely. Maybe a clod of caked earth hit me? Very carefully I removed my hand from my hip and glanced at the palm: it was dry! I glanced forward – Tarasov, who had just been groaning, suddenly leaped to his feet and darted at full speed to a nearby shrub. I rushed after him, but my every step was very painful, and something else was making my running difficult, Somehow I reached the shrub. Lying there I discovered that the heel and the sole of my right boot were partly torn. I tore them off completely and shortly thereafter started my next rush to the next group of bushes standing by the far edge of the meadow.[27]

Kobylyanskiy found himself with a group of other Soviet soldiers in a narrow gully that ran back to the east towards the Mius. The German tanks soon withdrew a short distance, but a Stuka attack followed. It was only when a sudden thunderstorm broke, preventing further German air attacks, that the retreating Soviet troops were able to pause and reorganise.

In an attempt to get the German attack moving forward faster, Obergruppenführer Paul Hausser, commander of II SS Panzer Corps, wanted to use his reserve formation – the *Der Führer* panzergrenadier regiment of *SS-Das Reich* – in a new attack and outlined his plans late on the first day of the operation. Manstein was dubious about whether a single regiment could restore momentum where several panzer divisions had failed to make rapid progress, but Hausser replied in a long exchange that the capture of key high ground would unlock the Soviet defences and was given permission to proceed. Obersturmbannführer Sylvester Stadler, commander of *Der Führer*, was promised whatever fire support he needed and proceeded to carry out a careful reconnaissance before deciding that the best chance of success was by making a surprise attack before dawn on 1 August with little or no fire preparation – salvo rocket launchers would be used to put down a smoke barrage to protect each flank of the attack while the panzergrenadiers advanced as silently as possible. Preparations for the attack were almost abandoned when the Soviet troops launched a surprise attack of their own, but the front line was restored in sufficient time for the plan to proceed.

The German panzergrenadiers duly set off, screened by the smoke barrage, and reached the Soviet lines without being detected. Here, fighting broke out at close quarters; the Soviet defenders called down an artillery barrage to prevent further German troops moving up to their lines, but the bulk of *Der Führer* was already in the Soviet positions. About 30 minutes after the fighting began, Soviet tanks appeared, but in the meantime German assault guns had also moved up in support and fighting became generalised. For much of the morning, Stadler was isolated in the front line when his radio developed a fault and he had no contact with higher commands, but by late morning the Soviet counterattacks slackened and ceased. From the high ground he had captured, Stadler could observe much of the battlefield and, with contact once more restored, was able to call in air strikes against the withdrawing Soviet troops.[28]

Elsewhere, the Tiger tanks of *SS-Das Reich* were also involved in the attack. The SS divisions each had their own *Kriegsberichterzug* ('war reporters' section'), and one member wrote a vivid description of the Tigers in action, and the perils of operating without close infantry support:

> Our mission was to take by storm the high ground, which was studded with formidable bunkers, mortar positions, machine-gun nests, anti-tank obstacles and trenches, to crush everything that opposed us and to make a breach in the well-armed enemy front line for the infantry that would follow us.

Forming a firing line with barely 100m between each tank, the colossi rolled forward across no-man's land and closed with the enemy's field positions, leaving behind them the Bolshevik riflemen who were unable to flee at the last minute and made straight for the objective. We left behind us the killing zone of heavy defensive fighting, the labyrinth of enemy trenches that were stacked with corpses. Helmets, rifles and shell-cases crunched under our tracks like glass. Shells exploded in front of and next to us as the enemy tried to set up a curtain of fire. They couldn't stop us. Anti-tank shells rang out as they struck frontal armour and the hull. Buzzing like wicked insects, the shots of anti-tank rifles flew past and ricocheted into the sky leaving faint marks. Now as the anti-tank fire intensified and a couple of Bolshevik tanks appeared on enemy high ground, we halted for a while and with a few shots destroyed a couple of guns we spotted, left the T-34s burning, and then we rolled onwards.

At this moment our vehicle commander, an Oberscharführer from Carinthia who would be wounded for the ninth time two hours later, took overall command. The platoon leader's vehicle had run over a mine and had been disabled. It was left behind to provide covering fire and act as a strong bastion against any possible surprises.

Now we had just four Tigers and had no time to hang around. We engaged the dense crowds of enemy infantry with machine-gun fire while driving at full speed. During brief halts we fired our explosive shells against mortar and anti-tank gun positions. It all went so quickly that only fragmentary details were left in our memory, no overall picture but rather like an impressionist watercolour, a disorderly confusion of death and destruction overlaid by the thick, sweet smell of corpses. Right over there lay the commissar with his cap next to him, wearing blue trousers and a pistol clutched in his hand, pointing down into the ravaged earth. Weapons and equipment lay all around. The enemy riflemen hopped back and forth in the cornfield before us like frightened animals, driven back by fear and forwards by their orders.

We reached the bottom of a shallow dip, emerging from a cornfield and rolling towards the crown of Hill 280, our next objective, across the open steppe. The speed of our advance left us weak-kneed. We had barely noticed the shell-strikes, the bursting detonations of enemy artillery rounds …

We reached the heights at 0900. The fighting raged on. We advanced tentatively, engaging tanks and anti-tank guns, earthworks and firing points. At that moment, our vehicle ran over a mine. As if struck by a huge fist, the tank reared up. I saw the driver fall from his small seat. We stopped. The engine was no longer running. Slowly, the black smoke of the great explosion spread. Thank

God, nobody was wounded. The main gun and machine-guns were operational. But the turret wouldn't turn properly. Just as the gun-aimer called out, 'Now the others will have to look after us', two neighbouring vehicles ran onto mines. That was the signal for the enemy infantry. The riflemen moved into the high corn and moved towards us. We fired, of course. But we were pinned down far in front of our own lines and needed help. The middleweight and light tanks that had attacked further to the right and were meant to advance towards us didn't come any closer. We could see them four or five kilometres away engaged in heavy fighting with the enemy defences. Two of them were ablaze. We had no time to pay much attention to them. All eyes stared ahead anxiously. The enemy riflemen were dangerously close. They set up mortars, wanting to set us ablaze by striking the thin deck armour. We dealt with five with well-aimed shots. Then the turret machine-gun jammed. One fellow charged towards us over a short distance carrying something heavy. The radio-operator's machine-gun couldn't cover him. He came within 100m, 80m, and we fired an explosive round at his feet at 50m. He didn't bother us any more but he wasn't alone. New groups constantly appeared and probed towards us. We fired while we could, coordinating our close defence and sending warnings to our neighbours by radio and by waving. After about an hour we also had enemy infantry behind us. We couldn't see them, or defend against them. If they showed any initiative, they would have us sooner or later. But they seemed afraid. Or perhaps they had other orders. They didn't succeed in carrying them out. A new wave of tanks appeared behind us, drove up to us, and allowed the withdrawal of the stricken Tigers. We came back under our own power. The driver had worked out that the tank would still run in fourth gear. All we could do was resume the attack. Just a few metres forward and the commander was wounded in his hand by shrapnel. We took him back and drove back into battle with a new commander.

At 1600 we too were pulled out. The repair section would repair us by the following morning.

Didn't we wish to admit that we had been shaken a little? A few tanks deep in enemy territory, immobile, didn't amount to much. They could easily have become our coffins or even crematoria. That wouldn't have been a happy ending. It did no good to dwell on it. Get a grip, laugh a little, and move on – that was best.[29]

The hill that had cost *SS-Totenkopf* so many casualties and the high ground captured by *Der Führer* proved to be key positions in the Soviet defences, and lacking the strength to retake it with a counterattack, the Soviet units had little option other than to start a general withdrawal towards the Mius. Now that they held the high ground overlooking the west bank of the river, the Germans could call down artillery fire and air attacks on the Soviet rearguard and the units struggling to cross, inflicting substantial losses. The final advance to the old front line along the Mius involved little hard fighting. By the time that the battle died down, the Germans claimed 18,000 prisoners and the destruction of hundreds of Soviet tanks. However, casualties were substantial, with *SS-Totenkopf* alone recording nearly 1,500 dead, wounded and missing in just three days of fighting; as the battle died down, the division reported that it had only 23 tanks operational, and six of these were command vehicles without main armament.[30] When they reached the Mius, a group of soldiers made a grim discovery, as one wrote in his diary:

Just above the trench we have occupied lies a dead German soldier who has been lying there for who knows how long. The ground must have softened before countless Russian boots trampled him. Is this really the man's face? Was it stubbornness, brutality, lack of feeling, hatred, or revenge that made them step on you, my unknown friend, and stamp you into the Russian soil until you were barely recognisable? Only the buttons of your uniform jacket allowed us to find you. We couldn't loosen the hard earth with our entrenching tools. Tomorrow, mate, we'll dig you out.[31]

German units that had been in the sector throughout the initial Soviet attack and the German counterattack that followed had suffered badly. From 17 to 31 July, 16th Panzergrenadier Division calculated that it lost nearly 4,600 dead, wounded and missing. Although it was not present for much of the first Soviet attack, 23rd Panzer Division too suffered about 1,800 dead, wounded and missing. Whilst there was some relief for 16th Panzergrenadier Division on 2 August when about 950 reinforcements arrived, they represented only 20 per cent of its losses, and most of the new men were relatively inexperienced.[32]

The fighting on the Mius had been compressed into a comparatively small area, with both sides making extensive use of artillery and air support. The scale of destruction was therefore considerable, as Vogelsang wrote:

I had the opportunity to take a look at the Krutaya gully. The impression was simply grim and was of the most dreadful picture of destruction that I had ever seen. For weeks, bombs and shells of all calibres had struck its floor and slopes. Not a single tree or shrub was undamaged. Huge bomb craters gaped in its slopes, swampy pools glimmering faintly in them. Torn up trees and shredded equipment were strewn far and wide in an impassable mess. Broken trailers, wrecked vehicles, the corpses of horses torn open, the maimed bodies of men, the smoke-blackened remains of burned out ammunition stores, shreds of uniforms, smoking tank wrecks, overturned guns – all as if a giant had mindlessly raged and whirled through everything and stamped it all into unrecognisable heaps with its huge boots. All over the destruction was the stifling haze of smoke, dust and rotting corpses.[33]

The Soviet forces that had been driven back across the Mius were from Second Guards Army, commanded by Lieutenant General Iakov Gregorovich Kreiser. He was removed from his post and sent to take command of Fifty-First Army. Rumours circulated amongst the Soviet troops that *Stavka* had refused to issue any medals to soldiers who had fought bravely in the battle, but after a short delay the medals duly appeared.[34] The attack by the Red Army might not have achieved a substantial gain in territory, but it had served a purpose, dragging German reserves into a wearing battle in the south at a time when they might have benefited from a pause to rest and refit. The German counterattack on the Mius commenced less than two weeks after II SS Panzer Corps was pulled out of the fighting in the Kursk salient, and much of that time had been spent redeploying from one location to another. Even as the fighting died down along the Mius, the tired panzer divisions were aware that a further long march awaited them before they went into action once more in their role as firefighters. The human fatigue, the wear and tear on equipment, and the loss of irreplaceable experienced personnel would all take a toll, and it was inevitable that a stage would come when they could no longer prevail as they had in the past. With its huge resources, the Red Army could afford to keep applying pressure on different parts of the front, confident that a breakthrough would come, as Vasilevsky later wrote when he summarised the operations that were carried out all along the Eastern Front in the second half of 1943:

> Not one of these operations was to begin or end at the same time. They were to overlap one another in time, being consecutive only in a very general sense. This would force the enemy to split up his reserves, bringing them from one sector to another, trying to block the enormous breaches being made in his front by Soviet troops first in one place and then another.[35]

Phasing these operations had another benefit for the Red Army: its logistic services would not need to support simultaneous operations, but would be able to switch resources from one sector to another.

Immediately after the battle, Gruppenführer Walter Krüger, commander of *SS-Das Reich*, wrote a detailed critique of the operation for Hausser, the commander of II SS Panzer Corps. The terrain on which the battle had been fought was favourable to the Soviet forces and prevented armoured units from manoeuvring freely, thus depriving them of their main advantage. The slowness of their attack, he argued, gave the Soviet units sufficient time to create new minefields along their axis of advance, adding further to the difficulties they faced, and the division's tanks ended up functioning as little more than infantry support – a role that was better served by assault guns, and in any case panzer divisions didn't have sufficient infantry resources to function in such a manner. As had been the case in the fighting in the Kursk salient, the Red Army made good use of defence in depth with extensive use of artillery and anti-tank guns, and it was almost impossible to achieve any degree of surprise in the attack – the long approach march had been clearly visible to Soviet aircraft and the forming-up areas had also been under observation. Normally, movement by night might have prevented observation, but the short summer nights and the distances that had to be covered made this impossible. The delay required to repair vehicles prior to launching the attack was put to good use by the Soviet units, with prisoner interrogations suggesting that in some places the Red Army had been able to double the number of men in the front line. Reconnaissance had been inadequate, particularly in identifying the Soviet artillery positions so that they could be silenced once the attack began. The long approach march by road had a deleterious effect on the division's armoured vehicles – Krüger reported that half of them were not operational at the end of the long drive. He was also critical about the manner in which artillery was used in a general bombardment of the enemy front line, describing this as a waste of ammunition; prisoner interrogations suggested that little damage was done to the Soviet positions. Similarly, coordination with Luftwaffe units had been inadequate, and Krüger felt that it was important for decisions about timing and precise location of attacks to be made wherever possible by the commander on the ground.[36] The logic of his comments is inescapable, and almost identical criticisms could have been levelled by any senior commander, whether in the SS or the Wehrmacht, against Hitler and his constant interference, though few if any would have dared to do so.

The influence of Reichsführer Heinrich Himmler, head of the SS, would ensure that the Waffen-SS divisions received lavish supplies to recover from their losses, though their constant use in the hottest parts of the front line would lead to the loss of increasing numbers of experienced personnel, whose replacement would be almost impossible. The Wehrmacht divisions were less fortunate in terms of supply and faced a harder path to recovery. In addition, the Soviet bridgehead near Izyum remained in place. Manstein had hoped that the Red Army would take several weeks to recover from the fighting near Kursk; but time was rapidly running out.

CHAPTER 3

OPERATION *POLKOVODETS RUMYANTSEV*

Whilst the Germans struggled with limited resources, constrained by their industrial difficulties and the impact of British and American bombing, the Soviet Union's relocated industries, safely out of reach of the Luftwaffe, continued to produce tanks, guns and other weapons on a scale that dwarfed even Speer's best efforts. The supply of material from Britain and the United States was also of considerable benefit, and whereas the Wehrmacht was forced to restructure formations in response to shortages, the Red Army continued to re-examine its performance and make appropriate modifications. The field armies that had fought the Germans in 1942 had been stripped of corps headquarters, largely due to the losses of the previous year, but by the end of that year they were being reintroduced, increasing the flexibility of the armies and allowing them to be enlarged. Supporting elements, both combatant (e.g. artillery) and support (e.g. signals) improved steadily, and it became increasingly commonplace to attach additional brigades and regiments to armies in order to help them carry out specific operations. These new armies reaped the benefits of this approach in the fighting in the Kursk salient, where they were reinforced with additional anti-tank forces in anticipation of the German attack. Nevertheless, the losses they suffered were substantial, and Manstein's assessment that it would take considerable time to restore them to full strength was by no means over-optimistic. However, the Red Army did not have to wait until the battered divisions of Voronezh Front had been replenished. The forces of Steppe Front, deployed across the base of the salient, were still fresh, and Voronezh Front's depleted Sixty-Ninth Army and Seventh Guards Army were transferred to Steppe

Front as soon as the attempts of Fourth Panzer Army to continue the offensive began to slacken. In return, Voronezh Front received the relatively fresh Twenty-Seventh Army and II and X Tank Corps from Steppe Front.

As a result of these rearrangements, Vatutin's Voronezh Front now fielded no fewer than seven armies over about 86 miles (138km), with two tank armies. In keeping with the doctrine of adding additional punch to help field armies achieve their objectives, he had four tank corps, an artillery corps, five anti-aircraft artillery divisions, and a large number of brigades and regiments providing additional artillery, anti-tank, mortar and engineer capabilities. Nevertheless, the recent fighting had left its mark, and despite fielding a total of nearly 2,000 tanks and assault guns, Vatutin's armies were all below establishment strength, with rifle divisions averaging about 75 per cent of their full complement.[1]

Now that the German attempt to attack the Kursk salient had been defeated, *Stavka* was able to release Steppe Front, commanded by General Ivan Stepanovich Konev, to operate on the southeast flank of Vatutin's Voronezh Front. Largely as a consequence of transferring substantial forces to Vatutin and receiving weakened armies in return, Konev's front was significantly below its nominal strength, with perhaps two thirds of its establishment.[2] Nevertheless, it could contribute a further 450 tanks to the coming operation. To the south of Konev's front was Fifty-Seventh Army, the first formation of Southwest Front, with a further 100 tanks, intended to contribute to the coming operation, and a further two armies were held in reserve. The total strength of the Soviet forces amounted to about 900,000 men with over 2,800 tanks; by contrast, Manstein had about 300,000 men supported by 560 tanks.[3] The previous year's great offensives – *Uranus*, *Mars*, *Saturn* and *Star* – had all been given astronomical codenames; the operations of 1943 were named after great Soviet generals. *Kutuzov* had already driven back Army Group Centre to the north of the Kursk salient; *Polkovodets* ('General') *Rumyantsev*, which was the codename assigned to the coming drive towards the Dnepr, was named in honour of Pyotr Alexandrovich Rumyantsev, who had fought with distinction in the Seven Years War and the Russo-Turkish Wars. The operation was intended to capture important cities in northern Ukraine – Belgorod, Kharkov and Akhtyrka – but its ultimate aims were more ambitious. If the German line could be broken, there was the prospect of a swift advance to the Dnepr and then down the valley of the river towards the south, threatening complete encirclement of Army Group Centre and Army Group A. This was largely what Manstein had anticipated when planning his 'backhand' operation at the beginning of the year – he had wanted to allow the Red Army to make such an attack, while he concentrated his armoured assets on its northern flank and then launched a counterstrike into the rear flank of the advancing Soviet forces. The fighting in the Kursk salient, together with the powerful attacks by the Soviet Southwest and Southern Fronts, seems to have distracted him from his previous astute awareness of the fact that the ultimate weakness of Army Group South's position lay on its northern flank; whilst Hitler remained obsessed with the economic, political and industrial importance of the Donbas, any major setback in the north would have disastrous consequences for the entire army group.

As had frequently been the case with previous major operations, Stalin dispatched Zhukov to oversee preparations prior to the operation's start date of 3 August. In what was increasingly a hallmark of Soviet planning, Zhukov's intention was to strike at the seam between two German commands – in this case, Fourth Panzer Army and *Armee Abteilung Kempf*, with the expectation that the retreating Germans would then fall back on diverging axes, allowing the Red Army to penetrate swiftly with its massed armour. The immediate objective for the Red Army was the recovery of Belgorod and Kharkov, scenes of bitter fighting the previous winter. The preparatory phase was an opportunity for Zhukov to make new acquaintances:

In preparing the operations of the troops of Steppe Front, I had to get acquainted with the commander of Fifty-Third Army, General [Ivan Mefodevich] Managarov, whom I did not know before.

Managarov made a very good impression on me, although I had to work intensively with him on the plan for the army's offensive. And when the work was finished and we sat down to supper, he picked up an accordion and played some merry tunes beautifully. Our fatigue seemed to fall away. I looked at him and thought: such commanders are particularly loved by their troops, who will follow them into fire and water.

I thanked Managarov for the excellent accordion playing and expressed the hope that he would play artillery music for the enemy just as effectively on 3 August.

Smiling, Managarov said: 'We will try, we have plenty to play.'

I liked Lieutenant-General [Nikolai Sergeyevich] Fomin, the artillery commander, who was well acquainted with the methods of using artillery means in the offensive. Together with Colonel General [Mikhail Nikoleyevich] Chistyakov [another artillery expert] … he did a very detailed and effective job of distributing artillery, providing ammunition, and carrying out all preparations for an effective artillery attack.[4]

The artillery preparations were indeed impressive, giving the Red Army a massive concentration of firepower with which to crush the German defences at the beginning of the operation. Voronezh Front would deploy about 113 guns and 129 mortars per kilometre of attack front; Steppe Front fielded only marginally smaller resources.[5] The concentration of tanks was also impressive – the Soviet tank armies would deploy their armour at a density of 70 tanks per kilometre of front.[6]

The Germans were defending lines that – in most areas – they had held since the end of the winter fighting, and extensive positions had been established. In most sectors, there were at least two continuous lines of such positions, but the infantry units occupying them were not numerous or strong enough to make best use of them. In nearly every sector, the German infantry divisions were forced to put all three regiments into the front line, rather than holding one regiment back for counterattacks or to act as a reserve. Nor did higher commands have access to sufficient reserves to throw into the battle. As already described, the attention that Manstein and Hitler turned to the Red Army's attacks on the Mius and at Izyum were based upon the assumption that these attacks represented the main effort of the next phase of Soviet operations, and that the forces that had fought against the Germans during *Zitadelle* were too badly degraded to launch a major strike in the northern parts of the Ukraine, meaning that German armour could be used elsewhere and then rushed back to this sector in time to intercept a Soviet attack. Both of these assumptions were incorrect, and the diversion of armour to the south would prove to be a major disadvantage in the fighting that followed.

As was almost always the case, the scale of preparations for the coming offensive was such that it was inevitable that German reconnaissance would be alerted. Manstein was provided with a steady stream of information from which he surmised that the Red Army intended to try to encircle the German forces in Kharkov and Belgorod. On 2 August, in order to try to create an armoured reserve that could be used in counterattacks, Army Group South ordered 3rd Panzer Division, which had been supporting Hollidt's Sixth Army to the south, to head north immediately. The remaining divisions of II SS Panzer Corps were also alerted, and a request was sent to *OKH* for the return of troops that had been transferred to Army Group Centre. Far too late, Manstein realised that his assumptions about the time it would take the Red Army to recover from the damage inflicted during the fighting in the Kursk salient were incorrect. He now had to scramble to avoid a potential disaster.

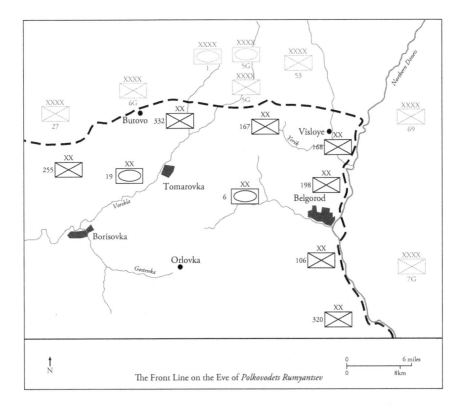

The Front Line on the Eve of *Polkovodets Rumyantsev*

Even if the troops required by Manstein had been released promptly, there was insufficient time for them to reach the endangered sector before the storm broke. On 3 August, after receiving the codeword *Uregan* ('Hurricane'), the Soviet artillery began the offensive with a carefully planned bombardment. Initially, there were five minutes of heavy shelling of the German defences, followed by a 30-minute pause during which combat engineers went into action to start clearing minefields and wire entanglements. Then, air and rocket attacks were directed at key positions, followed by a further 70 minutes of heavy bombardment. Finally, the rocket artillery struck the defences for a further ten minutes before the ground attack began.[7]

Using the prerogative of the attacker to the full, the Red Army had concentrated a powerful strike against the German defences to the northwest of Belgorod. Here, the German 332nd and 167th Infantry Divisions felt the full weight of the Soviet bombardment, and when concentrated forces of Fifth

Guards Army moved forward, they made rapid progress through the first line of German defences, as did the troops of the Soviet Sixth Guards Army to the west. The first serious resistance occurred only after the attacking troops had penetrated over a mile into the defences, when a series of Luftwaffe attacks attempted to stop their advance. Showing their increasing mastery of operations, the commanders of the leading Soviet formations had already brought forward their second echelon units to maintain the momentum of the attack and the leading formations of the Soviet First Tank Army, which was acting in support of Fifth Guards Army, were also fed into the attack, often bypassing areas where German defenders were still holding up the advancing Soviet infantry and pressing on to the south. General Mikhail Efimovich Katukov, commander of First Tank Army, later described the moment when his forces moved forward en masse:

> The magnificent advance of the Soviet tanks as they joined the breakthrough was imprinted indelibly on my memory. We advanced along the right side of a corridor about 5km [three miles] wide with the two corps each in a column. To our left, Fifth Guards Army moved forward alongside us. We were covered by squadrons of 'Yaks' [Yakovlev Yak-3 fighters] overhead. We had visual contact between our columns. During the entire war, none of us had seen such a concentration of Soviet tanks on such a narrow section of the front.[8]

Fifth Guards Tank Army, which was supporting the eastern flank of Fifth Guards Army's attack, began to move forward during the afternoon, further disrupting the German defences. Despite starting the battle in comparatively good shape, the German 332nd and 167th Infantry Divisions had effectively ceased to exist as coherent units by the end of the day.

By nightfall, Fifth Guards Army had advanced up to nine miles (14km) from its starting line, and in some sectors the leading elements of the supporting tank armies had pushed on even further. Despite these successes, the attack was not proceeding smoothly in all sectors. The Vorskla River ran across the line of advance, and despite the best efforts of the Soviet combat engineers, crossings were not established sufficiently quickly or in enough areas for the leading tank corps to cross en masse. To make matters worse, there was only a single road running from the Vorskla towards the key town of Tomarovka, and energetic German counterattacks held up the first units that attempted to advance down the road. This bought sufficient time for the German 19th Panzer Division, which was the local armoured reserve, to move into Tomarovka. One of the division's panzergrenadier regiments had already been deployed in support of

332nd Infantry Division, and the second panzergrenadier regiment now took up positions in the northeast part of Tomarovka; late on 3 August, both German regiments launched powerful attacks against the leading Soviet units in an attempt to recapture the road that ran east from Tomarovka to Belgorod. Heavy fighting continued throughout the night, with casualties accumulating on both sides for little gain.

Mansoor Abdullin was a soldier with 66th Guards Rifle Division who had risen through the ranks, taking part in the battles to encircle Stalingrad and the fighting in the Kursk salient. When his division embarked upon its attack into the Ukraine, he was appointed as commander of the division's *Komsomol* battalion, composed mainly of young communists. These young enthusiastic men often arrived at the front with minimal training, as Abdullin described:

> The average number of *Komsomol* members in the battalion varied from battle to battle, from 240 to 280. It was very fluid. I had a lot of work to do and there was never enough time. The fighting was brutal with heavy losses. Every night fresh replenishment drafts arrived in the battalion. Each *Komsomol* member had to be registered. The task assigned to each of them was the same: to do as much as they could in the war, especially as their lives might be cut short at any moment. They should aim to kill at least one Fascist! If they were lucky, they should kill two Fascists: one for themselves and one for a comrade who did not manage to kill a single reptile!
>
> ... By nature I am of a soft and impressionable nature – neither a ruffian nor a fighter, but in the war I destroyed and wanted to destroy the Fascists. 'You have time to kill the one that you have to kill before you die!' – thus I inspired newcomers to the front.
>
> But how painful it was, reducing me to tears, to utter despair, when I saw with my own eyes our dead soldiers who had just arrived as replacement companies. My true nature then burst out. My comrades in arms felt similarly and appreciated my honesty.[9]

By the end of the day, the Soviet attack had opened a substantial breach in the German line. Even if 19th Panzer Division managed to hold on at Tomarovka, there was now a substantial gap from there to the east. To make matters worse, the Soviet Sixth Army was advancing directly towards Tomarovka from the north. Here too, the Soviet troops were held up by waterways, on this occasion a tributary of the Vorskla, but by nightfall they had advanced to within two miles of Tomarovka. A little further to the northwest, the small town of Butovo lay immediately behind the German defences and the initial Soviet artillery bombardment was not as effective as further east. The German defenders, part of Generalmajor Adolf Trowitz's 332nd Infantry Division, were able to bring the Soviet advance to a halt just to the south of Butovo. The German 255th Infantry Division, a little to the west, was fortunate to have a battalion of Tiger tanks assigned to it, and these joined an energetic counterattack late in the day. Lieutenant General Ivan Mikhailovich Chistiakov, commander of Sixth Guards Army, threw his second echelon troops into the fighting but the stubborn German defences continued to hold up his advance:

> Only after we captured an officer from the headquarters of 332nd Infantry Division did I find out the reason for the delay. During interrogation, which I personally conducted, the captured major showed on the map where they had an intermediate position, which was not known to us ...
>
> After the entire first defence line was overrun, the enemy seemed to come to his senses and began to offer us stubborn resistance along the second defensive line. To contain our offensive, he clung to every grove and fought for every farm ...
>
> At noon, our troops approached Tomarovka. My 51st and 52nd Guards Rifle Divisions fought desperately in this area and tried to take the town on the march, but unfortunately they did not succeed in this.
>
> For a long time we couldn't secure Tomarovka. There were numerous stone buildings there, and the enemy skilfully used them as cover for machine-guns, cannons and tanks. We approached Tomarovka rapidly on August 3, and since I could not break into it, it was necessary for me, with the commander of the Fifth Guards Army, General [Alexei Semenovich] Zhadov, to bypass it. We went to the west, and his men to the east. The terrain here was difficult – ravines, small rivers with swamps, and we couldn't move forward.[10]

Chistiakov had expressed doubts about the ability of his army to achieve its objectives, as many of its divisions had suffered substantial losses in July defending the southern part of the Kursk bulge. While he tried to get his troops moving forward, he had a difficult encounter with Zhukov, who suddenly appeared in Sixth Army's command post. Zhukov demanded to know why General Andrei Grigorievich Kravchenko's V Guards Tank Corps, which had been assigned to Fifth Guards Army, wasn't helping the attack on Tomarovka. Chistiakov began to explain that the tanks were still struggling forward over the river crossings in their path, but Zhukov brusquely cut him short, ordering him to assign the tank corps to First Tank Army immediately, and departed with a comment that he had expected better from an experienced commander like Chistiakov. The embattled commander of Fifth Guards Army contacted Katukov and explained Zhukov's orders. Katukov might have been expected to welcome such reinforcements, but he was not remotely enthusiastic, aware that an additional tank corps would place huge strain upon the support services within his army and would merely add to congestion in his sector. In any event, he currently had no need of such reinforcements. The two army commanders and Kravchenko hastily met to try to resolve the issue but parted without any solution:

> With a heavy heart, I returned to my command post. Here the commander of the armoured and mechanised troops of the army, Colonel [Konstantin Sergeyevich] Lipatov, reported to me that the tank corps had begun to overcome the swampy banks of the Vorskla River.
>
> 'Is Marshal Zhukov aware of this?' I asked.
>
> 'No, he's in the dugout talking on the radio to the commanders of Voronezh and Steppe Fronts.'
>
> Taking advantage of the fact that Marshal Zhukov was busy, General Kravchenko and I went to the Vorskla River, where the Chief of the Engineer Troops, General [Emilian Evanovich] Kulinich, reported to me, 'Two crossings have been made for the tanks, and the third is nearly complete. In 20 or 30 minutes it will be ready. One tank brigade has already crossed.'
>
> I returned to my command post. There Marshal Zhukov was studying coloured maps of the operation. Before I could report how things were going, he asked, 'Has the corps been moved?'
>
> 'I'm dealing with it,' I replied. However, I did not tell him where I was sending it. Zhukov looked at me sternly.
>
> 'Good, Comrade Commander, sometimes it is possible and necessary to use the neighbouring sector.'
>
> While he spoke, I kept wondering whether I should say that the corps was still deploying in its originally intended sector, which was closer, more convenient and easier for us, even though we had lost two hours. I didn't say anything then, and later, when the task had been completed, I told Zhukov, 'In the end, I deployed the tank corps according to the original plan.'
>
> 'Why didn't you say anything?'
>
> 'I was too embarrassed.'
>
> It would be more accurate, of course, to say that I was afraid and hoped for a good outcome in which 'the victor is not judged', because of his success.[11]

This passage offers a fascinating insight into relationships in the Red Army. Zhukov had a deserved reputation for being obstinate and domineering, but ultimately remained focused on achieving victory; if a subordinate like Chistiakov didn't follow his instructions but still achieved success, he was unlikely to object, but had the deployment of V Guards Tank Corps not proceeded well, the consequences for Chistiakov would have been severe. Interestingly, Zhukov makes no mention of this incident in his memoirs.

One of the German armoured formations that was in the path of the Soviet attack was 6th Panzer Division, which had led the attempt to break through the Stalingrad encirclement in December 1942 and had then been in almost constant combat through the winter as Manstein first struggled to prevent a complete collapse of the German front line and then conducted a devastating counterattack. After being brought back to strength – including the addition of a company of 'Cossacks' recruited from the local population – the division took part in *Zitadelle*, under the command of Generalmajor Walter von Hünersdorff. Formerly the commander of the division's panzer regiment, Hünersdorff was a popular figure in the division and had always led from the front, and there was widespread dismay on 17 July when he was shot in the head by a Soviet sniper:

> Fragments of the helmet that Generalmajor von Hünersdorff was wearing penetrated into his brain. The unconscious general was taken by a Fieseler Storch [a light reconnaissance and liaison aircraft] to Kharkov. Dr. Tönjes, a senior neurosurgeon, operated on him, but the 45-year-old General died of his wounds that day in the army hospital. His wife, who as a sister in the Red Cross ran the soldiers' association in Kharkov, was with him.[12]

It was a bitter blow to lose a respected and highly energetic commander who had been awarded the Oak Leaves to the Knight's Cross just a few days before. His replacement was Oberst (soon promoted to Generalmajor) Wilhelm Crisolli, who had distinguished himself in leading a battlegroup of 8th Panzer Division on a heady advance into Lithuania in the first days of the German invasion, reaching and securing the vital crossings over the River Daugava in an operation that was the epitome of armoured warfare and the German principle of *Auftragstaktik*, by which a mission was assigned to a commander and he was then left to execute the mission in the most appropriate manner with little or no interference from above. Whilst 6th Panzer Division was fortunate to acquire such an experienced and skilled commander, the continued loss of battle-tested personnel at every level was a troubling trend; just as Speer juggled with inadequate resources to keep Germany's war industry functioning, the Wehrmacht had growing concerns about the loss of personnel like Hünersdorff, and perhaps even more so the casualties amongst NCOs and junior officers.

Deployed under the command of *Armee Abteilung Kempf*, 6th Panzer Division had been alerted as soon as the Soviet artillery bombardment began. It sent its armoured battlegroup forward immediately and the German tanks were soon in action against their Soviet counterparts; two further battlegroups were organised and dispatched to the front line as the day progressed in an attempt to prevent the collapse of 167th Infantry Division. The reports from the front line were grim, as the division diary recorded:

> The division commander was up front and established contact with the commander of 167th Infantry Division. He reports that elements of the reconnaissance battalion have been routed and are fleeing back. It is essential to bring up all the [division] artillery behind the anti-tank ditch in order to catch the fleeing troops. 4th Panzergrenadier Regiment is in position either side of the main road. The enemy is thrusting south there. Division headquarters received a radio signal from a reconnaissance patrol near Visloye: 'Infantry are fleeing back to the south.' Division headquarters has radio contact with the armoured battlegroup. It has been ordered to advance to Hill 218.5. Soviet tanks have penetrated there.[13]

The panzer division's reconnaissance battalion was intended purely for scouting, but as the war continued the equipment of these battalions became steadily heavier and they were frequently used as battlegroups. The partial rout of 6th Panzer Division's reconnaissance battalion was a singularly unusual event, but there was little time to dwell on the matter. The panzer regiment found itself increasingly hard-pressed, as its war diary recorded:

> As the enemy had occupied Gonki, the tanks had to push through to the south in order to cover the redeployment that had been ordered. Under heavy enemy artillery fire, the high ground to the east was held until our artillery and rocket launchers could withdraw. Oberleutnant Bonke was killed here. Enemy aircraft dominated the sky and made constant attacks on the withdrawing units with bombs and fixed weapons.[14]

In the early evening, the panzer regiment attempted a new counterattack but found its left flank was exposed and, watching helplessly as powerful Soviet columns drove on towards the south, the German tank crews withdrew into a position for all-round defence. The Soviet units waited until first light the following morning before attacking, taking advantage of morning mist to shield their advance. After suffering further losses, the German tanks withdrew to the south.

The troops that were opposing 6th Panzer Division were from Managarov's Fifty-Third Army, part of Konev's Steppe Front. Its exploitation force consisted of Lieutenant General Mikhail Dmitrievich Solomatin's I Mechanised Corps and – on the instructions of Konev – this entered the battle during the afternoon of 3 August; the powerful Soviet forces spotted by 6th Panzer Division's tanks were probably parts of the corps. Whilst the mechanised corps was able to make fair progress towards Belgorod, its early commitment deprived Fifty-Third Army of its armoured reserve. Consequently, when the left flank of the army struggled to make any progress against strong German defences along the line of the Yerik River, which had been reinforced by 6th Panzer Division's panzergrenadiers, Managarov had no powerful armoured unit to throw at the German lines. Nevertheless, whilst the attacks here and further east along the course of the Northern Donets made little or no headway, the Red Army had enjoyed a successful day. Along large stretches of the front line, the attackers had penetrated deep into the second line of German defences. The few German reserves available locally had been committed, and momentum remained firmly with the Red Army. Whilst Tomarovka remained in German hands, it had effectively been bypassed.

The German defenders of Belgorod were grouped together as XI Corps, under the command of General Erhard Raus, and after the customary heavy artillery bombardment, the first Soviet attacks against the German 320th Infantry Division, on the right wing of XI Corps, succeeded in establishing small bridgeheads across the river during the morning of 4 August. A determined counterattack in the middle of the day eliminated most of these footholds, but fighting continued all day. Raus later described an unusual development in the battle on the southern flank of 320th Infantry Division's positions:

In the gap between the battalion defending the gorge and the battalion on the hill, soldiers in German uniforms carrying German equipment appeared and, in good German, reported the arrival of reinforcements, come to aid the threatened sector in the nick of time. Understandably, the troops received this news with great joy, and the story spread through the battalion with lightning speed. Before the battalion commander had time to ascertain the strength and origin of this seemingly providential reinforcement, the Soviets launched an assault along the battalion's entire front. In minutes the situation became critical, and the battalion committed every last man to the front line.

This was the moment when the 'German' soldiers from the newly arrived companies poured out of the woods in dense columns and opened a murderous hail of fire against the battalion's flank and rear. Through the confusion that followed, shouts rang out: 'Here are Germans!' 'Don't fire!' 'Cease fire!' 'Madness!' 'What's going on here?' For precious minutes no-one among the defenders comprehended what had happened. Abruptly, all firing ceased as these new 'Germans' had become hopelessly intermingled with the defenders. Now they unleashed ear-splitting yells of 'Urrah! Urrah! Urrah!' and attacked at close quarters. In this bewildering situation it was impossible to distinguish friend from foe, and everyone in the forest began to fight everyone else. No-one seemed to be able to help, or even to disentangle the chaos.[15]

According to Raus, the commander of the German battalion was able to extract most of his command to a secondary line of defence, from where – reinforced by assault guns – he was able to mount a successful counterattack the following morning and recapture his positions. This account is not corroborated in any other record of the fighting, and Raus's memoirs are often inaccurate; he was commander of 6th Panzer Division the previous winter and led it in its attempts to break the Stalingrad encirclement, and his account of the chronology of the fighting is not consistent with the division's war diary. The accuracy of his account of this incident is therefore open to question, but it is perhaps relevant that the panzergrenadier division *SS-Wiking* reported a similar incident when it encountered a small group of Soviet soldiers in German uniform.[16] It is almost impossible to assess how widespread such attempts to masquerade as Germans were, though both sides frequently made use of captured armoured vehicles to try to take their opponents by surprise.

Raus regarded such conduct as criminal, in that it was contrary to the Hague Conventions. However, whilst Tsar Nicholas II had been instrumental in initiating the conferences that led to the conventions, the Soviet Union did not become a signatory and therefore was not bound by them. It should also be remembered that the conduct of German forces in the Soviet Union fell far short of the standards required under the conventions, and it is inconceivable that a senior officer like Raus was unaware of the atrocities committed not only by SS and paramilitary units, but also by the army. Given that both the orders from Hitler and the conduct of German forces in the Soviet Union were contrary to the Hague Conventions, it is at best rather selective of Raus to accuse the Red Army of not abiding by these rules.

The main Soviet effort had been deliberately directed at the seam between two major German formations – to the west was Fourth Panzer Army, and to the east was *Armee Abteilung Kempf*. If a gap could be created in the German line, it was likely that the two German armies would withdraw along diverging axes, thus making further Soviet advances far easier. Throughout the night, ammunition and fuel was brought forward and engineer units toiled to improve bridges to allow movement to continue. The reduction of the German strongpoint at Tomarovka was a clear priority and the town came under heavy air and artillery bombardment at first light on 4 August. Vatutin, commander of Voronezh Front, had stressed to Chistiakov the importance of taking Tomarovka as soon as possible and the commander of Fifth Guards Army did his best to eliminate the German defences:

> On 4 August, our artillery and aviation attacked targets before the front of my army and its neighbour, after which the troops of Sixth Guards and Fifth Guards Armies, in cooperation with First Tank Army, attacked Tomarovka. After heavy fighting on 5 August, parts of 52nd Guards Rifle Division managed to break the stubborn resistance of the enemy and penetrate into the northern outskirts of Tomarovka. The neighbouring unit now bypassed the enemy, resulting in battles on the northern and eastern outskirts. Other units that bypassed the town – 67th and 71st Guards Rifle Divisions – became engaged in fighting for the western and southern outskirts of Tomarovka.
>
> My 52nd Guards Rifle Division fought tenaciously to capture Tomarovka, but unfortunately without success. Seeing how difficult the situation was, I ordered the commander of 51st Guards Rifle Division, which was advancing from the northwest, to bypass Tomarovka to the west. General Tavartkiladze, who had commanded 51st Guards Rifle Division both at Stalingrad and in the defense on the Kursk salient, was able quickly and skillfully to change the direction of the attack to his regiments, after which he struck at the enemy who had held the western and southwestern part of Tomarovka.[17]

Despite these efforts, the defenders of Tomarovka continued to hold out; during the night, the rest of 19th Panzer Division had arrived, together with 255th Infantry Division. Several units of First Tank Army were diverted to the west in an attempt to break the deadlock and, partly through their intervention, the German positions in Tomarovka were now threatened from the southeast and south in addition to the pressure from Chistiakov's forces, but the price that the Red Army paid was a dilution of the armoured thrust by the two tank armies towards the south.

The key point of the attack was inevitably the relatively narrow sector in which the two Soviet tank armies had been committed, and here the battered remnants of the German 167th Infantry Division, reinforced by 6th Panzer Division, spent much of 4 August being driven back. Eventually, as the day drew to a close, the Soviet forces were brought to a halt, but they had created a gap of 12 miles (20km) between the western flank of *Armee Abteilung Kempf* and the right wing of Fourth Panzer Army at Tomarovka. Despite having to divert forces to support the attack on Tomarovka, Katukov's First Tank Army was still advancing and, even if Tomarovka should continue to hold, the Soviet tanks were now feeling their way past it and moving on to the south and southwest. German reconnaissance detected this advance, but in the confusion of the battle, the scale of the forces that were now between Fourth Panzer Army and *Armee Abteilung Kempf* was not clear. In addition to Katukov's tanks, Rotmistrov's Fifth Guards Tank Army advanced steadily at first, leaving its infantry support struggling to keep up. Later in the day, the Soviet tanks ran into a defensive line set up along the line of the Gostenka River, where further parts of 6th Panzer Division had taken up positions. Supported by the timely appearance of German dive-bombers, the panzergrenadiers were able to stop the Soviet drive. Rotmistrov later described the events of the day:

At 0500 on 4 August, Fifth Guards Tank Army continued its offensive, trying as quickly as possible to turn a tactical success into an operational one. The beginning was promising. By 0900 the leading units had already reached Orlovka and Kazichev. But here they were stopped by 6th Panzer Division, reinforced by elements of other enemy formations. With desperate tenacity, the Nazis clung to each advantageous position, and there were a lot of them. There was a multitude of heights and deep gullies. Rivers, including the rugged Gostenka valley, represented a serious obstacle for our tanks. The enemy had time to mine all the approaches to them and to dig in tanks and anti-tank guns on high ground with all-round fields of fire.

Major General [Alexander Vasilevich] Egorov's XVIII Tank Corps ran into the enemy's defences in terrain where it was impossible to manoeuvre, and was forced to suspend the offensive. I also received alarming reports from the commander of the XXIX Tank Corps' Major General [Ivan Fedorovich] Kirichenko. Enemy resistance intensified with each passing hour and his corps was suffering losses, especially from frequent raids by fascist aircraft. Kirichenko asked for assistance in the form of artillery fire and aircraft.

We called in air support. *Sturmoviks* dived on the enemy, bombing and shelling his positions, but with relatively little result. The Germans were dug in deeply, met our attack with heavy fire, and in some locations even made counterattacks.

I decided to move artillery forward and enter the second echelon of the army – V Guards Mechanised Corps – into the battle. The corps commander, Major General [Boris Mikhailovich] Skvortsov, was ordered to strike at Kazichev and Udy, bypassing the left flank of the enemy's 6th Panzer Division and to reach the Zolochiv district by the end of the day.

But Skvortsov's mechanised corps hadn't reached its start line to join the fighting when a radio message arrived from the commander of Voronezh Front, ordering me to turn his troops towards Belgorod. We learned only later that Managarov's Fifty-Third Army General, advancing to the left of Fifth Guards Tank Army, had moved its I Mechanised Corps, commanded by Major General Solomatin, towards Belgorod. To provide assistance to the troops of Steppe Front, General Vatutin asked me to strike with V Guards Mechanised Corps in the neighbouring sector.[18]

Without V Guards Mechanised Corps, Rotmistrov's two tank corps continued to struggle. However, that evening, when Rotmistrov and his subordinates analysed the day's fighting and modest progress, they learned that III Mechanised Corps from the neighbouring First Tank Army had crossed the Gostenka six miles (10km) west of Orlovka and was continuing to develop the advance towards the south and southwest. Unconsciously following the maxim that Zhukov had described to Chistiakov, Rotmistrov decided to take advantage of the gains of his neighbouring army. XVIII Tank Corps was to angle its advance to the southwest, bypassing Orlovka and advancing to Gomzino, in order to turn the flank of 6th Panzer Division and thus unlock the stubborn German defences; in order to coordinate this move with the various supporting units of Fifth Guards Tank Army, General Kuzma Grigorevich Trufanov, Rotmistrov's deputy commander, was sent forward to oversee operations on the western flank. At the same time, XXIX Tank Corps was to keep up pressure on the German defences in and around Orlovka, pinning the Germans in place and preventing their withdrawal. It would be assisted in this by the arrival of the infantry of Fifth Guards Army, which had been left behind initially by the rapid advance of the Soviet tanks but had now caught up.

While Vatutin's subordinates struggled to widen the breach they had made in the German line, the neighbouring Steppe Front was fighting its way closer to

Belgorod. Despite committing their armoured reserves, Konev's armies advanced only slowly through the tough German defences. With casualties mounting, Konev ordered Fifty-Third Army and I Mechanised Corps to direct their efforts to overcoming the German defences as fast as possible in order to make the continued German occupation of Belgorod impossible. The night of 4–5 August passed with the constant roar of engines as artillery and tanks moved into position for the following morning, and essential ammunition and fuel was brought forward. A little to the southwest, Soviet forces made the first of several attempts to force their way across the Northern Donets and thus to approach Belgorod from the southeast.

The German troops in Tomarovka had held out far longer than the Red Army had expected, and the strongpoint effectively contained the western flank of the Soviet advance. Throughout 5 August, the third day of the battle, heavy fighting raged around the town as Chistiakov tried in vain to storm the defences from the north. But even if the Germans continued to cling to the ruins of the town, they were in danger of being surrounded. Attempts by Fifth Guards Army to attack Tomarovka from the east made slow progress, but the Soviet 13th Guards Rifle Division, heavily supported by units of First Tank Army, advanced into what was effectively open space, driving southwest and penetrating to an area south of Borisovka.

To make matters worse for the German units in Tomarovka, they were now threatened from the northwest, where the Soviet Twenty-Seventh Army, commanded by Lieutenant General Sergei Georgievich Trofimenko, began its attack. Trofimenko made his initial assault with two rifle divisions, holding back IV Guards Tank Corps in reserve; once the German defences had been breached, the tanks would be unleashed to drive on towards Akhtyrka. During 4 August, aggressive Soviet reconnaissance had alerted the Germans to the likelihood of a major attack, and during the night Soviet combat engineers worked to clear mines and other obstacles from the area that the reconnaissance units had captured. At dawn on 5 August, the massed artillery of Twenty-Seventh Army struck the German defences of XLVIII Panzer Corps, manned in this sector largely by 11th Panzer Division. When the Soviet infantry advanced, it soon ran into determined resistance from the German armoured formation; despite having been reduced to about 50 tanks in the July fighting on the southern side of the Kursk salient, 11th Panzer Division remained a formidable force, albeit one not suited to defending an extended sector of the front line. In mid-morning, Trofimenko ordered Lieutenant General Pavel Pavlovich Poluboyarev's IV Guards Tank Corps forward. As had been the case in other parts of the Soviet operation, the terrain came to the aid of the Germans; although Soviet combat engineers had built bridges over the Vorskla River, the crossings weren't strong enough to take the weight of tanks and there was a delay whilst the bridges were strengthened. During the early evening, sufficient tanks crossed to allow the advance to resume and by the end of the day, Trofimenko had penetrated eight miles (13km) into the German defensive belt. Generalmajor Johan Mickl, commander of 11th Panzer Division, launched several counterattacks to drive back the Soviet tanks, but in vain. There was now a real danger of Tomarovka being encircled.

The German defenders of Tomarovka were increasingly imperilled, but the situation soon became even worse when the Red Army expanded its offensive to the west. Colonel General Kirill Semenovich Moskalenko's Fortieth Army, on Trofimenko's western flank, commenced a two-hour bombardment at first light before attacking through a smokescreen, a relatively new innovation in Soviet operations, as a report to Vatutin described:

> A system of four smokescreens was used. This facilitated the initial task of the army and, fully blanketing the [German] units defending Terebreno, covered the approach of attacking units from the enemy's aimed fire, the resupply of ammunition to forward positions, and the deployment of artillery observers for directing fire. By blinding the enemy, the smokescreen disrupted his fire plan, thereby allowing Terebreno and other pockets of resistance to the south to be bypassed.[19]

Moskalenko's troops made rapid progress through the defences of XLVIII Panzer Corps, and a battlegroup from 7th Panzer Division was thrown into the battle; it had little impact upon the momentum of the Soviet units. By the end of the day, almost all available German reserves were fully committed, whereas Moskalenko still retained considerable forces with which to increase pressure upon the defences.

Whilst the fighting at Tomarovka held up one shoulder of the Soviet attack, the resistance of 6th Panzer Division and 167th Infantry Division continued to constrain the eastern shoulder. However, Vatutin was aware that both of his tank armies had now penetrated the German defensive lines and he urged them both forward. First Tank Army's drive to the southwest would coincide with attacks by Twenty-Seventh Army further to the west, creating an encirclement around Tomarovka and Borisovka, while Fifth Guards Tank Army would advance a little to the east, threatening the flank of 6th Panzer Division and 167th Infantry Divisions.

Rotmistrov's advance alongside Katukov's army was rapidly stretching the resources of *Armee Abteilung Kempf*. Both 6th Panzer Division and 167th Infantry Division were fully committed defending Orlovka, and although it was possible for both formations to detach small formations in order to extend their flank to the southwest, the greater resources of the Soviet forces ensured that they continued to outflank the Germans. Manstein had ordered III Panzer Corps to the area, but although the corps headquarters had arrived in Zolochiv, 3rd Panzer Division – the main combat unit of III Panzer Corps – was some distance away to the south of Kharkov. At best, it would take another day before the German division was available for a counterattack.

Meanwhile, Konev's Steppe Front was fighting its way closer to Belgorod. The defenders – from 168th and 198th Infantry Divisions – had pulled back during the night into their last line of defences, and now faced a renewed Soviet attack. The attempts by Seventh Guards Army to fight its way across the Northern Donets to the southeast of Belgorod failed as the German 320th Infantry Division continued to use the rugged terrain to good effect, bloodily defeating every attempt to penetrate its lines; but on the other flank, Konev was pleased to receive reinforcements in the shape of V Guards Mechanised Corps, transferred from Rotmistrov's Fifth Guards Tank Army. In bitter fighting, the ring around Belgorod grew ever tighter, but the threat from the Soviet armoured advance towards the rear of the German positions could not be ignored. It was impossible for 6th Panzer Division to extend its flank any further, and rather than face certain encirclement, General Erhard Raus, commander of XI Corps under whose aegis the various units fighting around Belgorod were operating, gave the order to abandon the city. By early evening, Belgorod was in Soviet hands.

During the hectic fighting of the previous winter, the Red Army had captured Belgorod after the collapse of the Hungarian divisions defending the line of the Don, but even as the spring thaw began and made the landscape almost impassable for all vehicles, the divisions of II SS Panzer Corps had succeeded in recapturing the city. Now, it was once more under Soviet control. The liberation of Belgorod coincided with the recapture of Orel, further north, and guns were fired in salute in Red Square in Moscow. It was the first such salute of the war. Most of the city centre was in ruins, partly as a consequence of the repeated battles for Belgorod in 1943 but also because of demolitions carried out by the retreating Wehrmacht. Prior to the war, the city had a population of about 34,000, but when the Red Army took control in the summer of 1943, this had fallen to less than 200.[20]

The intention of the Red Army had been to try to encircle the German XI Corps in and around Belgorod, but the stubborn resistance of 6th Panzer Division and 167th Infantry Division to the west of the city, combined with the failure of Steppe Front's Seventh Guards Army to force the lines of 320th Infantry Division along the Northern Donets, allowed the Germans to withdraw intact. It is also notable that Hitler was heavily distracted by the growing crisis in Italy, where King Victor Emmanuel III had dismissed and imprisoned Mussolini and despite public statements that his nation would continue to fight alongside Germany, had opened secret negotiations with the Western Allies. Consequently, Hitler failed to declare Belgorod a 'fortress' that was to be held until the last man, and Raus was able to extract his divisions. They had suffered substantial losses, particularly 167th and 168th Infantry Divisions and 6th Panzer Division, but they remained intact. Soviet losses were far higher.

At about the same time, the bitter defence of Tomarovka was also coming to an end. Threatened on all sides, the German forces took their last opportunity to escape to the southwest. As had been the case in Belgorod, the German divisions managed to withdraw relatively intact, but their losses were heavy. Pulling back to Borisovka, the various elements of the German LII Corps took up positions around the town, with 255th Infantry Division occupying a horseshoe of defences facing north, while 19th Panzer Division deployed facing east and southeast. To the west, covering the region where Twenty-Seventh Army would advance, were 7th and 11th Panzer Divisions.

Katukov described the role played by his tanks in the final capture of Tomarovka:

A fairly large tank battle rapidly developed. The right flank brigade of XI Tank Corps and elements of XXXI Tank Corps engaged the German tanks in a pincer attack. At the same time, V Guards Tank Corps under Major General [Andrei Gregorovich] Kravchenko advanced on my right behind Tomarovka on a parallel axis. As soon as his leading elements were engaged, Kravchenko turned his brigades against 19th Panzer Division.

The Nazis fled. The roads to the west, south and north were closed to them. And then our assault aviation assets appeared in time to support the Soviet tank crews pressing in from three sides. The final battle did not take long. The enemy division was soon defeated, leaving more than 50 tanks on the battlefield. The commander of 19th Panzer Division, Generalleutnant [Gustav] Schmidt was killed by a shell fragment. His staff car with documents and personal belongings was brought to my command post by our tank crews.

A large group of German soldiers and officers surrendered. In Tomarovka we captured 45 serviceable Tiger tanks ready for battle. Apparently, they had just been repaired.[21]

The captured tanks were almost certainly not all Tiger tanks, but their loss was a serious blow. According to the accounts of other German officers from 19th Panzer Division, Katukov's account is incorrect and Schmidt was not killed by Soviet fire. He and his staff found themselves encircled during the fighting and when their ammunition was almost exhausted, he and his adjutant shot themselves before the rest surrendered; however, whether this occurred during the withdrawal from Tomarovka or shortly after in the fighting near Graivoron is not clear. At about the same time, a group of Soviet tanks almost overran the headquarters of General Hermann Breith's III Panzer Corps. Breith was wounded in the fighting, and it was only the timely intervention of soldiers from the corps signals battalion that drove off the Soviet troops. Despite his wound, Breith remained with his command.[22]

Chistiakov's troops were also heavily involved in the final reduction of Tomarovka. His infantry continued fighting for the town throughout 6 August, mopping up the last of the German resistance. When his units reported that the fighting was over, his relief was evident:

I called Vatutin and joyfully reported to him this event. He said, 'Well, at last you, Zhadov and Katukov have dealt with Tomarovka. Three army commanders have fought for three days and three nights to take this small town.'

I replied, 'The enemy had prepared for all-round defence in Tomarovka for a considerable time.'

'I know, I understand. On behalf of the Military Council of the Voronezh Front and personally from myself, I express my gratitude to the troops who participated in the liberation of Tomarovka. Medals are to be awarded immediately to those who distinguished themselves.'

This was done, although it must be said that in the conditions of street fighting it is difficult to identify the exploits of individual soldiers and subunits. I am convinced that dozens of our guardsmen performed feats in Tomarovka that are worthy of conferring on them the title of Hero of the Soviet Union, but they did not catch the eye of the authorities.[23]

With the frustrating resistance on either flank of the Soviet tank armies now easing, Vatutin believed that he had achieved a decisive breakthrough. The next objective was Kharkov, which like Belgorod had changed hands twice during the winter fighting; despite Hitler's declaration in early 1943 that the 'fortress' was to be held at all costs, Obergruppenführer Paul Hausser, commander of II SS Panzer Corps, refused to risk the encirclement and destruction of his units and abandoned the city before retaking it just a few days later. Vatutin was now determined finally to recapture Kharkov and issued new orders to his armies late on 5 August, even as the fighting for Tomarovka was continuing. Zhadov's Fifth Guards Army was to advance towards the southwest, attacking Borisovka and cutting the road to Graivoron, thus severing the line of retreat of the formations pulling back from Tomarovka to Borisovka. At the same time, Chistiakov's Sixth Guards Army would attack directly towards Borisovka, while Twenty-Seventh Army to the west advanced on Graivoron. Finally, First Tank Army was to drive southwest to Bogodukhov while Fifth Guards Tank Army advanced south to prevent the Germans from establishing a strong defensive line around Kharkov.

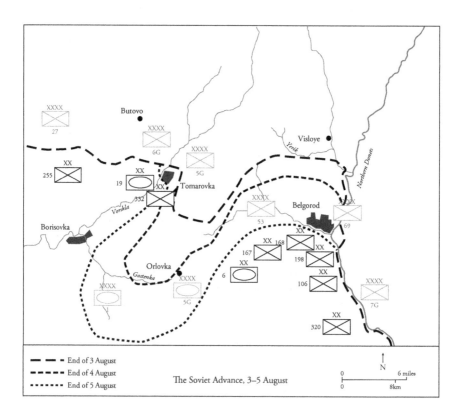

The Soviet Advance, 3–5 August

- ▬ ▬ ▬ End of 3 August
- ▬▬▬▬ End of 4 August
- •••••••• End of 5 August

N

| 0 | 6 miles |
| 0 | 8km |

On 6 August, Konev and Zhukov agreed a plan for Steppe Front's attack towards Kharkov. It is an indication of the losses suffered by the Red Army in the fighting for Belgorod that Konev estimated that he needed 35,000 men and over 300 tanks to bring his front back to full strength.[24] For the moment, he would have to manage without reinforcements, and his troops launched attacks towards Kharkov on 6 August. Despite heavy rain, which made many of the roads almost impassable to wheeled traffic, Fifty-Third Army drove back the German 168th Infantry Division, but Solomatin's I Mechanised Corps failed to break through as anticipated. It took the full strength of the corps to drive back the Germans in Mikoyanovka, but there was little chance to exploit the success; the retreating German infantry took up strong positions to the south of the town. In anticipation of a threat to Kharkov, the Germans had organised a series of defensive lines and fell back in an orderly manner when required.

Chistiakov also discussed the next steps with Zhukov and then issued orders to his troops. Attacking early on 6 August, his XXXII Rifle Corps rapidly closed with the eastern edge of Borisovka, fending off repeated German counterattacks. At the same time, the leading elements of First Tank Army, with infantry, artillery and anti-tank support, penetrated to Khotmyzhsk, roughly midway between Borisovka and Graivoron. Here, they surprised a small German group in the town, swiftly capturing them and several locomotives that they were guarding and triggering furious counterattacks. Although all the Soviet tanks were destroyed or disabled by the end of the day, the Soviet force, under the command of the energetic Captain Ivan Nesterovich Moshchenko, continued to hold on – despite their intrepid commander being wounded – until reinforcements arrived in the early evening.

With Soviet forces astride the Borisovka-Graivoron road and threatening Borisovka from all sides, it was clearly futile to continue to defend the Borisovka position and General Eugen Ott, commander of LII Corps, issued orders late on 6 August for his troops to withdraw before it was too late. The German line to the west had come under huge pressure earlier in the day when Twenty-Seventh Army's right flank launched a powerful attack on 11th Panzer Division. Weak in infantry, the panzer division was rapidly forced back most of the way to Graivoron, while the leading elements of First Tank Army approached the town from the southeast; with the two Soviet forces almost within touching distance, the German LII Corps was already effectively surrounded, even if it could withdraw the 24 miles (40km) to Graivoron.

Ott's attempt to extract his corps began before nightfall. The main body, consisting of 19th Panzer Division and 255th Infantry Division, set off towards the southwest along the main road from Borisovka to Graivoron, while 332nd Infantry Division followed a parallel route a little to the south. While these troops attempted to reach safety, 11th Panzer Division, supported by parts of 57th Infantry Division, was ordered to prevent the Soviet pincers closing on Graivoron.[25] At first, the withdrawal benefited considerably from dense fog that formed along the valley of the Vorskla, which ran slightly north of the Borisovka-Graivoron road. The first clash occurred near Golovchino in the early hours of 7 August when the main German column ran into Soviet infantry and was forced to turn away to the north; a second clash shortly after, involving elements of 19th Panzer Division, ended in a similar fashion.[26]

Unfortunately for the Germans, 7 August dawned bright and sunny and the fog of the preceding night rapidly dispersed. Chistiakov's troops pressed into Borisovka from the north while the German divisions urgently attempted to determine the positions of the Soviet forces that blocked their line of retreat. The main obstacle was 13th Guards Rifle Division, part of Zhadov's Fifth Guards Army, and in mid-morning the Germans concentrated their forces for a major attack. Under constant artillery fire and air attack, the German columns managed to make their way through Golovchino, but were then forced to detour to the west before they could bypass the Soviet infantry and regain the road. They now encountered elements of Trofimenko's Twenty-Seventh Army, which attacked Golovchino and Graivoron even as the retreating German troops were attempting to pass through the towns. Heavy fighting continued all day with substantial losses on both sides as the Soviet Twenty-Seventh and First Tank Armies' pincers met at Graivoron; taking advantage of the confusion of the battle, much of the German LII Corps was able to infiltrate through the Soviet encirclement and escape to the south.[27]

Despite the escape of considerable German forces, the outcome of the battle was a substantial success for the Red Army. Zhadov claimed that, in combination with the troops of Chistiakov's and Katukov's armies, his men killed some 5,000 Germans and took 2,000 prisoners, as well as capturing about 40 tanks. It should be borne in mind that such figures of captured equipment in Soviet accounts often include half-tracks; nevertheless, LII Corps had suffered serious losses, though as Zhadov wrote, it came at a price:

> The victory over the enemy was great, but it cost us dearly. We lost many remarkable guardsmen from our ranks, who gave their lives for the freedom of their native land.[28]

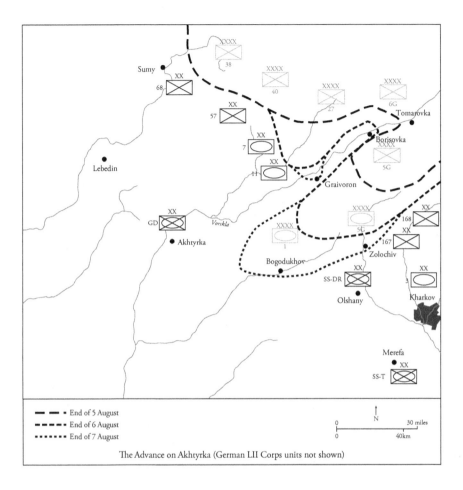

The Advance on Akhtyrka (German LII Corps units not shown)

The heavy fighting around Tomarovka, Borisovka and Graivoron might have cost Voronezh Front's armies substantial casualties, but perhaps the most importance consequence of German resistance was that much of Vatutin's infantry was tied down in the battles, with the result that the two tank armies that had broken through between the German Fourth Panzer Army and *Armee Abteilung Kempf* lacked the infantry support to hold the ground that they had seized. Indeed, the manner in which troops from several armies had been drawn into the fighting around Tomarovka, Borisovka and Graivoron caused consternation in *Stavka*. Late on 6 August, a signal was sent to Vatutin:

119

From the position of Zhadov's Fifth Guards Army it is evident that the army's assault group has become scattered and the army's divisions are operating in divergent directions. Comrade Ivanov [the current code name for Stalin] orders that the assault group of Zhadov's army be led compactly, without dissipating its forces in several directions. This applies equally to Katukov's First Tank Army.[29]

The deployment of the armoured formations of the SS in the area marked the end of II SS Panzer Corps. It had been created when the SS units were reorganised as panzergrenadier divisions – in reality, they were equipped on a scale that gave them more firepower than Wehrmacht panzer divisions – and under Hausser's command had been used to great effect in the German counterstroke in March 1943 that restored the front line after the disaster of Stalingrad. One of its divisions – *LSSAH* – had already been sent west, and the others were now subordinated to Wehrmacht corps commands. Hausser and his corps headquarters were sent to Italy, where they oversaw the disarming of Italian troops after the withdrawal of Italy from the war.

With 3rd Panzer Division now assembling near Kharkov and *SS-Das Reich* a little to the west, Manstein had at least an opportunity to strike a blow at the Soviet armour before their infantry support could arrive, and thus reduce, if not eliminate, the gap between Fourth Panzer Army and *Armee Abteilung Kempf*. The two divisions were assigned to III Panzer Corps, which was tasked with launching the counterattack; in addition, Manstein was able to promise Breith that he would receive *SS-Totenkopf*, which was still en route from Sixth Army's sector along the Mius valley. These forces had all been in the area to the south of Kharkov before being dispatched south to deal with the Soviet penetration across the Mius, but Hitler's interference in Manstein's intentions (first to reduce the penetration near Izyum before addressing the penetration in Sixth Army's sector) and Manstein's overestimate of the time it would take the Red Army to recover from losses sustained during *Zitadelle* notwithstanding, the hard facts were that the Germans did not have adequate armoured forces to deal with the multitude of crises that were now erupting. And, of course, the transfer of these divisions to try to intervene in the fighting to the northwest of Kharkov left the rest of Army Group South, facing the Red Army across the Donets and Mius, deprived of any panzer divisions – only the limited forces of small detachments of assault guns would be available to deal with any resumption of Soviet attacks across the Mius.

Helped considerably by the growing partisan movement, *Stavka* was aware of the limited resources available to Manstein and intended to take every step possible to increase his difficulties. Zhukov and Vasilevsky spoke to Stalin on the day that Belgorod fell and proposed that, in addition to continuing the attacks to recapture Kharkov, Southwest and Southern Fronts should commence offensive operations as soon as possible, with a view to meeting Vatutin's forces thrusting down from the north. At the very least, the Germans would be forced to retreat towards the Dnepr, and at best, it might be possible to encircle and destroy considerable German forces. Stalin was not enthusiastic about attempting an encirclement and told Zhukov that it would be better for the moment to concentrate on driving back the Germans and weakening them further before doing so, but nevertheless there was general agreement that attacks across the Donets and Mius should begin in order to tie down German forces. When formal orders appeared, it seemed as if Stalin had modified his views, as Vasilevsky wrote:

On 6 August ... Zhukov and I received a directive from *Stavka* ... The directive said that *Stavka* had approved the plan Zhukov had put forward for Voronezh and Steppe Fronts to destroy the enemy in the Kharkov area. Moreover, the right flank of Fifty-Seventh Army of Southwest Front had been transferred to Steppe Front so as to help the main grouping take Kharkov by an enveloping movement south of Kharkov. In the meantime, Southwest and Southern Fronts were to prepare and then to carry out operations to liberate the Donbas. The former was to spearhead an attack to the south in the direction of Gorlovka and Stalino from the banks of the Northern Donets; the latter was to strike from Voroshilovgrad and the Mius to the west, linking up with its neighbour in the vicinity of Stalino. The date of 13–14 August was set for these two fronts to be ready for carrying out their mission. I had to give *Stavka* the operational plan for approval on 10 August. I was also made responsible for their further coordination.[30]

The oversight roles that Zhukov and Vasilevsky took up reflected an arrangement that had worked well throughout the war. Broadly, Soviet formations were one step away from German formations – thus a Soviet corps was roughly equivalent to a German division, a Soviet Army was roughly equivalent to a German corps, and a Soviet front was roughly equivalent to a German army. The coordination role therefore was essentially equivalent to German army group commanders, but the arrangement was far more ad hoc. Zhukov and Vasilevsky had the further benefit of not having to deal with constant nit-picking interference from above; Stalin might make suggestions, but the level of trust between the three men was far greater than existed on the German side.

Whilst Manstein was aware of Soviet forces moving forward in the breach that had opened between Fourth Panzer Army and *Armee Abteilung Kempf*, he had no accurate information about how many Soviet units, and of what size, were involved. Nevertheless, the breach had to be closed if the front line was to be restored, and he confirmed his orders for the assembling III Panzer Corps to strike from the south and southeast, while Fourth Panzer Army's XLVIII Panzer Corps would counterattack from the west. Whether the depleted divisions of the latter corps, weakened in *Zitadelle* and then suffering further casualties during the first days of the Soviet offensive, had the strength to launch such attacks remained to be seen, particularly as their defensive duties would have to be passed to other, equally hard-pressed units.

CHAPTER 4

AKHTYRKA AND BOGODUKHOV

In his memoirs, Manstein makes a passing comment that the Russian recovery from their losses in *Zitadelle* was largely achieved by the transfer of forces from other sectors of the Eastern Front. There is some truth in this, but it also reflects a continuing frustration for Manstein. He had saved the disastrous situation that he inherited in the wake of the encirclement of Paulus's Sixth Army in Stalingrad by taking considerable risks in shuffling units within Army Group South in order to counter the Russians. Like several other senior German officers, he believed that the appointment of a military figure as commander-in-chief of the entire Eastern Front would allow for such redeployment of resources to be carried out on a far greater scale, but Hitler refused to agree to such a change; the best that Manstein had achieved when he had raised the issue during the winter was a passing suggestion from the Führer that the only potential candidate for such a post was Göring. The ability of the Russians to switch troops from one sector to another – and the inability of the Germans to match this – unquestionably made the mismatch in resources worse than it might have been.

The battles for Kharkov and the region immediately to the west took place simultaneously, but they are separated into consecutive chapters in this account for the sake of clarity.

On 6 August, even before Stalin issued his rebuke to the tank army commanders for needlessly dispersing their formations, Katukov tried to regroup his units in order to concentrate his forces. He had started the operation with 542 tanks, of which fewer than 300 were still running; whilst losses from German action had been substantial, many other vehicles had suffered breakdowns or been left behind due to terrain difficulties, and the supporting engineer units were labouring around the clock to effect repairs.[1] By mid-morning, First Tank

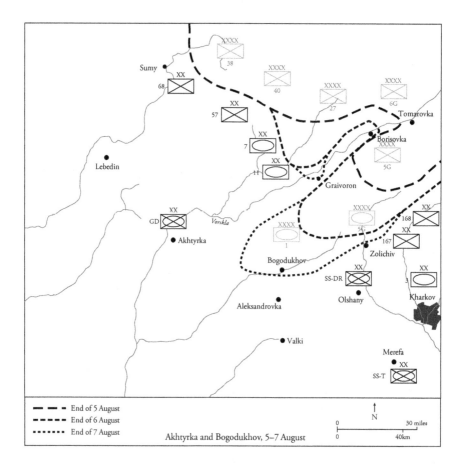

Akhtyrka and Bogodukhov, 5–7 August

Army was moving forward again, though large parts of XXXI Tank Corps remained tied up in fighting around Borisovka and Graivoron. Kravchenko's V Guards Tank Corps – finally transferred from Chistiakov's army to Katukov's command – was also absent from the drive to the south, dealing with the remnants of 19th Panzer Division and 11th Panzer Division to the west. Nevertheless, by the end of the day VI Tank Corps and III Mechanised Corps had advanced a further 20 miles (34km) towards Bogodukhov. A little to the east, Rotmistrov's Fifth Guards Tank Army was having a somewhat harder time. Its leading element – XVIII Tank Corps – penetrated to Zolochiv early on 6 August where it ran into the first units of the German 3rd Panzer Division. A little to the northeast, XXIX Tank Corps had been ordered to drive in the flank of the German units pulling back from Belgorod, but it too encountered elements of 3rd Panzer Division and the advance stalled. By the end of the day, V Guards Mechanised Corps, which had been diverted to help capture Belgorod, began to arrive in support of the two tank corps and Rotmistrov issued fresh orders for a resumption of attacks on 7 August. Even if the German forces intended for a counterattack by III Panzer Corps could concentrate in time, they would have their hands full stopping further Russian advances, let alone mounting a significant counterattack.

Katukov launched VI Tank Corps towards Bogodukhov on 7 August, with most of the rest of his tank army advancing immediately to the east. It took until mid-afternoon for the troops to regroup, refuel and rearm, but by early evening they had pushed the Germans back to the outskirts of the town, as Katukov wrote:

> The town was defended by rear area units, which did not expect such a sudden appearance of Soviet tanks, and therefore we captured a rich haul of loot. Whole warehouses of food, engineering equipment, and building materials were seized, and were later sent to Kiev to help restore the Ukrainian capital.
>
> We also seized large fuel reserves in the town – about 700 tons. Unfortunately, it was not possible to use it. The day after the capture of Bogodukhov, the Germans attacked the city with a squadron of bombers, which struck first at the fuel depots. The earth was shaken by deafening explosions. Bogodukhov was enveloped in a veil of black smoke. I had to order attempts to extinguish the fires to be abandoned.[2]

Lieutenant General Andrei Levrentovich Getman, commander of VI Tank Corps, described his men's performance in the battle with pride, as they liberated another town from German control:

> Corps headquarters decided that 200th Tank Brigade should advance from the northwest and 22nd Tank Brigade from the east in the first echelon. The second echelon consisted of 6th Motorised Rifle Brigade and 112th Tank Brigade.
>
> Before the battle, I visited the brigades to check on their preparations for the attack and talked with the soldiers and commanders. In 22nd Tank Brigade I encountered a brave and enterprising officer, Lieutenant Ivchenko, who was well known to me. He was a native of Bogodukhov, and before the war he worked here in a furniture factory and was elected a deputy of the City Council. He left to fight the enemy, leaving his mother, his wife with his one-year-old child, and his

sister and her family in the city, which was soon captured by the enemy. It is easy to understand the feelings of a soldier who for two years did not know about the fate of his loved ones and who was now triumphantly returning to his native city.

'Are you worried?' I asked.

'I'm worried, Comrade General,' the lieutenant sighed frankly. 'I don't know what's happened to my family. But now,' he said, his eyes flashing with determination, 'now I will find out. I'll be the first to enter the city.'

And he kept his word. When Colonel Vedenichev's 22nd Tank Brigade broke the resistance of the enemy at 1600 and penetrated into Bogodukhov, the leading tank was that of Lieutenant Ivchenko. Soon the tanks of 200th Brigade appeared on the streets in the northwest part of the city. The enemy garrison tried to continue the resistance, but after suffering heavy losses and fearing encirclement and complete destruction began to retreat hastily to the south after a two-hour battle.

By 1800 on August 7, Bogodukhov was cleared of the enemy. The entire population of the city joyfully met the liberating soldiers. The streets blossomed with wildflowers and flags, enthusiastic greetings were heard everywhere.

The invaders had inflicted a great deal of grief. The population had suffered looting and was starving, young people had been sent to Germany as forced labour, and many patriots were shot by the Hitlerites. And Lieutenant Ivchenko sought his family amongst the inhabitants of Bogodukhov who had survived the occupation. When his tank stopped at 10 East Street, a woman with a child ran out to meet him. It was his wife and son – all that remained of his large family. It turned out that his mother died of hunger, and the rest of the relatives died of other causes.

The soldiers of the corps went to new battles filled with hatred of the enemy and the determination to cleanse him from their native land.[3]

During this period, trains continued to ferry German troops to the region from far and wide. Some units had a long journey from Army Group Centre around the Kursk salient, while others, like *SS-Totenkopf*, made their way north from the battlefields on the Mius. When they received orders to pull out of the front line and to prepare for entrainment, the soldiers of *SS-Totenkopf* speculated on where they would be sent. Previously, the division had fought in the northern sector before suffering badly during the fighting around the Demyansk pocket in 1942, and there were rumours that they would be returning to Army Group North; the rumour that caused the greatest stir, inevitably, was a suggestion that the division was returning to Germany for a period before being returned to front-line duty. A sense of resignation and disappointment reigned when they realised that they were once more heading towards Kharkov, where they had fought the previous February and March. As they drew closer, many of the units were unloaded and continued by road:

> The closer we came to Kharkov, the greater the numbers of Soviet attack aircraft overhead. They flew to their hearts' content. Our Luftwaffe was conspicuous by its absence. Smashed vehicles were strewn along the main road, the 'Panzerstrasse Ost'. They were mainly tankers, which the Russian low-flying planes had targeted and were now burning, sending up clouds of smoke that could be seen far and wide ...
>
> Near Staritovskaya the Russians were firing on the main route with artillery from beyond the Donets. We detoured around the shelling through a huge field of corn. Under the blazing sun, we travelled the 300km [180 miles] to Merefa.[4]

Given the manner in which they had been equipped – far more generously than Wehrmacht panzer divisions – and the quality of the recruits who passed through the SS training establishments, the SS divisions had considerable justification for regarding themselves as an elite force, but this brought its own consequences. There was a tendency to expect superhuman efforts from them and casualties continued to accumulate. As they headed back towards the Kharkov region, the officers of the divisions would have been aware that since they had been reorganised as panzergrenadier divisions and had arrived on the Eastern Front in February 1943, their losses had been substantial – over 600 officers and nearly 19,000 other ranks killed, wounded or missing.[5] Whilst Himmler ensured that a steady stream of reinforcements arrived to make good the casualties, these new drafts could not directly replace the experienced troops who had preceded them. Such a high casualty rate would inevitably have an impact on the fighting power of the SS divisions.

As will be described in the next chapter, the German 3rd Panzer Division had now arrived and took up positions on the approaches to Kharkov, allowing the exhausted 6th Panzer Division to pull back for some much-needed rest, and other German units were also beginning to make their presence felt. SS-Das Reich continued its duel with Major General Semen Moiseevich Krivoshein's III Mechanised Corps, and the Russians were driven back to the outskirts of Bogodukhov. Getman, commander of the Russian VI Tank Corps, left a single motorised rifle brigade to defend Bogodukhov and dispatched two brigades past the western flank of SS-Das Reich where the gap between Armee Abteilung Kempf and Fourth Panzer Army remained open. By the end of the day, his leading troops were about 12 miles (20km) south of Bogodukhov, astride the Merchik

River at Aleksandrovka. Further progress was hindered by timely demolition of bridges over the river by German rear area units, but swift interrogation of captured German soldiers revealed details of the German troops that were being dispatched to the area; the Russians learned that a 'strong' corps of SS troops was on the way.[6] This intelligence was passed back to Getman and thence to Katukov, who decided that it was vital to cut the railway line running to Kharkov from Poltava in order to disrupt the arrival of German reinforcements. Getman was ordered to concentrate his forces as rapidly as possible in order to strike at the railroad. At the same time, the first units of *SS-Totenkopf* were deploying to try to protect the open flank of *SS-Das Reich*:

> It was so hot that we had just our camouflage jackets on our bare bodies. Dirty rivulets of sweat and dust ran in thick black streaks from our foreheads to the collars of our jackets and our hair, still full of the dirt of the foxholes of Hill 213.9 on the Mius and the dust of the road journey, lay heavy and straggling across our faces … enveloped in giant clouds of dust, we bumped along small roads. The sun blazed down mercilessly. It burned through our camouflage jackets and made our heads hurt. We would have loved to stop, seek out a sheltering tree, lie down in soft green grass, and eat a juicy red tomato, a sweet melon or a plump apple … but we drove on in column. We were just links in a chain. We had to wait for a mechanical breakdown. Then we climbed down off the vehicles to lie on the grass, but even on the road verges there was nothing but dust – dust everywhere. It lay like fine grey flour on leaves and flowers and on the grass stalks. It was in our eyelashes and our beard stubble, it clung to our jackets and penetrated the very pores of our skin.
>
> But at least there were often cornfields nearby. The young corn was juicy and quenched our thirst. Still clutching the heads of corn, we drove on. Remorselessly, the column ground on towards a new combat mission.[7]

In an attempt to get an accurate assessment of the yawning gap between the western flank of *Armee Abteilung Kempf* and the eastern flank of Fourth Panzer Army, *SS-Das Reich* organised a reconnaissance patrol consisting of just two armoured cars; Untersturmführer Scheller, the commander of the patrol, was to try to reach Fourth Panzer Army and report back by radio on his progress. For the first day of his mission, Scheller managed to stay in touch, carefully avoiding clashes with Russian units, but thereafter contact was lost and it was assumed that the patrol had been destroyed. But on the third day of the mission, a radio signal was received from Scheller. His armoured cars returned to the division a few hours later and reported that they had successfully made contact with Fourth Panzer Army, and provided detailed information about Russian columns that they had observed. The joy at the safe return of the patrol was tempered by the news that the gap to Fourth Panzer Army was now 33 miles (55km) wide.

Rotmistrov's troops attacked Zolichiv on 8 August, and Lieutenant Colonel Puzyrev, commander of 181st Tank Brigade, later gave him a personal account of the fighting:

It was already past midnight [on the night of 7–8 August] when the tankers reached the outskirts of the town, with their lights turned off. The dim light of the moon cast mysterious shadows on the roadside bushes and ravines. Somewhere to the rear, artillery fire rumbled, lighting up the horizon with crimson flames.

By 0400 the brigade was assembled on the town outskirts and Puzyrev ordered it to halt, and for engines to be turned off. The battalion commanders and their deputies gathered at the brigade commander's tanks, waiting for his orders.

'At first I hesitated, Comrade Commander,' Puzyrev confessed to me. 'I did not know what forces were in the town. I was worried about becoming entangled in streetfighting and considered waiting until dawn before sending in reconnaissance units. We listened. It was quiet, unusually calm, and we couldn't even hear any dogs barking. We concluded that the enemy was sleeping and finally I decided to break into the town, spreading confusion among the fascists. The main thing was swiftness of action.'

It was a bold decision, but courage was needed to capture the town. The brigade commander issued orders: 'Start your engines. We'll surprise the Nazis. Act with determination, but be careful. Forward to Zolichiv!'

The engines roared and the tanks burst into the town. Awakened by the rattle of caterpillar tracks and the roar of gunfire, the half-stripped Nazis wildly tumbled out of the houses and were mown down like sheaves of corn by machine-gun fire. Officers rushed into the streets trying to organise resistance. But our tank companies moved in parallel through the streets, shooting and overrunning trucks, staff cars, tractors, field kitchens and other equipment.

Fascist gunners hastily deployed an anti-tank battery at the church. Junior Lieutenant Baratynsky spotted this. His tank crossed the square at high speed and crushed the enemy's guns in just a few moments.

As it grew light, the resistance of the Hitlerites began to increase. The brigade commander reported to the corps commander by radio and was ordered to hold on in the town by all means possible. Concerned that the enemy might receive reinforcements by rail, Puzyrev decided that he had to capture the railway station.

The tanks of Captain Vergun and Senior Lieutenant Shkurdalov rushed to the station, scattering the Nazis along the way. They were still two or three blocks from the station when Shkurdalov suddenly realised that in the mayhem of the battle, he had used up all his ammunition. The last round was loaded into the gun. Then an open car appeared and rushed past the tank. Shkurdalov could see a German senior officer's cap in the car. 'Oh, hell, he'll escape!' he thought and fired his last round. His crew shouted in delight as the car was blown to pieces.

At this point, an enemy tank appeared out of an alley. 'Forward!' shouted the commander to the driver. The T-34 crashed into the German tank, pushing it into a ditch. The road was open, and Shkurdlov and Vergun moved forward.

When it was fully light, the battle broke out with renewed vigour. The enemy managed to bring up tanks and assault guns. An enemy armoured train approached the station. It became increasingly difficult to resist the pressure of the Hitlerites. But then T-34s appeared on the high ground north of Zolichiv. After driving the enemy from Shchetinovka and Uda, the main forces of XVIII Tank Corps had hurried to the aid of 181st Tank Brigade.

Towards the evening, the Nazis were finally thrown back to the southwest. For their courage and fearlessness in these and previous battles, Vergun and Shkurdalov were awarded the title of Heroes of the Soviet Union by decree of the Presidium of the Supreme Soviet of the USSR.[8]

It isn't clear which senior German officer was in the car that came under fire from the Russian tanks near the railway station, and the account is full of the characteristic rhetoric of the era. In the confusion of battle, it was often impossible to know for certain the details of the fighting, and both German and Russian first-hand accounts tend to exaggerate the effectiveness of their own side. Nevertheless, by the end of the day Zolichiv was firmly in Russian hands.

On the western end of the battlefield, Hoth's Fourth Panzer Army received valuable reinforcements in the shape of Generalleutnant Walter Hörnlein's Panzergrenadier Division *Grossdeutschland*. Intended to be one of the premier divisions of the Wehrmacht, *Grossdeutschland* had an unusual establishment for a panzergrenadier division, with additional battalions of assault guns and Tiger tanks, giving it a combat power more akin to a panzer division, and despite suffering substantial losses during the fighting in the Kursk salient, it fielded 140 tanks and assault guns. Whilst this was below its establishment strength, it still represented a powerful force, but a shortage of railway capacity delayed the arrival of the division. By dawn on 8 August only 50 of its tanks had arrived. The complexity of moving the heavy Tiger tanks added to the difficulties of rail transport; the tanks had to have their 'driving tracks' – weighing about six tons – removed and replaced with narrower 'loading tracks'. Once the tank was loaded onto its freight car, the heavy 'driving tracks' were loaded alongside, and on arrival at their destination the crews and maintenance teams had to reverse the process.[9] As the first formations of *Grossdeutschland* began to move up to the front line, they passed retreating remnants of LII Corps, some of whom shouted at them to go home and stop prolonging the war. Tasked with closing the breach in the German lines from the west, *Grossdeutschland* formations had their first major clashes with Russian units on 8 August to the west of Bogodukhov and succeeded in fending off the first attacks, which were little more than reconnaissance probes; however, other Russian units managed to reach some of the railway stations designated as detraining points for *Grossdeutschland*, with the result that units would have to detrain further west and proceed by road to the battlefield, adding to the delays in concentrating the division.

Throughout 9 August, Getman and VI Tank Corps attempted to capture enough of the south bank of the Merchik at Aleksandrovka to allow his combat engineers to build bridges. In addition to his formations, he had the benefit of flank support from the first of the rifle divisions that were struggling to catch up with the Russian armour. Despite this concentration of forces, the intended thrust across the Merchik failed to make any headway; *SS-Totenkopf* had taken up positions south of the river during the night and beat off every attempt by Getman's troops to force a crossing. It was a day of considerable frustration for Vatutin, as his infantry armies were forced to spend most of it reorganising their units after the heavy fighting around Borisovka, but by nightfall they had moved several divisions far enough forward that the tank armies would once more be able to concentrate their forces. The clear presence of powerful new German forces led to Zhukov and Stalin concluding that the critical moment of the campaign had arrived – Kharkov had to be captured before the Germans could stabilise their line and repair the breach between Fourth Panzer Army and *Armee Abteilung Kempf*. Accordingly, new orders were issued during the evening:

> *Stavka* considers it essential to seal off Kharkov by the immediate capture of the main roads and railways leading to Poltava, Krasnograd and Lozovaya, thus accelerating the liberation of Kharkov.
>
> To achieve this aim, Katukov's First Tank Army must cut the main communications in the Kolyagi-Valki area, while Rotmistrov's Fifth Guards Tank Army, outflanking Kharkov on the southwest, must cut communications in the Merefa area.[10]

As the war dragged on, both the Germans and Russians made use of armoured trains. There had been a number of such trains in the First World War, but during the inter-war years it was generally believed that they lacked the mobility to be of much use in future conflicts. Nevertheless, the Wehrmacht kept a small number of such trains in service and these were deployed during the invasion of Poland in 1939, where their performance was poor. Several new trains were assembled in preparation for the invasion of the Soviet Union, often using armoured trains captured from the Polish and Czechoslovakian armies, and during the fighting of 1941 there were numerous engagements involving both German and Russian trains; the latter proved to be fairly effective in defensive fighting and many captured trains were then deployed by the Germans, usually by adding their rolling stock to existing trains. Many of the trains were fitted with turrets from older German tanks and in some cases from captured Russian tanks, and three such trains – 11, 28 and 62 – were deployed in the Kharkov area.[11] One of these trains now went into action in an attempt to retain control of the railway line running west from Kharkov when a group of about 16 Russian tanks was reported to have penetrated the lines of *SS-Das Reich*. Arriving suddenly at first light on 9 August, the train opened fire on the tanks at close range, rapidly driving them back.[12]

There was further fighting to the west as Trofimenko's Twenty-Seventh Army was ordered to advance on Akhtyrka in order to protect the flank of the Russian advance. In its path was *Grossdeutschland*, still awaiting the arrival of several of its units, and after his first probes towards Akhtyrka were beaten off late on 8 August, Poluboyarov ordered his IV Guards Tank Corps to carry out extensive reconnaissance the following morning. He soon realised that although the Germans were able to establish strong positions in his path, they lacked the numbers to extend their line to the south. Accordingly, he ordered one of his tank brigades to try to outflank *Grossdeutschland* from the south while the other two tank brigades applied direct pressure on the German defences. Heavy fighting continued all day, with elements of *Grossdeutschland* often finding their lines of communication severed, but determined counterattacks once more opened the roads. By the evening, it was clear that the German defences couldn't be held much longer without risking the encirclement of the units that were fighting the Russians, and orders were issued to pull back towards Akhtyrka.[13]

The new defensive line of *Grossdeutschland* was similar to the positions it had occupied through 9 August; the individual strongpoints were formidable, but there were substantial gaps between them. Constantly outflanked to the south by the tank brigade that Poluboyarov had dispatched in that direction, the Germans were forced back to the outskirts of Akhtyrka, where the last elements of *Grossdeutschland* detrained during the day. As 10 August drew to a close, the German defensive line had pulled back to the outskirts of the town.

On the same day, VI Tank Corps from Katukov's First Tank Army finally managed to force its way across the Merchik at Aleksandrovka. The leading brigade managed to advance about ten miles before it ran into *SS-Totenkopf* near Vysokopolye, where it paused to concentrate its resources before attempting an assault. Another detachment took advantage of the bridgehead secured at Aleksandrovka to push directly south to Kovyagi in order to try to cut the railway line running west from Kharkov, as Getman described:

We prepared a special demolition group under the command of Senior Lieutenant Trofimov of 22nd Tank Brigade, a *Komsomol* commander known in the corps for his courage and resourcefulness. He had proved himself on more than one occasion to be a brave and experienced commander. Thus, during the fighting for Verhopenya, Senior Lieutenant Trofimov led a handful of fighters and successfully repulsed the onslaught of superior enemy forces trying to seize the bridge across the Penne River. Now he volunteered to carry out a responsible task in the enemy's hinterland.

The other participants of the forthcoming sabotage on the enemy's communications lines were also suited to the task. The group included several soldiers of the same brigade who volunteered, and combat engineers led by Lieutenant Vedeneev from the 85th Independent Engineer Battalion.

Taking explosives with them, the group infiltrated to the enemy's rear area after the onset of darkness. The brave men covered 12km [seven miles] carrying their heavy loads on their backs. Finally they reached the railway 4km west of the station at Kovyagi. This was the site planned for the explosion. As they watched an armoured train carrying Nazi markings heading towards Kharkov, Senior Lieutenant Trofimov noted with regret: 'It managed to slip through. Well, too bad, we will assume that this is the last for the time being.'

After securing the area, he chose two sites where it would be particularly difficult and time-consuming to repair the railroad track. Then they laid their charges and moved away. At 0200, two powerful explosions were heard. When the dense cloud of dust and smoke cleared, Trofimov and Vedeneev went back to check on their handiwork. Content that the railroad was destroyed over a considerable length, the 15 brave men hurried back and returned to the morning without loss.

The same night, it was possible to blow up the railway track in yet another section. This was done by the tank crew of Senior Lieutenant Maslov, commander of one of the platoons of 125th Tank Battalion.

After crossing the river, the battalion – part of 112th Tank Brigade, which had the task to seize the railroad – advanced south. However, as it approached the villages of Dergachi and Maryino, the brigade met with strong resistance from a group of tanks with infantry from the remnants of the enemy's 3rd Panzer Division. Leaving 124th Tank Battalion to deal with the enemy, Colonel Leonov ordered the commander of 125th Tank Battalion, Major Orekhov, to advance rapidly to the station [at Kovyagi], occupy the nearby high ground, and cut the railway there.

Going around Dergachi and Maryino to the east, Orekhov's battalion approached the station from the northeast before dawn. Maslov's company was the first to approach the railroad. On the orders of his commander, Sergeant Pshenichnikov skilfully laid his explosives and soon a large section of the railroad track was blown up.[14]

It is likely that the German units encountered by 112th Tank Brigade were from *SS-Totenkopf* rather than 3rd Panzer Division, which was fighting some distance to the northeast. The day's fighting had resulted in substantial losses for the SS division, necessitating reorganisation:

We no longer had individual companies [in the panzer regiment's I Battalion]. The surviving tanks of 1st and 2nd Companies were combined in a battlegroup, and the rest of the tanks formed a second battlegroup. To our joy, Obersturmführer Riefkogel returned from hospital. He took command of the first battlegroup. Supplies were brought right up to the front line and orders for the first attack were issued. *Kampfgruppe Riefkogel* was to clear the ground as far as Kolyagi of the enemy. We had just four tanks ... We ran into a Russian *Pakfront* [a coordinated defensive line of anti-tank guns]. Nitsche's tank went up in flames before we overcame the five Russian anti-tank guns ...

Two hours later Riefkogel was wounded for the seventh time. A few ground attack aircraft fired on our tanks with machine-guns. A fragment struck him in the head. Then the regiment commander, Sturmbannführer Bochmann, and the battalion commander, Meierdress, arrived. In front of the assembled tank crews, they presented Riefkogel with the Knight's Cross, which had been awarded to him on 11 July. Riefkogel was then sent to the aid post in a Kübelwagen. Once more, we had no battlegroup commander. There was a further reshuffle, as we learned that the commander of the second battlegroup, Obersturmführer Altemiller, had been killed. We had lost the last company commander from 1st Battalion. The two battlegroups were now combined and placed under the command of the former adjutant, the Viennese Obersturmführer Herbatscheck, for future operations.[15]

Like the units just to the north of Vysokopolye, the Russian spearhead in Kovyagi was in a precarious position. All of the leading formations of First Tank Army faced powerful German forces and the bulk of their supporting units were still struggling to cross the Merchik. If the Germans could launch a counterattack, they would be very vulnerable. *SS-Totenkopf* continued to mount local attacks throughout the day with some success, but paid a heavy price. An NCO in an improvised group of tanks and assault guns recalled:

Wherever we encountered the Russians as we drove our tanks through fields of summer flowers and corn, above which only our turret cupolas were visible, we overcame them. In a tank duel, Hauptsturmführer Nerpel was killed by a direct hit. He had led the company for just three days.[16]

By the end of the day, *SS-Totenkopf* had eliminated most of the Russian bridgeheads on the south bank of the Merchik, but clashes with the tanks that had crossed between Alekseyevka and Kolvagi continued into the night without either side gaining ascendancy.

To the east, Rotmistrov's Fifth Guards Tank Army had been tasked with attacking towards the southeast in order to cut the lines of communication from Kharkov. Throughout 10 August, its men struggled to make significant progress but, although they gained ground, it was at considerable cost; in addition to 3rd Panzer Division and *SS-Das Reich*, they now also faced *SS-Wiking*, and the Russian advance ground to a painful halt about six miles (10km) north of Olshany.

On 11 August, the leading brigade of VI Tank Corps attempted to capture Vysokopolye. After heavy fighting, the Russians succeeded in seizing the town, but just as *Grossdeutschland* had been unable to create a continuous defensive line to stop the Russians from outflanking it, the Russians now found themselves in a similar position. During the afternoon, *SS-Totenkopf* launched counterattacks that cut the road from the north, isolating the Russian tank brigade. After suffering heavy losses, the Russians pulled back from Vysokopolye to await reinforcements. After these arrived, fresh attempts were made to capture the town, and the fighting continued throughout the following day without a clear conclusion.

Meanwhile, Poluboyarov attempted to capture Akhtyrka and attacked the town early on 11 August. Most of *Grossdeutschland* had now assembled, but the Germans were still not sure of the precise locations of their enemies, particularly to the southeast. The division's assault gun battalion was one of the last units to arrive and its commander was ordered to occupy a village just to the east of the town. Only a third of the battalion was immediately available, and the Germans took up positions before dawn. They could hear Russian tanks driving past their northern flank towards Akhtyrka and threatening to isolate the battalion. Dispatching his wheeled elements back to Akhtyrka by a southern route, the battalion commander ordered his small group of assault guns to attack the Russian force that had bypassed him; for the loss of one assault gun, he claimed to have left five T-34s ablaze as he fought his way back to the town.[17] Other Russian units attacked the panzergrenadiers deployed by *Grossdeutschland* to the northeast of Akhtyrka and drove them back, but as the day drew to a close it was clear to Poluboyarov that he lacked the strength to complete the capture of the town. The following day, Trofimenko and Poluboyarev discussed the situation briefly and agreed to screen Akhtyrka with Poluboyarev's infantry, while his armour was sent in a sweep south of the town to try to secure crossings over the Vorskla and then outflank *Grossdeutschland*.

To the northwest of Akhtyrka, the German 7th and 11th Panzer Divisions of XLVIII Panzer Corps had an increasingly difficult time holding back the Russian Fortieth Army. The panzer divisions had never been intended for this sort of defensive fighting and lacked the infantry to hold extended positions. Russian forces were able to make several deep penetrations into their lines, but additional reinforcements – a regiment from 88th Infantry Division and a battlegroup created around the remnants of 19th Panzer Division – arrived just in time. By withdrawing a short distance, 7th Panzer Division was able to release sufficient units to join 11th Panzer Division in a counterattack that restored the line by recapturing the town of Belka. After a brief pause, Moskalenko threw his Fortieth Army at the German lines again but failed to break through, grinding forward perhaps a mile or two over three days.[18]

The Russian tank armies had become strung out during their advance, and to their rear the infantry and support and rear area units continued to labour forwards, recovering damaged tanks as they did so. The advance of First Tank Army's leading elements had cut the railway line running west from Kharkov, and whilst the loss of the railway was a significant blow to the Germans, these

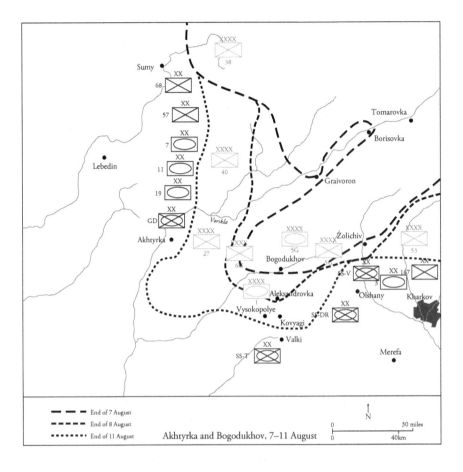

Akhtyrka and Bogodukhov, 7–11 August

advanced units were now exposed to a counterattack. Breith, commander of III Panzer Corps, ordered *SS-Totenkopf* and *SS-Das Reich* to deal with them. On 11 August, the two SS divisions attacked, the former from the south and the latter from the east. The following day, Katukov ordered his troops to pull back towards the Merchik in order to buy time to concentrate his forces; the reinforced battalion at Vysokopolye found itself encircled by *SS-Totenkopf*, as Getman later wrote:

> Once isolated, the Soviet soldiers did not lose their heads. They fought defiantly against superior enemy forces. First the tankmen of Senior Lieutenant Maslov's company went into action. Hardly had they managed to dig in when a column of

enemy tanks appeared on the road that ran along the railroad tracks. Maslov radioed his men to prepare for battle and continued watching. At this moment, two fascist tanks separated from the column and made a detour, obviously intending to cut off the only line of retreat for our tanks.

Carefully taking aim, Maslov fired. The shell struck the turret of one of the enemy tanks [attempting to outflank him]. The second shot set the vehicle ablaze. His third projectile broke the tracks of the other, leaving it helplessly turning in one place.

Seeing that three more enemy tanks were approaching, the commander decided to change his position. His T-34 quickly withdrew to the corner of an empty stone building. The manoeuvre proved timely, since a moment later the Nazis opened a heavy fire, but at his old position. Now one of their tanks bypassed the building behind which Maslov's tank was hiding and began to turn its turret towards its target. However, Maslov again fired first. The 'Tiger' began to smoke and backed away. The second shell finished off the fascist beast: it was enveloped in flames.

On the left, two more machines of the enemy were ablaze. This was the work of the crew of Sergeant Epishkin in the neighbouring tank, firing from cover. The nerve of the Hitlerites broke. The remains of the column pulled back.

The rest of the company also repulsed several attacks by the enemy. In the afternoon, Major Orekhov, on orders from the commander of the brigade, began to withdraw the battalion to the north to a more advantageous position. Manoeuvring skilfully, the tankmen fought their way through to the southern bank of the Merchik, where by the end of the day the main forces of the 112th Tank Brigade were concentrated. Motorised infantry was sent to support them ...

It was harder for 1st and 3rd battalions of 6th Motorised Rifle Brigade, which also found themselves cut off [near the railway]. They had been reinforced with anti-tank guns and had the task of maintaining positions on this section of the railway. Being attacked by numerically superior enemy forces, they fought off his violent attacks for three days.[19]

Whilst Getman was understandably proud of the manner in which his men fought their way back to the Merchik, the reality was that the forces that had reached the railway line west of Kharkov lost over half their tanks and equipment as the Germans drove them back. He had been given control of 163rd Rifle Division to strengthen his flanks and one of its regiments was also cut off; Getman dispatched 12 tanks from 200th Tank Brigade to its aid, but eight were destroyed before they could reach the trapped infantry.

During the fighting of February and March 1943, Vatutin – and higher commands – had repeatedly disregarded evidence that the Germans were concentrating their forces for a counterstrike against the advancing Red Army, preferring the more optimistic interpretation that the German redeployments were a prelude to a retreat to the line of the Dnepr. Now, Vatutin received reports as early as 8 August about the growing strength of German units to the west of Kharkov, but again made the wrong assessment, assuming that they were intended to strengthen the German defences and perhaps provide armoured cover while the battered infantry divisions pulled back to new defences. *SS-Totenkopf* inflicted a serious check on First Tank Army on 11 August, and to its east *SS-Das Reich* also moved forward in strength, yet even at this stage Vatutin continued to misinterpret events. In the path of *SS-Das Reich* was III Mechanised Corps, which at first was driven back by the Germans. It took the deployment of XXXI Tank Corps to stop the SS division towards the end of the day, but the attacks by both *SS-Totenkopf* and *SS-Das Reich* had inflicted considerable damage. Katukov estimated that the units that were deployed in front of the two German divisions had perhaps 134 tanks between them, with a few more tanks trying to retreat back to Russian lines from various small encirclements.[20] The infantry formations of Fifth and Sixth Guards Armies were still struggling forward, but for the moment the tank and mechanised corps were on their own. The only intervention that Vatutin and Zhukov made was not to counter the German blow, but to try to accelerate their own advance. Rotmistrov was summoned to a meeting with Zhukov:

At the time designated by Zhukov, I drove to a small village. The officer who met me asked me to leave my car in the village and to follow him. We went down a country lane into a dense pine forest. There were several military vehicles here, well camouflaged and parked in a deep depression. It was gloomy and quiet. But from one car came the sound of an accordion. I was pointed at that car.

Zhukov, wearing a white shirt, was sitting on a chair, slowly stretching the accordion's bellows. I greeted him, saying, 'That's good music!'

'Is it?' smiled the marshal. 'Managarov is a great master. I have to listen to him when I visit his army.' He put aside the accordion and took a deep breath. 'But I play when I'm in the mood, or to escape from sad thoughts, or sometimes to concentrate – it helps.' He stood up and asked me to supper. I thanked him but declined, as I had eaten en route.

'Then let's come to the point,' said Zhukov, and walked over to a large map on a table. He showed me how the situation around Kharkov was developing, incidentally noting that there was intelligence about the Germans redeploying the resources of part of the SS Panzer Corps to the Orel sector to counter that attacks of our Bryansk Front. The marshal looked at me, his face stern and frowning. 'Personally, I don't believe it.' He put his hand on the map. 'They can't do that when the battle for Kharkov is continuing. It should not be forgotten that the Hitlerites are sophisticated masters of disinformation. We learned this in March. The first to fall for their bait was the command of Southwest Front [Vatutin], which believed that the enemy's regrouping was for a withdrawal of his troops to the west bank of the Dnepr. And these SS, with powerful air support, suddenly launched an armoured attack from the Bogodukhov area against our troops which had just liberated Kharkov and Belgorod.' Zhukov walked along the table and, turning to me, continued. 'So there are fears that the enemy will try to repeat this manoeuvre or cut off and dismember our troop formations to the west of Kharkov. We cannot allow this.' The marshal thought for a moment, and then circled an area southeast of Bogodukhov with a red pencil and spoke again. 'General Rodimtsev's XXXII Guards Rifle Corps, part of Zhadov's army, is here. You are tasked to concentrate your army, screened by this corps, so that once artillery preparation is complete and the infantry attacks, you can launch a powerful armoured strike on a narrow front, bypassing the German forces around Kharkov. How long will it take you to redeploy your army?'

I thought for a moment, and then answered, 'It's only possible to relocate safely at night. I estimate it will take roughly three days.'

'Is it impossible to do it in two?'

'No, Comrade Marshal, we can't do it in that timescale. It's 0200 now. I will be back at my headquarters by 0400. I will meet the corps commanders at 0500 and leave with them to reconnoitre the new area. They will also need time to speak to their brigade commanders. XVIII and XXIX Tank Corps can move on the first night, V Mechanised Corps the following night. It will also take time to transfer the rest of the army units and rear area formations.'

Zhukov agreed with my assessment.[21]

It is characteristic of Soviet historiography that Vatutin was blamed for the over-optimism that contributed so much to Manstein's successful counterattack of March 1943, but it should be remembered that all levels of command, including Zhukov and Stalin, accepted Vatutin's assessments without question. Indeed, many of the overly ambitious orders to push on and to try to destroy Manstein's armies before the spring thaw emanated from *Stavka*.

The redeployment of Fifth Guards Tank Army brought the two tank armies of Voronezh Front together again, but as Rotmistrov pointed out, it would take time. Whilst it would increase the strength of the Russian forces in the path of the SS counterattack, it was actually intended as an offensive step in order to unhinge the German defences. Early on 12 August, the first elements of Fifth Guards Tank Army began to deploy in their new sector south of Bogodukhov in expectation of supporting Rodimtsev's infantry when it attacked later that morning, but instead found themselves in the path of the SS assault, as Rotmistrov described:

I agreed with Rodimtsev, who I knew to be an experienced and courageous commander, that the attack would commence at 0600 after a 45-minute artillery preparation, and that our tank corps would follow his infantry. We established observation points to coordinate our units, and my command post was ahead of the main forces of the army.

At 0400 the command to mount up was given, and the forest was filled with the noise of engines. Red signal lights were lit and the tank corps moved to their deployment areas.

I also went to my command post in good time. Here, at about 0600, I received reports that the formations had concentrated and were ready for their attack. But General Rodimtsev wasn't in my command post, and instead of the thunder of our artillery we heard the roar of German aircraft engines. A few minutes later, fascist aviators bombed Bogodukhov and the village where XXXII Guards Rifle Corps' headquarters was located. Moreover, scouts reported to me that the vehicles about 500m from my command post were German tanks, which I could see for myself through binoculars. I immediately leaped into my jeep and drove to Rodimtsev, and found him very agitated. The house in which he had slept was ablaze. Other houses, villages, fences, everything in the village, was burning. 'Alexander Ilyich! What happened? Why didn't you attack?' I asked him.

'The artillery wasn't ready,' Rodimtsev answered agitatedly. 'And you can see what's happening now!'

I returned to my command post. I saw a bleak picture through my binoculars en route: German tanks attacking in a broad flood, fascist aircraft bombed mercilessly. Our infantry hurriedly withdrew, even fleeing in panic here and there. Only our anti-tank guns continued a desperate, unequal battle. I immediately gave the commanders of XVIII and XXIX Tank Corps uncoded instructions by radio to deploy their vehicles and artillery to repel the enemy tanks and mechanised infantry. Things began to improve; Rodimtsev's infantry took refuge behind the tanks of Fifth Guards Tank Army.

Instead of advancing, we had to defend ourselves. Zhukov had foreseen the actions of the enemy. We soon learned that we were under attack by *SS-Das Reich* and *SS-Totenkopf*, supported by other elements of the SS Panzer Corps.

That day, the battlefield resembled the scenes of the fighting at Prokhorovka. Our tanks and those of the enemy were ablaze everywhere, broken anti-tank guns and armoured personnel carriers, motor vehicles and motorcycles abandoned, farm buildings and haystacks ablaze, blue-black smoke everywhere.

Despite heavy losses, the enemy continued to attack aggressively. Fascist aircraft in groups of 30 or 40 constantly bombed our army's formations and parts of Rodimtsev's corps. One group of aircraft dropped its bombs and flew off to be replaced immediately by another, which continued the bombing. Our aviation was nowhere to be seen for some reason; it was probably concentrating its efforts on attacks on the approaches to Kharkov.

XXIX Tank Corps had a particularly hard time, receiving the enemy's main blow. At the price of considerable losses, the Hitlerites managed to drive the corps back and captured Kiyana. The corps formations were in difficulties trying to resist the superior forces of the enemy as they had not prepared for defensive fighting and had deployed on my orders for an attack. But the tankmen fought hard, defending their lines to the last possible moment. The crews of knocked-out tanks fought on foot.

When I arrived at the headquarters of [Major General Ivan Fedorovich] Kirichenko [commander of XXIX Tank Corps], 32nd Tank Brigade and four tanks of XXV Tank Brigade had retreated to a line between Gavrish and Ratino. Taking advantage of this withdrawal, 16 fascist tanks (six of them Tigers) formed a column and moved towards the railway crossing. It seemed that there was nothing to stop them and the Nazis were about to cut the railway line. However, the commander of 2nd Battalion of 32nd Tank Brigade, Captain Vakulenko, decided to engage the enemy tanks in an ambush. Six T-34s, under cover of a railway embankment, approached the crossing and took up positions. Unaware of the danger, the Nazis crossed the railway in close column and were suddenly met by the accurate fire of our tankmen. Our vehicles fired from both sides at a slight angle against the side and rear armour of the fascist tanks.

The platoon commander, Lieutenant Parshin, set fire to the enemy's leading tank with the first round. Then two more tanks were ablaze. Having stalled the advance of the entire enemy column, Parshin's platoon engaged the Tigers, which opened fire indiscriminately, not knowing how many Soviet tanks were opposing them. It was possible to knock out two Tigers, and the rest hurriedly withdrew, still firing.

For his repeated battle exploits, Lieutenant Viktor Stepanovich Parshin was awarded the title of Hero of the Soviet Union by decree of the Presidium of the Supreme Soviet of the USSR on 15 January 1944.[22]

By the end of 12 August, all of Rotmistrov's tank corps were in the front line, alongside Rodimtsev's infantry. Further west, the battered formations of First Tank Army were also in defensive positions, supported at last by the infantry of Sixth Guards Army. The German advance had for the moment been halted, but Rotmistrov received orders during the evening that revealed the lack of understanding of the situation on the ground: Vatutin wanted him to attack towards the southwest to relieve the pressure on First Tank Army, while Konev demanded an attack towards the southeast to support Managarov's Fifty-Third Army's advance on Kharkov. Correctly assessing that any such redeployment of his units would leave the Germans with an open advance into the rear of First Tank Army from where they could threaten Fifth and Sixth Guards Armies, Rotmistrov simply told his subordinates to remain on the defensive for the time being. As the night wore on, he received further news:

In the evening, Generals [Pyotr Grigoryevich] Grishin [a member of Fifth Guards Tank Army's military council] and [Vladimir Nikolayevich] Baskakov [Rotmistrov's chief of staff] came to see me. They reported that they had held a conversation by telephone with Lieutenant General [Matvei Vasileyevich] Zakharov, chief of staff of Steppe Front. He informed them that on 9 August, *Stavka* had decided to transfer Fifth Guards Tank Army to Steppe Front. Zakharov confirmed the orders of the front commander, categorically demanding the transfer of the army to Fifty-Third Army's sector, from where it was to attack rapidly to Novaya Vodolaga to cut off the enemy's line of retreat from Kharkov towards the southwest.

'Pavel Alexeyevich, you must come to some decision,' Grishin said.

'I have already made a decision to take up defensive positions while clarifying the situation, Pyotr Grigoryevich.'

'But if you don't execute the orders in a timely manner, you could be arrested and shot,' said Grishin excitedly.

'If we withdraw and the Germans occupy Bogodukhov, they will definitely judge me and shoot me. You understand that if that happens, the rear area of the entire left wing of Voronezh Front will come under enemy attack.'

In support of Grishin, Baskakov said that perhaps higher commands had a clearer overall picture. 'The commander of Steppe Front,' he said, 'requires us to carry out a task similar to that set for the army by Marshal Zhukov, that is to strike against the enemy's Kharkov group from the southwest.'

'True, Vladimir Nikolayevich, but with a very significant difference: Zhukov expected the enemy to be on the defensive, and our army would attack and break through the enemy's defences. Things have turned out differently: a powerful German armoured force is attacking and we have to defend ourselves.'

After these arguments, I took the following decision: I sent a cipher message to Zhukov. I reported the situation in the army's area of operations to him and that I had received contradictory orders from the two front commanders. In conclusion, I informed him that if no new orders were issued by him by 0600 the next morning, the second echelon of the army – V Guards Mechanised Corps – would deploy as per Vatutin's orders, and at 0800 both armoured corps would follow if possible, but I would not be responsible for acts of fate. After signing the signal, I suggested that Grishin and Baskakov also sign it. They exchanged glances. The pale Grishin said in a formal tone, 'You do not take account of our opinion, Comrade Commander, so we abstain from signing this document.'

'That's your choice,' I replied calmly, and ordered the cipher clerk to send the signal immediately to Khukov.[23]

This incident sheds an interesting light on the Russian command, and the manner in which it worked. The purges of the 1930s were still fresh in the minds of senior officers, particularly those like Grishin who played a more political role. Rotmistrov, on the other hand, relied on his good personal relationship with Zhukov (and perhaps more importantly with Stalin) to protect him from any fallout.

As Chistiakov's Sixth Guards Army finally caught up with the leading armoured formations, the army commander received reconnaissance reports of a German force advancing along the Poltava-Vysolopolye road. Chistiakov passed the information to Vatutin and the two men agreed a plan to strike at the German force with a single rifle corps and V Guards Mechanised Corps from Rotmistrov's army. When he learned of the plan, Zhukov was unenthusiastic, but Vatutin's enthusiasm carried the day, with VI Tank Corps from Katukov's First Tank Army also ordered to advance once more.

Throughout 12 August, SS-Das Reich ground forward in the face of tough resistance from Rotmistrov's men. On the division's left and right flanks, battlegroups from SS-Totenkopf and SS-Wiking respectively provided support, but compared to the rapid counterattacks of the preceding winter, there was little sign of a decisive breakthrough and by the end of the day the chief of staff of

III Panzer Corps recorded that he regarded the chances of a major operational success as unlikely.[24] In its report to III Panzer Corps late on 12 August, *SS-Das Reich* commented that it had captured or destroyed 70 Russian tanks, but given that the area had seen extensive fighting in the preceding days, it is likely that at least some of these were vehicles that had been knocked out in earlier actions.[25]

Along the line of the Merchik, the *SS-Totenkopf* battlegroups continued to try to eliminate the remaining Russian pockets on the south bank, encountering local civilians and realising once more that the loyalties of ordinary people were sometimes hard to predict:

At the edge of the wood to the northwest of the village we established numerous positions. We cut a hole in the roof of one of the houses and created an excellent observation post. From here, our view extended far into the enemy hinterland as far as the high ground either side of the Merchik. The land in front of us consisted of cornfields and wildflower meadows. In order to have a clear field of fire, we mobilised the inhabitants of the *Kolkhoz* [collective farm]; with their sickles they cut the corn and brought it in. It turned into a hefty harvest. I was astonished how many Russians turned out to work. We quickly established good relations with them. They repeatedly asked us anxiously if the 'Russki-soldiers' were coming. We couldn't answer their questions. Who knew what was going to happen to us? During the afternoon our observers in the roof reported horsemen. They halted on the road by a house. We watched them anxiously through our binoculars. They dismounted at the house. The occupants of the house pointed towards us. One of the immobilised [German] tanks in the area in front of us fired its 75mm gun … The house collapsed and the Russian scouting group was buried in the rubble.[26]

The 'Russians' who turned out to work for the Germans were of course Ukrainians; as already described, the mobilisation of younger inhabitants for service in the Red Army in 1941 resulted in the remaining population consisting largely of older people, who tended to be more likely to hold anti-Soviet views, but the civilians in the house where the Russian cavalry dismounted seemed less favourably inclined to the Germans. The reality was that many civilians probably sided with whoever they believed they needed to support in order to survive life in a war zone.

On 13 August, the Russian VI Tank Corps' attack began. During the preceding night there were repeated probing attacks of the German defenders, which consisted mainly of the reconnaissance battalion of *SS-Totenkopf*. With its forces now stretched along a front line of about 30 miles (50km), the SS division was not in a good position to deal with a major Russian onslaught. Ably supported by Chistiakov's rifle divisions, the Russian tanks made repeated attacks and, despite extensive support from the Luftwaffe, the Germans were driven from their original positions. In mid-morning a determined counterattack by a regiment of panzergrenadiers restored the situation somewhat, but the Russian pressure forced Gruppenführer Max Simon, commander of *SS-Totenkopf*, to pull back his left flank. Taking advantage of this, the Russian VI Tank Corps was able to advance and recapture Vysokopolye. However, the battlegroup that reached the town soon found itself isolated and most of its tanks were destroyed in fighting that continued into the night. V Guards Mechanised Corps arrived in the sector later in the day but was unable to exploit the earlier Russian successes. Despite securing crossings over the Merchik, it was recalled as crises developed elsewhere.

SS-Das Reich attacked the same day towards Bogodukhov from the south, supported by elements of *SS-Wiking*. After taking part in the counterattacks on the Mius, the latter division, commanded by Obergruppenführer Herbert Gille, had been rushed to Kharkov; its involvement in the fighting to eliminate the Russian penetration across the Mius had not been a happy one, particularly after the division's panzergrenadiers were ordered by General Sigfrid Henrici, commander of XL Panzer Corps, to make a costly attack to recapture an area of wooded terrain. One of the officers of the SS division recorded in his diary an angry exchange between Gille and Henrici, with the former expressing a strong wish never to serve under the latter's command again.[27] Relations between SS officers and Wehrmacht officers were often difficult, particularly at higher levels; Manstein had insisted on placing Wehrmacht liaison officers in SS formations during the fighting the previous winter in an attempt to ensure that his instructions were followed, despite which several SS units still became involved in streetfighting in Kharkov contrary to his express instructions. As the men of *SS-Wiking* made their way to Kharkov, the same SS officer who had witnessed the row between Gille and Henrici recorded his impressions:

> There was traffic on the road like on the *Kurfürstendamm* [a major thoroughfare in Berlin]. The closer you got to the city, the crazier the traffic on the road. The Luftwaffe ground personnel and the agricultural managers [from Erich Koch's *Reichskommissariat*] were in a hurry to leave the city…
>
> It was strange to see an unending column of vehicles composed of military personnel of all branches waltzing past you in an effort to get to safety.

146

Heading in the other direction was a very thin membrane trying to hold up the Russians.

We passed Kharkov … In the city, they were still in the process of loading up all industrial infrastructure on trains. That meant the situation was pretty rotten.[28]

After an artillery bombardment, the SS units attacked in strength. The Russians were driven back, exposing the flank of Rotmistrov's Fifth Guards Tank Army; any notion of using Rotmistrov's tanks for a concentrated attack was now completely out of the question. As the day wore on, the German advance was brought to a halt as Vatutin, belatedly realising the strength of the German attack, rushed troops from Fifth and Sixth Guards Army to the area. The *Germania* panzergrenadier regiment of *SS-Wiking*, supported by a tank battalion, attacked on the eastern flank of *SS-Das Reich* and was involved in heavy fighting around the village of Klenovoye, where an initial attack was brought to a standstill by well-camouflaged defenders. In mid-afternoon, the Germans tried again:

3rd Company screened off to the west of the southern edge of Klenovoye towards reported [Russian] armoured forces. I moved with 1st Company on the left; the assault guns were in the middle. On the right, there was Beck with his 2nd Company. The [infantry] battalion moved with us. Battalion is saying a bit much, since the companies only had 25 men each. With a certain amount of grim fury in our bellies, we worked our way forward through the cornfield. The Russians were firing like crazy again … It was my misfortune that there was a steep *balka* in my attack sector. I held a course more towards the centre and moved along the *balka* in an effort to find a bypass or a bridge.

I reached the first houses with the assault guns. The Russians then started to fire with increased fury from the opposite slope. The assault guns moved back because of the fire. Since I was powerless all by myself, I initially pulled out of the line of sight of the enemy by seeking concealment behind a house. I had barely reached that spot when a man from the assault gun battery came running up to me and asked for assistance in towing out his vehicle. So, out again into the fire to recover the vehicle, which had driven into the middle of a manure pile. The men worked feverishly to attach the tow cable. When everything was ready, we gave it a jerk and it was freed up again. I was unable to find a crossing point [across the *balka*]. There was nothing to be seen of my company, either. Since I was all by myself moving up front and was also unable to locate my infantry, I moved back along the *balka*. All of a sudden, I saw tank tracks. That meant that my guys had gone behind me through the *balka*. Time to get moving and follow them!

It was like a roller coaster. It went down, steeply for 10m. The engine, in first gear, started to howl. I had barely reached the bottom and wanted to climb up the other side when the engine spluttered a few times and then fell silent. All the efforts on the part of the driver to get the engine turning over were in vain. Great!

The Russians were hopping around on a bridge about 500m away. An anti-tank gun was constantly firing down the *balka*, and I was in a mousetrap, immobile. A terrific situation. I cussed and cursed. But the engine refused to stir. Gradually, the whole crew started to sweat. After 15 minutes, the overheated engine finally came to life. The radiator temperature measured 110°C.

Slowly, like a snail, my vehicle climbed up the slope in front of us. I had barely arrived at the top when I saw my company in firing order and stuff exploding all around it. Enemy artillery was impacting in between them. What a sight! ... There was nothing to be seen of our friends, the [panzer]grenadiers, far and wide.

I decided against moving into the locality without an infantry escort. To remain where we were was nonsense, since we had not reached the actual attack objective.[29]

The panzergrenadiers of the second battalion of *Germania* had been intended to support the tank attack, but the battalion commander, Hauptsturmführer Hans Juchum, disappeared in the mayhem and was later found dead. He was a popular figure in the division, being only the second infantryman to be awarded the *Nahkampfspange in Gold* (the 'close combat clasp in gold') just days before; he was also awarded the Knight's Cross posthumously. In his absence, the battalion failed to advance with the tanks, a breakdown that would have been unlikely earlier in the war, but by mid-1943 even the 'elite' SS divisions were struggling to maintain an experienced core of officers.

Alongside the units of *SS-Wiking*, the battlegroups of *SS-Das Reich* had made better progress, but the steady stream of reinforcements arriving in the Russian lines brought their advance to a halt late on 13 August. The estimates of destroyed Russian tanks – *SS-Das Reich* and *SS-Totenkopf* claimed a total of over 80 kills between them for just one day's fighting – are probably as wide of the mark as other such estimates, but the day belonged largely to the Germans. During the evening, the officers of the SS divisions became aware of Hitler's latest order: Kharkov was to be held at all costs, and 'the most severe measures' were to be taken against any units that failed to obey.[30] Whilst the SS units were fighting to the west of Kharkov, the order nevertheless brought back unpleasant memories of the previous winter when they had been given a similar order; it took the strong will of Hausser, commander of II SS Panzer Corps, to risk the Führer's wrath by opting to save his units from near-certain destruction and to abandon the city.

Despite the confident manner in which he had faced down his chief of staff and military council representative, Rotmistrov spent the hours before dawn wondering why he hadn't heard from Zhukov and was issuing orders at first light when the marshal appeared in his command post:

'Where is Skvortsov [the commander of V Guards Mechanised Corps], and can you recall him?' asked the marshal.

'About 25–30km to the southwest. I have communications with him.'

'What tasks have been assigned to him?' I gave him the details. 'And if the Germans attack now, what will you do?'

'If we halted their onslaught yesterday, Comrade Marshal, a new attack today will not be so terrible for us. The tank corps are prepared for determined defence, and Skvortsov's corps could strike a blow in the enemy's flank. In addition, I have strong reserves.'

'That's good,' Zhukov said, adding, 'but still, if it is possible, order Skvortsov to return to his original position.' I immediately obeyed the marshal's order. He then suggested, 'Write on my behalf to *Stavka* – everything, as you understand the situation, and that I agree with you.' The report was written, signed and sent. 'Have you had breakfast?' asked the marshal suddenly.

'No.'

'Well then, let's have breakfast, I'm pretty hungry,' said Georgi Konstantinovich, unbuttoning his tunic. During breakfast, I received a cipher signal from Konev. It said very laconically, 'You will answer with your head if Bogodukhov falls.' Zhukov read it and smiled silently.

Georgi Konstantinovich was clearly pleased that he had foreseen the direction of the German armoured group's attack and admired the steadfastness with which our tankmen blocked the enemy's path … He asked me to convey his gratitude to the army's personnel and left, promising to contact Konev when he had returned to his headquarters and to clarify our further tasks.

After Zhukov left, Grishin and Baskakov appealed to me for permission to add their signatures to my previous signal, as Pyotr Grigoryevich [Grishin] put it, 'for the sake of posterity.'

'You're welcome to,' I laughed, 'but posterity will preserve only the encrypted signal, with just my signature.'[31]

The political instincts of Grishin and Baskakov served them well; they both enjoyed long careers in the army after the war.

Mansoor Abdullin's division was involved in the fighting in which locations changed hands repeatedly. Despite the constant threat of the sudden renewal of combat, soldiers found some items they found in towns and villages too tempting to resist:

> After the artillery fire, the regiment rose to attack. The fascists left Chervonyi Prapor and we entered the village and the neighbouring industrial plant.
>
> There was a lot of alcohol, both refined and untreated, in bottles and barrels, in small tanks and larger tanks on a railway spur. There was no discussion about what everyone poured into his flask as a 'reserve'. No matter how much you tried to convince each other that, for example, the Germans might have poisoned the alcohol, it seemed that our heads didn't accept this: how could we liberate an alcohol plant from the Germans and not get drunk? This option seemed unnatural to us. Our damnable self-delusion was constantly at work!
>
> In short, we were ordered to leave the village and the industrial plant and dig in. I don't know how it went in other battalions, but many of us had time to 'get wet'. Even some platoon leaders were tempted. Quarrels broke out. Someone yelled, 'I killed hundreds of Fritzes, I'm not afraid of anyone!' Someone else grabbed his weapon. This might have been part of the enemy's plan. Thirty fascist tanks, some armed with flamethrowers, suddenly rushed at us at top speed.
>
> It's hard to remember how it went. When sober and on firm feet, we could orient ourselves and manoeuvre. Many remarkable, heroic combatants perished in the sticky fire of the flamethrowers. It was all the more humiliating that the fascists obviously didn't doubt the success of what they conceived when they retreated from Chervonyi Pravor.[32]

After a day of heavy fighting, the German armoured groups paused to reassess the situation – although they had inflicted substantial losses on the Russians, they had gained little ground. To the west, Chistiakov's troops were in action on the flank of First Tank Army, trying to outflank *SS-Totenkopf* in a series of advances that saw the leading elements push about eight miles to the southwest. This forced the German division to extend its flank still further, and in order to release troops for this – particularly to allow *SS-Totenkopf* to concentrate sufficient forces for a counterattack – *SS-Das Reich* had to take over sections of the line to the east and assigned a reinforced panzergrenadier regiment to *SS-Totenkopf* to help with its attack. The drive by Chistiakov into the gap that still remained between the

German forces of *Armee Abteilung Kempf* around Kharkov and Fourth Panzer Army to the west forced a reappraisal of German plans, not least because, by advancing in this direction, the Russian Sixth Guards Army was increasingly strung out. Accordingly, the two SS divisions were ordered to counterattack into Chistiakov's eastern flank with a view to taking advantage of the manner in which the Russian units had become dispersed, but also to try to close the troublesome gap.

The constant fighting took a heavy toll on the units of both sides, but one area where the Germans continued to have an edge over the Russians was the efficiency of their tank recovery and repair teams. A steady stream of repaired tanks allowed *SS-Totenkopf* to bring its panzer regiment back towards at least a level where it could function effectively. In the early evening of 14 August, the regiment's II Battalion launched a counterattack:

There was heavy firing to our right. The sunflower meadow came to an end. Before us was a village. We rolled through it. The inhabitants told us that Ivan had recently left the village with 12 tanks. At the other end of the village we took up firing positions and fired on the seething Russian infantry. We set off after them. Tanks from our battalion were advancing to our right, too. We turned to the northwest and drove in a broad wedge formation through an ever-broader valley. In the distance I could see the buildings of a sugar refinery. There – about 2km in front us were Russian tanks. More and more appeared. We counted 30, then 40. They came directly towards us. We drove on against them. Now they disappeared into a meadow. We could see the stalks of sunflowers, taller than a man, disappearing as if cut by an unseen scythe as they were pulled down by the Russian tanks' tracks. They left the cover of the field. Now they appeared to spot us and tried to take shelter behind bushes to the left. The command of our officer, Bochmann, rang in our ears: 'Tigers and Pz.IVs: free to fire! Range 1600m! Pz.IIIs turn to the right! We'll take them in a pincer.' There was a clanking like falling church bells. We drove to the right flank and then pushed forward. The Tigers and Pz.IVs moved forward towards the enemy, firing as they did. The first plumes of smoke from burning T-34s climbed high into the air. The valley was full of the thunder of tank guns and the crash of bursting shells. We drove into a firing position and joined the battle with our Pz.IIIs. A few Russian tanks tried to escape. They were brought to a halt by our concentrated fire.[33]

The Tiger tanks with *SS-Totenkopf* were first deployed the preceding winter as the division's panzer regiment's 9th Company. Although the unit had never exceeded

15 tanks, the survival of these vehicles in combat was impressive; the battles around Kharkov in March 1943 resulted in the loss of only two, and just one was lost during *Zitadelle*. The range of their guns also allowed them to engage enemy tanks before other German tanks could come into action, and a disproportionate number of the Russian tanks claimed as kills by the panzer regiment of *SS-Totenkopf* were attributed to the Tiger crews. The claims of other SS units during the fighting near Bogodukhov were questionable; Sturmbannführer Walter Kniep, commander of the assault gun battalion of *SS-Das Reich*, was awarded the Knight's Cross after his battalion intercepted a Russian armoured penetration and drove it back, allegedly destroying 51 enemy tanks for the loss of just a single vehicle.[34]

SS-Totenkopf and *SS-Das Reich* resumed their attempts to reach Bogodukhov on 15 August. At first, the newly arrived infantry of Sixth Guards Army proved to be brittle and the German armour made rapid progress, particularly in overcoming the Russians who had repeatedly attacked the reconnaissance battalion of *SS-Totenkopf* in the preceding days, but resistance stiffened steadily as the day continued. For the battered SS companies that had fought in the Merchik sector for the previous few days, the advance provided a welcome respite and boost to morale:

> We formed up in an assault formation. Everything that remained of the reconnaissance battalion was gathered together, and Pz.IIIs and Pz.IVs also appeared. We had no idea of our objective. We had already become accustomed to not being filled in on the overall situation. We followed orders, ready to make decisions and to act independently. Higher commands referred to us as 'experienced *Einzelkämpfer*' ['individual soldiers', i.e. capable of acting in this manner]. We moved out: four tanks leading, then the half-tracks following. Everything else fell in behind.
>
> Our unit looked impressive. We hadn't seen this for some time; it felt really good and restored our faith in the strength of our division.[35]

Whilst the support provided by the Luftwaffe appears to have varied – on some days, German accounts described powerful support, while on others they lamented the absence of friendly aircraft, particularly fighters – German artillery constantly inflicted heavy losses on the Soviet units. Abdullin and his comrades were not alone in finding the frequent, heavy bombardments more than just an irritation:

The fascist artillery constantly harassed us with their fire. They hammered us whenever they spotted us!

It turned out that a fascist 'Hunchback' spotter plane was directing their fire. We called it that because it really was 'hunchbacked'. The aircraft was single-engined, heavily armoured and very slow moving. It would hang over our positions and watch the flight or 'undershoot' of shells.

In the mortar company there was a PTR anti-tank weapon [*Protivo Tankovoye Ruzhyo*, literally 'anti-tank rifle'] and when the Hunchback was hanging over us, I opened fire on it with the PTR. I really wanted to shoot down this plane and record its destruction in my combat record. In addition to a medal, the soldier who downed an aircraft was given a period of home leave. I confess that in terms of morale, I was sick of the war by that time. Tired both physically and mentally. You couldn't just quit the war of your own accord, I understood this. But a break to get ten or 20 days to sleep in silence, drink some fresh milk from a cup, time to go fishing!

I shot at the Hunchback and deafened myself and stirred up the whole company. Everyone was annoyed by my attempt. Most annoying for me was the heavy recoil of the PTR against my shoulder. The shot missed by perhaps half a metre. My head almost burst with the concussion. But every time I missed, I fired again with greater anger. After ten shots the plane suddenly 'dived' and disappeared apparently without any visible damage. And a week later, when we had received reinforcements and we drove the fascists from their trenches and carried out an attack deep into their defences, we saw my Hunchback, riddled with shots from the PTR and burned out. I must have hit it loads of times! I was very pleased that I actually destroyed it, but then I had to try to prove that this downed Hunchback was mine.

'Mansoor, you shot him down!' said one person, enthusiastically congratulating me.

'Maybe someone else shot it down?' asked others doubtfully.

… In the regiment, then in the division, officers of anti-tank units were told to shoot at Hitlerite planes with PTRs. Earlier we were bombed with impunity by Hitlerite aircraft, but now in every raid the fascists lost one or two planes in our division's combat zone. Only it was difficult to know who to reward and who should be given home leave under the terms of the incentive scheme. But the gunners now always fired on aircraft with their PTRs, even though it wasn't easy – the main thing was to destroy enemy aircraft collectively and hurry the advent of final victory, when we would all get home leave.

I didn't receive a personal award for the downed Hunchback because it wasn't possible to prove that it was brought down by me and not someone else ... Our regimental commissar, Vladimir Georgievich Egorov, told us: 'For you, the *Komsomol* and party organisers in the battalions, your reward is the fact that you are Comsorgs [*Komsomol* leaders] and party organisers! Be humble and do not think about your personal rewards. But do not forget to present awards to the rank and file for their heroic deeds!'[36]

It isn't clear which aircraft was involved in this incident. Most of the reconnaissance aircraft that were used by the Luftwaffe in such a role were either relatively light, unarmoured planes like the Fieseler Storch, or were twin-engined. The account also shows the great difficulty in allocating 'kills' to individual gunners, regardless of whether the target was a plane or a tank. Many of the undoubtedly exaggerated claims of enemy losses that both sides made were the result of more than one person being credited with destroying an enemy vehicle or aircraft.

Two of Chistiakov's divisions were badly mauled as they fought their way back to the safety of the Merchik in the face of the SS attack. The mixed force of Russian tanks and infantry in Vysokpolye was overwhelmed, but the German advance couldn't be sustained; as previously mentioned, *SS-Totenkopf* had been forced to extend its western flank to avoid being compromised, lessening the forces available for the attack, and *SS-Das Reich* had barely 50 tanks and assault guns still running. Nevertheless, several groups of Russian infantry and many of the tanks of VI Tank Corps were encircled. The front-line commanders on both sides pressed for a pause in operations to allow them to recover their strength – Vatutin's artillery commanders estimated that it would take two days to bring forward their guns and ammunition – but despite recognising the need for a pause, Zhukov urged Rotmistrov to make one more effort. If he could concentrate the diminished strength of his tank corps a little to the east, he might be able to prise open the seam between *SS-Das Reich* and *SS-Wiking*. The fears of the artillery commanders proved to be justified; the initial bombardment on 17 August failed to inflict much damage on the German defences, and the leading elements of Rotmistrov's tank formations soon ground to a halt. When Skvortsov's V Guards Mechanised Corps was thrown into the battle, there was limited progress but at the cost of heavy casualties, and Rotmistrov broke off the attack.

SS-Totenkopf was tasked with the destruction of the encircled Russian forces. Several isolated units were swiftly overrun, but not without further German losses:

The grenadiers and combat engineers complained once more about casualties. The losses were partly because wounded Russians allowed our men to approach closely, often pretending to be dead, and then viciously attacked them from behind.[37]

Such tactics were condemned by both sides when carried out by the enemy, but lauded when carried out by their own men. Inevitably, this resulted in many wounded being shot out of hand. It is also likely that such accounts were used to justify the killing of wounded men by both armies.

Fighting slackened in the Bogodukhov and Kharkov sectors as both sides tried to catch their breath and reorganise; the remaining units encircled by the SS were either destroyed or managed to slip away to the north. *SS-Totenkopf* was ordered to drive towards the northwest, but ammunition shortages and the high casualty rate in its formations made such progress almost impossible. Attempts to establish a bridgehead over the Merla ended in failure, compounded by a Stuka attack that dropped more bombs on the Germans than the Russians.

It is a sign of the intensity of fighting in this sector that 17 August was regarded by the Russians as a day of comparative calm. Konev, commander of Steppe Front, visited Rotmistrov to clear the air over recent disagreements and to consider plans for the next phase of fighting. Rotmistrov later wrote:

I liked him, he was undoubtedly one of the most outstanding Soviet military leaders. I had deep respect for him and for the courage, detail and wide scope of his plans, his ability to explain simply yet exhaustively the plan and the tasks he assigned to the troops, and for his determined perseverance in accomplishing planned tasks. Subconsciously, I emulated him when assigning tasks to my subordinates.

At this meeting, Ivan Stepanovich [Konev] said that he was pleased that General Zhadov's Fifth Guards Army had been transferred to Steppe Front. 'We will take Kharkov, the second city of the Ukraine,' he said, trying to give the words added solemnity.

'Thank you for your confidence, Comrade Commander,' I said, wondering if Fifth Guards Tank Army was to be used in the assault directly towards the city.

'Wait, hear me out,' smiled Konev. 'They considered pulling you out and redeploying you with Shumilov's Seventh Guards Army [on the northeast approaches to Kharkov]. This would have led us into the Kharkov tractor plant, where the tanks would lack the space to manoeuvre.' He looked at me and seeing the consternation on my face, added reassuringly, 'Don't worry. I have decided to assign you a more difficult task. Let the infantry attack the factory. You and your tankmen are to advance on the right flank of Managarov's [Fifty-Third] army, where you will strike towards Korotich and Lyubotin in order to cut the enemy's line of retreat from Kharkov towards Poltava, and to prevent the Germans from bringing up reserves from the Bogodukhov area.' Konev's face broke into a mischievous smile. 'Do you think I'm worse than Vatutin? Tanks against tanks – he used you against the German tank units near Prokhorovka [during the Battle of Kursk] and I am doing the same here.'

'But my army is not in the same state. Even with repaired vehicles, I doubt I can deploy 200.'

'Don't complain! For every tank you deploy, the Germans will have to deploy two or three.' Konev looked at his watch and hurried off, refusing my offer of dinner. 'Until we take Kharkov, I will not eat,' he joked as he said goodbye.[38]

Konev's parting words are curious. Despite the clear advantages enjoyed by the T-34 over older German tanks, it was surely an exaggeration to suggest that each Russian tank was worth two or three German vehicles, particularly given the presence of long-barrelled Pz.IVs and Panther and Tiger tanks. Rotmistrov would of course have the attacker's prerogative of being able to concentrate his forces at a point of his choosing, but given the run-down state of his units, it was still surely asking too much that they take on numerically superior German formations.

Manstein had originally intended for the SS assault on Bogodukhov to coincide with a thrust by Fourth Panzer Army from the west, led by *Grossdeutschland* and 7th and 11th Panzer Divisions. The two Wehrmacht divisions had been badly degraded in the recent battles, but *Grossdeutschland* remained a formidable force, and in addition the Germans had *Schwere Panzer Abteilung 503* with 13 Tiger tanks available. The planned attack was delayed when reinforcements needed to release 7th Panzer Division from its defensive duties – 112th Infantry Division and 10th Panzergrenadier Division, both transferred from Army Group Centre and laboriously brought south by train – were repeatedly delayed. For the attack, Hoth assigned the armoured formations to General Walther Nehring's XXIV Panzer Corps; the weakness of 11th Panzer Division resulted in a further change in plan, with 10th Panzergrenadier Division now designated for the attack group whilst 11th Panzer Division remained on defensive duties.

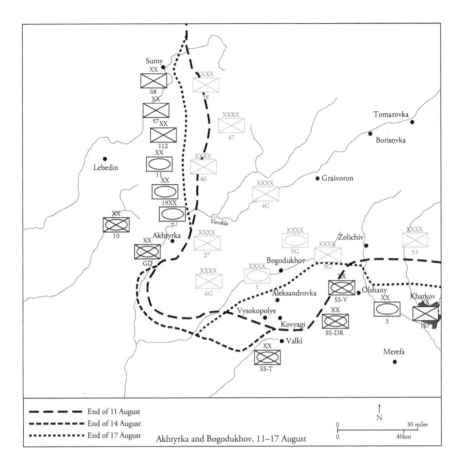

Akhtyrka and Bogodukhov, 11–17 August

In an attempt to disrupt the clearly visible German preparations, Vatutin ordered Moskalenko's Fortieth Army to resume its attacks further west, but he had ordered Moskalenko to release X Tank Corps for use elsewhere, markedly reducing the striking power of Fortieth Army. For three days from 13 August, Moskalenko's infantry struggled to make any progress and advanced barely two miles, attacks repeatedly foundering under heavy German artillery fire.[39] As Moskalenko's attack faltered, Vatutin issued fresh orders on 15 August for Forty-Seventh Army, on Moskalenko's western flank, to mount a joint attack with Fortieth Army on 17 August towards the southwest; it was hoped that this would unhinge the German defences and make the German positions at Akhtyrka untenable, thus eliminating any threat of Fourth Panzer Army counterattacking towards the east. At the same time, Twenty-Seventh Army was to resume direct attacks on Akhtyrka, but the badly depleted infantry divisions of Trofimenko's army were in no state to launch such an attack. Nevertheless, the main attack would be made by a formidable concentration of resources; about ten Red Army divisions with over 250 tanks would attack two battered German divisions.[40] Such a concentration of strike power was almost irresistible, and after a heavy artillery bombardment early on 17 August, the Russians swiftly broke through the German defences and advanced rapidly towards the Psel River. A weak battlegroup from 11th Panzer Division counterattacked with German infantry late in the day but could do little to restore the situation, and the Russians advanced up to seven miles (12km).

The speed and strength of the Russian advance was a serious setback for Hoth's Fourth Panzer Army. The armoured units concentrating around Akhtyrka could be used to launch the planned attack to the east and southeast, or could be sent west to deal with this new Russian advance – to attempt both ran the risk of launching two attacks with inadequate forces to achieve either objective. After careful consideration, Hoth decided to continue with his planned attack. If contact could be restored with Eighth Army (formerly *Armee Abteilung Kempf*), it might be possible to release sufficient forces to intercept this new Russian threat, but in the meantime it was best to concentrate as much power as possible to ensure success. Preparations for the attack were finally complete late on 17 August; reinforced by an independent brigade of Panther tanks, an assault gun battalion, and the Tigers of *Schwere Panzer Abteilung 503*, *Grossdeutschland* would lead the attack while 7th Panzer Division took over the defence of Akhtyrka and operated to safeguard the northern flank of *Grossdeutschland*. As the attack unfolded, 10th Panzergrenadier Division was to deploy to the right of *Grossdeutschland* while Geman infantry units concentrating near Poltava attacked from the southwest. At the same time, III Panzer Corps in the east would resume its attempts to attack with *SS-Totenkopf*, which had finally been able to hand over some of its front line to 223rd Infantry Division and could therefore concentrate its forces better.

The commander of 7th Panzer Division, General Hans Freiherr von Funck, who had commanded the unit throughout the war against the Soviet Union, was replaced by Generalmajor Hasso von Manteuffel just before the attack began. Manteuffel had commanded one of 7th Panzer Division's infantry regiments before being assigned to a command with Rommel's Afrika Korps, but illness resulted in him being flown home before the German forces in North Africa surrendered. He now returned to 7th Panzer Division, a popular and respected officer.

At the same time that Russian forces threatened to push forward across the Psel, the right flank of Army Group South came under renewed pressure along the Mius and around Izyum. There had been low-level fighting throughout August, with constant artillery harassment of the Germans and occasional raids by small groups of tanks and infantry. In order to strengthen First Panzer Army further to the north, 23rd Panzer Division was pulled out of the Mius line in early August with orders for 16th Panzergrenadier Division to follow in the middle of the month. Whilst these units – despite their losses earlier in the year, which had still not been made good – would provide welcome reinforcements for Mackensen's First Panzer Army, their departure left the Mius line with almost no armoured formations. The Russian attempts to penetrate across the river in July had been stopped largely through the efforts of 16th Panzergrenadier Division, and it was highly questionable whether the infantry divisions that remained would be able to hold back any renewed attack.

Vasilevsky had been sent to the southern sector by Stalin to coordinate a renewed attack; at the very least, it would tie down German forces and prevent their transfer to the Kharkov area, and at best it might be possible to overwhelm defences that had already been weakened by the movement of German armour to the north and achieve an important breakthrough. After a short period of preparation, Southwest Front and Steppe Front attacked on 16 August at several points. There was heavy fighting along the entire front line but with only modest gains; Vasilevsky spent the entire day with Major General Vasily Vasilyevich Glagolev's Forty-Sixth Army, and early the following morning received a tetchy signal from Stalin:

> You have not yet taken the trouble to send *Stavka* reports on the operation … and your assessment of the situation. A long time ago I commanded you as the *Stavka* representative strictly to send *Stavka* special reports at the end of each operation day. Almost every time you have neglected to do your duty …
>
> I warn you for the last time that if you ever fail to do your duty to *Stavka* again you will be removed from your post as Chief of the General Staff and recalled from the front.[41]

Vasilevsky had enjoyed a singularly cordial relationship with Stalin, and was dismayed by such a rebuke and contacted his deputy, Colonel General Alexei Innokentyevich Antonov, who reassured him that the signal had been prompted more by the poor progress of the new attacks rather than as a direct criticism of Vasilevsky. It is characteristic of Vasilevsky's somewhat reticent, accommodating and modest character that he concluded his assessment of this incident thus:

My feeling is that the lack of any indulgence to a *Stavka* representative was justified in the interests of efficient control of hostilities. Stalin very attentively followed the course of events at the front, quickly reacted to all changes in them and firmly held control in his own hands.[42]

The attack by Fourth Panzer Army would fall mainly upon the weak divisions of the Russian Twenty-Seventh Army, which had somewhat half-heartedly been concentrating its troops in order to launch the attack it had been commanded to make on Akhtyrka. As a result, it had deployed almost all of its strength in the front line, with no operational reserve available to deal with a German attack, despite being aware of German preparations. Artillery had been positioned in readiness for a Russian attack, and in any case ammunition was in short supply, and matters were made worse by almost all of Vatutin's air assets being committed to support the attacks by Fortieth and Forty-Seventh Armies to the west.[43] After a brief artillery bombardment, *Grossdeutschland* attacked on 18 August, rapidly penetrating the lines of the Russian infantry in its path. An officer of the division's assault gun battalion found himself advancing on a village where his men had fought just a short while before, when the division first deployed in the area:

> Only two assault guns struck light mines and suffered track damage. The rest chanced upon a gap and were able to veer right north of the village and eliminate the anti-tank and machine-gun fire which flared up at the edge of the village. The rest of the assault guns were able to follow the tracks of those that had got through … we attacked southeast with mounted elements of the fusilier regiment … We were able to seize the enemy artillery positions about 4km [2.5 miles] south of Bolshoye Osero after a brief firefight.[44]

Other elements of *Grossdeutschland* were less fortunate; most of the Tiger tanks with the division found themselves in a dense minefield, resulting in a dozen being disabled by track damage. Nevertheless, progress was swift and the Russian defences were rapidly overwhelmed. Some were encircled, while others pulled back in disarray. By chance, Zhukov was in Vatutin's headquarters when news of the German attack arrived, and the two men worked feverishly to find reinforcements for Trofimenko's stricken army. By the end of the day, they had ordered Trofimenko to deploy two tank corps and an infantry division to launch a counterattack against *Grossdeutschland* from the south, while another infantry division attacked from the north. Vatutin had also just been given Fourth Guards Army as a reserve force and he ordered Lieutenant General Grigory Ivanovich

Kulik – demoted from the rank of marshal in 1942 for failing to prevent the German capture of Rostov and now working to restore his reputation – to hold his men ready to intervene in Twenty-Seventh Army's sector. Finally, Katukov and Rotmistrov were ordered to release whatever armoured forces they could to support Trofimenko.

The day saw two notable Russian casualties. Major General Pyotr Ivanovich Krainov, the political commissar of Chistiakov's Sixth Guards Army, was badly wounded when his car came under attack from German aircraft; he was, according to Chistiakov, a popular figure in the army. His replacement, Major General Konstantin Kirikovich Abramov, stayed with Sixth Guards Army until the end of the war, repeatedly distinguishing himself by joining the troops in the front line, and was even credited with destroying German tanks by personally using an anti-tank rifle.[45] The second was Major General Dmitri Chrisanforovich Chernienko, commander of XXXI Tank Corps. Part of Katukov's First Tank Army, the corps was one of the formations dispatched to intercept the German thrust from Akhtyrka, and first had to disengage from the front line facing the SS divisions to the southeast. There hadn't been time to constuct proper field positions and Chernienko and his staff were sheltering in an improvised dugout; when the general took advantage of a break in the fighting to climb out of the dugout to stretch his legs, he was caught in a sudden German bombardment and killed.[46] A day later, Colonel Mikhail Trofimovich Leonov, commander of 112th Tank Brigade, was killed when his command post came under heavy fire.[47]

Despite the failure of the Tiger tanks of *Grossdeutschland* and *Schwere Panzer Abteilung 503* to get past the Russian minefields, Fourth Panzer Army's attack had gone well, with the leading elements penetrating about 15 miles (24km). In the southeast, there was heavy fighting as *SS-Totenkopf*, reinforced with two infantry regiments, attempted to advance towards the approaching forces of Fourth Panzer Army. On this occasion, it was possible to secure crossings over the Merla. Abdullin's regiment was in the path of the attack and suffered heavy losses, but as was often the case with both armies, the conduct of a decisive leader could have a profound effect on the outcome of the fighting:

Tanks appeared suddenly, moving swiftly and spreading confusion, and the two neighbouring regiments began to retreat. If the regiments to the right and left retreated, it was difficult to hold on and not rush to the rear as it was so dangerous to stay where we were. But other soldiers had a different belief: we couldn't be the ones to start a retreat. Whoever did so faced a tribunal. Let someone else start, and then we would see what happened.

We party organisers were distributed to the left and right flanks of the battalion and ran off along the trench in different directions. I didn't know that it was the last time I would see Pyotr Vasilyevich [Vasilyev, the battalion commissar].

The tanks were already close to us. Two of our anti-tank gunners fired, but missed. The tanks responded with their guns and put them out of action. Our lads started to throw grenades, but they were completely ineffective. They hurriedly threw the grenades without aiming. In one place our outposts were already wavering. I rushed there and returned them to their trenches – otherwise the tanks would crush them, like in another company where the soldiers leaped from their trenches and found themselves under caterpillar tracks.

We continued the fight, setting fire to some tanks with grenades and firing on them with submachine-guns, driving the German infantry away from the tanks.

The situation grew more complicated every minute; our neighbouring regiments continued to retreat. I too didn't want to end up in an impossible situation; ammunition in our sector was running low. But I could see that it was too soon to retreat and shouted myself hoarse: 'Hold on! It's desperate, but hold on!'

Then a company *Komsorg* ran up to me and gave me Lieutenant Vasilyev's field bag and party card. That's another commissar killed, I thought. Farewell Pyotr Vasiyevich. 'Where's the battalion commander?' I asked.

'He was carried back, wounded.' The deputy battalion commander had been killed three days ago. In such a situation, the rules were that the commander of the first infantry company had to take command of the battalion. But there was no time to search for him!

'Komsorg! Your orders! Why are you silent?' shouted the commander of the second company.

In this difficult moment, as if emerging from the ground, the giant figure of our regiment commander, Major Bilonov, appeared. With him was his adjutant, Lieutenant Kolya Korsunov. 'Boys, not one step back!' His thunderous voice shook the trench almost as if it was the rumble of thirty tanks hurrying to our rescue.

Though it eased my mind that the situation no longer depended on me, seeing our regimental commander still left me unhappy. We will die now, I thought, we won't be able to retreat.

Bilonov was a man of unbelievable courage. He couldn't be forced to retreat under any circumstances. This man had made up his mind, and we were with him. Even now, decades later, I struggle to understand the phenomenon of this man's personality. He picked up an abandoned anti-tank rifle from the ground and mechanically opened the bolt. He looked around for cartridges – there! He drove a cartridge into the chamber. At this moment, in a flash, a fascist tank appeared in front of him, stopped, and fired with its turret gun and with several bursts of its machine-gun. It was clearly a formidable threat and was about to attack. The only position that Bilonov could find was an ancient oak tree, overgrown with lichen, right next to him. Putting the PTR on a cross of branches, he took aim at the side of the tank. The range was no more than 50m.

The tank crew, of course, noticed the Soviet officer aiming at them with the anti-tank rifle and began to turn the turret with its main gun and machine-guns in our direction. I was to the commander's right and Korsunov to his left. The barrel of the tank gun seemed to become shorter and was soon staring at me with its black pupil. I knew that this was death: the pupil went up and down, left and right, as if lining us up more accurately for a photograph. I was nailed to the ground and nothing could force me to flinch to the side. It seemed that Bilonov would die anyway now, so what difference did it make what he thought of me at this last moment? But such was the power of this man's personality that it was unbearable that even at the end, he should think of me as a coward!

The regimental commander was taking careful aim. I was prepared to accept death along with my regimental commander and his adjutant, Kolya Korsunov. Now all three of us would die instantaneously.

The explosion was so loud that I did not immediately comprehend where the sound came from. The tank shooting or the PTR? But I could see that I was alive and well, as were the regimental commander and Kolya! So had Bilonov fired the first shot? The regimental commander fired again and I noticed that he was wounded in his right hand. The tank caught fire! Kolya and I wanted to take the wounded man to a place of safety but he stayed there and we had to bandage him. We were wrong, Bilonov understood that in this difficult situation the men should see their commander under fire with them.

The Nazis hurriedly jumped from their burning tank but machine-guns turned the energetically leaping Fritzes into rag dolls. The appearance of Bilonov in the front line at the critical moment – now I understood his care when aiming at the tank in front of the battalion – and the destruction of the fascist tank made our battalion do the impossible: soon the other five tanks that I could see began to pull back. The fascists were withdrawing! The neighbouring regiments also managed to reverse their movement. Our division returned to its previous positions.

The next day I attended a meeting of the regimental party department, where they unanimously entered my name in the regiment's book of heroes of the war.

Major Pavel Semenovich Bilonov, with his right hand bandaged, was presiding, and I sat next to him. After the party department meeting, we conducted Bilonov to the field hospital.[48]

In costly fighting, the Russians were able to prevent any major German advance, using swampy terrain to good effect. Nevertheless, there remained a very real danger that the two German forces – now less than 20 miles (33km) apart – would succeed in linking up and thus isolating much of Twenty-Seventh Army and Sixth Guards Army. On 19 August, the main units that were threatened with encirclement – IV Guards Tank Corps and two rifle divisions – attempted to counterattack against *Grossdeutschland* from the southwest and hectic fighting continued for much of the day. At the same time, the northern flank of the German advance came under attack by other elements of Trofimenko's Twenty-Seventh Army, but 7th Panzer Division, which had advanced out of Akhtyrka the previous day, was able to beat off the attacks with ease. The first elements of Kulik's Fourth Guards Army were arriving though, and there was no guarantee that the Germans would find things so straightforward in the coming days.

On 18 August, Vasilevsky oversaw further attacks along the Mius and Donets after extensive regrouping and reorganisation of Southwest Front's units. Despite heavy artillery preparation, the attacks near Izyum made no headway and the following day, some Russian armoured groups managed to achieve local penetrations but these were all eliminated by German counterattacks. After discussing the poor prospects of success with Malinovsky, the commander of Southwest Front, Vasilevsky agreed to switch the point of effort. It was inconceivable that the Germans could maintain such strong defences all along the front, and he ordered forces to be transferred to Eighth Guards Army. When he explained his plans to Stalin by telephone, the latter was displeased, making several disparaging comments about the failures both of Vasilevsky and Southwest and Southern Fronts. In particular, Vasilevsky's report that no new attack would be possible before 27 August seemed to cause particular resentment. However, Stalin had little choice but to agree. In the meantime, local attacks continued but achieved little other than further casualties; 16th Panzergrenadier Division reported on 24 August that with the support of an attached battalion of assault guns, its panzer battalion and artillery succeeded in knocking out 140 enemy tanks; this is likely to be a substantial exaggeration, even after allowing for multiple hits on the same vehicle and temporarily disabled Russian tanks being counted as 'kills'. However, the division's status report shows no German tank or assault gun losses during the day.[49]

There was better news for Vasilevsky and Stalin from further south, where Southern Front also renewed its attacks on 19 August. Fifth Shock Army enjoyed a particularly successful day, advancing about six miles (10km), and released IV Guards Mechanised Corps to exploit the penetration, rapidly pushing forward and cutting the railway line running southeast from Stalino (now Donetsk). With all available armoured resources diverted to the Kharkov area, the Germans had little with which to restore the situation.

The area where *Grossdeutschland* was still trying to advance to the southeast saw further heavy fighting. Both sides attacked on 19 August, advancing in some areas and being driven back in others. The gap between the two German forces attempting to isolate the Russian Twenty-Seventh and Sixth Guards Armies was now barely ten miles, but *SS-Totenkopf* had struggled to make any progress; about 1,400 new recruits arrived to restore the division's strength, but it would take time for them to be brought up to the standard required for action on the Eastern Front. In order to try to disrupt the German attack, Vatutin ordered the forces that had been concentrated in the area to counterattack and drive back Fourth Panzer Army's armoured group and there was heavy fighting on 20 and 21 August, forcing *Grossdeutschland* into an increasingly defensive posture. Like the panzer divisions, *Grossdeutschland* had two infantry regiments, named the Panzergrenadier Regiment and Panzerfusilier Regiment, and the former was in the thick of the defensive fighting. A company of the division's anti-tank guns was operating in support:

At about 1000 [on 21 August] several Russian tanks with infantry drove past us on the road. Because of a shortage of ammunition we weren't permitted to open fire on such a target. Then it was quiet again. In the afternoon our runner came with mail and some ammunition ... then at about 1400 it began.

German aircraft – He 111s – dropped countless high explosive bombs right in front of our position, several dangerously close, but there was still nothing to be seen of the enemy. Because the terrain before us fell away somewhat and there was a ravine running across in front of us, we suspected that this was where the Soviets were making their preparations.

The Soviets attacked suddenly at 1530; they tried to outflank us. This time the enemy attack was made without mortar support and also without artillery. Our gun tractor came over immediately in order to limber so that we could withdraw if necessary. But things did not happen as we expected. Five minutes after the attack began our platoon runner ... was killed by two bullets in the head. Gefreiter Drescher and I jumped for cover. In doing so Gefreiter Drescher was shot in the heart and I in the shoulder, both with explosive bullets. We both passed out from loss of blood. I soon regained consciousness and tried to get out of the hole. With my Russian sniper's rifle in my hand, I realised that I was almost paralysed, then I passed out again.

When I woke up again … I saw that Gefreiter Drescher … was wide awake even though he was bleeding heavily from his chest. Blood was running down from under my jacket. How I got out of the hole I don't know; I merely watched as Gefreiter Willi Müller … pulled me behind the gun tractor. Another two minutes and I would have ended up like Gefreiter Drescher, who was stabbed to death with bayonets in his hole by the Russians.

In spite of the heavy fire Gefreiter Müller dragged me to a grain shed, where the seriously wounded of 3rd Company lay … Our artillery intervened at about 1600 and gained some breathing room for us. Things were apparently not too good with the grenadiers either. When we drove away in the gun tractor I could see groups of grenadiers with raised hands being led away by the Soviets. Overturned and burning vehicles, empty gasoline cans, knocked-out tanks and dead, friend and foe, wounded heading for the rear, blown-up and abandoned guns, all this I saw on my way back.[50]

Despite coming under heavy pressure, the grenadier regiment was able to cling to its positions. A little to the south, the leading elements of 10th Panzergrenadier Division probed forward towards where they hoped to establish contact with *SS-Totenkopf*. To date, the SS division had made little headway despite inflicting substantial losses on the opposing Russian forces, but attempts were made to create a stronger force in the hard-won bridgehead over the Merla during the night of 19–20 August and at first light reconnaissance platoons set off towards the north and northwest. There was bitter fighting in and around Kolontayev with heavy losses on both sides and it took the arrival of the tanks of *SS-Totenkopf* in the afternoon to swing the battle in favour of the Germans, but the first attempt to push on beyond the village ended in early evening when the German armour ran into well-positioned Russian anti-tank guns. Another column dispatched by the reconnaissance battalion had better fortune:

Suddenly the ominous message 'Tanks! Tanks!' rang out. Five tanks were advancing towards us. One drove right up the slope on the main road. What had seemed to be just a heap of straw was also now moving. Bundles of straw fell off to the side. A second tank drove towards us, but lower down, next to the road. I drove into cover with our vehicles behind a haystack. Other vehicles also headed that way as if by herd instinct. The first tank was already approaching our road. It was only 600–700m from us. It had to open fire at any moment. 'Let's get away from the crowd,' said Unterscharführer Ehgartner to me. We drove to one side. There was still no gunfire. The tanks came closer and closer, more of them appearing on the high ground. 'Guys, they're German tanks!' A sigh of relief! They were Pz.IIIs and Pz.IVs, with half-tracks and even an armoured ambulance, almost a complete regiment. I was ordered to establish contact. I set off across country to the high ground and passed through Kotelevka. From the other side the first tank clattered into the village. It was from *Grossdeutschland*. Its turret hatch opened. An Oberleutnant waved me over and sent me onwards. I was told, 'Go to the *Graf* ['Baron']' and pointed at a command tank. I assumed that the unit was led by a certain Major Graf. I reported formally to him. He seemed rather ungracious to me and ordered, 'Report to your commander that the Russian tanks have been shot up and he can advance.' I snapped to attention and said, 'Yes, Herr Major!' He looked me up and down. 'I am no major, I am Oberst Graf von Strachwitz! Take note!'[51]

Hyazinth von Strachwitz was the commander of the panzer regiment of *Grossdeutschland* and was famous throughout Germany as an energetic tank commander with a reputation for leading from the front, having served with 1st Panzer Division at the outset of the war. He entered the Soviet Union in 1941 with 16th Panzer Division and was repeatedly in the thick of the action, being wounded twice before the end of July – despite being hospitalised on August when his latest wound became infected, he discharged himself and returned to his men. Still with 16th Panzer Division, he was involved in the advance on Stalingrad but was badly burned in October when his tank was knocked out. When he recovered from his wound, he took command of the *Grossdeutschland* panzer regiment, and whilst one account suggests that he may have been involved in a plot to arrest or kill Hitler in February 1943, others suggest that his aristocratic beliefs as a Prussian would have made an assassination unthinkable.[52]

With the link-up between *SS-Totenkopf* and Fourth Panzer Army, the Russian 166th Rifle Division and IV Guards Tank Corps, both of which had suffered heavy losses, were now completely cut off to the southwest. However, Vatutin's attacks on Fourth Panzer Army were too heavy for any forces to be released to destroy the encircled Russians, but the tempo at which the Russian attacks were mounted brought its own problems – the lack of artillery preparation noted in the *Grossdeutschland* report was a direct consequence.[53] While the Panzergrenadier

Regiment of *Grossdeutschland* was heavily engaged to the north, the Panzerfusilier Regiment fought a bitter battle for Kaplunovka and Parkhomovka to the south and was forced out of the former when outflanked; the Russian III Mechanised Corps managed to capture the latter at dawn on 21 August but was so badly reduced in strength that it could do no more than defend the ground that it had gained. Nevertheless, Fourth Panzer Army's advance had effectively ground to a halt.

As is described later, *Armee Abteilung Kempf* had now been transformed into Eighth Army under the command of General Otto Wöhler. As the pressure from the Russian Fortieth and Forty-Seventh Armies continued to press back the German defences, it was clear to Hoth, Wöhler and Manstein that time was running out for the counterattack that had been intended to restore continuity to the front line, particularly as there were no forces available to destroy the Russian formations that had been cut off by the advances of *Grossdeutschland* and *SS-Totenkopf*. On 19 August, several Soviet units converged on Lebedin. III Guards Mechanised Corps (a different unit from the mechanised corps fighting for Parkhomovka) and LII Rifle Corps approached from the northeast while II Tank Corps attacked from the east, forcing the Germans to abandon the town late in the day. On the left flank of Moskalenko's Fortieth Army, his XLVII Rifle Corps was heavily engaged with the German 11th and 19th Panzer Divisions. The Luftwaffe carried out several attacks, succeeding in hitting the headquarters of 206th Rifle Division in a raid that killed the division's commander and chief of staff, but the battlegroups from the German divisions continued to come under heavy pressure and, despite their heavy losses, the Russian units reached the banks of the Vorskla just two or three miles from the northwest outskirts of Akhtyrka late on 20 August.

The threat to the rear of the German forces that had advanced from Akhtyrka was now acute and required urgent attention. In an attempt to shore up the line, Hoth ordered 10th Panzergrenadier Division, which had recently linked up with the leading elements of *SS-Totenkopf*, to move to the northwest to support the hard-pressed 11th and 19th Panzer Divisions, effectively abandoning any possibility of further attacks towards Wöhler's Eighth Army. Bitter fighting erupted the following day around Dovshyk, Chupakovka and Oleshyna; despite Vatutin's constant urging, the advance ground to a halt. Whilst the Russian attack had forced the Germans to divert forces away from their counterattack, it had failed to break through and unhinge the German defences, and *Stavka* expressed its displeasure in a signal dictated personally by Stalin to Shtemenko, as the latter described:

He [Stalin] armed himself with a red pencil and, pacing up and down along the table, dictated the first phrase:

'The events of the last few days have shown that you have not taken into account past experience and continue to repeat old mistakes both in planning and in conducting operations.'

After this there was a pause while Stalin collected his thoughts. Then, in one breath, as they say, a whole paragraph was dictated:

'The urge to attack everywhere and capture as much territory as possible without consolidating successes and providing sound cover for the flanks of the assault groups, amounts to a haphazard attack. Such an attack leads to the dissipation of forces and materiel and allows the enemy to strike at the flank and rear of our groups which have gone far ahead and not been provided with cover on their flanks.'

The supreme commander stopped for a minute and read what I had written over my shoulder. At the end of the phrase he wrote in his own hand, 'and to slaughter them piecemeal.' He then went on dictating:

'Under such circumstances the enemy succeeded in breaking out in the rear of First Tank Army ... then he struck at the exposed flank formations of Sixth Guards Army ... and finally, profiting by your carelessness, the enemy on 20 August struck southeast from the Akhtyrka area at the rear of Twenty-Seventh Army and IV and V Guards Tank Corps.

'As a result of these enemy actions, our troops have suffered considerable and quite unjustified losses, and the advantageous position for smashing the enemy's Kharkov grouping has been lost.'

The supreme commander stopped again, read what I had written, struck out the words 'profiting by your carelessness', and then continued:

'I am once again compelled to point out to you inadmissible mistakes, which you have more than once perpetrated in carrying out operations, and I demand that the task of liquidating the enemy's Akhtyrka grouping, as the most vital task, should be fulfilled in the next few days.

'You can do this because you have sufficient means to do it with.

'I request you not to be carried away by the task of outflanking the Kharkov area on the Poltava side but to concentrate your attention on the realistic and concrete task of liquidating the enemy's Akhtyrka grouping, because unless this enemy group is liquidated Voronezh Front can have no success.'

Upon concluding the last paragraph, Stalin glanced through it, again over my shoulder, emphasised the meaning of what was written by inserting after the words 'I request you not' the words 'to dissipate your strength' and ordered me to read the final text aloud ... [Then he] nodded and signed the paper.[54]

When Manstein had counterattacked in March 1943 and caught the overextended Red Army by surprise, Vatutin was singled out for criticism by Shtemenko and others, but the reality was that practically everyone in the army's command structure shared the belief that the Germans had been too badly beaten at Stalingrad and along the Don to recover. On this occasion too, Vatutin was blamed for over-extending his lines, but on 12 August Stalin had personally ordered Vatutin to advance towards Poltava and Kremenchug, the very action that now attracted his criticism.[55] Other senior Red Army commanders had been reassigned, dismissed or even executed for such failures, but Stalin's assessment of Vatutin appears to have been that, despite his tendency to over-optimism, he was an aggressive, innovative commander, and he remained in post.

Both sides were committing their dwindling armoured assets to the battle to the west of Kharkov. Rotmistrov's tank army could field 111 tanks against an almost identical number of German tanks and assault guns, and neither side enjoyed a decisive advantage. There were confused actions as small units clashed, often at night, in an area where there were substantial pockets of Russian troops operating behind the German front line, as a group of soldiers from *SS-Totenkopf* in the village of Kolontayev discovered before dawn on 21 August when they heard engines approaching and assumed that they were German reinforcements:

> The sentry by the road was still pondering whether [the lead vehicle] was a Pz.III or Pz.IV when suddenly a flare rose steeply into the sky. At the same time the commander of the leading tank shouted '*Idi Szuda!*' ['Come here!'] at the sentry who stood as if petrified. In the flickering light of the flare, he now recognised the typical Russian armoured hull of the vehicle from whose turret the commander was calling. Now everything was clear. In a flash he ran to the regimental commander's battlewagon and raised the alarm … chaos broke out everywhere … It was an unpleasant awakening during the night. Ivan had broken into Kolontayev. He shot up the houses and fired on everyone he encountered. We grabbed our weapons and poured out of the houses … At first we couldn't work out who was firing. Gradually, the situation became clearer. T-34s with mounted infantry, self-propelled guns, trucks and jeeps with mortars mounted on them pressed into the village … We opened fire immediately. We had the advantage of being able to fire from the cover of the buildings. We blazed away at the Russian column with submachine-guns, machine-guns and rifles. Some of the vehicles came to a halt. Their crews emerged and tried to flee. There was great confusion. Tank guns roared at the edge of the village. Ear-splitting explosions followed …[56]

Confused fighting continued all night, but as it grew light the Germans began to take control. Most of the Russian tanks managed to escape, though some were abandoned when they ran into boggy ground. Several hundred Russians were taken prisoner, many of them wounded. The German company in the village also took heavy losses, including the battalion commander, Sturmbannführer Heinrich Krauth.

There were fierce clashes all along the front line held by *SS-Totenkopf*, with most of the Russian units coming from IV Guards Tank Corps. Rottenführer Georg Hax of the reconnaissance battalion wrote in his diary:

[The enemy] now attacked across the entire breadth of the valley without preparatory fire. A wildly firing T-34 rolled along the road and broke through our infantry. A nearby 37mm anti-tank gun popped up at the closest possible range from behind a dungheap and hit the tank on its closed turret hatch.

The steel giant halted. Now our infantry guns fired together on the iron hull until smoke obscured it. The Russian infantry that had been following it ran back. Then we realised that our heavy machine-gun on the crest was no longer firing. We could no longer go towards it by the most direct route. The squad leader worked his way around to the position. Our comrades lay there, shredded by countless shells, in and around their foxholes. Even in death, the gunner clung to his machine-gun, which was now no more than a piece of mangled metal. The squad leader returned and just stammered, 'All dead!'[57]

By first light on 22 August, the Russians had completed their preparations for a major new assault in their attempts to break into the German defences that ran west from the Kharkov area, with 233rd Rifle Division and V Guards Mechanised Corps on the right flank of the bridgehead over the Udy and 107th and 28th Guards Rifle Divisions and XVIII Tank Corps on the left. A further two rifle divisions would lead the main attack, with a final rifle division held back in reserve. At 0500, the battle began with the customary heavy artillery bombardment, and fighting rapidly erupted all along a frontage of about 12 miles (20km). Given the number of tanks concentrated in the area and the importance of the battle, the fighting was as intense as any such clash in the entire war, with air power on both sides being used to try to overcome the enemy. The town of Korotich became a key focus and the German defenders were isolated by 24th Guards Tank Brigade, but when tanks from Solomatin's I Mechanised Corps penetrated into the town, a German counterattack enveloped and overwhelmed them. V Guards Mechanised Corps was driven back by an armoured battlegroup of *SS-Das Reich* and the beleaguered garrison of Korotich clung to the ruins in the face of repeated Russian attacks. Rotmistrov's tanks managed to penetrate as far as the Poltava-Kharkov road and deny its use to the Germans, but every attempt to exploit this success failed in the face of accurate fire from the German Panther tanks.

Russian armour also penetrated into Lyubotin, but a unit from a panzergrenadier regiment of *SS-Das Reich* was close by:

Dismount, trucks to the rear, attack, report to [Hauptsturmführer Alfred] Lex, the battalion commander. The first casualties from Stalin organs [*Katyusha* rockets]. A solitary assault gun stands at the first road fork after entering the town and fires to the right. 'Thank God you're here!' we hear as we go past.

We attack along the road that runs right to the railway embankment. Two platoons and a heavy support group, that's the entire company. It goes well up to the town centre. But we must seize the railway embankment ...

But now it heats up in the town square, where two medium mortars are firing and the heavy machine-guns are covering to the right, and three T-34s appear from the left with crowds of Ivans! Suddenly they are amongst us, 80 against eight. My machine-pistol jams on the third burst. It becomes cat-and-mouse around the houses. A T-34 fires from behind the embankment and then suddenly rolls back. Hauptsturmführer Lex – who has been with us for a while – shot its commander when he peered out, trying to orient himself. After half an hour the crisis is past.[58]

In the face of this determined resistance, the advance of Rotmistrov's tanks was relatively modest but nonetheless critical; as is described in the next chapter, it made it impossible for the Germans to continue to cling to Kharkov without a serious risk of encirclement. However, further objectives lay ahead and Rotmistrov continued to try to achieve a breakthrough with his tank army, despite its brutal losses. To make matters worse for the Russians, *SS-Das Reich* received welcome reinforcements in the shape of its panzer regiment's I Battalion, which had been in the west undergoing re-equipment with Panther tanks. Although it had been intended as a medium tank – a direct response to the Russian T-34 – increases in the armour of the Panther during its development resulted in the vehicle weighing 44 tons when it entered service, meaning that special railcars were required for its transportation. Forced to detrain before its intended destination as a result of a preceding train being hit by Russian bombers, one Panther company found itself assigned to support 3rd Panzer Division. Even during training, the shortcomings of the new tank became apparent; its 75mm gun was a deadly weapon, capable of striking with accuracy at ranges in excess of 2km, but there were serious reliability issues with its engine. The relatively small engine compartment of the tank resulted in the engine being a tight fit, making maintenance difficult, and the engine ran at higher engine RPM than older designs – in combination with poor quality lubricants, this led to overheating and even engine fires. Nevertheless, the first Panthers of *SS-Das Reich* went into action early on 22 August led by the battalion commander, Hauptsturmführer Hans Weiss:

Our company commander at that time, Obersturmführer [Joachim-Günther] Schöntaube, gathered I Platoon together and gave us a few good words of advice. Roughly, he told us that during the night, I Platoon with supporting panzergrenadiers was to capture an important hill. It was expected that the following day the enemy would attack. It was likely the enemy attack would be supported by tanks. As we now had a tank that, in contrast to the old Pz.III, was superior to the T-34, we would soon deal with them. 'I wish you the best of luck in your first action with your new Panthers!'

At this point we didn't know just how much we would need that luck. After the platoon was ready for combat, we drove to the aforementioned hill between Starya Lyubotin and Kommuna under cover of darkness. One Panther was left behind en route due to mechanical problems.

We occupied the hill with four tanks on 22 August at about 0100. Untersturmführer Mühlbeck directed us to each position. The grenadiers of *Der Führer* Regiment were already in the positions, and complained bitterly that we would draw the fire of enemy artillery onto the hill with our engine noise, thus disturbing the grenadiers' restful night. They couldn't know just how much they would need us the following day ... During the night we heard loud engine noises from the enemy's direction. Rottenführer Slavik ... said, 'Not so bad, at most that's two or three tanks. Engines always sound louder at night.'

... At first light we saw a village (Kommuna) about 1km in front of us ... In that moment hell broke loose. An enemy bombardment struck the hill. It was only due to the instincts of our driver that we avoided being hit. Whenever he changed position, a shell landed on our previous position shortly after. I don't know how long the bombardment lasted. When the smoke dispersed a bit, we saw them advance out of the village before us ... In my entire deployment in Russia, I had never seen the likes of what we saw before us.

Roughly 80 Russian tanks attacked our hill. Now we discovered how good our new 75mm guns were. The first tank was destroyed at 2,000m range. The Russians too appeared to be surprised. The engagement lasted between two and three hours. An artillery shell had struck the muzzle-brake of the gun on the tank of the platoon commander, Untersturmführer Mühlbeck, and the recoiling barrel broke his right forearm and collar-bone, and he was also lightly wounded on the head.

After a fierce battle, 23 Soviet tanks, three trucks and two anti-tank guns lay smashed on the ground ...

Mühlbeck's tank had taken further hits. Despite repeated advice via the radio to abandon his tank, he refused and remained with us.[59]

There was also heavy fighting in the sector held by *SS-Totenkopf* and, in a brief pause, Rottenführer Hax and his comrades took the opportunity to collect supplies and speak to a small group of prisoners that they had captured earlier:

Amongst them there is also an officer. We call him Fedor, and Geimer translates. We discover that he is from an armoured artillery unit. His battery was bombed by German aircraft. We pass this information on. A little later orders arrive for a raiding party to be sent out against this battery. From there, we are to push on further to Mikhailovka. There, we should find a battalion that wants to surrender but has been prevented from doing so by its commissar. Unterscharführer Ehgartner leads the raiding party. They are guided by Fedor, who has volunteered to help us. He leads us to his battery position. It has been abandoned. An intact 120mm self-propelled gun remains. Fedor immediately climbs onto it. A little later its engine fires up. We load up as many shells and cartridges as we can. Fedor explains how to handle the gun. Then we drive on to our next objective, the village of Mikhailovka. The Russian gun leads. The village appears before us. Positions have been established about 200m from its edge. The 'Soviet Star' emblazoned on the gun is visible at a distance. Cautiously, we approach the positions. Now we see movements in them. A few Russians leave their foxholes and come out to meet us. They clearly think that they have their own troops before them. We wave back and roll on a bit. Now the Ivans become uncertain. We take up position on some high ground. Now the penny drops for the Russians. They can see that we have them cold. A few run from the village. Ehgartner raises his arm: 'Fire!' Our captured gun thunders. Our *Schwimmers* [*Schwimmwagens*, cross-country vehicles analogous to jeeps] burst into the enemy positions. Our machine-guns blaze away.[60]

Supported by other troops from *SS-Totenkopf*, the raiding party rapidly overran the village and took many of the men prisoner. There is no mention in the account of whether the commissar who had allegedly prevented a surrender was found, or what fate he suffered; given the orders to execute all commissars immediately, it is likely that he would have tried to slip away undetected.

In another attack, the Germans found that even their mighty Tiger tanks were not invincible:

We drove through Lupochovatye, turned towards a hill and moved forward in a broad company wedge formation. Soon fountains of earth started to rise up in front of us. A little later there were the first impacts amongst our tanks. They couldn't be coming from ordinary anti-tank guns. The leading Tiger was hit. Damn! We couldn't see where they were firing from. To my left, Oberscharführer Robbi's tank halted. He stuck his head out of the turret to search the landscape ahead. Then there was an impact next to him on the turret. The cupola was blown off. 'Robbi, man, they've got you!' I thought in a flash. Before us a Tiger was burning, and our tanks to right and left were also hit. We pulled back and assembled on the rear slope. Two Tigers had been shot up. We tank commanders were shocked. What could have happened? Our infantry moved forward. We attacked again. This time we wanted to take the Russians in the flank. So we moved along the hill to the north and then turned west.

To our right, our assault guns were moving forward. We waved enthusiastically to them to press on. Then there was a flash in front of us. The enemy guns were under the cover of bushes and clumps of trees. We marked it all up on a map and roared forward. There they were: anti-aircraft guns, well camouflaged. All calibres were present from long-barrelled guns to flak machine-guns, apparently an entire anti-aircraft regiment. But we were now approaching from the side. And now we charged in! Our guns roared and our machine-guns blazed at the crews who struggled to turn their guns quickly and to aim at us. Too late![61]

By 25 August, Rotmistrov's formations – which had started the operation with over 540 tanks and assault guns – could field just 50 fighting vehicles and he had to call a pause to operations. The remaining tanks were consolidated into a single tank corps and the other units pulled out of line to allow them a chance to recover their strength. The local balance of power was now with the Germans – the tank strength of *SS-Das Reich* was 78 tanks and assault guns, including 21 Panthers and six Tigers, and although *SS-Totenkopf* was in somewhat poorer shape, their collective strength was now greater than the forces arrayed against them.[62] Further west, Chistiakov attacked in an attempt to rescue the units that had been cut off when *Grossdeutschland* and *SS-Totenkopf* met to the southeast of

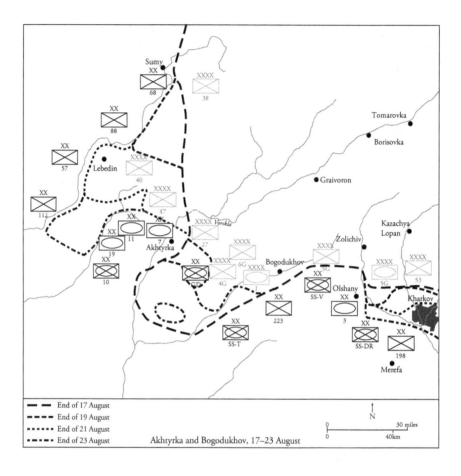

Akhtyrka and Bogodukhov, 17–23 August

Akhtyrka. Using III Guards Tank Corps and 51st Guards Rifle Division, he managed to reach them without heavy fighting; the German units had also suffered heavy losses, and a member of the *SS-Totenkopf* panzer regiment noted that men who had been serving as gunners and loaders were now acting as tank commanders, with personnel from the division's rear area units drafted in to replace them as loaders.[63] Perhaps in response to the criticism directed at him by *Stavka*, Vatutin urged his western flank to complete the envelopment or destruction of the Germans around Akhtyrka. The advance of Forty-Seventh Army effectively came to an end when it reached the Psel, but Fortieth Army continued to advance towards the southwest. When it tried to turn to the south and southeast towards Zenkov, it ran into the German 34th Infantry Division,

176

recently arrived from Army Group Centre, and its leading elements were driven back in disorder. Nevertheless, the position of *Grossdeutschland* and 7th Panzer Division in and around Akhtyrka was becoming increasingly vulnerable, and on 24 August, Manteuffel – who had been wounded earlier in the day – ordered his men to pull back from the town. With the German front line now considerably shortened, it was possible to extract most of *Grossdeutschland* from the front line in order to create an armoured reserve.

Fighting began to ebb in intensity as both sides took a much-needed breath. By contrast, Soviet efforts further south to expel the Germans from the Donbas continued without pause, and Vasilevsky conscientiously kept Stalin updated on the slow, painful progress of South and Southwest Fronts as they ground their way forward. The Izyum sector remained largely quiet with Soviet resources concentrating on achieving a breakthrough further south; if this were successful, this would leave the German First Panzer Army in a salient projecting towards Izyum and there might be an opportunity before the end of the year to put pressure on this from both north and south. Taganrog fell on 30 August, with some of the defenders being surrounded and wiped out, but elsewhere Army Group South managed to extract its forces in relatively good order. Kobylyanskiy and his comrades were once more in the thick of the fighting, often moving during the short night hours as they attempted to bring the withdrawing Germans to battle. As is the case with accounts written by soldiers of all nations, the enemy vehicles they encountered were almost always reported to be the most formidable opponents possible:

Our march along country roads was interrupted several times at some intersections because the regiment's advance guard hesitated over which road to take … As a result, it was already daylight when we approached the hamlet of Vishnevy, and an unexpected German reconnaissance plane performed a circle above our march column …

Suddenly, there was an alarming announcement: a column of German tanks and trucks was moving toward Vishnevy! A lot of orders rang out, and all of our infantrymen ran down the gentle slope of a shallow, 1.5km-long ravine covered by blooming sunflowers. About 300m from the hamlet outskirts, they began furiously digging in. My platoon (with only one gun because the other two guns of our battery were under repair at the time) was ordered to engage the enemy over open sights. The second platoon (also with only one gun) was directed to a relatively safer covered position.

The gun crew commander, Vladimir Tetyukov, and I chose an apt place for laying direct fire right on the nearby edge of the slope. Then we gave the sign to our horseman, Suyunov, to bring up the gun and shells. Three more crewmen joined us: the gunner, Ismaylov; the charger, Khorkov; and the shell carrier, Yusupov. Suyunov brought up the gun and shells, and then he drove the limber to shelter behind a nearby house. In a few minutes the five of us hurriedly prepared the emplacement, set up the gun, and brought up and opened the shell boxes. We had just begun to dig foxholes for ourselves when a German tank with a dozen or more soldiers aboard appeared from behind a hillock on the opposite side of the ravine.

The tank was crawling slowly, and we were waiting for its manoeuvre. But in a minute two more tanks came into view, and then we saw a few more tanks and self-propelled guns. They were all moving slowly toward the ravine. If nothing was done about it, within five or six minutes the 'Tigers' and 'Ferdinands' would crush our still un-entrenched infantrymen. On the other hand, if we opened fire, we would be challenging a dozen armoured monsters to an unequal duel. There was no time for reflection; the situation required immediate action.

In spite of the mortal risk, I gave the order, 'To action!' The gun crew, directed by Tetyukov, prepared the shot, and I, while looking through my binoculars, estimated the distance to the leading 'Tiger' and called out the number to set the sight. A few seconds passed, and the laying was completed. Tetyukov's order sounded, 'Fire!' And in a split second a thundering roar pierced the seeming deathly quiet that had dominated the ravine …

Crouched on one knee … I looked through my field glasses for the point of explosion. What a horror! The shell exploded far to one side of the tank. I ran up to the panorama sight and took a short glance at the scale – there's the problem! Instead of the usual 30.00, it was set to 29.00. Evidently through his nervousness, Ismaylov had missed the proper setting by a whole point! Tetyukov adjusted the setting correctly, and the second shot rang out. This time the shell exploded exactly on the leading tank's track. And the soldiers who were sitting on it instantly disappeared as if being blown off by a strong gust of wind. The 'Tiger' stopped moving, and we could hear the rattle of the German submachine-guns. Meanwhile, we redirected our aim to a neighbouring self-propelled gun and hit it with our next shot. But at the same moment, a German shell flew over our heads with a threatening hiss – overshot by about 50m. We began to prepare to fire another round.

A sudden burst of tremendous force deafened me. Everything around was shrouded in suffocating propellant gases and rising dust. I lay on the ground, my head pounding. I raised it a little and took in a terrible view. Our gun was tilted unnaturally to one side. Ismaylov was lying beside it, writhing in pain while holding his head. Khorkov was slowly and carefully getting up off the ground. Yusupov was on his knees, and only Tetyukov was lying motionless. I walked up to the lifeless body of the gun commander – an enemy shell fragment had struck him in the temple. Ismaylov had a head wound, but it wasn't serious – a fragment just grazed his skin. Shell-shocked, Khorkov began to vomit. Somehow I bandaged Ismaylov's wound and sent Yusupov, who hadn't been wounded, for Suyunov.

Then I looked over our gun. The shell had exploded beside the now-shattered left wheel. The gun shield was pierced in many places, and the aiming gear was damaged, too. When Yusupov and Suyunov returned, we took out the panorama sight, and the four of us (Khorkov couldn't help) carried Tetukov's still-warm body to the hamlet outskirts.[64]

Despite losing his gun commander and the last gun of his platoon, Kobylyanskiy judged the action a success – the German tanks were halted long enough for the infantry to dig in, and from Vishnevy the gunners watched the Germans pull back. It is likely that, given the scarcity of German armour, the German unit was anxious not to get drawn into a protracted fight; almost any show of determined resistance would probably have had the same outcome.

For Manstein, the outcome of the battle to the west of Kharkov must have brought mixed feelings. On the one hand, the Red Army had been thwarted in its attempts to exploit its early successes and the two tank armies had failed to burst through into open space; losses inflicted upon the Russians were also substantial. However, the German armoured formations had also failed to break through the Russian lines when they launched their counterattack. Much had been achieved in February and March 1943 by Wehrmacht units launching sudden, powerful counterattacks that allowed for units to be switched to other critical points in the front line, and – particularly following the failure of German armour to prevail in the fighting around the Kursk salient – it seemed as if it would no longer be possible for such tactics to guarantee success. It was increasingly clear that the Red Army had learned how to blunt the German armoured attacks and this would further tip the balance against the Wehrmacht in the coming months.

CHAPTER 5

KHARKOV

After recapturing Belgorod in early August, the Red Army was anxious to press on to the south as fast as it could in order to secure Kharkov before the Germans could reorganise their defences. Similarly, the Germans needed to slow the Soviet advance as much as possible. Reinforcements in the shape of armoured formations were on their way, but they would take time to arrive.

One of the units in the front line trying to hold back the Soviet onslaught, 6th Panzer Division, was in poor shape after the heavy fighting around Belgorod. It was now assigned to III Panzer Corps and pulled back perhaps half way to Kharkov, covering the Belgorod-Kharkov road from attacks from the northwest. The normally reliable troops of the division's panzergrenadier regiments began to show signs of strain in heavy fighting that raged throughout 6 August, and Oberst Martin Unrein, commander of 4th Panzergrenadier Regiment, had to intervene personally at one stage to prevent a rout. It was a measure of the strain that the division was under and the losses that it had suffered, but for the moment it continued to hold the line.[1] Given just a short break from combat, it would rapidly recover its tank strength as repaired vehicles were returned to service, but there were no other armoured formations available to replace it and its fighting power continued to decline daily.

The advance of the Soviet Fifty-Third Army from Belgorod towards Kharkov had slowed almost to a standstill after the capture of Mikoyanovka. Managarov, the army commander who had entertained Zhukov with his accordion, tried to organise a mobile group to break through the lines of the German 168th Infantry Division with the intention of reaching Dergachi and thus cutting the line of retreat of the German defenders; at the very least, this would force a substantial withdrawal, and at best might trap some of the stubborn defenders in an encirclement. Despite penetrating the first line of German defences, the group – about four tank battalions, a tank destroyer regiment, and two infantry battalions – failed to reach its objective, coming to a standstill at the village of Kazachya Lopan. Further Soviet units were fed into the fighting, and Kazachya Lopan finally fell late on 8 August, but the cost of the ground gained was disproportionately high. Once more, the Germans withdrew to new positions a little further to the south.

On the eastern flank of the Soviet force that captured Bogodukhov was Krivoshein's III Mechanised Corps, which had been ordered to bypass the town and cut the railway line running to the southeast. It ran headlong into the reconnaissance battalion of SS-Das Reich, which was advancing in the opposite direction in two columns. Krivoshein ordered one of his mechanised brigades and a tank brigade to attack immediately while a further mechanised brigade moved to attack the Germans from the west and another tank brigade was held back in reserve. The SS reconnaissance battalion would have normally been inadequate to hold back such an attack, but it was substantially reinforced by a battery of assault guns, an independent tank company, and a rocket launcher battery – all Wehrmacht formations that were already in the area. As darkness fell on 7 August, SS-Das Reich, which still had most of its elements en route, ordered the battlegroup to pull back a short distance; the first units of Der Führer panzergrenadier regiment were now in position to relieve the strain on the reconnaissance battalion, and with the support of one of the armoured trains operating in the Kharkov area and the assorted Wehrmacht units that had aided the reconnaissance battalion throughout the day, the Soviet III Mechanised Corps was brought to a halt.

For the troops of 6th Panzer Division further to the east, there was little respite as heavy fighting continued, but an energetic counterattack briefly threw the Soviet troops back, allowing the tired German troops to pull back unmolested a short distance into new defensive positions. However, the respite proved to be short-lived, and the Soviet forces launched powerful attacks before dawn on 8 August, once more leading to panic amongst 6th Panzer Division's panzergrenadiers. Major Franz Bäke, commander of one of the panzergrenadier battalions, hastened to the front line to restore order and it was possible to conduct a reasonably orderly withdrawal to a new defensive line. Rounding up disparate elements of the division, Bäke once more drove the attacking Soviet units back, and 6th Panzer Division was finally able to gain some breathing space and was pulled out of the front line for much-needed rest and replenishment. The units of 3rd Panzer Division now took its place.[2]

As the troops of the Red Army advanced, they took advantage of brief opportunities to enjoy a moment of indulgence, as Abdullin found when he encountered some comrades:

I was walking past a group of our guys who had settled down in a trench. Without bothering anyone else, they were eating. They had Schnapps and a captured wurst. 'Ah, Mansoor! Sit down, *Komsorg*!'" They poured me a glass of Schnapps and offered me some wurst but I refused, spitting it out and saying, 'Don't pour me this German rubbish.' The guys were all older than me, and two or three had medals, one of them 'For Courage'.

I took a drink and we sat, talking about this and that. All of a sudden, one said, 'Comrade, are you averse to another glass?'

'Go on,' I said. They poured it but then there was no more. They began to look at each other questioningly and a bit dramatically, rummaging through their kit and saying there was still a bottle left. I should have stayed silent but I blurted out a question: 'Where did you get it?'

'Look, we'll show you. There's more. But look, the Fritzes are firing heavily and already two of our guys haven't returned.' I sat and thought, they hooked me. I was treated and must repay them. If I don't, they will start a rumour that I was afraid. 'Don't do it, *Komsorg*,' they said, trying to persuade me.

But I understood the intonation. 'It's necessary.' The lads were the foremost of the brave soldiers. There was more at stake than a bottle of Schnapps.

The Schnapps had come from a half-track in no-man's land, 100m away across a meadow. I took off my rucksack and groundsheet, and jumping lightly out of the trench, I rushed like a hare to the half-track without stopping, swerving and leaping. By the time the Germans opened up with a machine-gun, I was already in dead ground.

I took two bottles from a box in the half-track, caught my breath and paused for thought. I had to cover the return leg differently. The Germans were waiting for me. What did they expect me to do? There were two bodies lying close to our trench. They would try to bring me down at the same point. Consider, Mansoor! I told myself it was time and rushed straight to the corpses of our two soldiers who were now my objective. I reached the deadly zone, bullets were already tearing up the ground in front of me – and I fell at the feet of the corpses as if slain. I went limp and relaxed and didn't move for an age, my eyes half-open.

Komsorg was the title of a local Komsomol in peacetime.

Next to my nose, on the boot of one of the dead soldiers, crawled a bug. The insect continued on its way, unaware that there was war all around, and that perhaps another person at whom it looked without seeing would now cease to live.

Did they believe that I was dead? Had they taken their finger off the trigger? Turned away? I sprang up, three leaps – and I fell into our trench alive and unharmed. The machine-gun fired again, but too late.

Where was my group? The trophy wurst rolled on the ground. It turned out that the guys were convinced that I was lying dead in no-man's land. They were troubled by their conscience that through their fault, a *Komsomol* had died senselessly.[3]

At the beginning of the second week of August, when *Stavka* was urging the tank armies operating to the west to push forward and to sever the German lines of communication running west and southwest from Kharkov, Steppe Front was ordered to increase its efforts to break through along the line of the Donets to the east and southeast of Kharkov. This was territory that had been covered at speed when the Red Army had pursued the badly mauled German infantry divisions in January 1943, but conditions were very different in August. During the winter, the frozen river had been easy to cross, and the Germans – heavily outnumbered – were too busy pulling back to construct strong defences. Now, they were occupying carefully sited positions, albeit in smaller numbers than they might have wished. In particular, they had artillery support that was positioned to fire on any crossing points over the river and repeated attempts to secure bridgeheads were eliminated by heavy bombardments followed by counterattacks by local German units. The experiences of the previous winter in particular had made the Germans aware of the importance of destroying any Soviet bridgehead, however small, as quickly as possible, as the Red Army had proved highly adept at rapidly reinforcing such bridgeheads until they became the starting points of new attacks.

Meanwhile, Managarov's Fifty-Third Army continued to try to force its way along the Belgorod-Kharkov road. On 10 August, the increasingly frustrated army commander ordered Solomatin to concentrate his I Mechanised Corps and advance to outflank the German defences to the west. The objectives were ambitious; in addition to redeploying over the muddy roads, Solomatin would have to advance up to 24 miles (40km) to the very outskirts of Kharkov. Unable to get all of his brigades into position in the stipulated time, Solomatin attacked with two brigades and ran straight into 3rd Panzer Division, which rapidly brought his troops to a halt; the German division's artillery regiment reported that it fired over 2,800 rounds during the day, a record for the unit, and the division claimed to have knocked out 46 Soviet tanks. Briefly, 3rd Panzer Division's reconnaissance battalion was encircled, but was saved from being overrun by the timely appearance of Stuka dive-bombers; it managed to withdraw to safety under cover of darkness.[4] Konev and Managarov could only watch with growing frustration as the thrust stalled with substantial casualties for little gain. *Stavka* had ordered Konev's front to capture Kharkov as soon as possible, but Konev had concerns about getting drawn into urban fighting:

> We had a great desire at that time to liberate the city definitively, preventing the enemy from recapturing it. To achieve this, it was necessary to smash the enemy and drive him from Kharkov, causing as little damage as possible to the city. In no circumstances could we allow the city to become the scene of hand-to-hand fighting. This would lead to the complete destruction of the urban area. This was well known to us from the example of Voronezh.
>
> … Of course, it would have been preferable not only to drive the enemy from the city, but also to surround him. However, it must be said that bypassing such a large city as Kharkov and creating a complete encirclement with our troops would also lead to great destruction. This became clear when we were still advancing on the city. The enemy still possessed large tank forces at that time and manoeuvred them constantly, making the encirclement of Kharkov a difficult task for the front.[5]

Late on 10 August, Konev sent further instructions to Managarov, requiring him to advance the following day to cut the railway line between Zolichiv and Kharkov, while I Mechanised Corps advanced to Gavrilovka, about six miles (10km) to the west of the city. Grimly aware that his forces were too weak for such rapid gains, Managarov nevertheless urged his troops forward, but made almost no progress. The German defensive ring around the north of Kharkov continued to hold tight – as Konev had noted, the defenders shuffled their limited armoured resources from one area to another as required. However, the Soviet Fifty-Seventh Army, on the northern flank of Southwest Front, was transferred to Konev's Steppe Front so that it could cooperate with the attack on Kharkov, threatening the city from the southeast and on 9 and 10 August succeeded finally in forcing crossings across the Northern Donets. Even if the German line continued to stop Managarov's advance, the city was increasingly threatened by this new advance.

Raus describes a curious incident that he attributed to 168th Infantry Division:

The 168th Infantry Division, missing for several days, was found in a well-concealed area when I made a personal reconnaissance trip north of Kharkov. The division commander, Generalmajor Walter Chales de Beaulieu, explained that he had understood his unit was to act as corps reserve and that he had therefore withdrawn to the forests 40km [24 miles] behind the front. Though I recognised that this general had suffered a nervous breakdown, there was no time to be lost. After castigating his conduct in no uncertain terms, I ordered him to commit his division as the covering force in the next position to be occupied.[6]

It is clear from other accounts that 168th Infantry Division was actually heavily engaged in fighting on the eastern flank of 3rd Panzer Division, which leaves the accuracy of this account open to dispute. The division had suffered heavy losses in the winter fighting for Kharkov and had been brought up to strength with fresh drafts, but there was little question that the quality of these new recruits was far short of the standard required for effective functioning on the Eastern Front, a problem that would worsen steadily as the war continued. In an attempt to remedy this, units at different levels attempted to set up 'combat schools' where the recruits could be taught the realities of fighting and surviving in the front line, but often there wasn't sufficient time to send recruit drafts through these schools before the pressing needs of the front-line units took priority. After serving in a number of staff officer roles and two spells as a regiment commander, Beaulieu had taken command of 168th Infantry Division in June 1943. It is perhaps significant that he remained in post until 10 November; if his nerves had failed as badly as Raus implies, it seems likely that he would have been replaced sooner. As will be described below, a similar incident occurred with another German infantry division, and it is likely that Raus identifies the wrong division in his account.

Despite the stubborn resistance of the German troops deployed around Kharkov, the Red Army was slowly picking its way through the series of defensive positions. In particular, there was a growing risk of encirclement and when the German 282nd Infantry Division, one of the formations on the eastern side of the defences, reported that the Soviet Fifty-Seventh Army had achieved deep penetrations in its ranks, Kempf ordered 6th Panzer Division to move to the southeast of Kharkov and place itself under the command of General Franz Mattenklott's LVII Corps. One regiment of 282nd Infantry Division reportedly pulled back to the city itself without receiving any orders to do so, and rumours circulated that 'higher commands' – presumably Hitler – had considered imposing the ancient Roman punishment of decimation, or the execution of one man in every ten, selected at random, by his comrades.[7] This was presumably the sort of policy that followed from Hitler's decree that Kharkov was to be held to the last man, and severe measures were to be taken against units and men who failed to obey. Fortunately for the soldiers of 282nd Infantry Division, no such orders were ever issued – given the pressing need for every available soldier, it would have been absurd to inflict such losses in the name of punishment – but Generalmajor Wilhelm Kohler, the division commander, was dismissed and Generalmajor Hermann Frenking dispatched to replace him. When Soviet troops broke through the wavering lines of the infantry, Mattenklott issued orders to 6th Panzer Division:

> Early on 12 August, *Kampfgruppe* Crisolli [the division's armoured battlegroup] is to destroy the enemy who has penetrated to Sorokova by mounting an attack either side of Hill 209.3 and is to prevent any further advance of the enemy towards Kharkov. The *Kampfgruppe* is to be withdrawn [from the front line] as soon as this mission has been completed and is once more to hold itself in readiness. Close contact with 282nd Infantry Division is to be maintained.[8]

Crisolli sent his troops into action, as a report from 282nd Infantry Division recorded:

> In the early hours of the morning, the gap [in the lines] was closed by the insertion of *Panzeraufklärungsabteilung 6* ['6th Armoured Reconnaissance Battalion', from the panzer division]. At 1000 the enemy broke into the central positions of the [infantry] division with 30 to 40 tanks followed by infantry. Despite heavy fire from anti-aircraft guns [often used as infantry support weapons] the enemy penetrated as far as the artillery positions, where seven tanks were destroyed by the artillery. Through the use of heavy anti-aircraft guns and a flank attack by an armoured group from 6th Panzer Division, the penetration was cleared by assault guns and Hornets. The armoured group from 6th Panzer Division counterattacked and reached the previous front line. After this group was withdrawn … our infantry fell back and the front line was penetrated at various points. The gaps were closed by 1500.[9]

The *Hornisse* or 'Hornet' was a derivative of the Pz.IV tank chassis; it mounted a long-barrelled 88mm gun, the best anti-tank weapon available to Germany at the time, in a turretless mount and was sent to the Eastern Front with *Schwere Panzerjägerabteilung 655* for use during *Zitadelle*. Despite its relatively thin armour, it was a lethal tank killer and its deployment with 6th Panzer Division gave the armoured battlegroup some welcome additional firepower. Soviet accounts of the fighting repeatedly describe actions against 'Ferdinand' assault guns; although one Ferdinand-equipped battalion was deployed in the Ukraine in the late summer of 1943, it is likely that many of these Soviet accounts actually refer to the Hornets of *Schwere Panzerjägerabteilung 655*; both vehicles used the same 88mm gun, but the Ferdinands were far larger and had armour that was impervious to all but the heaviest Soviet guns. Just as many German accounts describe every Soviet tank as a T-34 and the accounts of Germany's enemies often describe all German tanks as Tigers, it was inevitable that in the heat of battle, troops would assume that the vehicles opposing them were the most formidable that their opponents had.

After its intervention in 282nd Infantry Division's sector, 6th Panzer Division was once more withdrawn to function as corps reserve. Its deployment east of Kharkov reduced the armoured forces available elsewhere, where the necessity of stopping the advance of Voronezh Front had forced the Germans to commit their armoured reinforcements – 3rd Panzer Division, *Grossdeutschland*, and the SS divisions – as soon as they arrived rather than concentrating them for a decisive counter-blow. The original intention had been for *Grossdeutschland* to strike against the western flank of the Soviet advance while III Panzer Corps attacked from the southeast, but both forces had committed their armour to defensive battles and now struggled to concentrate it for a counterattack. Already degraded by the fighting in the Kursk salient and then in the battles on the Mius, the German divisions of III Panzer Corps were significantly below strength; even though the two Soviet tank armies had also suffered substantial losses, they still outnumbered the Germans at this stage. Historically, the German units would still have been confident of success, relying on their greater tactical and operational skill, but the Red Army had made huge strides in these fields; there could be no foregone conclusions about the outcome of the fighting.

The German perimeter to the north and east of Kharkov continued to be gradually pushed back, but the well-organised defences inflicted punishing casualties on the Red Army units. Early on 13 August, Soviet artillery was close enough to start shelling German supply dumps and other installations in the city itself, and towards the end of the day Managarov's troops finally reached Dergachi, where they ran into a battlegroup of 3rd Panzer Division and were fought to a standstill. The losses they had suffered now forced a pause in operations; with his divisions reduced to less than half their establishment, Managarov could do little more than mount reconnaissance probes the following day, but despite inflicting far heavier casualties than they suffered themselves, the German units were also badly degraded, and even these smaller attacks were sufficient to put the fast-waning strength of 3rd Panzer Division under heavy strain. Despite his impatience to press on and capture Kharkov, Konev had no choice but to allow Fifty-Third Army a few days to regroup and rest; it was ordered to resume its advance on 18 August at the latest. The other Soviet armies attacking from the northeast and east were in no better shape, and it was only to the southeast of the city that the joint efforts of First Guards and Fifty-Seventh Armies made major progress, with the German 39th Infantry Division suffering particularly badly. Once again, 6th Panzer Division was thrown into the battle to stop the German lines in that sector, under the overall control of General Anton Dostler's XLII Corps, from collapsing. After a day of heavy fighting, Dostler reported the precarious situation of his corps to Kempf late on 13 August, asking for an additional division to restore the situation. Kempf responded glumly that he had no reinforcements to offer, let alone a full division, and had already sent Dostler a small group of assault guns, his only reserves. Dostler then advised Kempf that many of his artillery units were running out of ammunition; in anticipation of further Soviet advances, some of the ammunition stocks in Kharkov had already been destroyed, worsening the supply situation for the troops in the front line. Kempf responded by reminding Dostler that Hitler had issued a *Führerbefehl* – 'Führer order' – that Kharkov was to be held at all costs. The exchange highlighted the difficulties created for field commanders by such arbitrary decrees, and the verbal gymnastics they sometimes used to handle the gulf between operational reality and Hitler's edicts:

> Dostler: Yes, we have received the *Führerbefehl* and made our decision [to obey it].
> Kempf: A *Führerbefehl* is an order and not a decision. You always answer in the affirmative if I ask whether you can hold your line, and also if you might be overrun.
> Dostler: It is possible that we can hold.
> Kempf: Possible, but is it likely?
> Dostler: I would rather not split hairs. My chief of staff has the same opinion as me that it is likely that the enemy will break through our lines.
> Kempf: Then we are of the same mind. It is conceivable that the *Führerbefehl* will result in the enemy breaking through the centre of your corps, with the result that XI Corps [operating to the north of Kharkov] and 282nd Infantry Division will not be able to withdraw from Kharkov.[10]

Dostler would end the war having shown a rigid adherence to orders from Hitler. In March 1944, when he was in command of LXXV Corps in Italy, his troops, operating with a group of Italian fascists, captured 15 US Army personnel who had landed on the coast behind German lines. Although the men were in uniform, Kesselring – the overall commander of German forces in Italy – ordered the implementation of Hitler's instruction of 1942 that all commandos should be treated as spies and executed, and Dostler passed this command on to the garrison in La Spezia, where the US soldiers were being held. The officers of the German garrison protested and repeatedly asked that the order should be rescinded. One of Dostler's staff officers refused to sign the execution order and was summarily dismissed, and the prisoners were duly executed on 26 March 1944. Six weeks later, Dostler was captured and subsequently tried for the unlawful killing of the US soldiers; he was found guilty and executed by firing squad on 1 December. Kesselring, who had ultimately issued the orders for the execution, was tried for war crimes against Italian civilians, including mass executions, and was found guilty; he too was condemned to death by firing squad, but the sentence was commuted to life imprisonment, at least partly because many senior figures in the west campaigned on his behalf, claiming that he had been an 'honourable opponent', despite the manifest evidence of his war crimes. In 1952, he was released from captivity on medical grounds, and died in 1960.

By the end of 13 August, much of 6th Panzer Division had been pulled out of the front line to act as Dostler's reserve. Its rest was short-lived and the following day, Crisolli's men were once more in action dealing with determined Soviet attacks. By nightfall the situation was increasingly desperate, as a division signal reported on the division's hugely depleted strength:

> As a result of the continuing heavy losses, it will not be possible to continue holding the line that has been ordered, and moreover if the shortage of artillery ammunition continues it is questionable whether continued defensive fire will be possible. Tank strength: one Pz.II, three Pz.IIIs, two Pz.IVs, one command tank.[11]

There was further fighting on the morning of 14 August as Soviet troops pressed into the eastern outskirts of Kharkov, but the remaining tanks of 6th Panzer Division were able to bring the attack to a standstill, largely as a result of substantial support from the Luftwaffe. During the afternoon there were further Soviet assaults, which were all ultimately driven off with heavy losses on both sides. To the north of the city, 3rd Panzer Division reported coming under a Soviet artillery bombardment that was reminiscent of the First World War in its intensity, but made only local withdrawals.[12]

Formations in both armies were close to exhaustion, but the Soviet attacks on the east and southeast approaches to Kharkov continued on 15 August, supported by air strikes. Working closely together, tanks and infantry penetrated into the edge of Kharkov, where the motorcycle battalion of 6th Panzer Division had been deployed. By the afternoon, the houses the Germans had been holding were largely in Soviet hands, and the exhausted defenders were faced with the daunting prospect of having to withdraw across open ground to a group of abandoned hospital buildings. A final attack by Soviet tanks with infantry riding aboard threatened to overrun the motorcycle battalion and it took a last-ditch intervention by the division's anti-tank battalion to stop the advance. As the Soviet units pulled back to lick their wounds, the Germans counted 25 destroyed and disabled enemy tanks.[13] At the same time, pressure continued on 3rd Panzer Division, particularly its left flank, guarding the northwest approaches to Kharkov. During the afternoon, more Soviet aircraft appeared overhead, but instead of dropping bombs, they released a rain of leaflets:

> Comrades of 3rd Panzer Division! We know that you are brave soldiers. Every second one of you wears the Iron Cross. But every second one of us carries a mortar.[14]

The exhausted soldiers in the depleted panzergrenadier companies needed no reminder of the bombardment capabilities of the Red Army, but whilst Managarov's divisions were able to harass the Germans with bombardments and sharp probing attacks, they were still regrouping and gathering their strength for a renewed attack.

Armee Abteilung Kempf was originally created as an improvised group from the debris of retreating German units and reinforcements arriving from the west during the winter fighting. It was now renamed Eighth Army. Kempf was replaced as commander by General Otto Wöhler. Kempf had questioned Hitler's order to hold Kharkov to the last man, and it is likely that – recalling the manner in which a similar order had been ignored during the preceding winter by army and SS officers alike – Hitler decided to replace him before any act of insubordination could occur. Wöhler had served as chief of staff with Eleventh Army under Manstein's command and then as chief of staff with Army Group Centre for much of 1942 before taking command of I Corps in Army Group North, and had led a determined defence during fighting around Lake Ladoga near Leningrad during the summer of 1943. He and Manstein knew and respected each other, and although he had experienced no particular difficulties with Kempf, Manstein was content with the change in command. To date, Wöhler hadn't experienced the need to disobey Hitler's orders, but he would soon be put to the test in his new position.

One of Kempf's last acts as commander was to visit the SS divisions on the left flank of his units, where he agreed further reorganisation for the attack towards the northwest. Soviet pressure on *SS-Totenkopf* continued throughout 14 August, and the exhausted troops of the reconnaissance battalion were increasingly hard-pressed:

> Out there on the high road the Russians were on the march with infantry and anti-tank guns drawn by oxen. Their direction of march was towards us. What was actually going on? New orders: 'The company will pull back.' It was hard not to lose our sense of direction as the march was carried out in a zigzag fashion. None of the lower commanders had a map. I suspected that the company commander himself didn't have one. The only information we heard was 'There must be a village over there' or 'We should take up positions on that hill over there.' The company had never operated in such a depressed and defensive manner. Villages and streams, hills and valleys existed purely as tactical locations.[15]

After its brief pause to bring up supplies and reposition its artillery, Managarov's Fifty-Third Army tried once more to break the German defences to the north of Kharkov, attempting to penetrate the seam between 3rd Panzer Division and 168th Infantry Division on 18 August. Late the previous day, Wöhler had visited the panzer division and in response to a question from one of the officers about the feasibility of mounting a prolonged defence in the face of escalating losses, he replied, 'What will happen is what has to happen.'[16] This slightly ambiguous reply was greeted by the headquarters staff of 3rd Panzer Division with relief as an indication that Wöhler would not make a pointless stand in Kharkov, but might equally have been interpreted as confirming the need to adhere to Hitler's instructions. In any event, the Soviet attack made little progress at first, but a second, heavier attack was launched during the afternoon; perhaps aided by the unusual timing of the attack, the leading units rapidly broke through the first line of defences and penetrated to the Udy River immediately outside Kharkov. With its armoured strength reduced to just 13 tanks and one of its panzergrenadier regiments able to field the equivalent of perhaps two companies of infantry, 3rd Panzer Division was unable to mount a counterattack to restore the front line and was limited to fighting a delaying action. To date, timely intervention by the Luftwaffe had repeatedly blunted Soviet advances, but on this occasion the attacking troops penetrated into dense woodland, which offered them considerable protection from aerial attack. Throughout the night, Managarov moved reinforcements forward to try to sustain his advance and his troops reached Peresechnaya, a mere eight miles (13km) from the northwest edge of Kharkov. Fighting continued into the night, particularly on the western flank of Managarov's advance where *SS-Wiking* came under attack along its front line and particularly its right flank. Like most German formations, *SS-Wiking* still had numerous tanks that had long been regarded as obsolete, such as the Pz.III with its 50mm gun. An officer with the division's panzer regiment described one of the actions as he struggled to hold the line with four tanks as he found himself being outflanked by a group of six T-34s and an assault gun, but fortunately for the Germans the Soviet tanks were concentrating on threats from the south and thus turned their turrets away from the German tanks:

> It was our misfortune that we had only one Pz.IV with the good 75mm main gun … The second round was a hit, and the Soviet tank started to develop smoke soon thereafter. [Untersturmführer Paul] Senghas [the commander of the Pz.IV] immediately shifted targets, and the second one was ablaze after a few rounds. The first tank that had been hit was also consumed by flames when it started to back up.
>
> Unfortunately, Zäh and I were unable to participate in the engagement with our 50mm vehicles, since our main guns wouldn't reach that far. We limited ourselves to keeping the Soviet infantry off Senghas' back. We were unable to prevent a Soviet anti-tank gun from setting the successful tank alight. Too bad, since Senghas was doing such a great job. The last 75mm vehicle of the company burned out …
>
> On top of everything else, however, Senghas was wounded pretty badly. He left the engagement with his upper arm shattered by a shell. It was only with great difficulty that the knocked-out crew could be evacuated and brought to safety.[17]

Despite his wounds, Senghas recovered and returned to the division, and served in its ranks until the end of the war.

Another company of the panzer regiment of *SS-Wiking* was in action close by. The Soviet forces commenced their attack with a two-hour artillery bombardment just before dawn, and the German tanks moved forward rapidly in support of the thin infantry line, as Untersturmführer Gustav Waber described:

Field Marshal Ewald von Kleist, seen here in 1941. (Photo by ullstein bild/ullstein bild via Getty Images)

Generaloberst Hermann Hoth. (Photo by Heinrich Hoffman/ullstein bild via Getty Images)

Field Marshal Georg von Küchler, seen here in 1938. (Photo by ullstein bild/ullstein bild via Getty Images)

Field Marshal Erich von Manstein. (Photo © CORBIS/Corbis via Getty Images)

General Ivan Stepanovich Konev. (Photo by
Universal History Archive/UIG via Getty Images)

General Rodion Yakovlevich Malinovsky, seen
here in 1944 as Marshal of the Soviet Union.
(Photo by Popperfoto/Getty Images)

Colonel General Fedor Ivanovich Tolbukhin.
(Photo by Keystone/Hulton Archive/Getty
Images)

General Nikolai Fyodorovich Vatutin, seen here in
1944. (Photo by Sovfoto/UIG via Getty Images)

A Soviet 107mm mortar unit prepares to fire. (From the fonds of the RGAKFD in
Krasnogorsk via Stavka)

Two Waffen-SS men inspect the remains of a Soviet T-34. (Nik Cornish at www.Stavka.org.uk)

Soviet infantry run past an abandoned German armoured train. Armoured trains were widely used by both sides on the Eastern Front as a means of covering vulnerable sectors of the front line and providing mobile artillery cover. (Courtesy of the Central Museum of the Armed Forces, Moscow via Stavka)

Hundreds of thousands of Ukrainians were forcibly (and voluntarily) evacuated by the Germans as they fell back. Only very isolated communities or those who fled into hiding escaped this fate. Here, a Soviet tank crew is welcomed by liberated farmers. (Courtesy of the Central Museum of the Armed Forces, Moscow via Stavka)

German front-line trenches on the open steppe. The only topographic features that provided potentially solid defensive lines were the rivers, but successful defences of these depended on there being positions to hold, which was rarely the case. (Nik Cornish at www.Stavka.org.uk)

Repairing the tracks on a German Panther type D. Mechanically delicate, the Panther required a considerable amount of time to be spent on maintenance. Unfortunately, time was not a luxury available to the units operating this type and many were abandoned. (Nik Cornish at www.Stavka.org.uk)

Soviet infantry fighting in the ruins of a city. (Courtesy of the Central Museum of the Armed Forces, Moscow via Stavka)

House to house fighting in Kharkov. These men are scouts, *razvedchiki* (note the hooded camouflage smocks), elite infantrymen deployed ahead of the main attack forces to probe enemy positions. (From the fonds of the RGAKFD in Krasnogorsk via Stavka)

German infantry hitch a ride on a *Sturmgeschütz* III assault gun. (Nik Cornish at www.Stavka.org.uk)

This Soviet column was attacked by a Luftwaffe air strike when crossing a tributary of the Dnepr River. Two early model T-34s can be seen to right of centre. (Nik Cornish at www.Stavka.org.uk)

Waffen-SS infantry take their positions in and around a ruined farmhouse.
(Nik Cornish at www.Stavka.org.uk)

Red Army men in the front line, armed with PPSh-41 submachine-guns and a selection of hand grenades. (From the fonds of the RGAKFD in Krasnogorsk via Stavka)

A Waffen-SS counterattack. Infantry follow a *Sturmgeschütz* III assault gun of *SS-Das Reich* into action. (Nik Cornish at www.Stavka.org.uk)

Soviet engineers build a landing stage under fire. (Nik Cornish at www.Stavka.org.uk)

German infantry dig foxholes to defend a hamlet to their rear. To the left an NCO
can be seen keeping watch for approaching Soviet troops. A bemused civilian watches nervously.
(Nik Cornish at www.Stavka.org.uk)

A group of Soviet infantry attacks up hill, closely supported by an M1910 Maxim machine gun.
(Nik Cornish at www.Stavka.org.uk)

A Soviet attack with SU-76 self-propelled guns and supporting infantry.
(Nik Cornish at www.Stavka.org.uk)

German Stuka dive-bombers in winter camouflage. By late 1943 the Luftwaffe could still achieve local air superiority, but experience and improvements in training had improved the capabilities of the Red Air Force immeasurably. (Nik Cornish at www.Stavka.org.uk)

Aircraft production in the USSR increased massively when compared with Germany during 1943. This factory is producing Il-2 Shturmovik ground attack aircraft. (Nik Cornish at www.Stavka.org.uk)

Soviet scouts celebrating in the outskirts of Kiev. As the capital of Ukraine and the third biggest city in the USSR, its liberation provided a huge morale boost. (From the fonds of the RGAKFD in Krasnogorsk via Stavka)

Soviet BA-10 armoured cars advancing west of Kiev. By this time there were very few of these vehicles still in service, having been replaced in the reconnaissance role by light tanks. (Nik Cornish at www.Stavka.org.uk)

'Scorched earth' tactics involved rounding up cattle and other foodstuffs and herding them to the west. Nothing which could prove to be of even minimal use was to be left to the advancing Soviets. Here, a German officer supervises such an action. (Nik Cornish at www.Stavka.org.uk)

Ukrainians had suffered horrifically during the famines of the 1930s and many initially welcomed the advance of the Wehrmacht. However, as the realities of Nazi occupation became apparent, more and more of the population became sympathetic to the partisan movement. Here, Ukrainians are being rounded up for allegedly supplying food to the partisans. (Nik Cornish at www.Stavka.org.uk)

Sometimes the German attempts to 'scorch the earth' were too late and the Soviet advance caught them out. Here, Soviet troops march into a recently liberated town whilst buildings burn all around them. (From the fonds of the RGAKFD in Krasnogorsk via Stavka)

When we reached the hilltop and looked down into the valley, our hair stood on end. It was swarming with enemy tanks. When the first T-34s had approached close enough, we greeted them with our long 75mm guns. Although we scored hit after hit, we were unable to take on all of that onslaught.

Individual T-34s were already infiltrating and attempting to effect a breakthrough. Then, in our hour of need, three Tiger tanks came to our aid from a neighbouring army unit. During their approach they started to sweep away the T-34s that had broken through with their long 88mm main guns.[18]

Despite the best efforts of the tank crews of *SS-Wiking* – Waber and the Tigers claimed an improbable 84 enemy tanks destroyed on 18 August – the SS division was forced to pull back its flank. It seemed as if the stubborn German ring to the north of Kharkov was finally beginning to give way. Manstein had gambled on being able to eliminate the gap between Eighth Army and Fourth Panzer Army quickly, thus freeing armoured resources for use elsewhere, but all of the divisions that had been committed to the battle around Bogodukhov and Akhtyrka had ground to a halt and there was no possibility of releasing any of them to aid the defences of Kharkov. Grudgingly, Hitler granted permission for Kharkov to be abandoned 'in the event of an extreme emergency'.[19] The exhausted formations fighting around the city were now under increasing pressure from the Red Army after the brief pause, as Raus reported to Wöhler from the headquarters of XI Corps late on 20 August:

The enemy attack has shifted to the left flank of the corps … Without question, his objective is to break through the front and encircle Kharkov from the west and northwest …

Under constant heavy artillery, mortar, rocket and tank fire, and due to the incessant day and night bombardment of the front line … by enemy aircraft and the bitter defence against enemy attacks, the regiments, which have been in continuous combat for the past six weeks, especially those of 198th and 168th Infantry Divisions and 3rd Panzer Division, have been bled dry. Not many more enemy attacks can be withstood in the present positions.[20]

As Kempf had advised Dostler shortly before being replaced by Wöhler, there were few reinforcements available. By contrast, the wrangle between Konev, Rotmistrov and Zhukov was finally settled on 20 August, when the latter agreed to Fifth Guards Tank Army being released to Steppe Front's control. Late that day, Fifth Guards Tank Army handed over its sector of the front line to Fifth

Guards Army and redeployed to the east so that it could operate on the same axis as Fifty-Third Army, and the following morning XVIII Tank Corps was in position with V Guards Mechanised Corps still en route; XXIX Tank Corps had to be left behind in Bogodukhov to cover against any further German attacks. On the morning of 21 August, XVIII Tank Corps attempted to secure a crossing over the Udy River; the river was not a particularly wide obstacle, but its muddy banks and flood meadows, softened by summer rainstorms, resulted in many tanks getting bogged down, and a combination of German minefields and artillery fire stopped every attempt by the Soviet troops to expand the bridgehead. As German anti-tank guns began to pick off the tanks struggling through the mud, the attack was abandoned and the armoured units were withdrawn across the river.

During the following night, 28th Guards Rifle Division and 84th and 252nd Rifle Divisions – all from Managarov's Fifty-Third Army – laboured to increase the size of the bridgeheads that they had already captured, while combat engineers deployed a substantial bridge across the Udy while under heavy German artillery fire. On the other side of the front line, Breith's III Panzer Corps effectively abandoned its attempts to break through to Bogodukhov and shifted elements of SS-*Das Reich* further east to try to bring some relief to the battered remnants of 3rd Panzer Division and 168th and 198th Infantry Divisions. To that end, the SS division had concentrated nearly 60 tanks and assault guns in Lyubotin by the end of 21 August. The arrival of the re-equipped I Battalion of the panzer regiment with 42 Panther tanks provided a much-needed boost, both in terms of firepower and morale. This concentrated almost all the armoured assets of Wöhler's Eighth Army; the Germans had correctly identified the threat posed by Soviet forces pressing south and cutting the roads running west and southwest from Kharkov, thus effectively encircling the city.

It was the intervention of Rotmistrov's tank army that effectively broke the deadlock around Kharkov. Although the Soviet armoured units managed only a relatively modest advance to Korotich, this was sufficient to force a decision, particularly as attempts to throw back the Soviet units with counterattacks were to no avail. There was every likelihood that a Soviet breakthrough either in this sector or to the east and southeast of Kharkov could lead to the encirclement of the German forces holding the ring around the city, and as Manstein later wrote in his memoirs, he had no intention of sacrificing Eighth Army purely to hold a fortress designated as such by Hitler.[21] Artillery ammunition was running out and without the use of massive defensive bombardments the increasingly depleted infantry divisions would surely collapse sooner rather than later. After a brief discussion of the situation with Wöhler and Raus, whose XI Corps was most at risk of encirclement, Manstein ordered the city abandoned. Given their proximity to Kharkov and the presence of Soviet aircraft over the city, it was inevitable that the Red Army would become aware of German plans for a withdrawal and in an attempt to tie down the German troops, Konev ordered the ring of infantry to press into Kharkov late on 22 August. There were repeated clashes in the urban areas between German units and the leading Soviet elements and partisan groups. The Soviet 183rd Rifle Division, part of Fifty-Third Army, reached the city centre during the morning of 23 August; although Konev claimed that his armies destroyed most of the German forces in Kharkov, the reality was that Wöhler's Eighth Army withdrew in good order, taking up a new line along the Udy River. Konev's men were greeted with near-universal jubilation by the remaining civilian residents of the city as they took control:

During the five months of their second occupation [i.e. after they recaptured Kharkov in March 1943], the fascists carried out further destruction in Kharkov. They set fire to or blew up hundreds of the best buildings and stripped the city of everything, even tram rails, furniture, stores and firewood. In the hospital district, the Nazis murdered 450 wounded soldiers and officers of the Red Army. Everywhere there were ruins. There were only 190,000 people left in a city where more than a million used to live. According to incomplete data, the Hitlerites liquidated over 60,000 Kharkov residents in their concentration camps and sent more than 150,000 to Germany [as forced labourers].

23 August was the day of liberation for Kharkov. Before I reported to Stalin about the situation at the front and the liberation of Kharkov, I spoke to [Alexander Nikolayevich] Poskrebyshev [head of the 'Special Section', or intelligence services, of the Central Committee of the Communist Party]. He replied, 'Comrade Stalin is resting, I will not disturb him.'

I decided to call him myself. My first calls were unanswered. I told the telephone operator to try again, and that I would answer for the consequences. Finally, I heard a familiar, hoarse voice.

'I'm listening.'

'Comrade Stalin, I report that the troops of Steppe Front have liberated the city of Kharkov today.'

Stalin replied immediately. 'Congratulations. We offer you our warmest congratulations.' It is worth noting that as he worked at night, Stalin usually rested at this time [during the afternoon]. I knew this, but nevertheless the recapture of Kharkov was such an important event that I wanted to report to him personally about the completion of the operation.

That evening, Moscow saluted the soldiers of Steppe Front for liberating Kharkov with a 224-gun salute.[22]

The German defences to the north of Kharkov had proved to be stubborn and the Red Army paid a heavy price to overcome them – no fewer than eight distinct defensive lines had to be overcome, and the Germans fell back from one line to the next in an efficient, coordinated manner, largely preventing the Soviet attackers from exploiting exposed flanks.

The square in the centre of Kharkov had been named *Platz der Leibstandarte* by the Germans in honour of *LSSAH*, the SS division that led the capture of the city in March; it now reverted to its Soviet name of Dzerzhinksy Square. Much of the city was in ruins after the heavy fighting of the winter, and twice in five months the Germans had withdrawn from it, carrying out extensive demolitions on each occasion. Nearly three quarters of the buildings of Kharkov had suffered partial or total destruction and its industrial capability had been reduced to almost nothing – before the war, it had been a centre of tank production, with the first T-34s being assembled in its factories, but a large proportion of the military industry had been evacuated to the Urals before the arrival of German troops in 1941, and almost all of its industrial installations that had been left had been deliberately destroyed by the retreating Wehrmacht.

The population had also suffered huge losses. Before the war, the city had been home to about 900,000 people, rising rapidly as the Germans advanced across the Ukraine in 1941 and tens of thousands of people fled before them. A census in 1939 showed that there were nearly 126,000 Jews in the city, nearly 18 per cent of the population, but it isn't known how many fled before the Germans arrived, and how many Jews from areas further west were caught in Kharkov when the city fell. Compared to some regions of the Soviet Union, the Jewish population of Kharkov was relatively integrated, with most Jews regarding Russian as their first language and many marrying non-Jews. Despite this, there was a long history of violence against Jews by Ukrainian and ethnic Soviet citizens and the rising profile of Jews after the Bolshevik Revolution – they were more likely to be better educated than other ethnicities and therefore more likely to be appointed to high office in place of the traditional aristocratic families that had run civil and military affairs during the reign of the tsars – led to considerable resentment. There were similar anti-Jewish thoughts amongst non-Jewish populations elsewhere in the Soviet Union, particularly where Soviet control had been imposed upon the population against its will, for example in the Baltic States; in all the occupied territories, the deliberate association of Jews and communists by the Nazis was repeatedly used to justify anti-Jewish measures.

Kharkov changed hands several times in the war. In October 1941 the troops of the German LV Corps had first captured the city. Mikhail Usyk was an academic who lived there and kept a diary throughout the German occupation:

24 October: At noon, from the window of the corner room, I saw the Germans for the first time on Veterinary Street, turning into Pushkinskaya Street towards Technological Street. People poured out onto the streets. To greet them? No, to stare at them. Who are these conceited conquerors? Why are they here? Who invited them into our country?

A German plane flew low overhead, dropping leaflets. They fell mainly far away, but one whirled and landed in the next courtyard. Sanin [his son] fetched it. '... Stalin's criminal policy ... German troops are liberating you ...' His eyes flashed.

Lies, lies, it seems to me. They are not liberators, but slavers, come to enslave and exterminate our people. We will wait and see.[23]

Six days later, he was in Dzerzhinsky Square when he saw a crowd gathering outside a building and staring up at a balcony:

And all of a sudden, a scene unfolded before my eyes: two big Germans in helmets, with police badges on their chests, throwing a rope around a man.

I was standing about 70–75m back, and could not see the whole man. He was obscured by the balcony wall. I could only see his black, oily hair. Yes, they were going to hang him, without a doubt. My skin was cold. The rope was around his neck. The Germans lifted the man and, holding the rope around his neck in their hands, lowered him down. The rope was secured to the bar of the balcony.

There were murmurs in the crowd. Women cried hysterically. The man convulsed once, twice, and then hanged there dead. On his chest in Soviet and German was a placard: 'Partisan.'

A woman in the crowd raised her hysterical voice in prayer.

[He was] a hero. The body of the hanged man was still dangling there in the evening, shaken by the wind and drenched by the rain.

I walked home with a huge weight on my chest.[24]

Throughout its period of occupation the city remained outside the authority of *Reichskommissariat Ukraine* as it was too close to the front line, but as Usyk witnessed, killings began almost immediately after the Germans took control. Field Marshal Walther von Reichenau had issued orders to all troops in the German Sixth Army that reinforced and expanded upon the infamous *Commissar Order* issued by Hitler in June 1941, which required all those suspected of being political commissars or having other involvement with communism to be executed on capture, and many such suspects were hanged or shot by Wehrmacht troops in response to an order from LV Corps:

> The victors [of the battle for Kharkov] may use any means to restore and maintain law and order in Kharkov.
>
> Disorderly elements, saboteurs and partisans, who can be found exclusively amongst the Jewish population, must be punished by death. Similarly, public execution by hanging should be carried out and the victims left hanging for purposes of intimidation. The executed bodies are to be guarded by auxiliary police [i.e. pro-German Ukrainians]. Jews, Jewish shops, and Jewish businesses should be clearly marked.[25]

The retreating Red Army had buried several bombs in the city with long time fuses, and many of these exploded on 14 November. There were extensive casualties, including Generalleutnant Georg Braun, commander of the German 68th Infantry Division, and Wehrmacht troops promptly rounded up about 200 civilians, mainly Jews; they were summarily hanged from balconies. A further thousand civilians were imprisoned in a hotel on Dzerzhinksy Square as hostages.[26] Matters worsened when the SS arrived and all Jews were ordered to wear distinctive armbands with the Star of David. As was the case elsewhere in the occupied parts of the Soviet Union, military authorities were ordered to take note of any tendency by the local population to take measures against the Jews. Ivan Fedorovich Bogdanov, the director of the Kharkov Mechanical Engineering Institute, recalled that when the first German troops entered his apartment, they had only two questions: whether there were any weapons in the building, and whether there were any Jews.[27]

On 14 December, all Jews in Kharkov were ordered to assemble near the tractor factory in the city suburbs. Many non-Jewish citizens took advantage of the opportunity to denounce Jewish neighbours who tried to avoid the order; most of those who showed any form of resistance were shot on the spot. Anna Iosifovna Chernyenko was a Jewish woman married to a non-Jewish Ukrainian and taking a few possessions with her – some bed linen, a change of clothes, and perhaps sufficient food for a week – she and two neighbours joined the ragged columns of people heading for the tractor factory. Her husband Ivan accompanied her for much of the journey before she persuaded him to turn back – she would rather that he survived and she didn't have to witness his death at the hands of the Germans. The guards swiftly confiscated what little the Jews had brought with them, and crammed them into the huts that had formerly housed the factory workers:

> We looked out of the window ... a Russian brought a basket full of boiled potatoes, a piece of bread, some radishes and carrots, intending to sell them. The Germans spotted him and fired. He fell with a thump. When I saw this, I thought I would die. He had a red cap on a bald head. I then saw it wasn't Ivan. He lay groaning. The Germans approached and stamped on him. Blood poured everywhere and he died. I turned away.
>
> ... The Jews began to pray. Everyone tried to think about what they could do. At 2pm, we saw a group of men and women, aged between 18 and 20. The Germans ran into the barracks and began to beat and shout at them. One Jew didn't want to give up her ring. She was dragged out almost by her finger. She screamed and cried when her finger was broken ...
>
> One had a hungry child and had a small tin of oil that she was going to give to the child. It was taken away. She begged and cried, but they refused to give it back, shouting 'Shut up, Jewess!' and other terrible things. They took the tin and left.
>
> On the third day, they let us have some water ... The smell was suffocating, with 60 people in a small room ...
>
> We managed somehow, getting water and buying potatoes from those who had them. And in the snow, we made fires and cooked them on bricks. When the latrine buckets were taken out in the morning, the Germans forced the Jews to pour them onto the food.[28]

Some 20,000 Jews were gathered under the eyes of *Sonderkommando 4a*, part of *Einsatzgruppe C*. Several hundred Jews were too sick or frail to travel to the designated area and personnel of *Sonderkommando 4a* gathered them in a synagogue in the city where they were left to die of hunger and cold. Sometimes at random, groups of Jews were ordered out of the huts near the tractor factory and shot, and on other occasions they were marched to a ravine at Drobitsky Yar, just outside the southeast outskirts of the city, where they were machine-gunned.

In an attempt to speed up the process the commander of the SS group, Standartenführer Paul Blobel, made use of modified vans. Up to 50 people at a time were loaded into the vans, which then drove slowly around Kharkov; the exhaust fumes were channelled back into the vans, killing those in the cargo compartment through a mixture of carbon monoxide poisoning and suffocation. Most of the dead were dumped in Drobytsky Yar; in an attempt to save ammunition, the SS frequently threw children into the ravine whilst still alive, calculating that the winter cold and starvation would kill them. Anastasia Zakharovna Osmachlo, a non-Jewish Ukrainian woman, witnessed the massacre and was inadvertently caught up in the killings:

> When I learned of the murder of Soviet citizens ... I went to see what was happening there together with my son Vladimir, aged 12, and another 11 people from the village. In the valley [Drobytsky Yar] we discovered a pit several tens of metres long, ten metres wide and several metres deep. Many bodies of those who had been shot were piled up in the pit. When we had looked at the bodies we decided to go home. But we had not yet had time to leave the valley when three trucks arrived carrying German soldiers. The soldiers stopped us. They took us to the pit and one of them began to shoot at us with a machine-gun. When my son fell I fainted and fell into the pit. When I recovered I found myself lying on dead bodies. Later I heard the cries of women and children whom the Germans were bringing to the pit and shooting. The bodies of those who were shot fell into the pit where I lay.
>
> I was in the pit from morning until 4 or 5pm and saw how, throughout the day, the Germans kept bringing groups of people to the pit and killing them. Before my eyes several thousand people were shot. Were they Jews? ... When the Germans had finished the slaughter they left the place. From among the corpses groans and cries went up from the living wounded. About half an hour after the German soldiers had left the place I crawled out of the pit and ran home. My son and the other people who had come with me from the village had been shot.[29]

By early 1942, it is estimated that there were over 30,000 corpses in the ravine and the 'ghetto' that had been established near the tractor factory had ceased to exist by the middle of January.[30] Anna Chernyenko was fortunate and managed to escape and returned to Kharkov. She was briefly reunited with her husband Ivan, who was seriously ill, and then hid in the cellar of a friend for several days before moving to another hiding place. Here, she became unwell with pneumonia and the terrified residents of the block told her to leave before her coughing alerted the Germans. Finally, she hid in the apartment of another friend in Sumy for 18 months until liberated by the arrival of the Red Army.[31]

In addition to the deliberate killing of Jews, communists and others, there was also a high death rate from starvation. Food was already running short for the population by mid-December 1941, and Usyk noted in his diary that the weekly bread ration – 400g for Ukrainian and Soviet workers and only 200g for non-workers – contrasted with 1.5kg for non-working ethnic Germans and 2kg for working ethnic Germans. Those who helped in police duties and killings received an additional bread ration.[32] However, whilst these were the official rations, they rarely appeared in full or even at all. Food became a little more plentiful during the summer of 1942, but only for those who had money or other goods that they could trade. Usyk learned about some of the deaths from starvation and wrote in his diary that about 500 had died in December 1941, rising to 1,603 in January 1942, 2,133 the following month, and 2,699 in March.[33] To make matters worse, the water supply was badly disrupted as a result of damage to the city's power system, and many residents had to fetch water by hand – it was only in August 1942 that Usyk once more had running water in his apartment.

During the entire period of German occupation, starvation resulted in a total of about 80,000 deaths, and as Konev described, many civilians were rounded up by the Germans and forcibly removed from the city as forced labour, often being sent to Germany and elsewhere. In the first four months of 1942 alone, Usyk recorded that about 16,400 people had been taken away from Kharkov. The total figure of such enforced labour was approximately 120,000 rather than the 150,000 quoted by Konev; few of them returned. Only those who were deemed physically unable to work could escape being called up for labour, and many tried to get certificates from doctors to protect their family members. In some cases, they had to pay substantial bribes, thus reducing still further the money they had for buying food. Even possession of medical certificates did not guarantee protection; when an engineer produced his certificate of exemption, the German soldier in charge of the work detail read it and then beat the engineer senseless.[34] Within a very short time, most people who could gain access to horsemeat had put aside any pre-war fussiness and took what they could get, and it wasn't long before other meats were also tried, as Alexei Alexeyevich Migulin, a professor of biology, recalled:

After the arrival of the Germans, I found two dead horses lying in a meadow. I lived in the village of Lipovaya Roscha, 10km [six miles] from anywhere else.

The Germans started killing dogs. At first we refused to consider them, but in the end we ate more than two dozen dogs. Their meat was better than horsemeat. Once the Germans had killed their own dog, a fat, very tasty German shepherd, and we were delighted. We had wonderful cuts of meat all week.[35]

Although the Germans tried to control the access of the public to news about the progress of the war, sporadic reports reached the citizens about events elsewhere. Throughout the second half of 1942, these reports largely confirmed German accounts of the advance of the Wehrmacht to the Don and into the Caucasus, but Usyk and others tried to take solace in observing the manner in which the garrison troops in Kharkov appeared to be increasingly resorting to alcohol and were downcast by the apparently endless war. As they ran out of money and items of value that they could barter, the city's inhabitants suffered ever more from starvation with many choosing to work for the Germans just to survive, taking posts as labourers, administrators, and even working in the brothels that were set up for Wehrmacht personnel. If the mood of the city towards the communist authorities had been ambivalent before the war, Nina Andreyevna Veretenchenko wryly noted, it changed as the German occupation continued – one of the jokes that circulated was that Hitler was far stronger than Stalin – in two decades, Stalin had failed to persuade the people to love him, but Hitler taught the people to love Stalin in just a few months.[36]

Inevitably, some collaborated with the Germans to survive, as an academic who worked in the university described:

As for Zhelikhovsky, I must say that the Germans showed great skill in identifying people who were losing their political focus. Zhelikhovsky lived in the same apartment block as me. He was very busy in the university, but he increasingly looked to his self-interest. He provided for several families, several women. He did not leave the state farms for weeks at a time, where he was working, and carts [of provisions] came to his apartment constantly. He was seen less and less in Kharkov and, finally, completely disappeared. I believe that Zhelikhovsky proved himself to be someone without any morality both personally and politically. It was said that the Germans had taken him west as a valuable specialist.

Vetukhov made an even more disgusting impression. He worked in the Zemstvo [a council of the local government] and lived in the same block as me with his family and there wasn't a day when carts didn't call there. Literally, everything was his apartment. It was a hard time, in winter. My wife asked his mother to share something with us as a good neighbour. When she entered the apartment, she saw that the next room was full of bags, there was a pile of butter blocks on the table, and several hams …

Apparently, the Germans knew what sort of person they were dealing with, and took him to Kiev on the eve of their retreat. His family left the house and headed in the same direction.[37]

Inevitably, the lack of reliable reports on affairs elsewhere led to wild rumours. In late 1942, Kharkovites discussed an alleged mutiny of German soldiers and sailors in France, which had apparently been bloodily suppressed. The first hard evidence of German setbacks came on 16 January 1943 when a column of tattered, exhausted Italian troops marched through the city, the survivors of the rout of the Italian Eighth Army on the Don. By early February, the departure of many German administrative personnel and increasing air attacks by Soviet planes raised morale as it became clear that the Red Army was approaching. By the middle of the month the front line was rapidly getting closer, as Usyk recorded:

14 February 1943: Morning. When I write these lines, the air and windows shake to almost continuous explosions. The fascists are apparently destroying all public buildings, venting their anger at their doom. Explosions started at 3am and it is now 5.45am.

6am: There are fires all around … Artillery is firing, nobody knows whose.[38]

The arrival of Red Army troops shortly after led to great rejoicing, but it was short-lived. When the Germans recaptured Kharkov in March 1943, many – including Usyk – left with the retreating Red Army, and the depleted population was left in a city that the Germans had deliberately wrecked as they withdrew just a few weeks before. When the Germans were finally expelled in August, there was still more destruction, and as the procurator of the city's art gallery glumly recorded, about 700 pieces of art were dispatched back to Germany – almost all of them small pieces, with the larger works being left in the building where they were destroyed when it was set ablaze. Nina Ivanovna Pukalova was an older resident who survived both German occupations, and had little doubt that the second occupation, while shorter, was also far more brutal:

The second time the Germans came [to Kharkov], they didn't behave like an army, just as beasts. They kicked open doors and fired indiscriminately, then entered the apartment and if they saw a man, took him out and shot him. They explained this by saying 'We do not know if he was a military man or not. The military do not always wear uniforms.' One person was sitting [in his apartment] in Iskrinsky Lane with his three children and they shot him. On Lenin Street they shot 26 people. They were hiding in a basement. The German soldier didn't enter the basement, but threw in a grenade and shouted 'Get out!' They emerged and were shot.[39]

As they prepared to leave in August, the Germans once more killed and destroyed, often indiscriminately, as a doctor later described:

The second time [the Germans] came [to Kharkov], they were just beasts, particularly the SS ... When they left, they threw grenades into the small houses and stabbed people with bayonets. Then came to our friends' place, where just the old woman and the old man lived. He had served as a police administrator and was old and disabled. They were sitting at the table at Staro-Moskovskaya Street. Their son sat with them, making cigarettes. The SS went in, looked around, and said to his son, 'Komm, komm.' ... They took him into the corridor and immediately in front of their parents – bang, their son was no more. Then they went to the next house. The person who lived there had worked for me. He was killed on the spot. In the next house after that, they caught a woman. She held her children in her arms. They shot her, too, in the stomach. It was hard enough that they destroyed buildings, that they did not appreciate any culture – but it was even harder to see their brutal behaviour towards people.[40]

Constantly hunted by the occupying Germans, Communist Party officials gathered information about German atrocities and when the opportunity arose, tried to escape to the east to report on what was happening. The reaction of Red Army soldiers, many of whom had families in areas now controlled by the Germans, can easily be imagined:

In Novy Liman, 93 out of 96 houses were set ablaze. Only three remained. A squad of 20 Germans arrived in a truck and told the people that they had an hour to leave before their houses were torched. Trucks and wagons arrived and the Germans loaded them with the possessions [of the residents] and then fired on the people.

The same thing happened in Volokhovoy Yar. Most of the population did not have a chance to take food or clothes.

... Two women were shot [in Pisarevka] and 28 women, who had gone to the state farm looking for food, were rounded up and put in a cold barn. They were detained there for five hours and then they were beaten in turn and from there sent to Chuguyev with a group of prisoners, where they were put in an unheated room. They spent the night there and were released in the morning ...

Two people went to Volokhovy Yar in search of bread ... A patrol captured them and took them to its base. The command was given to shoot them. These people were taken back to their apartments and were shot in the courtyard with their wives watching, and they were told that they were not permitted to bury the corpses for three days ... Olga Mahonko lived there [in Volokhovy Yar], a 26-year-old collective farm worker with two children, her husband was in the Red Army. A German soldier entered her house where she was sleeping on the stove [a common practice in the Ukraine during the cold winter]. He clambered onto the stove and tried to rape her. She lost consciousness through fear. She is now insane. The women collective farmers gathered and went to the commandant and told him about the case. He replied to them that it was an inevitable consequence of war ...

The prison in Kharkov is full of prisoners of war. On 19 December [1941], about 120–140 prisoners were taken along the Grigorovskoye Road, and 11 prisoners who were lagging behind through weakness from malnutrition were shot. Their corpses were thrown to one side. They lay there for four days. The prisoners are terribly mistreated. Those who stop along the road are beaten with rifle butts. A German officer who works in the prison said: 'I was in Holland and Belgium, and finally I arrived here, but what I see here, I have not seen anywhere else. I'll shoot myself or go mad. In all my life, I have never seen such a brutal, inhumane attitude.' He asked to be released from working in the prison. The same officer said that prisoners were not fed, were held in unheated cells, were not allowed to sleep, and were beaten and humiliated. Dozens of prisoners die every day.[41]

Not all Germans behaved with brutality towards the citizens of Kharkov. Ivan Pavlovich Korolev, a senior technician in the city's cryogenic laboratory, was ordered to dismantle various items of equipment so that they could be sent to Germany. In February 1943, the Germans left an aerial bomb in the laboratory and told the staff that they should keep clear until the bomb had exploded, but somewhat to everyone's surprise there was no detonation. When the Red Army took control of the city, sappers examined the bomb and found that its fuse had been removed, rendering it harmless. During the second German occupation, Korolev was once more put under the command of a German technical officer, Hauptmann Ebert, who distributed letters from people who had voluntarily travelled to Germany; these letters painted a favourable picture of life there, resulting in several Ukrainians wishing to leave when the Germans prepared for the abandonment of the city in August:

> Ebert stressed that he would only accept volunteers. In general, he was not a stupid man. When he left, he said something interesting:
> 'Farewell, stay with my blessing, and tell the Reds that there are good people amongst the Germans.' Most of our institute was saved from destruction because there were people like Ebert.[42]

After the expulsion of the Germans in August 1943, the Soviet authorities gathered extensive evidence of the atrocities that had been carried out during the periods of occupation, and much of this was later used in the trials of Germans accused of war crimes. But despite the clear evidence for the manner in which the Jews had been singled out, Stalin ordered that their suffering should not be portrayed as any different from that of other Soviet citizens who were the victims of the Germans. Even before the end of the war, it was Soviet dogma that the people of the Soviet Union had suffered uniquely at the hands of the hated fascists, and this would have been undermined by any suggestion that a particular subgroup had suffered more than the rest. Recognition of the treatment of the Jews became mainstream historical teaching only after the fall of the Soviet Union. There were other steps taken to ensure that accounts complied with official dogma; Usyk's diary has many pages removed, almost certainly because they contained entries describing events that did not portray the communists in a favourable light.

The German withdrawal to the line of the Udy was carried out without major incident; the Soviet forces pursuing them, particularly Rotmistrov's armoured units, had suffered heavy losses in the fighting. The rearguard of the German forces was largely from 6th Panzer Division, and when it reached the river, its personnel were alarmed to find that the last bridge had collapsed when two Hornisse tank destroyers attempted to cross at the same time. A group of eight tank destroyers and the better part of an infantry battalion were stranded briefly on the wrong side of the Udy, but had little difficulty in fending off the relatively weak Soviet attacks that developed through 24 August. During the following night, the bridge was successfully repaired and the rearguard withdrew to safety.

Operation *Polkovodets Rumyantsev* was at an end. Following the series of winter offensives mounted by the Red Army – *Uranus*, *Little Saturn*, and the advances from the Don to the Donets – both *Kutuzov* to the north of the Kursk salient and this operation to the south demonstrated how far the skill of Soviet planners had come. The reconquest of Belgorod and Orel had been planned at short notice, but whilst the operation encountered difficulties, these were not due to problems in the manner in which the plans were drawn up; the strength of German resistance and the arguments over when Rotmistrov's Fifth Guards Tank Army would be released to Konev's Steppe Front could not have been anticipated until the operation unfolded. The revised composition of tank armies was a considerable step forward, though they continued to experience problems as their pace of advance left them far ahead of supporting infantry and artillery; it remained to be seen whether these problems could be resolved by better use of the tank armies, or whether further changes to their composition would be needed.

Soviet-era historiography consistently treats both *Polkovodets Rumyantsev* and *Kutuzuv* to the north of the Kursk salient as inseparable parts of the Battle of Kursk itself. From the Soviet perspective, the intention was always to switch to offensive operations once the Wehrmacht had been halted in defensive fighting, and whilst the assault towards Belgorod and Kharkov was devised with considerable speed immediately before its execution, there had always been an intention to carry out some such operation, as Zhukov later wrote:

The main plan for the counteroffensive of Soviet troops at the Kursk bulge, developed and approved ... by the supreme commander in May, was amended and repeatedly discussed in *Stavka* during the defensive battle. This was the plan for the second stage of the defeat of the enemy in the areas of Orel, Belgorod and Kharkov and was part of the plan for the entire summer campaign of 1943.

The first stage – a defensive battle in the fighting at Kursk – was completed on Central Front on 12 July, and on Voronezh front on 23 July. The different timings of the end of defensive operations on these fronts are explained by the scale of the battle and the losses suffered. It should also be taken into account that on 12 July, Central Front received significant assistance from Bryansk and Western Fronts, which launched an offensive against the enemy's Orel group. This led to the Hitlerites moving seven divisions rapidly from the troops operating against Central Front.

The second phase of the battle – the counterattack – was also not started simultaneously.

Thus, in the Belgorod area, the counteroffensive began on 3 August, 20 days after the counteroffensive of Central, Bryansk and Western Fronts, which required less preparation time, since the planning of the counteroffensive and its comprehensive logistic support were largely worked out in advance and merely refined during the defensive battle.

In the second case [i.e. south of Kursk], more time was required for preparation, since the troops of Steppe Front, which were being launched into the counteroffensive, did not have a fully developed plan of action drawn up in advance. Being in *Stavka* reserve, they could not know the specific missions and initial areas for their counterattack and the specific enemy against whom they would have to act.[43]

The scale of the entire scheme of operations – the defensive phase in the Kursk salient and the counteroffensives that followed – was immense:

Significantly greater forces were involved here than in the previous large counteroffensive operations. For example, 17 small combined arms armies without tank formations took part in [the battle of] Moscow, and 14 combined arms armies, one tank army and several mechanised corps took part in [operations] in the Stalingrad area. In the counteroffensive near Kursk, there were 22 powerful all-arms armies, five tank armies, six air armies and large long-range aviation forces.[44]

The Red Army's casualties in the fighting for Belgorod, Kharkov and Akhtyrka were heavy. By the time that the operation came to an end, the rifle divisions of Konev's Steppe Front and many of those of Vatutin's Voronezh Front had been reduced to as little as 25 per cent of their establishment strength; it is estimated that losses came to over 250,000 dead and wounded.[45] Over 1,800 tanks were lost, though a proportion of these would be recovered from battlefields and returned to combat in the coming weeks.[46] German losses were numerically lower, at 30,000 dead, wounded and missing, a reflection of the manner in which Manstein and his subordinates managed to pull back rather than risk encirclement. In addition, the Germans lost about 240 tanks, and matters were worsened by the fact that the engineer units with the panzer divisions were equipped largely with tractors designed to cope with the older Pz.III and Pz.IV tanks rather than the far heavier Panther and Tiger tanks – unless another Panther or Tiger was available to help tow away the damaged vehicle, or it was possible to attach several tractors, any damaged heavy tanks had to be abandoned.

These losses have to be seen against the context of the resources available to both sides. Whilst Soviet casualties for what amounted to less than four weeks' combat were heavy by any standard, the tank losses would rapidly be made good by the immense production capacity of the Soviet armaments industry, whereas the Germans would feel their losses far more severely. During the months of July and August, the Red Army had expended a staggering 42 million artillery rounds; this compared with German munitions production for the entire year of just 56 million rounds.[47] The casualties in personnel for the Red Army were a painful blow, particularly as they included many experienced officers and NCOs, but similarly the German units also lost irreplaceable personnel. Manstein was aware that the Eastern Front was rapidly becoming a tomb for the Wehrmacht's officer corps – from the beginning of *Zitadelle* to the end of August, his units had lost seven division commanders, 38 regimental commanders, and no fewer than 252 battalion commanders.[48] The loss of so many experienced men was a massive blow, and those who remained were increasingly pessimistic about the ultimate outcome of the conflict; one wrote that the Wehrmacht was doomed to follow what amounted to a *Totenritt* ('death ride') to the bitter end.[49] And whilst the Red Army had been brought to a halt, the Wehrmacht had almost no reserves available for future crises. It was increasingly clear to the Germans that despite the declaration of the Badoglio government in Rome that it would continue to fight alongside its ally, it was only a matter of time before Italy sought an armistice (negotiations were actually already under way in secret), and the German units in Italy, Sardinia and Corsica were generally weak and would require further reinforcements. With such a threat, it could not be assumed that reinforcements would always be available for the Eastern Front. Any new crisis was likely to have grave consequences.

CHAPTER 6

ATTRITION: FROM THE MIUS AND DONETS TO THE DNEPR

The arguments between Manstein and Hitler about the conduct of the war on the Eastern Front repeatedly returned to the same issue: the presence of German forces in the eastern parts of the Ukraine, particularly the Donbas region. For Hitler, control of this region was an economical and political necessity: economically, its coal and mineral resources were deemed by him to be essential for the German war effort and depriving Soviet industry of access to them would greatly limit the ability of the Soviet Union to continue fighting; politically, any withdrawal from this area would weaken the allegiance of the Balkan nations to the Axis and would alienate Turkey. This latter point was largely an irrelevance as there was never any significant chance of Turkey entering the war on the Eastern Front on either side, but Hitler often returned to it. Therefore, argued Hitler, it was essential that Germany remained in control of this region. For Manstein, control of any territory was the outcome of the military position and if it was not possible to provide sufficient military resources to ensure a favourable outcome, all economic and political considerations were largely irrelevant. Since the first winter of the war with the Soviet Union, the Germans had repeatedly faced the same problem: the geography of the rivers of the eastern Ukraine and the position of the front line meant that the Red Army was constantly facing southwest – any significant advance would threaten to push at least part of Army Group South towards the Sea of Azov or the Black Sea, and consequently the German positions that were furthest east – in the Donbas – were always under some form of threat. As August came to an end, these arguments resumed once more. The forces available to Army Group South –

particularly on the southern flank – were too weak to hold back the Red Army, and Manstein demanded that Hitler make a choice: either he had to provide sufficient troops to restore the military balance; or he had to grant Army Group South permission to pull back to a shorter defensive line.

Whilst the military logic of this was impeccable, Manstein must have known the limitations of both options. The German military structure was by this stage of the war extensively compartmentalised, with different commanders in the field knowing little about the deployment of troops in other areas, but nonetheless Manstein would have had at least unofficial contacts with his equivalents in Army Group Centre (Field Marshal Günther von Kluge) and Army Group North (Field Marshal Georg von Küchler). He would therefore have been aware that even if Hitler could be persuaded to transfer troops from other sectors of the Eastern Front to the Ukraine, it was almost impossible to release these forces without leaving those other sectors fatally weak. Consequently, he must have known – at least in general terms – that reinforcements on the scale that he needed were very unlikely to be available unless they could be brought from the west. This effectively left only the option of freedom of movement, and it is likely that Manstein merely included the choice of substantial reinforcements in order to make the case that, as these were not available, there was no alternative but to concede ground and pull back towards the Dnepr – but the experience of the previous winter, when Hitler had shown huge reluctance to abandon any ground even when Sixth Army was dying in Stalingrad and the rest of the front line was in tatters, must have made clear to Manstein that there was little or no prospect of Hitler agreeing to a substantial withdrawal now.

Nevertheless, Manstein had no choice but to make the attempt. Hitler responded to his latest demand by travelling to Vinnitsa for a face-to-face meeting and arrived on 27 August. In an attempt to strengthen his hand, Manstein had summoned his army commanders to the conference as well as a corps commander and a division commander. He informed Hitler that the units of Army Group South had lost 133,000 men since the beginning of the year and had received only 33,000 replacements; even if these men had been experienced soldiers, it would still mean that three out of four casualties had not been replaced, but the fact that most of the replacements were raw recruits made matters still worse. Anticipating Hitler's response, Manstein went on to describe the losses suffered by the Red Army, acknowledging the damage that had been inflicted upon the Soviet units, but added that in comparison to the Wehrmacht, the Red Army showed greater ability to move substantial forces from one sector to another to create local superiority and furthermore had the industrial resources to make good most of the losses of materiel that had been suffered – the German occupation of the Donbas was clearly not having a significant effect on the Soviet war effort. The previous winter, the greatest threat to the Wehrmacht had been that the Red Army would exploit the collapse of the armies of Germany's allies – the Romanians, Italians and Hungarians – and would sweep down to the Sea of Azov and the Dnepr crossings, isolating all German forces in the Ukraine and thus destroying Army Group South entirely; had this happened, it would have been almost impossible for Germany to continue fighting. Given the failure of *Zitadelle* and the subsequent Soviet advance to recapture Kharkov, this threat remained in place:

> I presented Hitler with the clear alternative:
> Either of quickly providing the army group with new forces – in any case not less than 12 divisions – and exchanging our tired divisions with others from quiet stretches of the front;
> Or of abandoning the Donets area to release forces within the army group.[1]

As had been the case the previous winter, Hitler repeatedly tried to divert the discussion into pointless arguments of a technical nature, such as the performance of the newest German tanks and statistics for mineral production across the entire Reich, but Manstein had learned from previous meetings and studiously avoided getting drawn into such sterile discussions. As the meeting drew to a close, Hitler promised to provide Army Group South with reinforcements from other parts of the Eastern Front, and discussion of rotating worn-out units to quieter sectors was postponed until the next day.

The unreality of being able to find 'quieter sectors' was revealed in full the following day when news began to arrive of renewed Soviet attacks on Army Group Centre. Kluge reported that he too needed reinforcements just to survive, while Küchler said that he couldn't spare any troops whatever. The only source of reinforcements was therefore from the west, and Hitler refused to release any of the troops held there until the Western Allies revealed their hand – would there be further landings by British and American troops in Italy, or the Balkans, or even southern France? The most that Hitler was prepared to accept was the creation of a fortified line along the Dnepr, to which the Wehrmacht would ultimately be allowed to fall back – but until this line had been built, it was important to continue to hold the Red Army at bay further to the east. In any event, Hitler was ambivalent even about authorising the construction of these defences, officially part of the *Ostwall* on which he now hoped the Red Army could be bled to defeat; the existence of defensive positions to the rear of the existing front line, he told his entourage, would result in soldiers simply retreating to them rather than holding their current positions.

The *Ostwall* was intended to create a fortified region along the entire length of the Eastern Front. The first considerations for the construction of such a defensive line took place in early 1942, when the Wehrmacht was still catching its breath following its near-destruction during Zhukov's counterattacks in front of Moscow. General Friedrich Olbricht, chief of the *Allgemeines Heeresamt* (General Office of the Army), discussed the setbacks of the previous two months with General Friedrich Fromm, head of the *Ersatzheer* ('Replacement Army'), and the two men proposed at a conference in January that a defensive line stretching 1,200 miles (2,000km) should be constructed. They estimated that it would require 250,000 men to construct the line and that it could be built within just 100 days. Further details were developed in February before the proposal was put to Hitler, who forbade any such work to take place on the grounds that it would have a negative effect on Germany's allies; also, Hitler argued – an argument that he would use repeatedly – the existence of a strong line in the rear of the field army would encourage officers and men to opt for withdrawals rather than moving forward.[2]

Even if Hitler had been minded to approve the construction of the proposed defensive line, it is highly unlikely that Germany had the resources for the work. Fromm and Olbricht had planned to use the men of the *Ersatzheer* for labour, but moving sufficient materials would have required a huge amount of railway capacity at a time when Germany was barely able to provide enough trains to supply the Wehrmacht in the occupied parts of the Soviet Union. As the war turned against Germany, there was once more consideration of building a defensive line, but the obvious route for the line – along the Dnepr – was at the time far behind the front and Hitler was hugely resistant to such a move. He grudgingly gave permission for work to commence during 1943, but repeatedly delayed giving final approval – by the time that he did so in August 1943, it was too late.

In some sectors, such as near the Baltic coast in the north, the 'Tannenberg' positions in Estonia proved to be formidable defences and the Red Army suffered major casualties attempting to force them.[3] Elsewhere, the *Ostwall* existed more in Hitler's imagination and on maps than it did on the ground, with few positions being built. The segment that was to run along the Molochna River to the east of the lower Dnepr – the 'Wotan' line – was one such sector, and the few positions that had been created were vulnerable to being outflanked if the Red Army were able to secure crossings over the Molochna and Dnepr. But even if the designated line had not been flawed by considerations of terrain, Hitler's proposal to bleed the Red Army to defeat against an impregnable line of defences contained an insurmountable flaw: it could only succeed if the Wehrmacht had sufficient troops to man such a line along the entire length of the Eastern Front. Even if there had been no foes to face in the west, Germany simply did not have the manpower to produce enough infantry divisions for the task, especially as the Soviet commanders could choose where they concentrated their forces for an attack. As Speer so accurately described, Hitler's thinking remained embedded in his experiences of the First World War, and he clearly hoped that the creation of a long line of entrenchments in the manner of the Western Front of the previous conflict was the answer to his desire not to concede territory in order to undertake the sort of mobile defence that the military professionals wanted.

It must have been clear to a strategist of the calibre of Manstein that Germany now lacked the ability to wage the war to a successful conclusion. In the First World War, the Entente Powers had decided at an early stage on a strategy of striking major blows on Germany from all sides – ultimately, the Germans would run out of resources with which to counter these blows, and a breakthrough would be achieved at some point or other. Germany now faced a similar situation, with the Red Army apparently capable of raining blows on the Eastern Front that stretched the resources of the Wehrmacht to and beyond any reasonable limit – once the Western Powers added their contribution, the end of the war would surely come quickly. But the strong instincts of loyalty continued to prevent senior German commanders from taking any action that might alter the outcome. In fairness, there were numerous reports from front-line units that Soviet prisoners often included large numbers of youths or old men, and this was frequently interpreted as a sign that the Soviet Union was approaching the end of its vast manpower reserves. Similarly, captured bags of mail suggested widespread food shortages throughout the Soviet Union.[4] *Fremde Heere Ost* ('Foreign Armies East'), the German military intelligence section dealing with the Soviet Union, was by this stage of the war widely discredited due to its failures in 1941 and 1942, and its reports that Soviet human resources were far from exhausted were disregarded by Hitler and others. If the Red Army could be ground down and forced to pay a further huge price in terms of men and equipment, Stalin would surely be forced to sue for peace.

The state of the Wehrmacht along the Eastern Front was woeful. The fighting of July and August had cost Army Groups Centre and South 10,000 officers killed, wounded or missing – a devastating loss of experienced, irreplaceable men.[5] Every formation was below establishment strength, and many infantry divisions had been forced to reduce their three regiments from three battalions each to just two battalions. Despite this, they were still expected to hold a length of front that would have been difficult for a full-strength infantry division. Artillery batteries in many divisions had been reduced from four guns per battery to three guns, and a shortage of horses and trucks meant that these guns were increasingly immobile – almost any Soviet penetration beyond the German front line could lead to gun positions being overrun, and even if the Soviet troops were driven back, the precious guns would have been lost. Almost since the onset of the war in the east, the Germans had made use of volunteers from amongst the hundreds of thousands of Soviet prisoners of war they captured – known as *Hilfswillige* ('voluntary helpers', or *Hiwis*) in a variety of roles. Many such volunteers were only attempting to escape the brutal conditions and starvation of prison camps, but others were motivated by a mixture of issues – some were hostile to the Communist regime, while others believed that the Germans would win the war and wished to be on the winning side. At first, these men were used in rear area roles, helping with transport, hard labour, horse welfare etc., and their numbers grew steadily in an attempt to offset the shortage of German troops. One veteran later wrote:

> In my division we counted about 300–400 of these Russian auxiliaries. They joined us during the first winter … They helped in transporting the wounded and worked in workshops, and some worked as interpreters … [Many of them] went into captivity with us … in May 1945 in Austria. And then began a very difficult period, because the Red Army was looking for them. [We helped many escape into the countryside.] When my division's veterans meet today there are always between 30 and 35 of these auxiliaries who survived the war.[6]

As the war began to go badly for Germany, many *Hiwis* disappeared, presumably finding their way back to the Soviet side of the front line; they would have been treated with grave suspicion by the Soviet authorities, and many would have been sent to penal units. But others were simply returned to front-line service by unit commanders desperate to keep their units operational. Most of the *Hiwis* who did not desert during 1943 remained loyal to the Germans until the end of the war.

As a consequence of its numerical weakness, the German defensive line became increasingly brittle. Defensive doctrine, defined in military manuals published in 1933, had not been changed officially, though inevitably there had been changes in practice to reflect the realities of war. But these changes were implemented at a local level, with the result that each division, corps and even army tended to devise its own changes. The principles of defensive warfare for the Wehrmacht were based upon defending in depth, manoeuvring to a favourable position, using sudden, intense fire to shock and stop the enemy, and then launching a powerful counterattack to restore the front line. There were now too few troops available for a defence in depth and Hitler's refusal to countenance even local withdrawals made effective tactical manoeuvres almost impossible – in any event, the Soviet formations were usually more mobile than their German equivalents. It was only when it was usually too late that Hitler could be persuaded to approve a withdrawal to a shorter line – by which stage the losses suffered in trying to hold the original front line meant that the new line was also untenable. Shortages of ammunition and guns made the sudden 'fire strike' against attacking formations difficult to achieve, and whilst counterattacks were still a hallmark of German defensive fighting, the weakness of units greatly reduced the effectiveness of these attacks. Armoured formations were increasingly used to launch counterattacks to restore the front line, but this ensured that they too became chronically weakened. It was only a matter of time before the line collapsed at one point or other, and at that stage the relative immobility of the German infantry might result in catastrophe.[7]

To make matters worse, partisan activity was worsening. The hotbed of partisan attacks was further north in Army Group Centre's rear areas, but there had been plenty of activity in the Ukraine throughout 1942. Compared to further north, this was relatively low-key and consisted of isolated attacks by small groups, mainly in pursuit of getting food or weapons. Throughout 1943, this activity increased markedly, particularly with attacks on railway lines, bridges and against trains – such attacks tripled compared to 1942. The partisan groups became larger and better organised, placing a further demand upon German troops.

Taking advantage of Hitler's grudging acceptance at the end of his visit to Vinnitsa that, in circumstances where there was no alternative, units were permitted to make local withdrawals, Manstein ordered Mackensen and Hollidt on 31 August to conduct a mobile defence rather than tie down the precious panzer and panzergrenadier divisions in positions that would inevitably be outflanked when units elsewhere came under pressure. On 3 September, he travelled to East Prussia where he met Hitler once more to discuss plans for future operations. On this occasion, Manstein attempted to prevent Hitler from making unchallenged comments regarding other sectors of the Eastern Front:

I asked Field Marshal von Kluge to accompany me, as I wished to act conjointly with him in getting our forces distributed in a way which would take account of what the enemy so obviously had in mind. At the same time we wished to broach the need for rationalising the overall leadership – i.e. for getting rid of the *OKW-OKH* duplication in the eastern theatre of war. The previous day I had written General Zeitzler a letter demanding that something finally be done to effect a real concentration of effort at the decisive point on the Eastern Front. In view of developments on adjacent wings of Army Groups South and Centre, I had said, it was essential that we take the precaution of assembling a strong army forward of Kiev. If the arrival of reinforcements from other theatres were delayed until our western opponents committed themselves by a landing on the continent, we should be too late in the east. In any case, it should not be too difficult to guess the Western Powers' general intentions from the disposition of their naval forces and shipping space. Zeitzler told me that when he showed the letter to Hitler, the latter had fumed in rage and averred that all I was interested in doing was conducting ingenious operations and justifying myself in the war diary.[8]

Once again, the meeting degenerated into arguments in which the two parties talked almost entirely at cross purposes, with Hitler complaining repeatedly about the manner in which Manstein was allowing Sixth Army to withdraw from the Donbas. Zeitzler pointed out that there was little question any longer of holding onto the region – the only matter that remained to be settled was whether an army group was to be sacrificed in a futile bid to prevent its loss. The main issue that Manstein – and with somewhat greater reluctance, Kluge – wished to discuss, namely alteration of the command structure, was barely considered before Hitler dismissed it. Nor was there any possibility of reinforcements from Army Group North or from the west, Hitler told his field marshals. Despite this clear evidence that Germany simply did not have the resources to continue fighting on so many fronts, nobody appeared willing or able to face such a reality. With great reluctance, Hitler finally gave permission for Seventeenth Army, at the southern end of the Eastern Front, to pull back across the Kertch Straits into the Crimea and to abandon the Taman Peninsula. This 'bridgehead' had been held since the withdrawal of German forces from the Caucasus following the disaster at Stalingrad in a vain hope of being able to launch a new offensive at some point in the future, but nobody other than Hitler had ever regarded such a possibility as being achievable. There had been constant requests for Seventeenth Army to be allowed to withdraw, and on 14 August Zeitzler thought he had secured agreement from Hitler, only for the order to be rescinded almost immediately, with Hitler once more citing the political impact on the Balkan region of such a withdrawal. Now that permission was finally granted, General Erwin Jaenecke's Seventeenth Army pulled back to the Crimea in an efficient and orderly manner – preparations had been in place for months, and there was little that the Red Army could do to prevent the withdrawal.

The demands upon German resources were growing steadily. In addition to the constant pressure upon the Eastern Front, a new crisis developed in the west when British forces landed in Calabria in southern Italy on the same day that Hitler faced his two army group commanders. The intention of the British was to tie down German forces in the extreme south of Italy and then to trap them by conducting landings further north; correctly assessing the situation, Kesselring, the commander of German forces in Italy, ordered his troops to pull back and to hinder the advance of the British by destroying bridges and blocking mountain passes. There was now clear evidence that the British and Americans were concentrating their plans on the Italian peninsula – this became even clearer on 9 September when American forces landed at Salerno – and forces held in readiness in southern France and elsewhere might have been made available for the Eastern Front, at least for a short time. However, such a policy could only be effective if it was part of an overall strategy, for example to use the units from Western Europe to create a mobile force that could strike quickly and effectively on the Eastern Front and could then be withdrawn and used elsewhere. When his grand plan to win the war in 1942 by securing the lower Volga and then seizing the Caucasus oilfields failed, Hitler failed to come up with any strategic vision for how the war could be won, or even how defeat could be avoided. The Battle of Kursk would ultimately have been irrelevant if the Germans had won – it only made sense in its original context, i.e. as a follow-on from the winter fighting and a means of bringing the battered Soviet tank formations to battle once more with a view to destroying them. Once the plan started to suffer delays, the likelihood of a strategic victory effectively disappeared. All that Hitler could suggest now was the creation of an *Ostwall*, which he hoped would somehow be manned and made impenetrable.

Such considerations almost irresistibly beg the question: given their high levels of training and experience in operational and strategic matters, these conclusions must have been clear to the senior officers of the Wehrmacht, particularly those like Manstein and Kluge. After the winter campaign, which was punctuated by a series of meetings in which Manstein saw very clearly the inability of Hitler to consider issues in a logical manner, Manstein should have had no doubts about the Führer's inability to formulate or accept plans that might save Germany from ultimate defeat. Whilst Kluge had not been party to these discussions, he had warned Manstein in November 1942 – when the latter was journeying south to take command of the growing crisis in Stalingrad and on the Don – that Hitler would interfere repeatedly in every redeployment of forces, so he too appears to have had little confidence in Hitler. Yet despite being peripherally involved in plots to unseat Hitler, Kluge repeatedly shied away from taking any decisive step. At one stage, he told the conspirators that, following Hitler's acceptance of responsibility for the disaster at Stalingrad, he had decided to give the Führer one last chance. The fact that Hitler had also made a substantial financial award to Kluge during the winter may have played a part in his decision, but the fact remained that despite being fully aware of the plots in Army Group Centre to arrest or kill Hitler, he repeatedly failed to throw his weight wholeheartedly behind the conspirators, or to arrest them. Instead, he appears to have chosen to wait to see which side would prevail. In July 1943, Carl Goerdeler – a leading conservative politician before the war and a member of the movement to overthrow Hitler – visited bombed cities and wrote to Kluge that 'the work of a thousand years is nothing but rubble'. He urged Kluge in vain to join the conspirators before it was too late.[9]

Manstein did even less than Kluge to take any steps to put the interests of Germany above his personal loyalty to Hitler. It is highly likely that he too was aware at least of the existence of conspiracies against Hitler – Klaus von Stauffenberg, who would try to kill Hitler with a briefcase bomb in 1944, visited Manstein during the winter of 1942–43 and probably tried to persuade Manstein to become the high-profile military figure that the conspirators needed to rally resistance to the Nazis. Instead, Manstein retreated to a purely military world in which the oath of allegiance that he – like all German officers – had given to remain loyal to Hitler was paramount.

Rudolf-Christoph von Gersdorff was an intelligence officer serving with Army Group Centre and had been involved in liaison work with *Einsatzgruppe B*, which was responsible for the mass murder of Jews, suspected communists, and other 'undesirables' in the central region of the Eastern Front. He was also aware of the atrocities committed by the Soviet Union, having supervised the excavation of the mass graves near Katyn, where the NKVD had slaughtered several thousand Polish officers and intelligentsia who had been taken prisoner by the Red Army after the Soviet occupation of the eastern parts of Poland in 1939. He was a close friend of Oberst Henning von Tresckow, one of the leading conspirators in the anti-Hitler circles in the Wehrmacht, and became an active member of the conspiracy in March 1943; he attended a visit to an armoury in Berlin where

Hitler was to inspect equipment captured in the Soviet Union, with explosives concealed in his coat and intending to act as a 'suicide bomber' to kill Hitler, but the plan failed when Hitler's visit was far briefer than expected and Gersdorff barely had time to disarm the explosives before they detonated.[10] Shortly before the meeting with Hitler attended by Kluge and Manstein, Gersdorff visited Manstein's headquarters and gave the commander of Army Group South letters that urged him to take action against Hitler. Kluge had told him to inform Manstein that once Hitler was removed from power, Kluge would back the appointment of Manstein as chief of staff of all the German armed forces.[11] Manstein makes no mention of this in his memoirs, but his diary includes some relevant entries. On the question of what he called 'internal difficulties', he wrote:

> Whether these exist, I cannot judge. In principle the army has nothing to do with such things. It has its oath and duty of obedience, and will always be that part that remains ever loyal. Any thought that military commanders should meddle in questions of political leadership would mean the undermining of the military chain of command ... In any case, Hitler is the only man who enjoys the trust of the people and the soldiers, and whom they believe in. No other would have this.[12]

The accuracy of Gersdorff's version of events – that he urged Manstein to hold a gun to Hitler's chest – is questionable, as the two men were not familiar with each other and both would have known that such talk could easily lead to their arrest and execution. Nevertheless, Manstein later acknowledged that he had received letters from conspirators, but had felt unable to respond to their urging – he believed that the removal of Hitler would automatically result in defeat for Germany, and that it was impossible for senior commanders to expect soldiers to lay down their lives and then to precipitate defeat by attempting a *coup d'état*. It should also be remembered that even at the time of the failed July Plot in 1944, there was widespread shock in Germany and in the Wehrmacht that such a treacherous deed had been attempted. Even with many of Germany's cities reduced to rubble and the clear evidence of the superiority of Germany's foes, belief in Hitler remained strong.

During this period, Vasilevsky continued to oversee the advance of Southwest and Southern Fronts on the Mius sector. Stalin's earlier criticism was now forgotten as the Soviet units slowly fought their way clear of the hilly terrain where their attack had foundered in July and on 2 September he contacted Vasilevsky to suggest assigning two tank corps to the attack. Vasilevsky agreed readily, proposing to use them with a cavalry corps to penetrate the German lines south of Stalino before angling northwest to meet units of Southwest Front, thus surrounding any German troops to the east of Stalino; to his chagrin, the plan failed to have the desired effect, with the forces of Southwest Front, largely from Sixth and Eighth Guards Armies, being brought to a halt by strong German defences. Hollidt's Sixth Army had suffered about 24,000 casualties in the fighting of July and early August, and had received only 3,300 replacements; by mid-August, Hollidt had no tanks at all, and the resumption of Soviet attacks was an unwelcome surprise – both Hollidt and Manstein had hoped and expected that the Soviet forces that had been driven back in August would take longer to recover.

The Red Army had followed its medium-term plan with considerable success, stopping the German attacks on the Kursk salient and then transitioning to offensive operations. Even before the end of the fighting for Belgorod and Kharkov, discussions about the next stage of operations in the Ukraine began in the second week of August, when Kharkov was still in German hands and the outcome of the current operation was still not clear. The next obvious objective would be to reach the Dnepr, particularly as there were intelligence reports that the Germans were preparing defensive positions along the river. Zhukov returned to Moscow on 25 August to discuss future plans with Stalin and others. He had already had preliminary discussions on how to proceed when General Alexei Innokentyevich Antonov, the first deputy chief of the general staff, visited the front line in the Kharkov sector:

In the opinion of the general staff, the German military command still had considerable forces for the continuation of the war with the Soviet Union, especially as according to all information available to us, Britain and the United States were still not going to commence major offensive operations in [Western] Europe. The landing of their troops in southern Italy on the island of Sicily did not make any significant changes in the alignment of the German forces at a strategic level, although of course the Hitlerite leadership had unnecessary worries.

The general staff believed – and with this the supreme commander agreed – that Germany was no longer able to undertake any major offensive on the Eastern Front. However, the enemy still had sufficient strength and materiel for the conduct of active defensive operations. This had actually been seen in our experience of the battles in the Bogodukhov, Akhtyrka and Poltava areas, where

German troops inflicted effective counterattacks and achieved temporary successes.

I fully agreed with Antonov's conclusions and also believed that the German command would demand a stubborn defensive effort from its troops in order to retain the Donbas and the Ukraine on the left bank [of the Dnepr].

According to the draft directives prepared by the general staff and partly already distributed to the fronts, it was planned to launch an offensive on all fronts facing the west and southwest [i.e. all those facing the German Army Groups Centre and South] in order to reach the eastern regions of Belarus and the Dnepr, where they would seize a bridgehead for continuing operations to liberate the Ukraine on the right bank.

From Antonov's report I realised that the supreme commander urgently demanded the immediate development of the [next phase of the] offensive in order not to allow the enemy to organise defences on the approaches to the Dnepr. I shared this attitude but I did not agree with the [proposed] form of our offensive operations, in which the fronts from Velikiye Luki to the Black Sea would make frontal assaults.

In fact, there was an opportunity (after some regrouping) to carry out operations to cut off and encircle significant enemy forces, which would facilitate further prosecution of the war. In particular, I referred to the enemy's southern group in the Donbas, which could be cut off by a powerful blow from the Kharkov-Izyum area in the general direction of Dnepopetrovsk and Zaporozhye.

Antonov replied that he personally shared this opinion, but the supreme commander demanded that the enemy should be expelled from our territory more quickly with frontal assaults.

Before Antonov left for Moscow, I asked him once again to report my thoughts to the supreme commander and to convey the request of the fronts for replenishment of the tank units with tanks and trained personnel, as their ranks had been thinned by the intense battles.[13]

The Moscow meeting started with a summary of the armaments production of Soviet industry and the predictions for the second half of 1943 – Zhukov records that it was anticipated that 35,000 aircraft and over 24,000 tanks and self-propelled guns were expected to be produced over the full year, far in excess of Germany's capabilities. After a series of reports on operations in different sectors of the Eastern Front, discussions turned to the Ukraine. Stalin explained that his call for a speedy offensive was motivated by a desire to expel the Germans from the Donbas before they had time to carry out a comprehensive 'scorched earth' policy, and that although a frontal attack on the Wehrmacht would inevitably result in further heavy losses, this had to be offset by the damage done to Soviet assets if the Germans were permitted to continue their widespread destruction. Zhukov was ordered to prepare a summary of how the offensive could be resumed and what would be needed, and when he presented his case that evening, calling for large quantities of troops, guns, tanks and ammunition to bring the depleted formations of Voronezh, Steppe, Southwest and Southern Fronts back to something approaching full strength, Stalin studied the requested quantities carefully, correlating them with the requirements of other sectors. Finally, he reduced them all by between 30 and 40 per cent, telling Zhukov that the rest would be provided when the formations involved reached the Dnepr.[14] The practicalities of balancing a multitude of demands clearly created problems for the Soviet Union as well as for Germany, but the overall level of supply was far greater. The reinforcements that the Red Army units designated to advance to and beyond the Dnepr would receive, were far in excess of what Manstein's formations could expect, even after the reductions imposed by Stalin. Unable to bring all the formations of Voronezh and Steppe Fronts back to full strength, Zhukov had no doubt about the arduous nature of the task that lay ahead:

> We had no opportunity for thorough preparation for the offensive to the Dnepr. There was great fatigue in the armies of both fronts from the recent continuous fighting. But all of us, from private soldiers to marshals, were eager to throw the enemy out of our land quickly, and to free the long-suffering Ukrainian people from the heavy oppression of the invaders, who vented their anger at their failures on the defenceless population.[15]

Whilst most soldiers and officers in the Red Army were unquestionably fired by a desire to expel the Germans and inflict revenge upon them for their misdeeds, it should be remembered that many Ukrainians – particularly those in the rural parts of the region – had been regarded as enemies of Bolshevism just a decade before and had been treated with arbitrary brutality by the authorities. Many of these people had little desire to see the communists return to the region, at least at the beginning of the war; however, the brutal reality of German occupation hugely undermined the potential support that the anti-communist parts of the population might have provided.

Vatutin's Voronezh Front would once more lead the way in the new offensive, as Shtemenko later wrote:

The proposals of Voronezh Front, which had been agreed with *Stavka*, and which Marshal Zhukov had signed, were ready by 8 September and presented to [Stalin] in map form. The front intended to attack by the shortest route and keep as straight as possible. In order to disperse the enemy's forces and divert their attention, our troops were to come out on the river simultaneously on the whole line of the offensive. Thirty-Eighth Army was to seize the crossings in Darnitsa, a suburb of Kiev. To make sure it was not late in doing so, three of its divisions were given motor support ... The distance of 160–210km [96–126 miles] ... to the Dnepr was to be covered in seven or eight days, from 18 to 26–27 September. The average rate of advance was to be between 20 and 30km [12 to 18 miles] a day.[16]

Fighting had merely reduced in intensity after the Soviet recapture of Kharkov, but continued along the entire front. On 25 August, while Stalin and Zhukov discussed future plans, the Soviet Twenty-Seventh Army retook Akhtyrka as Hoth ordered his men to abandon the exposed salient that stretched towards the town. The following day, Vatutin issued orders to his armies. He made clear that reaching the Dnepr wasn't sufficient; as large a proportion as possible of the German forces east of the river was to be destroyed before they could withdraw, and bridgeheads were to be secured across the Dnepr to allow for further exploitation, and to make its use as a defensive line impossible. This was particularly important as the west bank was generally higher than the east bank, and if the Germans were given time to establish positions along the river, an assault crossing would be a risky and costly undertaking. The right flank of Voronezh Front, consisting of Thirty-Eighth and Fortieth Armies, supported by Third Tank Army, I Guards Cavalry Corps, and three further tank corps would form the main strike group, with Forty-Seventh, Fifty-Second and Twenty-Seventh Armies advancing to their south. As had been the case with earlier operations, the initial breach in the German lines was to be made by the infantry armies; Third Tank Army and I Guards Cavalry Corps would then be deployed to exploit the success.[17]

On the front line, matters continued to move in favour of the Red Army. In the south, the armies of Southwest Front pushed forward across the Donets. The attempts to force the German lines between Izyum and Slavyansk were finally abandoned in the face of heavy casualties, but on the southern wing of the front Lieutenant General Dmitry Danilovich Lelyushenko's Third Guards Army managed to make significant progress. At the start of the attempt to force the Donets, Lelyushenko was concerned that his army was weak in armour, with only 5th Guards Mechanised Brigade's solitary tank regiment forming a 'mobile

The Soviet Advance,
Late August to Early September

group' for exploitation of any breakthrough, and even this formation was far
below establishment strength; Southwest Front had two formations, I Guards
Mechanised Corps and XXIII Tank Corps, in reserve, and Lelyushenko asked for
them to be assigned to his army but was turned down.

During the night of 1–2 September, the German units facing Third Guards
Army began to withdraw from their positions on the west bank of the Donets.

Immediately, Lelyushenko ordered his leading elements to secure bridgeheads and to pursue the Germans as rapidly as possible. Once again, Lelyushenko asked for the armoured units to be released from Southwest Front's reserves, and when his request was turned down a second time, he tried to improvise a mobile group by scraping together what vehicles he could find. Built around units of 279th Rifle Division, the group – with just five tanks, eight armoured cars and a mobile anti-aircraft battery – crossed the Donets at Lysychansk and rapidly pressed forward.

The German 16th Panzergrenadier Division and 17th Panzer Division were in the area in readiness to deal with a Soviet incursion and Eduard Moser, a senior NCO in the former's reconnaissance battalion, was ordered to take a scouting party south in order to establish contact with 17th Panzer Division across terrain where the precise whereabouts of friend and foe were almost unknown:

Near Krasny Dor I left my armoured car behind a hill and took a foot patrol into the village. Just 80m from a couple of tanks, which were refuelling, I fired my flare gun and could see two Soviet T-34s perfectly clearly. We reported again to division [headquarters] and moved a further 5km west. We passed through a boggy area at 2300 and crossed the Soviet line of advance, which had been chewed up by tank tracks. In pitch-black night we fumbled towards the south without any lights. After 5km we approached a village. I crawled forward but couldn't determine the nationality of the troops overnighting there. We quickly decided to drive in. There were vehicles and tanks everywhere! We turned off our engines and listened. A guard approached us and spoke – in Russian! So off we went.

We drove through the village and out of its southern edge. There were a few Russians on the edge of the road, and then just the country lane. After 5km we came to the next village. Once more we drove in and turned off our engines. Once more a curious guard approached, but this time he was a German. I was taken to the battalion command post and told an astonished major that the Russians were in the next village. Alert! Foot patrols were dispatched. A motorcyclist joined us and led my scouting party and me 15km [nine miles] further to the headquarters of 17th Panzer Division.

At 0130 on 2 September I stood before the commander of 17th Panzer Division, who was wearing the Knight's Cross with Oak Leaves and Crossed Swords. A handshake: 'Take a seat, *Kamerad*!' and a slug from a bottle of three-star Cognac. Then I gave him my news. As his division had only arrived here a couple of hours ago, he didn't know any of it.

So I was given a new task: to return to 16th Panzergrenadier Division with a letter that included a proposal for a combined attack at dawn, and to do this while it was still dark.

I headed north at 0330 along the direct road, which was only 20km [12 miles]. A wide road, in a pitch-black night, one vehicle close behind the other. There – in front of us, a tank – was it German or Russian? Was it a wreck? We drove past it on the left. After 2km another tank – once more we drove past! Our nerves were stretched tight. Then – without coming under fire – we were at the crossroads where the German attack was to commence the following morning. So we turned right to drive the last 2km to Michailovka. It was so dark that I couldn't see my hand in front of my face. The terrain passed on either side. Woods and bushes, as marked on the map. Then my armoured car tilted to the left, the turret swung in the same direction and we rolled over and our gun embedded itself in the earth! We had wandered into the roadside ditch. We didn't think we could recover it ourselves. So we continued on foot intending to return with a tractor from 60th Panzergrenadier Regiment. When I reached Mikhailovka, I could see that several houses were ablaze, the bridge had been blown, and a few civilians were running here and there trying to save what they could. No Germans were to be seen. What had happened here? Back to the scouting party! We harnessed the second vehicle, everyone climbed out, both engines roared – a jolt, a crack, the towing cable broke, but the vehicle was once more on its wheels.

I led the armoured cars on foot and eventually reached open ground, roughly where we had been shot at by aircraft the previous day. About 8km [five miles] further, we stumbled upon a column of horse-drawn wagons in the darkness. I crept forward again – and – thank God, they were Germans. We drove past and tried to find 60th Panzergrenadier Regiment, but couldn't do so. I then passed the contents of the letter to division headquarters by radio, and we finally got some sleep.[18]

Moser must have been mistaken regarding the decorations worn by the commander of 17th Panzer Division. The previous commander of the division, Generalleutnant Walter Schilling, had been killed in fighting near Izyum on 20 July, and his replacement was Generalleutnant Karl-Friedrich von der Meden; whilst serving as commander of 12th Infantry Division's reconnaissance battalion in August 1941, he was awarded the Knight's Cross, but had not been awarded the prestigious oak leaves or even rarer crossed swords. The proposed counterattack proved impossible to organise, and 16th Panzergrenadier Division spent 2 September improving its defensive positions in anticipation of further Soviet attacks.

The city of Lysychansk had been under German occupation since late 1941. It was one of the centres of coal mining that Hitler had been so determined to control, and when they liberated the city the soldiers of Third Guards Army came across further evidence of the manner in which the German occupiers had treated the local population. Local residents informed them that over 8,000 people had been herded to a local ravine shortly after the occupation began and executed there. Others had been taken back to Germany as forced labour.[19] There was little time to pause and dwell on such matters and Third Guards Army continued its advance, widening its bridgehead to the south throughout 2 September before pushing west. By the end of 3 September, Lelyushenko's leading troops had advanced about 18 miles (30km) in just one day. They were now about 33 miles (55km) to the east and northeast of Stalino – now Donetsk – and at the same time Southern Front's troops had fought their way across the Yelanchik River and were close to Amvrosievka, about 24 miles (40km) southeast of Stalino. Vasilevsky somewhat belatedly ordered Southwest Front to divert I Guards Mechanised Corps and XXIII Tank Corps from the Izyum-Slavyansk sector to Lelyushenko's army, which was to use them to bypass the northern edge of Stalino. At the same time, Southern Front's XI and XX Tank Corps and V Guards Cavalry Corps would advance past the southern outskirts; the two forces would then converge and trap any German troops that were in Stalino itself.[20]

In an attempt to hurry his troops forward, Lelyushenko had left his headquarters and created an improvised mobile command post. Vasilevsky spent much of 4 September trying to locate him, finally meeting up with him the following day; whilst he commended the commander of Third Guards Army for showing such personal energy, Vasilevsky was rather more critical of the manner in which Lelyushenko had allowed himself to be drawn into the minutiae of local battles and in the process had somewhat lost control of other elements of his army.[21] The two men rapidly drew up plans for how the new armoured forces transferred to Third Guards Army would be used: Lieutenant General Ivan Nikitich Russianov's I Guards Mechanised Corps was to advance towards Pavlograd, thus outflanking the stubborn defences that had held up attempts to advance between Izyum and Slavyansk, while Lieutenant General Efim Grigorevich Pushkin's XXIII Tank Corps advanced through Krasnoarmeisk (now Pokrovsk), somewhat closer to Stalino. Pushkin would then direct units towards the south, in order to link up with Southern Front's leading formations.

On 6 September, Lelyushenko unleashed his armoured reinforcements, and both corps made rapid progress, effectively dislocating the German defences along the 'Tortoise Line', which was intended to run along the valley of the

Kalmius River – in reality, it existed more on maps than on the ground. Within a day, the Soviet armour penetrated 30 miles (50km) beyond the German lines. As they approached Pavlograd, the spearheads were only 30 miles from the Dnepr, but with their infantry and artillery support struggling to keep up, the Soviet tanks were forced to pause for breath.

At the same time, Southern Front's leading units also continued their advance and rapidly approached Stalino. Kobylyanskiy was with the troops who marched towards the city on the first day of the renewed attack:

Just before retreating from Stalino, German special incendiary commandos had set hundreds of houses on fire, most in the central part of the city. There was a terrible illumination when our troops passed through the streets. There were hundreds and hundreds of residents standing alongside the road and heartily greeting us. I'll never forget an elderly, grey-haired man who continuously crossed himself and made low bows to us.

... The next morning, as we were already leaving the city, a group of local inhabitants stood by the road and greeted us. Unexpectedly, an old and absolutely scraggy man left the group and approached the battery column. He hadn't shaved for a long time and was wearing some dirty, cast-off clothes. The man drew up to our wagons and said in a low, sad voice, 'Lieutenant Brechko, I'm your blacksmith, Suchkov,' and began to cry. It was hard to recognise Alexei [who had been left behind in a hasty withdrawal a few months earlier] ... Later, Suchkov shared with us his terrible experience. The Germans had found him in the cowshed and had taken him prisoner. For almost five months he was kept in a prisoner-of-war camp. In mid-July the panic-stricken guards suddenly left the camp, and all the prisoners scattered ... Since then Suchkov had been a fugitive. Without any identity papers, he had been experiencing another terrible time. Constantly afraid to bump into a policeman, he was suffering from fear and starvation.[22]

Suchkov was wise to be cautious. Kobylyanskiy and his comrades took good care of their comrade and he took up his former role without attracting the attention of the ever-suspicious Soviet authorities.

Despite the best efforts of Vasilevsky and Lelyushenko, the plan to trap German forces in Stalino failed, not least when a battlegroup from 16th Panzergrenadier Division, led by Hauptmann Helmut Zander, engaged Colonel Fyodor Vasilyevich Chervyakov's I Guards Mechanised Corps in running battles to the north of the city. The Soviet units had swiftly gained control of Druzhkovka, but their attempts to accelerate the advance were repeatedly thwarted by skilful counterattacks from

Zander's group and a continuing shortage of infantry, artillery and most of all ammunition, but the resources available to Zander were limited – just a couple of panzer companies with supporting units – and it was always possible for Soviet columns to bypass him while he was engaged in battle. A little to the south, the Soviet XXIII Tank Corps had captured Kostantinovna on 1 September in bitter fighting that cost the lives of two Soviet battalion commanders from 135th Tank Brigade. The battle was only decided when the third battalion moved to cut off the lines of retreat towards the west from Konstantinovka, triggering an immediate German withdrawal. As the second week of September began, Lelyushenko's two armoured formations – I Guards Mechanised Corps and XXIII Tank Corps – finally began to accelerate their advance as they fought their way clear of the German units that had doggedly held them back.

Hollidt's Sixth Army was soon to be subordinated to Field Marshal Ewald von Kleist's Army Group A, which currently controlled Seventeenth Army in the Crimea, but for the moment Hollidt consistently followed the instructions issued by Manstein: there was to be no pointless defence of positions that could not be held without risk of encirclement and annihilation. At the outset of the new Soviet offensive, the advancing Soviet forces briefly isolated parts of Brandenberger's XXIX Corps on the coast of the Sea of Azov in and around Taganrog at the end of August. The trapped formations were mainly from 111th Infantry Division commanded by General Hermann Recknagel, but as a consequence of casualties suffered and inadequate replacements, the division amounted to little more than a battlegroup. As soon as he realised that he had been cut off, Recknagel ordered his men to abandon the town and fight their way through to the west. Fortunately for the Germans, they had been surrounded by units of IV Guards Cavalry Corps, a highly mobile unit but one that lacked the infantry strength to establish a secure perimeter around the encirclement. Most of the Germans managed to escape, but the fighting strength of the division was further reduced by the loss of heavy equipment. However, this proved to be an isolated incident, with most units pulling back before they could be encircled, but the only manner in which it was possible to achieve this was by constantly conceding ground.

After his adventurous journey to locate 17th Panzer Division, Eduard Moser was once more in action, seeing first hand how neither side was inclined to show any quarter:

We rolled east until suddenly we heard terrific firing near the town of Losovaya. We approached the town and stopped by an armoured vehicle where our battalion officer and his drivers were lying in a trench; they told us that the Russians had penetrated into the town along the railway line. We drove to within 300m of the railway line and opened fire. Soon we had shot up three Soviet trucks, which resulted in our supply officer giving us a bottle of Cognac. Now, the Russians tried to pull back, unsettled by our firing in their rear. I then drove on to the railway embankment and we were able to cause some confusion in the rear of the Russians. Then, when an assault gun from 9th Panzer Division, coming directly from the workshops, drove up to join us, we crossed the embankment and moved further forward. In the meantime, the Russians had cleared the field hospital in Losovaya, throwing the wounded from the windows and raping a nurse. Now they attempted to pull back past us. After an exchange of fire that lasted two hours we cleared the area and drove the last Russians into a gully from which they were later forced out. We captured two trucks, one towing a 76.2mm anti-tank gun, for the battalion and then pulled back to the division's workshops. In the trucks were food supplies from German supply dumps, and we had an enjoyable couple of hours.[23]

Lelyushenko's armoured forces had now finally overcome the German defences to the north and northwest of Stalino and advanced swiftly towards Pavlograd. By doing so, they threatened to break into the rear of First Panzer Army and Eighth Army to the north, and Sixth Army to the south. To make matters worse for Manstein, additional crises were developing further north. After their brief pause to bring forward reinforcements and supplies, the Soviet forces facing Fourth Panzer Army and Eighth Army were once more ready to resume their advance, and here the situation was almost the reverse of that faced by Hollidt's Sixth Army and Mackensen's First Panzer Army. From the shores of the Sea of Azov to the middle Donets, the German line was held mainly by infantry divisions with a few under-strength armoured formations supporting them; Fourth Panzer Army, by contrast, had a large number of panzer and panzergrenadier divisions, but few infantry formations, and those that were available were badly degraded and likely to collapse at the first serious setback. Consequently, most of the precious panzer divisions had to remain in the front line, holding extended sectors. This deprived them of one of their greatest assets: the ability to function as a mobile whole, blocking Soviet penetrations and destroying them in determined counterattacks. Their prolonged use in the front line placed them at a severe disadvantage as they lacked the infantry resources for such combat and on the occasions that they were extracted from the front line, they were too badly weakened to function as they had in the past. On 26 August, a crisis a little further north developed when Rokossovsky's Central Front unleashed an offensive against the southern flank of Army Group Centre with two Soviet armies. One of the attacks was bloodily brought to a halt, but the other broke through. Immediately, Rokossovsky committed Second Tank Army, his main reserve, and within a day a gap of 60 miles (100km) opened between Army Group Centre and Army Group South. The forces of Second Tank Army surged ahead almost unopposed, rapidly covering 108 miles (180km) and seizing crossings over the Desna River. Once again, Army Group South was faced with the prospect of being compressed against the coast of the Black Sea and the Sea of Azov.[24]

The fighting on the sector held by *SS-Totenkopf* continued throughout this period with only a modest reduction in intensity, and the division's resources became ever more badly stretched. Whilst both sides frequently shot enemy soldiers who had surrendered, many men were taken prisoner, even if only so that they could be interrogated. Occasionally, this led to adventurous attempts to escape, as a tank crewman in *SS-Totenkopf* described:

> In the fading light we saw a face in the sunflower field, a figure staggering towards us, a Soviet rifle with fixed bayonet slung over his shoulder. From his uniform we realised he was one of our comrades. We jumped out of the tank and ran up to him. When he reached us, he collapsed. We carried him to the tank and recognised him as Unterscharführer Fritz Sauer from 7th Company. His face was completely swollen and his front teeth were missing. We gave him something to drink. Slowly he rallied and told us: 'We had driven into a sunflower field with our company. The Russians who were dug in there threw a Molotov cocktail at my tank. The vehicle immediately went up in flames. We bailed out. The Russians promptly shot my comrades. They took me prisoner and took me to Michailovka. There they beat me and interrogated me. When Stukas attacked the village, I managed to get away.'[25]

Throughout this period, the heaviest Soviet attacks on *SS-Totenkopf* were directed at its flanks. At first the greatest pressure was on the left flank, where a substantial stretch of ground to the neighbouring 7th Panzer Division was held by the thinnest of lines. The division's reconnaissance battalion was hastily dispatched to the sector to reinforce the line, but the other flank of *SS-Totenkopf* was also under attack and in need of support. To make matters worse, the ground immediately behind the division was swampy with only one good road and bridge running across it. By the end of 28 August, the seam with 7th Panzer Division had been forced open and an attempt to restore the line with a counterattack by the *SS-Totenkopf* reconnaissance battalion and two tank companies failed; the best that could be achieved was to bring the enemy to a halt. During the night, the division organised some improvised combat teams from rear area units – its fighting units were all fully committed – and attempted a new counterattack early on 29 August. A key hill was recovered, but the German units were too weak to retain it and were forced to pull back to their start line. Throughout 30 August, there were repeated attacks by Soviet troops but all were beaten off; the cost was high, and by the end of the day *SS-Totenkopf* was forced to disband two of its battalions. Even if the SS division continued to hold, it was now in danger of being outflanked – on 31 August, its right hand neighbour, 223rd Infantry Division, was driven back with further heavy losses. By the end of the day, *SS-Totenkopf* reported that it was nearly 9,000 men below its establishment strength of 22,000 and of its intended strength of 182 tanks and assault guns, it could field only 48.[26] An armoured counterattack on the first day of September partly restored the situation on the division's right flank, but pressure remained everywhere along its extended front. The remaining ten tanks of the panzer regiment's I Battalion took up positions near the ruins of Kotelevka, a scene of bitter fighting for several days:

Suddenly the [Soviet] artillery fire eased. Then it stopped entirely. In the distance, either side of the high ground, we heard the deep growl of Russian tank engines. It seemed as if an entire tank armada was approaching. A little later the first armoured colossi appeared on the hill, whose highest point was about 1,000m from us. A radio order from Säumenicht warned us only to open fire when ordered. 'We'll let them come close to us!' we heard in our headphones. More and more enemy tanks appeared over the hill by the second. We counted ten, 20, 40, then we stopped counting. They approached us at speed. They seemed not to be aware of our positions. The massive enemy appeared about to crush us. Now the tanks were 500m away and still there was no fire order from Säumenicht. The tension increased steadily. This was the moment to hold our nerve. Then came the commander's voice: '*Lily* [the commander's radio callsign] to all: armour piercing rounds, free to fire!' Iron against iron, steel against steel, tank against tank! The first T-34s were blown into the air. Our bombardment was so sudden that before the Russians could return fire, 20 T-34s were already burning in front of our lines … all the foreground was covered with dust and smoke that obscured our sight. Whenever gaps appeared in the smoke cloud, we opened fire again. But now the Russians had rallied and joined in. A few of our tanks were hit and knocked out.

However, we enjoyed tactical superiority. More Russian tanks went up in flames. The tank battle lasted about an hour. Then suddenly there was silence. The clouds of smoke from the burning Russian tanks cleared. It was almost unbelievable. Before us on the landscape lay about 40 destroyed enemy tanks. Those who escaped from them fled back over the hill.[27]

Bitter fighting raged all along the front line held by *SS-Totenkopf* but, for the moment, the German division held firm. Nevertheless, casualties were steadily rising and the division's artillery regiment was running short of ammunition. Having driven back 223rd Infantry Division, the Soviet troops now began to infiltrate into the SS division's rear areas, and the ad hoc combat units improvised

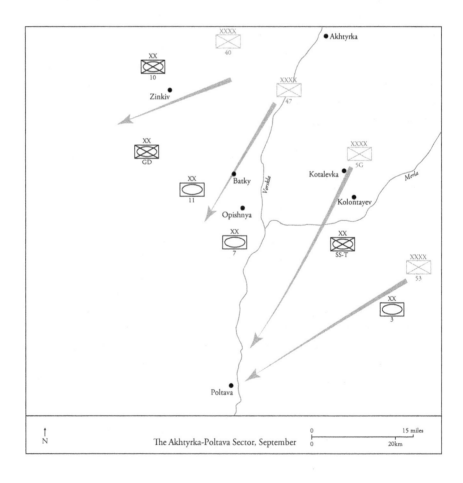

The Akhtyrka-Poltava Sector, September

from the rear area units dealt with the threat – whilst this was effective, it disrupted the activity of the rear area units, worsening the supply situation. Replacement drafts had been arriving in a trickle over the preceding days, but they had added nearly 2,000 men to the division's combat strength and were immediately sent into action as they arrived.

By 5 September, the position in the sector held by *SS-Totenkopf* was critical. The attacking Soviet forces had succeeded in taking the village of Slobodka on the division's eastern flank the previous day, and everything depended upon a counterattack by the division's reconnaissance battalion. The attack got off to a bad start when the battalion commander, Obersturmführer Quirin Fürter, was badly wounded; he had been leading the battalion for barely two weeks following the death of the unit's previous commander, Sturmbannführer Heinrich Krauth. Nevertheless, by the end of the day most of Slobodka was back in German hands, but attempts to complete the operation by clearing Soviet troops from the woodland to the west of the village were abandoned after heavy casualties. The failure of this attack left 3rd Panzer Division, now operating on the right flank of *SS-Totenkopf* after the retreat of 223rd Infantry Division, badly exposed. The losses suffered by 3rd Panzer Division in the fighting around Kharkov had been substantial, and the division was further weakened by the absence of one of its panzer battalions, which had been sent to France earlier in the year to be equipped with Panther tanks; it was destined never to rejoin its parent division, and was later incorporated into the new *Panzer Lehr* division. In its absence, 3rd Panzer Division used an armoured battlegroup equipped largely with Pz.IV tanks, shuttling this unit from one critical point to another to launch sharp, limited counterattacks against the Soviet forces that constantly pressed forward. Inevitably, losses of vehicles left the group badly weakened, but the division made a virtue out of necessity, switching tired tank crews with men who had previously lost their vehicles and thus giving the crews a much-needed opportunity to get a day or two of comparative rest in the rear areas of the division.

SS-Totenkopf had largely held firm for the first week of September, but its strength was rapidly diminishing; during this period it recorded the loss of a further 976 officers and men, with the majority of losses being caused by mortar and artillery fire.[28] The soldiers in the front line were increasingly exhausted but continued to beat off the Soviet attacks, as a non-commissioned officer in the division's panzer regiment recorded in his diary:

> The Russians attack again and again. There are often several attacks within a few hours. They penetrate into our infantry positions during the night. We are

constantly under way with our few tanks and are deployed in one sector after another. We now know the terrain around the *Kolkhoz* so well that we can engage the Soviet spearheads without being seen. Unterscharführer Hauler was killed in a counterattack. The tally of tank commanders and crews grows ever smaller. It is also steadily more difficult to bring forward supplies. The rear area is under constant artillery fire. The day is coming when we will have to give up Kolontayev and the swamp behind us.[29]

With the seam between Army Group Centre and Army Group South forced by the Soviet advance along the Sejm River, it became impossible to contemplate holding a defensive line to the east of the Dnepr. Although Hitler had belatedly ordered the construction of the *Ostwall* fortifications needed to turn the formidable obstacle of the Dnepr into an impregnable one, it would take several weeks for work to be completed, and it was essential to prevent the Red Army reaching the river for as long as possible. On 9 September, orders were issued for the abandonment of the existing front line; the following day, Eighth Army reported that it had lost contact with First Panzer Army to its south, with substantial Soviet forces penetrating between the two German commands. It would not be until 15 September – nearly a week after the retreat had already begun – that Hitler gave definitive permission for the withdrawal of Army Group South to the line of the Dnepr, with bridgeheads to be held on the east bank around Nikopol and Zaporozhye. As they pulled out of the positions they had defended at such a high cost, the soldiers of *SS-Totenkopf* looked back at the past few days:

> Now came the withdrawal from Kolontayev and the 'three bridges' and our fallen comrades. The fighting on the Merla had also resulted in marked losses for the heavy [artillery] battalion. Following the departure of numerous wounded men, its combat strength was reduced. The commander of 11th [Battery], Hauptsturmführer Kriebich, had left as a result of wounds …
>
> … During the night the regiment moved out. I could have wept when I looked across the fertile land that we had bought with our blood. Now it had to be given back to the enemy.[30]

The retreating Germans were ordered to do all they could to hinder the Soviet pursuit, but their ability to do this was often very limited. Oberscharführer Paul Schmidt, a platoon commander in the pioneer battalion of *SS-Totenkopf* who had been ordered to prepare the bridges near Kolontayev for destruction, recorded:

The grenadiers had already pulled back … I had been tasked with remaining in position until midday and holding off the Russians with harassment fire. In front of us on either side of the river the landscape was flat and then ascended gradually. We could see every enemy approach very clearly. Soon the Russians appeared on the heights, at first in a skirmish line, then lines of riflemen, followed by platoons and companies. We watched the enemy batteries going into position. I asked the forward artillery observer who had been assigned to us: 'Why aren't you firing? Surely you've never seen such worthwhile targets!' He replied, 'I have only ten shots available and can only use them in the most extreme emergency.'[31]

In heavy rain, *SS-Totenkopf* began its withdrawal towards the Dnepr, taking up new positions which the division was ordered to hold for at least a day before continuing the retreat. Many of the division's damaged tanks had been dispatched to the rear, leaving the companies in the front line desperately weak:

Now and again a repaired tank came forward to reinforce our battlegroup, but usually just for a few hours before a couple more broke down. The companies were scattered, with no company having more than two or three tanks in any location … All day we had been stuck in the woods to the west of the swamp, defending against one Soviet attack after another. The more we beat off, the more the Russians sent against us. All day we were unable to leave the tank as our front line was only 50m from the enemy. Our infantry cowered in foxholes next to us. They stood knee deep in water. When we suddenly had to move out to clear an enemy penetration, they stared after us with downcast expressions.[32]

Despite the best efforts of the pursuing Soviet forces, the Germans were able to conduct a generally orderly withdrawal, contesting positions when they could and successfully preventing Soviet breakthroughs that would have turned the withdrawal into a rout or might have threatened encirclement. Wöhler, the commander of Eighth Army, in which *SS-Totenkopf* was currently operating, issued clear orders on the ongoing withdrawal late on 14 September:

The tempo of the withdrawal is to be determined solely by the need to preserve the combat power of the troops. Where it is possible to allow the enemy to be engaged so that his strike power can be weakened without endangering the entire operation, this may be attempted.[33]

Another division to lose a battalion for re-equipment was 7th Panzer Division, deployed to the west of *SS-Totenkopf.* Unlike 3rd Panzer Division, it would ultimately be reunited with its new Panther battalion, though not until July 1944. By contrast, Soviet tank units simply received a stream of replacement T-34s to make good their losses; if a unit required major re-equipment, the Red Army had sufficient resources that it was able to pull a complete tank corps out of the front line, rather than leaving it weakened. The Wehrmacht might have been able to do this in earlier phases of the war, but the demands on its resources were now so serious that it was almost impossible to consider such a policy. Despite losing half their tank strength while troops underwent training with the new Panther tank, the hard-pressed panzer divisions had to remain in the front line. For the first third of September, 7th Panzer Division was in constant action, defending the Vorskla valley; like the other armoured formations fighting to hold back the Red Army, it was generally successful, but it paid a steadily increasing price in terms of irreplaceable losses.

After forming the main component of Fourth Panzer Army's attack towards the southeast in late August, *Grossdeutschland* was pulled out of the front line late on 26 August. The tired personnel enjoyed 24 hours of rest to the north of Poltava before they were alerted for deployment in the previous sector of operations. On 28 August, *Grossdeutschland* marched north to take up positions to the west of Akhtyrka between 10th Panzergrenadier Division and 34th Infantry Division to mount a counterattack, which gained a modest amount of ground before coming to a standstill in the face of heavy Soviet artillery fire. The three divisions were pulled back to a new line as the Red Army pressed ever closer to Zinkiv and *Grossdeutschland* was ordered to launch a new counterattack towards the northwest on 1 September; after two days of heavy fighting, the bulk of the division handed over control of the threatened sector to 112th Infantry Division and pulled back closer to Poltava, only to be ordered back to Zinkiv a day later to drive back Soviet units that had captured the town. No sooner was this mission accomplished than news arrived of another Soviet penetration, this time to the southeast at Batky, just north of Opishnya. This sector was defended by 11th Panzer Division, which had been forced to remain in the front line due to the lack of infantry divisions that could relieve it. Bitter fighting followed, with further heavy losses – some of the infantry companies of the panzergrenadier regiments of *Grossdeutschland* were down to no more than a dozen men. By the second week of September, Opishnya was in the front line and despite repeated counterattacks by the few remaining tanks of *Grossdeutschland*, had to be abandoned. A company commander from the division's Panzergrenadier

Regiment – the two infantry regiments of *Grossdeutschland* were named the Panzergrenadier Regiment and the Panzerfusilier Regiment – described the fighting towards the end of 12 September:

> The forward observer [of the division's artillery regiment] had contacted the rocket launcher [battery] and with their help I successfully repulsed the last enemy assault of this day. Finally it became dark. A patrol returned: the Russians were behind us again in the cornfield. This meant we had to be careful, and I set up an all-round position as a precaution.
>
> Later our Kübel[wagen] eventually appeared with the food and rations. Wolter was standing right beside me and we talked about the general situation. Then suddenly, a shower of Soviet mortar shells landed directly behind the Kübel. Those who had been hit cried out. There was no medic there, but Sturm immediately set about tending to the wounded. I was completely shattered. They all lay there – dead, wounded – all my good men! I ran from man to man like a hunted wild animal. The Kübel was finished, completely wrecked, and there were no vehicles to be had.
>
> Finally, finally, I obtained an armoured personnel carrier from Stöwer. Four of the wounded had already walked to the rear. We loaded Röhr, Rumey and Wurm into the APC. The latter cried out continually: 'Herr Leutnant! I'm dying, I'm dying!' Finally, after they were all gone, I was able to calm myself somewhat …
>
> I ascertained that after this loss I was left with a total of eight men, including those from the elements placed under my command. My entire company headquarters squad was gone; they'd all been killed.[34]

The entire regiment barely amounted to a single company: the following day, it reported that the combined strength of its two battalions amounted to just six officers and 51 men.

The Soviet Seventh Guards Army had been battering at the defences of Merefa, to the southwest of Kharkov, since the end of August, and finally secured the town on 5 September. Just as Lelyushenko's successful attack had turned the southern flank of the German defences between Izyum and Slavyansk, the fall of Merefa exposed the northern flank and made any prolonged defence of the Donets impossible. Similarly, the German defences further west were also outflanked and could not be held indefinitely. Immediately to the south of Merefa was the town of Taranovka, where 6th Panzer Division had been involved in bitter fighting the previous winter; it was once more fighting for the town, defending it against repeated Soviet attacks. As was the case with all the German units in the area, its losses climbed steadily and in the second week of September the division's war diary reported:

> In the heavy fighting of recent days, the formations deployed in Taranovka in particular have suffered heavy losses from artillery and mortar fire, and the three combat companies of 57th Panzer Pioneer Battalion have been so badly affected that the remnants, amounting to 25 men, had to be grouped together in a platoon and deployed with 4th Panzergrenadier Regiment. This leaves only the light pioneer column, bridging column and the combed-out troops from the rear units. The troops deployed in Taranovka remain tied down in heavy defensive fighting. At the moment, the division's tanks have been dispatched south to give relief.
>
> A staff company from 335th Infantry Division holding a sector between 114th Panzergrenadier Regiment and 57th Panzer Pioneer Battalion were still holding firm during the afternoon. Elements of the staff of 6th Panzer Division have been tasked with closing the gap [to the south of Taranovka]. The remaining elements of 4th Panzergrenadier Regiment are assembling in the nearby woodland. Three tanks remain operational.[35]

In order to allow Vatutin's Voronezh Front to advance on a more westerly axis than before, the Soviet attacks towards Poltava were now under the control of Konev's Steppe Front. Further to the west, Moskalenko's Fortieth Army had received welcome reinforcements in the shape of Getman's VI Tank Corps. Like all the units on both sides that had been in almost continuous action since the beginning of the *Zitadelle* offensive, VI Tank Corps was badly below establishment strength, with only 20 T-34s and 32 T-70s, but Moskalenko was nevertheless grateful for the additional strike power.[36] After a brief pause, Fortieth Army renewed the pressure it was applying on the German lines on 9 September and immediately enjoyed rather more success than it had in the tough, attritional fighting of the first week of the month, pushing on to the Sula River with its western flank. On Moskalenko's other flank, there was also encouraging progress as his XLVII Rifle Corps drove back the German 10th Panzergrenadier Division, gaining perhaps eight or nine miles (14km) by 13 September. These advances put the leading elements of Fortieth Army about 42 miles (70km) from the Dnepr and also created a gap in the lines of Fourth Panzer Army, with Hoth's western units falling back towards the Dnepr to the southeast of Kiev, while the eastern part of the army withdrew on a diverging axis inclined further to the south. To make matters worse, a further Soviet breakthrough at Lebedyn – to the southwest of Sumy – broke the eastern part of Fourth Panzer Army in two.

This was the sort of development that Manstein had feared. Hoth now had little control over his formations and his entire army was in danger of being destroyed piecemeal. All he could do was establish a garrison at Nizhyn, astride the road along which the Red Army was advancing towards Kiev, and when news arrived in Hitler's headquarters that this force had been driven back on 15 September, there was near-panic. Despite the heavy losses it had suffered as a consequence of Stalin's decision to launch a frontal assault towards the Dnepr without pausing to regroup, the Red Army was now close not only to reaching the key river but also potentially in a position to trap many of the retreating German formations before they could reach its safety.

Almost as quickly as the prospect of a substantial victory opened before Moskalenko, it disappeared as the Germans continued to contest every major town. Lokhovitsa, in front of Moskalenko's eastern wing, became the scene of bitter fighting as remnants of four German infantry divisions took up defensive positions in and around the town. The fighting that followed was bloody and frustrating, with substantial losses on both sides – but it was increasingly clear that the Red Army was paying a heavy price for Stalin's insistence on an immediate drive to the Dnepr without a pause to regroup and bring up reinforcements. Regardless of their losses, the Soviet troops pressed on, exhorted by Vatutin with the words 'They are burning our bread, we must attack!'[37]

Like all German divisions involved in the fighting, 10th Panzergrenadier Division was close to collapse. Throughout September, the division rarely had more than two assault guns and two heavy self-propelled anti-tank guns available. By the end of the month, the division's two grenadier regiments had only eight officers between them.[38] Morale was collapsing, with some soldiers openly saying that fighting on the Eastern Front meant certain death. Ten men were sentenced to death for cowardice, and Eighth Army headquarters issued orders for ten men who were presumed to have wounded themselves to be investigated. Following these measures, dissent within the division became less pronounced; whether this was due to fewer such cases or fewer cases being reported to higher authorities is impossible to determine. Other units in Fourth Panzer Army and Eighth Army began to show signs that morale was rapidly deteriorating – Hoth and Wöhler repeatedly found that in addition to struggling with inadequate resources, their problems were worsened by the unwillingness and inability of German infantry to put up any prolonged resistance when they came under pressure, particularly by tank formations. The only consolation for senior German commanders was that the Red Army's tank forces needed good roads both for their movement and critically for their supply services, and it was thus possible for the Germans to concentrate their very limited anti-armour resources to cover these roads. Whenever rain turned the non-metalled roads to mud, the Soviet advance slowed, giving the retreating German troops a welcome respite.

As they fought their way forward, Moskalenko's troops found more evidence of the manner in which the Germans had behaved during their two years of occupation of the region. After the recapture of the town of Gadyach, Moskalenko visited the location, much of which had been left in ruins:

> Here, on Zamkova Street, in the buildings of an agricultural school, the German Fascist command had established a torture chamber in which Hitler's executioners daily killed dozens of innocent people. Whoever was sent to this camp did not leave alive. With anguished hearts, we read the inscriptions left on the wall of Cell 20 by the captured Soviet soldier Sandro Chaturia: 'They beat me again, they beat me endlessly, I am exhausted. I feel like I am dying. I never thought that you could feel the approach of death in your heart. Well, this is the end. Farewell, comrades. Sandro did not disappoint you and did not betray anyone.'[39]

It is doubtful that an ordinary soldier would have known anything that would have been of sufficient importance for him to be beaten repeatedly in an attempt to extract the information; it is possible that he had been fighting with the partisans, or that this entry is to some extent exaggerated by Moskalenko for dramatic effect. Nevertheless, there were undoubtedly many atrocities uncovered by the advancing Red Army – civilians told Moskalenko's men in the town of Chornukhy, halfway between Gadyach and the Dnepr, that about 500 people had been marched away as forced labourers and another 700 had been executed and thrown into a common grave. Such a mass killing is likely to have been of Jews, but in keeping with Soviet historiography, Moskalenko makes no mention of the ethnicity of the victims.

However, the Red Army was far from blameless when it came to atrocities. During the fighting in the Crimea in 1942, Soviet troops surprised the Germans with an amphibious counterattack and found themselves fighting close to a building used by the Germans as a hospital that had not been evacuated, as a Red Army veteran later recalled:

> A group of about 50 marines were advancing quickly along Lenin Avenue. The Germans opened fire on them from the windows of the Stamboli dacha. The marines took off their packs and stacked them against the wall, and broke into the hospital by climbing onto them. They reached the second floor [first floor in

British parlance] fairly quickly but got stuck on the next floor. The Germans had barricaded themselves in and continued firing back. Infuriated by the resistance, the marines began killing the [German] wounded. I'll be honest with you – they threw many of them from the windows together with their beds ... They finished their business on the third floor too. In short, they shot them all – a heap of corpses was piled near the sea. Then the marines tackled the Romanian gun crews near the stone bridge across the railroad where a pair of small-calibre anti-aircraft guns had been positioned ... One clever Romanian who had fought for the Germans jumped from a window and landed on a pile of corpses. He was lying on the heap, raising his head from time to time, perhaps waiting for the right moment to try to escape. A marine came up to me, handed me a captured German rifle, and said: 'Listen, kid, why don't you shoot that Romanian? Look at what he's doing, pretending to be dead! He's still alive.'

I took the rifle from him, chambered a round and stopped, looking at the marine's belt buckle with an anchor engraved on it. 'But this is terrible!' I protested.

He smiled. 'Come on, don't mess about, kill him! He wouldn't spare you!'

I aimed at the head in the sheepskin hat and smoothly pulled the trigger – bang! I felt the recoil into my shoulder.[40]

Hitler visited Manstein in Zaporozhye on 8 September in what would prove to be the Führer's last visit to the Ukraine. Kleist, commander of Army Group A, was also summoned to the meeting, as was General Richard Ruoff, who had until recently been commander of Seventeenth Army. The relationship between Hitler and Manstein had never been warm; it was now decidedly icy with a veneer of politeness. In the safety of his headquarters in Rastenburg, Hitler increasingly tolerated his subordinates referring to Manstein as '*Feldmarschall Rückwärts*' ('Field Marshal Backwards') and mocked the messages from Manstein and others:

My generals only wish to manoeuvre rearwards: so much for their renowned operational art.[41]

As for Manstein's constant demands for troops, Hitler commented to his entourage that Manstein wanted them purely so that he could carry out more operational manoeuvres in order to enhance his personal fame.[42] He also repeatedly complained that when he did permit retreats, the benefits that his generals had promised from such withdrawals (such as freeing up troops) almost never appeared; this conveniently ignored the fact that Hitler's prevarication and delay in agreeing withdrawals greatly reduced their value. Nevertheless, by the end of the month Hitler commented to Goebbels that the withdrawals that had been authorised would shorten the front line by 200 miles (350km), releasing 34 divisions which could then be used as a mobile reserve.[43] These figures were largely figments of his imagination – the new front line might be shorter than before, but not by such a large margin. Nor would this result in liberating anywhere near as many divisions as Hitler now confided to his propaganda minister.

Manstein's pressing concern was the state of his northern flank, where the gap to Army Group Centre was covered by what remained of two divisions. With his armoured assets already committed, Manstein told Hitler that the only way that the gap could be closed was by an energetic attack from Army Group Centre towards the south; Kluge should withdraw to the upper Dnepr in order to shorten his front and thus release sufficient troops for such an operation. Neither Hitler nor Kluge were enthusiastic about such a proposal and claimed that such a withdrawal at short notice, on the eve of the autumn rainy season which would turn many of the region's roads to mud, was impossible. The previous year, Hitler had ordered all armies to hold larger stockpiles of food and ammunition closer to the front line in order to try to reduce the strain upon supply lines in the event of new crises, but these stockpiles would now be lost in a rapid retreat. Nevertheless, at Zeitzler's suggestion, Hitler agreed that Army Group Centre should assemble two panzer divisions and two infantry divisions in a new corps on its southern flank and use this force to close the gap with Fourth Panzer Army's northern flank. He also promised Manstein additional infantry divisions which could be used to reinforce the line of the Dnepr. Knowing Hitler's tendency to countermand such agreements after the end of the meeting or to prevaricate about implementing them, Manstein wanted the relevant orders to be issued before Hitler and his entourage left Zaporozhye, but this proved to be impossible. Manstein's fears proved to be well founded; the four divisions he had been promised as reinforcements for the Dnepr line did not appear, and the planned creation of a new panzer corps on Army Group Centre's southern flank was delayed repeatedly.

When he became aware of Hitler's failure to implement what had been agreed, Manstein contacted Zeitzler and asked him to inform Hitler that, in these circumstances, he could not guarantee the safety of the Dnepr line and that it was possible that the Red Army might break through the lines of his retreating formations and reach the river first, either seizing the vital crossing points and thus isolating large parts of Army Group South or securing bridgeheads on the west bank. The record of the telephone conversation shows both Manstein's growing frustration, and his awareness of Zeitzler's lack of any real authority. One division that had been sent to Manstein from Army Group Centre lacked an entire regiment, and one of the promised panzer divisions had just two operational tanks and 300 panzergrenadiers. Zeitzler replied that he had spoken to Fromm and Olbricht about securing larger numbers of replacement troops, but Field Marshal Wilhelm Keitel, head of *OKW*, vetoed the proposal. Manstein's response was both accurate and hurtful. It is an example of why so many of his peers found him a difficult personality:

> Manstein: Can you box?
> Zeitzler: Unfortunately not.
> Manstein: But do you understand anything about boxing? Do you know what a
> punch-ball is?
> Zeitzler: Of course.
> Manstein: You look like a punch-ball to me, struck on one side by Keitel [whose
> *OKW* was responsible for all theatres of war outside the Soviet Union] and on
> the other by the army groups [on the Eastern Front], while the Führer stands
> to one side as referee. But seriously: you simply aren't allowed to function as
> chief of the general staff![44]

He added a final, forceful message in a signal:

> The army group has been reporting ever since the end of the winter battles [i.e.
> since March 1943] that it would not be able to defend its front with the forces at
> its disposal and has repeatedly called, without success, for a radical adjustment of
> forces within the Eastern Front or between the latter and other theatres of war. In
> view of the importance of the territory being defended by Army Group South and
> the clearly foreseeable fact that the Russians would direct the main effort of their
> offensive against the latter, this adjustment was absolutely imperative.
>
> Instead, the army group has been divested of forces after *Zitadelle* and never
> provided with adequate or timely reinforcements when a crisis occurred.
>
> My motive in making these statements is not to fix *ex post facto* responsibility
> for developments in the west but to ensure that in future the necessary action will
> be taken in good time.[45]

This led to a fourth meeting, this time in East Prussia. Aware of Hitler's reluctance to concede territory, Manstein had held out the possibility of halting the Red

Army near Poltava and thus avoiding a retreat to the Dnepr, but this was only possible if the promised reinforcements arrived and Army Group Centre carried out the attack proposed by Zeitzler and Manstein. In the absence of such reinforcements, it would be impossible to hold such a forward position, and there was a considerable risk of the northern flank of his army group being driven south, away from Kiev. Such a development would render any prolonged defence of the Dnepr line impossible and might even lead to the encirclement and destruction of all of Army Group South. There was a further exchange of signals, in which Manstein expressed disappointment that, whilst his army group had always executed instructions from *OKH*, Army Group Centre appeared able to avoid doing so and was thus endangering the very survival of the 'loyal' Army Group South. He must have been aware that the reason for the delays in organising an attack by Army Group Centre was because such an attack would inevitably require a shortening of the front line and, presented with such a choice, Hitler preferred to accept without question Klug's statements that a rapid redeployment of troops as Zeitzler had suggested was impossible. Hitler reluctantly agreed to Manstein's demands for reinforcements, advising again that four divisions would be transferred from Army Group Centre, but the precise timing of this remained unclear and Manstein would have to wait to see whether they ever appeared. He now turned his attention back to the growing crisis along his front. The demands of trying to hold his army group together were huge, enough to tax even the most capable commander; to do so whilst having to fight constantly with Hitler for resources, repeatedly having to make the same points and extract the same grudging concessions which then disappeared before they could be enacted, required superhuman strength of character. These bruising encounters with Hitler had a fatal impact upon the relationship between the two men. Manstein's comment that he, at least, could expect his orders to be carried out was a barely disguised criticism of Hitler's inability to get Army Group Centre to abide by what had previously been agreed. For the moment, Manstein remained in post, not least because the magnitude of the crisis required the attention of the best operational mind in the Wehrmacht.

The withdrawal of German forces to the Dnepr line was detailed in orders that reached the army and corps headquarters of Army Group South on 15 September. From this point, the dogged retreat increasingly took on the characteristics of a race between the slowly withdrawing German forces and their pursuers. Given that there were so few major crossings over the Dnepr – at Kiev, Kanev, Cherkassy, Kremenchug, Dnepropetrovsk and Zaporozhye – it was vital to prevent the Red Army from achieving an armoured breakthrough anywhere, as the loss of any of these crossings might prove fatal to the entire army group. In addition to some 63 divisions with all their equipment and personnel, between 100,000 and 200,000 wounded and sick would have to be evacuated, together with the medical staff caring for them, and tens of thousands of Ukrainians would also be moved west (either because they voluntarily chose to leave with the Germans rather than face the consequences of a resumption of Soviet rule, or because the German authorities decided that they were of potential use to the advancing Red Army and could not therefore be left behind). As it pulled back, 19th Panzer Division came across scenes of confusion and huge wastefulness, which were doubtless repeated right across the region:

> In the towns, particularly at railway stations, there were large quantities of brand new agricultural machines that had been brought here from the Reich to help with agricultural work. This equipment had never been handed over to the farmers. Large stocks of grain had been gathered at railway stations but couldn't be transported to the rear, and thus could not be used in future for supplying the troops. Amongst our columns were ever larger numbers of refugees and marching columns of men of military age who – wherever possible – were taken with us or voluntarily left, so that they could escape Soviet military service or perhaps to save themselves.[46]

Hollidt's Sixth Army was to pull back towards the lower Dnepr, retaining a substantial bridgehead east of the river from Zaporozhye to Melitopol and thence the coast of the Sea of Azov, thus preventing the Red Army from isolating the German Seventeenth Army, the main formation of Army Group A, in the Crimea. In order to allow for closer cooperation between Sixth Army and Seventeenth Army, Sixth Army was now assigned to Army Group A. To its north, First Panzer Army was to withdraw over the Dnepr at Dnepopetrovsk and Zaporozhye, and Eighth Army was to defend the line from about 18 miles (30km) south of Kremenchug to a point a similar distance south of Kiev, while Fourth Panzer Army then took over control of the line from there to the junction of Army Group South with Army Group Centre's Second Army, roughly where the Pripet flowed into the Dnepr to the north of Kiev.[47] The armoured formations of Army Group South were to act as a rearguard for the retreat, particularly when covering the northern flank of Eighth Army; given the strength of the opposing Soviet formations, this would prove to be an arduous task. On 18 September, Hoth impressed upon his corps and division commanders the critical nature of the task:

The withdrawal of an army is one of the most difficult tasks it can be assigned. It must be executed successfully. If this does not occur, the outcome would be unthinkable. It must succeed ... The panzer army is determined to gets its formations back across the Dnepr without the loss of a single man or weapon.[48]

The losses suffered by *SS-Das Reich* during August had left the division badly depleted in armour; although the arrival of its Panther battalion provided a welcome boost in firepower, the new tanks suffered an alarming rate of mechanical failures. When Manstein authorised a withdrawal of his armies to the line of the Dnepr, there was concern that further breakdowns of the new tanks might result in them being abandoned on the battlefield and thus lost permanently, and a decision was made to pull most of the division's panzer regiment back to the Dnepr for replenishment and repairs. A single panzer company and the remaining assault guns from the division's assault gun battalion were grouped together as *Panzergruppe Holzer* and, together with the reconnaissance battalion, the panzergrenadier regiment *Der Führer*, the artillery regiment, and the combat engineer battalion, a force was assembled to act as the rearguard for III Panzer Corps. Very rapidly, the rearguard settled into a pattern of attack and defence, as was the case with the other units covering the German retreat. Elements of the reconnaissance battalion stayed in close contact with the pursuing Soviet forces, identifying their main concentrations and wherever possible their assembly areas for planned attacks. These were then subjected to a heavy bombardment by the division's artillery regiment, and *Panzergruppe Holzer*, accompanied by half-track-mounted panzergrenadiers, conducted short, sharp attacks to disrupt the Soviet troops and force them to break contact, while the artillery regiment pulled back. At the same time, the combat engineers prepared a new defensive line further to the rear, which was occupied by the rest of the rearguard. Covered by artillery fire and smoke barrages, *Panzergruppe Holzer* then withdrew to the rear of the new position. Each such cycle unfolded over perhaps two days with considerable success.[49] On occasion, Holzer's group used captured Soviet tanks, operating them until they were knocked out or suffered breakdowns.

In this manner, *SS-Das Reich* pulled back steadily towards the Dnepr. On 11 September, it was ordered to take up positions along the line of the Msha River, and to hold this position rather than continue its steady withdrawal while slower units made their way back to the Dnepr. To the relief of the division's troops, they found prepared positions waiting for them, complete with trenches, command and support bunkers, and minefields. Early the following afternoon, the position held by the division's reconnaissance battalion reported an attack by as many as 70 Soviet tanks with substantial infantry support. Artillery fire rapidly drove the Soviet infantry to cover and although the Soviet tanks pressed forward through steadily falling rain, they then encountered the German minefield and several were disabled. The rest continued forward, and the personnel of *Panzergruppe Holzer* were alerted, rapidly preparing their Panther tanks for action:

At top speed, the driver and commander took their positions. The radioman and gun-loader took hold of the engine crank handles. On the third attempt the engine finally fired. Everyone hastily took up battle stations. Radio switched on and contact made. Weapons loaded and checked. More and more [Soviet] tanks could be made out about 3km away. An order over the radio: 'Let the advancing Russian tank brigade come within 1000m! The fire order will be given then. No movement until then!'

In the meantime we learned over the radio that the advancing Russians consisted of an entire tank brigade of about 80 tanks (we had 14 against them, including two without working engines). The Russians were still driving quite slowly, deeply echeloned. Most of them were T-34s with a few KV-1s and KV-2s. It was later discovered that there were 86 tanks. Ludwig reported from the left that his attempts to get his engine started were ineffective. Two enemy tanks were already standing 600m in front of his hole [the disabled tank had been dug in]. The infantry division elements deployed to our right were already pulling back. A Leutnant came up with a weak company and reckoned that the great Soviet tank armada couldn't be held back. In response to Schäfer's suggestion that he and his men might let them roll past them and then give the Soviet infantry that was following a hot reception, he just shrugged. He couldn't hold his men back. After a radio conversation, the reconnaissance battalion and 15th Company of *Der Führer* tried to extend their line to the right into the abandoned sector as well as holding their own overstretched position. They fanned out to the right and let the Soviet tank brigade overrun their entire sector. Great chaps, our 'old' comrades, who we already knew well from earlier actions. Hubert Ludwig came on the radio again: two T-34s were stopped 400m from his tank in its hole. He asked for permission to fire and within a minute hit both T-34s. The Russians quickly realised something was up on their right flank. There was movement in their ranks. The rain had eased. Most of the T-34s angled a little to the right as they had only detected Ludwig so far. By doing so, they exposed their left side armour to us and could clearly be targeted. But they were also moving further away, and their characteristic grey clouds of diesel exhaust smoke could be seen clearly.

We now received permission across the radio waves to fire. The Russians became confused and couldn't spot us quickly. They fired without any control. Ernst Zittla, our loader, made a fervent wish with each round he loaded. Our gun-aimer, Heinz Schröder, was his old calm self. While our commander, Untersturmbannführer Emmerling, was already wriggling into the turret, everything remained calm and measured. By our second shot, we had set our first T-34 ablaze. A great 'fire magic' developed. We now tried to drive our tanks from their dugouts. But after two days of rain, that was exceedingly difficult. Our driver, Böck, was quite worked up at the thought of not being able to get our machine out of the dugout. He let the clutch engage too quickly a few times and stalled the engine. But after several attempts we finally managed it. Wimmer approached us from the right. He was in need of a tow and needed a new fuel pump.

Ever more Soviet tanks were ablaze. Every vehicle played its part in these hits. It was no longer possible to work out which tank had shot up which Russians. Herbert Ludwig constantly reported more hits from the left, and by the end of the battle 23 shot up enemy tanks were counted in front of his dugout.

We drove our vehicle behind the dugouts of the tank on the right flank (Wimmer) on which the towing hook and cables had already been attached. With much effort, we pulled the tank to a new firing position. It wasn't possible to tow it further as both the hook and two cables broke. In any case our ammunition was running very low. Then we took a hit on the left side of the engine compartment. It lodged in the fuel tank on that side (one of five). Fortunately it was already empty; there was no explosion. Shortly after we took a second hit on the left fourth wheel. We changed positions again.

Now we were told to drive to the battalion command post. Pull back! We set off for the rear and quickly reached the command post, which wasn't far away, after passing through a dip. We were refuelled and rearmed in great haste and a fuel pump and replacement towing hooks and cables were rapidly brought up and taken aboard. Then we quickly drove back up the steep hillside. As we drove up, we encountered a T-34 driving slowly forward from left to right about 100m away, presenting its right front corner. Obviously, we didn't expect to find it here behind the front line. After a few brief seconds of shock, during which the distance narrowed, our commander Lorenz Emmerling ordered: 'Ram and board!' The T-43 had stopped about 50m away and was turning its turret to the right towards us. Heinz Schröder shouted 'Halt!' and struck the Soviet tank with the round that was loaded in the gun directly on the turret ring. Two seconds later, before we could fire a second round, there was a sheet of flame from its turret, the body of its commander appeared from the hatch and fell forward onto the turret.

Our weapons, better and more powerful [than those of the Russians], combined with experience, courage and coordination, had once more given us victory over the 'comrades from another postcode'. Later, in a quiet moment, we could think back to this: how easily the result might have been reversed. But now we had no time for such thoughts. We had to hurry to the immobilised vehicle of Max Wimmer, which waited for us. He was still there and had taken hits from only light weapons.

The battle had long passed its peak, and almost all the enemy tanks had been shot up. The driver, Emil Engel, took the replacement fuel pump we had brought and changed it nonchalantly in record time under occasional fire.[50]

The Germans claimed to have destroyed 78 out of 86 Soviet tanks in the battle. They recorded one Panther destroyed, though several others were 'not fully operational' – it isn't clear whether this reflected the vehicles that had engine problems before the battle, or vehicles that suffered damage during the action. Nevertheless, even allowing for some distortion of the figures, the high level of training, excellent optics, and powerful guns of the German tanks gave *Panzergruppe Holzer* a decisive advantage, much as the tanks of *SS-Totenkopf* had enjoyed in the battle near Kotelevka.

The mechanical unreliability of the Panthers detracted greatly from their undoubted prowess in battle, and steps had to be taken to remedy this as quickly as possible:

Hauptsturmführer Alois Ennsberger, commander of the tank repair company of *SS-Das Reich*, was instrumental in recovering and repairing the division's tanks. Working calmly day and night, he succeeded in bringing all the damaged tanks – these came to 65 Panthers and a few Tigers – back over the Dnepr to safety. Recovery of tanks sometimes took place beyond the front line held by the rearguards that were covering the retreat, and Ennsberger had to organise all-round defence while doing so.

In view of the reports of the alarming breakdown rate of these newest tanks, the battalion commander (Sturmbannführer Hans Weiss) was ordered by Eighth Army to go to Speer's Armaments Ministry in Berlin to give an update on these serious problems, which had affected the Panther battalions of various army panzer divisions in a similar manner, and to get replacement engines for the tanks.

As a result, 65 new Panther engines were prepared within a few days and brought by the Luftwaffe in large gliders directly to the air base near Kirovograd, near where the tank repair company had set up workshops in large warehouses. Here, the Panther engines were replaced at high speed through the professional brilliance of all concerned.

After just ten days, two companies of Panthers were returned to the division for further deployment.[51]

The use of gliders to transport equipment to the front was not a new innovation. Germany produced a number of glider designs, originally when plans were being made for the invasion of Britain in 1940. One of the largest was the Messerschmitt Me 321, capable of carrying 200 troops or 20 tons of cargo, but it was of limited value due to its lack of manoeuvrability and its sheer size – it required specialised equipment to move it when it was on the ground, and it proved difficult to find aircraft capable of towing it. One option was to use three Messerschmitt Me110 fighters operating as a team, known as the *Troikaschlepp*, but this was fraught with danger and required highly skilled pilots to coordinate their movements. In 1941, one such flight ended in disaster when the towing fighters collided with the resultant destruction of all three Me110s and the glider, with the loss of nearly 130 lives. Rather more effective was the DFS.230, a smaller glider that was built in large numbers – although production ceased in 1943, it remained in service until the end of the war and was used both in aerial assaults, such as the capture of the Belgian Fort Eben-Emael and during the invasion of Crete, and as a cargo carrier, particularly when supplying German formations in the Demyansk and Stalingrad encirclements. It could carry only nine troops or 1.2 tons of cargo, but it was possible for it to be towed by most of the Luftwaffe's larger aircraft, and even by smaller planes like the Messerschmitt Bf109 fighter. The unit that ferried engines for *SS-Das Reich* was *Verbindungskommando(S)4* ('Communications Command 4'), which operated a mixture of DFS.230s and the larger Gotha Go242 glider – the latter could carry up to four tons of cargo – and several different towing planes. Even in the cargo role, the gliders sometimes found themselves under attack; although they were equipped with a small number of machine-guns for defensive use, their survival was dependent upon their towing aircraft, as Karl Sandvoss, a junior officer in the unit's DFS.230 squadron, described:

During this operation [flying munitions to an airfield in support of the *Zitadelle* offensive] two towed aircraft came under attack from Russian fighters. We were flying in close formation, fortunately at low level, and were to the north of

Kharkov. Hauptmann Faè, our squadron commander, was in a Ju87 towing the first glider, and to his left was the second with Unteroffizier Schöner, and I was in a glider. Suddenly, tracers flashed past us as Russian fighters flew past at the same altitude. Flames burst from the oil cooler of Hauptmann Faè's machine and then everything happened very quickly. We detached, pushed the stick forward and headed down at speed. The undercarriage was torn away and rounds struck us in the rear while we were still sliding; by the time the fighters made a third pass, we had already run a short distance from the machine. Hauptmann Faè's machine was ablaze, but he and his tail gunner were able to escape unharmed. The other Ju87 had dived into the next valley and was able to reach Kharkov safely. Our DFS.230 was unusable but we were fine. The infantry nearby loaned us a truck, and we drove our cargo of bombs to Kharkov.[52]

The engines for the Panther tanks weighed about 1.2 tons; the transport of the engines required by *SS-Das Reich* would therefore have required over 20 DFS.230 gliders. Given the congestion on the railways, exacerbated by constant partisan attacks, air transport was the only realistic option for rapid delivery of the engines to the front line.

The unreliability of the new Panthers was probably not merely due to mechanical issues associated with a vehicle operating near the limits of what was technically possible. Soon after he became armaments minister, Albert Speer was forced to tackle the problem of Germany's labour shortage – he estimated that, by 1942, German industry needed one million more workers. The solution was forced labour from the occupied territories, but this brought its own problems – many of those dispatched to Germany, particularly from the occupied areas of the Soviet Union, spoke no German. In the First World War, Germany and other combatant nations had made extensive use of women workers, but Nazi officials repeatedly blocked Speer's suggestions of increasing the employment of German women in industry, largely on ideological grounds; he estimated that even as the war dragged on, 1.5 million German women continued to work as domestic helps, and a further half a million women were brought from the Ukraine and elsewhere to work alongside them at a time when labour shortages in the war economy were causing serious problems. The indiscriminate recruitment of forced labour in the more industrialised parts of German-controlled Europe, such as France, proved to be counter-productive as it left French factories – often producing materiel for Germany – unable to function properly, and although Speer again tried to intervene, he was only partially successful. To make matters worse, internal rivalries in the Third Reich also exacerbated labour shortages.

Himmler created a network of SS-controlled labour camps and his subordinates repeatedly arrested foreign labourers working in factories for trivial or non-existent offences and dispatched them to these new camps, a practice that Speer estimated cost him up to half a million workers a year.[53] The foreign labourers who did work in the mainstream war industry understandably showed little enthusiasm for hitting production targets and many resorted to acts of sabotage, though the impact of these acts is hard to assess – there is little evidence of planned, deliberate campaigns of sabotage, and although a report produced by the RSHA estimated that there were nearly 7,000 cases of sabotage per year, closer investigation showed that most of these were either acts of negligence or relatively minor incidents.[54] Nevertheless, a group of Soviet officers who were held in a German prison camp near Munich created the *Bratskoje Sotrudnichestvo Voiennoplennych* ('Fraternal Cooperation of Prisoners of War' or *BSV*) in 1943 with the intention of creating widespread disruption within Germany, but although it managed to establish links between different camps, the organisation was unable to organise the scale of disruption it had intended and a wave of arrests and executions in 1944 effectively eliminated it.[55] It is likely that the unreliability of many German industrial products at this stage of the war was more due to the crippling shortage of suitable raw materials, resulting in the use of substandard lubricants, softer alloys, etc. than deliberate sabotage, though language problems undoubtedly led to work being carried out incorrectly.

The recovery of damaged tanks continued to play an important role in helping *SS-Das Reich* maintain its operational strength. On 13 September, a Panther was knocked out by a direct hit on its engine compartment, but that evening it was nevertheless recovered so that repairs could at least be attempted. At the same time, combat engineers were ordered to proceed across the recent battlefield and place demolition charges on all the Soviet tanks that had been knocked out to ensure that, even if Soviet engineers recovered them, they would be unable to return them to service. Any hope that the personnel of *SS-Das Reich* might have had of being able to stay in their current positions for a prolonged period of defence disappeared on 14 September with new orders from III Panzer Corps for the division to pull back to the next designated line of defence. It had been outflanked on both its northern and southern wings and staying in its current location invited isolation and encirclement. Accordingly, the division's armour launched a sharp attack to allow the infantry to disengage, and the Soviet attempts to pursue seemed a little half-hearted; the crews of the *SS-Das Reich* panzer regiment speculated that the range of their Panther tanks had made a marked impression upon their opponents.[56]

Poltava was a growing centre of industry when the war began, with a population of about 130,000. It fell to the advancing Wehrmacht in September 1941, and its Jewish population – about 10 per cent of its pre-war population, though many had left before the arrival of the Germans – suffered internment in a ghetto as wretched as any other in German-occupied areas before being massacred by personnel from *Einsatzgruppe C* in two operations, the first shortly after the occupation and the second in late November 1941. The city now became the scene of further bitter fighting as the northern wing of Konev's Steppe Front tried to bypass the city and strike towards the Dnepr while the southern wing was launched towards Dnepopetrovsk. On 21 September, Managarov's Fifty-Third Army reached the eastern outskirts of Poltava and the first attempt to take the city failed. Reinforced by Zhadov's Fifth Guards Army, Managarov tried again two days later – unless Poltava could be taken quickly, the German bulwark there would act as a substantial hindrance to Konev's forces that were attempting to bypass it. On 22 September, the second attack began, with Zhadov's troops crossing the Vorskla close to where Peter the Great's army had crossed in the great battle that took place near Poltava in 1709 during the Great Northern War. By the end of the day, the Red Army had secured much of the west bank of the river and began to penetrate into the city itself. Fighting continued through the night, with the Germans resuming their dogged withdrawal rather than risking encirclement and destruction in Poltava, and during 23 September the Red Army completed the recapture of the city. The triumphant soldiers were greeted by the surviving civilian population with tales of slaughter, and in one case the advancing Soviet troops claimed that they arrived in time to prevent a large group of civilians being burned alive in a school.[57] Whilst there can be no doubt that such incidents occurred, it seems somewhat unlikely that the Germans would have carried out an atrocity like this while in the process of abandoning the city – their thoughts and energies would have been devoted more to escaping to the west before they were overrun by the advancing Red Army.

Mansoor Abdullin's XXXII Guards Rifle Corps was one of the units that crossed the Vorskla in order to be able to approach Poltava from the west and thus possibly encircle the defenders. Prior to the war, he had been a miner in southern Siberia, and some of his experiences from that life now came back to him:

> The river was not particularly wide – no more than 100–120m. And it was shallow enough to be waded. But adjacent to the river [on the eastern bank] was a marshy floodplain at least 1km wide. Where and how to force the Vorskla? With

the help of the local population, scouts determined that the most suitable place to force a crossing was via a gravel road and bridge that crossed the entire floodplain. The approaches to the bridge had to be seized to prevent the Fascists from destroying it. The gravel road across the floodplain was high, raised about 5–6m with steep slopes. If you rolled off, the swamp would suck you in.

Calculations showed that with a relative speed of 15km/hour [9mph i.e. running], each soldier would need 5–6 minutes to cross 1km. And if you could achieve twice this speed? Then you reduced the time in the killing zone to three minutes.

The lot of crossing the bridge and seizing a bridgehead on the right bank fell to our regiment. Our battalion led and we began to prepare. The division sent us some vehicles and two-horse carts. We had volatile *Komsomol* meetings where we discussed how best to execute the order with minimum losses. We would have to move under strong artillery fire from the Hitlerites – the embankment and bridge were well targeted. Yes, the Fascists wouldn't skimp on shells and few of us would manage to reach the far shore. I had never experienced such a thing. Here it was, the hour when everyone would test their fate. Only the lucky would survive! It would be difficult to come out of the continuous fire intact. Everyone knew this, but nobody changed their behaviour. I didn't see even a small hint of doom in anyone.

I felt as if I were in a cell. I mentally replayed the 'movie' of all my experiences. I thought it was the last day that I would be breathing. I thought about what was inevitable. Where could you run from the embankment? Nowhere. There was swamp on the left, swamp on the right. The road led only one way – forwards. And how could we go forwards? Through a solid wall of explosions?

I decided to cross with the horses in a two-wheel cart. I knew one vital feature of horses: they would not stray from their path into the most severe snowstorm or blizzard. The horses would never turn off the road even if there were explosions all round. If only the explosions didn't kill them! Horses wouldn't get lost in the darkest night! I had seen how they found their way through mines without lamps.

I chose a pair of Mongolian horses with a strongly built cart. Moiseyev, the driver, asked 'What, man, do you have faith in the horses?'

'Oh yes,' I said to the driver. 'Horses are reliable. I worked in the mine as a digger and I know horses well. Never let you down! Horses are the most intelligent of animals.'

Moiseyev listened to me and was clearly pleased; he lived all his life around horses. I had clearly struck a chord with him and he exclaimed in a singular way, 'That's right, man! Horses are smarter than humans! They can't speak, but they understand things better than us!' We had plenty of food in our rucksacks and we settled down to share a bread roll. Moiseyev suddenly looked at me questioningly and asked, 'Listen, were you at Stalingrad?'

'I was,' I replied.

His eyes widened. 'What is your name? Abdulov?'

I answered, 'Not Abdulov, Abdullin.'

'I was in your mortar company!' exclaimed Moiseyev. 'I remember the commander of the company, Butenko, I think. I remember Suvorov with a beard. And then I was sent to the transport team from the mortar company on account of my age.'

I had already remembered this. 'Yes,' I said. 'You were all transferred from the company, four older men, into the transport team.'

Moiseyev's smile faded and he said, 'They were all killed in the Kursk salient.'

I immediately remembered my seven friends whose deaths also caught up with them in the Kursk salient. Frankly, I wasn't happy that I found myself talking with Moiseyev about them here, before the deadly attack across the Vorskla.[58]

Together with a third 'Stalingrader', an Armenian called Grigory (or 'Grisha') Hambardzumyants, Abdullin and Moiseyev decided to attempt to cross the Vorskla together. They waited as the first elements of the battalion moved off and German artillery began to fire:

We dashed out onto the road and the horses, understanding their task, pulled up their short, shaggy tails and took off at a gallop. Ahead of us were other wagons, some got caught in the shelling, and we barely managed to keep up, even though we were meant to maintain a precautionary interval of at least 20m.

Moiseyev dropped the reins and clung tight to the side of the cart so he would not be thrown out. Grisha and I jumped off and lightly, holding onto ropes tied to the front of the car, we raced alongside. It was easy to run, nothing to do but breathe: above us, earth and sand and marsh weed, our noses clogged by dirty, wet dust, smoke and methane blown away as it rose from the swampy mess. Shells struck around at such a rate that anything thrown into the air didn't have time to fall back to earth. Explosions hurled it up again and again.

Ahead the road was narrowing. The cart jumped about, just about ready to break up. I had already thought that we should have tied our ropes to the horses' harnesses. Now the wagon would fall apart and the horses would run off alone. Without them we would be lost! And the horses raced on faster, through the thick dust and smoke where I could see only the occasional glint of a horseshoe.

The cart racing ahead of us disappeared before my eyes and our horses raced into a cloud of dust and disappeared. Had our cart been hit by a shell? But the rope, the end of which was tightly bound around my fist, continued to pull me and I continued to run blindly. The acrid smoke burned in my throat. This nitrogen oxide was a very poisonous gas. My mouth was full of earth and sand. In the rare moments I opened my eyes I still couldn't see anything, but our horses were still whole and without getting lost rushed on like devils.

Just don't fall! We had to be wary of craters. One or other leg thrust into a hole every now and then but I was used to it. But if there was a blockage up front and the horses jumped – would I jump over? My body felt coiled like a spring and I thought I could jump over anything.

Run, skip, rush on, the embankment seemed endless. But then under my feet were the wooden boards of the bridge! We were ready to cross to the right bank! Press on now! But would we make it? 'Moiseyev!' I screamed, 'Hold the reins! We mustn't blunder into the Fritzes! Turn either right or left along the shore, there isn't an embankment here.'

Moiseyev grabbed the reins and somehow pulled the left rein and managed to turn off the road along the shore. Grisha and I grabbed our things from the cart on the run, letting go of the ropes and dropping into the thick grass, pressing ourselves against the cool ground for a second.[59]

Despite the intense artillery fire, much of Abdullin's battalion managed to storm across the river. The bridge disintegrated under shellfire but the river was fordable and the crossing continued across the wreckage, reinforced by shattered vehicles, guns, carts, and even the corpses of horses and men.

SS-Totenkopf was now part of XI Corps, which had been tasked with withdrawing through Kremenchug and holding a bridgehead on the east bank until all the retreating elements had reached safety. There were several defensive lines that were held for perhaps a day before being abandoned during the withdrawal, all given female names – *Lili Marlene, Laura* etc., but these terms merely referred to the designated positions and none of the lines were at all fortified. The autumn rainy season had begun, with repeated and often prolonged rain making the landscape increasingly difficult for vehicle movement. The heavy road traffic during the retreat had already put a great strain on the relatively poor roads of the Ukraine, and the rearguard units struggled through the mud to reach their designated positions. Rumours abounded amongst the exhausted German troops about what they could expect when they finally reached the Dnepr; a junior officer from the headquarters of XXIV Panzer Corps visited

10th Panzergrenadier Division and later gave his corps commander a dispiriting report:

> The men are struggling through the mud. They haven't had any sleep for days, there's not a dry stitch on their bodies. They've been in action for weeks. But they're holding out. The Dnepr is attracting them like a mirage. Oberstleutnant de Maizière, the chief of operations, said to me: 'The men are looking forward to a well-built defensive line. They're looking forward to bunkers and troop quarters where at long last they will be able to hang on.'[60]

The reality of course was very different, as the first troops reaching the Dnepr were discovering; given Hitler's near-endless delays in giving permission for the construction of the *Ostwall*, efforts to date had concentrated on just a few points. Elsewhere, the German troops would have to construct their own positions, a task made much harder by the increasingly muddy terrain. On 22 September, Manstein had another exchange of signals with Zeitzler, stating that much of the ground being held by Army Group Centre – specifically around Velikiye Luki and Smolensk – was of no importance and could be abandoned without significant detriment, releasing troops that could be sent to the Ukraine. Manstein's frustration boiled over in the closing signal:

> [When Army Group South has succeeded in crossing the Dnepr] we can't just stare out over the river and believe that nothing can now go wrong just because we have crossed it.[61]

In other words, without more troops, the line of the Dnepr provided only illusory safety.

The Soviet forces that bypassed the southern edge of Poltava pressed on towards Kremenchug, hot on the heels of *SS-Totenkopf*. The German rearguards had fought a skilful delaying action, but given the scale of the operation, it was almost inevitable that the Red Army would succeed at some stage in isolating and encircling some of their opponents. On 25 September, the panzergrenadier regiment *Eicke*, named after a commander of *SS-Totenkopf* who was killed during the fighting near Kharkov in early 1943, was cut off. Despite having almost no armour-piercing ammunition available, the remaining panzer battalion of *SS-Totenkopf* – it too had dispatched a battalion west to be re-equipped with Panthers – tried to break through to the encircled panzergrenadiers. Gruppenführer Max Simon, the division commander, was in the encirclement and during the night he led a breakout to the nearby panzer battalion and the regiment made good its escape, albeit at the cost of having to abandon several vehicles.

Before the war, many Ukrainians had been lukewarm at best about Bolshevik rule, particularly in the rural areas that had suffered so badly during the famines of the 1930s. As had been the case in Kharkov, a period of German rule changed their attitude markedly, and it seems that most of the population genuinely welcomed the Red Army soldiers as liberators. Vasily Grossman was a journalist who travelled with the Soviet 75th Guards Rifle Division as it drove on towards the Dnepr:

Old men, when they hear Soviet words, run to meet the troops and weep silently, unable to utter a word. Old peasant women say with quiet surprise: 'We thought we would sing and laugh when we saw our army, but there's so much grief in our hearts that tears are falling.'

… Every soldier, every officer and every general of the Red Army who had seen the Ukraine in blood and fire, who had heard the true story of what had been happening in the Ukraine during the two years of German rule, understands to the bottom of their souls that there are only two sacred words left to us. One of them is 'love' and the other one is 'revenge'.

… According to what prisoners said and letters found on dead German soldiers, the Germans considered themselves the representatives of a higher race forced to live in savage villages. They thought that in the wild eastern steppes one could throw culture aside.

… On a windy and overcast morning, we met a boy on the edge of the village of Tarasevichi, by the Dnepr. He looked about 13 to 14 years old. The boy was extremely thin, his sallow skin was tight on his cheekbones, large bumps protruded from his skull. His lips were dirty, pale, like a dead man's who had fallen face flat on the ground.

His eyes were looking in a tired way, there was neither joy nor sadness in them. They are so frightening, these old, tired, lifeless eyes of children. 'Where is your father?' 'Killed,' he answered. 'And mother?' 'She died.' 'Have you got brothers or sisters?' 'A sister. They took her to Germany.' 'Have you got any relatives?' 'No, they were all burned in a partisan village.'

And he walked into a potato field, his feet bare and black from the mud, straightening the rags of his torn shirt.[62]

The 'scorched earth' policy as the Germans retreated added a final layer to the misery of the rural Ukrainian population; the area had been devastated by Stalin's famines in the 1930s, and the welcome that many Ukrainians gave to the Germans in 1941 was soon forgotten when the brutality of German occupation policies became clear. In 1943, the towns and villages in a strip of land perhaps 20 miles (33km) wide on the east bank of the Dnepr were deliberately ravaged to create a region where the Red Army would struggle to find shelter and where destroyed bridges, roads and other infrastructure would greatly hinder its ability to organise a new offensive operation. This policy was the basis of one of the charges made against Manstein and others after the war, i.e. that they had inflicted unnecessary suffering on the civilian population. In his memoirs, Manstein was utterly unrepentant about the subject:

> In pursuance of instructions specially promulgated by Göring's economic staff, the zone was to be emptied of all provisions, economic goods and machinery which could assist Soviet war production. In the case of my own army group, this measure was confined to essential machinery, horses and cattle. Naturally there was no question of our 'pillaging' the area. That was something which the German Army – unlike certain others – did not tolerate. Strict checkpoints were set up to ensure that no vehicle carried misappropriated goods. As for the effects and stocks of factories, warehouses and *Sovkhozes* [Soviet collective farms], these were in any case the property of the state and not of private individuals.
>
> Since it was Soviet policy, whenever any territory was recaptured, immediately to embody all able-bodied males under 60 into the armed forces and to conscript the whole of the remaining population for work of military importance, often in the battle zone itself, the supreme command had directed that the civil population would also be evacuated ... a considerable proportion of the Russian [sic] population joined our withdrawal quite voluntarily in order to escape the dreaded Soviets ... Although the war caused these people a great deal of misfortune and hardship, the latter bore no comparison to the terror-bombing suffered by the civil population in Germany or what happened later on in Germany's eastern territories.[63]

Manstein's statement that the Wehrmacht did not indulge in pillaging may have been true of the front-line formations, which were largely too busy fighting for their lives, but as has already been described, other organisations were actively involved in looting from places like Kharkov, where many art treasures were removed and others destroyed. It is unlikely that ordinary Ukrainians made much distinction between the men of front-line units and those from rear area units – and in particular the SS and the various occupation authorities – who behaved with unchecked brutality. Nor does Manstein acknowledge the widespread starvation that was a direct consequence of German occupation policies, and his casual failure to distinguish between 'Russians' and 'Ukrainians' is symptomatic of the manner in which so many made similar mistakes. His distinction between goods that belonged to the 'state' and goods that belonged to ordinary people doesn't stand up to scrutiny – in the Soviet Union, the population was dependent upon these goods for survival, regardless of whether they were technically the property of the state or of individuals. However, his point regarding the impact of the bombing of German cities by British and American aircraft is a reasonable one. In addition, it should be remembered that when it withdrew towards the east in 1941, the Red Army too had carried out a policy of deliberate destruction, largely for the same reasons that the Germans now used.

There can be no doubt that some Ukrainians were anxious to accompany the retreating Germans rather than await the return of Soviet rule, but the friendly greetings that some of the German rearguards received were more due to mistakes, as an officer in the tank company of *SS-Totenkopf* commented – after several days of watching German units withdraw to the west, villagers sometimes assumed the armoured rearguard elements were actually the spearheads of the pursuing Red Army.[64] Nevertheless, many civilians did take to the road, sometimes in an attempt to avoid their livestock being taken by the retreating Wehrmacht. An artillery officer from *SS-Totenkopf* came across one such column:

A slowly rising hill to the right of the road obstructed our view of the terrain. I therefore steered the Kfz.15 [similar to a jeep] to the top. As far as we could see far across the land, it was free of the enemy. But what we could see in a large hollow right next to the road left us speechless: a huge town of wagons, hitched up like in the Wild West, around a great herd of cattle. Many men and women, who had stopped moving when the Kfz appeared on the hill above them stared at us. Hundreds of pairs of eyes, full of anxiety, were turned in the direction of the two solitary Germans. A village elder, perhaps also the local partisan leader, and all the inhabitants of his village had taken to the bushes to allow the front line to pass over them so that they could then return to their village. Our Kfz.15 sat over the silent Soviet encampment for some time. What should be done? Nothing at all! We drove on – we almost expected to hear them breathing out in relief.[65]

The discussions and debates about the possible illegality of the 'scorched earth' policy still lay in the future. For the moment, the most pressing issue was the Wehrmacht's withdrawal to the Dnepr, whilst it tried desperately to prevent any

Red Army units from reaching the river first. When General Pavel Rybalko's Third Guards Tank Army succeeded in slipping past the dogged rearguards and rushed towards the Dnepr, it seemed as if the German withdrawal might end in disaster. For the Soviet soldiers, it was a much-needed sign that Stalin's insistence on immediate frontal attack and pursuit was paying off; to date, casualties in Voronezh, Steppe, Southwest and Southern Fronts had been many times greater than those suffered by the Germans. One estimate put the casualties suffered in the fighting between Chernigov in the north and Poltava to the south at nearly 420,000 men.[66] A major success was needed to end the campaign, and Rybalko's advance appeared to offer just such an opportunity.

CHAPTER 7

THE DNEPR BRIDGEHEADS

Lieutenant General Pavel Semenovich Rybalko's Third Guards Tank Army was transferred to Vatutin's Voronezh Front shortly after the beginning of the drive to the Dnepr in an attempt to increase the rate of progress. Due to congestion on the roads behind the advancing Red Army, worsened by the damage done by the retreating Germans and repeated Luftwaffe air attacks, it took until 19 September for the troops to reach their assembly area; the weather was also a problem, with increasing rain heralding the arrival of the autumn muds. Like all Red Army formations in the campaign, the units of Third Guards Tank Army were all below strength. The standard of their equipment was varied; the heavy tank units in particular gave cause for concern, as they were made up largely of vehicles that were showing marked signs of wear and Rybalko was doubtful that they would be able to cover the distance to the Dnepr.[1] Nevertheless, Vatutin ordered him to prepare immediately for a high-speed advance to the river, and Rybalko dispatched a small reconnaissance group, disguised in SS uniforms, to scout the line of advance.

The scouting party of seven reached the Dnepr without incidents and succeeded in crossing the river through a mixture of swimming and the use of an improvised raft. After capturing a German NCO, they returned safely to their unit and made their report: there were few German formations in the path of Third Guards Tank Army, and the Dnepr in this sector would be simple to cross provided that the Germans did not have time to secure the west bank. Rybalko immediately unleashed his forces. From their starting point around the town of Pyryatin to the Dnepr was a distance of about 46 miles (75km); starting late on 20 September, Major General Konstantin Alexeyevich Malygin's IX Mechanised Corps covered the distance in a little under a day. It was followed by 51st Guards

Tank Brigade, the leading formation of VI Guards Tank Corps. Despite being substantially below strength, the Soviet units were in a threatening position when they reached the banks of the Dnepr roughly midway between Kiev and Kremenchug. The only German units in the area consisted of about 120 personnel from an anti-aircraft training unit based in nearby Cherkassy and the reconnaissance battalion of 19th Panzer Division.

Immediately, the Soviet troops began preparations to establish a bridgehead on the west bank of the Dnepr. The task was assigned to Major Harun Umarovich Bogatyrev, the deputy commander of 51st Guards Tank Brigade, and with the assistance of a group of local partisans he sent the first group across the river in small boats. A small German detachment on the west bank brought them under fire but was unable to stop their progress and, by the end of 22 September, the village of Grigorovka was in Soviet hands. A steady stream of reinforcements followed through the night; for the moment, it was impossible to transport any heavy equipment over the Dnepr, but construction of a larger ferry began. The first elements of Moskalenko's Fortieth Army, following close behind Rybalko's armour, also began to assemble along the Dnepr and, over the following days, secured a series of bridgeheads upstream of Grigorovka. Moskalenko hurried to the scene:

> The Dnepr! How many thoughts and feelings it evoked in me on that memorable day when together with the advanced units of the army, Major General [Konstantin Vasilevich] Krainyukov and I went to the bank of the river and gazed at it silently, unable to find words for the joy of this long-awaited moment. Before my mind's eye there was a picture of our retreat from the Dnepr during the grave days of the early autumn of 1941. The enemy was stronger than us then ... but even when the enemy was triumphant, believing that he had captured the Dnepr 'for a thousand years', we knew, we believed: we would return.[2]

The leading units of Third Guards Tank Army and Fortieth Army had reached the Dnepr at an advantageous location. Here, the river formed a curve, known as the Bukrin bend, projecting to the northeast; as they formed up along the eastern shore, the Soviet units found themselves in an ideal setting for forcing a river crossing – the German-held bank effectively formed a salient projecting towards the northeast, allowing the Red Army to fire into the selected area from three sides. Nevertheless, the following days saw the development of what amounted to a race: could the soldiers of Vatutin's leading armies cross the Dnepr in strength and unite their bridgeheads before German reinforcements could hurry to the

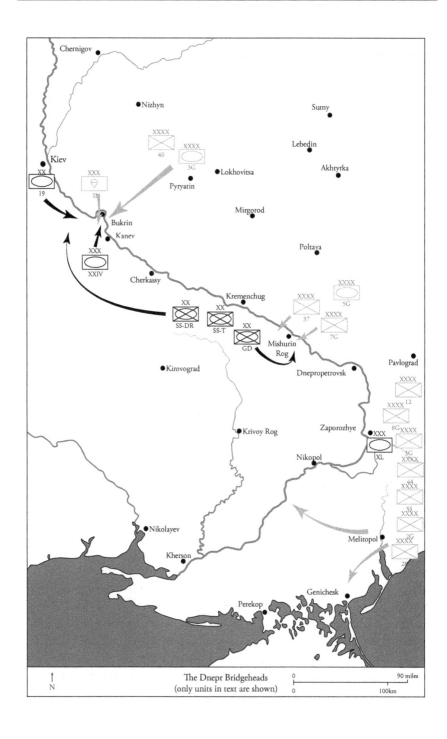

The Dnepr Bridgeheads
(only units in text are shown)

N

0   90 miles
0   100km

area, eliminate the small footholds that had already been gained, and then secure the west bank? Combat engineer units with the two Soviet Armies hurried to the riverbank, bringing with them a steady stream of boats of differing sizes. While aircraft of both sides launched attacks to try to give their ground troops much-needed support, the Red Army units steadily reinforced what became known collectively as the Bukrin bridgehead and continued to widen their hold on the east bank of the Dnepr. At the same time, *Stavka* prepared the deployment of a new innovation on the Eastern Front in an attempt to gain a decisive advantage.

The Red Army had formed its first parachute unit in early 1933, steadily increasing the strength of these formations until five airborne corps had been established by the beginning of the war with Germany. Like airborne forces of all nations, the paratroopers regarded themselves as an elite, and their personnel were meant to have at least three parachute drops during training; the rapid enlargement of the airborne forces had an impact upon this, and by the start of hostilities many of the airborne forces had only made jumps from training towers rather than aircraft. Also, unlike airborne formations of other nations, most of those who served in the Soviet units had simply been assigned to be parachutists when conscripted rather than volunteering. Most were happy to serve in this role, but some were understandably nervous about parachuting. However, they were given a simple choice: if they refused to jump, they were dispatched to penal companies.

Most of the airborne units were used as infantry in the months that followed the German invasion. The one occasion when they were deployed in strength in their designated role was in the Soviet *Rzhev-Vyazma* Operation of January 1942 when about 2,000 troops were dropped in an attempt to encircle German troops south of Vyazma. The drop did not go as planned, with only 1,300 men being able to form up in coherent formations. A further drop followed a short time later but was also disrupted by German defences; ultimately, the surviving paratroopers were able to link up with Soviet ground forces and reach safety, though they remained in sporadic combat with German units for several weeks before ending their isolation. Many of the Red Army's airborne units saw action in the heavy fighting that has already been described, but they functioned as infantry formations. On 16 September, a new II Airborne Corps – a total of about 10,000 troops – was created under the command of Major General Ivan Ivanovich Zatevakhin, the deputy commander of Soviet airborne forces, for a possible mission to seize a bridgehead across the Dnepr. Initial plans changed rapidly as the campaign unfolded, but just three days later Zhukov gave approval for the operation. As Vatutin's troops reached the Dnepr, Zatevakhin's paratroopers would be dropped on the west bank.

A year later, when pursuing German forces back towards a river on the far side of the Reich, the Western Allies would also make repeated plans for the use of their airborne forces, finally dropping three divisions in and south of Arnhem in an attempt to secure a bridgehead across the Rhine before the Germans could withdraw to it and set up defences that might prove to be difficult and costly to overcome. Rapid rewriting of complex plans was a potentially dangerous exercise, increasing the risk of confusion and error; in the case of airborne operations, the close cooperation required between ground and air formations added to the complexity of planning and hence to the risk of mistakes occurring when plans were drawn up at speed. Operation *Market Garden*, the attempt to seize bridges and open the road from south of Eindhoven to Arnhem, was badly compromised by the shortage of transport aircraft for such a large air drop, with the result that there were critical delays in bringing all the airborne forces into action. Similarly, the more modest plans for an air drop to secure the Bukrin bridgehead also ran into problems with the provision of transport planes, many of which were located far from the assembly points of the airborne troops. The high tempo of operations since the beginning of Operation *Polkovodets Rumyantsev* led to widespread

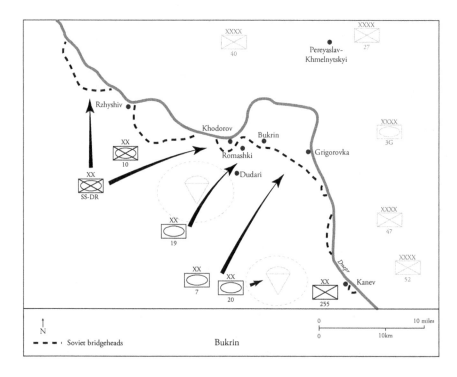

Bukrin

shortages of aviation fuel, and aircraft availability was further compromised by shortages of spare parts. During the deployment of airborne forces near Vyazma, it had been anticipated that transport aircraft might be able to fly two or even three missions in a single night, but this had proved impossible; yet the same requirements were written into the plans for the new operation without any detailed consideration of why it had not been possible to carry out so many flights the previous year.

The haste of operational planning also had an impact upon the preparation of the paratroopers, with many officers having little or no idea of where they were going or what their missions were. Officers down to battalion level received details only the day before departure, and scrambled to draw up plans for their subordinates. In some cases, these plans became available only once the paratroopers were already on their way to the drop zones aboard transport aircraft, or even after they had landed. Frequently, these plans and orders were far too vague to be of any value, merely reiterating training doctrine about regrouping after the air drop and establishing appropriate perimeters. The plans called for two thirds of the designated force to be deployed in the first drop, not least because there were insufficient aircraft for all the troops to be dropped in one mission. The landings would be made at two locations, with one brigade parachuting to the southeast of Rzhyshchiv, at the northwest end of the Bukrin loop of the Dnepr, and another brigade landing west of Kanev, at the southeast end. It was expected that the two brigades – together with any additional reinforcements that were later dropped – would secure a front of about 24 miles (40km) and might have to function for up to three days before they were relieved by Vatutin's ground forces, which would support the airborne formations with artillery fire. In anticipation of the rapid arrival of ground forces, the paratroopers were not issued with digging equipment or anti-tank mines, or even waterproof outer clothing.

As was the case with *Market Garden*, radio communications would play a critical part in coordinating movements and the development of the operation, but there were too few radio sets amongst the paratroopers, and the sets that they had were supplied with a very limited number of batteries. Additional communications problems were caused by the confusion of implementing plans in a hurry; one radio operator found himself on a plane with the codebooks and spare batteries, while his partner, who had the radio, was hustled into a completely different aircraft. At the last minute, delays in getting the personnel of 1st Guards Airborne Brigade to the right location resulted in 3rd Guards Airborne Brigade being assigned to its mission. None of the officers of the latter formation had been briefed about their objectives, and there was frantic activity while maps and orders were distributed, often as the men were filing into the transport planes. Whilst there had been aerial reconnaissance of the drop zones, the intelligence about the German forces in the area was very limited.

The air transport assets of the Soviet forces were modest. The Douglas DC-3 was purchased by the Soviet Union in small numbers for use by Aeroflot before the war and a license was then granted for production of a Soviet version, the Lisunov Li-2. Nearly 240 aircraft had been built in a factory in Moscow by the beginning of the war with Germany, all for civilian use, and production ceased until January 1942 while the factory was relocated to Tashkent in what is now Uzbekistan. A total of 180 such aircraft were available for the Bukrin operation, and it was expected that they would fly two missions on the first night. In addition, ten Il-4 medium bombers would be used to transport supplies – each could carry nearly two tons of cargo – and 35 gliders, a mixture of Antonov A-7s and Gribovsky G-11s, were to carry light artillery and anti-tank guns. Most of the aircrews involved had little or no experience of carrying paratroopers, and to date had flown only in a purely cargo-carrying role.

The first drop, scheduled for late on 25 September, was to be carried out by 65 aircraft. Logistics teams laboured hard to prepare the planes, but despite their best efforts there were only 48 aircraft available at the designated time. There were further problems when pilots refused to take the expected load of 20 'units' – either paratroopers or an equivalent amount of cargo – citing safety reasons. Hastily, changes were made, largely by leaving behind some of the supplies intended for the first drop.[3] Most of the planes managed to fly two missions, but of the planned 500 flights by both transport aircraft and supporting fighters, only 298 were successfully completed. Nevertheless, 3,050 paratroopers of 3rd Airborne Guards Brigade and 1,525 of 5th Guards Airborne Brigade were dropped. The airfields were scenes of frenzied activity, with returning aircraft often ending up at the wrong airfield and columns of trucks trying frantically to move paratroopers to wherever the planes might be available. Fuel trucks had less fuel aboard than expected, resulting in paratroopers being ordered off one plane and onto another. The 45mm anti-tank guns destined for 3rd Guards Airborne Brigade remained stranded on the airfields, largely because they had not been prepared for transport in time.[4] About 2,000 paratroopers, some 30 per cent of those intended for the first drop, were unable to reach the bridgehead. To make matters worse, the weather over the Bukrin region deteriorated during the night, with low cloud and increasing rain; when the rain stopped, fog rapidly developed. The first troops to be landed were meant to set up visible signals to guide later drops, but few managed to do so, and these were generally not visible to the pilots. The only landmark that they had to guide them was the Dnepr itself, and the proximity of the river to the drop zones should have been sufficient to ensure at least a degree of accuracy; due to a lack of training in airborne operations and generally poor skills in night-time navigation, many pilots rose to higher altitudes and increased speed to evade any German anti-aircraft guns in the area, with the result that some drops were made up to 24 miles (40km) from the designated drop zones. It was estimated that only 5 per cent of the paratroopers actually landed in the drop zone; 23 per cent landed within six miles (10km); and 14 per cent landed over nine miles (15km) away. Some were unfortunate enough to land in the Dnepr itself, where they drowned as they struggled to release themselves from their parachute harnesses. Two aircraft dropped their men on the wrong side of the river, and 13 flew back to their bases without making a drop at all.[5]

The arrival of the Soviet Third Guards Tank Army and Fortieth Army on the banks of the Dnepr had not gone unnoticed by the Germans. The reconnaissance battalion of 19th Panzer Division, one of the few German units in the area, had already raised the alarm, and substantial forces were moving to the area. The rest of 19th Panzer Division, which had crossed the Dnepr at Kiev, was ordered south with all speed and its main column watched in amazement as Soviet transport planes roared overhead, manoeuvring wildly to avoid anti-aircraft fire even as the paratroopers attempted to make their jumps:

The half-track battalion of 73rd Panzergrenadier Regiment [from 19th Panzer Division], with elements of the division staff … was followed by the main body of 73rd Panzergrenadier Regiment and 74th Panzergrenadier Regiment. Behind these forces came the rest of the division, including 19th Panzer Regiment. After the troops had reached Dudari, the first Russian parachutists jumped from a transport plane flying at an altitude of 600–700m above the small village. While these paratroopers were still in the air they were brought under fire by machine-guns and a 20mm anti-aircraft gun. Between a half-minute and a minute later, the second plane flew over and thereafter at similar intervals other planes followed, flying in single file; only occasionally did two planes appear side by side.

The paratroopers came under fire while they were still in the air … As a result the fourteenth or fifteenth plane turned off in a northerly direction and dropped its parachutists near Romashki. These parachutists were immediately brought under fire by men of the supply columns, repair teams, and maintenance sections of 19th Panzer Reconnaissance Battalion.

> The jumps ... steadily became more irregular ... the paratroopers were dropped without any plan. Wherever they landed they were immediately attacked.[6]

Some of the first wave of pathfinders – the paratroopers who were meant to signal the planes that followed to safe drop zones – managed to fire signal flares as arranged, but to their dismay the Germans immediately started firing flares too in order to confuse the approaching pilots, as Matvey Tsodikovich Likhterman, a radio operator in 3rd Guards Airborne Brigade, later recalled:

> We were dropped from a height of about 1,000m. While we were descending we did not come under fire from the ground. I landed in a ravine. It was pitch black, even though my eyes were sharp. I could hear dogs barking nearby, which I thought meant that I was near a settlement. I came across two paratroopers from other aircraft. We looked at each other, waiting for the signal flares. About half an hour passed. Three rockets soared into the sky. A minute later, three identical rockets appeared to our left, then to our right, and in five minutes from all sides, flares of the same combination of colours flew up and it was impossible to tell who was firing them and where the assembly point was. I told the others, 'We have to wait, this looks very suspicious.' We were hiding, and it was silent. We heard the roar of an aircraft in the sky. And then it began! Hundreds of tracer rounds flew up. It became light as day. Anti-aircraft guns barked. A terrible tragedy was unfolding over our heads. I can't find the words to describe it. We watched the whole nightmare. The tracers of incendiary bullets tore into parachutes, and their fabric instantly burst into flames. Dozens of burning torches appeared immediately in the sky. Our comrades burned in the sky and died before they could fight on the ground. We saw everything. Two shot-up 'Douglas' planes came down before their men could jump. The guys poured from them and fell, too low to open their parachutes. A Li-2 crashed 200m from us. We rushed to the plane but there were no survivors. During this terrible night, we came across a few more paratroopers who had miraculously survived. All the area around us was covered in the white patches of parachutes. And corpses everywhere, dead and burned.[7]

This sector of the Dnepr sector was intended to be defended by the German Eighth Army. XXIV Panzer Corps, which had been the southern element of Fourth Panzer Army before Hoth's forces were split into three, had pulled back to the Dnepr bridge at Kanev and had then been assigned to Eighth Army; as its formations withdrew over the river, they were assigned to take up positions along the Dnepr on Wöhler's northern flank. One of its last units to reach the Dnepr crossing was the exhausted 10th Panzergrenadier Division. With one of its panzergrenadier regiments reduced to fewer than 80 men, the division was close to the end of its strength:

The division had to defend the wide, deep bridgehead in front of the railway bridge at Kanev and protect several infantry divisions that were crossing the Dnepr. Only after that could the division gradually reduce the bridgehead and send freed-up elements of the division across the 1,500m bridge. Finally, only one battalion was to shield the bridge against powerful enemy forces. For this task, I suggested the particularly mobile armoured reconnaissance battalion to the division commander [Generalleutnant August Schmidt]. It would have strict orders to hold its positions until the last elements of the division had crossed the river. Only then could this battalion be given permission to move.

The dangers of this mission were obvious. After this suggestion, Schmidt sat silently at the table for a long time with his head in his hands. Then he suddenly smashed his fist against the table and said, 'Damn it, you're right. I must do it. But it's simple for you – you just have to suggest it to me. But I have to give the orders; and also, I then have to write letters to the bereaved, and I know their wives personally.'

I would never forget that moment. He made me aware in this clear case of the difference between an adviser and a responsible leader. After all, it's far easier to suggest something than to order it with full responsibility. The armoured reconnaissance battalion executed its mission with far fewer losses than we had feared. After the bridge had been demolished, the last elements crossed to the west bank in assault boats and rafts.[8]

There was little prospect of rest for the men who reached the west bank, and together with the rest of Nehring's corps they now hurried to the Bukrin sector. After one of its panzer battalions was dispatched to France to be re-equipped with Panther tanks, 7th Panzer Division had withdrawn across the Dnepr at Kremenchug and was now also ordered thence, joining XXIV Panzer Corps' remnants of three infantry divisions, 20th Panzer Division and 10th Panzergrenadier Division. As they moved towards the Soviet bridgehead, the Germans were repeatedly surprised to encounter small groups of paratroopers who had been dropped far from their designated drop zones; most of them were swiftly captured or killed. In some cases, the Germans found paratroopers actually descending from the sky around them. About 10 per cent of the Soviet airborne troops who were dropped were killed or captured before midday on 26 September. The first infantry units of XXIV Panzer Corps were already in position, and their main bodies were en route – all undetected by the Red Army.

Hitler had issued an order on 25 September stressing the threat posed by the Soviet bridgehead, and the importance of destroying it as soon as possible by bringing all available forces to bear. Faced with the repeated failure of Hitler to deliver the reinforcements that he had repeatedly promised, Manstein replied the following day by reminding Hitler that Army Group South had made ten requests for reinforcements – some by signal, some at the conferences with Hitler. He added that Army Group South had also pointed out the discrepancy between orders to hold bridgeheads on the east bank whilst finding sufficient troops to defend the river line and concluded with the terse comment:

> After all these orders [to try to hold the Dnepr line despite the failure of Hitler to provide the promised reinforcements], the order of 25 September [i.e. to reduce the Soviet bridgehead as a matter of urgency] can do nothing other than give the impression that the high command believes that the army group leadership lacks both operational foresight and the energy to deal with the emerging crises.[9]

There is no record of any response from Hitler.

To the east, the Soviet commanders waited in vain for news from their airborne forces, while in the bridgehead itself the paratroopers struggled to orient themselves and to reach their assembly points. Nevertheless, the immediate balance of strength still lay with the Red Army, and forceful measures – a rapid crossing of the Dnepr and delivery of the remaining elements of the airborne forces – might yet have saved the day. Instead, further airdrops were postponed pending clarification of the situation. Within the bridgehead, there was huge confusion. Battalions and companies were intermingled, with officers finding themselves surrounded by men who they did not know. Lieutenant Colonel Goncharov, commander of 3rd Guards Brigade dropped in the northwest sector, was wounded during the first fighting; he was later evacuated in a small aircraft. The commander of 5th Guards Brigade in the southeast sector, Lieutenant Colonel Pyotor Michailovich Sidorchuk, found himself alone for two hours after landing before he encountered anyone – a soldier of 3rd Guards Brigade, who had landed in the wrong drop zone. By dawn on 26 September, he had managed to gather just five soldiers; fortunately, one of them had one of only five operational radio sets in the entire bridgehead, and Sidorchuk was able to send a report to higher commands, describing the chaos.[10] It would be nine days before he met the men who had jumped from the same aircraft. During the morning, the paratroopers began to coalesce into ad hoc groups, but these were not substantial; the largest, near Kanev, consisted of about 600 men. Many of the supplies that had been dropped for them were lost or captured by the Germans, who left some of them in the open and staged ambushes to capture any paratroopers who attempted to retrieve them. In many cases, the supplies that the paratroopers managed to locate consisted of supplies that were intended for other specialist functions. Thus, ordinary soldiers came across signals equipment or ammunition for anti-tank guns, while gunners found canisters of small-arms ammunition.

The paratroopers were engaged primarily in a struggle to survive, gathering together wherever they could; attacking the Germans was, for the first day, a secondary concern. Far from landing in an area with few or no German troops, the paratroopers were soon outnumbered by the assembling Wehrmacht units, which began a systematic search for their enemies. Likhterman was amongst those trying to evade discovery:

The Germans pursued us through the countryside and gradually wiped us out. They hunted us with dogs. I buried the notepad [with his radio codes] on the second day. At first there were three of us, then we formed a group of 12 paratroopers. We managed to escape from the roundup for four days but then our luck ran out. We had spent three days trying to escape from the constricting circle of our pursuers, but we were tightly surrounded. We emerged from a ravine and stumbled upon a group of about 70 men led by Major Zhernosekov, a battalion commander. The Germans were on all sides … One of the paratroopers lying next to me shouted, 'The battalion commander shot himself!' After the war, Zhernosekov's widow came to a veterans' meeting. I told her about this battle. She didn't want to believe me and said that her husband couldn't have shot himself. We stood with her and wept together. I survived that battle. We broke up, but there were 14 of us left in a group. Among us was an officer, a commander of a machine-gun company, and again we hid, fired back, and broke through towards the Dnepr, but things looked hopeless. We had no food, no water, we ate corn and potatoes from the fields, we couldn't light fires. We took ammunition from the dead. It was impossible to enter any village as ambushes had been set for us everywhere. We never heard any sounds of battle, like an attempted breakthrough towards us from the front line. The Germans and Vlasovite Cossacks hanged captured paratroopers on telegraph poles along the roads. Placards were hung on them: 'Greetings to *Komsomol* members from the Vlasovites'.[11]

General Andrey Andreyevich Vlasov commanded the Soviet Second Shock Army in an attack to try to lift the siege of Leningrad in 1942. His army was surrounded and he was eventually captured by the Germans. During captivity, he became an increasingly outspoken critic of Stalin and was ultimately permitted to organise the *Russkaya Osvoboditelnaya Armiya* ('Russian Liberation Army' or ROA). At the time of the Bukrin fighting, this army did not exist, but the Germans had made extensive use of his name in propaganda material and many Red Army personnel routinely described any former Soviet citizens fighting on behalf of the Germans as 'Vlasovites'. Many paramilitary formations had been recruited from Ukrainian and Russian men in the occupied zones, and these were often involved in massacres of Jews and others. It is likely that the men encountered by Likhterman were from one such unit; elsewhere in the interview, he describes them as being members of the Turkestan Legion. Although the Germans raised 16 battalions of troops from Turkic men found both amongst Soviet prisoners of war and in the occupied territories, these units were deployed exclusively in the west.

Likhterman and his small group found themselves encircled again and surrendered. A fellow soldier betrayed Likhterman as a Jew and he was fortunate to find an opportunity in the confusion to lose his documents. Together with the other paratroopers in his group he was taken to a prison camp near Uman, where he passed himself off as an ordinary Russian rifleman under the pseudonym of Mikhail Garin. As the fighting approached Uman, the prisoners were force-marched west into Romania, where he managed to escape and encountered advancing Soviet forces. He then had to endure rigorous interrogation – the Red Army routinely treated any men who had been taken prisoner as suspicious. Whilst some men who had escaped German captivity were executed, larger numbers were sent to fight in penal battalions, which were used to attack German positions and to draw defensive fire while regular soldiers launched their attack. Survival rates in a penal battalion were low, and only a few men survived long enough to earn redemption.

The Germans rapidly concluded that the airborne formations were too badly scattered, and had suffered too heavy casualties, to be a significant threat. The priority was to destroy the Red Army's bridgehead on the west bank of the Dnepr before significant armoured forces could cross. The bulk of *SS-Wiking* withdrew across the Dnepr via Cherkassy on 27 September, precisely two years after the leading elements of the division had crossed the river at Kremenchug heading in the opposite direction. The first units were immediately dispatched to the Bukrin bend where they became involved in the sweep to eliminate the Soviet paratroopers south and southwest of Pekari. General Walther Nehring, commander of XXIV Panzer Corps, later made a crisp and accurate assessment of the Soviet airborne assault:

> The airborne operation bore clear signs of amateurism. The enemy leadership lacked the essential understanding of their troops, of time and space, of the possibilities for [successful] execution and an accurate assessment of the German defenders.[12]

Confident that the situation was largely under control, Nehring ordered the first tentative attempts to drive the Soviet troops back across the Dnepr to be halted until he had assembled a more powerful force. Wöhler and Manstein agreed – the former had visited the sector and had spoken to several division commanders, and the terrain was judged to be difficult for armoured forces. The attack would need good artillery support and it was likely that the Red Army would have positioned anti-tank guns in anticipation of such an attempt by the Germans. The new plan called for a mass attack on 28 September, but Manstein remained concerned about the prospects for success, particularly as Wöhler wished to attack the Soviet bridgehead from both the northwest and the southeast; Manstein questioned whether there was sufficient strength to mount such an attack.

Everywhere, the Red Army was approaching the Dnepr. The German retreat had been conducted with considerable skill in the face of immense adversity and there had been little opportunity for the pursuing Soviet forces to trap any significant formations east of the great river, but there was widespread dismay amongst the German troops when they crossed to the west bank to find that few if any positions had been prepared for them. Generally, the German policy of withdrawing during the night and then holding a new line for the following day, launching counterattacks when possible, was an effective one, but it took a huge toll on the troops who were constantly marching, digging new positions, or engaged in combat. Nor were the pursuing Soviet troops the only danger for the tired Germans who reached the west bank. Like other members of the Wehrmacht's armoured forces, the men of one of 12th Panzer Division's panzergrenadier regiments had been in near-constant combat and were just relieved to have a moment to pause and catch their breath:

> Exhausted but happy to have escaped from the front line, the company reached the regiment's assembly area in Pylypcha [about 50 miles or 84km southwest of

Kiev] during the evening of 24 September. The supply columns and regimental staff had been positioned in the village, which was about 15km [nine miles] behind the front line. The men in the combat companies ... simply wished to be able to sleep in peace in what was their first quiet night for two weeks. When the dozing sentries had their weapons grabbed from them just a few hours later by Russians emerging from the darkness, this was why shouts of warning and a few shots were not taken seriously by other units. But then grenades detonated, vehicles started to burn, and the wounded began to call for medics! Finally, 3rd Company's ammunition truck, together with all the newly arrived weapons, was blown into the air with an enormous bang, and as machine-gun and mortar fire began, the most hardy veterans realised that they had to cope with partisans. In a short time a full-scale fight developed from the initial confusion. It continued until dawn and ended with the complete destruction of the battalion-strong enemy ... [The full scale of the fighting] only became clear during the course of the following day. The drivers of a transport unit who had been asleep in the cabs of their trucks were found with their throats cut. Many who had been with our staff and supply columns for many years had not survived this night.[13]

In mid-September, the Germans completed their evacuation of the Taman Peninsula, to the east of the Crimea. The Red Army claimed that it had driven them out, but the reality was that the German defences had obdurately repulsed every attack that the Soviet forces threw at them. Vasilevsky was still with Southern Front, overseeing its operations, and proposed moving the troops that had been attacking the German Seventeenth Army in the Taman Peninsula to the north coast of the Sea of Azov in order to aid the continuing attempts to reach the lower Dnepr. As they drove the German Sixth Army west from the Mius, both Vasilevsky and Colonel General Fedor Ivanovich Tolbukhin, the commander of Southern Front, had planned to seize crossings over the Molochnaya River, which runs down from the north through Melitopol to the Sea of Azov, as part of their pursuit operation rather than as a deliberate, formal attack. To their frustration, they discovered that – unlike the German troops falling back to the Dnepr – Hollidt's Sixth Army now occupied positions that had been prepared in advance and the leading Soviet formations, Fifth Shock Army and Second Guards Army, came to an abrupt halt when they reached the Molochnaya. The German defences in this sector, known as the Wotan Line, consisted of several layers of entrenchments and strongpoints with plentiful minefields and wire entanglements. Together with the swampy banks of the Molochnaya, this constituted a formidable barrier.

Strung out over the steppe during their advance, the depleted Soviet divisions were increasingly short of personnel, equipment, ammunition, food and fuel, and several attempts to seize bridgeheads were beaten off by the Germans with comparative ease. Prisoner interrogations revealed that amongst the German defenders were the troops of 4th Mountain Division, one of the units pulled back into the Crimea from the Taman Peninsula. In addition, Soviet intelligence reports identified other relatively fresh German formations. In late 1942, under pressure to release surplus personnel to the army, Göring had instead created a number of Luftwaffe field divisions, many of which were rushed to the Eastern Front to deal with the crisis created by the encirclement of Sixth Army in Stalingrad; the new divisions performed very poorly and were generally subordinated to regular infantry divisions after suffering heavy losses in their first battles, but some were more fortunate. One of them was 5th Luftwaffe Field Division, which had spent much of its existence guarding the coastline of the Crimea – a good opportunity for its officers and personnel to get to grips with being an infantry unit. The division was now sent to reinforce the defenders of Melitopol. Vasilevsky had wished to strengthen the Red Army units in the area by bringing over the forces no longer needed in the Taman Peninsula; to his chagrin, Kleist – the commander of Army Group A, operating on the extreme southern end of the German Eastern Front – had already put such a plan into effect.

The armies of both sides had paid a heavy toll in terms of casualties and material losses in the bitter fighting of the summer. After visiting the armies of Southern Front, Vasilevsky wrote a report for *Stavka* about the poor state of Fifth Shock Army and Second Guards Army. The other forces available to Tolbukhin were Twenty-Eighth, Forty-Fourth and Fifty-First Armies, which were only in slightly better shape. After the briefest of pauses for regrouping, Vasilevsky issued orders for another assault on the German lines to be made on 26 September. In particular, two artillery divisions – at full strength, each of these would have fielded 72 76mm guns, 72 122mm howitzers, 36 152mm howitzers, and a mortar brigade with over 100 120mm mortars – and an independent mortar brigade would be used to assist the breakthrough. Separate artillery divisions were not a feature of the manner in which the Wehrmacht or western armies organised their forces, though as will be described later, the Germans experimented with such a formation, creating 18th Artillery Division in October 1943 around elements of 18th Panzer Division; this was prompted by an express order from Hitler to create such a unit with good mobility, which could be used to provide additional offensive and defensive support where required. As a precaution, it included a battalion of infantry in its establishment for protection of the artillery units, something that proved its value on several occasions when the infantry managed to hold off attacking Soviet troops long enough for the division to withdraw its heavy weapons. The Germans soon abandoned the project, but the Red Army continued to use such formations through the war and they remained part of Soviet military organisation for many years after.

There were only three days for the forces of Southern Front to prepare for the new attack, as Lieutenant General Sergei Semenovich Biryuzov, Tolbukhin's chief of staff, later recalled:

> This assault was to thrust through the enemy's defensive positions on the Molochnaya River north of Melitopol, encircle and destroy the main force of the enemy's Melitopol group, and further develop the offensive towards the Crimea on the heels of the enemy who would be retreating to Perekop and the lower Dnepr.
>
> The main attack was to be carried out by Fifth Shock Army, Forty-Fourth Army and Second Guards Army, reinforced with tank and cavalry corps ... To develop any successes on this axis, Fifty-First Army was held in reserve by Southern Front. We assumed that it would be deployed when the enemy's defences had been penetrated to their full depth. A supporting attack was to be made south of Melitopol by forces of Twenty-Eighth Army. It was given a limited task: tie down the enemy.
>
> ... I summoned the new chief of the operations department, Colonel [Alexander Pavlovich] Tarasov, who had just joined us from Karelian Front, and assigned him specific tasks, warning him that we had to work quickly. 'When should I finish all of this?' he enquired.
>
> 'By 6am tomorrow morning.'
>
> Tarasov went pale. For a few moments he couldn't say a word. Then he recovered a little and firmly stated, 'I cannot deal with this amount of work in such a short time. It will take at least a few days.'
>
> 'In a few days, it won't be of any use to anyone.' My close assistant was so upset that I felt sorry for him. 'Come, let's go for dinner,' I said to Tarasov, feeling that at that moment, he needed camaraderie and kindness.[14]

According to the plan that was rapidly drawn up – after a 'comradely' dinner, Tarasov spent the night producing the detailed planning that Biryuzov had requested – the first two days would see an advance of about 12 miles (20km), at which point three mobile groups would be unleashed to break into the rear of the

German positions. One was to drive forward to reach the lower Dnepr opposite Kherson; the second was to attack towards the southwest to reach the Perekop Isthmus connecting the Crimea to the mainland; and the third was to reach the lakes a little further to the east. By doing so, the mobile groups would isolate the German Seventeenth Army in the Crimea and would envelop any defenders in Melitopol and further south. At the same time, the seizure of the Perekop Isthmus before German troops could reach the area opened up the possibility of striking into the Crimea and thus preventing the Germans from establishing a defensible position. The advance to the lower Dnepr was seen as a prelude to an advance over the river with the intention of opening the road to Nikolayev and Odessa. After reviewing the plans, *Stavka* made only minor amendments – instead of bringing troops up from the Taman Peninsula as reserves, it was suggested that they should be used to launch an amphibious operation into the eastern parts of the Crimea.[15]

When the operation began on 26 September, it ran into tough resistance and gains were minimal, despite a heavy initial barrage. Stalin and Vasilevsky discussed matters by telephone late on 28 September. Stalin informed his subordinate that the greatest effort in the Ukraine would be made further north: Vatutin's Voronezh Front was to advance across the Dnepr and capture Kiev before continuing to the west; Konev's Steppe Front would cross the Dnepr and strike towards Kirovograd and Krivoy Rog; and Malinovsky's Southwest Front would concentrate on destroying the German bridgehead at Zaporozhye. Southern Front was to continue its attacks to isolate the Crimea.

There was a small, though important, development along the Molochnaya. During the fighting to the north of Melitopol, the Soviet units identified several German units that had been moved to the threatened sector from further south. Biryuzov correctly identified this as evidence that the German Sixth Army had no further reserves available and had only been able to reinforce its line by shifting troops from one zone to another. However, when he brought this to Tolbukhin's attention, the front commander replied that the failure to break through was due to inadequate efforts by the armies operating to the north of Melitopol. He was particularly critical of Lieutenant General Vasily Afanasevich Khomenko, commander of Forty-Fourth Army, and dispatched Biryuzov to Khomenko's headquarters to oversee matters:

We found Khomenko in a very dejected state. What had happened to his usual daring, even arrogance? This army commander had a striking characteristic: when everything went well for him, he was excessively cheerful and was able, as the saying goes, to move mountains; if operations failed, Khomenko immediately became upset and seemed lost. In addition, I had noticed earlier that he was not sufficiently trained in operational matters. This latter was apparently because his previous service had mainly been with border troops.[16]

Despite this assessment, Biryuzov returned to Tolbukhin's headquarters and reported that the lack of progress by Forty-Fourth Army was not due to failures on the part of its troops or its command, but because of the strength of German defences. Tolbukhin remained unconvinced and continued to criticise Khomenko. Nevertheless, the assaults were stopped on 30 September to allow time to regroup.

Further north, almost constantly engaged by the pursuing Soviet forces, *SS-Das Reich* pulled back towards Kremenchug, and as news came of the Soviet airborne operation at Bukrin, the panzergrenadier regiment *Der Führer* and its associated support formations were ordered to cross to the west bank of the Dnepr as soon as possible and then proceed towards Kanev in order to take part in the operations to prevent the Red Army from establishing a bridgehead. While the troops struggled to reach and cross the Dnepr, hindered more by the heavy traffic than Soviet intervention, Krüger (the division commander) and Obersturmbannführer Sylvester Stadtler (the commander of *Der Führer*) were summoned to Hitler's headquarters in Rastenburg to be awarded medals. Fortunately for the division, they were only briefly absent, returning to the Dnepr region on 27 September, but Krüger took advantage of the opportunity to speak frankly to Hitler. Replacement drafts were inadequately trained, he reported, and replacement of equipment was also far from what was needed. Perhaps taking advantage of the privileged status of the SS, Krüger went on to say that it was pointless and wasteful to designate places like Kharkov as 'fortresses' to be held at all costs when the tactical situation on the ground made such orders unworkable. The two men had also seen first-hand the lack of preparation of the planned Dnepr defences, and Hitler silently listened to their assessment of the situation. After a lengthy dinner, the two men were invited to further discussions, and Stadtler commented that the war appeared to be lost and that despite the sacrifices made by the men in the front line, the situation couldn't be altered. There was, apparently, a stony silence, which Hitler broke by inviting the two SS officers to return the following day when Zeitzler and Göring would be present.

On 28 September, the conversation resumed early in the morning and Zeitzler pointed out that the lack of preparation of the Dnepr positions owed much to Hitler's very tardy approval of the fortified line. Whilst both field officers were grateful of the chance to speak so openly to the highest command, they returned to *SS-Das Reich* with a strong feeling that Hitler had little understanding of the tactical realities that they faced, or of the ordeal of the overstretched soldiers in the front line.[17]

In addition to moving tens of thousands of head of cattle and other commodities deemed to be valuable to the advancing Red Army, the withdrawing Germans took with them prisoners that they had captured in their repeated anti-partisan operations. Nikolai Gavrilovich Kolesnik was a young soldier who was wounded in the German advance on Voronezh in 1942, and managed to escape captivity on his second attempt. He was recaptured a year later:

> On 25 September they loaded us and some prisoners of war into rail cars, 95 per car, and sent us west ... They took us to Mauthausen concentration camp ... They formed us into groups of ten men and began to beat us with sticks from both sides, making sure nobody evaded them. We were on a flat area surrounded on all sides by ditches. We had to run from one end of this area to the other. While we were running, we had to remove all our clothing and throw it into the ditches. Then they pulled the hair off our head and other parts of our bodies more than shaved it and doused us with some kind of disinfecting substance.
>
> We were subjected to a conveyor-like medical inspection. They made a pencil mark on everyone's chest. A red cross: you went to the barracks. A blue cross: you went to the hospital. A black cross: you went to the crematorium. They put a red cross on my chest. They led us to the 'bath' where they poured icy water over us for five minutes, after which they sent us to the quarantine block. This was intended for 1,200 people but there were many more than that packed in ...
>
> In the morning they drove us, naked, out into the freezing air and in place of shoes issued us with wooden clogs for our feet. I remember how the square was paved with cobblestones, and how it was almost impossible to stand upright on them in clogs. We hugged each other in the cold but they beat us to separate us and forced us to run in circles on the square. In wooden clogs![18]

Kolesnik survived the dreadful regime in Mauthausen – discipline was enforced by the harshest of measures, food was inadequate, and any who became significantly ill were thrown into freezing pools of water to drown – until March 1945, when he escaped with nine other inmates. They were recaptured and taken back to Mauthausen, where they were hung from chains on the camp gates as an example to others. Before they could be executed, the prison guards fled. The following day – 4 May 1945 – the Red Army liberated the camp.

The remaining German bridgeheads across the Dnepr were steadily shrinking. On 26 September, the perimeter around the Kremenchug bridgehead was barely seven miles (12km) from the crossings. Raus issued orders to his XI Corps for all units that could be spared to be sent to the west bank. Throughout 27 September there were constant clashes between the rearguard and their pursuers; both sides were too depleted and exhausted to be able to achieve a decisive outcome, but the retreating Germans knew that any mishap at this stage could easily result in the Red Army's spearheads reaching the vital bridges before the evacuation was complete, as a junior officer in *SS-Totenkopf* wrote:

> Shortly before we reached the river crossings at Kremenchug the situation once more became critical. Russian tanks pressed us hard and in some places broke through. Unsettling rumours about enemy paratroopers and tanks on the Dnepr bridges troubled the soldiers.[19]

Under almost constant air attack, the Germans began to evacuate the bridgehead. With the news of the parachute landings at Bukrin, there was a great deal of uncertainty about what the troops would find awaiting them on the west bank. During the afternoon and evening, the Red Army made a determined attempt to overwhelm the rearguard but were beaten off. As darkness fell, most of *SS-Totenkopf* withdrew across the bridges. The heavy weapons that had been brought across the river now took up firing positions to support the rearguard; only elements of *Grossdeutschland*, *SS-Totenkopf* and 320th Infantry Division were left in the bridgehead. In the early afternoon, a group of perhaps 25 Soviet tanks made a determined attempt to reach the bridges and were repulsed with considerable difficulty, and Soviet infantry pushed through the southeast flank and reached the artillery positions of the few guns of *SS-Totenkopf* still on the east bank. A resolute counterattack drove the Soviet troops back, allowing the guns to withdraw across the river. At the same time, pioneers from all the German divisions still east of the Dnepr laid extensive minefields in Kremenchug. There was near-complete disregard for conventions about putting up warning signs and mines were laid on roads, in gardens, and even within buildings. The lack of any clear signs resulted in German vehicles occasionally suffering serious damage as they set off the mines, adding further to the road congestion.

Likhterman might have complained of little sign that the Red Army's ground forces were trying to reach the paratroopers who had survived the disastrous airborne operation in the Bukrin bend, but the reality was that Fortieth Army and Third Guards Tank Army were struggling to bring sufficient men across the Dnepr just to hold their existing bridgeheads, let alone launch determined attacks towards the west. Luftwaffe formations made repeated attacks on the troops assembling to cross, disrupting attempts to build rafts and ferries large enough to transport tanks. The troops who had managed to cross the river remained in isolated pockets, unable to coalesce into a single large bridgehead. The panzergrenadiers of *SS-Das Reich*, supported by the division's artillery and reconnaissance battalion, attacked the bridgeheads from the northwest on 28 September after a long march from Kremenchug, circling to the west in order to be able to make their assault. Although a number of villages were taken, German casualties were disproportionately high for the amount of ground gained. The capture of Khodorov allowed the Germans to bring the attempts by Soviet pioneers to build a pontoon bridge across the river under artillery fire but attempts at further advances foundered in the face of determined resistance. Unterstürmführer Gerhard Schmager was the commander of the motorcycle company of *Der Führer* and was now ordered to make an attack against the rear of the Soviet position in an attempt to unlock the defences:

In the gathering dark, the company had to move past the enemy along the Dnepr and then turn back in order to take him in the flank and rear. As soon as the motorcyclists had begun their full attack after a short preparation period, green flares were to signal to the two battalions deployed frontally to begin their attack.

Some woodland and a few awkward ravines were crossed almost silently. The darkness helped us approach without being spotted. About 45 minutes after the assignment of the mission the sweat-soaked motorcyclists were in the rear of the enemy at the bottom of the slope where Ivan sat, 25m above them. Pushing and supporting each other, dragging their weapons and ammunition with them, the motorcyclists climbed the slope as quietly as possible in the darkness. Sometimes, we heard a repressed curse. Occasional firing could be heard from the sector of II and III Battalions.

Ivan had no idea what was brewing to his rear.

The preparation area consisted of a few square metres of ground. The last instructions were issued in whispers. The motorcyclists took a few deep breaths. The green flares climbed into the night sky and slowly descended – the men of 15th Company *Der Führer* stormed forward with a wild 'Hurrah!' and furious roars, which echoed back eerily from a nearby slope. It sounded like the battle cry of more than a hundred men – the actual combat strength of the company was one officer, six NCOs and 39 men! Hurling hand grenades, firing on the run with machine-guns and machine-pistols and yelling at the top of their voices, the motorcyclists ran up to the completely dumbfounded and startled enemy ...

At the same time the two battalions used the enemy's confusion to begin their frontal attack. Ivan was no match for this night attack. Total surprise was achieved. The nocturnal action lasted barely 15 minutes and then 15th Company was firmly in control of the hill.

The positions were searched and secured rapidly. A weak counterattack made immediately after the capture of the hill was swiftly repulsed. Together with the men who had arrived from II Battalion, we threw boxfuls of hand grenades at the enemy who had appeared below at the riverbank until finally there was silence.[20]

Whilst Schmager and his comrades celebrated their success and took up new positions, *SS-Das Reich* was ordered to make a further attack against another ridge a little further to the southeast. Given the losses that the battlegroup had suffered during the day, there was no likelihood of success and the attack was cancelled. In the following days, much of *SS-Das Reich* – in particular the panzer regiment, which had almost no operational tanks left – was pulled out of line and sent a short distance to the west for much-needed rest.

On 29 September, Nehring launched his counterattack from the southeast with 7th and 20th Panzer Divisions, supported by 72nd Infantry Division. At first, the Germans made good progress, but as they approached the Dnepr they came under increasingly heavy fire from Soviet guns on the far bank. Ultimately, the attack broke down before the bridgehead could be completely destroyed. The delay in launching the attack might have allowed Nehring to concentrate his forces, but it also gave the Red Army time to move personnel across the river; elements of 51st Guards Tank Brigade and 69th Mechanised Brigade from Rybalko's Third Guards Tank Army were now on the west bank and carried out an ambush near Grigorovka, effectively bringing the German attack to a standstill. Rather than get drawn into an increasingly bloody battle for little gain, the Germans decided to leave the Soviet forces on the west bank and to screen off their bridgehead. The Soviet forces had meanwhile constructed a bridge capable of carrying tanks and reinforced their bridgehead with substantial forces; Vatutin now tried to use these to break out, but two attempts to do so ended with heavy losses. Realising that the opportunity that had seemed to present itself for a rapid advance via the Bukrin bridgehead towards the River Bug, a further 132 miles (220km) to the southwest, had disappeared with the arrival of XXIV Panzer Corps, Vatutin called off a planned third assault. Troops from the Soviet Twenty-Seventh Army began to cross into the bridgehead, allowing Rybalko's armour to be withdrawn for use elsewhere. If it wasn't possible for Voronezh Front to break through the German troops facing the Bukrin bridgehead and attack towards Kiev, it was time to consider making an attempt from a small crossing that had been secured at Lyutezh, a little to the north of the Ukrainian capital. On the German side, the reduction in intensity of fighting allowed 7th Panzer Division to be pulled out of line.

Despite the sweep by the Germans to eliminate the Soviet airborne forces, several pockets continued to function. The paratroopers in the northern landing area suffered from being in relatively open terrain; they were in groups that were too large to hide and too weak to engage the Germans in open battle. The southern landing area was more heavily forested, allowing Sidorchuk to organise the men he gathered together into three battalions. On 6 October, a signalman with an intact radio joined the group and Sidorchuk could finally establish proper communications with Red Army units on the east bank of the Dnepr.[21] It was now possible to organise supply drops to the airborne forces, and after surviving several German attempts to wipe them out, Sidorchuk's men moved further south to the Tagancha Forest, where they encountered further small groups of paratroopers from the disastrous landing. From here, Sidorchuk mounted a series of attacks on nearby German units, triggering counterattacks that led to confused fighting. Nevertheless, largely through encounters with other groups of paratroopers, Sidorchuk's brigade was still able to field over 1,200 men by early November.

The airborne assault in the Bukrin bend was one of the largest airborne operations conducted by the Red Army in the war. Stalin was scathing in his criticism of the manner in which the operation was planned and executed:

> The attempt to make a mass parachute drop at night is evidence of the incompetence of its authors. As experience has shown, a mass parachute drop at night even on one's own territory entails great difficulties.[22]

There were many reasons for the failure. Senior commanders had little experience of airborne operations, and the lessons of the deployment of paratroopers at Vyazma had not been analysed to any useful degree. The need to plan and execute the operation at speed made it impossible for sufficient planes and supplies to be brought to the right locations, and reconnaissance of the intended drop zones was inadequate. Similar criticisms could be made a year later following the failure of *Market Garden* to secure a bridgehead over the Rhine. The Germans, too, had poor results from airborne operations; although the invasion of Crete, largely by paratroopers, was ultimately successful, the airborne forces suffered heavy losses in the attack. Before the war, some enthusiasts had anticipated the use of parachute formations to capture key locations quickly before defenders could organise themselves, thus paving the way for the advancing ground forces, but the reality of deploying the paratroopers from slow-moving transport aircraft proved to be a different matter for all nations. Even the relatively successful parachute drops in Normandy in 1944 were bedevilled by confusion when the two US divisions were not dropped as tightly as intended, and the one airborne landing that was an unequivocal success – the airborne assault in conjunction with ground forces crossing the Rhine in 1945 – took place against an enemy who had largely been defeated. On no occasion was an airborne operation that was conceived in haste a success.

News now arrived of Soviet forces crossing the Dnepr either side of Mishurin Rog, 28 miles (45km) downstream of Kremenchug and at the boundary between Eighth Army and First Panzer Army; this was in keeping with Stalin's instructions to Konev's Steppe Front to cross the river and then push on towards Kirovograd and Krivoy Rog. Wöhler wanted to mount an immediate counterattack with whatever armoured elements of *SS-Totenkopf* were available together with troops from 106th Infantry Division; Raus protested that *SS-Totenkopf* was too weak to provide support for such an operation and suggested using elements of *Grossdeutschland* instead. Wöhler agreed to the changes. Meanwhile, the Kremenchug bridgehead had contracted to the immediate area around the road and rail bridges. While troops were crossing on 28 September, Soviet aircraft attacked the road bridge; one bomb triggered some of the demolition charges, partly destroying the bridge, and henceforth it was only possible to bring heavy weapons back across the river via the rail bridge. Nevertheless, despite the best efforts of the Soviet forces closing in on the bridgehead, the evacuation proceeded smoothly. That evening, both bridges were destroyed. One battalion of German infantry lost its way back to the river and the planned final phase of the operation was delayed to give the retreating men time to reach the banks, where a small fleet of pioneer boats had been positioned. Under sporadic mortar fire, the last German troops boarded the boats in the late evening accompanied by the commander of the *Grossdeutschland* panzergrenadier regiment, who had been in command of the last forces in the bridgehead.

Abdullin and his comrades were amongst the first troops to enter Kremenchug. Like many veterans of the Red Army, Abdullin casually termed all former Soviet citizens who had served in uniformed services for the Germans as 'Vlasovites':

In Kremenchug, which we entered on 29 September, we liberated a camp in which several thousand Soviet prisoners of war were tortured. Partisans and underground workers who were captured were also held here. The Fascists in this camp used the cruellest methods of torturing and killing prisoners. The gallows here were unusual – the Fascists hanged people on iron hooks, by a leg, or a hand, or all limbs simultaneously, just for a laugh. The executioners were Vlasovites. Hundreds of people had been hanged, but we managed to bring out twelve to fifteen alive.

I later saw an episode that I have remembered all my life. On a street, a group of women was leading several Nazis. Everyone had an axe or a pitchfork, a poker or a stick. The women were very agitated, shouting and making a lot of noise in Ukrainian. I couldn't understand everything. But they stopped near a pit and began to push the Nazis into it, and several Vlasovites were thrown in too. One Fascist tried to resist, squealing, 'In my house! *Kinder!*' And the women shouted back at him: 'And what do we have? Puppies? So what? Push him in!'

And no power on earth could have forced me to stop this just punishment of the Fascist executioners. In Kremenchug the Fascists mined everything that might attract our attention. A *Komsorg* of the neighbouring battalion picked up a Russian balalaika that was on the ground – and killed himself, and 17 others with him. I saw a new bicycle leaning against a wattle fence in an alley, and my boyish passion, which had never left me, to ride a bicycle carried me straight to it. I hurried to the bicycle, its metalwork sparkling, but a senior lieutenant rushed forward trying to outrun me. Feeling aggrieved, I tried to tell myself I didn't really want it. I turned around and walked back towards the street. Suddenly there was an explosion behind me! I turned around: no senior lieutenant, no bicycle – just a smoking crater in place of the fence where the bicycle had been leaning.

Leaving their shelters, the residents of Kremenchug hurried back to their city and their homes and throughout the city there were the rumbles of explosions…

[A few days later] I recalled visiting a small church in Kremenchug. The Fascists had tried to destroy it several times. They had tried to blow it up and set it alight. Its wooden parts had burned away but the church was still standing. In the courtyard of the church I met an old man.

'Who are you, old man?'

'The priest.'

We sat and talked … The priest wasn't in his robes but in a padded old shirt and did not look at all like a religious minister. It was interesting to meet him without these ceremonial things which I wouldn't really have understood. And what to say? Even in my childhood I had been told that everything that would happen in the world was foreseen in the Bible. Everything that was and will be in the world was in the scriptures, only in words that were incomprehensible. Well, I was curious and said, 'If everything is predicted in the Bible, then surely this war is predicted, eh?'

'Yes, yes, my son.'

I was surprised that he didn't try to fool me with any ingenuity – the most important thing for him seemed to be that I was worried and tormented. 'How long will this war last?'

I was sure that he would just shrug his shoulders. But he thought, as if counting or remembering, and said to me, 'About 48 months.'

What guided the priest in saying this? Of course, not the Bible. I understood this. Most likely he was prompted by intuition or common sense. Now, sitting on the left bank of the Dnepr, thinking about this figure of 48 months, I counted, and it seemed that if this figure was to be believed, we had reached the Dnepr in the middle of the war.[23]

The Germans regarded the withdrawal to and from the Kremenchug bridgehead as a considerable success. The Red Army tried to claim that it was a substantial victory, but the figures quoted by Soviet-era writers as justification for their claims are not impressive: Konev wrote that the elimination of the bridgehead resulted in the capture of 21 anti-aircraft guns, 26 machine-guns, several motorcycles and barges, 640 tons of grain, and 300 head of cattle, and that the fighting cost the Germans 2,700 dead and wounded.[24] Given the tens of thousands of cows and other livestock moved to the west, this seems like a modest haul. Nevertheless, celebratory salvoes of artillery were fired in Moscow to mark the occasion, and several units were raised to 'Guards' status and awarded the additional title of 'Kremenchug' to recognise their role in the fighting. With barely a pause, Konev and other commanders began the next phase of their advance: a thrust across the Dnepr south of Kremenchug. If the Germans had expected that there would be a pause in operations, they were to be disappointed.

On 5 October, Abdullin's division made an attempt to cross the Dnepr to the north of Kremenchug near the village of Vlasivka. At the selected point, Peschany Island – a relatively flat strip of land about two miles long – was in the middle of the stream and it could be used as a staging point for the crossing. It divided the Dnepr into two channels, with a 700m channel between the Soviet infantry and the island and a smaller channel from the island to the German-occupied bank. The infantrymen were given a few days to prepare, stitching their greatcoats into big bags, which they filled with straw as flotation aids. Abdullin was an accomplished swimmer, but many of the men would struggle, particularly as they were in full combat kit and boots; Abdullin had his submachine-gun, a pistol, grenades, and ammunition. Others were encumbered with even heavier equipment.

Unknown to Abdullin and his comrades, the Germans had deployed troops on Peschany Island. The Soviet soldiers began to enter the water late on 5 October, deliberately starting some distance upstream. Abdullin estimated that he was more than halfway to the island before the silence was suddenly broken by German artillery. The shells plunged down around the swimming men, killing many and leaving others disoriented. Abdullin helped a soldier who was struggling to stay afloat to reach the island:

Finally our feet touched the bottom and we stood. It was shallow. Explosions illuminated the figures of our soldiers running from the shore onto the island. The flashes showed pandemonium. An explosion! Again an explosion! The air around me was full of sand that couldn't fall to earth … Amongst the sand raining down from the sky were fragments like wet pieces of bark. Pieces of human bodies …

While we were floundering across the Dnepr, all our regiments had become mixed up and nobody could find their own. Where's our unit? Where's the battalion commander? The thoughts flashed through my head, together with the stupid answer: Look at the sand! Look at the sand! The sand was almost completely covered with bodies, alive or dead you couldn't tell … Sand was all over me, in my mouth too. It blasted my face and flayed my skin away as if it were sandpaper … A blast wave knocked me to the left. There was no time to fall before another blast wave hurled me to the right. I was shaken in all directions and then fell. I squirmed, drowning in the wet sand like a crab. Sand and water wrapped my beaten and exhausted body. I just wanted to lie down. But I couldn't put my head down, I would choke. But was it any better to expose it? The blast waves tried to tear it off …

A comrade from 13th Division was searching for his men but couldn't find anyone, he fell next to me and shouted in my ear: 'I'm Sasha – Sasha Koleskinov! Let's stay together! Do you understand? We can help each other! Do you understand?'

'Got it!' I screamed. The Fascists hammered away at the island. They gave us no respite. What to do next? Our guns wouldn't fire – all the parts were jammed with sand, as were our grenades. The muzzle of a half-buried Maxim gun was sticking out, our shovels glinted – the only weapon that didn't fear sand …

Sasha and I decided to move along the island towards the right bank of the Dnepr. It was quieter, there were no explosions, it was 'dead ground'. We ran, jumping over people lying like seals. We stopped, we were alone. But what was this – in front of us, machine-guns were firing! They spat out red flames! So the Fascists were on the island? That was why the shells weren't bursting over here – the Nazi artillerymen wouldn't fire on their own! That's it! The Germans were here on the island!

... It was a bad, bad situation. It began to grow light. The Fascists intensified their shelling ... The Fascist shells rained down but they couldn't kill us all. They resumed again and again after five-minute pauses. They shelled us for 20 minutes, then paused again for five minutes ... I think of the most difficult battles in the Kursk salient and there was nothing more difficult or dangerous than this. Near Prokhorovka, near Dragunsk, on the road of death over the Vorskla, and now here, this island on the Dnepr! An island grave! With its unjust cruelty and doom, it eclipsed all my experience of the battles from the Volga to the Dnepr.

Unarmed, stunned, half-blind, confused, scattered, dying hopelessly under the cruel Hitlerites' artillery fire ... we had no contact with the left bank. The only thing we were achieving was drawing the fire of the Fascist artillery, stopping the Hitlerites from using it elsewhere. But perhaps this was the strategic plan? Perhaps we were not dying here in vain? It seemed as if the Hitlerites wanted to destroy us quickly so they could move their guns to another sector. Only they couldn't wipe us out and with renewed vigour and anger they resumed their shelling.

The day passed. When night fell the Nazis stopped firing ... [rather than swim back to the east bank] my plan was that we should stop looking for our own men. We were all here together – put together a shock group of five hundred and attack the Fascists' trenches here at dawn on the other shore of the island. There we would be safe from the artillery. But how could we attack without automatic weapons or grenades? Our guns would have to be the blinding sun in the eyes of the Nazis! Our grenades would be suddenness and speed! We would fall on the Fritzes in their trenches! We would kick them, tear at them with our teeth! We would take their machine-guns, set up all-round defence, and dig in. In addition to Sasha, other soldiers listened to my plan. Some thought it unrealistic but everyone agreed to take part. All options here on the island were the same, you would still die – and it was better to die in a fight than lying on wet sand.

We gathered quickly – more than 500! We moved quietly as close as possible to the German trenches and burrowed into the sand. The signal for attack would be when my group stood up. It was not yet dawn when the Fascist artillery opened up again. They ploughed up the ground behind us where the wounded lay, then moved the shelling to the middle of the island, where we were. A strong blast hit my head. It seemed as if at least a ton of sand buried me before I could close my eyes. My head was ringing, my eyes burning, it was dark, I felt I was lying under a giant weight. With all my strength I pressed upwards to escape. My head jerked up easily and only then did I realise that there was no weight on me. But I couldn't hear or see anything. I blindly dug at the sand until water flowed into it, I grabbed it with a handful of silt and splashed it against my eyes. I had to see! It splashed against my red-hot, inflamed eyes and I could distinguish a bloody, muddy glimmer of light. First red, then lighter and lighter.

Sasha raked at the sand and splashed cleaner water in my eyes. I tried to blink – how it hurt! I blinked and blinked, and it improved. But there was still dead silence. As before, there were explosions all around. I could barely see them and not hear them at all. Sasha pushed my nose into the sand when I had to duck, then lifted me by the collar when he could …

I looked to the east and saw the sun rolling up over the horizon. Sasha poked his thumb under my nose … he made a running gesture on the sand with two fingers – to attack. I nodded approval. I got up – I was glad my legs would hold me! We stood up, ten or 15 of us, as we had agreed. We did not have time to take three steps before an avalanche of 500 jumped out of the sand and followed us in a black storm towards the Fascist trenches. I saw open, screaming mouths. I screamed and though I could not hear my own voice, I felt the pain as my scream tore at my throat. I was rushing across the sand towards the frightened faces of the Germans …

Many amongst those running with me were falling. But the sun blinded the Germans and they fired inaccurately. I saw a German had already dropped away from the firing point and was climbing the opposite side of the trench. An officer's mouth was open as he shouted, he fired a pistol and the soldier jumped back into the trench. But he couldn't shoot them all – others had already climbed out and were running. We jumped on top of the most determined Germans, or simply those paralysed by fear. We struck them with feet and fists, we pulled away their weapons. A soldier sat astride a Fritz, riding him back and forth. I used my jammed submachine-gun like a cudgel and finally grabbed a functioning gun from a dead Fascist, and now I wasn't afraid and shot at the escaping Fritzes.[25]

Abdullin and his comrades held their position for five days, exchanging fire with the Germans to either side. Then, as his hearing began to recover, the Soviet soldiers found that the Germans had abandoned the island. They returned to the left bank, where to their relief they learned that an attempt had been made to recall them two days before. A small group of men from the neighbouring division had actually succeeded not only in reaching the island, but had also crossed the second channel and had reached the German-held bank with the aid of local partisans.

Abdullin wrote that he learned some 30 years later that the entire operation had been a feint, intended to divert German attention from other attempts to cross the Dnepr, but the memoirs of Zhadov, whose army controlled the units involved in this attack, suggest otherwise:

> In order to force the Dnepr, XXXII Guards Rifle Corps' 13th and 97th Guards Rifle Divisions were designated for the first attack; for XXXIII Guards Rifle Corps, 6th Guards Airborne Division and 95th Guards Rifle Division. Each corps had a division in reserve.
>
> ... The first attack was by 95th Guards Rifle Division, but it was unable to penetrate the enemy's dense barrage. At first it seemed that things were going better in 6th Guards Airborne Division's sector. Mixed groups of scouts and sappers ... forced the Dnepr and established themselves on Bolshoi Island. However, all attempts to exploit this small success failed. Battalions of the first echelons of these regiments couldn't reach the island. In XXXII Guards Rifle Corps' sector the divisions in the first echelon captured small islets ... and the island of Pechany.
>
> Thus, the army failed to capture bridgeheads on the west bank of the Dnepr. Only isolated islands to the north of Kremenchug were captured.
>
> What was the reason for our failures? Firstly, I must emphasise that the army's formations reached the Dnepr without their full complement of personnel and combat equipment. The army was short of ammunition. Communications were very stretched. After all, by that stage the troops had fought for more than 300km [180 miles] from Belgorod. The broken roads and railways and the blown bridges were still being repaired, making it difficult to bring forward materiel. Finally, we must admit that we underestimated the enemy's defences on the west bank of the Dnepr, believing that we would be able to dislodge him from his positions with the forces we had available and we would be able to seize bridgeheads.
>
> For seven days, the army's units were involved in heavy combat on the captured islands. It was particularly hard for [the men] on Peschany Island. A sandy part of the island, captured by the Guards, was completely open and entirely visible to the enemy. Trenches dug in the sandy ground crumbled from the frequent impact of shells and mortars and filled with water. Weapons were clogged with sand.

Soon it became clear to us that the captured islands were of no tactical significance, as they did not allow for further deployment of units and the continuation of the offensive. In the battles on these islands, we suffered considerable losses.[26]

It seems that the account heard many years after the event by Abdullin was an attempt at rationalising facts after they had occurred: had the operation been a success, it would have been lauded as a great triumph; and if it failed to establish a bridgehead on the west bank, it had never been intended to do so and was merely a feint. After a brief period for rest, Abdullin and the rest of his division crossed into a bridgehead that had already been established. Just a few weeks later, he was badly wounded by an artillery shell. He endured a long evacuation across the Dnepr and then by truck away from the combat zone without any pain relief, and then suffered surgery without anaesthetic. Despite the severity of his wounds, he recovered sufficiently to volunteer to return to the front line, but his request was declined. He spent many years after the war trying to track down Sasha Kolesnikov, the soldier who had fought with him on the island, but in vain.

In an attempt to allow the division's exhausted troops an opportunity for rest and recovery, *SS-Totenkopf* established a 'rest camp' in the village of Onufriyevka, a little to the south of Kremenchug. The men were rotated regularly, spending only a couple of days in the camp, but it was a welcome break from the arduous work of digging new fortifications – particularly when the troops had withdrawn to the Dnepr in the expectation of finding positions already constructed – and the opportunity to spend a couple of nights sleeping under a roof was hugely welcome. Bath wagons gave the troops their first opportunity since the withdrawal past Poltava to clean themselves and their uniforms; de-lousing facilities were also provided:

How were they to use this first day of peace and quiet? Of course, they had to do what had been in their hearts for so long, namely to write a detailed letter home. How long was it actually since they had last been able to write? They had no idea. In any case it was a long time. Since the morning of 5 July [the beginning of *Zitadelle*] they had been in the vortex of a furious defensive battle and had been in such a breathless series of operations that they hadn't ever had a moment to sleep and wash. They were the 'fire brigade' for the southern part of the Eastern Front. Wherever the fires broke out, they were summoned. Wherever men were needed, they had to get there as fast as possible.

They lived from hour to hour, fully caught up in the moment and during desperate counterattacks, constant redeployment, tough defensive battles and moving to new positions, had barely had any opportunity to pause for thought, let alone sufficient time for a long, thorough letter.[27]

The Dnepr runs southeast across the Ukraine until it reaches the city of Dnipro, which during the Soviet era was known as Dnepropetrovsk. Here, it curves south for about 45 miles (75km) to Zaporozhye, where it curves again to run southwest to the Black Sea coast at Kherson. It was the intention of the Germans to hold strong bridgeheads at Dnepopetrovsk and Zaporozhye, from where the front was to run due south to Melitopol in order to protect the narrow land bridge to the Crimea. Mackensen's First Panzer Army, on the southern flank of Army Group South, and the neighbouring Sixth Army – now under the command of Army Group A – had been ordered to pull back towards the great Dnepr bend, with the latter remaining east of the river in order to hold the line running to Melitopol. Like the German formations pulling back further north, XL Panzer Corps, withdrawing towards the Zaporozhye bridgehead, continued to conduct as orderly a withdrawal as possible. However, the increasingly rainy weather left the roads – already degraded by the passage of rear area units – almost unusable for the retreating men. Ernst Schwörer was a soldier serving with 16th Panzergrenadier Division, which struggled to hold back the pursuing Soviet forces, and described an engagement on 17 September:

We immediately took cover. In the flat terrain, there was a solitary hill only about 10m high, which had to be the next position – the Russians thought so too. 76.2mm shells and mortar rounds constantly struck it. Jäger and Heuermann were wounded immediately.

Eight tanks appeared and attacked the village. Thank God that four of our Pz.IVs were already in cover behind us. We hadn't noticed them. There was a small area of bushes behind us and they were lying in wait there.

A march battalion [a replacement draft] had been deployed in front of us. When they saw the Russian tanks, they pulled back and the Russian tanks followed them with machine-gun fire. Confident of success, the Russian tanks drove up at a fair pace about 40–50m behind the infantry, thinking that they would soon wrap up the battalion. But their nice drive was spoiled when our Pz.IVs opened fire and shot up the column of eight tanks, one after the other. The last one was hit first, so that the ones further ahead wouldn't notice.

And from the last tank to the leader, all were set ablaze. It was good for us and we were delighted. Eight blazing wrecks lay barely 200m in front of us. Our tanks remained in cover and couldn't be seen. The retreating march battalion rallied, and then the Russians appeared. They swarmed forward like monkeys. The landscape was covered with men. They ran up to the German positions, which had been reoccupied by our infantry, as fast as they could. When they were 100m away, the infantry began to fire. The tanks also joined in. On this occasion, the Russians didn't shout 'Urrah!' and just ran up to the German lines. Machine-guns reaped a dreadful harvest. Despite this, ever more Russians came up through the village into the fire of our machine-guns and the tanks. We also called in fire from our artillery; a few shells exploded in the village, but unfortunately there was never enough ammunition.

The attack was finally beaten off at 1400. The Russians carried their wounded away. We did nothing to stop them. The infantry too fired no shots, even though they were only 300–400m away.[28]

The action shows the difficulties that the Soviet forces faced – if they pressed too hard, they were vulnerable to such ambushes, yet if they were more cautious, they allowed the Germans to conduct both an orderly withdrawal and the 'scorched earth' policy that Stalin was so keen to avoid.

After disengaging from the pursuing Soviet forces, 16th Panzergrenadier Division and the rest of XL Panzer Corps pulled back to Zaporozhye where they were to form a local reserve. With a degree of resignation, the troops learned that Hitler had declared that the bridgehead was to be held to the last man. This sector fell within the domain of First Panzer Army, which had been falling back towards the Dnepr bend and the crossings at Dnepopetrovsk and Zaporozhye; the former bridgehead was to be abandoned once the troops had withdrawn. Schwerin, the commander of 16th Panzergrenadier Division, later wrote:

For those who have never been in a tightly constrained bridgehead without room for manoeuvre and questionable chances of being able to get out of such a witches' cauldron intact, it is probably impossible to grasp the constantly increasing strain on morale. This was particularly true for commanders. How could they explain to their men what was expected of them, and why? In the case of the Zaporozhye bridgehead, it was impossible to explain. It is worth noting that in no account of the war is any reason given for the creation of this bridgehead … not a word from the army and corps commanders responsible for the Zaporozhye sector. It was simply that in his order for Army Group South to fall back to the Panther Line on the west bank of the Dnepr, Hitler had called for the creation of several bridgeheads, of which only Zaporozhye and Nikopol remained. Given Hitler's mindset, it is likely that he clung to the mistaken belief that we could later use the bridgeheads to launch a major counteroffensive. Manstein had probably made clear to him that this was completely illusory, as the Russians had reached the Dnepr at several points in the sectors of Eighth and Fourth Panzer Armies and in places had crossed. North of Kiev there was a gap of 50km [30 miles] to Army Group Centre, and there were no reserves to close both existing and new gaps.[29]

Hitler's justification for holding onto a bridgehead at Zaporozhye was that the presence of powerful German units on the east bank of the Dnepr would act as a strong disincentive to the Red Army if it were to try to drive back German forces further south with the intention of isolating the Crimea. If such an operation was attempted, the bridgehead could be used as the start point of a powerful counterattack into the northern flank of the Soviet advance. This reasoning made considerable sense, but only if sufficiently strong forces could be concentrated in the bridgehead. Futhermore, if this concentration was achieved at the cost of leaving the Dnepr line weak at other points, there was a strong likelihood that instead of being a threat to the Red Army, the bridgehead could become a target for attacks aimed at its isolation; by forcing the Dnepr further north, or by exploiting the bridgeheads at Mishurin Rog, Soviet forces would be able to cut the bridgehead off and then destroy whatever forces had been concentrated there.

The forces committed to the Zaporozhye bridgehead were substantial – XL Panzer Corps and XVII Corps with a total of seven infantry divisions, 9th Panzer Division and 16th Panzergrenadier Division, collectively designated *Armeegruppe Henrici*. Although all the divisions had suffered losses in the recent fighting, they were still in comparatively good shape and would have been better employed to defend the line of the Dnepr. Whilst Zaporozhye was a substantial industrial centre, with a particularly important hydroelectric dam, its industry was barely functioning and the city could have been abandoned without any detrimental impact upon the German war effort; the facilities in the city could have been rendered unusable to prevent the returning Soviet authorities from benefiting from them. In any event, the Red Army had tried to wreck the turbines in the hydroelectric power plant when it retreated through the region in 1941, and only limited capacity had been restored by the summer of 1943. Henrici had no intention of allowing his troops to be sacrificed because Hitler couldn't bring himself to abandon what he deemed to be a prestigious location or a possible springboard for a future counterattack. Accordingly, Henrici ordered Schwerin to make preparations to blow the dam in order to cover a withdrawal. In the meantime, the infantry divisions were ordered to hold their positions, supported by the panzer and panzergrenadier divisions, the assault guns of several *Sturmgeschütz* battalions, and the Ferdinand tank destroyers of *Schwere Panzerjäger Regiment 656*.

The threat of the Zaporozhye bridgehead being outflanked and threatened with isolation was already significant. While attention was centred on the Bukrin bend, the Soviet Thirty-Seventh Army had secured two bridgeheads over the Dnepr southeast of Kremenchug near Mishurin Rog. If these were to coalesce into a single bridgehead, the Soviet forces would be in a position to thrust towards Krivoy Rog and beyond. It was therefore essential for the Wehrmacht to eliminate these bridgeheads if at all possible; similarly, it was vital for the Red Army that they be reinforced and enlarged as quickly as possible.

SS-Totenkopf had informed higher commands that it was too weak for an immediate attack to destroy the Mishurin Rog bridgeheads, and there had been suggestions, both from the commander of the division and from Raus, that *Grossdeutschland* would be better equipped to launch a counterattack. The reality was that *Grossdeutschland* wasn't in much better shape: the heavy losses of the summer battles had left many companies reduced to less than platoon strength, and there was an acute shortage of officers, with some companies now commanded by relatively junior NCOs. At the end of September, the division's panzer regiment reported that it had only ten Tiger tanks and one other tank available for action, though its assault gun battalion could still field 25 vehicles, 80 per cent of its establishment strength.[30] The infantry divisions that had pulled back across the Dnepr were also far below their theoretical strength, with most having perhaps 50 per cent of their notional strength and many being even weaker – despite which, Hitler behaved as if they were at full strength and expected them to hold segments of front line that would have been challenging even had they been fresh and completely replenished. The Soviet units that had crossed the Dnepr near Mishurin Rog were relatively few in number but had already pushed far enough to the west to disrupt German traffic; a second bridgehead, to the southeast of Mishurin Rog, was rather more substantial with elements of at least five fresh Soviet divisions in a hilly region between the river and the town of Anovka. The German forces in the area were ordered to eliminate the bridgeheads immediately, and the weary columns of *Grossdeutschland* began to move south.

The contrast between the opposing units in the battle couldn't have been greater. All of the German formations were badly degraded by the recent fighting; by contrast, Lieutenant General Mikhail Nikolayevich Sharokhin's

Thirty-Seventh Army had been held in reserve as the second echelon of Konev's Voronezh Front and its units were almost at full strength. They had been awaiting their turn to join the fighting, and had moved forward swiftly to replace the exhausted Sixty-Ninth Army. The first crossings were made late on 28 September; the troops of 92nd Guards Rifle Division suffered heavy losses when their boats were spotted by the Germans and bombarded by artillery, but 62nd Guards Rifle Division had better success, first securing an island in midstream before pressing on to the west bank.

The initial intention of the Germans was for *Grossdeutschland* to eliminate the smaller northern bridgehead first, but only a single battalion from its Panzerfusilier regiment had deployed when orders were changed. The attack on the northern bridgehead would now be carried out by 23rd Panzer Division, to which the *Grossdeutschland* battalion was temporarily subordinated; the rest of *Grossdeutschland* was to proceed further south in order to strike against the larger bridgehead near Anovka. Late on 30 September, the division's Panzergrenadier regiment attacked through the villages of Zapolichki and Ivashki, into the southern flank of a group of Soviet infantry that had been advancing towards Anovka. A further attack scheduled for the following morning had to be

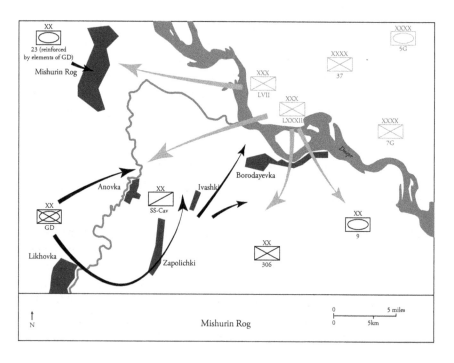

300

postponed as much of the division was still en route from Kremenchug. Later in the day, sufficient forces had arrived for an attempt to be made, and there was further progress through the hills and ravines that lay between *Grossdeutschland* and the Dnepr. Ivashki and the hills immediately to its north were taken, and as darkness fell the leading German elements – a group built around the remaining Tiger tanks – had managed to push east to the village of Borodayevka, less than two miles from the pontoon bridges over which the Soviet forces were bringing reinforcements and supplies. By contrast, the rest of the division, attempting to attack north along the Dnepr into the southern flank of the bridgehead, made little headway despite supporting attacks by the neighbouring 306th Infantry Division.

Bitter fighting continued for control of Borodayevka throughout 2 and 3 October, with the Germans unable to advance beyond the western parts of the village and the Soviet troops unable to dislodge their opponents. Further German reinforcements in the shape of 9th Panzer Division had arrived on the eastern flank of 306th Infantry Division – both divisions had been pulled out of the increasingly pointless Zaporozhye bridgehead and sent northwest – but attempts to advance along the Dnepr continued to be foiled by stubborn defences. In the meantime, the units of *Grossdeutschland* that were deployed along the hills from Ivashki to Borodayevka continued to suffer heavy losses as Soviet reinforcements were thrown into determined attacks. To make matters worse for *Grossdeutschland*, the western end of the line – near Ivashki – was held by a formation of SS cavalry under the command of Standartenführer Hermann Fegelein, a talentless and widely detested protégé of Heinrich Himmler whose troops had repeatedly failed in combat against the Red Army, preferring to spend their time massacring civilians that they claimed were either partisans or had been collaborating with partisans. Originally known as the SS Cavalry Brigade, the formation had steadily been enlarged through the war – often suffering catastrophic casualties and then being rebuilt – and was now officially the SS Cavalry Division. Despite receiving favourable treatment in terms of equipment and replacement drafts, Fegelein's men continued to perform poorly and the left flank of *Grossdeutschland* was repeatedly threatened when the SS units retreated in the face of almost any Soviet attack. In a desperate attempt to shore up the line, Hörnlein – the commander of *Grossdeutschland* – was forced to improvise combat teams using his division's rear area personnel; this had a detrimental effect on the performance of his division, as these men were no longer able to carry out their normal tasks of bringing forward supplies, evacuating wounded, and repairing damaged equipment.

The attempt by 23rd Panzer Division to penetrate the northern flank – originally intended to wipe out the northern bridgehead altogether – led to heavy fighting. Although the Germans managed to reach Mishurin Rog, they lacked the strength to move further, and the daily stream of Soviet reinforcements into the bridgehead steadily tilted the situation in favour of the Red Army. *Grossdeutschland* made a final attempt to drive into the southern flank of the bridgehead on 8 October with an infantry attack supported by the division's surviving Tiger tanks. As they advanced, the Tigers soon found themselves far ahead of their accompanying infantry and Soviet troops that had allowed the tanks to pass by now reappeared, attacking the Tigers from the rear and stopping every attempt by the German infantry to come to their aid. All of the German tanks were destroyed, effectively reducing the tank strength of *Grossdeutschland* to zero.

The intention of the Germans in attacking the Mishurin Rog bridgeheads had been to eliminate them quickly so that the German armoured units could be moved to deal with other threats. Instead, the bitter fighting around the bridgehead resulted in the already weakened panzer and panzergrenadier divisions suffering further losses for little gain, and tied them down at a time when other Red Army units were seizing bridgeheads elsewhere. About ten miles (17km) to the southeast of the Mishurin Rog battles, elements of the Soviet Seventh Guards Army had crossed the Dnepr at Domotkan. Lacking sufficient troops to screen off or eliminate this threat, the Germans attacked the bridgehead repeatedly from the air, and eventually ground troops arrived to block further Soviet advances. Meanwhile, Konev had no intention of allowing his bridgehead at Mishurin Rog to be sealed off and steadily reinforced it, moving depleted units back to the east bank and replacing them with relatively fresh formations. One such was Rotmistrov's Fifth Guards Tank Army, which had been recovering from its losses in the battles around Kharkov and Akhtyrka. Nevertheless, it remained far from its establishment strength, as Rotmistrov made clear to Konev when the two men met:

> 'It's good, we will fight together again,' Ivan Stepanovich [Konev] firmly clasped my hand with a friendly smile. 'You can't imagine how much we need your tanks now!'
>
> 'I understand, Comrade Commander. But I am obliged to report that instead of the 600 tanks that the army requested, exactly half – 300 – have arrived by today, and the weapons and equipment intended for V Guards Mechanised Corps are still somewhere in the rear echelons.'

'You're complaining already! But this isn't like you, Pavel Alexeyevich,' Konev said without any reproach in his voice, 'we've been spoiled with all this equipment. I'm sure you haven't forgotten that in the battles near Moscow, you didn't have more than a dozen tanks in the brigade, and you fought the Germans not with numbers, but with skill. Don't worry: the rear echelons will move up, and the missing tanks too. They will be needed during the development of the offensive to sustain the strike power of your army.' [Konev] went to the open window and looked thoughtfully at the ruins of the village, the fruit trees burned and shredded by shrapnel. I saw his heavy fists clenched and his face was red with anger. Turning sharply to me, he said with great conviction, 'Now, one of our most important tasks is to prevent the evil Fascists from exterminating the Soviet people in the territory they hold, to stop them stealing and destroying our people's property, and destroying towns and villages. And to do this, it is necessary to smash and pursue the Hitlerites without rest, give them no time for brutality and robbery. *Stavka* has decided: to advance without any operational pause, to cross the Dnepr quickly and to liberate the Ukraine on the right bank.'[31]

Rotmistrov might have grumbled that his tank army was not at full strength, but he must have been aware that the arrival of 300 tanks represented a huge change in the local balance of power. The German divisions clustered around the bridgehead on the west bank had been unable to reduce the Soviet foothold to date, and the Red Army would have known – through a mixture of prisoner interrogations, reconnaissance activity, and radio intercepts – that the German armoured formations were close to the end of their strength. Konev's assessment was surely correct; the later arrival of half of Rotmistrov's tanks might prove to be a blessing, in that it would allow momentum to be sustained.

Konev's impatience to drive the 'evil Fascists' from Soviet territory looks at first glance as typical of the rhetoric used in Soviet accounts after the war, but it is a theme that recurs in contemporary letters as well as accounts written later. Everyone in the Red Army, from the highest officials to the lowest soldiers, knew about the widespread destruction left by the retreating Wehrmacht. The spirit of vengeance this engendered was then blended with an urgent need to prevent further depredations, particularly as so many serving soldiers had family members who were still in occupied areas.

Rotmistrov would also have been aware that his troops had not been re-equipped to the same standard as earlier in the year. Instead of the tried and trusted T-34s with which the men had become familiar, many units received other vehicles, as Sergey Andreyevich Otroschenkov, a newly promoted junior lieutenant in command of a tank company, described:

We received new tanks – the British Mk.II, Mk.VI, and Mk.VII Valentines. I had a Mk.VII with a 40mm gun and coaxial machine-gun. The traversing gear was hand-driven; the elevation gear was shoulder driven. We had only armour-piercing rounds, no fragmentation rounds ... There were several things about the Valentine I liked. It had an epicyclic traversing gear, and could turn at any speed, like driving a car. In our T-34s we had to slow down, squeeze a lever and then accelerate for the friction couplings to work. The British tank also had a good interior.

In late September ... we crossed the Dnepr in the Valentines to the south of Kremenchug near a village called Mishurin Rog. The left bank was flat while the opposite right bank was steep. Our infantry quickly forced the Germans out and the village was virtually intact. The engineers constructed a pontoon bridge. We crossed the river and attempted a breakthrough. After 3–4km we became involved in drawn-out battles for several large villages – Popelnastoye, Zelyonoye, and Zhyoltoye. The Germans had fortified them. The muddy season and minefields prevented effective manoeuvring. The sappers worked on minesweeping around the clock, but we still suffered heavy losses from anti-tank mines. The Germans used their Tiger tanks effectively in defence. They would position the tank on high ground with good overview and strike us at a range of 1.5–2km. Our guns couldn't reach them at such a range. We tried to attack Popelnastoye for two days, but in vain. Eventually we decided to capture the village in a night-time mass attack. We penetrated into the village in darkness and an attritional battle began. After heavy close-quarter combat, the Germans abandoned the village. The brigade moved further. After liberating Zelyonoye and Zholtoye we approached the town of Pavlovsk. The Germans pinned us down here. It also turned out that the Fascists had recaptured the villages we had liberated. Due to the danger of encirclement, we withdrew and had to force the Germans out of Zholtoye and Zelyonoye once more.[32]

The Valentine was one of many British and American tanks to be sent to the Soviet Union. Many of these tanks were regarded by the Red Army as markedly inferior to the T-34, but the Valentine was an exception, and at the request of the Soviet government it remained in production until the end of the war.

Having secured *Stavka* approval for a drive towards Krivoy Rog, Konev drew up his plans. The next phase of the operation would be an attack by Fifth Guards

Army and Thirty-Seventh Army. As they advanced towards Pyatikhatky, Rotmistrov's army would be inserted between them to take Krivoy Rog, and at the same time was to try to break through towards the northwest and if possible to reach Kirovograd and Alexandriya, thus making it impossible for the Germans to remain in position along the Dnepr. Zhukov had joined Konev and Rotmistrov and gave his personal approval for the plan; if it proved successful, any lingering hope of the Wehrmacht making a prolonged stand along the Dnepr would be extinguished. However, there was a large element of risk in the operation, especially as it called for Rotmistrov to deploy his tanks on diverging axes.

All along the Dnepr, Soviet troops were securing bridgeheads. *SS-Wiking* pulled back across the river via the crossings at Cherkassy and, with elements of 57th Infantry Division, it was ordered to eliminate positions seized by the Red Army on 'Foxtail Island' in the middle of the Dnepr stream. Obersturmführer Willi Hein later described the operation:

> In an operation entailing a number of casualties, without an inkling of the strength of the enemy on the island, II/*Nordland* [the regiment's second battalion] succeeded in getting a foothold on the tip of the island ... The situation became extraordinarily serious for our soldiers ... [causing] the division to consider the use of tanks.
>
> Only three Pz.IIIs with elevated exhaust stacks were available. The crews – Hein, Bock and Schnell – were selected, and a ford site was reconnoitred in the raging torrent during the night of 8 October. Oberscharführer Bock moved ahead with a long stick. The hulls of the vehicles sloshed full of water. The risky undertaking succeeded during the final hours of the night. The enemy did not appear to have taken notice of the undertaking, since barely a single round disturbed the operations by the submarine tanks. There was a short discussion of the situation with the commander of III/*Westland*, and the attack was scheduled for 7am.
>
> Our artillery fired smoke ... Trying to avoid too much battle noise, we crossed a slope that was more like a wall and landed in the middle of the enemy. Anti-tank guns were overrun with the tracks crunching as steel collided with steel. The main guns and machine-guns were giving it everything they had. ... The combat vehicles were rocked back and forth by the impossible ground conditions, the expressions on the men's faces frozen, with sweat pouring out of every pore. A few of the crew may have whispered to themselves: 'Tracks, don't break!' The Russians were taken completely by surprise. Whoever was unable to escape ... was taken into captivity.[33]

The deployment of the tanks secured the German foothold on the tip of the island but the rest remained firmly in Soviet hands, including the section of the island that was connected to the east bank by a submerged bridge. Gille, the commander of *SS-Wiking*, ordered a further attack, as a veteran later recalled:

> As a result of the preceding fighting the combat strength of the regiment at this time was roughly 40 men, and my 6. Company had about 20 men. It should be mentioned that relations between Gille and Dieckmann were very strained, as Gille was actually an artilleryman and had little sympathy for we grenadiers. Thus the grim line '*Kennt Ihr Gille, der Massenmörder mit der Brille*' ['Do you know Gille, the mass murderer in spectacles'] was passed amongst us. A bad expression, but characteristic of soldiers in the third year of war against the Soviet Union.
>
> When August Dieckmann received this new order, he donned his best uniform and said something like, 'If the last men of my regiment are killed here, I want to be amongst them.' Thus we set off to attack on 12 October and received murderous artillery and small arms defensive fire. During this, Dieckmann was mortally wounded by a Soviet sniper. August was the best regimental commander that *Westland* ever had ... I was shot through the right thigh by the same sniper and I see the scars every day when I dress. This attack too failed. The fighting strength of the regiment was reduced to about 20 men.[34]

Meanwhile, the first fighting around the Zaporozhye bridgehead occurred on 22 September, when 16th Panzergrenadier Division's panzer battalion led a sharp attack to drive back the leading Soviet spearheads approaching from the northeast. Nearer the Dnepr, parts of the panzergrenadier division's reconnaissance battalion were surprised by the appearance of Red Army troops; some of the men from the motorcycle company had to abandon their machines and swim to the far shore, under fire from the Soviet units. Other elements of the division were left isolated north of Petro-Mikhailovka, and were only able to rejoin the bridgehead the following day after Schwerin sent his panzer battalion to link up with them. Probing attacks followed in the next days as the leading Soviet formations attempted to determine the strength of the bridgehead, but the next major attack was made by the Germans, when a battlegroup from 9th Panzer Division and 16th Panzergrenadier Division was inserted into the seam between 306th and 123rd Infantry Divisions with the intention of penetrating to the Red Army's artillery positions. The attack rapidly ran into surprisingly strong defences and was abandoned before it suffered heavy losses. A further joint attack was planned for 29 September immediately south of Zaporozhye; on this occasion, the

Germans enjoyed rather more success, driving back the Soviet forces and restoring a previously held line. The following day, 9th Panzer Division and 306th Infantry Division were withdrawn to help with the growing crisis at Mishurin Rog.

The withdrawal of 9th Panzer Division from the Zaporozhye bridgehead at the end of September left 16th Panzergrenadier Division, with the subordinated tank destroyers of *Schwere Panzerjäger Regiment 656*, as the sole armoured division in the bridgehead. The intention was for it to act as a reserve for mounting counterattacks, but the increasing casualties of the German infantry divisions on the east bank meant that some of its personnel had to be deployed in the front line. This exposed them to further attrition so that even if they could be extracted, their strike power was much reduced. To date, Soviet attacks had been hindered – sometimes even stopped – by the use of heavy artillery fire, but ammunition was running short and on 5 October Henrici issued instructions that such heavy bombardments were to be used only when absolutely necessary.

One of the units that was deployed against the Zaporozhye bridgehead was Eighth Guards Army, commanded by Lieutenant General Vasily Ivanovich Chuikov. His troops had achieved great fame when, known as Sixty-Second Army, they had defied the Wehrmacht and had managed to cling to the ruins on the Volga shore in Stalingrad until the great Soviet counteroffensive in late 1942 surrounded the German Sixth Army. In honour of its heroic defence of the city, Sixty-Second Army was renamed Eighth Guards Army. Its approach march to the Dnepr was across land devastated by the retreating Germans:

> We moved towards the Dnepr literally across scorched earth. All the villages had been torched, bridges and railway tracks blown up. The population had been forcibly abducted to the west of the Dnepr. The terror inflicted by the Fascists was worse than ever before … Colonel Mikhail Ivanovich Semiryaga told me that after the liberation of Chervonoarmeiskoye, local people reported that there was a large mass grave in the park.
>
> Here, the Nazis had shot several thousand Soviet soldiers who had been surrounded in March 1943, together with local residents in whose houses the Soviet troops had sheltered. Our sappers began excavating the graves to give the heroes honourable burial. During the excavation, the residents of the town and surrounding villages gathered around. We all witnessed a tragic scene. By scraps of clothing or shoes, many recognised their loved ones and relatives and rushed straight to the pit and kissed their remains. Immediately, there was a meeting at which the soldiers vowed to fight even harder against the enemy to drive him quickly from Soviet land.

The rain was falling. The steppe was a black, charred plain before us. Even the foliage on trees in gardens had been burned. Not a single house was left, not a single wooden structure. Thousands of head of livestock, killed by the Germans, lay on the fields and along the roads, making a foul stench.

The population had been deported and those who could not leave their homes had been shot in the roadside ditches.[35]

With Major General Alexei Ilyich Danilov's Twelfth Army to the north and Lelyushenko's Third Guards Army to the south, Eighth Guards Army now prepared to reduce the bridgehead.

Despite the German counterattacks that repeatedly restored the front line, the days of the bridgehead's existence were drawing to a close. To complicate matters further, there were intelligence reports that there was a group of partisans in Zaporozhye in German uniforms, and Henrici ordered that Russians and Ukrainians who had volunteered to work with the Wehrmacht – *Hilfswillige* or *Hiwis* – were to be detained and their identities checked. One group of suspected partisans was detained, but the expected attempt to capture the Zaporozhye bridges or to attack a German headquarters failed to materialise. It is difficult to know whether this threat was real or imagined, but Hauptmann Gerhard Tebbe, commander of 16th Panzergrenadier Division's panzer battalion, later recalled an odd incident:

One day, a few Waffen-SS soldiers reported to my command post and asked for transport back to their unit. Two motorcycles with sidecars together with their riders were made available. They never came back! When my motorcyclists didn't return, I investigated and discovered that there weren't any Waffen-SS units in our area.

Several years later I read in a Russian publication that the Russians had deployed soldiers wearing Waffen-SS uniforms to prevent the demolition of the dam.[36]

The surrender of Sixth Army at Stalingrad had resulted in 22 German generals becoming prisoners of war. They and other senior officers were kept in a separate camp from other prisoners near Krasnogorsk where they were provided with a large library of books in German. In addition to well-known works of fiction and non-fiction, they were given brochures that introduced them to socialism and communism. In April 1943 the officers were moved to the Susdal monastery near Vladimir where they met several German exiles. Inevitably, some officers remained devoutly loyal to Hitler, but others began to question their previous allegiance and during the summer, when the officers moved once more – this time to Voikovo – they had divided broadly into three groups: those who were openly looking to a future for Germany without Hitler and the Nazi Party; those who had turned their backs on Hitler but had yet to declare this publicly; and the diehards who continued to greet each other with loud exclamations of 'Heil Hitler!' In July 1943, a group of German exiles and a small number of Wehrmacht officers who had been captured earlier in the war founded the *Nationalkomitee Freies Deutschland* ('National Committee for a Free Germany', or *NKFD*). The manifesto of this committee was published in a newspaper that was distributed to the inmates of Voikovo:

> No foreign enemy has brought us so much misfortune as Hitler.
>
> The facts prove that the war is lost. Germany can only drag on at the cost of inhuman sacrifice and deprivation. The continuance of this pointless war means the end of the nation. But Germany must not die! …
>
> If the German people take courage in time and demonstrate by their acts that they want to be a free people and are determined to free Germany of Hitler and win the right to decide about its future fate and its place in the world, that is the only way to save the existence, the freedom and the honour of the German nation.
>
> The German people need and want immediate freedom. But Hitler concludes peace with no one. No one will also deal only with him. That is why the formation of a true German government is our people's most urgent task.[37]

Whilst the German people might have needed freedom, it was an exaggeration to suggest that they generally wanted Hitler and the Nazis to be overthrown. Even a year later, when news of the failed attempt to assassinate Hitler spread through Germany and the Wehrmacht, there was widespread horror that such an attempt could have been made. But for the prisoners in Voikovo, schooled in the traditions of the German general staff and therefore having almost no experience or understanding of politics, this manifesto and other similar documents had a profound effect. Nevertheless, most German officers found it almost impossible to overcome their traditional antipathy of communism – at least at this stage – and refused to join the *NKFD*. In August 1943, several prisoners created the *Bund Deutscher Offiziere* ('League of German Officers' or *BDO*) and helped write propaganda material that was used by the Red Army to try to subvert German troops fighting against the Red Army. Henrici later wrote about the appearance of a document written by General Walther von Seydlitz-Kurzbach, the founder of the *BDO*:

A leaflet in German that had been dropped by air was sent to corps headquarters from one of our units. In it was a letter to the commander of the division on the dam in the middle of the bridgehead [123rd Infantry Division under Generalleutnant Rauch] with roughly the following text:

'Dear Erwin,

I have repeatedly tried to contact you via emissaries, but your men always fire on them. That's why I now choose this route.'

There then followed references to specific shared experiences at a military training centre (probably to demonstrate the credentials of the sender of the document). There was then a completely inaccurate description of the 'hopeless' situation of the division in the bridgehead – 'A new Stalingrad awaits you' – and finally a proposition: 'Come over to us with your entire division. For this eventuality, I have secured honourable and especially favourable conditions for you and your division from the Russian high command. [Everyone will receive] honourable treatment and will keep their personal belongings. Officers will keep their sidearms. The division will remain united and will be put to work as a unit. At the end of the war, you will be the first to return home ...' It was signed by Seydlitz.[38]

Such letters would appear with increasing frequency in the months that followed. In their memoirs, Germans describe how they regarded the letters as contemptible, but men who surrendered after receiving these letters would hardly have boasted about them. For those who did try to take advantage of the special terms being offered, disappointment lay ahead. They were treated like all other prisoners.

On 1 October, the encircling Soviet forces made their first major attacks on the Zaporozhye bridgehead, commencing with a heavy artillery bombardment across the entire front. Despite the intensity of the shelling, the attack made little headway; the first lines of defences were overrun at several locations, but ammunition shortages prevented the Red Army's artillery from providing further support. Soviet troops penetrated the lines of the German 123rd Infantry Division in the northeast sector of the bridgehead, forcing local withdrawals. An armoured counterattack partially restored the front line and by the end of the day the Germans had recovered most of the ground that had been lost in the morning. A similar Soviet attack on 2 October was repulsed. Casualties had mounted on both sides with almost no movement of the front line.

By this stage, the existence of Soviet bridgeheads across the river elsewhere made the continued presence of *Armeegruppe Henrici* on the east bank increasingly pointless. The only real justification for the bridgehead had been as a concentration point for strong mobile forces that might attack into the northern flank of Soviet units advancing further south, and the requirement to strengthen the line elsewhere had made it impossible to concentrate such forces – even those already in the bridgehead had been weakened with the withdrawal of 9th Panzer Division. Concluding that the long-term viability of the bridgehead was non-existent, Henrici ordered the destruction of key buildings and equipment in Zaporozhye. The losses suffered by all the German units in the bridgehead, combined with casualties sustained during the retreat towards the Dnepr, ensured that it was only a matter of time before it was impossible to restore the front line with counterattacks, and the lack of any tactical, operational or strategic justification for the bridgehead was becoming increasingly clear to all. However, there remained the difficult issue of Hitler's insistence that the bridgehead be held at all costs. Even at this stage of the wear, disregarding such an order was only possible in the most extreme emergency, and Henrici had no option but to allow matters to develop further.

Meanwhile, Vasilevsky and Tolbukhin met to consider how to resume their attacks on the Molochnaya line. After analysing the recent fighting, and most importantly the redeployment of Sixth Army's troops to the defences north of Melitopol, they decided to switch their point of emphasis to the south, assigning Major General Ivan Dmitrievich Vasiliev's XIX Tank Corps to Twenty-Eighth Army. There were some concerns that the Soviet armour would struggle, as their line of advance was crossed by both a highway and a railway line about three miles (5km) west of the Molochnaya, both on raised embankments, and he was assigned additional artillery, anti-tank and engineer battalions to try to improve the chances of success. On the night of 9–10 October, Vasiliev's tanks crossed the Molochnaya into the small bridgehead that had been seized on the west bank by Twenty-Eighth Army in the earlier attack; shortly before the operation was to begin, Southern Front learned that due to limitations in the crossings over the Molochnaya, barely half of XIX Tank Corps was in position. Nevertheless, Tolbukhin decided to continue. As it began to grow light on 10 October, the Germans became aware of the movement of Soviet armour. Luftwaffe units attempted to attack the tank concentrations, but were largely thwarted by the deteriorating weather – initially, there was thick fog, and this was replaced by drizzle and then wet snow. At 1045 a heavy artillery bombardment commenced and XIX Tank Corps plunged forward. Almost immediately it was confronted by a German armoured counterattack; as Vasiliev's brigades began to hesitate and stop, a renewed artillery barrage from the Soviet guns and rocket launchers allowed the advance to continue, passing the flank of the blocking German force.

Tolbukhin had assigned IV Guards Cavalry Corps as a reserve force for this attack and it was ordered forward to support the advance.

As the German lines began to give way, the Soviet Fifty-First Army, brought forward from reserve, battered its way into Melitopol. In an attempt to stiffen resistance, Hollidt – the commander of the German Sixth Army – had brought elements of 73rd Infantry Division, which had been holding the line between Melitopol and the coast, into the city; much of the regiment that was transferred was destroyed in a heavy artillery barrage on 12 October, while the Soviet XIX Tank Corps advanced through the area where the German infantry had been deployed prior to being ordered to Melitopol. Bitter fighting continued in Melitopol until 23 October, when the Germans were finally driven out of the city, but not all events were going in favour of the Red Army. A little earlier, after many delays the Soviet Black Sea Fleet had made an attempt to shell German positions in the Crimea as a prelude to carrying out amphibious landings with the troops from the Taman Peninsula. On 6 October, three destroyers – *Kharkov*, *Besposchadniy* and *Sposobniy* – bombarded Yalta and Feodosia, but as they headed back towards the east they were spotted by Luftwaffe reconnaissance aircraft hunting for them. Immediately, German dive-bombers were sent to attack the warships. In their first attack, the Stukas hit and badly damaged *Kharkov*, and a second attack shortly after crippled *Besposchadniy*. The two damaged ships were taken in tow by *Sposobniy*, which was thus forced to travel far slower than would otherwise be the case. The Stukas returned for a third raid and struck all three vessels and sank them. Rather than risk warships being lost in a similar manner in future, Stalin issued orders that vessels of destroyer size or larger were only to be committed to action with his express approval.

On 20 October, in recognition of the changes that had taken place during the year, the Red Army's formations in the Ukraine were renamed. Voronezh Front became 1st Ukrainian Front; Steppe Front became 2nd Ukrainian Front; Southwest Front became 3rd Ukrainian Front; and Southern Front became 4th Ukrainian Front.

Despite the failure of the Black Sea Fleet, the capture of Melitopol finally allowed the Soviet 4th Ukrainian Front to start a general advance towards the lower Dnepr. On 30 October, the leading elements of Twenty-Eighth Army reached Genichesk, and two days later they crossed the 'Turkish Wall', an ancient fortification across the isthmus to the Crimea. On 5 November, they reached the lower reaches of the Dnepr, effectively isolating the German Seventeenth Army in the Crimea. The battered remnants of Hollidt's Sixth Army pulled back across the Dnepr, with only the bridgehead at Nikopol left on the east bank. Biryuzov could take justified pride in the accomplishment of Southern Front; with pauses of only a few days, its soldiers had fought their way from the Mius to the Dnepr, a distance of about 305 miles (491km). They were now forced to call a halt, through a combination of German defences, the terrain, the deteriorating weather, and the near-exhaustion of the decimated formations.

Not all units of Southern Front had performed as well as expected. In particular, IV Guards Cavalry Corps was felt to have been slow in moving forward in the drive to isolate the Crimea, and Stalin dispatched an old comrade, Marshal Semyon Mikhailovich Budyonny, to prepare a report. Budyonny had established a reputation for personal courage and flair when commanding cavalry during the Russian Civil War and the subsequent Polish-Soviet War. Despite repeated questions about his fitness for high command, he was commander of Southwest and Southern Fronts at the beginning of the German invasion of the Soviet Union. Acting almost entirely on the basis of Stalin's instructions, Budyonny's command was nearly annihilated in the encirclements at Uman and Kiev and he was dismissed; however, his popular reputation was such that Stalin appointed him in a number of roles, finally as inspector of cavalry. Despite his past assertions that tanks could never replace horses in the army, he now arrived to pass judgement on the slow movement of IV Guards Cavalry Corps' units, which of course included several mechanised formations. As a result of his report, the corps commander, Lieutenant General Nikolai Yakovlevich Kirichenko, was sacked and replaced by Lieutenant General Issa Alexandrovich Pliev. Kirichenko was appointed commandant of the Higher Cavalry Officers' School.

Kobylyanskiy and his gunners were with the troops who took up positions on the lower Dnepr:

Our front line lay along the Dnepr's left bank, across from the city of Kherson, about 3km from Tsyurupinsk [now Oleshky]. Almost impassable floodlands of the narrow twisting Konka River, a tributary of the Dnepr, separated Tsyurupinsk from the Dnepr. For the first few days, it was impossible to shift our heavy guns any closer to the Dnepr because we couldn't find a longboat. So we set up temporary emplacements on the outskirts of Tsyurupinsk and began placing indirect fire on the Kherson freight train station. This was 'blind fire' using coordinates that we obtained from topographic maps. Nobody was able to control and correct our fire, and we couldn't judge its effectiveness, but we liked the routine of these days. The battery fought, as we say today, 'according to the clock'. In the mornings, we would move into our firing positions, and once having completed our fire missions for the day, we would return at dusk to Tsyurupinsk, where we spent the nights in the homes of local residents. It was a blissful time, as the hospitable hosts were happy to share their homemade wine and tasty snacks with us, their liberators …

As everyone knows, all good things must come to an end, and our 'fighting by shifts' didn't last long. The next day, Lieutenant Brechko located two local fishermen who owned longboats that they had hidden from the Germans in a reedy arm of the Konka River. That same evening, the fishermen landed their longboats near the town. Once darkness fell, we loaded both Kamchatny's and my fire platoons aboard the longboats, and they floated us to a position in the floodlands. From then on, small boats became the only means of delivering food and shells.[39]

After 2 October, there were a few days of relatively little activity around the Zaporozhye bridgehead, during which Konev met the commanders of the armies of his Steppe Front to discuss further operations. It was agreed that the divisions of Chuikov's Eighth Guards Army were generally in better shape than those of the other two armies and they would make the main assault; *Stavka* gave its approval, adding a stipulation that the bridgehead was to be eliminated by 15 October. While Chuikov's army prepared for its assault, there would be attacks to try to draw off the German armoured reserves whose counterattacks had frustrated the previous attempt to break into the bridgehead. To that end, Danilov's Twelfth Army attacked the northern side of the bridgehead on 8 October. The following day the German 125th Infantry Division, in the northern part of the bridgehead, was driven back at several points. A counterattack by 16th Panzergrenadier Division restored the situation but only at the cost of a panzergrenadier battalion becoming tied down in defending a sector of the front line, precisely the outcome that Konev and his army commanders had wished for.

The soldiers of Chuikov's Eighth Guards Army had been given additional rations and ample time to rest in order to recover from their approach march and the failed attack on the bridgehead. Chuikov visited the troops waiting in darkness to launch the new assault, and his account is typical of much of his writing – it portrays the atmosphere of the front line in vivid terms, but also contains many of the characteristic embellishments that pepper his memoirs:

> Not a single fire, not a single spark, not even the flare of a match or a flint lighter to be seen. The silence of the front line is a special silence. Guns fire here and there. Flares soar over the German positions.

They know about the preparations of our offensive and are ready for it. The only think they don't know is when. Today, tomorrow, at dawn, or in the evening, or in the middle of the day? The Fascists are nervous. Aircraft drop parachute flares. Everyone waits.

And yet there's silence. All movement has ceased. The troops are already at the start line, conversation has stopped, and if soldiers have gathered to joke or share a few personal thoughts before the battle, their conversation is in quiet tones, in a whisper – in short, everything is hidden.

I walked along the trenches where the men of the Red Army were waiting for the morning assault. Here, sheltering beneath a raincoat-tent, pulling his helmet low, was a submachine-gunner. A private. An older man, apparently from the more recent call-up. At first glance, I couldn't tell whether he was asleep or just lost in a reverie. I stopped, and the soldier got up. In the dark he couldn't see my rank.

We said hello, and I introduced myself. He made to salute, but I shook his hand. We sat down next to each other. Covering the light of the match with his hands, we lit up, hiding our cigarettes in our sleeves. 'Tomorrow, Comrade Commander?' asked the soldier.

I could guess what he was asking: would the assault come tomorrow, or was it being postponed for any reason? 'Tomorrow, soldier. Or perhaps I should postpone it? From your view as a soldier, is everything ready?'

The soldier thought for a moment. He took his time. He responded without hurry, thoughtfully choosing his words: 'In the opinion of the soldiers, Comrade Commander, we have already waited a long time! We can't see the arrangements of the fronts and armies. We're ready to attack, as soon as possible. The worst thing is not fighting, it's dreadful to wait, and there's nothing worse for a soldier than when they postpone a planned assault.'

'How so?' I asked, surprised. 'If the day passes and there is no attack, that's another day without risking your life.'

'But the attack will come! It's necessary, so why wait? I have summoned up my strength here, everything is like a spring ready to be released, but then it's postponed, and we have to prepare again. And killing? You can get killed in attack and defence. It's easier to get killed defending, and more stupid. When bullets fly, they don't choose who they hit. And in an attack, Comrade Commander, you have to think for yourself. When to get up, when to lie down, you can feel the battle!'

'So tomorrow isn't your first attack, soldier?'

The soldier sighed heavily. 'Not the first, Comrade Commander, but every time is like the first time. For me, it began with Kuporosnoye. An independent brigade of marines. Perhaps you remember, Comrade Commander?'

The Stalingrad fighting was unforgettable. And the marines proved themselves there. I knew that few of them had survived. 'So you've been in the ranks since that time?' I asked cautiously.

'I was in hospital in Stalingrad after Kuporosnoye.'

'On the other bank?'

'We didn't have time to transfer to the other bank. Our hospital was in a basement, in the Goloy gorge. So I stayed in the thick of it.'

'And tomorrow – what do you think about tomorrow?'

'There will be a battle, Comrade Commander, we'll move quickly, and we'll stay alive. Anyone who's frightened won't come out of it. There's a long night ahead to be afraid, but when we set off, there won't be time to be scared.'

Very few people were sleeping in the trenches. The autumn nights in the Ukraine are dark and silent, and the stars shone as if washed clean by rain.[40]

Early on 10 October, the Red Army's artillery hammered the German lines for 40 minutes. The attack that followed penetrated about a mile into the defences but could make little further progress as 16th Panzergrenadier Division's battlegroups were committed in a series of counterattacks. Fighting continued into the afternoon, with Soviet tank destroyer teams trying to use smokescreens in order to get close enough to the heavily armoured Ferdinands and Tigers to knock them out. The following morning, there was a shorter artillery bombardment – Chuikov commented that there was insufficient ammunition to repeat the previous day's preparatory fire – and a further attack was launched. Whilst the attacks were gaining ground, progress was slow and costly, and by the end of the third day of the assault both Chuikov and Malinovsky – the commander of Southwest Front – feared that they would not be able to achieve the objective set for them by *Stavka* to take Zaporozhye by 15 October. In a final attempt to achieve this, Eighth Army planned to throw its exhausted divisions forward one more time, this time with a night attack late on 12 October. The neighbouring Third Guards Army to the south had also failed to make much headway, despite committing the armour of XXIII Tank Corps, and it too paused for breath, reorganising its troops into assault groups consisting of perhaps a company of infantry supported by two or three tanks, a similar number of infantry support guns, and a platoon of sappers.

Henrici had already drawn up plans for the evacuation of the bridgehead. One particular problem was the presence of the Ferdinand tank destroyers; they were so heavy that their only route across the river was via the railway bridge in Zaporozhye aboard special railcars, and loading them aboard would take time as well as remove them from combat at a crucial point when their firepower was desperately needed. With the infantry divisions in the front line reduced to just a shadow of their former strength, a withdrawal to an inner defensive line closer to Zaporozhye was ordered, and was successfully completed by 13 October. Henrici later wrote an account of the decisions he had to make prior to the evacuation of the bridgehead, stressing the diminishing strength of his infantry formations, the lack of replacement drafts, and the shortage of ammunition. Matters were complicated by the consequences of demolition of the dam – there was a fear that this would create a large bulk of water rushing downstream into Sixth Army's sector, and it was therefore necessary for the water level in the river upstream of the dam to be reduced in stages prior to demolition. For Henrici, preparation of the river crossings for demolition and execution of his planned evacuation of the bridgehead – codenamed *Doppelkopf* – were inextricably linked, but he received permission from higher commands only for the former. Despite the numerous disasters that had befallen the Wehrmacht due to adherence to unworkable orders (of which Stalingrad was the greatest and most costly example), obedience to higher commands remained strong and Henrici asked again in mid-October, as pressure on the bridgehead intensified, to be given authority to order the execution of *Doppelkopf* if necessary. When First Panzer Army headquarters refused once more, he contacted Mackensen personally and said that he was prepared to be answerable for any consequences of an evacuation. Mackensen's response was suitably ambiguous: 'It's your neck that's on the block.'[41]

Henrici knew that time was running out. He immediately issued orders for *Doppelkopf* to proceed and was a little surprised when, just a day later, Mackensen's headquarters sent him a message: *OKH* had given approval for the evacuation of the bridgehead. Whilst Mackensen might have found it impossible personally to give an order contrary to Hitler's wishes, it seems he was prepared to make forcible representations to Zeitzler about the necessity to evacuate the bridgehead before it was overrun.

Doppelkopf was dependent upon 16th Panzergrenadier Division, which would act as the rearguard. The night attack by Chuikov's Eighth Army had made considerable progress towards Zaporozhye, but the Germans no longer intended to try to restore their previous positions. On 13 October the perimeter began to be pulled back to the *Heinrich* line around Zaporozhye itself. On the southern flank of the bridgehead, 333rd Infantry Division was to pull back to the east bank of the Dnepr from where its troops would be evacuated across the river by ferries during the following night; most of the division's artillery had already crossed to the west bank, from where it was able to provide fire support. A battlegroup from 16th Panzergrenadier Division was to provide cover for the withdrawal of 333rd Infantry Division, as Ernst Schwörer, a soldier serving with the panzergrenadier division's artillery regiment, later recalled:

> Towards evening [on 13 October] we left. Our mission took us to the southern part of the bridgehead. We had to cover the withdrawal of 333rd Infantry Division …
>
> We had barely set off along the road in column when bombs fell right close to the leading vehicles. There were several wounded, Leutnant Hernekamp was struck by shrapnel in the head and died shortly after …
>
> Everywhere, the slowly-flying Russian planes flew across the bridgehead and dropped masses of bombs. We felt as if someone was standing over us with a shovel and hurling them down; despite this, we had no further losses during the night march. We drove on through the burning buildings of Zaporozhye, a fascinating sight in the darkness. We had only driven a short distance before we came under tank fire. The Russians had broken through the southeast perimeter and stood just in front of our road. We pressed on towards our objective. Here, in the dark, we couldn't see anything, it was unreal.
>
> Finally, we reached Balabino. It was growing light and it had taken the whole night for us to travel just a few kilometres. Our battalion took up positions here and we waited to see what would happen.[42]

The tanks that had fired on Schwörer's column were from Lieutenant General Efim Grigorevich Pushkin's XXIII Tank Corps, which had exploited a further night attack by Chuikov's infantry and had made a significant penetration into the defensive line. A company of 16th Panzergrenadier's tank destroyer battalion was ordered to hurry south to intervene. It launched a counterattack at first light on 14 October and was able to restore the front line, but at the cost of becoming tied down in defensive fighting. In the meantime, Henrici's plan for an orderly evacuation was coming under increasing strain. Soviet air attacks repeatedly disrupted preparations for the destruction of the dam and the officer assigned to oversee this recommended that the dam be destroyed sooner rather than later – the longer the delay, the more likely it was that bombing attacks would kill his personnel or damage the wires running to the demolition charges. Soviet tanks were also reported to have advanced to within sight of the northwest parts of Zaporozhye on the heels of the withdrawing German infantry and were within three miles (5km) of the dam as Malinovsky and Chuikov urged their depleted and tired formations to make one last effort. Henrici issued instructions for the dam to be blown at 1700, but when he learned of this, Schwerin travelled from 16th Panzergrenadier Division's headquarters to meet Henrici. His protest was also sent by signal:

> The demolition at 1700 will be a total catastrophe not only in terms of the loss of vehicles and equipment, but above all because of its effect on the men on the east bank and their well-being.[43]

Technically, 16th Panzergrenadier Division was no longer under Henrici's command and was directly subordinated to First Panzer Army, but as a former commander of the division, Henrici informed Schwerin that he would not leave his former division in the lurch and would delay the demolition. It was agreed to postpone destruction of the dam until 2000. In the meantime, the defenders scrambled back to the last line of defence. Aircraft from both sides were constantly overhead, adding to the noise and chaos as the Red Army closed in on the burning city; the smoke from the numerous fires and the low overcast prevented accurate air attacks, but both sides suffered casualties nonetheless. After firing the last of their ammunition, the artillerymen of 16th Panzergrenadier Division withdrew across the river. The tank destroyer company that had been dispatched hastily to intercept the Soviet tanks threatening to penetrate into Zaporozhye was one of the last units to pull back:

> The guns were on the forward slope and thus came under fire from weapons of all calibres. One gun was abandoned when it was damaged but it was possible to destroy it. At 1600 the company broke contact with the enemy and pulled back over the dam to new accommodation in Chaiki. The 2nd Platoon, which together with II/60 [2nd Battalion, 60th Panzergrenadier Regiment] formed the rearguard, rejoined the company during the night.[44]

The railway bridge was demolished with explosives shortly before 1900. The rearguard formed by 16th Panzergrenadier Division, under the command of Hauptmann Helmut Zander, pulled back to the last line of defence, known as the Max line, around the eastern end of the dam. Constantly exchanging fire with the pursuing Red Army troops, Zander's men withdrew to and over the dam. At 2000, demolition of the dam began. Explosions continued through the night as different segments were destroyed.

After driving off the Soviet troops to its front, the battlegroup that had covered the withdrawal of 333rd Infantry Division in the southern part of the bridgehead was to pull back to the Dnepr where it was to use a pontoon bridge to cross to the west bank. In order to prevent the bridge from being swept away by the flood of water released by the destruction of the dam, it was partly dismantled and then hastily restored. The retreating German forces reached the east bank late on 15 October; they were hugely relieved to find that the bridge had been restored as intended and pulled back unmolested to the west bank, the last elements to withdraw.

Despite constant pressure, *Doppelkopf* was completed more or less as planned. The Red Army had done all it could to break into the bridgehead, but the losses it had suffered during the battles east of the Dnepr left its units weakened, and the damage inflicted to roads, bridges and other infrastructure by the retreating Germans made it impossible to bring forward ammunition and reinforcements at the pace that would have been needed to sustain high-tempo operations. The Germans could be satisfied that they had conducted a difficult retreat to and final evacuation of the Zaporozhye bridgehead with losses that, whilst substantial, might have been far worse. For the hard-pressed troops who now reached the west bank, there was little time for rest. Instead of the lavish defences that they had persuaded themselves they would find waiting for them, they had to take up positions in unprepared ground as the Red Army continued to keep up its pressure.

As it had advanced towards the east in 1941, the Wehrmacht had passed control of the area to the rear of the front line to the occupation authorities and the SS. Now, as the front line moved west, these bodies proved reluctant to hand back control. The approach of the Red Army led to increased partisan activity, as a result of both spontaneous acts and organised attacks coordinated by the Red Army, and the disruptive effect of such attacks began to have an impact upon the conduct of operations, not least because front-line commanders were forced to release troops that they couldn't spare in order to mount anti-partisan operations. To make matters worse, there was little or no coordination between such operations and the activities of security units operating for the occupation authorities and SS. On 16 October, Zeitzler's staff sent a signal to Heinrich Himmler, under whose authority the SS was operating, for urgent discussions on how command and control of such operations could be organised. Specifically, Zeitzler wanted a single body given control of the rear areas, and logically this should be the Wehrmacht. Somewhat predictably, Himmler had no intention of allowing control of the rear areas to pass from his authority and the request fell upon deaf ears.[45]

The soldiers and officers of the Wehrmacht had expected some degree of reprieve once they reached the Dnepr. Rumours about the strength of the *Ostwall* had circulated widely, but as already described the defences were very limited due to the lateness of Hitler granting permission for their construction. In previous years, the autumn rains had led to muddy conditions that made movement of large formations difficult, if not impossible, and this too had been a factor in the expectations of the Wehrmacht – surely the Red Army would have to halt operations at least until the winter froze the ground and allowed for vehicles to move freely. But the Red Army had no intention of giving the Germans any such breathing space. Despite their huge losses, Stalin's armies were confident and determined. They had driven the hated enemy from the central regions of the Ukraine. They too knew that the Dnepr could be fortified and turned into a formidable defensive line; they had to attack before the Germans could do so.

CHAPTER 8

KRIVOY ROG

If the Dnepr was to form the bulwark against which the Red Army hurled itself in vain and was bled to defeat, the Wehrmacht either had to eliminate the bridgeheads that the Soviet forces had seized when they reached the river, or render them harmless by screening them off. The terrain around the Bukrin bend allowed Nehring's troops to achieve the latter, but the larger bridgehead to the south of Kremenchug was a different matter. The attacks to reduce the bridgehead ground to a halt in the face of determined resistance in terrain that favoured defence; unlike the fighting at Bukrin, the Red Army was able to reinforce its troops on the west bank relatively rapidly, and as has already been described, Konev had no intention of allowing the Germans to screen off the sector. If his forces could break out of the bridgehead, the Dnepr would cease to be a defensible position for the Wehrmacht. There was also the possibility of trapping and destroying substantial German forces; the retreat to the Dnepr by the Wehrmacht had been carried out with considerable skill, but there was every likelihood that the divisions that had pulled back to the river would now attempt to make a stand there and the losses already inflicted upon them made it more likely that the Red Army would be able to achieve penetrations in the German lines.

The operation that Konev had in mind was to break out of the Dnepr bridgehead at Mishurin Rog and push east to Kirovograd (now Kropyvynytsyi) and Krivoy Rog, broadly along the seam between the German First Panzer Army in the south and Eighth Army in the north. The full weight of his forces could then be turned south, pinning First Panzer Army in the lower Dnepr and thus inflicting major damage on its units, if not surrounding them entirely. Such attacks had repeatedly shown that there was a tendency for units to pull back towards their centre of gravity; consequently, Konev could expect units of Eighth Army to pull back towards the northwest, while First Panzer Army would retreat towards the southwest. The gap that would open between the two would help the Red Army achieve further penetrations against the open flanks of both German armies. His plans were aided by Hitler's insistence that Nikopol, a short distance downstream from Zaporozhye, had to be held at all costs. The city was the centre of manganese mining and one of the few sources of this metal under German control; the Führer repeatedly told Manstein and others that this supply of manganese was essential for German production of steel alloys and armaments production would be severely hit if the mines were recaptured by the Red Army. Manstein and his staff already regarded the Dnepr as an unsuitable line for prolonged defence, not least because the Red Army had crossed it at so many points, and wished to pull back to a shorter line, allowing them to concentrate their resources more effectively, but Hitler was adamant: Nikopol had to be retained. In addition, the plains to the southeast of Nikopol were also deemed vital, as these provided the land link to the Crimea. The retention of the Crimea was another essential requirement as far as Hitler was concerned, as he feared that Soviet bombers would be able to operate against Romanian oil installations from the western parts of the peninsula. Whilst Manstein might have been minded to abandon Nikopol, he was ambivalent about the Crimea in his memoirs; on the one hand, it was increasingly difficult to justify an exposed line running to the southeast to cover Kherson and the land corridor to the peninsula, but on the other hand, his personal role in capturing the Crimea and in particular the fortress of Sevastopol made him reluctant to abandon territory for which his troops had paid a heavy price in 1942.

The initial attack against the German forces was made by Seventh Guards Army and Thirty-Seventh Army on 15 October. Just as the Germans had found when they attempted to reduce the bridgehead, the terrain was favourable for defence and despite heavy artillery preparation the attackers made little progress – in most sectors, they penetrated into the first line of German defences but were then either contained or driven out. Rotmistrov's tanks had begun to cross the Dnepr the previous evening and several senior officers met to discuss how to proceed. Fighting had died down and it seemed that the Germans had concluded that the day's serious business was over; in an attempt to take them by surprise, Konev's subordinates decided to commit Major General Kuzma Grigorevich Trufanov's XVIII Tank Corps, the first element of Rotmistrov's Fifth Guards Tank Army, to the battle. Originally, the intention had been to hold the armour in reserve until the infantry of Seventh Guards Army and Thirty-Seventh Army had created a breach, but the determined German defence had effectively derailed this plan. Zhadov, the commander of Fifth Guards Army (which was supporting the attack of Lieutenant General Mikhail Stepanovich Shumilov's Seventh Guards Army), claimed in his memoirs that the plan to send forward the armour in a surprise attack originated with Trufanov; Rotmistrov by contrast wrote that it was his idea, and Konev didn't even mention any discussion with his subordinates, merely writing that he personally decided to commit Rotmistrov's troops. Regardless of whose idea the plan was, two brigades of XVIII Tank Corps moved forward and after a brief artillery bombardment attacked the German lines. The constraints of the terrain over which the attack was conducted forced Trufanov to concentrate his men on a frontage of only a mile, and at the same time allowed the Germans to concentrate their defensive firepower, but Rotmistrov estimated that Trufanov's XVIII Tank Corps' leading units managed to advance about 15 miles (25km) by the time it was fully dark. To Rotmistrov's dismay, Trufanov was badly wounded when his jeep came under fire from German infantry that had been bypassed by the advancing Soviet armour. His deputy, Colonel Alexander Nikolayevich Firsovich, took command immediately but the changes in command combined with the confusion caused by advancing through difficult terrain left the tank brigades spread out and unable to coordinate. Much of the night was spent restoring contact between the units and moving them into position.

On the morning of 16 October, Wöhler's Eighth Army received orders to pull *SS-Totenkopf* out of the front line so that it could be sent to support XI Corps, which was on the northern flank of Konev's assault. Wöhler replied to Manstein's headquarters that it would be impossible to comply with this order in just one day – it would take longer for the neighbouring infantry divisions to shorten their lines sufficiently to release troops that could be used to fill the gap that would be created by the departure of the SS division. In response, a battalion improvised from the personnel of Eighth Army's *Waffenschule* – a training establishment set up to train new recruits in the use of heavy weapons and thus remedy some of the deficiencies in basic training that had resulted from the need to get soldiers to the front line as quickly as possible – was ordered to the front line so that at least a start could be made in withdrawing *SS-Totenkopf.* At first, only the division's reconnaissance battalion, reinforced by the six remaining tanks of the panzer regiment, could be released to First Panzer Army. To make matters worse, even as orders were issued, the Soviet forces facing *SS-Totenkopf* launched attacks in an attempt to tie down the German troops; these attacks were repulsed with energetic counterattacks.[1]

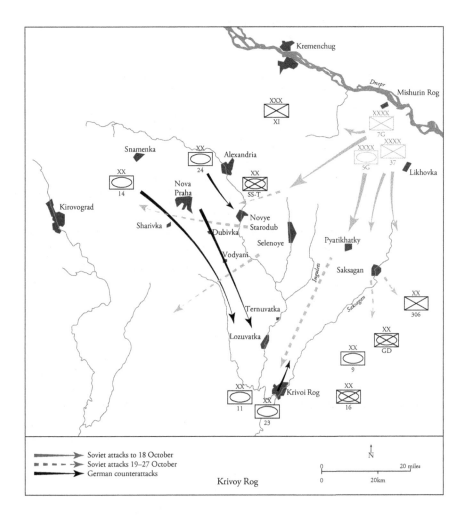

Krivoy Rog

The badly depleted units of *Grossdeutschland* were on the southern flank of Konev's assault. After months of continuous combat with inadequate replacements of personnel or equipment, the fighting strength of even a powerful armoured formation like *Grossdeutschland* – its establishment strength was significantly greater than that of the Wehrmacht's 'regular' panzer divisions – was a shadow of its former self; one company of *Grossdeutschland*'s reconnaissance battalion consisted of a single officer, two NCOs and six soldiers.[2] For a while, *Grossdeutschland* did its best to hold back the Soviet assault, making skilful

325

tactical use of the terrain, but by the end of 15 October it was forced to pull back to a shorter line. It was the beginning of an almost continuous, if dogged, withdrawal from one ridgeline to the next. Whenever circumstances allowed, the remaining tanks and guns of the division were used to good effect to engage the Soviet spearheads and inflict losses upon them, but the imbalance of forces was too great for anything more than a series of delaying actions. The equally depleted 9th Panzer Division fell back in a similar manner. Unless reinforcements arrived rapidly, it seemed as if Konev's 2nd Ukrainian Front would be able to exploit its breakout far to the west and southwest.

It was now the turn of 9th Panzer Division, to the west of *Grossdeutschland*, to come under pressure. Generalmajor Erwin Jollasse had been appointed commander of 9th Panzer Division only at the beginning of October, and less than three weeks after he took up his post he was badly injured in a fall. He was replaced by the commander of the division's 10th Panzergrenadier Regiment, Oberst Johannes Schulz, who had to deal with a new crisis just a few days later. A powerful tank and infantry attack drove back the right flank of 9th Panzer Division and although the intervention of the assault gun battalion of *Grossdeutschland* brought the Soviet advance to a halt, 9th Panzer Division's forces were too weak to recover the previous front line. Consequently, the entire front line had to pull back again. After a brief pause to bring up reinforcements and supplies, the Soviet units attacked again over the following days and rapidly put 9th Panzer Division's panzergrenadiers to flight. The *Grossdeutschland* reconnaissance battalion was able to form a thin screen in front of the advancing Soviet troops, and the division's assault gun battalion attempted to restore the situation. The boundary between the two divisions ran along a raised railway line, which was a mixed blessing – on the one hand, any Soviet tanks attempting to cross it found themselves in an exposed position where they could easily be engaged, but on the other hand it was difficult for Major Peter Frantz, commander of the assault gun battalion, to be sure what was going on beyond the railway line. He decided to investigate, crossing the railway line in his assault gun accompanied by a second vehicle:

> I saw friendly anti-tank guns and artillery driving at full speed toward the rear and fleeing infantry, here and there a squad regrouping. I managed to stop a Feldwebel who in a brief report told me that the Russians had overrun our lines with numerous tanks and broken into the village behind a hill which lay in front of us. However, since I could see no indication of direct enemy action on the hill, I decided to drive up to the hill with my escorting gun and see what was happening

… Just as I was about to get my first look over the hill, I realised that there were fast-moving T-34s (in this situation it was impossible to say how many) coming through the corn at full speed only 10m away. What was there to do? To take up the battle frontally made no sense, for the speed of the T-34s was too high and they were almost abreast of my position. Signal to my escort: turn around and tag along with the Russian tanks as if nothing was happening. We drove down the hill with the very fast T-34s in sixth gear. Looking around from my hatch I saw the face of the Russian commander of a T-34 driving only 20m behind me. We looked into each others' eyes and I now expected to see him close the turret hatch and train his gun on us. Nothing of the sort happened … We rolled onward and I succeeded in reaching a valley to our right, which I had earlier chosen as my objective. It fell away somewhat more steeply and in this way offered a degree of cover to the left, in the direction of the attack. On reaching the valley I turned around and opened fire on the T-34s, which were abeam and somewhat ahead of me. My escorting gun now likewise opened fire from the same position and direction. In a very short space of time we succeeded in halting seven T-34s in flames.[3]

Whilst this account may seem improbable, similar tricks were described by other German fighting vehicle drivers and appear to have been remarkably successful. Although Frantz describes seeing the commander of the T-34s, most Soviet tanks operated with the commander inside the vehicle and the turret hatch closed, which greatly reduced visibility. It should also be remembered that this incident happened in a field of high corn with vehicles moving over – presumably – bumpy ground at speed.

Georgi Nikolayevich Krivov was a young tank commander in the ranks of the advancing Soviet troops, about to have his baptism of fire:

We drove to the western edge of the copse and it began to grow dark. They ordered us to prepare to attack. We hoped that we wouldn't attack in the evening but I still sent Bodyagin [one of the crew] forward to see if the company commander intended to attack. We feverishly began to prepare the tank for battle: we wiped the lubricant grease from the shells, checked the engine and the chassis. At that moment Bodyagin ran up waving his arms. Thus we went into our first battle, without any reconnaissance. Ahead of us was a hill, and we had no idea what was beyond. It would have been better to send the officers up first to see where the German defensive line was. Apparently we were trying to achieve surprise. We were even ordered not to speak on the radio.

I heard the tank to my left, and then an engine roaring to the right. Slowly we climbed up the hill through the pouring rain. In my periscope I could see the dark grey earth and the cloudy sky. When we reached the top of the hill, the first impression was one of wonder. The huge ball of the sun seemed to be sitting on the horizon. I looked closer – there was flat ground about 800m ahead. Everything was quiet. I remembered that the 'old men' [veterans] had said that as soon as I saw the German positions, I should open fire immediately. The effect of this fire was of course zero, but we listened to the experienced men. Suddenly, from several places at once, there were the bright flashes of anti-tank guns. I tried to aim at one of them at least. But I couldn't. It was impossible to aim on the move, with first the sky, then the earth flashing before my eyes! I needed a short halt. But in my mind were the words of the older guys: if you stop and take too long, he [the enemy] will have plenty of time! The fighting compartment was full of powder smoke from the constant shooting, our eyes were watering and our throats were parched. It was good that the turret hatches were ajar as we would have perished otherwise, and Bodyagin constantly threw the spent shell-cases out of the hatches. Our physical tension seemed to have reached its limit. But I calmed myself, saying it wasn't going to last forever, there had to be a respite!

The tank to the left caught fire, two more vehicles were burning to the right. Bodyagin shouted, waving his arms. The shell-case extractor hit the back-plate and then flew forward, and the front edge struck behind the recoil mechanism. Bodyagin couldn't deal with it – his hands were burned from throwing out the shell-cases while I was firing ...

I fired the machine-gun. It was now night – you couldn't see a damned thing. We seemed to have passed the German defensive line but we didn't know where to go next. I asked the radio operator: 'Where are the others?'

'I think they went to the right past the trees and then we lost radio contact.'

I said to the driver-mechanic, 'Drive to the right.' Slowly, we crawled forward. I could see a dark haystack. I decided to fire a couple of shells at it in case someone was hiding there. But of course there wasn't. We were amongst the darkened houses of a village and stopped and I asked the crew, 'What shall we do?' Everyone was silent. We turned around and retraced our path through the village, still not saying a word. We passed the haystack and switched off our engine. We could hear snatches of conversation but couldn't distinguish if it was in Russian. Suddenly someone came up to us ... as if emerging from the earth the silhouettes of three of our soldiers appeared laden with grenades.

I jumped down from the tank immediately. 'Who are you?' they asked.

'We're driving back from the attack.'

'Why are you driving away from the Fritzes? We nearly attacked you with our grenades!' It turned out that they were scouts moving up to the village to see if there were any enemy soldiers there. We smoked and then headed in different directions. Thus our battle ended. When we returned to the battalion, I found almost none of those with whom I had gone into battle – they had all been set alight. Some of the most experienced had survived but our young replenishment draft was almost completely destroyed.[4]

As the Soviet attacks opened up a gap between First Panzer Army's northern flank and Eighth Army's southern flank, there were further arguments about the ongoing deployment of *SS-Totenkopf*. On 17 October, Manstein ordered that the division should remain with Eighth Army instead of being transferred to Mackensen's First Panzer Army; however, it was to be used to try to close the gap between the two armies. Along roads that had turned to mud in the autumn rains, *SS-Totenkopf* struggled to concentrate its forces for the planned counterattack. Despite the brief period of rest in Onufriyevka, the division was still in a badly weakened state, having received no replacement drafts or new equipment. As delays in concentrating its limited resources continued to force a postponement of any counterattack to close the gap in the German lines, Manstein intervened. The attack was to be delayed until the arrival of reinforcements so that it could be launched with sufficient strength to achieve the desired outcome.

The tired and battered elements of 16th Panzergrenadier Division, which had been the last unit to withdraw from the Zaporozhye bridgehead, were now arriving to help shore up the defensive line. Schwerin, its commander, later wrote in terms that few were prepared to speak aloud in 1943:

When a unit comes out of a chaotic inferno, such as the situation through which the *Windhund* division [the nickname of 16th Panzergrenadier Division] had had to fight through in Zaporozhye, drained and fought out, exhausted and weakened by heavy losses – yet successful and justly proud of an exceptional achievement – then, one might think, it has earned some rest, time for physical and mental recovery. That at least was the hope of the *Landsers* – their division commander knew that they would once again be disappointed. There would be no rest …

Since Stalingrad, the initiative over events in the front line had passed to the Russian leadership. The Germans were forced to limit themselves to defensive and counterattacking measures. This was due to the losses of the German combat formations, the impossibility of replacing senior personnel and the material losses of the preceding summer in all theatres of war, the expected creation by the Western Powers of a new theatre in France, the excessive mental demands made on troops due to the excessive duration of the war and the increasingly open hopelessness of the *Landsers* that the war could be won – in short, the total overstretching of the Wehrmacht by land, sea and air. Particularly important was the diminution of confidence in Hitler's leadership, which through his rigid insistence on defending every square foot of land destroyed what remained of the superiority of German troop leadership, particularly in the armoured formations and the artillery. Hitler's constant intervention in details at the front, which could not be understood or judged from the distant Führer Headquarters, created uncertainty in all commands, as any local initiative was stifled and there were only 'orders from above' and the general maxim of commanders in the conduct of combat was to 'cover their backs'. Consequently the German soldier lost more and more of his sense of superiority over the Soviets. He degenerated into a simple broadcaster of orders. The *Führerbefehl* ['Führer orders'] were the bogeymen of all senior and junior officers, not least because they were associated with the constant threat of court martial and the severest penalties. But as the enemy dictated the course of the fighting and prevented the execution of sometimes improper and pointless orders, the troops became accustomed to falsification of reports. They somehow had to deal with orders from above that were impossible to carry out, in order not to be found guilty later of non-execution of orders. This not only led to incorrect representations of the tactical situation, but also extended to loss and inventory reports about personnel and materiel. From the autumn of 1943 onward, these were more or less meaningless.

How then could the war be conducted successfully? By judgements of courts-martial and death? Of course, the war-experienced *Landsers* were also aware of all this. They weren't fools. They were tired of sacrificing themselves in futile warfare and only wanted to get home safely. They therefore placed their trust in their officers, who they thought would bring them through ...

There would be no rest, but renewed heavy fighting that would decide whether the division would come through the coming retreat or perish. It would have to use its last strength to avoid destruction. The *Landsers* had no idea about that. They did what they were used to doing after hard fighting: sleeping, cleaning clothes, weapons and equipment, putting them in order, writing letters, sitting with their comrades in the evening, chatting and sleeping again – and then it all resumed once more. They grumbled, but resigned themselves to what they couldn't change. One knew the seriousness of the situation and actually expected nothing else. Of course, it wasn't possible to bring the units back to full combat strength. There weren't sufficient replacements, and they were sent to the Eastern Front only in small numbers. But they included many familiar faces that we now saw again. After returning home [to recover from wounds] they cut through the hustle and bustle of rear area administration to return to their old units and their comrades-in-arms. They were aided by the division's rear area units and tactical roadsigns. They muddled through with much cunning and deception past all the rear area heroes at railway stations and assembly areas. Now they returned, we celebrated our reunion enthusiastically ...

[The units had constantly experienced] relocation forwards when attacking, locally improvised or planned counterattacks, retreats, organised withdrawals from contact, replacing or reinforcing other weakened units – in short, constantly on alert, and in the colder autumn weather without a roof over their heads in the open fields. They were constantly digging new foxholes and positions, being driven from them and retaking them – constantly in combat or at least expecting enemy attacks, repeatedly under fire from enemy artillery, machine-guns and mortars, confronted by and often relentlessly pursued by enemy tanks.

The artillery had it a little better. They were often able to set up their firing positions in the shelter of a village or collective farm. As a result the gun crews could at least take turns at warming themselves and sleeping. But their forward observers were usually up front with the infantry in the dirt. They got only an hour of sleep at a time and even then they were often only half-asleep. It's no surprise that the worn-down infantry gradually became apathetic, losing its energy and could no longer summon any desire for combat. The division commander knew this. He knew that he could only really count on the artillery, tanks and assault guns. If they were absent, the infantry would no longer hold, as they were physically and mentally exhausted. But it would get even worse.

But one should not think that the Russians had it much better. They were probably driven forwards by their political officers. But when they ran into the storm of our artillery barrage they fell or fled, sometimes in panic and en masse. They greatly feared our tanks and wouldn't stand when attacked by them. For the Soviets too, the war had gone on too long. The men extracted from recaptured villages were poorly trained and equipped, often not at all. They too were thus no longer enthusiastic about fighting. Here and there we encountered female battalions. Some of them were fanatical in combat, more so than the men.[5]

The Russians had deployed a number of women's battalions in the First World War, much to the horror of friends and foes alike; General Alfred Knox, the British military attaché in Petrograd, remonstrated with a Russian officer that the existence of such battalions was shameful for all Russian men. During the Second World War there were several squadrons of fighters and bombers in which all the personnel, including the ground crews, were female, and female snipers had been in the front line almost from the beginning of the war; a total of nearly 2,500 served in this role. Many also provided personnel for anti-aircraft units, and some served as tank drivers and machine-gunners. Maria Vasilyenevna Oktyabrskaya was a Ukrainian woman whose husband was an officer in the Red Army and before the war she trained as a military nurse, and learned to drive a number of army vehicles. After her husband was killed in the opening months of the fighting, she sold all her possessions and donated the money to pay for a T-34, requesting that it be named *Boyevaya Podruga* ('Fighting girlfriend') and that she be allowed to drive it. Her request was approved by the State Defence Committee who recognised the propaganda value of such a gesture, and she was given five months of training before deploying to the front line – this was unusual, with most tank drivers receiving only rudimentary training before being sent to their units. She joined II Guards Tank Corps and first saw action in October 1943. She rapidly won the trust and admiration of her comrades, often jumping out of her tank when it was disabled in order to carry out repairs while under fire, and on one such occasion in early 1944 she was badly wounded by shrapnel while trying to repair a damaged track. She died of her wounds two months later. She was not the first woman to serve in a tank crew; Alexandra Grigoryevna Samusenko had joined the army at an earlier date and took part in the Winter War of 1939–40 against Finland, and served with First Guards Tank Army. She died in March 1945 after being crushed by a vehicle during the night. In 1942, a rifle brigade with all-female personnel was formed and completed training the following year, but was not deployed as a complete formation; instead, it was broken up and its components used mainly for rear area security work.[6] It is conceivable that small groups of these women found themselves in the front line, and that documents found on their bodies or on prisoners suggested to the Germans that all-female infantry units existed.[7]

This is not the only part of Shwerin's account that is open to question. There can be no doubt that the ability of German infantry to resist was greatly reduced for all the reasons he describes, but even up to the rank of middle-grade officers, faith in Hitler remained strong.

After breaking out of the bridgehead and shaking off the stubbornly resisting German units in its path, the Soviet XVIII Tank Corps gained speed and reached Pyatikhatky on 18 October, where its sudden appearance seems to have taken the

Germans by surprise; Rotmistrov wrote that a train loaded with Panther tanks was waiting to unload in the railway station and fell into the hands of the Soviet armour.[8] The only significant resistance came from a handful of tanks – the last remaining tanks of 23rd Panzer Division – under the command of Hauptmann Werner Euler, and a Luftwaffe anti-aircraft battery. Too weak to hold the town, Euler's little force conducted a skilful fighting withdrawal through the town. There were several hospital trains in the railway station and at least one was left behind as the Germans pulled back. The following day, Euler returned to Pyatikhatky, escorting a locomotive down the track with his two remaining Panthers; they succeeded in reaching the hospital train, but found that all of the men in it had been killed by Soviet troops.[9]

Almost as significant as the capture of the tanks at the railway station was the seizure of the main ammunition supply dump for *Grossdeutschland*, where about 220 tons of supplies fell into Soviet hands. Until now, the weakened German units had at least been supplied with adequate ammunition – indeed, their reduced numbers meant that ammunition that would have been inadequate for full strength formations left them well supplied – but in addition to their other problems, the Germans now began to find that supplies of vital artillery and tank ammunition started to run low. Equally importantly, the advance to Pyatikhatky placed the Soviet tanks in a position from where they could outflank the retreating elements of *Grossdeutschland*, which were forced to increase their rate of withdrawal to the south.

Otroschenkov and his tank crew were in one of the Soviet tank formations that had broken out of the bridgehead. The fighting was often very confused, as he later recalled:

Once the whole battalion was involved in hunting a Tiger. The battalion had occupied half of the village of Dmitrievka. It was a large village, divided in two by a river. We were on one side, the Germans on the other. South of the village, on our side of the river, was an abandoned MTS [*Mashinno-Traktornaya Stantsiya* or machine and tractor station, a collective workshop for maintaining machinery from surrounding farms] where there was a reserve of fuel. In the afternoon we refuelled there. Near the station was a small bridge. That night, a Tiger crossed the bridge and drove to the MTS, refuelled, and set off for home. The nights were dark in the Ukraine and you could barely see anything. In addition, the late autumn landscape was dark. The Tiger lost its way and instead of returning to its bank it drove to our part of the village. It moved along the main street, along the defensive line behind our advanced tanks. On the left flank there was a battery of

SU-85s [85mm self-propelled guns, similar to German assault guns] attached to the brigade and they didn't notice it, and then it reached our battalion.

A soldier came running to the house where we were and reported, 'Comrade battalion commander, a German tank is approaching from the MTS!' We ran out as it passed us, driving slowly down the street toward the brigade headquarters. The brigade headquarters was on the edge of the village furthest from the MTS. Godin, the commander of the brigade's reconnaissance unit, was on duty that night. The battalion commander called him: 'Godin, a Tiger's coming your way!'

He replied, 'A Tiger? Where?'

'Go out and take a look, it's probably reached you already.'

Godin ran out of the brigade headquarters. The tank stopped at the headquarters, realised it was lost, turned around and drove back the same way.

At that moment, a *Sushka* [nickname for the SU-85] was approaching the German, that is, heading towards him from the left flank. The self-propelled gun passed our house and then passed the Tiger. Their tracks even scraped each other. The night was pitch-black! Between our house and the next was a Valentine tank, facing the street. I jumped into the gunner's seat and prepared to fire at the command of the battalion commander. Nothing could be seen. When the Tiger came up to me, Ivan gave the order and I fired. It was a 40mm round. There was just a shower of sparks from the Tiger's turret and it drove on. While I was loading a second round, the German drove around the corner of the house, and the driver didn't turn to approach me. I had fired my shot and it was gone. And the Tiger made its way home without any further problems.

How many jokes were circulated in the brigade – the whole battalion couldn't catch a solitary Tiger. It seemed to many that here it was, we could almost have seized it with our bare hands. But people aren't machines, and can't always act without mistakes.[10]

As they advanced, the soldiers of the Red Army frequently ran into rear area units of the Wehrmacht, many of which had been hastily organised into ad hoc battlegroups. On 18 October, there occurred a series of actions that exemplified the pitiless brutality of the Eastern Front. The village of Selenoye was the location of a makeshift hospital for wounded and sick personnel of *SS-Totenkopf*; in addition, the division's replacement battalion, composed of fresh drafts from Germany who were undergoing additional training prior to being sent to the division's combat units, and a school for experienced soldiers about to be promoted to NCOs were also in Selenoye. In an attempt to cover the withdrawal of the wounded, the replacement battalion was ordered to dig in around the village outskirts while the men of the NCO training course took up positions in the village itself. Unterscharführer Scholz was one of the wounded men:

As there was only one truck available, we gathered together all the usable *panje* wagons [a small cart drawn by a single horse]. At about 0300 some of our wounded and ill men were loaded aboard. All the rest would have to run. It was a sad scene as we set off. Almost all of us were without weapons. It seemed to me as if our slow departure took forever. Along with a few other comrades, I was tasked with forming a rearguard and thus ensuring that nobody was left behind. Hour by hour, our miserable column stretched out ever further. The partly healed wounds of some men burst apart. The walking wounded shuffled on, exhausted … Eventually towards evening a few motorbikes with sidecars came up to us, took the worst cases and drove off. They then came back and continued until we had all been moved to safety. Most of us were given makeshift accommodation in a school. It was clear to everyone that the wounded men owed their lives to our comrades in the replacement battalion.[11]

Armed only with rifles, a few machine-guns, and some anti-tank mines and grenades, the soldiers in Selenoye prepared to face the Soviet troops, aware that villagers had probably told their enemies that the German forces had minimal resources. The first probe by Soviet infantry was beaten off by an energetic flanking counterattack:

But then tanks moved up. Armed with their rifles, our men [of the replacement battalion] were powerless against the steel giants. Here and there, the tanks rolled over the foxholes of the young soldiers, turning and crushing their bodies into the Russian earth. Only a few of those who leaped from their foxholes were able to reach the shelter of the edge of the village. Most were killed or wounded by Soviet machine-gun and rifle fire. The terrain was perfect for the attacking Soviets. Their guns dominated the flat, open ground.[12]

As the fighting reached Selenoye itself, the trainee NCOs became embroiled in the desperate battle:

At first we tried to separate the Russian infantry from their tanks. The landscape was just teeming with Russians. We lost several men. With our limited means we knocked out several tanks, including one that the company staff sergeant disabled with a saucepan full of grenades after it got stuck in the mud.[13]

As they fell back through the village, the SS soldiers discovered to their horror that there were still many wounded men in the buildings; it was impossible to take them to safety and they had to be left behind. After a march that lasted all night, frequently dodging other Soviet formations, the exhausted survivors reached the lines of 11th Panzer Division. One wounded man who pretended to be dead later escaped from Selenoye and reported that the wounded men had all been shot.

It should be remembered that whilst the soldiers of the Red Army regarded all German soldiers as 'Hitlerites', they had a special hatred of the SS. The men who captured Selenoye would have seen first-hand the devastation left behind by the retreating Wehrmacht, and many would have lost friends and family members in the war. Originally, *SS-Totenkopf* was raised from concentration camp personnel, a fact that would have been known to the Soviet soldiers, and identification of SS troops was relatively straightforward; army and Luftwaffe personnel wore the distinctive eagle-and-swastika insignia on their chests, while SS troops wore it on their sleeves. It was almost commonplace for German soldiers wearing a 'bird on their sleeve' to be shot rather than taken prisoner.

Early on 19 October, 16th Panzergrenadier Division was ordered to move to defend the approaches to Saksagan, to the southeast of Pyatikhatky, where it found the remnants of the SS Cavalry Division that had fought under Fegelein's command in the battles around the Mishurin Rog bridgehead. After a singularly unimpressive record as commander, Fegelein was wounded in late September and replaced by Gruppenführer Bruno Streckenbach. Unlike his predecessor, Streckenbach had prior military experience, having served briefly in the First World War and then with the *Freikorps* in 1919. He was involved in attempts to overthrow the Weimar Republic's government in 1920 and 1923, and in 1933 was appointed head of the Hamburg *Staatspolizei*, the immediate predecessor of the Gestapo, despite his having no experience of police work. In 1938, Himmler appointed him inspector of the *Sicherheitspolizei* ('security police' or *Sipo*) and he led one of the *Einsatzgruppen* during the invasion of Poland; he then became commander of both the *Sipo* and the *Sicherheitsdienst* ('security administration' or *SD*) in Krakow, Lublin, Radom and Warsaw, in which role he was heavily involved in mass killings of Polish civilians. In late 1942, Streckenbach requested transfer to the *Waffen-SS* and was appointed commander of the SS Cavalry Division's anti-tank battalion. He now took command of the depleted division while Fegelein, his predecessor, recovered from his wounds. After their arrival in Saksagan, the soldiers of the SS Cavalry Division carried out a counterattack towards the north, driving off the approaching Soviet units for the moment and thus safeguarding the left flank of *Grossdeutschland*.

Henrici and the staff of XL Panzer Corps also arrived in the area on 16 September. There was a series of discussions between Henrici's staff and Generalleutnant Theodor Busse, Manstein's chief of staff; Henrici wanted to use *SS-Totenkopf* and 11th Panzer Division to launch an immediate counterattack, while Busse and Manstein preferred to concentrate more forces before attacking. *SS-Totenkopf* was still badly weakened with just 20 tanks available – two Pz.IIIs, eight Pz.IVs, six Tigers, and four command vehicles – and 11th Panzer Division was even weaker. There was little prospect of such a modest force making any significant impression, and Henrici reluctantly decided to wait.

Shortly after taking up their positions, the soldiers of 16th Panzergrenadier Division spotted the leading elements of Rotmistrov's troops approaching from the northeast and drove them off with a short artillery bombardment. The division was a shadow of its former strength; the six grenadier regiments had fewer than 300 men each and the panzer battalion fielded only six tanks. Fortunately, Major Rolf Brede's *Sturmgeschütz-Abteilung 236* was attached to the division, and its 14 assault guns provided a welcome boost in firepower. Subordinated to Generalleutnant Hans-Karl von Scheele's LII Corps, it joined a number of other depleted units assigned with blocking the Soviet advance and was further assigned to *Gruppe Buschenhagen* together with 15th Infantry Division, the remaining personnel of the SS Cavalry Division, and parts of 9th Panzer Division. The units of *Gruppe Buschenhagen* took up positions facing north; to the east, they had contact with neighbouring German units, but the western flank of LII Corps was entirely open and there was little that Scheele could do to prevent Rotmistrov's forces from penetrating further to the west and southwest. With low cloud making aerial operations difficult, neither side had a clear idea of the other's location, leading to surprise encounters, as Leutnant Wenzel Borgert from 16th Panzergrenadier Regiment's tank hunter battalion recalled when he carried out a patrol with three self-propelled guns:

In the only crossroads in the village we unwittingly encountered a group of between 80 and 100 Russian soldiers who had taken cover and suddenly fired on us at the crossroads from all sides with submachine-guns. Unfortunately, in the heat of the moment, our driver damaged the gearshift and the vehicle stopped. We jumped out and – as we weren't expecting the enemy, we hadn't prepared our weapons for action – we fought our way through the encircling Russian soldiers with our fists. We managed to break through the ring and ran back to Ordo-Vasilyevka. Despite the blasts of machine-gun fire at close range, Unteroffizier

Schwarz, the driver and I weren't wounded and reached the banks of the Saksagan River about 1km to the northeast.

After a short pause, during which I fired on the Red Army soldiers who were following us with my pistol, we caught our breath and decided to follow the river to the rest of our men, about 3km away. After I had emptied several magazines for my pistol, we ran along the bank. After about 200m Schwarz leaped into the river, despite the calls from the two of us for him to continue with us. As we couldn't defend ourselves against the pursuing Russians, it wasn't possible for us to wait for Schwarz or call to him. The driver and I ran back to our vehicle, during which several rounds passed through our coats but by good fortune we weren't wounded. When we reached the vehicle we immediately got it going and drove 3km back to Rai-Pole in order to help Schwarz. We shot at the Russians who were fleeing from our tank-hunters but couldn't take any prisoners as they ran off wildly.

Together with an armoured car from the reconnaissance battalion that meanwhile had arrived we reached Rai-Pole and at its edge we found Schwarz's wet coat, with holes from submachine-gun fire and bloodstains at the bottom. In its inner pocket, Schwarz had stowed the secret radio documents that had previously been in his webbing and we assumed that in order to avoid them falling into enemy hands, he had taken these out of his webbing and put them in his coat pocket and then dropped his coat thus hiding the radio codes from the Russians.

From this we concluded that although Schwarz was clearly wounded, he could still walk and followed the enemy in our vehicle to Novo-Chigirinovka, about 4km north of Rai-Pole. Here we came under strong anti-tank gunfire and had to turn back to Ordo-Vasilyevka. On our return we interrogated residents of Rai-Pole who confirmed that the German NCO had been taken away by two Russians with his legs bandaged …

On 22 October we drove north from Krinitchki in our vehicle as part of a counterattack, reaching the river about 500m south of Rai-Pole. As the Russians withdrew from Rai-Pole for a second time, we took the opportunity and together with our comrades we searched both riverbanks for further traces, unfortunately in vain.[14]

It had been the intention of Scheele, the commander of LII Corps, to use 16th Panzergrenadier Division in a concerted counterattack towards the north, ideally with the aim of reaching and recapturing Pyatikhatky, but the constant pressure from Rotmistrov's troops and the consequent gradual retreat of 9th Panzer Division, *Grossdeutschland*, and 306th Infantry Division led to an abandonment of this plan. Instead, *Gruppe Buschenhagen* was deployed behind the left flank of LII Corps to prevent it being bypassed and ultimately encircled.

Almost as soon as Rotmistrov's tanks managed to break out of the fragile German defences around the bridgehead, the weather turned rainy, bringing the infantry of Thirty-Seventh Army and Seventh Guards Army almost to a standstill. Wishing to exploit the breakthrough to the maximum extent possible, Zhukov intervened and instructed the two fronts further south to release two tank corps and several rifle divisions, which were to be sent to Konev's 2nd Ukrainian Front. In the meantime, Konev did what he could to reinforce the bridgehead by stripping the rest of his front line of all but the minimum number of units required to maintain continuity. Fifty-Third Army was ordered to concentrate its resources in order to advance towards Alexandria and Kirovograd, which meant that until Thirty-Seventh Army and Seventh Guards Army caught up, Rotmistrov's Fifth Guards Tank Army was left to push on towards Krivoy Rog potentially with its flanks unprotected. In an attempt to address this, Konev ordered V Guards Mechanised Corps – the last formation of Rotmistrov's Fifth Guards Tank Army, which had finally arrived with at least some of the tanks whose absence Rotmistrov had earlier lamented – to cover the right flank of 2nd Ukrainian Front, but in the heat of battle, Rotmistrov was not informed. When the two men had discussed the delay in its initial arrival, Konev had suggested that this might actually work in favour of Fifth Guards Tank Army, as the corps would provide welcome reinforcements and thus allow the advance to be sustained longer than might otherwise be the case; now, the two tank corps were left to press on alone.

Freshly promoted to Colonel General, Rotmistrov had ordered his XVIII and XXIX Tank Corps to continue their advance. Progress slowed as the two formations battled forward over a landscape crisscrossed by steep-sided gullies, many now filling with water from the autumn rains. They worked their way about 18 miles (30km) during the next three days and on 23 October the leading elements of XVIII Tank Corps attempted to seize Krivoy Rog in a rapid attack. Although a group of about ten tanks with infantry riding aboard managed to penetrate into the outskirts, brushing aside the improvised defences manned by Wehrmacht rear area personnel, they ran into the Tiger tanks of *Schwere Panzer Abteilung 506*. Despite being at reduced strength – the unit could field fewer than ten tanks – Major Gerhard Willing's heavy tanks, supported by a Luftwaffe anti-aircraft unit, rapidly destroyed the T-34s and drove off their accompanying infantry. Willing, who had commanded the battalion since its formation in July 1943, pushed on in pursuit of the hastily withdrawing Soviet forces, accompanied by a *Sturmbattailon* ('assault battalion') improvised from the personnel of a training unit located in Krivoy Rog and was able to recapture the defensive line that Rotmistrov's spearhead had penetrated so easily, thus preventing the early loss of Krivoy Rog with its substantial supply depots.

At the same time, the formations of the German LII Corps were forced to withdraw to the south bank of the Saksagan River. The pursuing Soviet units allowed them no pause for rest, rapidly seizing a small bridgehead; although the artillery regiment of 16th Panzergrenadier Division subjected the bridgehead to a heavy bombardment, it proved impossible to eliminate it. Interrogation of Soviet prisoners confirmed what the German commanders had already suspected: fresh Red Army units were now deploying in the region, in this case the first elements of 62nd Guards Rifle Division and 64th Mechanised Brigade.[15] On 24 October, after the customary heavy bombardment, the Soviet VII Guards Mechanised Corps, facing 16th Panzergrenadier Division, attempted to break out of the bridgehead over the Saksagan. The initial attack made good progress, particularly due to the presence of dense fog that shielded the advancing Soviet troops from German artillery observers, but a determined counterattack supported by the assault guns assigned to the division restored the previous line.

Otroschenkov, whose battalion had been the butt of jokes following its failure to intercept the Tiger tank that strayed into its midst, was involved in the fighting and saw at first hand how fatigue amongst the Soviet troops – many of whom had been in action since midsummer, with breaks that lasted just a couple of days at a time – was leading to a deterioration in combat performance:

> I don't remember the name of the village that we were ordered to take. A Tiger was hiding behind the houses. The self-propelled guns destroyed it and we entered the village early in the morning. The battalion commander immediately sent Lieutenant Popov's tank to the outskirts through which we had entered to cover our rear. There were no [friendly] troops behind us.
>
> Suddenly there was noise, confusion, shooting. Six Germans appeared with automatic weapons. They fell on the tired men and shot at them. Soldiers are all the same, they wanted to sleep. Sometimes our side showed so much carelessness, sometimes they did. But the Germans were clever fighters and this time we can say that we were lucky.
>
> The position in the village was not good. There was a hill on the other side of the village and we climbed it. From there it was clear that a battle was raging about 5km [three miles] away for a large neighbouring village. German assault guns were defending it. In all we had six or seven tanks, nearly all on the hill. We drove to the village and stopped by a building. The sounds of fighting had died

down and it was quiet. Those who had food started to eat and Ivan [the battalion commander] sat down, placing his bare feet in a bowl of water. I found a German *Panzerfaust* and began to examine it.

The woman of the house entered and told us: 'The Germans are here!' We leapt from the house and saw an assault gun. It drove past our house and its garden and stopped in the street about 20m away. Its back was towards us. I was young and enthusiastic – I had the *Panzerfaust* in my hands and thought, I should try it.

I aimed and fired. It was a simple device, I thought, and it was later copied. Our anti-tank grenade launcher was very similar. My shot hit right on the hatch at the back of the superstructure. The assault gun burst into flames. Everyone who was in it was killed except the driver. He leaped out of his hatch on the front and ran off, but was shot down.

We investigated how this had happened, because we had left a tank on the outskirts. We examined it. We found that a German assault gun had struck its turret with a round. The engine was intact and running, but the turret couldn't be used as equipment inside was damaged. The worst thing was that Lieutenant Popov's crew had escaped. There was no blood inside, which suggested that the tank was unmanned at the moment it was hit. Such was our carelessness. They had fled and hadn't warned us. Our security police searched for them but I didn't see them again. We were ordered immediately to the neighbouring village, where the German assault guns had taken up positions. We left this village – at this time, there was no front line in the usual sense. We would take a village and push on, and the Germans would retake it behind us.[16]

By 25 October, the pressure on *Grossdeutschland* had eased a great deal, allowing the division's units to stop their steady withdrawals. For the next few days, there were a few local attacks but the Germans had little difficulty in beating them off. As was often the case, the Soviet units now tried to identify the weakest part of the German line and on 28 October attacked 306th Infantry Division to the east of *Grossdeutschland*. The weakened infantry units were forced to pull back, and *Grossdeutschland* made a small withdrawal the following day in order to ensure that the front remained continuous. There was further pressure the following day, but it was only when elements of 16th Panzergrenadier Division arrived to reinforce 306th Infantry Division that the line stabilised. In an attempt to shore up the weakened infantry unit, the remnants of 328th Infantry Division were subordinated to it; it is a measure of the losses suffered by the Wehrmacht's infantry formations that the remaining personnel of 328th Infantry Division formed just two battalions instead of the nine in its establishment. Whilst General Karl-Erik Köhler, the commander of 306th Infantry Division, doubtless welcomed these reinforcements, the weakness of the German infantry was not simply a matter of numbers. The anti-tank establishment of the divisions had not really changed since the beginning of the war, and by 1943 the Red Army's attacks almost always involved mixed groups of infantry and tanks, supported by powerful artillery. In such circumstances, the ability and will of the German troops to resist was very limited. In an attempt to address this, Germany had begun development of anti-tank weapons for the infantry in 1942 and the first such device, the *Faustpatrone 1*, began to reach front-line units in August 1943. It consisted of a warhead with 400g of explosives in a shaped charge and was fired from a launch tube by a single cartridge of propellant. The penetrating power of the shaped charge was sufficient – if it struck at the right angle – to burn through about 140mm of armour, enough to defeat a T-34, but a range of only 30m meant that this weapon was of limited use and an upgraded version was in development almost from the outset. This became the *Panzerfaust* family of single-use weapons; the first versions had a warhead of 2.9kg and could penetrate 200mm of armour, allowing them to deal with T-34s with ease, though the sloping armour of the tank often prevented the *Panzerfaust* warhead from detonating at the ideal angle. As the war progressed, further versions were introduced, increasing the range of the *Panzerfaust* to over 100m. In skilled hands, it proved to be a potent tank killer and as Otroschenkov demonstrated, it was easy to use. Another infantry anti-tank weapon was the *Raketenpanzerbüchse* or *Panzerschreck*, often known to German troops as the *Ofenrohr* ('stove pipe'). It was developed after German troops came into contact with American-made bazookas and was designed to fire the 88mm rockets used in rocket artillery; it too could penetrate the armour of almost any tank that the Germans would face during the war, but the amount of smoke that the weapon produced when fired meant that it couldn't be used effectively within buildings or bunkers, and as soon as it was fired its position was revealed, forcing the anti-tank team to move to a new firing position, something that was not easy given that the operator had to wear a gas mask without its filter and a form of poncho for protection against the heat of firing. The *Panzerschreck* had a better range than the *Panzerfaust* from the outset, accurately hitting targets up to 150m away, but neither weapon was available in large quantities in late 1943.

There were repeated attempts to concentrate the resources of 16th Panzergrenadier Division on the western flank of LII Corps, but this required reinforcing 306th Infantry Division so that the units of Schwerin's division that were shoring up the infantry could be released. With Soviet forces across the Dnepr and rapidly capturing Dnepropetrovsk and other key cities, Mackensen's First Panzer Army could release forces to be concentrated further west; one such unit was 62nd Infantry Division, which was now sent to fight alongside 306th Infantry Division, allowing the latter to defend a shorter segment of front and – hopefully – finally releasing the elements of 16th Panzergrenadier Division so that they could form a stronger concentration to the west. At the same time, the remnants of the SS Cavalry Division were subordinated to 9th Panzer Division.

With the exception of the preparations prior to *Zitadelle* and the attempt to break into the Kursk salient, Manstein's tenure of command – first of Army Group Don, then of Army Group South – had been marked by a need to juggle inadequate resources in the face of multiple threats. This had nearly led to complete disaster in the winter of 1942–43, and only the timely arrival of reinforcements, consummate skill at every tier from the command of the army group down to the tactical level, and over-optimistic Soviet assessments prevented the Red Army from achieving a potentially war-winning position. After the end of the fighting in the Kursk salient, Manstein contended with pressure all along the Mius and Donets as well as the powerful attack from the north against Belgorod, Kharkov and Akhtyrka, followed by the difficult withdrawal to the Dnepr in the face of superior enemy forces. Now, with his troops finally behind the river, he once more faced multiple threats. In addition to the developing crisis caused by Konev's thrust towards Krivoy Rog, there was perhaps an even greater danger to the north of Kiev, where the Red Army had a bridgehead perilously close to the capital of the Ukraine and had also succeeded in creating a breach between the northern flank of Army Group South (Fourth Panzer Army) and the southern flank of Army Group Centre (Second Army). For the moment, Manstein had to concentrate on the threat that was developing in the south; Konev's front, which Manstein regarded as 'by far the most active on the enemy side', was rapidly reaching a position that would allow it to isolate First Panzer Army in the Dnepr bend, and also to strike south to isolate Seventeenth Army in the Crimea and Sixth Army a little to the north.[17] To prevent this, Manstein urgently needed armoured reinforcements, and for once his demands were answered. With the weather across Europe rapidly slipping towards winter, Hitler had concluded that an invasion of the European mainland by the British and Americans was now very unlikely, at least until the spring of 1944; there was therefore an opportunity to send troops east to try to stabilise the situation.

After a period of being re-equipped, *LSSAH* was heading east again. During its time in Italy, it had been involved in operations to disarm Italian units.

On 19 September, two NCOs of the division were captured by Italian anti-fascist partisans in the village of Boves. Immediately, a company of panzergrenadiers attempted to rescue them without success, and Sturmbannführer Joachim Peiper, commander of the *Lötlampe* ('*Blowtorch*') battlegroup, set off for the village with two companies. Several hundred homes in Boves and neighbouring Castellar were set ablaze; in a trial in 1968, Peiper and other *LSSAH* veterans claimed that this had occurred as a result of fighting, but testimony from Italian witnesses suggested that buildings had been set alight deliberately. In his report of the action, Peiper described how a small detachment of his battlegroup had driven into Boves and then come under fire from both partisans and Italian troops and had called for help. When the rest of the battlegroup attempted to move to their aid, the first attempt to reach them was abandoned after several men were killed or wounded by gunfire from the upper floors of buildings into the open-topped half-tracks. Peiper reported that he pulled back to allow his men an opportunity to prepare their vehicles for fighting in a built-up area and ordered a small detachment of artillery that was with the battlegroup to open fire on Boves to try to suppress the small-arms fire that had forced him back; it was this shelling, he asserted, that led to the fires that destroyed much of the village.[18]

None of the Italian accounts make any mention of troops from the Italian Army being involved in the incident. Italian partisans claimed that, after they arrived in the village, the SS prevented villagers leaving and ordered the village priest and a local businessman to tell the partisans to hand over the two prisoners within two hours. The two men were brought to Boves, but by that time the SS had already killed several Italian civilians, and as the day progressed the village was set alight – by contrast, Peiper claimed that the two captives escaped whilst their guards were distracted. A total of 24 Italian civilians died, including several who were caught inside burning buildings.[19] It is possible that Peiper used the incident to make a brutal example of the villages to intimidate the local population, much as he had done in the occupied regions of the Soviet Union. The division had previously been involved in a number of acts of violence against civilians. In the very first campaign of the war, its personnel were involved in the shooting of about 50 Polish civilians in Błonie at a time when *LSSAH* was being criticised for its poor combat performance; although the commander of 29th Motorised Infantry Division reported the killings and General Walter von Reichenau, the commander of Tenth Army to which both *LSSAH* and 29th Motorised Infantry Division were subordinated, attempted to investigate, Himmler asked Hitler to place SS troops outside the jurisdiction of the Wehrmacht and no action was taken against the troops involved.[20] It was only one of several incidents in which personnel from *LSSAH* killed Polish civilians and other units complained that the SS formation had a tendency to set ablaze almost every village that it passed through. Peiper and his battlegroup in particular had been involved in the mass shooting of civilians and the destruction of their villages on the Eastern Front, usually as revenge for attacks on German personnel, though on some occasions there was little or no direct link between the attacks and the civilians who were punished, and in many cases the alleged attacks against German units appear to have been exaggerated after the event, perhaps to justify the revenge attacks.

Charges were brought against Peiper and other *LSSAH* veterans about the Boves incident in a Stuttgart court in 1968, and the court acknowledged the marked differences in the German and Italian accounts of what had taken place. However, it concluded that there was insufficient evidence against Peiper or any other individuals, deciding that Peiper's warning to Italians just days earlier, that any attempts to interfere with the activities of his troops would be met with harsh measures, was inadequate evidence of itself to have any weight in the proceedings. There was a further trial of *LSSAH* personnel in Osnabrück in the same year concerning the killing of several Italian Jews in the same area; the conclusion of the court was that the soldiers had carried out killings but had concealed these from their superiors, who could not therefore be held accountable for the deaths. In any event, it was not possible for the proceedings to continue because the case was deemed to have occurred too long ago – at the time, a statute of limitations was in place that meant that this case was 'timed out'. After the war, Peiper eventually settled in France, and in 1976 his house was attacked on the night before Bastille Day and set ablaze. Peiper's body was found in the ruins. It is presumed that his death was a revenge killing for one of Peiper's war crimes, particularly as his battlegroup had resorted to arson on so many occasions.

LSSAH was now reorganised as a panzer division, and arrived back on the Eastern Front with a formidable strength of 95 Pz.IVs, 96 Panthers, 27 Tigers and 46 assault guns – a total of 264 vehicles. This should be compared with the total of 300 tanks deployed by Rotmistrov's Fifth Guards Tank Army at the beginning of the drive towards Krivoy Rog.

The other 'refreshed' division that was sent east, 1st Panzer Division, arrived with 95 Pz.IVs, 76 Panthers, and a handful of flamethrower tanks. Originally raised in 1935 from personnel of 3rd Cavalry Division, 1st Panzer Division regarded its status as one of Germany's first armoured units with great pride. It had been heavily involved in fighting in Army Group Centre in the last weeks of 1942 – in the six weeks before it was withdrawn and sent west on Christmas

Day, the division lost nearly 1,800 men, including two battalion commanders. Leaving behind what few tanks they still had, the division's personnel travelled by train to northern France, where they were issued with captured French tanks as a temporary measure – the division constituted the only armoured force available in the region in the (admittedly unlikely) event of an invasion of France from across the English Channel. These tanks were rapidly replaced by Pz.IVs and two of the division's four panzergrenadier battalions received half-tracks. Brought back to strength with replacement drafts and the incorporation of smaller, independent formations, the division trained hard to establish its normal levels of efficiency and was then dispatched to Greece; there were considerable fears that the Western Allies would invade Greece, a belief that was actively fostered by the British deception plan, Operation *Mincemeat*, part of the larger Operation *Barclay*. These operations were largely successful, with few if any German reinforcements being sent to Sicily. In Greece, 1st Panzer Division took part in further training and helped carry out sweeps against Greek partisans, who were increasingly active in a further attempt to create the illusion that Greece was the intended target of American and British invasion plans. One of the division's panzer battalions now returned to Germany to be re-equipped with Panther tanks while the rest of the division moved to Italy in order to take part in the German occupation of its former ally; here, the personnel received news that they were to return to the Eastern Front. With its re-equipment and training barely completed, the Panther battalion was also ordered east. The division commander was Generalleutnant Walter Krüger (not to be confused with the commander of *SS-Das Reich*), who had been in post since the beginning of the war with the Soviet Union; he was an experienced and skilled commander and, during the division's stay in Greece, he had tried to prevent his men from getting involved in reprisals against Greek partisans and civilians, with only mixed success.

In addition to these two panzer divisions, Manstein was promised three more. Two had been rebuilt after their original formations had been lost in the surrender of Sixth Army in Stalingrad. Although it was first deployed as an armoured unit in 1942, 24th Panzer Division prided itself on its historical ancestry; it was originally 1st Cavalry Division, tracing its lineage back to the mounted units of the Prussian Army, and in late 1941 it was withdrawn from the Eastern Front so that it could be converted into a panzer division. It fought with distinction in the advance to Voronezh in the summer of 1942 before being drawn into the street battles of Stalingrad where it was trapped in the encirclement. However, significant parts of the division, particularly many of its rear area units, were outside the city and thus survived. Together with men who had been on leave and by incorporating fresh drafts, the division was re-created in France in the spring of 1943, and placed under the command of Generalleutnant Maximilian Reichsfreiherr von Edelsheim, an experienced commander of armoured forces who had previously served with the division. His predecessor, Generalleutnant Arno von Lenski, had gone into Soviet captivity after the surrender of Sixth Army and would ultimately join the *BDO*. Shortly after the division was re-formed, it was sent to northern Italy where it took part in disarming the Italian Army. Now, it was ordered east without having had the chance to conduct any full-division field exercises, at the end of what had been a memorable break from the bitter fighting of the Eastern Front, and although its personnel were involved in a few actions against Italian partisans, the division's experience of Italy was clearly very different from that of *LSSAH*:

Night fell quickly. The full moon lit up the sharp silhouette of the hills in the darkness to the right in front of us. An old castle's bulky tower rose up, an ancient pine spread out its branches. Between them the moonlight fell on a truck. In the rear were a few soldiers, probably mountain infantry, singing songs of their homeland.

The following morning, the golden light of the autumnal morning sunlight spread across the mountains which had drawn closer during the night. Behind us was the fruitful plain of the Po, with our experiences of summer.

Do you remember when we came to this land on this very railroad? How long ago? It seemed like yesterday! When we detrained in the sticky heat and a string of armoured vehicles spilled from the small station at the edge of the Apennines into the surrounding fruit orchards and small farms, rapidly disappearing, hidden from the spying eyes of enemy planes. When we put up our tents under a few shady pines in the parks of beautiful castles and towns. And then began a lovely time with days full of sunshine, with glowing, unfamiliar heat and cool, bright nights, with the million chirps of cicadas, the laughter of girls, the clinking of glasses and the songs of the soldiers …

The last warm day of sunshine! … But we were needed in the immeasurable lands to the east. Soon we would once more be in the dreadful grip of war, and the loud roar of our guns, the ringing sound of steel on steel, the bright flashes of explosions and the faint groans of mortally wounded soldiers would be mercifully muffled by the vast, white cotton wool blanket of silently falling snow.

The plains lay behind us. One last time we looked back, to the rows of fruit trees in the delicate light of the sun, the rich fields of corn, the proud old towns with their beautiful cool churches in the land of carefree, friendly people with long-limbed, black-haired, laughing, graceful girls.

We were grateful that fate did not need us to bring the grey scars of war to this land.

The train laboured through the mountains of Styria.

Higher up there was already snow, a few commented that the leaves would soon be falling.

The memories of such a summer![21]

When it was re-formed, 24th Panzer Division's panzer regiment was to have three battalions, one each of Panthers, Pz.IVs, and assault guns. The Panther battalion was still in the process of forming and being equipped and trained, and the division headed east without it; the intention was for the Panthers to join the division at a later date, but ultimately they were sent to the Eastern Front as a stand-alone unit and were never reunited with the parent division.

The second 'new' unit promised to Manstein was 14th Panzer Division, which had also been rebuilt around elements of the division that were not isolated and destroyed in Stalingrad. It too was intended to have three battalions in its panzer regiment, but despite the strenuous efforts of Albert Speer and others, production of Panther tanks in particular continued to lag far behind levels required to satisfy all demands. This problem was worsened when the shortcomings of the first operational version of the Panther – *Ausführung D* – were found to be so serious that a new version (rather confusingly known as *Ausführung A*) was ordered. The weaknesses in the drive train were addressed with several modifications, and there were other changes to the design, particularly features of the turret. Hitler had already expressed a need for a more heavily armoured variant and the proposed Panther II was intended to start production in September 1943, but as the year progressed work on this new version effectively ceased while all attention was turned to improving production of the existing version. A total of about 850 *Ausführung D* variants had been produced before production switched to the *Ausführung A* and a large number of these had already been recalled to Germany once for major modifications in an attempt to address reliability problems. Whilst they waited for their new Panthers, the crews of 14th Panzer Division were given a mixture of tanks captured in 1940 in the French campaign – mainly Somua, Hotchkiss and Renault models. Some of these had been used by the Wehrmacht during the invasion of the Soviet Union in 1941, but the logistical difficulties of maintaining them, together with their obsolescence, led to their rapid withdrawal from service. However, they were useful for training purposes, though even in this role the chronic fuel shortages in the Third Reich reduced their value. By the time that 14th Panzer Division was ready to deploy on the Eastern Front again, it had just one battalion, mainly equipped with Pz.IV tanks and a single company of assault guns. The Panther battalion remained in the west, training with its French tanks while it awaited new vehicles, and the makeup of the proposed third battalion remained unclear. One proposal had been for it to be equipped with Tiger tanks, but it rapidly became clear that production would never suffice for this to be possible. In any event, reports from the fighting against the Red Army generally supported the continued deployment of Tigers in independent battalions, which could be assigned to whatever unit required them. Like their counterparts in 24th Panzer Division, the veterans of 14th Panzer Division who had not been encircled with Sixth Army in Stalingrad worked hard to bring the replacement drafts up to standard, but were severely hampered in their efforts by ongoing shortages of both fuel and ammunition. Nevertheless, the four panzergrenadier battalions received the new MG42 machine-gun with its very high rate of fire, though only a single battalion received armoured half-tracks. The wheeled transport for the other battalions remained inadequate until, in an attempt to improve the division's mobility, Heinz Guderian, the visionary panzer commander who was now serving as inspector-general of armoured forces, ordered the transfer of about 600 vehicles from the relatively newly formed 25th Panzer Division to 14th Panzer Division. But at the same time, the division suffered a setback in its long-term plans when the crews designated to form the third panzer battalion were transferred to *Schwere Panzer Abteilung 509*, a new Tiger tank battalion.[22]

Despite being at least one panzer battalion under strength, both 14th and 24th Panzer Divisions could still field about 100 tanks and assault guns each, significantly more than the badly worn-down divisions currently in the Ukraine. The commander of 14th Panzer Division was Generalleutnant Friedrich Sieberg, another experienced panzer officer; he was summoned to a meeting with Hitler immediately before his division travelled east, and the Führer attempted to impress upon him the importance of the battles currently raging in the Ukraine. As a man who had led 10th Panzer Regiment (part of 8th Panzer Division) at the beginning of the war and had since served in a training role where he was constantly appraised of the realities of the Eastern Front, Sieberg needed no lectures from Hitler about the critical nature of the fighting.

The final formation on its way to Army Group South, 25th Panzer Division, was created in February 1942 with units that had been deployed in Norway, originally for possible use in an invasion of Sweden. At first, the division – far from its theoretical establishment strength – was equipped with captured British and French weapons and in the summer of 1943 moved to France, where it received German equipment; almost immediately, as mentioned above, it was forced to hand over a large number of its half-tracks and trucks for use by other formations, including 14th Panzer Division. Although it was numerically strong, with a large number of Pz.IVs and Panthers, it had not seen action as a coherent unit. Its commander, Generalleutnant Adolf von Schell, had written a brief book entitled 'Battle Leadership' whilst in the United States in 1931, largely based on his experiences in the First World War, but even as his division boarded trains for the journey east it had been announced that he was to be replaced by Generalleutnant Georg Jauer, who was currently the commander of 20th Panzergrenadier Division. Due to problems replacing him in that role, Jauer was left in command of 20th Panzergrenadier Division and in his place Generalleutnant Hans Tröger was ordered to take command of 25th Panzer Division. Tröger had commanded 27th Panzer Division on the Eastern Front the previous winter before a spell in command of the *Schule für Panzertruppen* ('school for armoured troops'). He would not reach his new command until 20 November, and in the meantime Schell – who had not commanded any units in the field during the Second World War – would be in charge. He was suffering from glaucoma, a condition that he did not reveal to the army. As the division headed east, he briefly met Guderian in Germany; Guderian tried to persuade Schell not to travel to the Ukraine and to hand over command immediately, but in vain.

Inevitably, it would take time for these reinforcements to arrive. At first, Manstein had only the limited resources of his current armies at his disposal and he had to act rapidly in order to stop the Soviet advance. The Soviet thrust towards Krivoy Rog was clearly a major threat to Army Group South, but it also created an opportunity for a counterattack. The dogged resistance that held up the troops of the Soviet Thirty-Seventh Army left Rotmistrov's armour dangerously exposed, and Manstein resolved to use the reinforcements arriving from the west to strike against Fifth Guards Tank Army. At the very least, there was an opportunity to inflict sufficient damage upon Rotmistrov's formations to render them unable to mount further attacks in the coming weeks, and at best there was a possibility that the German units might be able to achieve something approaching their successes of March 1943 when similarly exposed Soviet tank units had been almost annihilated in Manstein's counterattacks. If the opportunity was to be seized, there would be little time for the new reinforcements to assemble before they were committed to action against the northern flank of Fifth Guards Tank Army, and the exhausted armoured units of First Panzer Army would have to gather their strength for an attack against Rotmistrov's southern flank.

Fortunately, Wöhler and Mackensen had already established good levels of cooperation during the withdrawal to the Dnepr and continued to do so. Wöhler ordered XL Panzer Corps to take control of the northern side of the Soviet advance in order to defend the approaches to Kirovograd; this corps would also receive the armoured forces arriving as reinforcements and was to use them to strike towards the southeast with the intention of inflicting as much damage as possible on Konev's front. At the same time, LVII Panzer Corps, commanded by General Friedrich Kirchner, was to take command of the units on the northern flank of First Panzer Army, with the task of preventing the fall of Krivoy Rog and if possible striking into the southern flank of the Soviet advance.

The troops that had stopped Rotmistrov's tanks from breaking into Krivoy Rog were the remnants of 11th and 23rd Panzer Divisions. Both divisions had been serving on the Eastern Front for some considerable time and were badly below strength, but they were fortunate to have experienced personnel. Generalleutnant Nikolaus von Vormann, commander of 23rd Panzer Division, had been in post since late 1942 and was a solid, dependable officer; his opposite number in 11th Panzer Division, Generalleutnant Wend von Wietersheim, was a similar personality. If Rotmistrov received sufficient infantry reinforcements from the divisions of Thirty-Seventh Army, the two divisions would be unable to put up prolonged defence, but against the armour of Fifth Guards Tank Army their anti-tank capability was effective enough to bring the Soviet troops to a standstill, particularly when defending an urban area.

In its advance from the start line of the offensive to Krivoy Rog, the Soviet Fifth Guards Tank Army had covered a distance of 60 miles (97km); from their starting strength of about 300 tanks, Rotmistrov estimated that XVIII and XXIX Tank Corps had only 75 operational tanks by the end of 23 October, a good indication of the difficulty in keeping vehicles running in such high-tempo operations.[23] Matters were probably made worse by the presence of several different types of tanks provided by the Western Allies. Whilst the modest engineering resources of Fifth Guards Tank Army would have been experienced at repairing T-34s and other Soviet-built vehicles, it is unlikely that they would have had many spare parts for the foreign-built tanks or much experience at maintaining them. In addition, the terrain – the two tank corps were constrained by the Ingulets and Saksagan rivers – was also not ideal, leaving Rotmistrov's troops with little room to manoeuvre effectively; even if they had been able to field more tanks, it would have been difficult to deploy them to full effect.

Krivov and his crew were in action in the front line near Krivoy Rog, once more involved in an encounter with a Tiger tank. Whilst Krivov and his crew were involved with tending to a wounded comrade, their platoon commander had already moved off towards the German lines:

We had to catch up with the platoon commander. We roared out of the village. To the left and ahead were bare fields, to the right there was a line of trees, and about 800m beyond it a line of hills, similar to mining waste spills. Ahead of me I saw the platoon commander's vehicle and two more tanks. Yermishin [the platoon commander] was walking to their right. I shouted to the driver-mechanic to speed up: 'Catch up! We must catch up!'

Then it seemed as if I saw a flash from one of the hills. Someone was shooting from there? ... 'Tiger on the left, Lieutenant, Tiger! Immediately to our left, in the ravine, you can only see its turret and radio antenna!'

I turned the turret. 'Armour piercing, Petya, armour piercing!' But the Tiger had already disappeared into low ground beyond a tree. I fired two rounds in his direction as a warning. The driver-mechanic yelled, 'Platoon leader Yermishin's tank is burning!' Two men emerged from the smoke-engulfed vehicle, then one more – the fourth didn't appear. The survivors jumped off and ran to the left towards the ploughed field. But the Tiger was somewhere over there ... I ordered, 'Grisha, take us to the right. The dead ground will cover us!' He quickly turned right but after about 20–30m we were hit. The shot came from the hills.

There was a sudden lurch. I was thrown forward, my face hitting the gun's breech and blood gushed from my nose, the pain from the bridge of my nose like a shower of sparks in my eyes. I shouted to the driver-mechanic, 'Turn the engine back on, start it!' He was already pressing the starter repeatedly but to no avail. We were stuck! The mechanic turned around and hopelessly spread his hands – and seeing something behind me let out a shout. I couldn't hear his words from the dull buzzing in my ears from concussion but I turned quickly. Tongues of flame were coming through the small cracks to the engine compartment. Instantly I felt the heat and the suffocating smell of burning oil filling the fighting compartment. 'Bale out!' I threw open the hatch and suddenly heard the sharp sound of an engine. It was really revving hard! But a burst from a large-calibre machine-gun explained everything – a plane was attacking us. We dived under the tank.

But we couldn't stay under the tank as the ammunition might explode at any minute. Bullets struck the armour, the wheels, and the tracks. The driver-mechanic shouted, 'Germans, Lieutenant!' We leaped out from under the vehicle and ran headlong towards the ploughed field where the guys had run from the burning tank a few minutes before. Kryukov was ten or 15 paces from me. The fire intensified. A terrible blast of bullets pressed us to the ground, making us crouch, wanting to spread out ... We had to pretend that we had been killed. We had to fall to the ground. I lay on the ground, taking shallow breaths. But the shooting stopped. The driver-mechanic had dropped alongside me, and thank God was still alive. After a few breaths, without a word we jumped up at the same time and rushed on. Everything was repeated: a furious fire, the eerie buzzing of rounds, grim thoughts about dying, but I noticed that the bullets were higher above our heads and I began to think we would survive. Again there was the roar of the aircraft engine. I fell to the ground and looked up at my approaching death. He banked towards us, almost touching the ground with his wheels, and I threw myself headlong into a furrow. He didn't see us or fire on us.

When it had grown quiet we got up. The tank was still burning. There was a powerful explosion, and we turned to see that in place of our vehicle was a shapeless mass. We descended into the low ground where we found a stream. We washed and rested. A little further along we came across some submachine-gunners [who had been riding the tanks into battle]. There were three of them ... In the ravine there gathered a few of our men, mostly submachine-gunners and our radio operator. I didn't know what had happened to the others. It seemed that Yermishin had jumped out but was missing. Perhaps they had shot him?[24]

To make matters worse for Rotmistrov, the German 14th and 24th Panzer Divisions had begun to arrive, and were allocated to XL Panzer Corps. The reconnaissance battalion of 24th Panzer Division reached Uman on 17 October and immediately detrained before moving forward towards Kirovograd; the rest of the division would continue by train in order to avoid the muddy roads and preserve fuel stocks. From Kirovograd, the battalion travelled on to Alexandria, from where it was ordered to probe towards the southeast on 20 October. To the left of the reconnaissance battalion was the German 376th Infantry Division, but to the right there was open space. The division's artillery, panzer regiment and panzergrenadiers had still not arrived and the first contact with the Red Army came on 23 October when a group of about 20 T-34s supported by infantry pushed forward into the village of Novyi Starodub. The Ingulets River ran past the village and at first the reconnaissance battalion was able to prevent the Soviet group from crossing the river from the east, but the following day the attacks were renewed and the German troops found themselves under attack from the south, east and north as Soviet tanks crossed the river and moved towards the rear of the defensive line, overrunning the battalion's command post. It took the hasty intervention of the first company of 24th Panzer Division's tanks, attacking from the northwest and pushing past Novyi Starodub, to drive off the T-34s, but pressure continued as Soviet infantry effectively encircled the village and put increasing pressure on the defenders. During 25 October, the leading elements of 24th Panzer Division's panzergrenadiers began to arrive and the Soviet troops were forced back. It was a tough baptism of fire for the reconnaissance battalion, largely composed of new drafts; both of its senior officers were killed in the fighting. Even after relative calm had returned on 27 October, a sudden Soviet bombardment struck the village, killing Rittmeister Ferdinand von Wrede, commander of one of the panzergrenadier battalions.[25] Despite these losses, the arrival of the German division had effectively blocked any Soviet drive towards Kirovograd.

The first elements of Sieberg's 14th Panzer Division began to arrive on the Eastern Front on 25 October. Given the uncertainty about the precise location of friendly and hostile forces, the first elements detrained in Snamenka, between Kirovograd and Alexandria; later elements, particularly rear area units, would continue by train all the way to Krivoy Rog. Sieberg, who arrived the same day, was ordered to use the division to secure the area between the Soviet thrusts towards Kirovograd and Krivoy Rog; together with 24th Panzer Division and *SS-Totenkopf*, it was assigned to XL Panzer Corps. Sieberg immediately dispatched his reconnaissance battalion towards the south, where it encountered and drove off a few small groups of T-34s. As the situation became clearer, Sieberg recognised that the Soviet spearheads were composed of mechanised and armoured formations, i.e. weak in infantry; consequently, they would need to be countered by similar armour-heavy formations. Following what had become almost standard practice in panzer divisions, the division's main armoured assets – the armoured battalion of its artillery regiment, its half-track panzergrenadier regiment, and a company of combat engineers – were attached to the panzer regiment, creating *Kampfgruppe Langkeit*. Such operational deployment had been rehearsed many times in France prior to the division's move to the east, and the battlegroup went into action on 28 October in an energetic attack, encountering and destroying several groups of Soviet tanks and infantry attempting to advance towards Kirovograd.[26]

Despite these successes, events not far away were adding to the growing pressure on Manstein's Army Group South. After reaching the Dnepr around Dnepropetrovsk, the units of Southwest Front – now 3rd Ukrainian Front – had been bringing forward supplies and reinforcements prior to attempting to force the river, and preparations were now complete. The first assault to secure a bridgehead over the Dnepr was at Verkhnodneprovsk, about 33 miles (55km) upstream from Dnepropetrovsk. On 22 October, troops of Lieutenant General Nikolai Alexandrovich Gagen's Fifty-Seventh Army crossed the river before dawn, rapidly securing a foothold outside the town. Vasily Ivanovich Kovalenko was a tank commander in a unit that was ordered to attempt a crossing:

We were on the Dnepr near Dneprodzerzhinsk, and on the far side of the river was the large village of Domotkan. We stopped. We needed a ferry, but there wasn't one. The Dnepr is wide there, about 800m. Many formations had gathered there, including a general with his headquarters. A group of German planes appeared and there were bomb explosions as they dived down on us. Nevertheless, a command was given to cross to the right bank under enemy fire. We built big rafts, sawed timber, hammered the rafts together under fire, drove tanks onto them and crossed to the far shore under bombardment. The planes sank some rafts and the tanks went to the bottom of the river, but the crews had been standing next to their vehicles and swam ashore swiftly. It was very dangerous – a small wave could tilt the wet raft and the tank would slip easily into the river. The whole river was alive with people and vehicles, and every crew tried to save their tank, standing on either side in order to try to level the raft at a dangerous moment, to balance it when it tilted. And all the time bombs rained down mercilessly on everyone. This is what the river crossing looked like. Many people were killed in the water and lost, and their relatives were left waiting for them to come home. No one would know how they died, or where they are now. They remained forever only in the hearts of their mothers … We were lucky, we were wet from the spouts of water and crossed immediately to the high west bank, and there we met German submachine-gunners. We had no air support and we had to wait for our infantry to cross. But it was good that we were at one end of a whole field of corn. It was very useful as camouflage. But [enemy] tanks attacked us, our tank was hit, the caterpillar torn away. Almost the whole crew was stunned by the impact. How I got out of the hatch I do not remember, or who helped me. It was already evening. Apparently, I was seriously concussed, since I couldn't think clearly. I remember the scene well: as in a dream, the Germans appeared as a running line of greatcoats and for some reason everything seemed small, like Lilliputians, and they shot at us. I stood near the tank, leaning on the caterpillar and the German submachine-gunner tried to cut me in half. Later it turned out that one bullet hit my right shoulder joint and the second bullet went under my arm. Apparently, I fell on my side, so all the blood that flowed from the wound soaked into my sleeve and clogged the wound. And at night the medics came and I remember a woman said: 'He's still alive, his heart's still beating.'[27]

Despite local successes like the one described above, the German forces were too weak to react decisively and Soviet reinforcements followed in a steady stream. To the south of Fifty-Seventh Army, Lieutenant General Vasily Vasilyevich Glagolev's Forty-Sixth Army crossed the river the following day, swiftly merging its bridgehead with that held by Gagen's men, and the two armies began to advance towards the southeast, intending to cut the German lines of communication from Dnepropetrovsk. At the same time, Chuikov's Eighth Guards Army seized a bridgehead south of Dnepropetrovsk at Voiskovoi and began to attack towards the northwest. The distance between the two bridgeheads was 40 miles (65km) with few German units able to intervene – Manstein had stripped the sector bare in order to release sufficient troops to deal with the threat to Krivoy Rog. Regardless of any orders Hitler might have been inclined to issue about holding the line of the Dnepr to the last man, Manstein acted quickly to prevent the troops in the region from being encircled and ordered the abandonment of the west bank between the two Soviet bridgeheads. On 25 October, the Soviet Forty-Sixth Army captured Dneprodzerzhinsk (now Kamianske) and advanced swiftly towards Dnepropetrovsk while Chuikov's troops approached from the south; by the end of the day, the city was in Soviet hands.

The bulk of Malinovsky's Third Ukrainian Front could now cross the Dnepr and concentrate on the right bank, from where Malinovsky was presented with two tempting options: he could drive southwest towards Krivoy Rog and link up with Konev's troops fighting to the north and northeast of the city; or he could attack south towards Nikopol, threatening the rear of what Hitler had decreed was a region vital for the German war effort. It marked the end of a long road of rehabilitation for Malinovsky. In May 1942, his Southwest Front had taken part in the disastrous attempt by Marshal Semyon Konstantinovich Timoshenko to recapture Kharkov. Although Zhukov and Vasilevsky had warned Stalin against allowing the offensive to proceed, Stalin had trusted his old friend Timoshenko to mount a successful attack and after the Red Army's defeat he told confidants that he had suspicions about the loyalty of Malinovsky. This appears to have been due to the fact that when serving in the Imperial Russian Army in 1916, Malinovsky spent some time in France as part of the Western Front Russian Expeditionary Corps, and the eternally suspicious Stalin feared that Malinovsky had kept in touch with acquaintances he had made in the west and might deliberately have sabotaged the attempt to take Kharkov. This ignored the fact that, at the time of his stay in France, Malinovsky was a lowly NCO and would have been exceedingly unlikely to have established contacts of any political significance. Stalin repeatedly showed great loyalty to his old comrades from the

Russian Civil War, and the suspicions directed at Malinovsky were probably due to his unwillingness to criticise Timoshenko. After commanding forces near Stalingrad, Malinovsky returned to the command of Southwest Front, which had now become 3rd Ukrainian Front; following the drive to and over the Dnepr, Stalin decided that he was unquestionably loyal.

For a brief moment, Malinovsky and his subordinate army commanders must have believed that they were about to win a dazzling victory. Only 45 miles (72km) separated the forces of 3rd Ukrainian Front from the German units around Nikopol to the south, and Krivoy Rog was only a slightly greater distance to the southwest. Accordingly, Malinovsky ordered his front to launch a powerful thrust towards the southwest with a view to exploiting both of these options. However, as Chuikov – temporarily away from his Eighth Guards Army for medical reasons – later wrote, the operation did not go according to plan:

The main axis of attack, towards Apostolovo [roughly midway between Krivoy Rog and Nikopol], was set on 29 October after XXXIII Rifle Corps had completed its assembly.

By 1 November, all units were across the Dnepr. In order to carry out the directives of the front command, [Colonel General Ivan Ivanovich] Maslennikov, the temporary commander [of Eighth Guards Army], aimed the army with its right wing on Apostolovo along the railway [from Dnepropetrovsk to Apostolovo] … if successful, Eighth Guards Army and Forty-Sixth Army would be in the flank and rear of the entire group of German units around Nikopol and would also open the road to Nikolayev and Odessa. The concept was correct, but required larger forces. If this axis had been chosen for a strike somewhat earlier, the operation would undoubtedly have succeeded.

It was the autumn muddy season. The army was short of tanks. Artillery units were constantly short of ammunition, which was difficult to bring forward across the Dnepr. After the successful battles to expand the bridgeheads, the offensive operations of the army were almost entirely fruitless. The enemy used a system of strongpoints with mobile defence in between. These strongpoints also served as ammunition depots. Consequently, the Nazis did not suffer from the muddy season as we did.

On 4 November, the right flank of the army attempted to attack along the railway line. Despite a 40-minute artillery preparation, the attack stalled after just 2–3km. The same thing happened on 5 November. At some points, the enemy mounted counterattacks. During the afternoon, after repulsing the counterattacks, the army's units moved over to a strong defensive posture.

I returned from the hospital shortly after the end of October. My Eighth Guards Army was manning fortified positions by then, the soldiers and officers were resting and replenishment was under way. On 12 November I met Malinovsky and Vasilevsky to find out what tasks they were assigning to the army. Alexander Mikhailovich [Vasilevsky] spoke first of the common mission of the front, indeed for several fronts, to seize Nikopol as soon as possible. The words 'Nikopol' and 'manganese' were now being used much as 'Donbas' had been used in the past. What tasks did he wish me to carry out?

'Advance to Apostolovo!' he told me.

... Before the war, few people had heard of such a small town in the Ukraine. Apostolovo now acquired paramount importance for the army. It would be impossible to break directly into the Nikopol bridgehead. The enemy had strong defensive positions there. We could not expect success with a frontal attack. But if we took Apostolovo, we would put the enemy in a catastrophic situation – the Nikopol garrison and the troops in the bridgehead would have their lines of communication cut and would be encircled.[28]

Since the start of the advance after the cessation of fighting in the Kursk salient, the Red Army had struggled with logistic issues. The sheer scale of operations consumed daunting quantities of ammunition and other supplies, and moving adequate stocks over degraded roads, particularly given the widespread destruction left by the retreating Wehrmacht, caused constant problems. As Manstein moved forces into position to launch his counterattack near Krivoy Rog, the Soviet units in the path of the planned operation were short of everything that they needed – men, equipment, ammunition, fuel and food. Rotmistrov's tanks were still close to Krivoy Rog, despite being driven out of the city by the Germans, but Thirty-Seventh Army was struggling to catch up with them. Konev joined Rotmistrov in Fifth Guards Tank Army's headquarters and the two men discussed ongoing operations; although he lacked support from Thirty-Seventh Army, Rotmistrov was receiving priority for air support from Lieutenant General Vasily Georgievich Riazanov's I Assault Aviation Corps, which at least prevented his units from having to pull back any further. From there, Konev visited the headquarters of Thirty-Seventh Army, where he urged Lieutenant General Mikhail Nikolayevich Sharokhin to show greater alacrity, promising his subordinate additional artillery support in order to deal with the threat of German armour.[29] In an attempt to alleviate the logistic problems of his front, Konev diverted air assets to a transport role, but was then surprised to have additional demands placed upon his severely overstretched logistic resources:

At the end of October, State Defence Committee member [Anastas Ivanovich] Mikoyan [who had responsibility for organising the transport of food and supplies], commander of Red Army rear areas General Andrei Vasilovich Khrulev, and chief of the army's food department Major General Dmitri Vasilevich Pavlov unexpectedly arrived at my command post in the village of Zalesye, 12km [seven miles] north of Pyatikhatky. They travelled to the command post from the railway station in Pyatikhatky on foot through the mud, which made it impossible to use cars.

Mikoyan wanted to know about our capacity for sending grain, which we had captured, from the front's reserves to the rear, as well as any grain harvested by the troops. The harvest around Kharkov, Poltava, Dnepopetrovsk and parts of the Kirovograd region was very rich in 1943. The retreating Hitlerites did not have time to destroy it completely, and the population couldn't move it. Therefore, on the decision of the front's military council, troops and rear area units were involved in gathering the harvest. The energetic enthusiasm of the soldiers working in the fields was something to behold. Most of the grain was sent to Moscow and Leningrad.[30]

Konev ordered his logistics officers and rear area commanders to assist in whatever way they could, and it was of course possible to load grain onto incoming trains and trucks once much-needed supplies for the front had been unloaded; nevertheless, regardless of the food needs of the Soviet Union, the diversion of soldiers to help with the harvest and the use of precious transport resources to move grain cannot have been welcome at a time when casualties continued to mount in the front line.

Meanwhile, deciding that for the moment he could afford to ignore the threat to his lines of communication from 24th Panzer Division, Rotmistrov ordered both tank corps, backed by air support, to make another attempt to take Krivoy Rog. Once the town had been taken, there would be ample time to turn to the northwest and deal with 24th Panzer Division, particularly after the infantry of Thirty-Seventh Army had arrived. At first light on 24 October, the Soviet artillery put down a brief, heavy barrage on Krivoy Rog before the tanks advanced. XXIX Tank Corps immediately ran into a strong German defensive position, ably supported by the anti-tank battalion of 11th Panzer Division, but XVIII Tank Corps was able to fight its way into the city. In his account, Rotmistrov described the heroic efforts of several of his men, but the reality was that towards the end of the day a German counterattack by the armoured battlegroup of 11th Panzer Division expelled XVIII Tank Corps from Krivoy Rog; the following day, the

Luftwaffe made heavy attacks on Fifth Guards Tank Army and succeeded in hitting Rotmistrov's headquarters. Several senior officers were killed or wounded.

Finally, 16th Panzergrenadier Division was able to establish contact with the defenders of Krivoy Rog, thus closing the gap that had existed between the right flank of LVII Panzer Corps and LII Corps. The division was badly weakened, with its six panzergrenadier battalions fielding an average of fewer than 200 men each, but despite being in almost constant action throughout the summer and autumn, its morale remained good. Dr Walter Jodzuweit, the division's medical officer, later described the conditions under which he and his subordinates worked:

> Unfortunately, none of our surgeons left me an account of his activity. Our surgeons changed quite frequently, probably because more than anyone else they were exposed to the most severe mental stress and physical strain during our assignments. The medical companies had set up operating vehicles for their surgical groups working in the main aid stations. These improvised vehicles were made by our staff and allowed for quick deployment. The field hospitals deliberately avoided setting up such mobile operating theatres. A field hospital was typically given a stationary setting as long as possible and was thus tied to solid buildings. School locations were therefore preferred because these buildings were the most suitable. We rarely found rooms with running water, which is a precondition for the surgeons to wash if the requirements of asepsis are to be fulfilled. In the turmoil of the war, the craftsmen of our unit then built a transportable washing station, according to the instructions of the surgeons, which provided the necessary flowing water. Self-help and improvisation throughout the war made our entire operating facility more and more complete, even though it could never reach the standards of a clinic in the homeland.[31]

Further attempts by the Red Army to take Krivoy Rog were unlikely to succeed, and on 26 October the Germans seized the initiative, with much of 23rd Panzer Division advancing north along the Saksagan River and turning the southeast flank of the Soviet XXIII Tank Corps. This put the German division in a position to operate against Rotmistrov's supply lines and possibly to cut right across them and link up with the forces of XL Panzer Corps pressing down from the northwest. The first units of SS-Totenkopf, which had been recovering its strength after pulling back across the Dnepr, arrived around Novyi Starodub on 28 October on a day that saw the first frosts of the approaching winter, and 24th Panzer Division was able to concentrate its resources in preparation for further battles. The Soviet forces facing it were from V Guards Mechanised Corps, which had been ordered by Konev to capture Novyi Starodub before continuing on to Snamenka, thus cutting the links between Kirovograd and Alexandria. A series of attacks and counterattacks developed in which both sides suffered losses, but those of the Red Army were heavier. Although small groups of Soviet tanks succeeded in moving past the western flank of 24th Panzer Division towards Kirovograd, Konev's attempts to thrust towards the northwest were effectively brought to a halt.

XL Panzer Corps now had the full weight of both 14th and 24th Panzer Divisions at its disposal. Despite its period of rest, *SS-Totenkopf* lacked the strength to launch major attacks and, together with 376th Infantry Division, was tasked with protecting the eastern flank of XL Panzer Corps. The two panzer divisions were ordered to attack towards the southeast; the fighting against V Guards Mechanised Corps had resulted in much of 24th Panzer Division becoming dispersed over a substantial area, but there was no time to regroup and concentrate resources. The reconnaissance battalion of 14th Panzer Division reported the presence of strong Soviet anti-tank units in the anticipated path of the attack, but the existing orders remained in force. The first task was to defeat the Soviet forces which, despite being halted by 14th and 24th Panzer Divisions, were still powerful and had concentrated substantial forces to the southwest of Nova Praha. On 28 October, a pincer attack was launched against Sharivka and drove the Soviet troops back; the Germans claimed to have destroyed 40 tanks. Fighting continued into the night as the Germans drove south, reaching Dubivka at midday on 29 October and Vodyane by the end of the day. Interrogation of prisoners suggested that in addition to V Guards Mechanised Corps, several formations of I Guards Mechanised Corps were also in the area and had suffered heavy losses.

The western flank of XL Panzer Corps remained vulnerable and the only force that could be spared to cover this was 14th Panzer Division's reconnaissance battalion. Sieberg ordered the battalion to launch an energetic advance, using its mobility to compensate for its lack of heavy armour and to try to simulate the presence of a larger force. In the meantime, the rest of the division attacked alongside 24th Panzer Division and achieved considerable success. As was often the case in panzer divisions, Sieberg had moved to the front line to accompany *Kampfgruppe Langkeit*, accompanied by Oberstleutnant Ferdinand von der Planitz, the division's operations officer. One of the numerous Soviet anti-tank guns that had been spotted by the reconnaissance battalion the day before fired on their vehicle and struck it with an armour-piercing round. Both men were wounded. Whilst Planitz was able to remain with the division, Sieberg was badly wounded and evacuated to a field hospital by air.[32] He died there on

2 November. His replacement was Oberst Martin Unrein, an experienced officer who had spent much of the war with 6th Panzer Division. It would inevitably take several days for him to take up his post. In the meantime, Oberst Karl-Max Grässel, commander of the division's 108th Panzergrenadier Regiment, took control.

Without pausing, 24th Panzer Division continued its advance on 30 October, reaching Lozuvatka, just a short distance to the north of Krivoy Rog.[33] The neighbouring 14th Panzer Division also had to switch the axis of its advance further south, and the first major obstacle the two divisions faced was a shortage of adequate roads, particularly as the autumn rains had turned much of the landscape to mud. Fortunately for the Germans, the prior deployment of 14th Panzer Division's reconnaissance battalion to cover the western flank now proved to be beneficial, as this unit had identified additional routes heading south and the entire division shifted its axis to the main road from Kirovograd to Krivoy Rog. Progress was rapid at first, but then slowed as the advancing German divisions encountered increasingly strong anti-tank defences.

At the same time, 16th Panzergrenadier Division was transferred to LVII Panzer Corps so that it could add its modest resources to the developing counterattack. Just a day later, it was transferred back to LII Corps and was immediately ordered to send a battalion – in reality, less than two infantry companies – and assault guns to the aid of 306th Infantry Division, which continued to be driven back; despite its reinforcements, the infantry division could field only 300 men. An armoured battlegroup from *Grossdeutschland* was also dispatched to the area, but a further withdrawal of the entire line was necessary. However, the successes of XL Panzer Corps were making such Soviet advances increasingly irrelevant, and the intervention of the reinforcements brought the Red Army's advances to a stop. The remnants of 306th Infantry Division were subordinated to 16th Panzergrenadier Division for the time being.

Konev had diverted V Guards Mechanised Corps towards the northwest specifically to protect the flank of Rotmistrov's tank army, and in its advance the German XL Panzer Corps had inflicted substantial damage on the Soviet formation. The German battlegroups were now operating with relative freedom and, as they approached Lozuvatka, they overran substantial artillery positions that had been used by Rotmistrov in his attempts to force his way into Krivoy Rog. Confident that his advance had closed the gap that had opened up between the defenders of Krivoy Rog and other German units to the northeast, Henrici – whose XL Panzer Corps had now been removed from the control of Eighth Army and assigned to First Panzer Army – ordered his two panzer divisions to turn east.

The first battlegroup of 24th Panzer Division reached Ternuvatka towards the end of 30 October, seizing a small bridgehead over the Ingulets. The following morning, the Soviet XVIII Tank Corps and the first elements of Thirty-Seventh Army, finally fighting their way forward from the northeast, set up a strong defensive line in the path of the Germans and progress slowed. On the first day of November, Edelsheim tried in vain to break through the Red Army's lines, encountering particularly stubborn resistance, and the attack finally halted despite intensive support from the Luftwaffe. Rotmistrov's account makes little mention of the German attacks, and he described how, with Konev's approval, he now pulled his two tank corps back a short distance to take up defensive positions where they could be supported by the leading units of Thirty-Seventh Army. A few days later, Fifth Guards Tank Army was pulled out of the front line to allow its units to be brought back to strength. To Rotmistrov's relief, most of the replacement tanks that arrived over the following days were T-34s, which would at least simplify the job of the repair teams. By 11 November, the army could field a total of 358 tanks.

Konev's attempt to break out towards the west was effectively at an end. Caught by the unexpected arrival of two fresh panzer divisions, his forces had failed to break through to Krivoy Rog and Kirovograd and had suffered heavy losses. From the German point of view, the counterattack launched by XL Panzer Corps was a gratifying success after the endless setbacks and the withdrawal to and over the Dnepr, but there was also a sense of missed opportunity. For a while, there had been a hope that the attack by XL Panzer Corps from the northwest might combine with an advance from the south by the forces of First Panzer Army and thus destroy Rotmistrov's Fifth Guards Tank Army entirely; the reassignment of XL Panzer Corps to First Panzer Army was intended to facilitate coordination of the attack. But the troops available to Mackensen's First Panzer Army were too badly degraded by their recent battles to launch a sufficiently strong attack, even though Mackensen – with Manstein's knowledge and approval – stripped much of his front line of all but a bare minimum of troops in an attempt to concentrate his resources.

Schwerin, the commander of 16th Panzergrenadier Division, later wrote about the year's fighting in which his division had been in constant action but had steadfastly achieved all that was demanded of it:

The attack by XL Panzer Corps, led by our former division commander General Henrici, into the deep flank of the enemy who had thrust from the north towards Krivoy Rog once more saved this industrial centre. In addition, the threat to the rear area of Army Group South was eliminated for the time being. The front along the Saksagan had been held. But at what cost! It is a military truism that troops who achieve great feats for a certain time are justly proud of their achievements.

That was true of 16th Panzergrenadier Division in a particular way in the Kalmyk Steppe [to the south of Stalingrad]. After that, the division was again able to perform at its best during the fighting withdrawal from the Manych and Don near Rostov. Every man knew how critical the situations were and their last strength was demanded – and given – to come out of those frequently desperate situations. When defending the Mius, the division achieved a special level of performance when it destroyed a Soviet Guards Tank Corps. The awareness of the troops of this, despite constant retreats and being outnumbered, led to a sort of euphoria. The period of rest and training on the Sea of Azov near Mariupol [during the second quarter of 1943] enabled the division once again to perform exceptionally well in the major defensive battles at Kuibyshev and Izyum …

The desperate battle for Zaporozhye and the ultimately successful evacuation of the bridgehead once more saw the division rescued from a life-threatening situation, but led to a particularly severe haemorrhage of personnel and for the first time there appeared signs of being overstretched. If we had had the opportunity for rest and replenishment at this point, then it would probably have been possible to restore the regiments to a reasonable level of efficacy for a few months. But instead there was not only no rest, there were also no longer any replacement personnel, and the division's internal reserves were completely exhausted.

In such circumstances, how could the companies be restored to fighting strength? In addition, men returning from leave told the troops about the devastating attacks of enemy bombers and the heavy casualties of the population. That was too much for our soldiers, who were from the Rhineland and Westphalia. The consequences were inevitable. The interminable, exhausting, and resource-depleting fighting retreat that followed led to the conclusion that it was no longer possible to create a continuous battle line along the Saksagan. The front line consisted only of strongpoints, and the gaps between them could barely be covered.

The Russians infiltrated everywhere. There was a constant need for counterattacks to seal off or clear penetrations. Tanks and assault guns were thus overstretched and decimated. They too were not replaced … The division was forced to embellish its situation reports. Many accounts of 'overwhelming enemy pressure' were fictitious in order to make a withdrawal to a new position or the straightening of a no longer defendable front line acceptable to higher commands.

We didn't expect much understanding from them. All requests resulted in the same stereotypical response: hold, hold, even when there was nothing left to hold because the infantry simply couldn't hold on any more. It became apparent that events on the battlefield were dictated by the Russians. Our own military command was forced to limit itself to more or less successful defensive steps or countermeasures due to weakness and physical overstretch. There was no longer anything else, because the infantry could no longer hold the line. They could only hold their positions if the attacking enemy was forced to ground or put to flight by artillery barrages or destructive bombardments, or if our own tanks and assault guns shot up the attacking enemy tanks and put the enemy to flight by mounting counterthrusts.

It wasn't much better for the Soviets. Their infantry was badly armed and equipped, above all poorly trained and also badly led. They were driven forward relentlessly en masse by the *Politruks* [political commissars]. Ever more new divisions, ever more new tanks, ever more new attacks! How could our drained troops, particularly the infantry, ground down to the lowest imaginable combat strength and as a result of their overstretch rendered apathetic, endure this in the long run? The division leadership was aware that the resistance of the troops would not cope with these burdens any longer. An attempt had to be made to save the remnants of the division from being finally wiped out. The general [i.e. Schwerin] decided to take a most unusual step. Confident of the high reputation with the Führer and the Wehrmacht high command of 16th Panzergrenadier Division from earlier, better days, he wrote a personal letter to Hitler … and asked him to transfer the division to the west. The soldiers, who were mainly from the Rhineland and Westphalia, as a consequence of the terror raids of the Americans and British, who had reduced their homeland to ruins and ashes, would consequently be burning to face this relentless foe. It was certainly a very remarkable letter and carried risks. The general did not place much hope in his attempt. But the attempt had to be made to save the division from being completely ground down and destroyed.[34]

The losses suffered by both sides in the fighting between the Dnepr and Krivoy Rog are difficult to ascertain with any certainty. Konev claimed that his front succeeded in stopping First Panzer Army's counterattack and destroyed about 150 German tanks; by contrast, 24th Panzer Division recorded the loss of just eight tanks and assault guns, and claimed the destruction of 201 Soviet tanks.[35] Regardless of the exact numbers, there can be little doubt that Konev's 2nd Ukrainian Front was badly hit by the fighting. Konev wrote in his memoirs:

I reported by radio to the supreme commander-in-chief [Stalin] on 23 November about the battles for the Dnepr, about how a great strategic bridgehead had been secured, and that the troops were fighting well and were in good spirits. But after being in continuous combat for about four months, the soldiers were physically tired and the units needed rest and replenishment. I asked for permission temporarily to adopt a defensive stance on the line that had been captured. Stalin expressed his full satisfaction with the performance of the front's troops and agreed with my proposal. However, he inquired about my immediate plans. I told him briefly that the front forces would still conduct operations to capture Chigirin, Alexandria, and the railway junction at Znamenka, would complete the liberation of Cherkassy, and would drive the enemy away from the Dnepr along the entire front. Stalin approved this plan and the conversation was concluded at this point.[36]

Despite being forced to abandon plans for any major attacks, Konev knew that his depleted units would rapidly be restored to something approaching full strength, as had already been the case for Rotmistrov's Fifth Guards Tank Army. By contrast, the German units that had taken part in the fighting around Krivoy Rog were unlikely to receive anything approaching adequate reinforcements. The German success in the battles was only made possible by the arrival of two fresh divisions from the west. In the absence of a continuing stream of such reinforcements, the balance of power would continue to tilt further and further in favour of the Red Army.

CHAPTER 9

KIEV AND ZHITOMIR

As the Red Army approached the Dnepr through August 1943, attention turned increasingly to Kiev, the capital of the Ukraine and the third largest city in the Soviet Union. In October 1941, a month after seizing the city, the German occupation authorities created a body known as the *Kievskaia Gorodskaia Uprava* ('Kiev City Administration' or *KGU*) to provide at least an appearance of local administrative authority. From the outset, the *KGU* was beset with difficulties; its first mayor was sacked after just a few weeks, and his successor was discovered to be collaborating with both communist and nationalist resistance groups and was executed at Babi Yar. In addition to responsibility for general administration, the *KGU* played a role in the dissemination of pro-German propaganda, education, public health, transport, communications, and housing. It even had its own police force, adding a further tier to the already complex and often poorly coordinated paramilitary structures in the occupied territories. These far-ranging responsibilities came with very little room for manoeuvre; almost every decision of the body had to be approved by the German occupation authorities, and the resources provided by them to the *KGU* fell far short of what was realistically required.

The retreating Red Army had damaged much of Kiev's infrastructure and parts of the city were without reliable water or electricity supplies in 1941. Restoring these was a priority and in the first year of the occupation the *KGU* managed to return three city power stations to something approaching normal capacity. In an attempt to alleviate the constant food shortages land was allocated to families within the city for them to grow vegetables, though the availability of seeds greatly limited this initiative. However, the primary function of the *KGU* was to help the occupying powers achieve their aims.

To that end, clear instructions were issued to the *KGU* about food requisitions; in order to allow for 'surplus' food to be sent to Germany, the number of 'unnecessary mouths' was to be reduced rapidly by the elimination of the Jewish population and other 'undesirables' and food supplies to urban areas were to be reduced drastically.[1] Families were forbidden from keeping more than one day's food and, when they finally appeared, ration cards only gave an allowance of 200g of bread per day – other foods were not provided. The *KGU* was also responsible for ensuring that sufficient workers were made available to the occupation authorities, both for work in the city and elsewhere. From April 1942, quotas for workers to be deported to Germany were imposed and over the following months about 120,000 people were sent west from Kiev. From the outset, the *KGU* tried to make such work sound as enticing as possible in brochures and newspapers:

> The best residents of the city of Kiev have shown their desire to volunteer to go to Germany to do work that is not yet available to everyone in Kiev, because not all of its enterprises that were wrecked by the Judeo-Bolsheviks have been rebuilt.
>
> I call on the young people of Kiev to go to work in beautiful Germany.
>
> Doing practical work in Germany, you will learn skills and, together with the cultured German people, use your energies and abilities to combat Bolshevism.
>
> Those eligible are young boys and girls aged 14 to 18. The first train with young people will leave Kiev on 4 May.[2]

Those who were sent to Germany soon discovered that the reality was very different from what they had been promised. They were kept in overcrowded accommodation and received inadequate rations, and were required to work long hours with severe punishments for any perceived misdemeanour. The families of those sent west received a modest supply of food, but this was suspended if their family members tried to run away from their place of work. Those who were injured or became sick were sent back to Kiev, where they rapidly spread the word about the reality of working conditions. As a result, recruitment dropped off rapidly. In an attempt to fulfil the quotas, the *KGU* introduced compulsory registration of all those aged from 16 to 65 with the intention of then selecting individuals for work elsewhere, with draconian punishments for anyone who did not comply.

The forcible deportation of workers left Kiev short of people to perform work in the city. At first, this had little impact as so much of Kiev's pre-war employment had effectively ceased with the departure of the Soviet authorities, but such was the scale of deportations that in late 1942 the *KGU* was forced to announce plans for children aged 11 to 14 to take up mandatory work. Orphans and children who had lost contact with their parents were rounded up and housed close to factories where they were taken for work; in some cases, these children were used as involuntary blood donors for the Wehrmacht.

Irina Khoroshunova wrote about a typical train taking child labour to Germany:

> They locked the children in the station for the night. They were put in an empty room and told to lie on the floor. Some children objected. They were beaten by the police. Vita [a member of her family] managed to escape and come home, and his mother Tasya was arrested for this. He cried all night, and in the morning he was taken back to the station.
>
> The entire platform was crowded with hungry, poorly clothed peasants. The train was packed with children. There were two carriages with Gestapo officers [all non-uniformed German police were usually described as 'Gestapo'] in front and two with [Ukrainian] police at the back. Groans and cries filled the station. And not only the station, but the whole city, the whole of the Ukraine.[3]

The authorities largely suspended education. This was partly in order to release people for labour, but it was also part of the overall plan for how the Ukraine was to be administered – the population would be used effectively as slave labour, and there was little need for such a workforce to receive more than rudimentary education. Many people attempted to evade the workforce quotas by claiming illness, and there was soon a burgeoning black market for letters from doctors. Others managed to get work with local occupation authorities; whilst it meant that they worked for the Germans, it ensured that they would not be sent to some uncertain destination. The police force of the *KGU* attempted to enforce the decrees of the mayor, but in addition played a substantial part in the mass executions of Jews, communists and hostages; it is estimated that 120,000 citizens of Kiev were killed during the occupation, with many tens of thousands more starving to death. As partisan activity increased, there were reprisal killings, with the Ukrainian police participating in the repression. On 27 May 1942, Khoroshunova recorded in her diary that after a partisan attack in nearby Brovary, all the men in the town were arrested and five selected at random and hanged. The population was warned that if there were any further incidents, one in ten of the male population would be executed.[4]

Within Kiev, it was almost as if there were two completely separate populations living alongside each other, but to all intents and purposes they might have been living in different worlds, as Khoroshunova described:

> One [part of the population] is German, well fed and satisfied. Attached to them are their hangers-on, those who do not care which god they serve. The second is ours, half-starved, most are very hungry, and this grows steadily worse and embraces more and more people.[5]

For those who had money, food could be bought in the markets, and restaurants had opened in many parts of the city, catering almost exclusively to the Germans and their supporters. The starving citizens of Kiev could not have afforded to eat there even if they had been permitted to enter. Nevertheless, during 1942 the Ukrainians noticed a distinct change in the mood of the Germans. Soldiers in Kiev told locals that the Wehrmacht might still be capturing cities in the east, but the British and the Americans would surely win the war. Despite the execution of hostages, the partisan movement continued to grow, leading to still more reprisals; on 18 August 1942, Khoroshunova wrote that a further 75 people had been executed in Brovary.

In early 1943, news of the German defeat at Stalingrad raised hopes in Kiev that the occupation might soon be over. Bedraggled, starving Italian soldiers fleeing the collapse of the Don front appeared on the streets, begging for food and shelter. But whilst some greeted with enthusiasm the news that the Red Army had – briefly – recaptured Kharkov, others were more concerned about the return of Soviet authority and particularly NKVD repression. In addition to those who had willingly collaborated with the Germans, there were large numbers of Ukrainians who had taken up work with the occupying authorities purely to survive, and many of these now feared that the NKVD would regard them as traitors. As Manstein's great counteroffensive of March 1943 brought the Soviet advance to an abrupt halt, it became clear that the liberation of Kiev was still some way off, and there was a further wave of repressions. Several members of Khoroshunova's family were arrested and, despite her repeated efforts, she was unable to determine their fate. She then started working for a German officer who wished to learn Russian, and was relieved to learn that he was strongly opposed to Hitler and the Nazis. On one occasion, he told her: 'We will pay in blood for everything we have done in your land.'[6] He volunteered to make enquiries about her missing family members, to no avail – they had almost certainly been executed in one of the many mass killings.

As the Red Army approached the Dnepr in 1943, the population of Kiev had fallen to about 186,000, only 20 per cent of the pre-war figure. In late August, Khoroshunova and other residents learned that the Germans were digging up the corpses of those killed and buried at Babi Yar and burning them in an attempt to conceal the killings. The operation was headed by Standartenführer Paul Blobel, who had been the commanding officer during the massacres in late 1941 and early 1942; prisoners from the nearby Syrets concentration camp provided the labour force for the exhumations and cremations, and were then executed and burned in turn. By mid-September, many German institutions were clearly making preparations for departure, and many anti-Soviet Ukrainians and *Volksdeutsch* (ethnic Germans, the descendants of settlers who had moved to the region decades or even centuries before) also decided to leave. The sound of artillery was now clearly audible and in October, as persistent rumours of a forced evacuation of Kiev circulated, Khoroshunova managed to get documentation via her German employer – she was working for the city library – to travel to Kamanyets-Podolsk. Here she was able to secure work in a German military canteen under the supervision of Gefreiter Alois Bukschik. On her first day, she discovered that, like the German officer she had met in Kiev, he was not a supporter of the Nazis and their ways:

He ordered me to sit at the table and set before me a huge dish of boiled chicken, which was still warm. He told me it was necessary to remove the meat from the bones, and then he said, 'Clean the bones, that's it, like that, and then you can *essen* all you want.' I didn't understand him and thought that I had just misunderstood his mixture of German and Russian. But he frowned and repeated the order again. 'Eat as much as you want. And take the best pieces, so that those dogs have less left for them.' He pointed to the mess-hall. And so, repeating the word '*Schnell!*' he made me eat.

It was so unexpected, an incredible contrast to the hunger and the years of starvation and everything that had happened, that at first I couldn't bring myself to eat. And yet, I ate. On this day I had little to do. When I was allowed to go home at about 7pm, Bukschik caught up with me on the stairs and put a loaf of real bread in my hands ...

By my third shift I had learned a lot about Bukschik. Usually after the main dining utensils had been washed and the dining room had been cleaned, he would sit on a high stool, put his feet on the crossbar and, propping his head in his hands, talk to us in Russian ...

Bukschik asked us whether we knew what was happening at the front and where the Soviet troops were. He was a Silesian German and did not conceal his hatred of Fascism, constantly saying he wished the Soviet troops would advance faster … He spoke Russian almost without an accent … In civilian life, he had been the manager of a small two-floor hotel in the Silesian mountains.

'When you win the war, I will return home to my hotel and write a sign: "The entrance of Fascist officers and dogs is categorically forbidden!"'[7]

In the Bukrin bridgehead, fighting continued as the Soviet units attempted to extend their perimeter. The first attempt to break out towards Kiev began on 12 October; by this stage, Vatutin's forces in the bridgehead consisted of six tank or mechanised corps and 14 rifle divisions, fielding almost 800 tanks and assault guns. The opposing German units – three panzer divisions, two panzergrenadier divisions and two infantry divisions – had barely 150 tanks. But whilst the Red Army enjoyed an advantage of 3:1 in infantry and 6:1 in armour, the difficulties of bringing forward supplies across the Dnepr, under constant air and artillery attack, greatly reduced the efficacy of the Soviet units. In addition, the Germans occupied strong defensive positions on favourable terrain. For three days, the Soviet forces struggled in vain to make any headway; Vatutin then called a halt to operations, but Zhukov insisted that a second attempt was made. On 21 October, after another artillery bombardment, the Soviet troops tried once more to break out and again foundered against the German defences. After a further three days of futile bloodshed, the attacks were halted. The effectiveness of Soviet artillery had been reduced by the difficulties in getting adequate supplies to the guns in the bridgehead, and fire support from guns on the east bank of the Dnepr was limited because of poor observation of where the shells were landing; the distance between the guns on the east bank and the troops in the front line on the west bank made effective coordination of fire with troop movements almost impossible. The fighting in the Bukrin bridgehead in September and October had cost the Red Army another 200,000 casualties for little gain. In the two attempts to break out of the bridgehead, the Red Army lost 250 tanks, though of course many could be recovered. But the Red Army could make good its losses, whereas the Wehrmacht could no longer do so, and the fighting tied down German formations, preventing their use elsewhere or even a much-needed period of rest. Finally, in a radio conversation with Vatutin and his army commanders, despite Zhukov's calls for a further effort – the Germans, he argued, must be approaching the end of their strength – Stalin called a halt to the futile attacks:

'Apparently, it is difficult for the troops of Comrades Moskalenko and Rybalko,' said the supreme commander [to Vatutin], 'to attack towards Kiev from this bridgehead. The terrain is very rugged, and this prevents large bodies of tanks manoeuvring effectively. The enemy is in good positions, and occupies high ground that dominates your ground. In addition, he has brought up substantial forces – panzer and motorised divisions, anti-tank units, and aviation assets. All of this you know yourself. All that remains is to come to a conclusion. That must be that you cannot strike from south of Kiev. Now look at the Lyutezh bridgehead, to the north of Kiev, in the hands of Thirty-Eighth Army. It is smaller, but the terrain is flat, allowing for the deployment of large numbers of tanks. From there it will be easier to capture Kiev.' After a pause, Stalin added, 'I suggest that you consider the question of transferring Third Guards Tank Army to the Lyutezh bridgehead, as well as reinforcing Fortieth Army. It is vital that it [Third Guards Tank Army] is withdawn at night from the Bukrin bridgehead and moved to the Lyutezh bridgehead. Fortieth and Twenty-Seventh Armies are to continue feigning an offensive along the previous axis. In short, the enemy must be deceived.'[8]

The first Soviet troops to reach the Dnepr at Lyutezh, about ten miles (16km) north of Kiev, were the men of 240th Rifle Division, part of Major General Nikandr Evlampievich Chibisov's Thirty-Eighth Army. Late on 26 September, the first attempt to cross the river – about 700m wide at this point – began. All three regiments of the division sent groups of men across on fishing boats and improvised rafts, and most were crushed by defensive fire from the German 88th and 208th Infantry Divisions. Before dawn on 27 September, a single platoon managed to secure a toehold on the west bank and held it through the day. During the following night, about 75 more men managed to reach the tiny bridgehead, followed by further reinforcements after dawn. The trickle of Soviet troops continued, and by the end of 30 September roughly two thirds of 240th Rifle Division had crossed, securing a bridgehead about two miles wide and one mile deep.[9] Supported by artillery on the east bank, these troops attacked repeatedly and finally achieved success on 2 October, seizing Lyutezh and reaching the Irpen River. Further expansion during the following week created a sufficiently large bridgehead for more troops to be brought across. The tanks of Kravchenko's V Guards Tank Corps began to cross on barges late on 5 October, going into action almost as they came ashore. Despite constant harassing fire from German artillery, the entire corps had succeeded in crossing by the end of 11 October.

One of the consequences of the Soviet attacks that separated Army Group Centre from Army Group South was that the most southern units of Army Group Centre's Second Army, grouped together as XIII Corps under the command of General Arthur Hauffe, were separated from the rest of Kluge's army group and now came under the command of Fourth Panzer Army and Army Group South. Included in XIII Corps was 8th Panzer Division, which like so many German armoured formations was badly degraded. Its two panzergrenadier regiments had been combined into two battlegroups, one with 659 men and the other with just 360 men and, collectively, these had less strength than a single panzergrenadier regiment. The other units of the division were no better. Like many panzer divisions, 8th Panzer Division had sent a battalion to the west to be re-equipped with Panther tanks, and its remaining panzer battalion fielded just four Pz.IIIs and three Pz.IVs. To make matters worse, the division had very limited mobility, with many of its trucks dating from equipment issued prior to the invasion of Poland in 1939. Nevertheless, as he repeatedly did, Hitler treated Oberst Gottfried Frölich's exhausted and depleted division as a full-strength unit and cited its transfer to Army Group South as part of the reinforcements that he had promised to Manstein.[10]

The first major attack out of the Lyutezh bridgehead came on 11 October. In terms of infantry, the Red Army enjoyed an advantage of 4:1, and although the two German infantry divisions facing the bridgehead were supported by small battlegroups from 7th and 8th Panzer Divisions, the Soviet forces had a substantial armoured advantage. With fighting raging south of Kiev around the Bukrin bridgehead and Cherniakhovsky's Sixtieth Army continuing to put pressure on the southern flank of Army Group Centre to the north, the attack by Thirty-Eighth Army came as an unwelcome shock to the Wehrmacht. Carefully directed at the seam between the German 208th and 82nd Infantry Divisions, the attack rapidly burst over the Irpen and threatened the railway running from Kiev to Korosten. However, the breakthrough was on a narrow front and the Germans were able to block every attempt by the Soviet LI Rifle Corps to widen the breach. In response, Chibisov pulled much of his armour back across the Irpen to help the struggling infantry; almost immediately, a German air raid struck the bridge that the Soviet tank formations had captured across the Irpen, severely damaging it. Fighting continued until 17 October, turning the bridgehead into a far stronger position than before. Nevertheless, it remained very cramped, with Vatutin, Rybalko and Kravchenko having their headquarters within a few yards of each other.

As directed by Stalin, Vatutin had turned his attention to the north, withdrawing Rybalko's Third Guards Tank Army from the Bukrin bridgehead and sending it north. The Bukrin bridgehead would continue to be held by Twenty-Seventh Army, which in accordance with Stalin's instructions made a series of apparently energetic attacks towards Kiev. To help deceive the Germans, Rybalko ordered his men to take deceptive measures, including the construction of mock-up tanks and leaving radio teams in place to continue transmitting with the same callsigns as if Third Guards Tank Army were still in position. Moving mainly at night, his troops removed their equipment from the bridgehead as quietly as possible and then drove to their new theatre of operations to the north. By the end of 1 November, they had taken up their new positions. To help ensure that the depleted tank army remained a potent force, it was now reinforced with the relatively fresh I Guards Cavalry Corps. In addition, Moskalenko left his Fortieth Army and took command of Thirty-Eighth Army, which would be responsible for opening the offensive. He took with him Major General Alexander Grigorevich Batiunia, his chief of staff.

The shift from Bukrin to Lyutezh was a logistic nightmare. The distance covered wasn't remarkable, but the roads running parallel with the river were in a very poor state and there were few crossings over the Desna River, which crossed the line of march. Fuel continued to be in short supply and the artillery units struggled with shortages of vehicles to tow their weapons. As had been the case during the fighting around Stalingrad, the Red Army constructed several bridges that were submerged just below the surface of rivers, in order to conceal them from the Luftwaffe. It was an extraordinary achievement, but the Germans had already anticipated that the next major Soviet effort would come north of Kiev. They too continued their preparations, in particular the transfer of the reinforcements that had been allocated to Manstein. As had been the case in the recent attempt by Konev to strike towards Krivoy Rog, the coming campaign would offer opportunities to both sides. The Red Army had the tantalising prize of Kiev before them, and perhaps of greater importance there was a possibility of turning the northern flank of Hoth's Fourth Panzer Army. This would create a gap between the German Army Group South and Army Group Centre, with opportunities for the Red Army to strike against either, or conceivably both. The Germans, too, were considering their options. The imminent arrival of fresh troops from the west would give an opportunity to counterattack and damage the Soviet armoured formations sufficiently to force a pause in the Red Army's operations, and such a pause was urgently needed to allow troops to be rested, and for replacement drafts to be assigned to depleted formations.

There were additional reasons for Hitler to hope for a pause in the constant withdrawals in the east. The U-boat war in the Atlantic had not gone well for Germany in 1943 for a variety of reasons. The British and Americans were using improved anti-submarine technology and growing numbers of convoy escorts made life progressively harder for German U-boat commanders. In October 1942, three crewmen from the British destroyer HMS *Petard* recovered Enigma coding material from the sinking *U-559* in the Mediterranean, allowing for coded German messages to U-boats to be intercepted; in March 1943, the Germans modified their Enigma machines, which prevented the Western Allies from decoding messages for nearly two weeks, during which the U-boats enjoyed a period of comparative success, sinking 476,000 tons of shipping for the loss of 12 U-boats. Just as had been the case in the First World War, the Germans placed great hopes on the ability of the U-boat arm to starve the British into defeat and to prevent the arrival of substantial US forces in Europe, and briefly it seemed as if the campaign was succeeding, with Britain beginning to suffer serious fuel shortages. But in April 1943 the pendulum swung sharply against Germany, with 235,000 tons of shipping being sunk for the loss of 15 U-boats. By May, matters were even worse; U-boat losses reached 43 – 34 in the Atlantic, nine elsewhere – or a quarter of the entire U-boat fleet, and Admiral Karl Dönitz called off attacks in the North Atlantic, declaring that the Battle of the Atlantic had been lost.[11]

Definitive defeat in this theatre of war would be tantamount to accepting that the entire war was irrevocably lost and the Germans did what they could to remedy matters. With increasing numbers of U-boats being sunk by air attack, Dönitz's vessels were equipped with larger numbers of anti-aircraft guns and a small number of type VII U-boats were designated 'U-flak' vessels. At first, these enjoyed some success, but it was relatively easy for RAF crews to postpone their attack until enough aircraft had arrived to allow for an overwhelming attack; improved anti-shipping rockets, capable of fatally damaging a submarine with a single hit, further benefited the aircrews, and the policy of trying to fight off air attack by staying on the surface was abandoned in November 1943. Improved torpedoes capable of acoustic homing were introduced, as were devices to help U-boats detect radar signals being used to hunt them, and better submarines were planned. It was hoped that some would be equipped with the revolutionary engines designed by Hellmuth Walter, allowing them to exceed 20 knots while submerged, and much hope was placed in the Type XXI U-boat. Although the design of this vessel – able to outrun many British and American naval escorts while still submerged, and also able to dive much faster than previous U-boats –

was effectively finalised in early 1943, production was repeatedly delayed and ultimately, although 118 were built, problems with reliability and other issues meant that only four ever saw service. Ultimately, the Battle of the Atlantic came down to a war of figures – if the *Kriegsmarine* was to win, it had to sink more shipping than could be replaced. This figure was put at 300,000 tons per month, increasing to 700,000 tons per month after the USA entered the war, and the achievement of such figures for more than a month or two was impossible. Nevertheless, Hitler continued to cling to the hope that the U-boat fleet could achieve a decisive result and turn the tide in Germany's favour. The Wehrmacht simply had to stop the Red Army while this victory was achieved.

Some German officers were becoming openly pessimistic about the prospects of being able to stop the Red Army. General Otto von Knobelsdorff, commander of XLVIII Panzer Corps, had briefly left his command for a short spell of home leave and in his absence the corps was led by Generalleutnant Dietrich von Choltitz. He had commanded an infantry regiment in the first phases of the German invasion of the Soviet Union; his troops took part in Manstein's assault on the Red Army's fortress of Sevastopol in 1942 and suffered heavy losses – by the end of the battle, the regiment had been reduced from a nominal strength of about 4,800 to fewer than 350 men, and Choltitz himself was wounded in the arm. He commanded 11th Panzer Division during the *Zitadelle* offensive and during his brief spell as commander of XLVIII Panzer Corps he told Oberst Friedrich von Mellenthin, his chief of staff, that he believed that the Red Army would overwhelm the Wehrmacht and would ultimately overrun Germany. He added that he intended to go to Berlin to make his views known to Hitler, and would resign if the Führer refused to change course. Mellenthin later wrote that he tried to dissuade Choltitz, but his commander was adamant and departed for Germany.[12]

Choltitz had met Hitler for the first time earlier in 1943 and the Prussian officer, a descendant of a long line of military ancestors, was deeply unimpressed by Germany's leader. When he reached Hitler's headquarters, he was met by Zeitzler, who listened with sympathy, but there is nothing to suggest that Choltitz's views were presented to Hitler. Nor did he resign his commission. He held commands in Italy and Normandy, and as military governor of Paris he was ordered by Hitler to destroy the city's bridges and major buildings. He did not do so, either deliberately or because he lacked the resources. After the war, Choltitz was not prosecuted for war crimes, despite being recorded secretly whilst being held in a camp for senior German officers admitting that he regarded the mass killing of Jews as the worst job that he had ever carried out, but that he had nevertheless followed his instructions to the letter; there was no corroborating evidence to support a prosecution.[13]

In the Lyutezh bridgehead, Moskalenko's new command – Thirty-Eighth Army – prepared to launch the attack that *Stavka* hoped would herald the final collapse of the German lines. Moskalenko had four rifle corps and V Guards Tank Corps at his disposal, together with the independent 1st Czechoslovak Infantry Brigade. As was increasingly commonplace in the Red Army, he had been given additional firepower in the form of VII Breakthrough Artillery Corps. The intention was to break out of the bridgehead towards the south, with the Svyatoshino district at the western edge of Kiev the main objective. This would require an advance of perhaps ten miles (15km) and would render impossible any continued German presence in Kiev. Once the breakout had begun, Third Guards Tank Army and I Guards Cavalry Corps would exploit the success by thrusting towards Fastov and Bila Tserkva, while Moskalenko's troops secured Kiev and then pushed on southwards, protecting the eastern flank of the armoured exploitation group. In order to prevent German forces attacking into the bridgehead and threatening the rear of this advance, the Soviet Sixtieth Army was to advance towards the southwest and guard the western flank. Moskalenko had a formidable concentration of forces at his disposal, but he chose to stack the odds even further in his favour by concentrating his initial assault on a frontage of less than three miles (6km), allowing him to achieve an artillery concentration of 380 barrels per kilometre.[14] Not everyone was in favour of such a plan:

On 1 November in Novopetrovtsi, in a building of the local farm collective, I had a meeting with members of my military council, the commanders of corps, divisions and brigades, including Colonel Svoboda, commander of the Czechoslovak Brigade, the heads of political departments, and the artillery commanders of the army, corps and divisions. The meeting was chaired by Vatutin, the front commander. In addition to him and Marshal Zhukov, there were members of the Front Military Council, Deputy Front Commander [Colonel General Andrei Antonovich] Grechko, and the front's chief of staff [Lieutenant General Semen Pavlovich] Ivanov.

When I reported on my plan for the operation and my decisions, in particular the narrow breakthrough sector, Georgi Konstantinovich [Zhukov] commented, 'And won't the enemy be able to concentrate their fire on the combat units in the breakthrough area?' But after discussion with Vatutin, who supported my decision, he too gave his consent. We worked on the operational orders and clarified which tasks had to be accomplished by the army. The meeting also gave its approval to the plans and then dispersed to examine the plans further and assign tasks to their troops.

As for my preference for a very narrow breakthrough, it was an unusual solution for the army but ensured success in that it would surprise the enemy. In addition, we took account of two more important factors. The first was that the forested terrain of the area of operations severely limited the enemy's line of sight. Secondly, the planned unfolding of the operation would not leave sufficient time for the enemy to take effective countermeasures.[15]

With the annual anniversary of the October Revolution – 7 November in the new calendar – approaching, there was understandable enthusiasm amongst Moskalenko's troops to celebrate the day in Kiev. The political officers of Thirty-Eighth Army's formations rapidly seized on this and used it as part of their inspirational and politically instructional rallies prior to the attack beginning. Whilst this overtly political activity might appear slightly unusual to western eyes, it had been widespread practice in the Red Army since its inception; Lenin and Trotsky had taught that the willingness of so many sons of Russia to die for the tsars was due to a lack of political awareness, and that it was vital that Soviet soldiers and workers understood the cause for which they were fighting and labouring. It should also be remembered that compared to the troops of the other major combatants in the Second World War, the Soviet Union still had significant numbers of barely literate or illiterate soldiers, and the only way of conveying complex political concepts to them was via public meetings. By contrast, the officer corps of Germany had effectively turned its back on politics prior to the First World War, and the historic loyalty of army officers to the Kaiser was transferred first to the state, and then to Hitler – this personal oath of loyalty was what stopped so many German officers from taking any action against Hitler. 'Correction' of this political naivety was an important task in prison camps where German officers were held prisoner. Moskalenko described the Soviet perspective on the overtly political rallies and messages:

I wish to emphasise that the words of writers during the Great Patriotic War played an important role in the development and strengthening of love for the socialist Motherland and hatred of the invaders within each Soviet citizen and every soldier in the Red Army. A great moral impact was provided by the works of Alexei Tolstoy, Mikhail Sholokhov, Alexei Surkov, Ilya Ehrenburg, Konstantin Simonov and our other writers and poets. They had a fine understanding of the thoughts and emotions of the Soviet people and wrote about love of the

Motherland in skilful, inspirational terms. Their articles, published mainly in *Pravda* and *Krasnaya Zvezda*, were reprinted in front-line and army newspapers.

On the eve of the offensive, Ilya Ehrenburg visited our army. His speech at the rally was published in the army newspaper 'For the Happiness of the Motherland':

'We must save Kiev. We must get ahead of the incendiaries. We must outrun death. Kiev awaits. It waits in deadly anguish. Without Kiev, there is no Ukraine. There is no homeland without Kiev. All of Russia is looking at us now. Here, beside the venerable Dnepr, formidable battles have raged. The fate of Kiev depends upon them. Our destiny too depends upon them. If we drive the Germans from Kiev, they will retreat to Germany. The Germans want Kiev to become their strongpoint. Kiev must become their grave.'

On the eve of the offensive, an order was issued to the troops by the Front's Military Council about the decisive assault on Kiev. It spoke of the great honour that would belong to the front's forces for the liberation of the Ukrainian capital. The battle for Kiev, the order stated, was a struggle for the liberation of all of the Ukraine, for the defeat of the enemy and their expulsion from Soviet territory.

Addressing the soldiers, the Front Military Council wrote:

'Comrades in arms! In the battles with the enemy you have shown majestic examples of courage, resolution and heroism. Many of your chests are decorated with medals and awards. About a thousand soldiers, NCOs, officers and generals of our front have been awarded the highest honour – Hero of the Soviet Union. You defeated the enemy on the Don. You defeated the German divisions near Belgorod. From the Don to the Dnepr, you marched triumphantly through the flames and destruction of war. You heroically crossed the Dnepr and have approached the walls of mighty Kiev.' When speaking about its liberation, the address told the troops: 'Do not spare your strength, nor your blood, nor your very lives … With a swift blow that will break up the enemy's troops, encircle them and take them prisoner. Those who do not surrender, destroy without mercy.'[16]

Ilya Grigoryevich Ehrenburg was born in Kiev to non-practising Lithuanian Jewish parents in 1891 and first came to the attention of the authorities when he was arrested by the Tsar's secret police in 1908; he was badly treated and held for several months before being allowed to leave Russia for exile in France, where he met Lenin and other communists. He returned to Russia after the 1917 revolutions and at first regarded the violent behaviour of the Bolsheviks as abhorrent, but gradually became closer to the Soviet leadership, writing novels and poetry as well as reporting on the Spanish Civil War as a journalist. His articles in Soviet newspapers became increasingly strident after the German invasion of 1941, culminating in a piece that appeared in 1942 in *Krasnaya Zvezda* under the one-word headline 'Kill!':

> The Germans are not human beings. From now on the word German means to use the most terrible oath. From now on the word German strikes us to the quick. We shall not speak any more. We shall not get excited. We shall kill. If you have not killed at least one German a day, you have wasted that day ... If you cannot kill your German with a bullet, kill him with your bayonet. If there is calm on your part of the front, or if you are waiting for the fighting, kill a German in the meantime. If you leave a German alive, the German will hang a Russian and rape a Russian woman. If you kill one German, kill another – there is nothing more amusing for us than a heap of German corpses. Do not count days, do not count kilometres. Count only the number of Germans killed by you. Kill the German – that is your grandmother's request. Kill the German – that is your child's prayer. Kill the German – that is your motherland's loud request. Do not miss. Do not let up. Kill.[17]

It should be noted that the original Russian text uses the masculine noun for 'German' and Ehrenburg maintained that his writing had always been about the armed invaders of the Soviet Union; in the same year as the 'Kill!' article, he also wrote that if a German soldier laid down his weapons and surrendered, he should not be harmed. However, once the fever of battle began, soldiers who had lost family members and comrades during the war, or whose families were enduring unknown privations behind German lines, were perhaps more likely to remember Ehrenburg's exhortations to kill Germans than to show leniency to prisoners.

The Wehrmacht had found it increasingly difficult as the war progressed to replace losses, both in terms of equipment and personnel; whilst the Red Army continued to receive large quantities of equipment, both from the prodigious output of Soviet industry and from the aid provided by the British and Americans, it too was struggling to replace troops, particularly those like tank crews who required a considerable degree of training. Ion Lazarevich Degen, a former crewman of an armoured train, had been retrained as a tank commander:

> [As for the quality of training,] I can only give one estimate: zero. In the tank training regiment, the crew received little food or training. I had nothing against the gunner, who could at least fire his gun. The driver had only eight hours of driving practice. But it was not just a matter of combat training – the crew was emaciated. I looked doubtfully at the gunner and wondered how that hopeless individual would be able to load 15kg tank shells in action, in combat, in terribly

confined conditions and on the move – where would he find the strength to lift a shell out of the ammunition store? I kept thinking about how to feed the crew.

Before boarding the train [for the front] we found an empty replacement fuel tank on trestles. We took it and filled it with gasoil. The gasoil tank taps weren't locked or guarded. We hid this tank under a tarpaulin, labelling it 'kerosene'. And thanks to that 'kerosene' my crew was finally fattened up. All the way up to the front, we would exchange some gasoil for sour cream, curds, milk, or bread. The guys perked up and regained their zest for life … For several days [after detraining] we followed the advancing front and during that time I was able to improve the crew in terms of battle training. We practiced all the way. The driver-mechanic built up hours of practical driving. Before the crew went into the front line we had some tactical training and a field firing exercise, where we did well, and I was pleased with my crew.[18]

The Soviet artillery bombardment began at 0800 on 3 November and lasted for about 40 minutes, with aircraft joining in and attacking locations further to the rear of the German positions. Moskalenko described the bombardment as highly effective:

The high density of artillery that we had created made itself felt. The enemy's defences were literally swept away. As we saw later, all his trenches, lines of communication, firing positions and bunkers were destroyed. As a result, reports began to arrive soon after the attack began that our troops had advanced easily up to 2km into the depth of the enemy defences. The few surviving enemy soldiers and officers fled. Many dead Hitlerites were found in the firing positions and trenches, together with large quantities of abandoned guns and ammunition.[19]

Amongst the aviators attacking German positions was the Ukrainian Georgi Timofeyevich Beregovoy, at the time a senior lieutenant. He survived the war as a pilot of the Il-2 *Sturmovik* with 185 combat missions to his name and then achieved fame as the commander of the *Soyuz 3* mission in 1968; at the time of his space flight, he was 47, the earliest-born man to have travelled into space.

It isn't clear whether the Soviet attack was a complete surprise for the Germans. The presence of a powerful concentration of Soviet troops in a small bridgehead was impossible to hide from the Germans, and Manstein had repeatedly stressed the danger posed to Army Group South by Red Army attacks against his northern flank, but the renewed fighting around the Bukrin bridgehead was seen as the likely forerunner of a major effort. The transfer of Third Guards Tank Army to the Lyutezh bridgehead had not been spotted and the generally difficult terrain on the east bank of the Dnepr near Lyutezh – which would make the task of reinforcing the bridgehead much more difficult – probably contributed to an assessment that the real danger lay south of Kiev. Nevertheless, although Moskalenko and others wrote that the attack took the Germans by surprise, the reality was that Army Group South had long anticipated further attempts to advance out of the Lyutezh bridgehead, and the war diary of Fourth Panzer Army recorded that the only question was whether this represented a major new advance or was intended purely as a local tactical attack.[20]

Whilst the first line of German positions might have been extensively damaged by shelling, the positions further back were still intact and the advancing Soviet troops soon ran into increasing resistance. The locally available reserves were rapidly committed, as was an armoured battlegroup from 20th Panzergrenadier Division. Further powerful units were also nearby – 7th Panzer Division, which had been constantly in action through the summer and autumn, had been enjoying a brief period as Fourth Panzer Army's reserve. Its units were quartered in the western parts of Kiev and were now called into action, launching an energetic counterattack. Despite this intervention, General Anton Dostler, now commanding the German VII Corps, had little option but to pull his units back – his main forces consisted of three badly weakened infantry divisions and a security division, none of which had sufficient numbers or firepower to hold back the Red Army.

Alexander Mikhailovich Fadin was a junior officer who had been serving as brigade staff liaison officer during the fighting around Belgorod and Kharkov. On 14 October, he was ordered to replace a tank commander who had been killed in action and went forward to find his new crew. At first, there was some friction between the crew – seasoned veterans who had a disconcertingly relaxed attitude to discipline, continuing to smoke after Fadin had called them to attention – and their new commander, but Fadin decided to tackle this head-on:

> I ordered, 'Stop smoking!' They dropped their cigarettes grudgingly. Stepping out of the line I turned around to face them and told them that I was not pleased to go into battle in such a rusty and dirty tank with an unfamiliar crew. 'Clearly, I don't satisfy you either, but the Motherland requires it and I will defend it in the way I've been taught and to the best of my abilities.' I saw the sneer begin to fade from some of the veterans' faces. 'Is the machine in serviceable condition?' I asked.
>
> 'Yes,' replied the driver-mechanic. 'But the turret rotation motor failed and we don't have any spare driving track links – only three guide links.'

'Fine, we'll fight with what we have. Aboard!' They followed the command, more or less. I climbed into the tank and told them we would go into position with Avetisyan's company. I took out the map and saw that the tank would have to drive to the village of Valky. On the way, at the outskirts of the village of Noviye Petrivtsy we came under artillery fire. So we hid the tank behind a building that had been damaged by shellfire to await dusk. When the tank was properly parked and the engine shut down, I explained to the crew where we were going and why I had done this.

'You're a good map-reader, Lieutenant!' said Golubenko, the loader.

'And apparently a good tactician too,' said Voznyuk, the radio operator. Only the driver Semiletov was silent. But I realised that the ice had been broken; they believed in me.[21]

Barely two weeks later, Fadin and his crew found themselves in the leading wave of Moskalenko's attack:

That night everyone slept well, apart from the duty observers. At 0630 on 3 November we were called for breakfast. When we were given our breakfast we didn't want to eat it in the dugout, preferring to go outside. Not far from us, 25–30m away, was our battalion kitchen trailer, with smoke and steam rising from it. As we sat at ease, the enemy opened up artillery fire. I just managed to shout 'Lie down!' One shell fell behind us, 7–8m away, but its shrapnel didn't hurt anyone. Another landed 10m away but didn't detonate, and as it tumbled away it hit a heedless soldier, broke off a wheel of the kitchen trailer, toppling it over together with the cook, tore off the corner of a house and came to a stop in the gardens on the opposite side of the street. After firing two or three more shells the enemy desisted. But we didn't feel like eating breakfast now. We picked up our few belongings and boarded our tank to wait for the advance to begin. Our nerves were tightly strung.

Presently, our artillery bombardment began and I commanded, 'Start up!' and when three green signal flares rose into the sky, I added, 'Forward!' A blanket of smoke and bursting shells was ahead, with occasional explosions from shortfalls visible. The tank jerked heavily – we had passed the first line of [Soviet] trenches. After a while I grew calmer. Suddenly to the left and right I saw other tanks advancing and infantrymen opening fire. The tanks on either side were firing in motion. I peered through the gunsight and saw nothing but heaped tree-trunks. I commanded the loader: 'Load shrapnel!'

'Yes, shrapnel!' replied Golubenko clearly. I fired the first round at the heap of tree-trunks, believing that it was the enemy's first line of defences. As I watched my round explode I felt completely calm, as if we were on a firing range shooting at targets. I started firing on running figures in mouse-coloured uniforms. I was excited by firing at the figures scrambling about and commanded, 'Increase speed!' We were amongst trees. Semiletov slowed down abruptly. 'Don't stop!'

'Which way do we go?'

'Forward, forward!' The old tank engine roared mightily while we smashed through a few trees, one after another. To the right was the tank of Vanyusha Abashin, my platoon commander, also smashing through the trees. I peered through the hatch and saw a narrow clear track running into the forest. I directed the tank over to it.

Ahead to the left, I heard tanks firing and the replying barks of the Fascists' anti-tank guns. I could hear the roar of tank engines to the right but couldn't see the tanks. My tank was advancing across a clearing. Careful, boy! I thought to myself and opened fire with the gun and machine-gun in turns around the clearing. It grew lighter between the trees and all at once there was a gap. Seeing the Hitlerites rushing around near the opening in the trees I fired a round. At once there was intensive machine-gun and submachine-gun fire from behind the high ground on the opposite side of the clearing. I caught a glimpse of a group of men between the hillocks and all of a sudden, a flash: an anti-tank gun. I fired a long burst with the machine-gun and shouted to the loader, 'Shrapnel!' And then we felt a blow and the tank stopped for a moment as if it had run up against a major obstacle, then moved forward with a sudden lurch to the left. Again, like on a firing range, I saw a group of men bustling about the [anti-tank] gun and fired a round at them. The gun and its gunners were torn apart.

Then I heard a shout from Fedya Voznyuk, the driver-mechanic: 'Commander, our right track is broken!'

'You and the radio operator, go out through the escape hatch and fix the track! I'll give you covering fire.' By now more tanks and, a bit later, riflemen were entering the clearing. Repairing the track with a guiding link took us about an hour. Besides, while spinning on its left track, the tank had become stuck in boggy soil and ahead to the left, about 10m away, there was a minefield set up by the Fascists on the drier part of the clearing. Therefore, we had to depart backward, which took about two more hours. We managed to catch up with our battalion when it was already dark where the Germans had managed to stop our tanks in front of their second line of defence. Through the whole night of 3 November and early morning of 4 November we were busy refuelling and replenishing our machines with ammunition, and had little rest.[22]

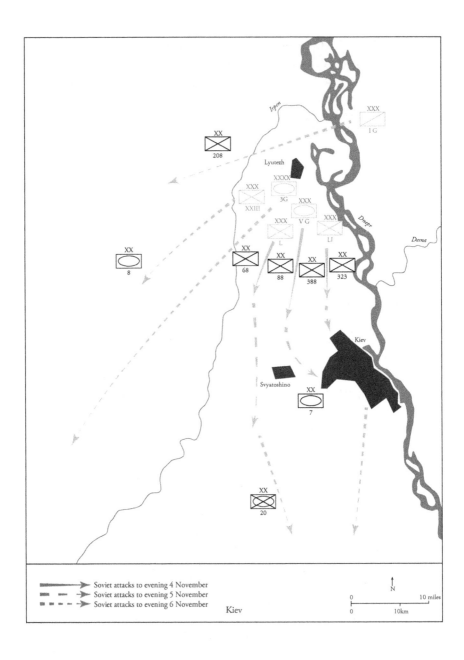

Irpen

XXX
1 G

XX
208

Lyutezh

XXXX
3G

XXX
XXIII

XXX
V G

XXX
LI

Dnepr

Desna

XX
8

XXX
L

XX
68

XX
88

XX
388

XX
323

Kiev

Svyatoshino

XX
7

XX
20

Soviet attacks to evening 4 November
Soviet attacks to evening 5 November
Soviet attacks to evening 6 November

Kiev

N

0   10 miles
0   10km

Moskalenko was pleased with the outcome of the first day's fighting and ordered his second echelon troops to be committed in order to retain momentum. Elements of Third Tank Army were assigned to his Thirty-Eighth Army and on 4 November, after a further artillery bombardment, the attack began again. Once again, Fadin and his crew were heavily involved:

At dawn on 4 November the battalion commander gathered all the tank commanders together for reconnaissance. Out of the 13 who had started the assault 24 hours earlier, only nine remained. We still had three self-propelled assault guns with us. We approached the trenches of the riflemen and Chumachenko [the battalion commander] told us, 'Do you see over there, 300m in front of us, the mass of tree-trunk obstacles?'

'Yes, we see them.'

'So, the enemy is behind those obstacles and is pinning down our riflemen. Now drive forward to this forest edge, line up and attack the enemy.' Why the Germans didn't shoot and try to kill us all, standing up in front of their defensive line, I don't know.

The tanks entered the forest edge, lined up and charged. We burst through the log obstacles and pursued the Germans through the forest clearings and thickets and before darkness fell we came out of the forest near the *Sovkhoz* [Soviet state farm] called Vinogradar, or 'Winegrower'. There we were faced by a counterattack of up to a battalion of German tanks, including Tigers. We had to retreat to the forest and establish a defensive line. When they reached the forest, the Germans sent three medium tanks forward while their main forces deployed in two columns to move into the forest. It was already dark but they were prepared to get involved in a night battle, which they usually hated.

I was ordered to secure the central clearing with my tank. To my right rear Vanyusha Abashin's tank was meant to cover me, and to my left I was covered by an SU-152 assault gun. The enemy reconnaissance patrol [the three medium tanks], which we had allowed past us, was advancing deep into the forest. The main forces were approaching. The roar of engines alerted us that a heavy Tiger tank was advancing quickly.

I gave an order to the driver-mechanic, Semiletov: 'Vasya, move forward a little at low speed – that tree in front of us is blocking me from firing head-on at the enemy.' After two days in combat I had forged a good friendship with the crew, who could read my mind from just a few words. After improving our position I saw the enemy tank. Without waiting for the driver to bring the tank to a halt, I fired the first sub-calibre round at the leading tank, which had already come within 50m of us. Immediately, there was a flash on the front of the enemy tank and all of a sudden it burst into flames, illuminating the entire column.

The driver-mechanic cried out, 'Commander, damn! Why did you fire? I haven't closed my hatch yet! The muzzle gases nearly blinded me!' In the heat of the moment, I had forgotten everything but the enemy tanks.

Before I even turned to him, Golubenko reported: 'The next sub-calibre round is ready!' Firing the second round I killed the second enemy tank, which was moving past the first burning tank. It also burst into flames. The forest was illuminated like broad daylight. I heard Vanyusha Abashin's tank firing, and from the left the dull, long sounds of the 152mm assault gun firing.

In the gun-sight I saw quite a few tanks were already ablaze. I cried out to the driver-mechanic, 'Vasya, move closer to the burning tanks, or the Fritzes will flee!' After moving close to the right of the first burning tank, I saw the next live target, a StuG III assault gun. One shot – and it was done. We pursued the enemy to the Vinogradar *Sovkhoz* where we stopped to regroup. We refuelled the vehicles with whatever we could find in preparation for a decisive attack on the city [Kiev].[23]

Of the nine T-34s that had been involved in the attack, two were lost during the day's fighting.

The SU-152 was a heavyweight assault gun with a 152mm howitzer mounted on the chassis of a KV-1 tank. Its 75mm frontal armour gave it good protection against many German weapons, though it should be noted that the 75mm long-barrelled guns on newer Pz.IVs as well as the 75mm guns on Panthers and 88mm guns on Tigers could penetrate this at ranges of over 1,000m; however, the vehicle had originally been intended to be used as a motorised howitzer rather than in direct action against enemy tanks. The crew compartment was cramped and there was only space for 20 rounds of ammunition, but the ability of its gun to blow the turrets off even Tiger tanks with a high explosive round earned it (and the slightly later ISU-152) the nickname of *Zveroboy* ('beast killer') amongst Soviet crews. The howitzer was not a very accurate weapon, requiring SU-152s to get perilously close to German tanks, but they were effective in ambushes like the one described by Fadin.

By the end of 4 November, the leading elements of the Red Army had reached the western and northwest suburbs of Kiev. Nevertheless, Rybalko's Third Guards Tank Army had struggled to achieve the planned breakthrough – low cloud and drizzle limited the air support available, and as Fadin's account shows, the terrain was eminently suitable for defensive fighting, allowing both sides to deploy anti-tank guns in lethal ambushes. Towards the end of the day Rybalko received orders from Vatutin to go forward to coordinate matters. He met his corps commanders and issued instructions for an evening attack: after a further artillery bombardment, all available vehicles were to advance, and in an attempt to overawe the German defences Rybalko ordered that the vehicles should have all available lights blazing and horns and sirens blaring. The attack was a success – the German defensive lines were finally overcome and the Soviet tanks reached and took Svyatoshino, immediately west of Kiev. Whether this was aided by the instructions to use headlights, horns and sirens is not clear – such a display would probably have made targeting much easier for German anti-tank gunners – but the road from Kiev to Zhitomir was cut.[24]

There was no prospect now of the Germans being able to continue to hold Kiev. While German troops fought with Rybalko's forces to the west and northwest of the city, an evacuation of the modest garrison was ordered. Once again, Fadin and his crew were in the first wave of the Red Army's attack:

We attacked and quickly seized the southern outskirts of Pushcha-Voditsa and reached Svyatoshino and the Kiev-Zhitomir highway. The road was guarded by an anti-tank ditch, dug in 1941, and we had to pass it in order to enter the city. We descended into the ditch but the tank then got stuck: the engine roared at maximum revolutions, with half-metre flames bursting from the exhaust pipes, showing how badly worn it was, but to no avail. I shouted to the driver-mechanic, 'Try reverse gear!' in an attempt to improve traction. We reached the first street [of Kiev] and had a further problem. The track that we had repaired in the woods had a 10cm 'tooth' and on the paved streets this lifted the right side of the tank, making it impossible to fire.

The battalion was ordered to move towards the city centre. The first tank reached a T-junction and suddenly, enveloped in flames, veered to the right and crashed into one of the corner houses. The troops riding it jumped off. Lieutenant Abashin and I opened fire on the enemy self-propelled gun. My second round struck its rear, immobilising it. It was a small setback and coming forward quickly, the battalion commander assigned Lieutenant Abashin as the lead tank. At the signal 'Forward!' we moved on and soon reached Khreshchatyk [in the centre of Kiev]. The city had been taken.[25]

It was the last battle in which Fadin and his crew would fight together. When his unit was ordered to move southwest, their tired tank became bogged down attempting to cross a small river. The repair crews that recovered the tank told

Fadin that it would not be possible to repair the tank in the field, and Fadin and his crew were dispersed to other tanks.

As Rybalko's tanks penetrated into Kiev, Moskalenko's Thirty-Eighth Army ground its way forward from the north into the city suburbs. On the 26th anniversary of the October Revolution, Moscow declared that Kiev had been retaken and was once more in Soviet hands. The recapture of Kiev was regarded as a great victory by the Red Army – it was the third largest city in the Soviet Union, and its capture by the Wehrmacht in 1941 had been seen as a major setback, not least because of the casualties suffered by the Red Army in the battles around the city. Rybalko's troops were met with ample evidence of the damage done to the capital of the Ukraine during the years of German occupation:

> There were ruins and fires everywhere, ugly piles of rubble where beautiful buildings had stood, avenues of chestnut trees and the famous poplars had been cut down or burned, Khreshchatyk was littered with rubble, statues of Marx, Sverdlov and others had been toppled. There were smoking tanks and self-propelled guns everywhere. At first not a soul was to be seen in this city of almost a million people. As they left Kiev, the Fascists had driven the inhabitants from the city. The survivors hid in cellars, in the crypts of cemeteries, or had escaped into the woods, and listened anxiously to the cannonade and explosions that thundered in the city. Only when it grew quiet did the people realise that the Red Army was back in the city. Exhausted by the atrocities of the occupiers and after all their humiliation and deprivation, the Kiev citizens hugged their liberators with gratitude.[26]

It should be noted that much of the destruction in central Kiev was a result of the fighting of 1941, and had been worsened by the delayed-action bombs left by the retreating Red Army. Air raids had added to the damage, and as it was the policy of the German occupation authorities that the great Slav cities would ultimately be erased from the face of the earth, the Germans had made little attempt to carry out any repairs – the Ukrainian authorities used their limited resources to clear some of the debris and managed to restore power and water to much of the city, but they did so in the face of German indifference. There is also no question that the retreating Wehrmacht carried out widespread demolitions.

The recapture of Kiev was only the first step of Vatutin's offensive and, throughout 6 November, Vatutin urged his troops to exploit their success by advancing towards the southwest. The German divisions in their path had started the campaign greatly below strength and were now in no condition to put up much resistance, and Vatutin issued fresh orders. Rybalko's Third Guards Tank Army was to continue towards the southwest, supported by elements of Moskalenko's Thirty-Eighth Army, but Moskalenko was also to organise a thrust towards Zhitomir, to the west. This represented a potential divergence of axes, but the ever-optimistic Vatutin believed that the Wehrmacht lacked the strength to take advantage. Moskalenko directed three rifle corps to continue towards the southwest, while V Guards Tank Corps and I Guards Cavalry Corps, with limited infantry support, were ordered to strike out to the west. In addition, Vatutin ordered Sixtieth Army to attack towards the northwest, dispersing his front's forces still further. Almost immediately, this divergence of axes created difficulties and Moskalenko reported that his units that were pushing south in the wake of Third Guards Tank Army were far too thinly spread to overcome even the limited resistance being offered by the Germans. In response, he was permitted to return V Guards Tank Corps to the southern axis; it was replaced in the drive towards Zhitomir by XXIII Rifle Corps and 7th Guards Tank Regiment. This latter formation was equipped with the KV-85 tank, which had been designed as an interim step – it consisted of the KV-1 chassis with a new turret, mounting the powerful 85mm gun, which was capable of penetrating the armour of a Tiger tank at ranges of 500m to 1,000m. However, this gun was in such demand (both as a towed anti-tank and anti-aircraft weapon and in the SU-85 assault gun) that only 148 KV-85s were built; they would ultimately be replaced by the IS-85 and the T-34/85. Design of what would become the IS-1 had started in early 1943 after the capture of a near-intact Tiger tank, and eventually about 130 were built. However, the need to be able to deal with Panthers and Tigers at longer range resulted in rapid development of the IS-2, which was armed with the bigger 122mm gun and entered service in the first half of 1944, allowing 85mm guns to be used for the production of the T-34/85, an upgraded version of the T-34 with a new, enlarged turret capable of carrying a more powerful gun.

On 7 November, the town of Fastov – about 35 miles (56km) southwest of Kiev – fell to Rybalko's tanks. The town was an important railway node and Manteuffel, commander of 7th Panzer Division, had been ordered to ensure that the town was held 'at all costs'. When he arrived in the town, Manteuffel found that there were no troops available with which to mount a meaningful defence – all he had at his disposal were a few anti-aircraft units and elements of formations retreating from Kiev. Concluding that it was impossible to carry out the instructions he had been given, Manteuffel ordered that the town should be abandoned; even so, he and his staff came perilously close to being captured by the advancing Soviet forces when they made good their own escape and returned to 7th Panzer Division.[27] The loss of Fastov and the advance of Soviet troops towards Zhitomir hampered still further attempts by Hoth to keep the increasingly scattered elements of his Fourth Panzer Army under coherent control. Despite these successes, Vatutin was criticised by Antonov, Deputy Chief of the General Staff, for not keeping his subordinate units under tight control. This resulted in a strong letter of protest and denial from Vatutin; in particular, the front commander went to some lengths to try to protect his chief of staff, Lieutenant General Semen Pavlovich Ivanov. Despite this, Antonov moved Ivanov from Vatutin's 1st Ukrainian Front to Transcaucasian Front.[28]

The German Fourth Panzer Army was in an increasingly desperate situation. The advancing Red Army had effectively divided it into three parts: VII Corps had retreated to the south; two further corps had retreated to the southwest; and other troops had been driven west by Moskalenko's forces that were advancing on Zhitomir. Manstein desperately needed powerful armoured reinforcements if he was to reunite his disparate forces. If the elements of Fourth Panzer Army were defeated and destroyed, the entire northern flank of Army Group South would be open for the Red Army to drive south, crushing and isolating Eighth, First Panzer and Sixth Armies. If such a catastrophe occurred, the entire southern wing of the German line on the Eastern Front would be annihilated, leaving the Red Army with every opportunity to turn north at its leisure in 1944 to advance north and northwest.

The armoured reinforcements that had been sent from the west had already made their presence felt in the fighting around Krivoy Rog, and Manstein had suggested to Hitler that they could be used to drive on to the southeast, striking into the flank of the Soviet forces that had isolated the Crimea. With the near-collapse of Fourth Panzer Army in the north, Manstein now wanted to abandon all such plans and concentrate on reinforcing Hoth so that a powerful counterattack could be launched at Vatutin's 1st Ukrainian Front. In particular, he regarded Rybalko's Third Guards Tank Army, advancing from Kiev to the southwest, as vulnerable and exposed. He proposed, therefore, to assign 1st and 25th Panzer Divisions and *LSSAH* to XLVIII Panzer Corps for this new operation; once the Soviet Third Guards Tank Army had been smashed, XLVIII Panzer Corps could turn west to strike into the rear of the Soviet forces advancing towards Zhitomir. At the same time, other German forces had to be deployed in the Zhitomir region to hold up the Red Army's thrust. It would take time to move all the pieces into position for such an operation, and in the meantime it was also vital to halt the Red Army before it pushed further to the southwest from Fastov. The loss of the town was serious enough; a further Soviet advance to Bila Tserkva and Berdichev would be catastrophic.

Manstein was aware from the outset that whilst the Red Army's successes against the southern flank of his army group were serious, and had isolated the German 17th Army in the Crimea, the greater threat to his position had always been in the north. Despite this, he had proposed the use of precious armoured assets in a counterattack in the south, largely in the hope that this could be accomplished quickly and the forces could be released for use in the north. To an extent, Hitler's refusal to countenance the abandonment of Nikopol meant that Manstein had little choice but to launch a counterattack to try to restore his line in the south. Now, when he wished to abandon the plan and strike in the north, he found himself opposed by Hitler. The Führer refused to abandon the counterattack, insisting that he had released assets from the west purely to take advantage of the opportunity to strike a blow in the south, and in an attempt to change Hitler's mind, Manstein travelled to East Prussia on 7 November. It was a measure of the setbacks suffered by the Wehrmacht that the journey from Manstein's headquarters to Rastenburg (474 miles or 763km) was significantly shorter than the flights Manstein had made the previous winter from Army Group South's previous headquarters in Zaporozhye (747 miles or 1,202km). But one thing had not changed. Hitler refused to change his mind:

> No success we might score at Kiev, he said, could be so effective that the armour up there would become free in time to help the southern wing. Neither the Crimea nor the defences on the Lower Dnepr would hold out as long as that.
>
> To this I replied that by adhering to the plan for operations in the Dnepr bend and Sixth Army's area we should be running far too great a risk on our northern wing, which would in turn affect the entire position of Army Group South and Army Group A. Much as I disliked forgoing the stroke south of the lower Dnepr, it was now absolutely essential that we intervene at Kiev with all three of the panzer divisions now arriving.
>
> Hitler retorted that there were both military and political reasons why we must achieve the success now offered to us in the area of the lower Dnepr. For one thing, the army must be made conscious that it was still capable of striking successful blows. For another it was vitally necessary to our war economy that we retain the manganese deposits of Nikopol. Furthermore, the enemy must not be allowed to regain the Crimea as a base for aerial warfare against the Romanian oilfields.
>
> While thoroughly appreciating Hitler's motives, I insisted that the risk on our northern wing was now becoming too great. If things went wrong with Fourth Panzer Army, the fate of Army Group South and Army Group A would be sealed sooner or later.

Hitler admitted the magnitude of the risk, but declared that it was one which must be accepted on our present situation and that he was prepared to shoulder the responsibility.[29]

Eventually, Hitler promised Manstein further reinforcements, most of which would never appear, and grudgingly allowed most of the armoured reinforcements to be diverted to the north. Nevertheless, 14th and 24th Panzer Divisions were to remain in the south. Nor was Manstein the only person to believe that Hitler's judgement was wrong. Heinz Guderian, the inspector-general of German armoured forces, later wrote:

> I took advantage of a conference on tank questions, held on 9 November 1943, to propose to Hitler that he give up the idea of numerous small-scale counter-attacks and that he concentrate all our panzer divisions available south of Kiev for the proposed operation through Berdichev towards Kiev. In this connection I proposed that the panzer division which was taking part in Schörner's defence of the Nikopol bridgehead [24th Panzer Division] be withdrawn, together with the panzer divisions of Kleist's army group which was holding the Dnepr in the Kherson area. I used my favourite old expression, *Klotzen, nicht kleckern* [equivalently 'a flood, not a trickle']. Hitler paid attention to what I said, but did not make his arrangements accordingly.[30]

Manstein wanted to use Bila Tserkva as a detraining point around which XLVIII Panzer Corps would deploy before launching its counterattack. In order to try to prevent the town from falling into Soviet hands, he ordered *SS-Das Reich* to move to the area from the Bukrin sector. It would take several days for the entire division to redeploy, and a powerful vanguard was dispatched:

> The Tiger company was ordered to entrain at the Bobrinsk railway station and on a foggy, damp, cold November morning the tanks set off along the road with III (half-track) battalion of *Der Führer* ...
> [Bila Tserkva] was reached at 2000 in complete darkness, and unloading of the tanks began immediately. The whole town was in turmoil. Evacuation trains were leaving the station, braziers had been lit, in which heaps of files were being destroyed; the town commandant and assorted German authorities were leaving. The Russian armoured spearheads were expected at any moment and men hastened through the streets with mindless anxiety. There was plundering and destruction, and nobody was there to organise resistance or bring order to the masses!

This was the situation in which we unloaded and found quarters at the northern edge of the town, as we were to carry out reconnaissance to the north and establish contact with German units there and locate the enemy …

It was snowing on the morning of 7 November and a cold north wind blew across the plain, puddles and ruts in the road were covered in a sheet of white ice. Our Tiger company, led by Kalls in place of the wounded Tetsch, formed up in its preparation area and after a short halt for maintenance moved on to the north towards the Russian tanks driving down the road from Fastov and Ksaverivka. The ignition of fuel and oil residues in the hull set one of the Tigers ablaze and it completely burned out with a long series of explosions. The crew was hurled from the hatches by the force of the explosions and miraculously was unhurt. About 5km north of Grebeniki on the road to Kiev, our tanks encountered the enemy and left six T-34s ablaze, but after about three hours had to pull back to the village in the face of superior numbers of infantry, destroying the bridge and establishing a new line south of there. Along the road, we had come across just eight German infantrymen from a construction battalion; that was the sum total of German troops here. They were hopelessly inferior to the Russian tanks.

At midday the snow turned to rain and the previously cold but dry weather turned to a steady downpour. While our eight brave infantrymen, who we first had to supply with food, dug in either side of the road from Grebeniki, the first shells landed on the high ground in front of us and sent their clouds of smoke into the grey overcast midday sky. Our tanks and vehicles stood exposed on the back slope covering the road to Kiev, along which we expected a new Russian armoured attack at any moment. When three Russian tanks pushed out of the village into no-man's land along the road, they were brought under fire at 1,000m range and in barely two minutes the concentrated fire of six Tigers left them ablaze; an hour later, a fourth Russian tank that crossed the road towards Slavia met the same fate when it was hit at 800m and burst apart with towering flames.

After these unsuccessful thrusts the Russians moved their point of main effort about 8km [five miles] further west and pushed towards Slavia with all their forces in order to penetrate our front there. Slavia was under tank and artillery fire all day, the situation there was critical.[31]

The Tigers and the SS infantry that followed might have brought the Soviet advance towards the south and southwest to a halt for the moment, but Moskalenko's thrust towards Zhitomir continued to make good progress.

The remnants of the German 8th Panzer Division attempted to intercept the Soviet forces but the division found itself heavily outnumbered, particularly when the Soviet I Guards Cavalry Corps turned its flank. Under constant pressure, 8th Panzer Division was driven back to Zhitomir; despite express orders to hold the city at all costs – it was intended to be a vital point from which Manstein proposed to launch counterattacks against Vatutin's forces – Frölich had no intention of allowing his battered division to be wiped out and ordered his men to give up Zhitomir. Together with its vital railway station and considerable stockpiles of German supplies, the town fell to the Soviet I Guards Cavalry Corps and XXIII Rifle Corps on 13 November.[32]

General Heinrich Eberbach had replaced Choltitz as commander of the German XLVIII Panzer Corps and was now ordered to take command of XL Panzer Corps but was wounded badly for the second time in a year, leaving him unable to command either formation. The man appointed to take command of XLVIII Panzer Corps was General Hermann Balck, who had been recovering from injuries suffered in Italy when his Fieseler Storch crashed while he was visiting units of his XIV Panzer Corps. Balck had led 11th Panzer Division with great success in the previous winter's fighting and had a reputation for being an outspoken man, full of self-confidence and energy. He appears to have had a good relationship with Hitler, and was generally popular with his subordinates, though many of his peers regarded him as a difficult individual. His account of his new assignment is typical of his strong sense of self-belief:

> I was assigned as commanding general of XL Panzer Corps, which was holding a bridgehead near Nikopol ... I flew first to Field Marshal von Manstein's army group headquarters. After dinner Manstein told me, 'I have just spoken on the phone with [Generalleutnant Rudolf] Schmundt [the Wehrmacht's chief of personnel]. You will take command of XLVIII Panzer Corps near Kiev. That's where the point of decision will be and that's where I need the best Panzer leader.'[33]

Manstein makes no mention of any such conversation in his memoirs; nor is there any other record that Balck was originally intended to replace Eberbach as commander of XL Panzer Corps.

Balck was delighted to be reacquainted with Mellenthin, chief of staff at XLVIII Panzer Corps; the two men had worked closely and happily together the previous winter when Balck's 11th Panzer Division had been subordinated to the same panzer corps. Almost immediately, Balck found himself disputing matters with higher commands. The planned counterattack was, he felt, poorly conceived – he wished to strike immediately towards Kiev in order to recapture the city before dealing with the various Soviet thrusts to the southwest and west. He was overruled by Hoth and Manstein and the original plan remained in force. Both Balck and Mellenthin were critical of this decision in their memoirs; Mellenthin wrote that it showed a degree of timidity, but as will be described, Moskalenko took steps to defend against an armoured thrust towards Kiev and it seems that on this occasion at least, Balck was wrong. Even if the comparatively fresh and powerful 1st Panzer Division and *LSSAH* had succeeded in reaching Kiev, it is highly unlikely that they would have had sufficient strength left to deal with all the Soviet forces that would then be to their west – indeed, such a move might have seen the two divisions isolated by a Soviet counterattack.

Amongst the German troops arriving were the first elements of Schell's 25th Panzer Division. Without waiting for the rest of the division to arrive, the first panzergrenadier units, organised into *Kampfgruppe von Wechmar*, were thrown into a hasty attempt to recapture Fastov. They came under heavy artillery fire and an energetic Soviet counterattack supported by tanks routed the panzergrenadiers, who fell back to their start line with heavy losses, both in terms of equipment and personnel. It was Schell's only battle in the field during the war, and represented a disastrous baptism of fire for the new division and a major blow to its morale. Barely able to read due to his deteriorating glaucoma, he headed back to Germany for medical treatment. In addition to trying to persuade Schell not to go to the Eastern Front, Guderian – in his role as inspector-general of armoured forces – had tried to prevent 25th Panzer Division from being sent east, as he believed that the division was not ready for service in the most demanding theatre of the war; he was overruled, and the men of 25th Panzer Division, who had been given little opportunity in division-sized exercises to perfect their cooperation and coordination, now paid the price.[34] As further elements of the division assembled, repeated attempts were made to push towards Fastov but any chance of swiftly capturing the town before the Soviet forces could reinforce their positions was gone. Despite having travelled east with something approaching a full complement of troops and equipment, 25th Panzer Division was reduced to little more than a battlegroup in its first week of combat.

Manstein originally intended to defeat the Red Army's forces with a pincer attack from north and south, but he lacked the forces for such an operation. The loss of Fastov and particularly Zhitomir necessitated an immediate response and it was decided to launch a counterattack with the forces of XLVIII Panzer Corps from the south. Inevitably, the Red Army spotted the arrival of German armoured forces and Moskalenko began to move specialist anti-tank units into position.

To prevent a direct attack on Kiev – Balck's preferred option – the independent 28th Anti-Tank Artillery Brigade deployed in and around Trypillya, on the bank of the Dnepr south of Kiev; a little to the east, Moskalenko positioned 9th Guards Anti-Tank Artillery Brigade. In addition, two anti-tank artillery regiments were sent to Obukhov, a little to the west, to create a second line of defences. The Red Army had learned a great deal about both offensive and defensive warfare, and perhaps more than any other army it had adapted both its units and doctrine appropriately.[35] Rybalko too anticipated a major German attack near Fastov, and his combat engineers busily mined the main approach routes to the town.

The weather was growing steadily colder, an unpleasant experience for the soldiers of 1st Panzer Division, fresh from their time in Greece and Italy. Many had not yet been issued with winter clothing. For the moment though, the muddy roads remained difficult for all vehicular traffic and the German units struggled forward for the planned counterattack. Balck's plan was to attack

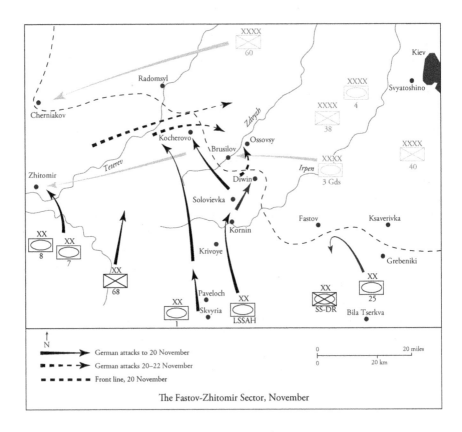

The Fastov-Zhitomir Sector, November

between Fastov and Zhitomir with 68th Infantry Division and 7th Panzer Division on the left, 1st Panzer Division in the centre, and *LSSAH* on the right. The various units of 25th Panzer Division and *SS-Das Reich* would extend the line to the west. Krüger, commander of 1st Panzer Division, had been anxious to wait for all of his units to concentrate but the division's Panther battalion was still en route. Further delays were not possible, and the attack would commence with the forces available.

Throughout 12 November, Krüger's armoured reconnaissance battalion clashed with Soviet units between Skvyra and Paveloch, and the following day, reinforced by 1st Panzer Division's panzergrenadiers, the reconnaissance battalion pushed towards the northwest. By the end of the day, Paveloch was in German hands. A little to the east, *LSSAH* had also been moving forward to secure good jumping-off positions for the planned counterattack and on 14 November, the assault began in earnest. At dusk, 1st Panzer Division reached Krivoye, an advance of about six miles (10km), and Krüger was heartened by the news that his Panther battalion had finally arrived, the first units detraining further south and immediately heading north to join the rest of the division. *LSSAH* also made good progress and during the evening Balck issued orders to his subordinates: the two divisions were to thrust north to cut the Zhitomir-Kiev road, while *SS-Das Reich* and 25th Panzer Division secured the corps' right flank.

Men and machines struggled forward through the night on muddy, badly degraded roads. At first light on 15 November the attack resumed with 1st Panzer Division rapidly pushing forward to Chodorkov, immediately to the east of the town of Kornin. *LSSAH* moved up alongside, taking Kornin and pushing on to the north. There was heavy fighting in the village of Solovievka, to the north of Kornin; *LSSAH* claimed to have destroyed 19 T-34s, whilst suffering losses of its own.

During the day, Hoth made what turned out to be a farewell visit to *LSSAH*. Vatutin and Antonov were not alone in receiving apparently unwarranted criticism from higher authorities. Hitler's anger at the loss of Kiev manifested itself in Hoth's dismissal as commander of Fourth Panzer Army. Like so many officers in the Wehrmacht, Hoth came from a traditional Prussian family and had served in the First World War. When Hitler turned the peacetime Reichswehr into the Wehrmacht, Hoth rose rapidly, commanding 18th Infantry Division and later XV Motorised Corps, which he led into Poland in 1939 and Belgium and France in 1940. He was the commander of *Panzergruppe 3* at the beginning of the invasion of the Soviet Union, leading the German drive across the Soviet Union towards Moscow and in November 1941 was assigned to command Seventeenth Army in the southern Ukraine. The following year, he became commander of Fourth Panzer Army, fighting in the campaign to reach Stalingrad both in the initial German advance on the city and later in the attempts to rescue the encircled Sixth Army. His command of Fourth Panzer Army was generally both skilful and free of errors – the occasions when Fourth Panzer Army failed were almost always due to the strength of the opposing forces rather than due to any errors on Hoth's part. He was now placed in the 'Führer Reserve' until April 1945 when he briefly held a meaningless post in central Germany.

There had clearly been discussions about replacing Hoth for several weeks. In a signal to *OKH* on 18 October, Manstein wrote:

> Generaloberst Hoth has led his army through the most difficult situations with initiative, skill and ruthlessness in every crisis. In the current critical situation, he is irreplaceable at the head of Fourth Panzer Army.[36]

This appears to have been triggered by a letter in which Hoth advised Manstein that, unless the German Second Army – on the southern wing of Army Group Centre – showed more energy in closing the gap between Army Groups Centre and South, Hoth would not be able to continue in command of Fourth Panzer Army. Hoth's position in command of an army that had been in a state of near-constant crisis since the abandonment of *Zitadelle* led to utterly unfair judgements by Hitler; shortly after Hoth was dismissed, Hitler confided in Zeitzler that he regarded Hoth as a 'bird of ill omen' and 'an instigator of defeatism of the worst sort.'[37]

Hoth was generally popular with his men, many of whom gave him the nickname 'Papa Hoth'. However, he was an unquestioning supporter of Hitler and in November 1941 issued an order to the troops of Seventeenth Army, requiring them to show no mercy to any who showed any degree of active or passive resistance to German occupation:

> These circles are the intellectual supports of Bolshevism, the bearers of its murderous organisation, the helpmates of the partisans. It is the same Jewish class of beings who have done so much damage to our own Fatherland by virtue of their activities against the nation and civilisation, and who promote anti-German tendencies throughout the world, and who will be the harbingers of revenge. Their extermination is a dictate of our own survival.[38]

After the war, Hoth was charged with war crimes in connection with the conduct of men under his command in the Soviet Union. He showed little repentance, arguing that it had been necessary to discourage German soldiers from showing their habitual 'good nature' and that if any Jews were killed as a result of his orders, these killings involved only those who had been resisting the German occupation; he even stated that it was common knowledge that Jews had been particularly heavily involved in acts of sabotage and espionage against the Germans.[39] He was convicted and sentenced to 15 years' imprisonment. He was released on parole in 1954, and died in 1971.

Hoth's replacement as commander of Fourth Panzer Army was Erhard Raus, who had led 6th Panzer Division in the attempts to break the siege perimeter of Stalingrad the previous winter and had then commanded an eponymous corps before commanding first XI Corps and then XLVII Corps. He was an experienced Eastern Front commander; his skills and experience would be critical in the weeks ahead.

While the command of Fourth Panzer Army changed hands, Balck's XLVIII Panzer Corps continued its counterattack. *LSSAH* had continued to probe forward during the night and early on 16 November its leading units penetrated through Turbovka to Divin on the eastern flank of the attack. On 17 November, still encountering relatively modest resistance, the two German divisions continued to push north. There were constant encounters with groups of Soviet tanks, infantry and cavalry, leading to confused fighting as these units clashed with German units to the rear of the main advance. Nevertheless, during the afternoon of 18 November, the leading units of 1st Panzer Division reached their objective, the road running from Kiev to Zhitomir. To the east, 25th Panzer Division also moved forward as flank protection, and Balck issued fresh orders. *LSSAH* was to turn to face east, whilst 1st Panzer Division attacked Zhitomir. At the same time, 7th Panzer Division and 68th Infantry Division would advance against Zhitomir from the southwest. Moving forward into position before dawn, Leutnant Werner Krusemarck, commander of one of 1st Panzer Division's panzer companies, had a lucky escape. Leading his platoon over a bridge across the Teterev River, he was unaware that the bridge had been partly demolished. Suddenly, his tank plunged through a hole in the bridge and fell about 25m to the muddy bank below. He and his crew escaped with cuts and bruises; their tank was rapidly recovered and swiftly repaired.[40]

On the eastern side of the advance, *LSSAH* had to fend off increasingly powerful Soviet counterattacks as elements of Rybalko's Third Guards Tank Army attempted to strike into the flank of XLVIII Panzer Corps. Elements of the SS division reached the Kiev-Zhitomir road at Kocherovo and awaited the next Soviet attack:

At the side of the road Rottenführer Schneidereit – a 24 year old from East Prussia – positioned his anti-tank gun. He now waited for dawn and Ivan.

And they came. At precisely 0630 the Russian artillery bombardment of the village began. It was followed by salvoes from Stalin Organs, which would now continue at regular intervals until evening. The air was full of the whistling, hissing, and howling enemy shells of all calibres. After the bombardment Soviet infantry, supported by tanks, stormed forward from all sides. Rottenführer Schneidereit also commenced work. Within half an hour he had shot up two T-34s with his anti-tank weapon and crippled two more, and they withdrew rapidly. The muddy, grey faces of the Soviet riflemen appeared over the embankment in front of the company. Machine-gun fire hammered at them and drove them to ground. Their loud shouts of 'Urrah!' fell away. The company was forced back by a second attack, once more reinforced by tanks, and Schneidereit was wounded. He bandaged the laceration from mortar shrapnel himself. He knew that the T-34s would approach precisely here. He was one of the experienced, unflappable NCOs whose long experience gave them an unfailing instinct for every situation in constantly changing combat ... The Russian attacks didn't cease. Almost without pause new waves stormed forward, fresh tanks tore up the ground, artillery rounds threw up fountains of earth over the grenadiers. Untersturmführer Müller, Schneidereit's company commander, was killed. One platoon commander after another, including Untersturmführer Brandstätter, was badly wounded. Towards midday the enemy forced a penetration. The Russians threatened to break through along the road and to fall upon the rear of our comrades on the opposite front of the encirclement [around Zhitomir]. Schneidereit now gathered a couple of men and a machine-gun that was still working and mounted a counterthrust, recovering his old position and his still undamaged anti-tank weapon. But artillery fire and rockets fell incessantly and the Russian infantry stormed forward. By the evening the strength of 8 Company was exhausted. There were no more officers or NCOs and almost all of the automatic weapons had failed; our artillery had almost used up its ammunition. Schneidereit's anti-tank weapon was also knocked out. As he tried to take it with him while changing position, it was hit and burst apart, and two of the fingers of his left hand were torn away. A rapidly applied bandage could barely stop the blood flow. His comrades urged him to go to the rear.

Then came an order that the company had to hold out until morning and would receive no reinforcements. The company? The men who were gathered in a hollow looked at each other. There were perhaps two small groups without any commanders. Only Rottenführer Schneidereit was left. When the Russians edged forward again and ventured across the first embankment, he took hold of a machine-pistol in his right hand, leaped suddenly from cover, took command of the remaining men of his company, led them forward, beat off the attack and once more secured the road. They had one machine-gun with them and found another. They fired away with their machine-guns all night, confusing the enemy about their numbers ... Eventually the firing died down. They took Schneidereit to the field dressing station where he sank into deep unconsciousness. For his decisive and exemplary leadership Rottenführer Schneidereit was awarded the Knight's Cross. Promoted to Unterscharführer, he was killed in April 1945 in the fighting near Berlin.[41]

The anti-tank weapon used by Schneidereit to such good effect was the *Schwere Panzerbüchse* ('heavy anti-tank rifle') *41*, a weapon with a tapered barrel – the internal diameter was 28mm at the breech, reducing to 21mm at the muzzle. This tapering resulted in high muzzle velocity, giving it excellent armour penetration for such a small weapon, but it had a short range and a very limited barrel life and required the use of hardened tungsten ammunition, which became increasingly difficult to produce in Germany as the war proceeded. Production of the gun ceased in 1943, but it remained in operation until ammunition supplies ran out.

Determined to push on before the Soviet forces in Zhitomir could organise their defences, 1st Panzer Division advanced in two battlegroups. They encountered repeated resistance along the road but overcame it swiftly. At the same time, the division's Panther battalion finally caught up and was immediately committed to the attack on the northern flank. It too advanced quickly, linking up with the leading elements of 7th Panzer Division advancing from the southwest. Despite constant clashes with defending Soviet troops, 1st Panzer Division swiftly drove into the eastern outskirts of Zhitomir. With 7th and 8th Panzer Divisions, the latter being the southern flank of XIII Corps – in reality, little more than modest battlegroups – and 68th Infantry Division closing in from the south and west, the outcome wasn't ever in doubt. Krüger was reluctant to send his tanks into the town in the gathering darkness and waited until the division's panzergrenadiers had caught up; concentric attacks were then made and by dawn on 20 November, the town was in German hands. The Germans described bitter fighting, but Moskalenko by contrast wrote that he had ordered his troops to avoid a pointless battle and the remaining Soviet forces pulled out of Zhitomir in good order. It is difficult to determine which account is more accurate, but the reality was that the important railway and road junction had been recaptured by XLVIII Panzer Corps. As a bonus, the Germans discovered that the supply dumps that had been captured by the Red Army just a few days earlier were still intact.

Hasso von Manteuffel, the commander of 7th Panzer Division, later described his division's attempts to take Zhitomir:

I had tried throughout 18 November to penetrate into Zhitomir but couldn't find a weak point in the enemy's defensive system. Under cover of an armoured group I tried to enter the town from the south. I failed – the bridge there could only be crossed by riflemen as the bridge over the Teterev to Zhitomir had been destroyed. With another battlegroup of the division leading, I made a similar attempt from the east and during the afternoon also from the north. We couldn't find any weak point that would allow us to push on with our forces. We also had to guard towards the east as our reconnaissance reported further [enemy] forces on the main Kiev-Zhitomir road; but our flank protection was able to stop them. About an hour before darkness I received a radio message: 'Manteuffel [to go] immediately to Schulz!' [Schulz was commander of the division's panzer regiment.] That was at the very least unusual and I was concerned what this meant, perhaps that something peculiar, probably a disaster, must have occurred, as I had spoken to Schulz just two hours earlier in his command post. When I reached Oberstleutnant Schulz, he said to me that in a local attack towards the town he had overrun a completely intoxicated anti-tank gun crew. (In fact, we later found in this and other gun positions a large number of empty champagne and cognac bottles!) This for me was a sign that despite the onset of darkness we should attack immediately. I sent a signal to all stations that everyone should prepare to attack the town and should follow Schulz's armoured battlegroup and me. I then sent a further radio message to everyone: 'Our Christmas presents await us in Zhitomir!' We – Oberstleutnant Schulz with five or six tanks, me with my half-track, and a panzergrenadier battalion of about 100 men – then pushed into the town metre by metre. Schulz was at the spearhead. The widespread fires at the eastern edge of the town helped greatly to light our way through the residential quarter, but even more important was the exemplary close cooperation between the few tanks and panzergrenadiers as they fought their way from one street to the next. Starting at 1700, we overcame resistance by 0300 the next morning and could then commence clearing the town of Red Army soldiers who had taken refuge in the houses. For me it left one of the strongest impressions of the war to date, with the readiness for combat and the impetuous urge to advance amongst the panzergrenadiers and tank crews as they raced to see who would be the first to enter the town. On foot, Schulz and I were with the leading groups and even today I recall how Schulz repeatedly shook my hand, amazed by what his men achieved.[42]

Leaving aside the natural pride of a senior officer in the achievements of his men, some points in this account are noteworthy. This was not the first – nor the last – time that Soviet troops would succumb to the temptation to indulge in consuming alcohol that they had captured. Nor was it the first time that German troops were surprised to find that precious transport capacity had been used for luxury goods; during the siege of Stalingrad, desperate men searching for food sometimes came across such caches. To an extent, Moskalenko's account of withdrawing to avoid heavy losses may be *post-facto* rationalisation, but the weakness of 7th Panzer Division – with its tank strength reduced to just a handful of vehicles and an entire panzergrenadier battalion able to deploy fewer men than a full-strength company – suggests that the Red Army did indeed pull back rather than make a prolonged stand in Zhitomir.

While the German forces had been thrusting north and then enveloping Zhitomir, the Soviet Third Guards Tank Army had been busy concentrating its forces. In addition to the troops of I Guards Cavalry Corps, which had led the advance to Zhitomir, Rybalko had positioned I, V and VII Guards Tank Corps in and around the small town of Brusilov, from where they threatened the flank of Balck's advance. With his usual energy, Balck issued orders for an immediate attack to destroy this group of Soviet formations; in addition to the divisions that he had used to recapture Zhitomir, he now had 19th Panzer Division available to him, and deployed this new force on his right flank with 25th Panzer Division. *LSSAH* was ordered to attack directly towards Brusilov from the southwest, while 1st Panzer Division was to turn the northern flank of the Brusilov concentration by thrusting directly down the road from Zhitomir to Kiev. With the axis of XLVIII Panzer Corps turning to the east, its northern flank was potentially exposed, and this area was to be screened by 7th Panzer Division and 68th Infantry Division. Having started the battle in a badly weakened state, 8th Panzer Division was effectively unable to take part in any further offensive action. It had enjoyed a moment of success during the recovery of Zhitomir, overrunning a Soviet rifle division and capturing a good haul of guns and prisoners, but it was at the end of its strength, as Oberst Joseph von Radowitz, commander of one of its battlegroups, described on 22 November:

> I report that after continuous operations of heavy fighting since the beginning of this month, the state of the troops has fallen so low that they can make no further major efforts. During the rearguard actions from Kiev to Zhitomir, the troops in the main had to withdraw on foot in the worst road and weather conditions ... in their current state, the troops cannot cope with a march of even a short distance.[43]

The division's medical officer also wrote a pessimistic report:

> Almost 100 per cent of the panzergrenadiers have foot problems. These are mainly
> due to overexertions of the joints, muscles and ligaments resulting in swelling ...
>
> In addition, due to the universal infestation with lice, particularly amongst
> the replacement drafts who have been here a while, there are numerous infections
> from scratching skin. These are often a consequence of the contamination of
> other skin conditions ...
>
> About 80 per cent of the combat strength are suffering from illnesses related
> to the cold. These include respiratory infections, rheumatic complaints, stomach
> and intestinal disorders, with many having severe diarrhoea, as well as bladder
> infections resulting in frequent incontinence ...
>
> In summary, it is necessary to report that from a medical perspective that no
> marching or related combat can be expected of the panzergrenadiers now or in the
> near future.[44]

It was therefore with considerable relief that Frölich – newly promoted to
Generalmajor – received orders to pull his division out of line so that it could get
some much-needed rest and a break from the constant mud of the front line. But
whilst he and his men could have a break from the wretched conditions they had
endured, it is worth remembering that the Wehrmacht's infantry divisions
suffered such an existence for month after month with no prospect of being
pulled out of the front line until their division had taken such heavy losses that
there was no point in them remaining in combat.

Balck complained in his memoirs that, whilst his divisions were now
finally heading towards Kiev, five days had been lost and the Red Army had
used these to organise defences in his path; in particular, he complained about
the concentration of Soviet armour in and around Brusilov.[45] Whilst he
continued to grumble about what he regarded as a lost opportunity, only a few
individuals shared his opinion. The assessment of the men of 1st Panzer
Division was that 'higher commands' were overly optimistic in their
expectations:

> The following days and weeks would show that in view of the actual ratio of
> forces, higher commands had once more set too high a goal. This was especially
> the case with an orthodox frontal attack with just modest mobile forces against
> the Dnepr bridgehead to the west of Kiev. Army Group and Fourth Panzer Army
> headquarters saw matters more realistically.[46]

It is worth noting that whilst Balck appears to have a good relationship with the commanders of *LSSAH* and 7th Panzer Division, matters were slightly more complicated in the case of 1st Panzer Division. In May 1940, Balck – with the rank of Oberstleutnant at the time – was commander of one of 1st Panzer Division's rifle regiments; the regiments were collectively under the control of a rifle brigade, whose commander was Krüger, with the rank of Oberst. A little over three years later, Balck and Krüger found themselves with roles reversed – whilst Krüger had risen to command of the division, Balck had overtaken him. Balck mentioned in his memoirs that this potentially difficult situation was managed due to the professionalism of both men, but it is clear that the relationship was not a warm one.

The main assault towards Brusilov was made by *LSSAH*. In its path were the Soviet units that had repeatedly tried to attack into the division's flank during the advance to isolate Zhitomir and in the face of a mixture of determined Soviet resistance, wooded terrain that made armoured manoeuvres difficult, and constant rain, the attack rapidly stalled. Elements of the division were still detraining to the rear and struggled forward along the muddy and degraded roads, competing for space with trucks carrying ammunition and other supplies, and vehicles loaded with wounded men moving to the rear. It was a dispiriting day for the SS division, with many of its men glumly reflecting that it was the first time they had failed to make headway in an attack of this nature. Regardless of the terrain and weather difficulties, the Red Army had learned from its experiences in the war and the German panzer formations could no longer expect to achieve rapid successes in the manner of earlier years.

The German forces that had captured Zhitomir fared rather better. Manteuffel's 7th Panzer Division advanced rapidly on the northern flank through essentially open ground, and 1st Panzer Division pushed forward a small distance along the Zhitomir-Kiev road; whilst Balck wanted the attack to begin immediately, it would take time for all of the forces sent into Zhitomir to move back towards the east. On 21 November, 1st Panzer Division resumed its attack. Cold rain was falling steadily, and the division struggled to make rapid progress through the woodland either side of the road where Soviet troops waited in ambush. The commander of the leading panzer company was badly wounded when his tank was knocked out and the division's Panthers found the wooded terrain difficult for effective operation, with the trees hindering their long-barrelled 75mm guns. As Krüger's division struggled towards the village of Kocherovo, it encountered further delays when the withdrawing Soviet troops destroyed a bridge over a small river. It took until the end of the day for the

Germans to secure the village, an overall advance of only three miles (5km). Krüger ordered his units to halt and regroup, a decision that greatly angered Balck when he heard of it. Immediately, he ordered 1st Panzer Division and 19th Panzer Division – which had also halted to the east of Brusilov – to press on through the night.

Perhaps taking their Soviet opponents by surprise when they resumed their attack, the men of 1st Panzer Division seized the village of Ossovzy and turned to the southeast. Fighting continued around Ossovzy for several days, but before dawn on 22 November, the two German pincers met and closed the ring around Brusilov. Three Soviet tank corps and a cavalry corps had been encircled, but the German armoured units – weak in infantry – lacked the troops to seal off the encirclement. Most of the Soviet troops escaped, albeit at the cost of abandoning their equipment. Fighting continued for several days until the pocket was finally reduced.

The haul from the Brusilov encirclement was substantial: the Germans counted 153 captured or destroyed Soviet tanks, together with 70 artillery pieces and 250 anti-tank guns. However, the modest haul of prisoners and examination of the dead revealed an interesting feature:

> It was characteristic of the Russian mentality that first of all the staffs, the officers, and certain specialists were taken out of the ring, while the bulk of the men were left to their fate. In the whole Brusilov area no staffs were captured nor was the dead body of a senior officer ever found. Thus the Russians saved the cadres for new formations. They were sent to the rear, where they received fresh troops and equipment, of which the Red Army seemed to possess an inexhaustible supply.[47]

Any hope that Balck still entertained of continuing the attack towards Kiev was dashed as heavy rain turned the landscape to mud. Balck experienced the difficulties of his troops first-hand on 26 November when he attempted to visit his units:

> While I was on my way to the northern wing of the corps, I had to be towed three times just to get to 19th Panzer Division. After that I got into a tracked vehicle, which promptly threw a track in the next village. Then I was able to get a bit further in a staff car, which finally also got stuck in the mud. Then I hiked on foot to 1st Panzer Division's headquarters and finally made it to my destination in another staff car. I made my way back well enough in another tracked vehicle. The trip took me 12 hours, while just a few days earlier the same trip had taken only three hours, including the staff meetings and briefings.[48]

Further attacks towards Kiev were clearly impossible, particularly as the weather deteriorated further. Meanwhile, Vatutin and his subordinates brought more forces up to strengthen their front line. Both Balck and Mellenthin bitterly resented the orders to strike towards Zhitomir first, and it is noteworthy that Moskalenko too regarded the time spent by the Germans in capturing Zhitomir and Brusilov as important. He was particularly grateful to the anti-tank units of his army for their performance, which saw the first large-scale use of 152mm and 203mm guns in direct fire against tanks. Although they fired only high explosive rounds, the concussion from these massive shells was often sufficient to damage the engines of tanks or injure their crew; damage to tracks would leave them immobile and easy victims for other anti-tank weapons. Whilst German accounts of the fighting emphasise the importance of the weather in preventing operations towards Kiev, Moskalenko was scornful of this version of events, particularly Mellenthin's comment that 'losses increased, as in this horrible mud nobody wanted to throw himself on the ground to avoid presenting a good target to the enemy':[49]

> One would think that the Hitlerites preferred to perish under bullets and shells rather than dirty their uniforms in the mud. The absurdity of this reasoning is obvious. I would also remind you that the number of infantry that participated in the enemy counteroffensive was relatively small. A feature of the enemy's offensive actions in those days was ... massive application of tanks, and in fact these did not have to lie down in the mud to avoid bullets and shells.
>
> Thus, the attempts of Hitler's generals to justify the failure of their offensive do not stand up to scrutiny. Indeed, the *Rasputitsa* ['rainy season'] at the end of November in the Kiev region was not severe that year. In the second half of the month the temperature fluctuated on average from plus 2° in the day to minus 4° at night. It snowed frequently and was often wet, and the earth froze at night and did not have time to thaw during the day. There was slush on the dirt roads, not enough to interfere with the movement of troops and equipment. As for the highway, which had a metalled surface, the weather had no impact on its condition.[50]

Moskalenko's account is somewhat at odds with the details of every German division's war diary, and it seems that even if the ground froze at night, the combination of warmer weather during the day and the constant movement of dozens of heavy vehicles made it very difficult for the Germans to operate. Had Manstein been permitted to concentrate all the panzer divisions in Army Group

South for this operation, it is possible that it might have enjoyed greater success, but driving the Red Army back across the Dnepr and recapturing – and then holding – Kiev was probably beyond the strength of the Wehrmacht.

The Red Army might have been driven back from Zhitomir and the threat of further advances towards the southwest might have been ended, but immediately to the north, there remained a considerable bulge to the west and Manstein was aware that this might easily form the starting point for a winter attack by 1st Ukrainian Front. Such an attack could easily break the tenuous link between Army Groups Centre and South, and accordingly Manstein and Raus decided to send Balck with his comparatively fresh armoured formations towards Radomsyl to reduce this threat. In addition, the Soviet advance had left a group of German infantry trapped in Korosten, and it was intended that this operation would allow the troops – 291st Infantry Division and *Korpsabteilung C*, effectively all that remained of General Kurt von der Chevallerie's LIX Corps – to break out to safety.

Balck's plan for the coming operation was to avoid the sort of frontal assault that had cost heavy casualties for *LSSAH* and in which the defensive skills of the Red Army were particularly effective. Instead, he intended to turn the northern flank of the Soviet Sixtieth Army, a task that was slightly complicated by the simple fact that the Germans were not entirely sure where this flank lay; their own troops in the area were so thinly spread that they could only provide approximate information. To avoid alerting the Red Army of their intentions, Balck and Mellenthin forbade reconnaissance operations. From its positions around Zhitomir, 68th Infantry Division was to attack towards the northeast; *LSSAH* was to be pulled out of the front line, moved northwest behind 68th Infantry Division, and then launched towards the northeast; and 1st Panzer Division was similarly to be moved so that it could attack north of *LSSAH*. Finally, 7th Panzer Division – somewhat strengthened with new drafts and a modest number of new and repaired tanks – would form the northern flank of XLVIII Panzer Corps in a wide sweep that would ultimately turn the flank of the Soviet line; to give Manteuffel's division additional firepower, a battalion of Tiger tanks was subordinated to it.

In his new role of commander of Fourth Panzer Army, Raus took every precaution to prevent the Red Army from realising what was afoot:

> General Balck's XLVIII Panzer Corps, with *LSSAH* and 1st and 7th Panzer Divisions was withdrawn from the front and assembled behind the centre of Fourth Panzer Army's defensive sector. Meanwhile, the approach routes – some

of which led through marshy, wooded terrain – were reconnoitred, bridges repaired, and the partisan units rampant in the woods dispersed by Generalleutnant Alexander Goeschen's 213th Security Division, which was responsible for this area. Immediately thereafter, the combat elements of all three panzer divisions moved out in broad daylight and marched along the main highway toward Zhitomir in order to deceive the Russians into believing that strong forces were being shifted to another sector of the front.[51]

The reconnaissance battalions of the various German divisions moved out on 5 December, accompanied by the engineer units that would repair roads and bridges. Moving mainly at night, the panzer divisions had already reached their forming-up areas, with road traffic during the day being used to simulate a withdrawal of the armoured forces further to the west. All German troop

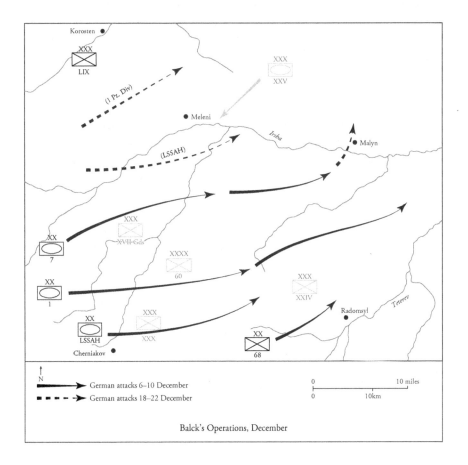

Balck's Operations, December

movements to their start lines took place to the west of the Zhitomir-Korosten road along smaller roads; these were unsuitable for the Tigers that had been attached to 7th Panzer Division, and these would have to wait until the Zhitomir-Korosten road had been seized before they could move north.

The weather was now getting colder, with regular frosts that hardened the ground. At 0600 on 6 December, *LSSAH* and 1st and 7th Panzer Divisions moved east across the Zhitomir-Korosten road. They did not expect strong resistance; the first thrust encountered several Soviet units that were preparing positions along the road and swiftly overran them. Throughout the day the German units pushed on, taking advantage of growing confusion in the ranks of the Soviet Sixtieth Army. The headquarters of Sixtieth Army was overrun during the afternoon, shortly after the army commander, Lieutenant General Ivan Danilovich Cherniakhovsky, had left with most of his personnel. By nightfall, the Germans had advanced 20 miles (34km) and they pressed on over the next three days. Increasingly, the armoured battlegroups had to pause while fuel shortages – a problem that had hampered Wehrmacht operations more and more at least since the summer of 1942 – were overcome, and thick fog in the sector where *LSSAH* was advancing also hindered movements. LIX Corps broke out of Korosten late on 6 December and rapidly made contact with the advancing panzers; Chevallerie was ordered by Raus to join the northern flank of the German advance, but his weakened troops could contribute little. The troops of 1st Panzer Division encountered increasing resistance every day but managed to keep their advance going. Finally, with no further clear objectives within range, Balck and Raus called a halt to the advance. The Soviet Sixtieth Army had suffered significant losses, and whilst the haul of prisoners and captured tanks and guns was perhaps modest, the threat of a Soviet drive towards Zhitomir from the northeast had been eliminated. Nevertheless, the panzer divisions had suffered a depletion of their strength, and it is worth noting that *LSSAH* finished the operation with just 28 tanks and assault guns still in the front line. Of these, six were Panthers; a remarkable 53 Panthers were with the workshop teams undergoing repairs, many for breakdowns rather than due to battle damage.[52] Moskalenko later wrote that the Germans failed to achieve surprise, and that the Red Army's intelligence service was aware of the shift in German positions and that this allowed the Soviet units to avoid major losses, but regardless of whether Balck achieved surprise, there can be no question that the operation resulted in a front line that was far better for the Wehrmacht than at the beginning of the operation.

Balck's advance had established a new front line that now ran north before turning west along the line of the Irsha River before inclining north again to the east of Korosten; the segment to the south of the Irsha was now held by XIII Corps, with Balck's panzer divisions behind the German infantry divisions. Reconnaissance suggested that there were strong Soviet forces near Meleni, 14 miles (23km) to the southeast of Korosten, along the Irsha. From there, they were in a position to attack towards the southwest, into the rear of XIII Corps, and Balck decided to use his divisions in an attack to eliminate this concentration. Once again, movements were carried out at night to avoid detection. The initial attack was to be made by 7th Panzer Division, which would secure a bridgehead across the Irsha at Malyn; *LSSAH* and 1st Panzer Division were to force a crossing further west, immediately to the west of Meleni. Here, they would link up with elements of LVII Corps advancing east from Korosten and together with 7th Panzer Division would launch convergent attacks to surround the Soviet forces along the river line.

The start date for the operation was 16 December, allowing the troops time to move, supplies to be brought forward, and at least some of the damaged tanks to be returned to service. Delays due to the weather, supply difficulties and the poor state of the roads led to a postponement of two days, but when they attacked on 18 December, the German forces made good initial progress; supported by a battlegroup from 1st Panzer Division, *LSSAH* rapidly gained its early objectives before supporting the advance of its westerly neighbour. Manteuffel's 7th Panzer Division also successfully crossed the Irsha, but even as the German spearheads turned towards each other, Soviet resistance stiffened. Over the next two days, the Germans made little progress, having to beat off repeated counterattacks of steadily increasing strength. On 21 December, troops from *LSSAH* discovered a set of maps on the corpse of a Red Army major, revealing that the Soviet forces in the area consisted of XXV Tank Corps and two rifle divisions; both Balck and Mellenthin later wrote that the maps revealed the presence of a total of three tank corps and three rifle corps, but this is at odds with the account in the unit history of *LSSAH*.[53] Regardless of the strength of the Soviet forces, they were sufficient to stop further advances by XLVIII Panzer Corps. There were further heavy clashes in the next few days; the Germans claimed to have destroyed dozens of T-34s, and an increasingly pointless battle of attrition slowly died down.

Manstein had placed great hope in a counterattack with the relatively fresh divisions that had been assigned to him, and it is questionable whether the gains made by Balck were as significant as Balck later claimed. The narrative adopted by the Germans was that their counterattacks prevented the Red Army from bursting through the northern flank of Fourth Panzer Army and turning southwest, an advance that would have been catastrophic for Manstein's army group. The Soviet version of events was that their attacks from the Lyutezh bridgehead resulted in the recapture of Kiev, and whilst the failure to hold Zhitomir was a bitter disappointment, the Wehrmacht's panzer divisions were drawn into fighting that cost them heavy casualties. Balck lamented what he regarded as timidity in higher commands that prevented him from launching an attack towards Kiev at the very outset of the operation, but it is questionable whether such an attack would have succeeded; far more accurate is Balck's criticism of the resources that had been used – wasted in his assessment – in creating 25th Panzer Division. This profligacy was then compounded by the premature deployment of the division in the front line before it had been given any opportunity to train its formations to the high standard required for the intensity of warfare on the Eastern Front:

> It is impossible to take a freshly stood-up division that does not have any combat experience, has not completed its training, and is under a commander who also does not have combat experience and throw that unit into the decisive point of a critical fight. It would have been better to reconstitute two or three old combat-proven divisions with the fresh troops, officers, weapons and equipment. 3rd, 8th, and 19th Panzer Divisions, which were all attached to my corps ... could have been the decisive factor had they been so reconstituted and then committed.[54]

As was almost always the case, the losses amongst Soviet units were far heavier, but the Red Army was in a better position to make good those losses than the Wehrmacht. The speed with which Vatutin's forces would recover their strength would be demonstrated again before the end of the year.

CHAPTER 10

YEAR'S END

Sigfrid Henrici, who had been commander of XL Panzer Corps as well as the other troops within the Zaporozhye bridgehead, became unwell immediately after his eponymous group had withdrawn to the west bank and had to return to Germany for medical treatment. His replacement as commander of the corps was General Ferdinand Schörner, who had been commander of XIX Mountain Corps. He was a particular favourite of Hitler and a committed believer in Nazi ideology; physically intimidating, he had a reputation for harshness and brutality that won him few friends amongst those under his command. An infantryman who served in one of Schörner's units later wrote:

> [He] placed loyalty to the National Socialist Party above his loyalty to the troops whose lives were entrusted to him. Schörner made a practice of punishing *Landsers*, NCOs, and officers with immediate transfer to the infantry for any insignificant infraction.[1]

It should be added that not all soldiers had a low opinion of Schörner. He was especially tough on rear area units, repeatedly ordering them to release some of their personnel for service in the front line, and like soldiers of most armies throughout history, the fighting men of the Wehrmacht generally regarded those who had managed to find comfortable posts far from danger with contempt. Consequently, Schörner's open scorn for such individuals earned him praise from some. His rigid, authoritarian attitude made him all the more attractive to Hitler and he was now transferred from the far north, where his troops had been fighting against the Red Army to the west of Murmansk, to take command of XL Panzer Corps.

By the end of October 1943, the Nikopol bridgehead started from the south bank of the Dnepr about 14 miles (23km) upstream of Nikopol and ran to just downstream of Bolshaya Lepetykha. It was about ten miles (17km) deep for most of its course, and covered an area where two streams – the Beloserka and the Rogatchik – ran northwest into the Dnepr; each stream was in a relatively deep valley and this would play an important part in the fighting to come, as the streams effectively divided the area into three zones. The autumn rains had turned the rich soil of the region into mud, and movement off the few roads in the area was difficult most of the time, and often impossible. The only bridges across the Dnepr were at Nikopol and Bolshaya Lepetykha.

The units that had retreated into the area consisted of three infantry divisions in Brandenberger's XXIX Corps, in the southern part of the bridgehead, and a further six in General Friedrich Mieth's IV Corps in the northern part. Originally, these units were to hold a line that ran north from Melitopol, but it proved impossible to stop the Red Army in that position, forcing a further retreat. Now that the front line was so close to Nikopol and – as far as Hitler was concerned – its essential manganese mines, Schörner was ordered to move his XL Panzer Corps headquarters and 24th Panzer Division to the bridgehead; the two corps already present were subordinated to his command, creating *Gruppe Schörner*.

The nine infantry divisions that held the perimeter of the bridgehead had suffered major losses during their withdrawal from the Mius line and had been in almost constant action. Most battalions numbered no more than 200 men, and much of the heavy equipment of the divisions, including most of their artillery, had been abandoned somewhere to the east. Ammunition was in short supply for the remaining artillery and morale amongst the troops was low. Until the arrival of 24th Panzer Division, the only armoured assets available to the defenders of the bridgehead were the remnants of two battalions of assault guns and a single battalion of tanks. All of these units were effectively committed to the front line, as the infantry divisions had utterly inadequate anti-armour resources of their own. It was only when 24th Panzer Division became available that the defences had any form of reserve behind the front line; until then, they had all of their troops committed to the defensive perimeter.

The Soviet forces facing the bridgehead were from 4th Ukrainian Front and consisted of Third Guards Army, Fifth Shock Army and Forty-Fourth Army. Between them, these three armies possessed eight rifle corps, each with between two and five rifle divisions. In addition to the armoured assets of each army, there were also two further units in reserve: XIX Tank Corps and IV Guards Mechanised Corps. Just like their German counterparts, many of the infantry and armoured

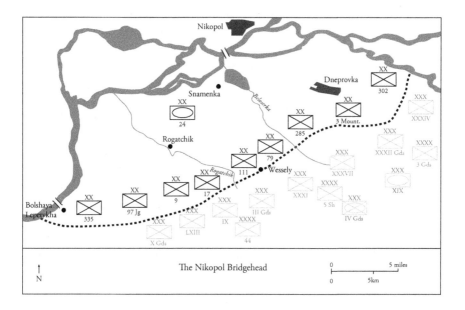

The Nikopol Bridgehead

units facing the Nikopol bridgehead were badly below establishment strength as a result of the constant fighting of the summer and autumn, but they were confident and flushed by victory. The devastated landscape over which they had passed had a profound effect on their personnel, leaving most soldiers in the Red Army with a strong desire to continue attacking in order to drive the hated Hitlerites from Soviet territory as soon as possible, and unlike their Wehrmacht counterparts, the Red Army units received regular replacement drafts, albeit not enough to replace all their losses. However, the training of these drafts was generally poorer than had been the case in previous battles and there was little time to allow these men time to learn from veterans. Increasingly, their German opponents reported the use of mass 'human wave' attacks as commanders attempted to make up for poor training by sheer weight of numbers. However, there were plenty of experienced, battle-hardened troops in 4th Ukrainian Front, and the balance of power lay very firmly with the Soviet forces.

The first test for *Gruppe Schörner* developed on 4 November, when the Soviet XXXI Rifle Corps attacked the centre of the bridgehead perimeter in an attempt to force the defences before they were fully prepared. As was often the case, the attack fell on the precise boundary between two different German commands, XXIX Corps to the southwest and IV Corps to the northeast, and penetrated to the village of Rogatchik. Schörner ordered 24th Panzer Division to restore the old front line as it represented the only realistic defensive perimeter for the bridgehead; after a careful reconnaissance on 5 November, the panzer division attacked energetically over the next two days with complete success. It even caught a Soviet rifle division moving its artillery forward and was able to destroy most of the guns.[2]

This Soviet attack was followed by a period of calm while 4th Ukrainian Front moved reinforcements up to the front line. The workshops of 24th Panzer Division were also busy repairing as many damaged vehicles as possible and on 19 November the division reported that it had 30 operational Pz.IVs and 23 assault guns – a marked reduction from the number when it arrived from Italy, particularly as the division had reported at the end of the counterattack north of Krivoy Rog that it had lost only six tanks and two assault guns. These figures highlight two factors that reduced the effective fighting strength of German units. Firstly, mechanical breakdowns were common, leaving tanks unable to move under their own power; secondly, the quoted losses were only those vehicles that were totally destroyed. Many tanks and assault guns were recovered from the battlefield but proved too difficult to repair, not least because of the constant and worsening shortage of spare parts; these vehicles were then written off at a later stage, but in the interim were counted as damaged rather than lost. When they were written off, these additional 'losses' are rarely added to the vehicles destroyed in combat. There were several reasons for this practice. Commanders in the field were aware of how unlikely they were to receive timely replacement vehicles, and therefore held onto wrecks in the hope that they might be repaired; the workshop teams often used wrecks as a source of spare parts; and there was a tendency at many levels to try to underplay losses.

Despite its modest armoured strength, 24th Panzer Division was still more powerful than the badly worn-down panzer divisions that had spent the summer and autumn struggling to hold back the Red Army's advance across the Ukraine. In addition, it received a welcome boost in firepower in the form of the heavyweight Ferdinand tank destroyers that had previously contributed to the defence of the Zaporozhye bridgehead. On 20 November, a sudden heavy artillery bombardment was followed by a powerful Soviet attack to the south of the Beloserka gorge, where the German 79th Infantry Division held a weakly manned line. The Soviet troops, led by elements of IV Guards Mechanised Corps, rapidly penetrated to a depth of about six miles (10km) and 24th Panzer Division was ordered to intervene. With its formations organised into two battlegroups, the division concentrated in Snamenka, and Edelsheim, the division commander, ordered *Kampfgruppe Müller-Hillebrand* to attack with the division's tanks and assault guns towards the point at which the Soviet forces had broken through the infantry defences. Once this attack had developed and effectively isolated the Soviet units that had made the penetration, Edelsheim would attack with *Kampfgruppe von Heyden* and would use the firepower of the Ferdinands to destroy the Soviet troops.

Oberst Burkhart Müller-Hillebrand made swift progress in his drive towards Wessely, where the German lines had been penetrated. The battlegroup reported the destruction of many Soviet tanks but was unable to restore the previous front line; at the same time, Oberstleutnant Hans-Wilhelm von Heyden screened off the Soviet penetration in preparation for a further attack to destroy it. The following day, Müller-Hillebrand resumed his drive and reached the Beloserka gorge. From there, the battlegroup turned to the southeast and attempted once more to restore the front line, labouring forward in the face of determined Soviet resistance and at least one further powerful Soviet attack. By the end of 22 November, the line was largely back to its original positions. The intention of both 24th Panzer Division and higher commands was to hand over the line as quickly as possible to the German infantry divisions so that the panzer division could remain mobile, but the infantry formations were too weak and Edelsheim was forced to leave a panzergrenadier battalion with the infantry divisions.

As the weather turned increasingly rainy and the state of the ground deteriorated further, the Soviet units abandoned further attacks. The forces that had made the penetration along the Beloserka gorge – elements of IV Guards Mechanised Corps – withdrew to the southeast and directly east across the gorge, leaving much of their equipment. The Soviet attempt to break up the bridgehead by attacking its centre had failed because of the timely action of 24th Panzer Division, and correctly assessing that the Germans had just one mobile division in the bridgehead, Tolbukhin now ordered his armies to mount simultaneous attacks at each end of the bridgehead. By doing so, the Germans would be forced either to divide the resources of Edelsheim's division, or to send it against just one penetration, allowing the other to make better progress. On 26 November, units from XIX Tank Corps broke through the infantry defences at the southern end of the bridgehead and rapidly approached the shore of the Dnepr, while at the same time elements of IV Guards Mechanised Corps attacked in the north and threatened the village of Dneprovka.

This latter penetration was deemed to be the more threatening. A single battalion of panzergrenadiers took up positions to block further advances and the bulk of the division moved up to take the Soviet troops in their exposed southern flank. Struggling through the mud, the tanks and Ferdinands attacked on 27 November and made limited progress, encountering well-organised lines of anti-tank guns. It was only when darkness fell and the Soviet gunners could no longer see the attacking German tanks so easily that it was possible to regain most of the front line. Meanwhile, *Kampfgruppe Müller-Hillebrand* had already been sent south as a precaution and counterattacked energetically on 28 November, rapidly restoring the position. However, the success was short-lived:

> Suddenly it all kicked off! From the command post, which was in some hedges, we saw eight, then 15, then 30 turrets approaching over the hill to the left of the 'Wart' [a name that the Germans had given to an ancient burial mound]. The storm broke with alarming speed. The long guns emerging from the dark bodies looked like poisonous spines, spitting fire and steel. They rolled forward over our line and my vision grew dark as a few of our men stood and tried to run, the most senseless thing that they could do. By now, the tanks had reached the high ground. Our command half-track was there in the open. At high speed the dark beasts rushed forward and past, through the hedges to left and right, on to our rear. They were a completely new type, better than the T-34, the spawn of hell. They moved so quickly that we couldn't warn the empty vehicles [to the rear]. They rushed through them like a wild hunt, barely 1,000m behind us in a hollow. Half-tracks raced the tanks across the frozen fields. The headlong chase finally stopped at the bridge [over the Dnepr] where anti-aircraft guns were positioned and shot up some of them.
>
> An anti-tank gun near us shot up eight, the other jammed just as the tanks passed it. The gun commander wept with frustration.
>
> Gradually, things calmed down. Our nerves relaxed and the men pushed their steel helmets back. On the wide plain were 30 tanks, ablaze. We could see over 60 just from where we were, knocked out yesterday and today![3]

It isn't clear what new model of tanks the Germans believed they had encountered. Whilst the German claims that over the previous two days they had destroyed 64 Soviet tanks and disabled another 12 may be exaggerated, there was no doubt that XIX Tank Corps had suffered heavy losses, and several days of relative calm followed. During this pause, news arrived of a new Red Army bridgehead across the Dnepr between Nikopol and Zaporozhye, and Edelsheim sent a battlegroup commanded by Oberst Gustav-Adolf von Nostitz-Wallwitz to try to drive the Soviet troops back; if this new bridgehead were permitted to develop, the Red

Army would be in a position to advance south along the west bank of the Dnepr and cut off the Nikopol bridgehead. As was frequently the case, the Soviet troops had wasted no time in bringing forward anti-tank guns and these, combined with well-positioned minefields, brought Nostitz-Wallwitz's attack to a halt.

On 19 December, Tolbukhin's troops attacked again, this time to the east of the Beloserka gorge, and advanced swiftly towards Dneprovka. The former *Kampfgruppe Heyden* had been disbanded to create the group led by Nostitz-Wallwitz and a second group under Oberst Walter Palm; this latter group was the first to move against the new Soviet attack, using a small group of assault guns to drive back the T-34s that had accompanied the attack. The other two battlegroups arrived during the afternoon and, late the following night, mounted a powerful counterattack to restore the front line. The personnel of the panzer division spent Christmas Eve and Christmas Day in the field; some units had erected small Christmas trees and a few men gathered around them to sing carols or to hear a Christmas address from their commanders, but a bitterly cold wind was blowing over a landscape covered with fresh snow and most men took shelter in their vehicles or bunkers. On 25 December, the Soviet XIX Tank Corps launched another attack close to where the previous attack had been beaten back; this latest attack also failed with further losses, including two T-34s that were captured intact. Although 24th Panzer Division's history, written by a former officer of the division, describes these as the more powerful T-34/85 – a T-34 chassis with a larger turret mounting the more powerful 85mm gun – this claim is unlikely, as the first of the new T-34/85s had only just left their factories and had been given to units that were still undergoing training with them; the new tanks wouldn't see action until the first months of 1944.[4]

The final attempts by 4th Ukrainian Front to penetrate into the Nikopol bridgehead during 1943 came on New Year's Eve, with attacks against the northern sector. These attacks too were repulsed in heavy fighting and the front line remained almost unchanged. Nikopol and its manganese mines remained in German hands, though the bridgehead was increasingly isolated. Its long-term survival would depend more upon events elsewhere than the futile assaults of Tolbukhin's troops, which merely added to the already enormous butcher's bill of dead and wounded. But the pressure upon the Nikopol bridgehead – and perhaps more importantly, the diversion of German forces to deal with the crises to the west of Kiev – meant that Hitler's cherished plan to inflict a major defeat upon the Red Army with a thrust to the southeast from Nikopol, which would also restore contact with the German Seventeenth Army in the Crimea, was never put into effect.

In almost every battle across the Ukraine – indeed, in almost every battle of the Second World War – the Red Army suffered higher losses than the Wehrmacht, and German hopes that the Soviet Union might finally run out of manpower were not entirely without foundation. In an attempt to stop the strength of front-line units falling too far, it was common practice for *Voenkomats* – an abbreviation of *Voennyi Komissaryat* or 'military commissariat' – to draft men found in the liberated areas into the ranks of the army. As these men had been under German rule for a period of time, the authorities regarded them with suspicion until they proved themselves to be loyal. Isaak Kobylyanskiy, whose 87th Guards Rifle Division had been pulled out of the front line prior to the fighting around the Nikopol bridgehead in order to recover its strength, described one such individual in a draft assigned to his battery:

The youngest among them was Slava (the nickname of Vyacheslav) Tsybulskiy. He was just 18 years old (some were in their mid-40s). His blond hair, blue eyes, athletic build, and neat appearance prompted positive feelings at first sight. I remember him as he just arrived at the battery wearing an old but clean military blouse, boots with black leg wrappings, and a field cap perched dashingly on his head … Everybody felt that the newcomer wanted to please his future commander.

I persistently asked the battery commander to place Tsybulskiy in my platoon, but Slava was made a telephone operator in the fire control and reconnaissance platoon. Over the next few days, we had a few short fights with the Germans who were retreating towards the lower Dnepr. As everybody supposed, Tsybulskiy proved himself to be a diligent, smart, and quite bold warrior. Soon we entered Tsyurupinsk, and for several days Slava was at the OP on the bank of the Dnepr.

One day, Tsybulskiy was sent back to Tsyurupinsk, where our battery rear services were located. Unexpectedly, Slava didn't return. The next morning, we found out that the chief of the regimental SMERSH [military counter-intelligence] group, Major Vignanker, had arrested him.

It turned out that in fact Tsybulskiy was a native of Tsyurupinsk. When the Germans came he served as a local policeman under them and was remarkable for his special devotion to the new rulers. Tsyburskiy headed the search for local Jews who were hiding from the Germans and the police. He personally escorted 70 poor Jewish old men, women and children to the place where they were to be shot, and actively took part in the executions. But by late September 1943, when the Soviet forces reached the Molochnaya River, Tsyburskiy realised that he had to disappear from Tsyurupinsk, where everybody knew of his monstrous crimes.

In due time he fled the town toward the northeast, as far as 250km [150 miles] away from Tsyurupinsk. Only there did Tsybulskiy present himself to the local *Voenkomat*. He was assigned to our division at the time when we were advancing on a westerly path. If our division had not been redirected toward the mouth of the Dnepr, Tsybulskiy would hardly have been unmasked … As soon as he reappeared in the town, some neighbours recognised him. In a few days after the arrest an open trial took place in the town. Many bore witness against Tsybulskiy. The sentence was death by hanging. He was executed in a small square in the centre of Tsyurupinsk.[5]

Not long after, when his 87th Guards Rifle Division celebrated the New Year, Kobylyanskiy witnessed an address by the division commander, Colonel Kirill Iakovlevich Tymchik, that further highlighted the impact of high casualties amongst Red Army units, particularly when experienced men were lost:

I would like to begin my toast by reminding you, comrade officers, of some well-known facts. One can restore a half-ruined hut within a few weeks. And it is possible to build a new apartment building within a year. Moreover, it takes about three years to rebuild a big factory or plant. However, a new man, who would be a skilled builder or a good defender of the motherland, could appear no earlier than in some 20 years.

Because of that I want you and I order you, comrade officers, to remember these facts and to always avoid the unnecessary expenditure of your soldiers' lives.[6]

Whilst Tymchik might have exhorted his men to avoid unnecessary losses, other Soviet commanders showed far less concern. Right up to the end of the war, senior commanders frequently used a callous form of slang when talking about casualties, asking each other how many matches they had burned, or how many pencils they had broken.[7]

But despite its terrible casualties, the Red Army proved to be remarkably resilient. Rotmistrov's Fifth Guards Tank Army had suffered heavy losses in the Kursk salient, yet just a month later it took part in the fighting near Kharkov, where once more it sustained serious damage. Then, when the Red Army burst across the Dnepr towards Krivoy Rog, the rebuilt Fifth Guards Tank Army was once more in the fore of the attack. The ability of the Red Army to recover from the heavy casualties inflicted upon its units undermined the Wehrmacht's strategy of trying to grind down its opponent, as Manstein was forced to acknowledge:

The extraordinary organisational performance in bringing in fresh reserves, and expanding war production, had not been expected by us. We were faced with a hydra that immediately would grow two new heads after one decapitation.[8]

Zhukov and Stalin remained concerned that the German armoured forces that had attacked Vatutin's armies in the fighting at Zhitomir and to the north might still be used in an attempt to recapture Kiev. In order to eliminate any such threat, Zhukov ordered Vatutin to prepare for a fresh attack towards Zhitomir and Berdichev. The forces that Balck had tried to destroy at Meleni had been concentrating as part of the preparations for this new offensive, which Zhukov hoped would throw the Wehrmacht back to the line of the River Bug. In a remarkably short time, replenished Soviet units – albeit not necessarily at full strength – began to assemble for a new attack.

Once again, Vatutin had powerful forces at his disposal: the operation would be mounted by First Guards, Eighteenth and Thirty-Eighth Armies, with First and Third Guards Tank Armies as the main strike force. Once the assault on Zhitomir and Berdichev had gathered momentum – and, crucially, had drawn in the German reserves – Sixtieth Army would join the attack on its northern flank; for this mission, it was assigned two tank corps and a cavalry corps, though these suffered heavy losses during Balck's attempts to take Meleni. Katukov's First Guards Tank Army had been in reserve for a few weeks and was rested and confident. With about 600 tanks and self-propelled guns of various sorts, it alone was stronger than the combined strength of all the panzer divisions in the sector and after it was assigned to Vatutin's front, its units began to form up immediately west of Kiev towards the end of November – further evidence that had Balck been permitted to mount an early attack towards Kiev, he would rapidly have faced overwhelming numbers. Katukov and his staff did what they could to blend their veterans with the new replacement drafts that had been used to bring the army up to full strength:

Usually, we selected tank crews in such a way that each crew had one or two experienced men. We tried to ensure that during training exercises, all of these people who didn't know each other developed good communications so that any of them could replace a comrade who was unable to continue at a critical moment. In short, we tried to turn each crew into a small but friendly team. It was difficult, painstaking work. We gave it our complete attention.[9]

Dispatched to reinforce Moskalenko's Thirty-Eighth Army, Katukov deployed his forces in two echelons. He planned to attack with VIII Guards Mechanised

Corps on the left and XI Guards Tank Corps on the right, with XXXI Tank Corps in reserve. Aware that there were several panzer divisions in the area – prisoner interrogation had revealed the presence of 19th and 25th Panzer Divisions immediately in front of Third Guards Tank Army, and there was a strong likelihood of Balck's XLVIII Panzer Corps being directed to the area – Katukov spent the eve of the battle conducting a map exercise with his headquarters staff. Colonel Alexei Mikhailovich Sobolev, the head of the division's intelligence department, played the part of the German command, and after analysing possible German countermeasures and counterattacks, Katukov issued fresh orders for the protection of the flanks of his army.

Moskalenko's army had received fresh drafts to try to bring its infantry divisions back to something approaching full strength, but of the 18,000 men who were added to Thirty-Eighth Army, most were men who had been impressed into the Red Army from the newly liberated areas, and had little or no military training. Despite these drafts, it is a measure of the Red Army's losses that Moskalenko's divisions remained weak. He reported to Zhukov that the divisions of LXXIV Rifle Corps had about 6,900 men each, but XXI Rifle Corps and XVII Guards Rifle Corps were in a far weaker state with between 4,500 and 6,000 men per division. Supply problems were also becoming serious; only 60 per cent of Moskalenko's men had received winter uniforms and shortages of boots were causing problems.[10] In an attempt to improve the chances of success, Moskalenko concentrated his artillery support on the right flank of his army, which was expected to make the main effort.

Energetic reconnaissance probes were made on 22 and 23 December and revealed that the local German forces were weak in infantry, and therefore greatly dependent upon mobile units to restore the front line in the event of a Soviet attack. Despite German attention being concentrated to the north, where Balck's XLVIII Panzer Corps tried to close its planned encirclement at Meleni, the build-up of Soviet forces – admittedly carried out mainly at night if possible – and the reconnaissance attacks couldn't fail to be recognised as the precursors of a new offensive, though it was not clear precisely where the blow would fall. Nevertheless, Raus issued orders on 22 December to the panzer divisions along the southern sector of Fourth Panzer Army to concentrate their forces in anticipation of their being needed for counterattacks. Early on 24 December, Moskalenko's artillery signalled the start of the new attack:

The silence of the December morning was suddenly shattered by a volley from the Guards mortar units. Ahead, where the enemy's positions were, the ground heaved with powerful explosions. The rumbles of detonations did not die down as our artillery roared.

This was how the eve of the third and last Christmas in Soviet territory began for the Hitlerites. On the first occasion in 1941, the Soviet armed forces ruined the invaders' festivities, smashing them near Moscow. The Nazis experienced the second Christmas in the encirclement in Stalingrad, dreaming in vain of escaping from the ring of our troops. And now, in December 1943, the Red Army once again assaulted them. But they had nobody to blame but themselves. Uninvited, they brought grief to the Soviet people and unprecedented suffering. But the hour of reckoning had come and it was time for the cruel enemy to receive vengeance in full.[11]

Some of the preliminary bombardments in the fighting in the Ukraine in 1943 had only a modest effect on German defences, but on this occasion – benefiting from the reconnaissance probes that had identified the main defensive positions – the outcome was rather more impressive. When they moved forward, Moskalenko's troops advanced at a steady rate of between one and two miles per hour and encountered little resistance until they reached a line from Brusilov to Turbovka. Here, they ran into counterattacks by battlegroups from 19th and 25th Panzer Divisions, both now functioning under the command of Nehring's XXIV Panzer Corps, but rapidly beat them off. It had been Moskalenko's intention to seize Brusilov before the end of the first day but the leading elements only reached the outskirts as darkness fell. As the Soviet reconnaissance patrols had discovered, XXIV Panzer Corps was weak in infantry and the two panzer divisions under its command were themselves far from full strength. One of 19th Panzer Division's battalions found itself encircled by the advancing Soviet forces near Lasarevka and was rescued by a counterattack led by Generalmajor Hans Källner, the division commander. Elements of the division pulled back to the edge of Brusilov. Here, there was a moment for the retreating men to catch their breath:

A small Christmas tree stood in the corner of the regimental command post. Someone stuck some candles on it. That was when we first realised that it was Christmas Eve. For a few minutes, while the candles burned, it was quiet. Soaked, sweaty, and shivering, the men – officers, NCOs and soldiers – sat and gave thanks. The door opened. General Källner entered. He also got caught up in the atmosphere for a moment, torn by the powerful breath of nostalgia ...

The general described the overall situation in broad outline. The enemy had achieved a deep breakthrough into the southern neighbour [25th Panzer Division] and was advancing further to the north. Brusilov was no longer [to be] held. Therefore, the division was to set out for Kabachin in the early morning.

There, on 25 December, we occupied a hedgehog defence. The snow was changing to rain. The vehicles often got stuck in the mud.[12]

Anxious to avoid falling behind his timetable, Moskalenko ordered an attack on Brusilov late on 24 December and the town was captured with barely a fight before dawn on Christmas Day. Throughout the day, the Soviet advance seemed to gain speed, but although Katukov later wrote that his army swiftly pressed forward against an increasingly ragged German defensive line, Moskalenko wrote that First Guards Tank Army was slow to advance and it was only after Vatutin intervened on Christmas Day that significant progress was made by the tanks.[13] There is perhaps a clue in this discrepancy in Katukov's account; he describes how he lost his temper with a staff officer who was painstakingly drawing up detailed maps and orders, something that Katukov regarded as a waste of time when the enemy was showing so little resistance.[14] On 26 December, First Guards Tank Army captured the town of Popilnya, roughly midway between Zhitomir and Bila Tserkva. Here, they were surprised when Ukrainian civilians, mainly women, burst from several trains in the railway yards and embraced the tank crews as liberators:

It transpired that five trains had been filled with 'cheap labour' in Popilnya railway station ready for dispatch to Germany, as well as several trains loaded with cattle. Just as the wagons with the 'slaves' were opened, a German train arrived at the station. The tank crews quickly disarmed the [German] guards. In the train wagons were Christmas presents for fascist soldiers – chocolate, wine, warm underwear, sweaters, and mittens. Judging by the labels on clothing and food products, the Hitlerite command gave its soldiers material looted from the enslaved countries of Western Europe.[15]

Immediately to the north of Nehring's XXIV Panzer Corps was what remained of 8th Panzer Division. It was involved in heavy fighting on the first day of the Soviet attack and like its neighbours to the south it lacked the strength for a prolonged struggle, pulling back to avoid complete destruction. On Christmas Day, there was the first bit of good news for the German defenders. Balck had already called off further attempts to destroy the Soviet forces at Meleni and Raus now ordered him to proceed with all speed to launch a counterattack into the northern flank of the Soviet thrust towards Zhitomir and Berdichev. In order to increase the forces at his disposal, Balck was to take control of 8th Panzer Division in addition to his other formations. Accompanied by Mellenthin, he arrived in Zhitomir on Christmas Day to find the town full of rear area units desperately making preparations to withdraw to the west. A local SS training unit had been reorganised to provide a small number of infantry companies, and additionally a new formation – the recently created 18th Artillery Division – had been ordered to join the defenders of Zhitomir; for the moment, the columns of guns and their ammunition trucks merely choked the already congested roads.

Even as they arrived, Balck and Mellenthin found themselves faced with an immediate crisis. After pulling back from Brusilov, 19th Panzer Division had been surrounded by the advancing Soviet troops, as had elements of 8th Panzer Division a little to the north. Balck ordered the two divisions to pull back towards the west, aiming to link up with *LSSAH*, which he had ordered to take up positions to the south of Zhitomir. The SS division had been heavily involved in the fighting further north but remained a formidable force and had received a fresh draft of replacement personnel, who had been assigned to the panzergrenadier regiments to restore their strength. At the same time that *LSSAH* deployed south of Zhitomir, 1st Panzer Division was to secure positions to the east of Zhitomir to stop any direct advance towards the town. During the morning of 25 December, XLVIII Panzer Corps headquarters received a despairing signal from 19th Panzer Division: its survivors were under heavy attack and had run out of fuel. Silence followed. There were discussions about what to do, with many calling for the elements of *LSSAH* that had arrived to be thrown into an attack to try to rescue the survivors of 19th Panzer Division, but Balck refused. Whilst failing to launch a relieving attack might result in 19th Panzer Division being lost, Balck feared the possible loss of much of *LSSAH* if it were sent into action before it could concentrate its strength. There was immense relief when, towards the evening, another signal was received: 19th Panzer Division was still intact, and was withdrawing 'in tolerable order'.[16]

The depleted forces of 8th Panzer Division had been organised into a battlegroup commanded by Major Berndt von Mitzlaff, with added support provided by the SS companies from the training unit in Zhitomir. A second battlegroup was led by Oberst Joseph von Radowitz, and elements of the division's reconnaissance battalion had been sent earlier to help 19th Panzer Division. These elements were now missing, and the rest of the division waited anxiously for news. Prior to the new Soviet assault, 8th Panzer Division's northern neighbour was *SS-Das Reich*, which like all German formations was badly weakened – in the four months from the beginning of August, the division had lost over 7,400 men killed, wounded or missing and replacements fell far short of this figure.[17] As a result of these losses, the division was reorganised on 17 December as *Panzer-Kampfgruppe Das Reich*. Krüger left the division a few days later and was replaced temporarily as commander by Obersturmbannführer Peter Sommer, the division's chief of staff. Sommer was a former army officer who had transferred to the SS earlier in 1943; he was a very unusual person to serve in the SS, as he was partly Jewish. The division was in the process of being pulled out of the front line and sent back to East Prussia when Vatutin's attack began, and it was decided that too many elements of the division had already left for it to return to the front line. Despite its absence, the direct Soviet advance on Zhitomir made only slow progress.

The first elements of *LSSAH* – mainly its reconnaissance battalion – arrived from the north in Zhitomir on Christmas Day and almost immediately went into action to deal with the nearest Soviet spearheads at Ivnytsya, about 15 miles (25km) east of Zhitomir. The small town lay on a railway line running from Zhitomir to Fastov and a German armoured train was assigned to help recapture Ivnytsya. The following day, even as this attack was being organised, other elements of *LSSAH* that were deploying to the south of Zhitomir encountered repeated Soviet attempts to take Volytsya, just six miles (10km) south of Zhitomir and astride the Zhitomir-Berdichev road. Ivnytsya was recaptured early in the afternoon. But when elements of the SS division probed further east, they were put to flight by another Soviet tank attack; the commander of one of the division's panzergrenadier battalions commented that the new drafts showed little resilience if they weren't supported by friendly tanks.[18] Nevertheless, there was some welcome news: one of the units of *LSSAH*, deployed immediately to the east of Zhitomir, made contact with what remained of 19th Panzer Division and the accompanying *Kampfgruppe von Radowitz*. After being bypassed by Soviet troops and nearly overwhelmed, the German troops had regrouped and withdrawn westward along small roads through the dense woodland in the area.

Meanwhile, 1st Panzer Division had been deploying to the east and northeast of Zhitomir. Balck hoped that once it had concentrated its forces, he would be able to use it in a powerful thrust towards the south, into the flank of the Soviet forces that were advancing on Zhitomir and Berdichev. The deployment of the division's forces was hindered more by the congestion of the roads with retreating German rear area units and civilians fleeing the fighting than by the Red Army. On Christmas Day, a probe eastward along the road to Kiev made contact with

8th Panzer Division's *Kampfgruppe von Mitzlaff*. Reinforced by a handful of Tiger tanks from *LSSAH*, the division beat off a group of Soviet tanks immediately north of the Zhitomir-Kiev road on 26 December, but attempts to launch a counterattack failed when they ran into a well-organised defensive line of anti-tank guns; this was precisely the German counterattack that Katukov had rehearsed with his staff, and for which he had ordered precautionary measures. Throughout the day, Krüger, the commander of 1st Panzer Division, tried in vain to start the attack towards the south and southeast, but by the end of the day it was all that his units could do to beat off the increasingly heavy Soviet attacks.

By the end of 26 December, 1st Panzer Division was approaching the end of its strength. It had suffered considerable losses both from enemy action and breakdowns during the fighting further north and had then intervened east of Zhitomir without a break; its panzergrenadier battalions were reduced to barely 100 men each and it had only four Panther tanks still running. Only its artillery regiment remained at anything approaching full strength and its heavy fire repeatedly brought Soviet attacks to a standstill. Throughout 27 December, Balck and Mellenthin awaited a fresh onslaught by the Red Army on Zhitomir, but to their surprise no significant attacks developed. In their memoirs, Balck and Mellenthin attributed this to the damage inflicted upon the advancing Soviet forces by 8th and 19th Panzer Divisions as they retreated, or caution once the Red Army became aware that XLVIII Panzer Corps was in the area, or perhaps the crushing firepower of 18th Artillery Division. The Soviet accounts are almost silent, merely mentioning that German resistance in the Zhitomir area was strengthening and that the advance on the town was left to Eighteenth Army while the main drive towards the southwest continued. By the end of 27 December, *LSSAH* had been forced to take up a defensive line extending some 21 miles (35km); its tank strength had shrunk to just five Tigers, 13 Panthers, 11 Pz.IVs, and 12 assault guns.[19] Early on 28 December, these few tanks were thrown into a flanking attack against a Soviet thrust and claimed the destruction of about half of the T-34s that had tried to advance across the Huiya River to the southeast of Zhitomir. Katukov later wrote that the main impediment to his advance was a shortage of fuel, worsened by the poor state of the roads, but on 28 December VIII Guards Mechanised Corps, on the left flank of Katukov's army, approached Kozyatyn, about 18 miles (30km) southeast of Berdichev. A small raiding group managed to penetrate the defences of the German 20th Panzergrenadier Division by circling around to the east of the town rather than attacking it directly from the north and a regiment of T-34s attacked during the night, driving along the railway line from the northwest with their lights on; the defenders apparently mistook the approaching column for a train until it was too late. By dawn on 29 December, the town was in Soviet hands. The troops who had advanced along the railway found a train of wagons in the station; when they opened the wagons, they found that they were full of prisoners of war captured by the Germans in previous battles.[20]

Lacking the strength to counterattack the Soviet forces, Balck had no choice but to pull back to a shorter line. Fortunately for the Germans, Vatutin's armies had suffered considerable losses and were unable to maintain the weight and momentum of their attacks. Nevertheless, Korosten fell to the Red Army on 29 December and Zhitomir was abandoned on the last day of 1943. In both Berdichev and Bila Tserkva, there were clashes between German rearguards and Soviet troops, but both towns fell that day.

Both sides later claimed the fighting as a victory. The German narrative, largely written by Balck and Mellenthin, was that after successfully defeating the first Soviet attempt to take Zhitomir in November, XLVIII Panzer Corps did a great deal of damage to Soviet units to the north of Zhitomir and repaired much of Fourth Panzer Army's front before turning south and stopping the renewed Soviet attack towards the southwest. The Soviet account highlighted that Zhitomir was recaptured and two panzer divisions effectively knocked out, and the front line was moved further away from Kiev, ending any possible threat of a German attack to recapture the Ukrainian capital. Whilst Balck might have thought that such an operation was possible in early November, it seems that there was no serious intention by the Germans to mount such an attack. It should be remembered that the operational orders issued by *Stavka* in mid-December called for an advance that would extend far to the west, perhaps reaching the River Bug, and such an advance was clearly not achieved, but the situation remained hugely in the Red Army's favour.

CHAPTER 11

A YEAR OF DECISION

At the beginning of 1943, German troops were besieged in Stalingrad and considerable German forces remained east of the Donets, albeit retreating towards the river. By the end of the year, the front line had moved far to the west, reaching and crossing the Dnepr. In some locations near Zhitomir, the Red Army had reached the 1939 frontier with Poland. Huge numbers of men had died or been wounded on both sides, and although the Wehrmacht remained a formidable force, there was a growing feeling on both sides that the end was getting closer.

From the moment that he took command of Army Group Don, Manstein was worried by the threat of a Soviet attack against the northern flank of his army group, which might result in all of his armies being pressed south and destroyed on the coasts of the Sea of Azov and the Black Sea. Although he had successfully avoided such a disaster, the year ended with the same threat hanging over his forces, albeit further to the west. There were still substantial gaps in the northern flank of Fourth Panzer Army and contact with Army Group Centre remained tenuous; if the Red Army were able to exploit this weakness in early 1944, a war-winning victory might be within its grasp. The previous winter, fighting drew to a close with the onset of the spring thaw and with the Wehrmacht – revived by a major transfusion of troops from the west – in the ascendant once more. In contrast, German forces barely survived in 1943 despite the arrival of more troops from elsewhere, and the initiative remained firmly with the Red Army.

Throughout the crisis that followed the encirclement of Sixth Army in Stalingrad, Manstein wanted to pull back the southern flank of his command in order to release units that could then be used to shore up the northern flank. On every occasion that he proposed such a move, Hitler objected on the grounds that

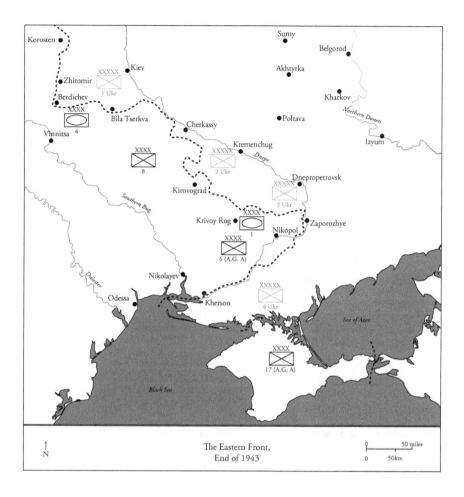

The Eastern Front,
End of 1943

0   50 miles
0   50km

the loss of terrain would be disastrous: it was vital to ensure a foothold on the lower Don so that a future attack towards the Caucasus could be launched; Germany needed the coal and minerals of the Donbas; the Nikopol area's manganese reserves were vital for the German war effort; and the loss of ground might have a disastrous political effect on Germany's Balkan allies and on Turkey. Such considerations paid no regard to the military reality on the ground. At the end of the year, these arguments between Army Group South and Hitler continued, with the Führer insisting that Nikopol should be held. Whilst the German troops tied down in the bridgehead were relatively modest, the bridgehead lay far further east than Manstein regarded as safe. Even at the cost of losing any possibility of restoring contact with Seventeenth Army in the Crimea, Manstein could see no alternative to abandoning the Dnepr bend and pulling back to a shorter line, and using the units that would be released to shore up his northern flank.

Relations between Manstein and Hitler deteriorated steadily through the second half of 1943. From the outset, Hitler had mixed feelings about his subordinate; he rightly held the field marshal in high regard for his operational skills, but was also aware that he couldn't exert influence over Manstein in the manner that he dominated other senior officers. Manstein's constant demands for a reorganisation of higher commands on the Eastern Front, with a single personality – and inevitably, this would be Manstein himself – in overall command led to growing resentment, with many of Hitler's entourage encouraging the Führer to believe that Manstein was more interested in personal glory than in serving Hitler. By the end of the year, a final breach between the two men was close, but still several weeks away.

The year had seen the much-delayed advent of new German tanks. The Panther had been intended to enter service in 1942 but first saw action in any significant numbers in the Battle of Kursk, and whilst Tiger tanks had been in action in 1942, they were now present in far larger numbers. Hitler had placed great reliance on these new tanks, repeatedly assuring those around him – both civilians and military figures – that the technical superiority of the Tigers and Panthers would greatly offset the numerical superiority of the Red Army. The reality was that the Panther remained an unreliable tank, with operational strength of front-line units declining rapidly from breakdowns once battle commenced. The Tiger was perhaps a more mechanically reliable vehicle but its size and weight limited its usefulness – most Ukrainian bridges were unable to bear its weight. In any event, it wasn't available in sufficient numbers to turn the tide in favour of the Wehrmacht. By the end of 1943, several panzer divisions had dispatched a battalion each back to Germany to be re-equipped with Panthers and Hitler continued to hope that once these battalions returned to combat, superior German technology would turn the tide; the commanders in the front line had no such illusions.

The Red Army started 1943 hoping to finish off the Wehrmacht in the wake of the encirclement of Stalingrad and had to endure a bitter lesson in the operational art when Manstein counterattacked in March and dashed Soviet hopes of a rapid victory. Throughout the preparations for the summer fighting around Kursk, Stalin repeatedly questioned whether the Soviet defences would be able to stop the imminent German attack; the assurances of Zhukov and others proved to be entirely correct, and despite suffering severe losses, the Red

Army defeated the last major German offensive operation on the Eastern Front. Thereafter, the speed with which Soviet units recovered from their losses and the huge resources of the Soviet Union allowed the Red Army to sustain a high tempo of operations. The additional help received from the United States and Britain was substantial; by mid-1943, the United States had sent 183,000 trucks to the Soviet Union, a figure that exceeded the entire production of trucks by Germany during the same period.[1] Although it avoided any major defeats on the scale of Stalingrad, the Wehrmacht could do little to stop the Red Army and was steadily driven west. Even more importantly, its strength haemorrhaged away at an irreplaceable rate, both in terms of men and the experienced cadres that had held it together in earlier campaigns. As Kobylyanskiy's division commander had stressed, replacing inanimate equipment was a relatively easy achievement – replacing troops, particularly seasoned veterans, was quite a different matter.

Total losses for the German armed forces on the Eastern Front in 1943 came to about 1,889,000 killed, wounded or missing – with wounded in this context being men who were unable to return to the front. Soviet losses were far higher, at about 8,145,000 – a ratio of about 4.3 Soviet soldiers for every German soldier.[2] This period covers the loss of the German Sixth Army in Stalingrad and the fighting in the Kursk salient, but throughout the year the Red Army continued to take far heavier losses than the Germans. After the annexation of neighbouring territories, the population of Germany was about 89.6 million people; these casualties therefore represent about 2.1 per cent of the total population. The population of the Soviet Union in 1941 was about 196.7 million people, and the casualties of 1943 represent about 4.1 per cent of the pre-war population. However, large numbers of Soviet citizens had died in 1941 and 1942, as a result of the fighting, starvation, and mass killings in the occupied territories; furthermore, the populations of areas like the Baltic States, Belarus and much of the Ukraine remained in German control, so the losses of the Red Army were a far greater proportion of the available population. There was therefore some basis for the hopes of Hitler and Manstein that the Soviet Union might be ground down by attrition, but as the year drew to a close there were no signs that Germany's foe was growing tired of the struggle. If anything, the growing evidence of German atrocities merely increased the desire for retribution on the hated Hitlerites. Such raw statistics also fail to take account of the manner in which the two opponents mobilised their resources for war. Even at this stage of the conflict, there were fewer German women working in roles that would release men for military service than had been the case in the First World War; by contrast, women formed a large proportion of the Soviet Union's industrial and agricultural manpower. For the moment at least, the Soviet Union could afford its higher losses.

The difference in losses of armoured vehicles was also considerable; the Wehrmacht lost 8,992 tanks and assault guns during the year, compared with 22,400 lost by the Soviet Union.[3] During the same period German industry produced 10,700 new vehicles, while Soviet factories turned out 27,300. In addition, nearly five million tons of military equipment – tanks, guns, aircraft and ammunition – arrived from the United States and Britain.[4] During the war, almost all new railway equipment in the Soviet Union came from the United States, and the importance of railways during the fighting for movement of reserves and supplies cannot be overstated. The bare figures suggest that the size of Germany's armoured forces actually increased during the year, but this ignores the loss of experienced crews. German military production was also running at an unsustainable level. Speer was able to increase the numbers of tanks, guns and planes being built, but reserve stocks of metals for steel alloys were running low. Hitler may have been obsessed with the importance of Nikopol's manganese mines, but tungsten – required for hardened anti-tank ammunition – was in far shorter supply.

The fighting in the Ukraine after the end of *Zitadelle* featured attacks on the German positions on the Mius and Donets, but the key battles were on the northern flank of Army Group South, just as Manstein had repeatedly feared. The first offensive – Operation *Polkovodets Rumyantsev* – tore a substantial hole in the front line between Fourth Panzer Army and *Armee Abteilung Kempf*, but every attempt by Vatutin to exploit this breakthrough was thwarted by German defensive measures. Critically, the shoulders of the breakthrough held firm and it was not possible for the Soviet tank armies to roll up the German front in either direction. The rate at which Soviet tank strength declined was alarming: Vatutin's Voronezh Front started the battle with nearly 2,000 tanks and self-propelled guns, but before the end of August the tank armies were almost completely exhausted and could barely scrape together a few dozen vehicles.[5] Nevertheless, the battles around and to the west of Kharkov had a major impact on the rest of the year. Several German armoured formations – particularly *Grossdeutschland*, 3rd, 6th and 11th Panzer Divisions, and *SS-Das Reich* and *SS-Totenkopf* – suffered heavy losses. At no point in the rest of the year would their strength approach the levels they had at the end of *Zitadelle*, which greatly reduced their capability to conduct anything more than delaying operations during the withdrawal to and beyond the Dnepr.

The repeated failure of armoured formations to achieve decisive breakthroughs was a recurrent feature of the fighting of 1943, from Kursk to the end of the year.

It has been suggested that this represents an end of the era of Blitzkrieg, but such conclusions are surely incorrect.[6] German successes in earlier years – and the successful attacks made by the Red Army against German and allied armies on the Don in the winter of 1942–43 – were characterised by a marked inequality between attackers and defenders, particularly in terms of armour and anti-tank capabilities. Furthermore, when breakthroughs were achieved in earlier years, exploitation was hugely aided by the defenders having few or no mobile reserves with which they could intercept the units that had broken through the front line. Additionally, in the case of the Wehrmacht, close cooperation between the Luftwaffe and ground forces contributed greatly to the destruction of what defences could be organised. During the fighting in the Ukraine in the second half of 1943, there were few if any occasions where either side achieved advantages in terms of force ratios when mounting an attack. Although Vatutin succeeded in creating a substantial gap between Fourth Panzer Army and *Armee Abteilung Kempf* in August, and by the end of the year Fourth Panzer Army's lines had several gaps in addition to the breach between Army Group South and Army Group Centre, exploitation of these gaps proved to be impossible for several reasons. There were insufficient armoured reserves available; the terrain was often suited for defence, allowing modest forces to hold up Soviet attacks; and in contrast to the situation in late 1942, Manstein had several panzer divisions available which could be dispatched to crisis points. Although aircraft from both sides intervened repeatedly in the fighting on land, neither side was able to establish lasting air superiority, though the balance steadily shifted against the Germans as the year progressed. In addition, the Red Army greatly improved its ability to defend against German armoured attacks. The lessons of previous battles had been thoroughly analysed and learned, and it was now routine for Soviet units to deploy powerful anti-tank units almost immediately after they gained ground, so that any German counterattack would run into tough defences.

One of the critical moments of the year was the decision by Stalin on how to proceed after the recapture of Kharkov. Zhukov wanted to pause and regroup before launching a thrust towards the lower Dnepr from the newly recaptured region in order to trap much of Army Group South against the coasts of the Sea of Azov and the Black Sea, but Stalin wished to attack without delay in order to prevent the Germans from destroying infrastructure, and also to deny the Wehrmacht any opportunity to catch its breath. The consequence of this decision was the terrible casualties suffered by the Red Army, and it is at least arguable that had Zhukov been permitted to carry out his planned operation, overall losses might have been lower; in addition, had Hitler refused permission for a timely retreat, there would have been at least a possibility, if not a probability, of trapping and destroying significant German forces before they could withdraw to the Dnepr. Such a Soviet operation would have been largely what Manstein had expected and feared but it would also have created the circumstances in which his oft-repeated desire for a 'backhand blow' – permitting the Red Army to strike towards the southwest and then launching a powerful counteroffensive from the middle Dnepr towards the southeast, into the rear and flank of the Soviet thrust – could be put into effect. Whether the Red Army could have reached the lower Dnepr with such a thrust, whether the Wehrmacht could have gathered sufficient resources to make such a counterthrust, and whether the Soviet forces could then have beaten off Manstein's counterthrust remain questions that will never be answered. Instead of an operation that carried a high degree of risk for both sides, but also created a possibility of a second Stalingrad – which might have proved fatal for the Wehrmacht – Stalin opted for the bloody frontal attacks that drove the Germans back to and over the Dnepr.

The ability of the Red Army to learn and improve through the war stands out in contrast to the Wehrmacht. Soviet doctrine, training and planning constantly attempted to learn from previous successes and failures, resulting in a steady improvement in performance. By contrast, official German doctrine barely changed, with adaptation to changing circumstances owing more to local arrangements and the experiences of a diminishing number of battle-hardened officers and NCOs than to any formalised attempt to assess and learn from events. It is arguable that the pressure upon the Wehrmacht left little time or opportunity to reflect on events and to learn from them, but the tone that was set from the highest level was critical. In 1941 and 1942, Stalin pressed his subordinates to explain why events had gone badly for the Red Army. By contrast, Hitler simply berated his subordinates for failing to show adequate resolve and determination. The only significant German innovations in terms of unit structure came in the form of the independent Tiger battalions, a number of independent Panther battalions, and the creation of the new artillery divisions. Whilst the first of these proved their worth on many occasions, the Panther battalions might arguably have been better used to bring existing panzer divisions up to strength, and the artillery divisions were a disappointment. Balck used the firepower of 18th Artillery Division to good effect in the defence of Zhitomir, but he was not impressed by the new formation:

> An artillery division was an absurdity that was established out of valuable army-
> level artillery units. If this unit had been committed to reinforce troop artillery

units, it could have had a decisive influence on the battle. As a division it had an independent combat mission that it could not accomplish, and it was doomed to fail. Reconstituted, the division reappeared later in Galicia. Now – interestingly enough – it was reinforced with an assault gun battalion, and as a result the division was used as a panzer division. Once again, it failed to meet expectations and it senselessly tied up precious equipment. It was all organisational madness, and it was not only Hitler who was guilty of such nonsense.[7]

The artillery division was created when it was recognised that, in contrast to British and Soviet formations, the only corps-level artillery units that could be used to provide an additional weight of firepower, whether in defence or attack, were rocket launcher battalions. By the time that 18th Artillery Division reached the front line, the weakness of the Wehrmacht prevented it from being able to function in its intended role – with the exception of the defence of Zhitomir – and it was almost never able to concentrate its guns as planned. Balck's remarks are a little wide of the mark; artillery in front-line units was sometimes weak, but its greatest disadvantage was its relative immobility. Most infantry divisions' guns were either horse- or truck-drawn, and whilst the Red Army was unable to achieve breakthroughs on the scale of the operations that led to the encirclement of Stalingrad or the destruction of the Italian and Hungarian armies on the Don, it was able to penetrate to the artillery lines of defending German divisions and thus often captured or destroyed division-level artillery. The weakness of German division-level artillery was therefore a consequence of its relative immobility and the weakness of defending infantry units, and had the guns of 18th Artillery Division been dispersed amongst front-line units, any benefit would probably have been temporary and greatly diluted. The reality was that the Wehrmacht needed stronger infantry defences, better mobility for division-level artillery, and formations like 18th Artillery Division that could be allocated to a corps or army to provide additional firepower – but such demands were far beyond the resources of Germany in 1943. Similarly, the use of independent Panther battalions in preference to reinforcing existing panzer divisions was to some extent a response to the increasingly apparent tendency of German infantry to pull back when threatened by armour unless they were supported by German armour. The anti-tank capability of infantry divisions was far too weak for the sort of fighting that the Wehrmacht faced in 1943, and there was a need both for better tank support for the infantry as well as better replenishment of panzer divisions, but achieving both (indeed, achieving either to an adequate degree) was now beyond the capacity of Germany.

With the war clearly going against Germany, the opposing nations continued to make plans for a successful prosecution of the war, and began to discuss the shape of the future. The Casablanca Conference of January 1943 between the British, Americans and Free French led to the proclamation that the Allies would continue the war until the unconditional surrender of the Axis Powers, and a conference in Cairo in late November 1943 between the British, Americans and Chiang Kai-Shek of the Republic of China explicitly extended this policy to include Japan. Stalin was invited to attend the conference but declined to do so, as the Soviet Union was not at war with Japan at the time. Two days after the end of the Cairo Conference, the British and American delegations travelled to Tehran, where they met Stalin and the Soviet delegation.

The meeting in Tehran had been planned for several weeks. According to Soviet sources, German military intelligence had deciphered American radio signals and had learned about the planned conference. In response, the Germans planned an operation codenamed *Weitsprung* ('long jump'), which would involve local agents – including some in Turkey – acting with a special group of operatives led by Obersturmbannführer Otto Skorzeny. The intention was to assassinate Churchill, Roosevelt and Stalin. The Soviet narrative is that a Soviet agent who was posing as a German officer in the western parts of the Ukraine revealed the plot to the NKVD, and that as a result several German agents who had been parachuted into Iran were discovered and captured, resulting in the mission being aborted. On 27 November, immediately after the western delegations had arrived in Tehran, foreign minister Vyacheslav Mikhailovich Molotov informed the British and Americans of the alleged plot and suggested that the American delegation should move to either the British or Soviet embassies. Both the British and Americans were highly sceptical about the plot but Roosevelt agreed to move to the Soviet embassy.

After the war, Skorzeny denied that there had ever been any serious intention to carry out such an assassination – although it was briefly discussed, it was soon dropped as unworkable. The Soviet account is questionable as it appears most German agents in Iran had been captured earlier in the year, and it would have been very difficult for the Germans to drop groups in the Tehran area – the city was at least 1,000 miles (over 1,600km) from the nearest German airfield, at the very limit of the range of aircraft like the Focke-Wulf Condor. It seems more likely that the entire 'plot' was an attempt by Stalin to get the American delegation to move to a location where it would be easier for Soviet agents to spy on them.[8]

Lieutenant General Sergei Matveyevich Shtemenko, chief of the Operations Directorate of *Stavka*, was at the conference; Antonov, who was effectively serving as Vasilevsky's stand-in while Vasilevsky was overseeing operations in the southern Ukraine, told him to prepare for 'a journey' just four days before it began but, other than advising him to ensure that he had adequate maps of all the fronts and a cipher officer with him, did not tell him where he would be going. The following morning, Shtemenko departed Moscow by train with Voroshilov, who despite failing to prevent the encirclement of Leningrad and being saddled with the blame for the poor performance of the Red Army in Finland in 1939–40, had survived in a political role. As the journey progressed, Shtemenko met Stalin and Molotov, who were also on the train, and still not knowing where he was headed, he travelled on to Baku, where aircraft were waiting to take them onwards.[9] Regardless of the existence of German plots, Stalin consistently showed a high level of caution and secrecy in his personal movements.

The Big Three met on 28 November. The conference ultimately ended with a commitment by the British and Americans to carry out an invasion of France in the coming year; the Red Army would make a simultaneous offensive in the east in order to create an intolerable strain upon German resources. Stalin proposed that the future eastern border of Poland should lie along the 'Curzon Line', a border that had originally been proposed by the British foreign secretary George Curzon at the end of the First World War. This effectively legalised the seizure of eastern parts of Poland by the Soviet Union in 1939. Churchill and Roosevelt agreed with the proposal, and it was decided – without any consultation with the Polish government-in-exile – that in return, Poland would be granted territories seized from Germany. There was also considerable agreement that Germany would be divided into zones of occupation after the end of the war, but there were moments of tension. In a dinner on 29 November, Stalin graciously acknowledged the importance of western aid to the Soviet Union, but also suggested that it might be necessary to execute 50,000 or more German officers in order to prevent a future conflict. Roosevelt tried to treat the comment as a joke and replied that surely a smaller number, perhaps 49,000, would suffice, but Churchill was offended. Only those convicted of war crimes should face punishment, he declared, and denounced what he called 'the cold blooded execution of soldiers who fought for their country'.[10] He stormed out of the room, and only returned after Stalin sent him an envoy who assured the British prime minister that the Soviet leader had intended the comment as a jest. Churchill was doubtful of this interpretation, believing that Stalin had been testing the water to see what the reaction of the western leaders would be. It is probably relevant that at this stage of the war, both the British and

Americans were aware that the NKVD had slaughtered about 22,000 Polish officers and intelligentsia in the Katyn forest in 1940. The graves of the victims had been revealed to the world by the Germans earlier in 1943, but Stalin had insisted that the Germans had carried out the killings. The Western Allies were aware through a mixture of decoded German signals and intelligence from Polish sources that the Soviet account was probably untrue – an analysis by Owen O'Malley, the British ambassador to the Polish government-in-exile, for Churchill made clear that it was almost certain that the massacre had been carried out by the Soviet Union rather than Germany. However, in the context of the war it was expedient for the British and Americans to behave as if the Soviet Union was blameless. Nevertheless, there was thus a clear precedent for Stalin's proposed massacre of German officers at the end of the war.

The retribution meted out by the Red Army to captured Germans was often arbitrary and brutal, but like soldiers throughout history, many Soviet men rapidly overcame their rage when they took prisoners and saw that their opponents were men just like themselves, often with no particular desire to be at war with anyone. Compared to 1944 and 1945, the numbers of men captured by the Red Army were modest. By the end of the year, approximately 200,000 Germans were being held, but this takes no account of the death rate amongst those who had been captured earlier. For example, although about 91,000 men were taken prisoner when the German Sixth Army surrendered in Stalingrad, a large proportion of these men died within weeks due to their malnourished state and the inability of the Soviet prison camps to cope with such a huge influx of sick and wounded men. Hitler repeatedly encouraged the belief that all men who surrendered were killed, but most soldiers in the front line in 1943 knew that this was untrue – the Soviet Union made extensive use of the prisoners to send radio messages and letters to the front line to encourage further surrenders, and even sent small groups of men to exhort their former comrades to lay down their arms. The lack of resources that had contributed to the high death rate after Stalingrad had largely been resolved by mid-1943, meaning that those men who made it to the prison camps were more likely to survive, albeit in harsh conditions.

In the first 12 months of the war between Germany and the Soviet Union, the death rate amongst Soviet prisoners of war held by Germany was appallingly high. About 2.8 million men died as a result of deliberate, widespread starvation and terrible conditions in the prison camps during this period.[11] Thereafter, as it became clear that there would be no early end to the war, conditions improved and prisoners were used as labourers. Nevertheless, by the time that the war ended, the death toll had risen to 3.5 million. The death rate amongst Germans in Soviet hands may have been severe, but there was no policy of deliberate starvation as had been the case on the German side during 1941–42.

Stalin's ability to learn from events was not restricted purely to military matters. A great deal of intelligence reached the Soviet leadership about the manner in which ordinary Soviet citizens had greeted the Germans as liberators in 1941, resulting in two policies. The first was an attempt to increase the status of regions like the Ukraine, with several prominent Ukrainians being appointed to high-profile roles within the Soviet government. Both defence and foreign affairs roles were created for the Ukrainian Soviet Socialist Republic, even if these remained entirely subordinate to Moscow. The former repression of the Orthodox Church was replaced by overt support, not least because Stalin and his colleagues recognised the potential role of the church in organising resistance in the occupied parts of the Soviet Union, and after the return of Soviet authority churches across the Ukraine were allowed to continue functioning. However, other aspects of the return of the Red Army were less pleasant. Many of the Ukrainians who had collaborated with the German occupation were executed within days of being captured, and whilst some – like the man in Kobylyanskiy's regiment – had some form of legal process, others were killed out of hand. Even before the Red Army arrived, local communist partisan groups compiled lists of those who had collaborated, ranging from men who had actively aided the Germans in killing Jews and others, through those who had denounced Jews and communists to the Germans, to women who had had sexual relations with the occupiers. On 7 February 1944, at the 9th Plenum of Soviet Writers in Moscow, writer Petro Panch told the gathering:

> The entire population that is now found in the liberated regions cannot, in essence, openly look in the eyes of our liberators, because it has become entangled in connections with the Germans to some extent … Some plundered flats and offices, others helped the Germans in looting and shooting, still others profiteered and engaged in commerce, while some girls, having lost a sense of patriotism, cohabited with the Germans.[12]

Such a statement could only have been made with official approval, and those who came under suspicion were subjected to years of persecution, arrest, imprisonment and even execution. Most of the Ukrainian population in the eastern parts of the Ukraine was pro-Soviet and gladly welcomed the return of the Red Army; as the war moved west, the percentage of those who came under suspicion increased steadily. The retribution of the Soviet Union fell upon its own citizens as well as upon the hated occupiers.

The year ended with the greatest possible contrast in moods in Germany and the Soviet Union. Most senior officers in the Wehrmacht remained grimly committed to the 'death ride' on which they had embarked, and few if any had faith in Hitler's assurances that the Soviet Union was running out of men or that the Battle of the Atlantic could be won. There was considerable talk – at least amongst Hitler's entourage – that the unlikely alliance of the Western Allies and the Soviet Union couldn't survive, but as a result of their deliberate aversion to political matters, the generals had no means of assessing this likelihood. Despite the huge setbacks endured during the year, the rank and file remained steadfastly loyal to Hitler, continuing to believe that new weapons or some other extraordinary change of fate would win the day. Nevertheless, the fighting power of the Wehrmacht had seen a radical decline relative to the fighting power of the Red Army. A year earlier, the Germans had been able to claim, with justification, that man for man the German forces were superior to their foes and the high standard of small- and medium-unit training and cooperation allowed them to overcome superior numbers. By the end of 1943, this was increasingly questionable. Whilst the new tanks might have technical advantages over their opponents, particularly with regard to their gunsights and firepower, the only sphere in which the Germans could still claim superiority was in tactical and operational command. But the high casualty rate amongst officers and NCOs was steadily eroding this advantage, and the Red Army was becoming increasingly skilled in such matters. The close relationships that had laid the foundations for small-unit cohesion in the Wehrmacht were increasingly a thing of the past. Historically, divisions had been raised predominantly from specified areas of Germany in order to encourage this sense of cohesion, but replacement drafts were now far more heterogeneous. By the end of 1943, harsh measures to ensure that discipline remained strong were far more widespread than ever before.

The brutal treatment of the civilian population of the territories occupied by Germany was a recurring theme throughout the year. As the Wehrmacht retreated, it tried to conduct a ruthless 'scorched earth' policy, and the discovery of atrocities spurred the soldiers of the Red Army to exact revenge upon any Germans they captured. The manner in which the German forces evolved their conduct towards the occupied areas has been the subject of considerable study in recent years.[13] The often-arbitrary mistreatment of civilians had many roots. Some soldiers unquestioningly accepted the Nazi ideology of the war in the east being a 'racial war'; others came to believe that the war was the only way of preventing Bolshevism from overrunning their homelands; and many were driven purely by military exigencies, with little or no regard for the consequences.[14] There was little consideration that it was German occupation policies that had created the increasing partisan movement, or that further attempts at repression merely exacerbated the problem. The few men in any position of authority who harboured such thoughts, like Kleist, had their hands full dealing with the deteriorating military situation. Far from protecting Germany by their conduct, the soldiers of the Wehrmacht continued to feed the implacable hostility of their opponents. Whenever the opportunity arose, the Red Army would take its revenge.

On the Soviet side, there was widespread optimism by the end of the year. More might have been expected at the beginning of the summer assaults given the near unprecedented concentration of offensive power for Operation *Polkovodets Rumyantsev*, but the heavy fighting of this operation was an essential precursor for what was to follow. In August 1943, the Wehrmacht remained a powerful force, and had to be ground down before decisive assaults could expect to succeed. The losses suffered during the year were terrible, but despite this the Red Army had actually grown in power. After the war, Vasilevsky wrote:

> The might of the Soviet Armed Forces was continuing to grow. During 1943 we had formed 78 new divisions. The troops operating at the front now comprised over six million officers and men, 91,000 guns and mortars, 4,900 tanks and self-propelled guns and 8,500 aircraft. Moreover, *Stavka* had considerable reserves of officers and men in its complement …
>
> Soviet fighting men had improved greatly in this time. They had been enriched by the new experience of strategic and operational-tactical skill and had learned more effectively to attack the enemy with a minimum number of casualties to themselves. All of this not only presented us with the possibility, but obliged us, to launch wide-scale offensive operations along the entire front from Leningrad to the Black Sea so as to liberate the entire Soviet territory from the enemy as soon as possible, paying particular attention to the flanks of the Soviet-German front.[15]

The comment that the Red Army had learned to keep losses to a minimum is open to question, and the figure of 4,900 tanks in the front line stands in stark contrast to the annual production of over 27,000, but in every other respect Vasilevsky was correct to look forward to the coming year. The process of exacting retribution from the hated invader had moved forward, but remained incomplete. Nevertheless, the conditions for a decisive blow against Germany had been created by wearing down the strength of the Wehrmacht in 1943. The harvest would be reaped in full in 1944.

NOTES

INTRODUCTION

1   M. Libardi and F. Orlandi, *Mitteleuropa: Mito, Letteratura, Filosofia* (Sylvi Edizioni, Turin, 2011), p.19. For an account of Bruck's contributions to the subject, see R. Charmatz, *Minister Freiherr von Bruck: Der Vorkämpfer Mitteleuropas* (Hirzel, Leipzig, 1916)

2   For a full account, see D. Olusoga and C. Erichsen, *The Kaiser's Holocaust: Germany's Forgotten Genocide and the Colonial Roots of Nazism* (Faber & Faber, London, 2010)

3   W. Thompson, *In the Eye of the Storm: Kurt Riezler and the Crises of Modern Germany* (University of Iowa Press, Iowa City, 1980), p.98–99

4   F. Naumann, *Mitteleuropa* (Reimer, Berlin, 1915)

5   R. Stackelberg, *Hitler's Germany: Origins, Interpretations, Legacies* (Taylor & Francis, London, 2002), p.188

6   R. Service, *A History of Modern Russia: From Nicholas II to Vladimir Putin* (Harvard University Press, Cambridge, MA, 2005), p.259–60

7   This is covered at length in V. Suvorov, *The Chief Culprit: Stalin's Grand Design to Start World War II* (Naval Institute Press, Annapolis, MD, 2008)

8   D. Glantz, *Stumbling Colossus: The Red Army on the Eve of War* (University Press of Kansas, Lawrence, KS, 1998), p.4; T. Uldricks, 'The Icebreaker Controversy: Did Stalin Plan to Attack Hitler?' in *Slavic Review* (Cambridge University Press, Cambridge, 1999), Vol. 58 III p.626–43

9   Quoted in U. Saft, *Krieg im Osten* (Militärbuchverlag, Walsrode, 2002), p.9

10   Dmitrov's diary, quoted in S. Sebag Montefiore, *Stalin: The Court of the Red Tsar* (Phoenix, London, 2003), p.318

11   G. Gorodetsky, *Grand Delusion: Stalin and the German Invasion of Russia* (Yale University Press, New Haven, CT, 2001), p.69–70

12   A. Kay, *Exploitation, Resettlement, Mass Murder: Political and Economic Planning for German Occupation Policy in the Soviet Union 1940–41* (Berghahn, New York, 2006), p.133

13   Ibid., p.133–34

14 For a discussion about the origins and development of *Generalplan Ost*, see P. Buttar, *Between Giants: The Battle for the Baltics in World War II* (Osprey, Oxford, 2013), p.52–57

15 A. Speer, *Inside the Third Reich: Memoirs of Alfred Speer* (Macmillan, London, 1970), p.115

16 A. Dallin, *German Rule in Russia 1941–1945* (Macmillan, London, 1957), p.102

17 Quoted in W. Lower, *Nazi Empire-Building and the Holocaust in Ukraine* (University of North Carolina Press, Chapel Hill, NC, 2005), p.24

18 O. Dietrich, *12 Jahre mit Hitler* (Isar, Munich, 1955), p.259; R. Meindl, *Ostpreussens Gauleiter: Erich Koch – eine Politische Biographie* (Fibre, Osnabrück, 2007), p.328

19 R. Pipes, *Russia Under the Bolshevik Regime* (Vintage, New York, 1995), p.232–36

20 Sebag Montefiore, *Stalin*, p.87

21 *Rossiyskiy Gosudarstvennyy Arkhiv Sotsial'no-Politicheskoy Istorii* (*RGASPI*, Moscow) 558.11.712.108

22 W. Newell, *Tyrants: A History of Power, Injustice and Terror* (Cambridge University Press, Cambridge, 2016), p.167

23 S. Mitcham, *The Rise of the Wehrmacht: The German Armed Forces in World War II* (Praeger Security International, Westport, CT, 2008), Vol. I, p.467

24 M. Burleigh, *Ethics and Extermination* (Cambridge University Press, Cambridge, 1997), p.68

25 K. Schmider, *Partisanenkrieg in Jugoslawien 1941–1944* (Mittler, Hamburg, 2002), p.282

26 J. Weiss, *Lemberg Mosaic* (Alderbrook, New York, 2011), p.173

27 V. Vyatrovych, R. Hrytskiv, I. Derevyanyy, R. Zabilyy, A. Sova, and P. Sodol, *Ukrayins'ka Povstans'ka Armiya: Istoriya Neskorenykh* (Chtyvo, Lviv, 2007), p.29

28 D. Moses (ed.), *Empire, Colony, Genocide: Conquest, Occupation and Subaltern Resistance in World History* (Berghahn, New York, 2008), p.388–90

29 Khoroshunova diary, 26 June 1941. The diaries of Irina Khoroshunova are available at www.gordonua.com/specprojects/khoroshunova_main.html

30 Khoroshunova diary, 25 September 1941

31 Ibid.

32 Ibid.

33 A. Hilgruber, 'War in the East and the Extermination of the Jews' in M. Marrus (ed.), *The Final Solution: The Implementation of Mass Murder* (Meckler, Westport, CT, 1989), p.96

34 M. Gilbert, *The Holocaust: The Jewish Tragedy* (Fontana, London, 1987), p.217–18

35 R. Evans, *The Third Reich at War* (Penguin, Harmondsworth, 2008), p.227

36 Khoroshunova diary, 1 October/2 October 1941

37 Khoroshunova diary, 14 October 1941

38 Lower, *Nazi Empire-Building*, p.107–08

39 Bundesarchiv Berlin, R6/70 17f

40 Quoted in Meindl, *Ostpreussens Gauleiter*, p.339

41 Mitcham, *Rise of the Wehrmacht*, Vol. I, p.468

42 R. Bartoleit, *Die Deutsche Agrarpolitik in den Besetten Gebieten der Ukraine vom Sommer 1941 bis zum Sommer 1942 unter Besonderer Berücksichtigung der Einführung der 'Neuen Agrarordnung'* (Magisterarbeit, Hamburg, 1987), p.108

43 Khoroshunova diary, 29 March 1942

44 Khoroshunova diary, 13 April 1942

45 A. Gogun, *Stalin's Commandos: Ukrainian Partisan Forces on the Eastern Front* (Tauris, London, 2015), p.36–37

46 See, for example, T. Snyder, *Germans Must Remember the Truth About Ukraine – For Their Own Sake* (Eurozine, Vienna, 7 July 2017)

47 Khoroshunova diary, 30 June 1942

48 Khoroshunova diary, 23 December 1942

CHAPTER 1

1 Quoted in W. Paul, *Brennpunkte: Die Geschichte der 6. Panzerdivision 1937–1945* (Biblio, Osnaück, 1993), p.288

2 Bundesarchiv-Militärarchiv Freiburg, RL 7-1 K1 TL II/42

3 For Speer's account of events, see Speer, *Inside the Third Reich*, p.273–79

4 Ibid., p.295

5 M. Kolomiyets, *Trofenyye Tanki Krasnoye Armii* (Eksmo, Moscow, 2010), p.109

6 S. Zaloga, *T-34/76 Medium Tank 1941–45* (Osprey, Oxford, 1994), p.19

7 P. Buttar, *Russia's Last Gasp: The Eastern Front 1916–17* (Osprey, Oxford, 2016)

8 A. Vasilevsky, and J. Riordan (trans.), *A Lifelong Cause* (Progress, Moscow, 1981), p.126

9 S. Zaloga and L. Ness, *Red Army Handbook 1939–1945* (Sutton, Stroud, 1998), p.78–79

10 F. von Mellenthin, *Panzer Battles* (University of Oklahoma Press, Danvers, MA, 1956), p.153

11 P. Rotmistrov, *Stal'naia Gvardiia* (Voenizdat, Moscow, 1984), p.123

12 Radio address given on 12 February 1943, in *The Public Papers of F. D. Roosevelt* (University of Michigan, Ann Arbor, MI, 2005), Vol. XII, p.71

13 A. von Hassell, S. MacRae, and S. Ameskamp, *Alliance of Enemies: The Untold Story of the Secret American and German Collaboration to end World War II* (Thomas Dunne, New York, 2006), p.151

14 E. von Manstein, and A. Powell (trans.), *Lost Victories: The War Memoirs of Hitler's Most Brilliant General* (Presidio, Novato, CA, 1994), p.445

15 T. Jentz, *Germany's Panther Tank* (Schiffer, Altglen, PA, 1995), p.130–32

16 M. Healy, *Zitadelle: The German Offensive Against the Kursk Salient 4–17 July* (History Press, Stroud, 2010), p.79

17   S. Shtemenko, and R. Daglish (trans.), *The Soviet General Staff at War 1941–1945* (Progress, Moscow, 1970), p.108–09

18   Vasilevsky, *Lifelong Cause*, p.255–56

19   D. Glantz and J. House, *The Battle of Kursk* (University Press of Kansas, Lawrence, KS, 2004), p.28–29

20   G. Zhukov, *Vospomimaniya I Razmyshleniya* (Olma, Moscow, 2002), Vol. II, p.131

21   Glantz and House, *Battle of Kursk*, p.64–65

22   V. Zamulin, and S. Britton (trans.), *Demolishing the Myth. The Tank Battle at Prokhorovka, Kursk, July 1943: An Operational Narrative* (Helion, Solihull, 2011), p.47

23   L. Clark, *Kursk: The Greatest Battle: Eastern Front 1943* (Headline, London, 2012), p.265

24   K. Münsch, *Combat History of Schwere Panzerjäger Abteilung 653* (Fedorowicz, Winnipeg, 1997), p.50–52

25   K. Frieser, K. Schmider, K. Schönherr, G. Schreiber, K. Ungváry, and B. Wegner, *Die Ostfront 1943/44 – Der Krieg im Osten und an den Nebenfronten* (Deutsche Verlags-Anstalt, Munich, 2007), p.188; Glantz and House, *Battle of Kursk*, p.297

26   Zhukov, *Vospomimaniya I Razmyshleniya*, Vol. II, p.174

27   Zamulin, *Demolishing the Myth*, p.114

28   M. Katukov, *Na Ostrya Glavnogo Udara* (Voenizdat, Moscow, 1974), p.219

29   P. Rotmistrov, *Tankovoe Srazhenie Pod Prokhorovkoĭ* (Voenizdat, Moscow, 1960), p.7

30   *Sovetskaia Voennaia Entsiklopediia* (Voenizdat, Moscow, 1977), p.612

31   For a detailed analysis of tank numbers and losses, see Zamulin, *Demolishing the Myth*, p.572–75

32   Rotmistrov, *Tankovoe Srazhenie Pod Prokhorovkoĭ*, p.86

33   J. Engelmann, *Zitadelle: Die Grösste Panzerschlacht im Osten 1943* (Podzun, Friedberg, 1981), p.151

34   *Tsentral'nyi Arkhiv Ministerii Oboroni* (Moscow) RF f332 op.4948, d6

35   D. Glantz and H. Orenstein, *The Battle for Kursk 1943: The Soviet General Staff Study* (Routledge, London, 1999), p.274

36   Manstein, *Lost Victories*, p.449

37   Vasilevsky, *Lifelong Cause*, p.275–76

CHAPTER 2

1   M. Zakharov, 'O Sovetskom Voyennom Iskusstve v Bitve Pod Kurskum' in *Voenno-Istoricheskii Zhurnal* (Voennoe izd-vo Ministerstva Oborony Soyuza SSR, Moscow, 1963), p.12–13

2   I. Kobylyanskiy, *From Stalingrad to Pillau: A Red Army Artillery Officer Remembers the Great Patriotic War* (University Press of Kansas, Lawrence, KS, 2008), p.88–89

3   N. Isayenko, *Vizyu Protivnika!* (Politizdat, Kiev, 1981), p.202

4   Ibid., p.211
5   F. Memminger, *Die Kriegsgeschichte der Windhund-Division: 16. Infanterie-Division (mot.) 1.7.40-1.10.41; 16. Panzer-Grenadier-Division 2.10.41-30.3.44; 116. Panzer-Division 30.3.44-18.3.45* (Pöppinghaus, Bochum, 1962), Vol. III, p.1729
6   Ibid., p.1729–31
7   Ibid., p.1735
8   Ibid., p.1735–36
9   Ibid., p.1737–38
10   Ibid., p.1739–40
11   Ibid., p.1759
12   Kobylyanskiy, *From Stalingrad to Pillau*, p.90
13   Manstein, *Lost Victories*, p.453
14   Ibid., p.403–04
15   Ibid., p.404
16   Speer, *Inside the Third Reich*, p.320–21
17   Ibid., p.389
18   Ibid., p.323–24
19   Traditionsverband der Ehemaligen Dritten Panzer-Division (henceforth abbreviated to TEDPD), *Armored Bears: The German 3rd Panzer Division in World War II* (Stackpole, Mechanicsburg, PA, 2013), p.175
20   O. Weidinger, *Division Das Reich* (Munin, Osnabrück, 1979), Vol. IV, p.235
21   Memminger, *Die Kriegsgeschichte der Windhund-Division*, Vol. III, p.1769
22   W. Vopersal, *Soldaten, Kämpfer, Kameraden: Marsch und Kämpfe der SS-Totenkopfdivision* (Biblio, Osnabrück, 1987), Vol. IIIb, p.438
23   Rottenführer Hax, quoted in Vopersal, *Soldaten, Kämpfer, Kameraden*, Vol. IIIb, p.439
24   Robert Gütlein, quoted in Vopersal, *Soldaten, Kämpfer, Kameraden*, Vol. IIIb, p.439–40
25   Rottenführer Hax, quoted in Vopersal, *Soldaten, Kämpfer, Kameraden*, Vol. IIIb, p.440–41
26   Kobylyanskiy, *From Stalingrad to Pillau*, p.92
27   Ibid., p.93
28   Weidinger, *Division Das Reich*, Vol. IV, p.250–55
29   Ibid., p.256–58
30   Vopersal, *Soldaten, Kämpfer, Kameraden*, Vol. IIIb, p.449–50
31   Ibid., p.452
32   Memminger, *Die Kriegsgeschichte der Windhund-Division*, Vol. III, p.1778–79
33   Ibid., p.1782
34   Kobylyanskiy, *From Stalingrad to Pillau*, p.95–96
35   Vasilevsky, *Lifelong Cause*, p.278
36   Weidinger, *Division Das Reich*, Vol. IV, p.268–70

CHAPTER 3

1   *Kurskaya Bitva v Tsifrakh* in *Voenno-Istoricheskii Zhurnal* (Voennoe izd-vo Ministerstva Oborony Soyuza SSR, Moscow, 1968), p.79–81

2   Ibid.

3   D. Glantz, *From the Don to the Dnepr: Soviet Offensive Operations December 1942–August 1943* (Cass, London, 1991), p.225

4   Zhukov, *Vospomimaniya I Razmyshleniya*, Vol. II, p.168

5   K. Kazakov, *Vsegda s Pekhotoi Vsegda s Tankami* (Voenizdat, Moscow, 1969), p.166–67

6   J. Erickson, *The Road to Berlin: Stalin's War with Germany* (Cassell, London, 2003), Vol. II, p.118–19

7   G. Koltunov and B. Soloviev, *Kurskaya Bitva* (Voenizdat, Moscow, 1970), p.282

8   Katukov, *Na Ostriye Glavnogo Udara*, p.244

9   M. Abdullin, *Stranits iz Soldatskogo Dnevnika* (Molodaya Gvardiya, Moscow, 1985), p.99

10 I. Chistiakov, *Sluzhim Otchizne* (Voenizdat, Moscow, 1985), p.161

11 Ibid., p.164–66

12 Paul, *Brennpunkte*, p.317

13 Ibid., p.324

14 Bundesarchiv-Militärarchiv Freiburg, *Kriegstagebuch des Panzerregiments 11*, 3 August 1943, RH27-6

15 E. Raus, and S. Newton (trans.), *Panzer Operations: The Eastern Front Memoir of General Raus, 1941–1945* (Da Capo, Cambridge, MA, 2003), p.225–26

16 Reported in *Illustrierte Beobachter* (Franz Eher Verlag, Munich), 30 December 1943

17 Chistiakov, *Sluzhim Otchizne*, p.165

18 Rotmistrov, *Stal'naia Gvardiia*, p.213–14

19 Quoted in K. Moskalenko, *Na Yugo-Zapadnom Napravlenii* (Nauka, Moscow, 1973), Vol. II, p.82

20 Y. Dudarenko, G. Perechnev, and V. Yeliseye, *Osvobozhdeniye gorodov: Spravochnik po osvobozhdeniyu gorodov v period Velikoy Otechestvennoy voyny 1941–1945* (Voenizdat, Moscow, 1985), p.599–600

21 Katukov, *Na Ostrya Glavnogo Udara*, p.245

22 TEDPD, *Armored Bears*, p.176

23 Chistiakov, *Sluzhim Otchizne*, p.166–67

24 Koltunov and Soloviev, *Kurskaya Bitva*, p.303–04

25 Bundesarchiv-Militärarchiv Freiburg, *Kriegstagebuch des LII Armeekorps*, 6 August 1943, RH24-52

26 I. Babikov and I. Samchuk, *Kotel Pod Tomarovkoi* (Voenizdat, Moscow, 1967), p.65–89

27 A. Krull, *Das Hannoversche Regiment 73. Geschichte des Panzer-Grenadier-Regiments 73 [vormals Infanterie Regiment 73]. 1939–1945* (Regimentskameradschaft 73, Hannover, 1967), p.326–27

28   A. Zhadov, *Chetyre Goda Voyne* (Voenizdat, Moscow, 1978), p.164
29   Shtemenko, *Soviet General Staff*, p.181
30   Vasilevsky, *Lifelong Cause*, p.278–79

CHAPTER 4

1   Glantz, *From the Don to the Dnepr*, p.393
2   Katukov, *Na Ostrya Glavnogo Udara*, p.246
3   A. Getman, *Tanki Idut na Berlin* (Nauka, Moscow, 1973), p.77
4   Hauptsturmführer Messerle, quoted in Vopersal, *Soldaten, Kämpfer, Kameraden*, Vol. IIIb, p.455
5   Weidinger, *Division Das Reich*, Vol. IV, p.279
6   Getman, *Tanki Idut na Berlin*, p.78
7   Quoted in Vopersal, *Soldaten, Kämpfer, Kameraden*, Vol. IIIb, p.458
8   Rotmistrov, *Stal'naia Gvardiia*, p.215–17
9   H. Spaeter, *History of the Panzerkorps Grossdeutschland* (Fedorowicz, Winnipeg, 1995), Vol. II, p.147
10   Shtemenko, *Soviet General Staff*, p.181
11   W. Sawodny, *German Armored Trains in World War II* (Schiffer, Atglen, PA, 1990), Vol. II, p.5–7, 37
12   Weidinger, *Division Das Reich*, Vol. IV, p.290
13   Spaeter, *History of the Panzerkorps Grossdeutschland*, Vol. II, p.154–55; Glantz, *From the Don to the Dneper*, p.303
14   Getman, *Tanki Idut na Berlin*, p.78
15   Quoted in Vopersal, *Soldaten, Kämpfer, Kameraden*, Vol. IIIb, p.463
16   Quoted in Vopersal, *Soldaten, Kämpfer, Kameraden*, Vol. IIIb, p.465
17   Spaeter, *History of the Panzerkorps Grossdeutschland*, Vol. II, p.158
18   Moskalenko, *Na Yugo-Zapadnom Napravlenii*, Vol. II, p.90
19   Getman, *Tanki Idut na Berlin*, p.79
20   Koltunov and Soloviev, *Kurskaya Bitva*, p.320
21   Rotmistrov, *Stal'naia Gvardiia*, p.219–20
22   Ibid., p.221–23
23   Ibid., p.225
24   Vopersal, *Soldaten, Kämpfer, Kameraden*, Vol. IIIb, p.468
25   Weidinger, *Division Das Reich*, Vol. IV, p.291
26   Vopersal, *Soldaten, Kämpfer, Kameraden*, Vol. IIIb, p.469
27   E. Klapdor, *Viking Panzers: The German 5th SS Tank Regiment in the East in World War II* (Stackpole, Mechanicsburg, PA, 2011), p.192
28   Quoted in Klapdor, *Viking Panzers*, p.192–93
29   Quoted in Klapdor, *Viking Panzers*, p.194–95
30   Weidinger, *Division Das Reich*, Vol. IV, p.293
31   Rotmistrov, *Stal'naia Gvardiia*, p.226–27

32   Abdullin, *Stranits iz Soldatskogo Dnevnika*, p.104–05
33   Quoted in Vopersal, *Soldaten, Kämpfer, Kameraden*, Vol. IIIb, p.475
34   Weidinger, *Division Das Reich*, Vol. IV, p.295
35   Quoted in Vopersal, *Soldaten, Kämpfer, Kameraden*, Vol. IIIb, p.480
36   Abdullin, *Stranits iz Soldatskogo Dnevnika*, p.105–06
37   Quoted in Vopersal, *Soldaten, Kämpfer, Kameraden*, Vol. IIIb, p.486
38   Rotmistrov, *Stal'naia Gvardiia*, p.228–29
39   Moskalenko, *Na Yugo-Zapadnom Napravlenii*, Vol. II, p.90–91
40   Glantz, *From the Don to the Dnepr*, p.334
41   Vasilevsky, *Lifelong Cause*, p.284–85
42   Ibid., p.285
43   Koltunov and Soloviev, *Kurskaya Bitva*, p.337–38
44   Spaeter, *History of the Panzerkorps Grossdeutschland*, Vol. II, p.163
45   Chistiakov, *Sluzhim Otchizne*, p.174–75
46   Katukov, *Na Ostrya Glavnogo Udara*, p.248
47   Getman, *Tanki Idut na Berlin*, p.80
48   Abdullin, *Stranits iz Soldatskogo Dnevnika*, p.109–12
49   Memminger, *Die Kriegsgeschichte der Windhund-Division*, Vol. III, p.1805
50   Quoted in Spaeter, *History of the Panzerkorps Grossdeutschland*, Vol. II, p.168
51   Quoted in Vopersal, *Soldaten, Kämpfer, Kameraden*, Vol. IIIb, p.502–03
52   See H. Röll, *Generalleutnant der Reserve Hyacinth Graf Strachwitz von Groß-Zauche und Camminetz: Vom Kavallerieoffizier zum Führer Gepanzerter Verbände* (Flechsig, Würzburg, 2011), p.182–84
53   N. Vorontsov, A. Biryukov, and A. Smekalov, *Ot Volzhshikh Stepei do Avstriiskikh Alp: Boevoi Put 4-i Gvardeiskoi Armii* (Voenizdat, Moscow, 1971), p.21
54   Shtemenko, *Soviet General Staff*, p.182–83
55   Vasilevsky, *Lifelong Cause*, p.284
56   Vopersal, *Soldaten, Kämpfer, Kameraden*, Vol. IIIb, p.505
57   Ibid., p.508
58   Weidinger, *Division Das Reich*, Vol. IV, p.305–06
59   Ibid., p.314–16
60   Vopersal, *Soldaten, Kämpfer, Kameraden*, Vol. IIIb, p.513
61   Ibid., p.513–14
62   Weidinger, *Division Das Reich*, Vol. IV, p.323
63   Vopersal, *Soldaten, Kämpfer, Kameraden*, Vol. IIIb, p.519
64   Kobylyanskiy, *From Stalingrad to Pillau*, p.99–102

CHAPTER 5

1   Paul, *Brennpunkte*, p.325–26
2   Ibid., p.326
3   Abdullin, *Stranits iz Soldatskogo Dnevnika*, p.102–03

4   TEDPD, *Armored Bears*, p.177

5   I. Konev, *Zapiski Komanduyushchego Frontom* (Nauka, Moscow, 1972), p.30–34

6   Raus, *Panzer Operations*, p.241

7   Paul, *Brennpunkte*, p.326

8   Bundesarchiv-Militärarchiv Freiburg, *Kriegstagebuch des Panzerregiments 11*, 11 August 1943, RH27-6

9   Bundesarchiv-Militärarchiv Freiburg, *Kriegstagebuch des XXXXII Armeekorps*, RH24-42

10 Paul, *Brennpunkte*, p.328

11 Bundesarchiv-Militärarchiv Freiburg, *Kriegstagebuch des 6. Panzerdivision*, 14 August 1943, RH27-6

12 TEDPD, *Armored Bears*, p.179

13 Paul, *Brennpunkte*, p.331–33

14 TEDPD, *Armored Bears*, p.180

15 Quoted in Vopersal, *Soldaten, Kämpfer, Kameraden*, Vol. IIIb, p.473

16 TEDPD, *Armored Bears*, p.181

17 Quoted in Klapdor, *Viking Panzers*, p.198

18 Quoted in Klapdor, *Viking Panzers*, p.199–200

19 Militärgeschichtliches Forschungsamt, *Das Deutsche Reich und der Zweite Weltkrieg* (henceforth cited as *DRZW*) (Deutsche Verlags-Anstalt, Stuttgart, 1979–2008), Vol. VIII, p.198

20 Bundesarchiv-Militärarchiv Freiburg, *Kriegstagebuch des XI Armeekorps*, 20 August 1943, RH24-11

21 Manstein, *Lost Victories*, p.456

22 Konev, *Zapiski Komanduyushchego Frontom*, p.37–38

23 E. Pivovar (ed.), *Gorod I Voyna Khar'kov v Gody Velikoy Oteuyestvennoy Voyiy* (Aleteya, St Petersburg, 2013), p.24

24 Ibid., p.27–28

25 Bundesarchiv-Militärarchiv Freiburg, *Kriegstagebuch des LV Armeekorps*, RH55-42

26 K. Margery, 'Kharkov' in *After the Battle* (Battle of Britain International, London, 2001), No. 112, p.8

27 Pivovar, *Gorod I Voyna Khar'kov*, p.113

28 Ibid., p.181

29 Quoted in *Doukumenty Obviniayut: Sbornik Dokumentov o Cudovisnyh Zverstvah Germanskii Vlastei na Vremenno Zakhvachennykh imi Sovetskoi Territoriakh* (Gos. Izd-vo Polit. Lit-ry, Moscow, 1945), Vol. II, p.308

30 A. Skoroboatov, *Harkiv u Casi Nimeckoi Okupacii 1941–1943* (Prapor, Kharkov, 2004), p.368–80

31 Pivovar, *Gorod I Voyna Khar'kov*, p.184–88

32 Ibid., p.29–30

33 Ibid., p.43

34 Ibid., p.236

35 Ibid., p.213–14

36   Ibid., p.174
37   Ibid., p.243
38   Ibid., p.94
39   Ibid., p.190
40   Ibid., p.344–45
41   Ibid., p.106–07
42   Ibid., p.336–37
43   Zhukov, *Vospomimaniya I Razmyshleniya*, Vol. II, p.165–66
44   Ibid., p.176
45   D. Glantz and J. House, *When Titans Clashed: How the Red Army Stopped Hitler* (University Press of Kansas, Lawrence, KS, 1995), p.297
46   Ibid.
47   Erickson, *Road to Berlin*, Vol. II, p.122
48   R. Citino, *The Wehrmacht Retreats: Fighting a Lost War* (University Press of Kansas, Lawrence, KS, 2016), p.252
49   Ibid., p.275–83

CHAPTER 6

1   Manstein, *Lost Victories*, p.458
2   *DRZW*, Vol. V, part 2, p.946; Vol. VIII, p.271–72
3   See Buttar, *Between Giants*, p.202–10
4   D. Irving, *Hitler's War* (Focal Point, London, 1991), p.535–36
5   *DRZW*, Vol. V, Part 2, p.944–56
6   Art of War Symposium, *From the Dnepr to the Vistula* (US Army War College, Carlisle, PA, 1985), p.84–85
7   T. Wray, *Standing Fast: German Defensive Doctrine on the Russian Front During the Second World War* (US Army Command and General Staff College, Fort Leavenworth, KS, 1983), p.168–77
8   Manstein, *Lost Victories*, p.461
9   W. Shirer, *Aufstieg und Fall des Dritten Reiches* (Pawlak, Herrsching, 1977), p.1013
10   R. Moorhouse, *Killing Hitler: The Plots, the Assassins, and the Dictator who Cheated Death* (Bantam, New York, 2006), p.192–93; B. von Scheurig, *Henning von Tresckow: Eine Biographie* (Ullstein, Frankfurt, 1980), p.146–49
11   R. von Gersdorff, *Soldat im Untergang* (Ullstein, Frankfurt, 1979), p.134
12   Quoted in M. Melvin, *Manstein: Hitler's Greatest General* (Orion, London, 2011), p.406–07
13   Zhukov, *Vospomimaniya I Razmyshleniya*, Vol. II, p.177–78
14   Ibid., p.180
15   Ibid., p.181
16   Shtemenko, *Soviet General Staff*, p.185

17 Moskalenko, *Na Yugo-Zapadnom Napravlenii*, Vol. II, p.100–02
18 Memminger, *Die Kriegsgeschichte der Windhund-Division*, Vol. III, p.1809–10
19 D. Lelyushenko, *Moskva – Stalingrad – Berlin – Praga* (Nauka, Moscow, 1987), p.188
20 Vasilevsky, *Lifelong Cause*, p.290–91
21 Ibid., p.291–92
22 Kobylyanskiy, *From Stalingrad to Pillau*, p.103–04
23 Memminger, *Die Kriegsgeschichte der Windhund-Division*, Vol. III, p.1814
24 K. von Tippelskirch, *Geschichte des Zweiten Weltkrieges* (Athenäum, Bonn, 1951), p.388–89
25 Vopersal, *Soldaten, Kämpfer, Kameraden*, Voll. IIIb, p.521–22
26 Ibid., p.530
27 Ibid., p.533
28 Ibid., p.541
29 Ibid., p.542–43
30 Ibid., p.545
31 Ibid., p.546
32 Ibid., p.547
33 Bundesarchiv-Militärarchiv Freiburg, *Kriegstagebuch des AOK-8*, 14 September 1943, RH20-8
34 Spaeter, *History of the Panzerkorps Grossdeutschland*, Vol. II, p.185–86
35 Bundesarchiv-Militärarchiv Freiburg, *Kriegstagebuch des 6. Panzerdivision*, 7 September 1943, RH27-6
36 Moskalenko, *Na Yugo-Zapadnom Napravlenii*, Vol. II, p.108–09
37 Glantz and House, *When Titans Clashed*, p.172
38 A. Schmidt, *Geschichte der 10. Division: 10. Infanterie-Division (Mot.); 10. Panzer-Grenadier-Division* (Fischer, Regensburg, 1984), p.197–201
39 Moskalenko, *Na Yugo-Zapadnom Napravlenii*, Vol. II, p.111
40 Transcript of interview with Stepan Georgievich Fedorovich, available at https://iremember.ru/memoirs/pekhotintsi/fedorovich-stepan-georgievich/
41 Bundesarchiv-Militärarchiv Freiburg, *Nachlass Zeitzler* 'Das Ringen um die Grossen Entschiedungen im Zweiten Weltkrieg', Vol. II, p.117
42 A. Seaton, *The German Army 1933-1945* (Littlehampton Books, Worthing, 1982), p.374
43 I. Kershaw, *Hitler 1936–1945: Nemesis* (Penguin, Harmondsworth, 2001), p.602
44 Bundesarchiv-Militärarchiv Freiburg, N507/106 14.9.1943
45 Manstein, *Lost Victories*, p.462–65
46 R. Hinze, *Die 19. Infanterie- und Panzer-Division* (self-published, Düsseldorf, 1988), p.582
47 Vopersal, *Soldaten, Kämpfer, Kameraden*, Vol. IIIb, p.551
48 Bundesarchiv-Militärarchiv Freiburg, *Kriegstagebuch des Panzer-AOK4*, 18 September 1943, RH21-4

49   Weidinger, *Division Das Reich*, Vol. IV, p.334–35

50   Ibid., p.344–47

51   Ibid., p.351–52

52   G. Schlaug, *Die Deutschen Lastensegler-Verbände* (Motor-Buch Verlag, Stuttgart, 1985), p.144

53   Speer, *Inside the Third Reich*, p.306–09, 436–38, 504–06

54   U. Herbert, *Hitler's Foreign Workers: Enforced Foreign Labor in Germany Under the Third Reich* (Cambridge University Press, Cambridge, 1997), p.346–47

55   Ibid., p.348–54

56   Weidinger, *Division Das Reich*, Vol. IV, p.355–56

57   Konev, *Zapiski Komanduyushchego Frontom*, p.56–58

58   Abdullin, *Stranits iz Soldatskogo Dnevnika*, p.112–14

59   Ibid., p.115–19

60   P. Carrell, *Scorched Earth: The Russo-German War 1943–1944* (Little Brown, Boston, MA, 1970), p.345

61   Bundesarchiv-Militärarchiv Freiburg, N507/106 22.9.1943

62   V. Grossman, A. Beevor (trans.), and L.Vinogradova (trans.), *A Writer At War: Vasily Grossman with the Red Army 1941–1945* (Pimlico, London, 2006), p.248–49

63   Manstein, *Lost Victories*, p.470–71

64   Vopersal, *Soldaten, Kämpfer, Kameraden*, Vol. IIIb, p.554

65   Ibid., p.561

66   *DRZW*, Vol. VIII, p.359

CHAPTER 7

1   S. Melnikov, *Marshal Rybalko: Vospominaniia Byvshego Chlena Voennogo Soveta 3-I Gvardeiskoi Tankovoi Armii* (Politizdat Ukrainy, Kiev, 1980), p.131

2   Moskalenko, *Na Yugo-Zapadnom Napravlenii*, Vol. II, p.124–25

3   I. Lisov, *Desantniki* (Voenizdat, Moscow, 1968), p.157

4   S. Sukhorukov, *Sovetskie Vozdushnye Dessantnye: Voenno-Istoricheskii Ocherk* (Voenizdat, Moscow, 1986), p.199

5   G. Sofronov, *Vosdushye Desanti vo Vtoroi Mirovoi Voine: Kratkii Voenno-Istoricheskii Ocherk* (Voenizdat, Moscow, 1962), p.31

6   E. Binder, 'Employment of a Russian Parachute Brigade in a Bend of the Dnepr Northwest of Kanev' in *Russian Airborne Operations* (Historical Division, US Army Europe, 1953), p.70–71

7   Transcript of interview with M. Likhterman (hereafter Likhterman interview), available at https://iremember.ru/memoirs/desantniki/likhterman-matvey-tsodikovich/

8   U. de Maizière, *In der Pflicht: Lebensbericht eines Deutsches Soldaten im 20. Jahrhundert* (Mittler, Hamburg, 1997), p.86–87

9   Bundesarchiv-Militärarchiv Freiburg, N507/106

10   Lisov, *Desantniki*, p.166
11   Likhterman interview
12   Bundesarchiv-Militärarchiv Freiburg, W. Nehring, *Einsatz Russischer Fallschirmverbände im Raum von Tscherkassy-Kiew am 24. Und 25.9.1943*, N543/172, p.214
13   G. Lubs, *IR 5 : Aus der Geschichte eines Pommerschen Regiments 1920–1945* (self-published, Bochum, 1955), p.595–96
14   S. Biryuzov, *Kogda Gremeli Pushki* (Voyenizdat, Moscow, 1961), p.208
15   Vasilevsky, *Lifelong Cause*, p.295–97
16   Biryuzov, *Kogda Gremeli Pushki*, p.212
17   Weidinger, *Division Das Reich*, p.367–69
18   Transcript of interview with N. Kolesnik, available at https://iremember.ru/en/memoirs/artillerymen/nikolay-kolesnik/
19   Vopersal, *Soldaten, Kämpfer, Kameraden*, Vol. IIIb, p.565
20   Weidinger, *Division Das Reich*, p.370–71
21   Lisov, *Desantniki*, p.171–72
22   Quoted in Shtemenko, *Soviet General Staff*, p.187
23   Abdullin, *Stranits iz Soldatskogo Dnevnika*, p.121–22, 123–24
24   Konev, *Zapiski Komanduyushchego Frontom*, p.60
25   Abdullin, *Stranits iz Soldatskogo Dnevnika*, p.126–32
26   Zhadov, *Chetyre Goda Voyne*, p.188
27   Vopersal, *Soldaten, Kämpfer, Kameraden*, Vol. IVa, p.6–7
28   Memminger, *Die Kriegsgeschichte der Windhund-Division*, Vol. III, p.1834
29   Ibid., p.1839–40
30   Spaeter, *History of the Panzerkorps Grossdeutschland*, Vol. II, p.207–08
31   Rotmistrov, *Stal'naia Gvardiia*, p.238–39
32   Transcript of interview with S. Otroschenkov (hereafter Otroschenkov interview), available at https://iremember.ru/memoirs/tankisti/otroschenkov-sergey-andreevich/
33   Klapdor, *Viking Panzers*, p.224–25
34   Private letter from Fritz Hahl to John Moore, made available on the Axis History Forum (forum.axishistory.com)
35   V. Chuikov, *Ot Stalingrada do Berlina* (Sovetskaya Rossiya, Moscow, 1985), p.372
36   Memminger, *Die Kriegsgeschichte der Windhund-Division*, Vol. III, p.1880
37   W. Adam, O. Rühle, and T. Le Tissier (trans.), *With Paulus at Stalingrad* (Pen & Sword, Barnsley, 2015), p.236
38   Memminger, *Die Kriegsgeschichte der Windhund-Division*, Vol. III, p.1888
39   Kobylyanskiy, *From Stalingrad to Pillau*, p.107
40   Chuikov, *Ot Stalingrada do Berlina*, p.378
41   Memminger, *Die Kriegsgeschichte der Windhund-Division*, Vol. III, p.1897–98
42   Ibid., p.1899–1900
43   Bundesarchiv-Militärarchiv Freiburg, *Kriegstagebuch des 16. Panzergrenadierdivision*, 14 October 1943, RH27-116

44 Memminger, *Die Kriegsgeschichte der Windhund-Division*, Vol. III, p.1904–05
45 P. Schramm (ed.), *Kriegstagebuch des Oberkommandos der Wehrmacht* (Bernhard & Graefer, Munich, 1982), Vol. VI, p.1202

CHAPTER 8

1   Vopersal, *Soldaten, Kämpfer, Kameraden*, Vol. IVa, p.16–17
2   Spaeter, *History of the Panzerkorps Grossdeutschland*, Vol. II, p.223
3   Ibid., p.230–31
4   Transcript of interview with G. Krivov (hereafter Krivov interview), available at https://iremember.ru/memoirs/tankisti/krivov-georgiy-nikolaevich
5   Memminger, *Die Kriegsgeschichte der Windhund-Division*, Vol. III, p.1918–22
6   A. Krylova, *Soviet Women in Combat: A History of Violence on the Eastern Front* (Cambridge University Press, Cambridge, 2010), p.164–68
7   For an account of the involvement of women in the Red Army, see G. Milanetti, *Gli Angeli Sterminatori: L'incredibile Storia delle Cecchine Sovietiche nell Seconda Guerra Mondiale* (IBN, Rome, 2017)
8   Rotmistrov, *Stal'naia Gvardiia*, p.248
9   G. Schrodek, *Ihr Glaube Galt dem Vaterland: Geschichte des Panzer-Regiments 15 (11. Panzer-Division)* (Schild, Munich, 1976), p.283
10 Otroschenkov interview
11 Vopersal, *Soldaten, Kämpfer, Kameraden*, Vol. IVa, p.23–26
12 Ibid., p.23
13 Ibid.
14 Memminger, *Die Kriegsgeschichte der Windhund-Division*, Vol. III, p.1926–27
15 Ibid., p.1930–31
16 Otroschenkov interview
17 Manstein, *Lost Victories*, p.481
18 R. Lehmann, *Die Leibstandarte* (Munin, Osnabrück, 1982), Vol. III, p.317–19
19 G. Schreiber, *Deutsche Kriegsverbrechen in Italian: Täter, Opfer, Strafvervolgung* (Beck, Munich, 1996), p.130–32
20 A. Rossino, *Hitler Strikes Poland: Blitzkrieg, Ideology and Atrocity* (University Press of Kansas, Lawrence, KS, 2005), p.109–10
21 F. von. Senger und Etterlin, *Die 24. Panzer-Division 1939–1945* (Dörffler, Eggolsheim 2004), p.157–58
22 R. Grams, *Die 14. Panzer-Division* (Podzun, Bad Neuheim, 1957), p.121–24
23 Rotmistrov, *Stal'naia Gvardiia*, p.250
24 Krivov interview
25 Senger und Etterlin, *Die 24. Panzer-Division*, p.159–60
26 Grams, *Die 14. Panzer-Division*, p.128–29
27 Transcript of interview with V. Kovalenko, available at www.iremember.ru/memoirs/tankisti/kovalenko-vasily-ivanovich

28 Chuikov, *Ot Stalingrada do Berlina*, p.393–94
29 Konev, *Zapiski Komanduyushchego Frontom*, p.75–76
30 Ibid., p.76
31 Memminger, *Die Kriegsgeschichte der Windhund-Division*, Vol. III, p.1937
32 Grams, *Die 14. Panzer-Division*, p.130–31
33 Senger und Etterlin, *Die 24. Panzer-Division*, p.161–62
34 Memminger, *Die Kriegsgeschichte der Windhund-Division*, Vol. III, p.1941–42
35 Konev, *Zapiski Komanduyushchego Frontom*, p.78; Senger und Etterlin, *Die 24. Panzer-Division*, p.164
36 Konev, *Zapiski Komanduyushchego Frontom*, p.78–79

CHAPTER 9

1   Nuremberg Trials Evidence File Documents (United States Library of Congress, 1949), Vol. I, p.714
2   *Gosudarstvennyi Archive Kievskoi Oblasti*, Kiev, Fond R-2356, 1/60, p.3
3   Diary of Irina Khoroshunova, 9 May 1942
4   Ibid., 27 May 1942
5   Ibid., 24 July 1942
6   Ibid., 28 May 1943
7   Ibid., 25 February 1944
8   Moskalenko, *Na Yugo-Zapadnom Napravlenii*, Vol. II, p.150–51
9   P. Carrell, *Scorched Earth*, p.356–57
10 W. Haupt, *Die 8. Panzer-Division im Zweiten Weltkrieg* (Podzun-Pallas, Friedburg, 1987), p.320
11 J. Costello and T. Hughes, *The Battle of the Atlantic* (Collins, London, 1977), p.281
12 Mellenthin, *Panzer Battles*, p.224
13 S. Nietzel (ed.), *Tapping Hitler's Generals: Transcripts of Secret Conversations, 1942–1945* (Frontline, London, 2007), p.196
14 Moskalenko, *Na Yugo-Zapadnom Napravlenii*, Vol. II, p.161–62
15 Ibid., p.163
16 Ibid., p.164–65
17 *Kraznaya Zvezda*, 24 July 1942
18 Transcript of interview with I. Degen, available at https://iremember.ru/memoirs/tankisti/degen-ion-lazarevich/
19 Moskalenko, *Na Yugo-Zapadnom Napravlenii*, Vol. II, p.166
20 *Bundesarchiv-Militärarchiv* Freiburg, *Kriegstagebuch Panzer-AOK3 3 Nov 1943*, RH20-4
21 Transcript of interview with A. Fadin (hereafter Fadin interview), available at https://iremember.ru/memoirs/tankisti/fadin-alexander-mikhailovich

22   Ibid.

23   Ibid.

24   Moskalenko, *Na Yugo-Zapadnom Napravlenii*, Vol. II, p.172; Melnikov, *Marshal Rybalko*, p.158–59

25   Fadin interview

26   Melnikov, *Marshal Rybalko*, p.160

27   H. von Manteuffel, *Die 7. Panzer-Division im Zweiten Weltkrieg* (Traditionsverband Ehemaliger 7. Panzer-Division-Kameradenhilfe, Krefeld, 1965), p.368

28   Moskalenko, *Na Yugo-Zapadnom Napravlenii*, Vol. II, p.179–80

29   Manstein, *Lost Victories*, p.486–87

30   H. Guderian, *Panzer Leader* (Joseph, London, 1952), p.315–16

31   W. Fey, *Panzer im Brennpunkt der Fronten* (Moewig, Munich, 1961), p.38 39

32   R. Forczyk, *Tank Warfare on the Eastern Front 1943–1945: Red Steamroller* (Pen & Sword, Barnsley, 2016), p.170

33   H. Balck, *Ordnung im Chaos* (Biblio, Osnabrück, 1981), p.355

34   R. Hinze, *To the Bitter End: The Final Battles of Army Groups North Ukraine, A, and Centre, Eastern Front 1944–1945* (Casemate, Philadelphia, PA, 2010), p.146

35   Moskalenko, *Na Yugo-Zapadnom Napravlenii*, Vol. II, p.187

36   Bundesarchiv-Militärarchiv Freiburg N507 Handakten Generalfeldmarschall von Mansteins, 18.10.43, p.23

37   E. Ziemke and B. Carruthers, *Stalingrad to Berlin* (Pen & Sword, Barnsley, 2014), p.212

38   Burleigh, *Ethics and Extermination*, p.69

39   V. Hebert, *Hitler's Generals on Trial: The Last War Crimes Tribunals at Nuremberg* (University Press of Kansas, Lawrence, KS, 2010), p.121–22

40   R. Stoves, *Die 1. Panzer-Division* (Podzun, Bad Neuheim, 1961), p.435

41   Lehmann, *Die Leibstandarte*, Vol. III, p.360–61

42   Manteuffel, *Die 7. Panzer-Division*, p.371–72

43   Haupt, *Die 8. Panzer-Division*, p.322

44   Ibid., p.323

45   Balck, *Ordnung im Chaos*, p.361

46   Stoves, *Die 1. Panzer-Division*, p.438

47   Mellenthin, *Panzer Battles*, p.230

48   Balck, *Ordnung im Chaos*, p.363

49   Mellenthin, *Panzer Battles*, p.230–31

50   Moskalenko, *Na Yugo-Zapadnom Napravlenii*, Vol. II, p.202–03

51   Raus, *Panzer Operations*, p.258

52   Lehmann, *Die Leibstandarte*, Vol. III, p.389

53   Ibid., p.403–04; Mellenthin, *Panzer Battles*, p.235; Balck, *Ordnung im Chaos*, p.372

54   Balck, *Ordnung im Chaos*, p.365

CHAPTER 10

1   G. Bidermann, *In Deadly Combat: A German Soldier's Memoir of the Eastern Front* (University Press of Kansas, Lawrence, KS, 2000), p.239

2   Senger und Etterlin, *Die 24. Panzer-Division*, p.170–71

3   Quoted in Bidermann, *In Deadly Combat*, p.177

4   Ibid., p.181–82

5   Kobylyanskiy, *From Stalingrad to Pillau*, p.109–10

6   Ibid., p.111

7   A. Beevor, *Berlin: The Downfall 1945* (Viking, London, 2002), p.228

8   Manstein, *Lost Victories*, p.489

9   Katukov, *Na Ostrya Glavnogo Udara*, p.270

10 Moskalenko, *Na Yugo-Zapadnom Napravlenii*, Vol. II, p.213

11 Ibid., p.220

12 O. von Knobelsdorff, *Geschichte der Niedersächsischen 19. Panzer-Division: Bis 31.10.1940 19. Infanterie-Division* (Podzun-Pallas, Friedberg, 1985), p.208–09

13 Moskalenko, *Na Yugo-Zapadnom Napravlenii*, Vol. II, p.226; Katukov, *Na Ostrya Glavnogo Udara*, p.274

14 Katukov, *Na Ostrya Glavnogo Udara*, p.275

15 Ibid., p.276

16 Mellenthin, *Panzer Battles*, p.238

17 Weidinger, *Division Das Reich*, Vol. IV, p.414

18 Lehmann, *Die Leibstandarte*, Vol. III, p.409–10

19 Ibid., p.411–12

20 Katukov, *Na Ostrya Glavnogo Udara*, p.279–81

CHAPTER 11

1   J. Keegan, *The Second World War* (Pimlico, London, 1997), p.467

2   N. Zetterling, 'Loss Rates on the Eastern Front during World War II' in *Journal of Slavic Military Studies* (Cass, London, 1996), Vol. IX, p.895–906

3   W. Dunn, *Kursk: Hitler's Gamble, 1943* (Praeger, Westport, CT, 1997), p.92–93

4   H. A. Jackobsen, *1939–1945, Der Zweite Weltkrieg in Chronik und Dokumenten* (Wehr und Wissen, Darmstadt, 1959), p.568

5   Glantz, *From the Don to the Dnepr*, p.394

6   See Citino, *Wehrmacht Retreats*, p.302ff

7   Balck, *Ordnung im Chaos*, p.402

8   For more discussion of *Weitsprung*, see L. Havas, *Hitler's Plot to Kill the Big Three* (Bantam, London, 1977); N. West, *Historical Dictionary of World War II Intelligence* (Scarecrow, Lanham, MD, 2008), p.140–41

9   Shtemenko, *Soviet General Staff*, p.189–93

10 R. Gellately, *Stalin's Curse: Battling for Communism in War and Cold War* (Oxford University Press, Oxford, 2013), p.177–78

11   D. Goldhagen, *Hitler's Willing Executioners: Ordinary Germans and the Holocaust* (Abacus, London, 2008), p.290

12   V. Hrynevych, 'Freedom without Liberation' in *The Ukrainian Week* (Ecem Media, Kiev), 8 February 2013

13   See for example O. Bartov, *Hitler's Army: Soldiers, Nazis, and War in the Third Reich* (Oxford University Press, Oxford, 1992)

14   For a detailed examination of this, see J. Rutherford, 'Life and Death in the Demiansk Pocket: The 123rd Infantry Division in Combat and Occupation' in *Central European History* (Cambridge University Press, Cambridge, 2008), Vol. 41.3, p.347–80

15   Vasilevsky, *Lifelong Cause*, p.307–08

BIBLIOGRAPHY

Bundesarchiv (Berlin)
Bundesarchiv-Militärarchiv (Freiburg)
Gosudarstvennyi Archive Kievskoi Oblasti (Kiev)
Rossiyskiy Gosudarstvennyy Arkhiv Sotsial'no-Politicheskoy Istorii (*RGASPI*, Moscow)
Tsentral'nyi Arkhiv Ministerii Oboroni (Moscow)
United States Library of Congress (Washington DC)

After the Battle (Battle of Britain International, London)
Central European History (Cambridge University Press)
Eurozine (Vienna)
Illustrierte Beobachter (Franz Eher Verlag, Munich)
Journal of Slavic Military Studies (Cass, London)
Kraznaya Zvezda (St Petersburg)
Slavic Review (Cambridge University Press)
The Ukrainian Week (Ecem Media, Kiev)
Voenno-Istoricheskii Zhurnal (Voennoe izd-vo Ministerstva Oborony Soyuza SSR, Moscow)

Abdullin, M., *Stranits iz Soldatskogo Dnevnika* (Molodaya Gvardiya, Moscow, 1985)
Adam, W., Rühle, O., and Le Tissier, T. (trans.), *With Paulus at Stalingrad* (Pen & Sword, Barnsley, 2015)
Art of War Symposium, *From the Dnepr to the Vistula* (US Army War College, Carlisle, PA, 1985)
Babikov, I., and Samchuk, I., *Kotel Pod Tomarovkoi* (Voenizdat, Moscow, 1967)
Bartoleit, R., *Die Deutsche Agrarpolitik in den Besetten Gebieten der Ukraine vom Sommer 1941 bis zum Sommer 1942 unter Besonderer Berücksichtigung der Einführung der 'Neuen Agrarordnung'* (Magisterarbeit, Hamburg, 1987)
Bartov, O., *Hitler's Army: Soldiers, Nazis, and War in the Third Reich* (Oxford University Press, Oxford, 1992)

Beevor, A., *Berlin: The Downfall 1945* (Viking, London, 2002)

Bidermann, G., *In Deadly Combat: A German Soldier's Memoir of the Eastern Front* (University Press of Kansas, Lawrence, KS, 2000)

Binder, E., *Employment of a Russian Parachute Brigade in a Bend of the Dnepr Northwest of Kanev* in *Russian Airborne Operations* (Historical Division, US Army Europe, 1953)

Biryuzov, S., *Kogda Gremeli Pushki* (Voyenizdat, Moscow, 1961)

Burleigh, M., *Ethics and Extermination* (Cambridge University Press, Cambridge,1997)

Buttar, P., *Between Giants: The Battle for the Baltics in World War II* (Osprey, Oxford, 2013)

Buttar, P., *Russia's Last Gasp: The Eastern Front 1916–17* (Osprey, Oxford, 2016)

Carrell, P., *Scorched Earth: The Russo-German War 1943–1944* (Little Brown, Boston, MA, 1970)

Charmatz, R., *Minister Freiherr von Bruck: Der Vorkämpfer Mitteleuropas* (Hirzel, Leipzig, 1916)

Chistiakov, I., *Sluzhim Otchizne* (Voenizdat, Moscow, 1985)

Chuikov, V., *Ot Stalingrada do Berlina* (Sovetskaya Rossiya, Moscow, 1985)

Citino, R., *The Wehrmacht Retreats: Fighting a Lost War* (University Press of Kansas, Lawrence, KS, 2016)

Clark, L., *Kursk: The Greatest Battle: Eastern Front 1943* (Headline, London, 2012)

Costello, J., and Hughes, T., *The Battle of the Atlantic* (Collins, London, 1977)

Dallin, A., *German Rule in Russia 1941–1945* (Macmillan, London, 1957)

Dietrich, O., *12 Jahre mit Hitler* (Isar, Munich, 1955)

Doukumenty Obviniayut: Sbornik Dokumentov o Cudovisnyh Zverstvah Germanskii Vlastei na Vremenno Zakhvachennykh imi Sovetskoi Territoriakh (Gos. Izd-vo Polit. Lit-ry, Moscow, 1945), two volumes

Dudarenko, Y., Perechnev, G., and Yeliseye, V., *Osvobozhdeniye gorodov: Spravochnik po osvobozhdeniyu gorodov v period Velikoy Otechestvennoy voyny 1941–1945* (Voenizdat, Moscow, 1985)

Dunn, W., *Kursk: Hitler's Gamble, 1943* (Praeger, Westport, CT, 1997)

Engelmann, J., *Zitadelle: Die Grösste Panzerschlacht Im Osten 1943* (Podzun, Friedberg, 1981)

Erickson, J., *The Road to Berlin: Stalin's War with Germany Vol. II* (Cassell, London, 2003), two volumes

Evans, R., *The Third Reich at War* (Penguin, Harmondsworth, 2008)

Fey, W., *Panzer im Brennpunkt der Fronten* (Moewig, Munich, 1961)

Forczyk, R., *Tank Warfare on the Eastern Front 1943–1945: Red Steamroller* (Pen & Sword, Barnsley, 2016)

Frieser, K., Schmider, K., Schönherr, K., Schreiber, G., Ungváry, K., and Wegner, B., *Die Ostfront 1943/44 – Der Krieg im Osten und an den Nebenfronten* (Deutsche Verlags-Anstalt, Munich, 2007)

Gellately, R., *Stalin's Curse: Battling for Communism in War and Cold War* (Oxford University Press, Oxford, 2013)

Gersdorff, R. von, *Soldat im Untergang* (Ullstein, Frankfurt, 1979)

Getman, A., *Tanki Idut na Berlin* (Nauka, Moscow, 1973)

Gilbert, M., *The Holocaust: The Jewish Tragedy* (Fontana, London, 1987)

Glantz, D., *From the Don to the Dnepr: Soviet Offensive Operations December 1942–August 1943* (Cass, London, 1991)

Glantz, D., *Stumbling Colossus: The Red Army on the Eve of War* (University Press of Kansas, Lawrence, KS, 1998)

Glantz, D., and House, J., *When Titans Clashed: How the Red Army Stopped Hitler* (University Press of Kansas, Lawrence, KS, 1995)

Glantz, D., and House, J., *The Battle of Kursk* (University Press of Kansas, Lawrence, KS, 2004)

Glantz, D., and Orenstein, H., *The Battle for Kursk 1943: The Soviet General Staff Study* (Routledge, London, 1999)

Gogun, A, *Stalin's Commandos: Ukrainian Partisan Forces on the Eastern Front* (Tauris, London, 2015)

Goldhagen, D., *Hitler's Willing Executioners: Ordinary Germans and the Holocaust* (Abacus, London, 2008)

Gorodetsky, G., *Grand Delusion: Stalin and the German Invasion of Russia* (Yale University Press, New Haven, CT, 2001)

Grams, R., *Die 14. Panzer-Division* (Podzun, Bad Neuheim, 1957)

Grossman, V., Beevor, A. (trans.), and Vinogradova, L. (trans.), *A Writer At War: Vasily Grossman with the Red Army 1941–1945* (Pimlico, London, 2006)

Guderian, H., *Panzer Leader* (Joseph, London, 1952)

Hassell, A. von, MacRae, S., and Ameskamp, S., *Alliance of Enemies: The Untold Story of the Secret American and German Collaboration to end World War II* (Thomas Dunne, New York, 2006)

Haupt, W., *Die 8. Panzer-Division im Zweiten Weltkrieg* (Podzun-Pallas, Friedburg, 1987)

Havas, L., *Hitler's Plot to Kill the Big Three* (Bantam, London, 1977)

Healy, M., *Zitadelle: The German Offensive Against the Kursk Salient 4–17 July* (History Press, Stroud, 2010)

Hebert, V., *Hitler's Generals on Trial: The Last War Crimes Tribunals at Nuremberg* (University Press of Kansas, Lawrence, KS, 2010)

Hérbert, U., *Hitler's Foreign Workers: Enforced Foreign Labor in Germany Under the Third Reich* (Cambridge University Press, Cambridge, 1997)

Hinze, R., *Die 19. Infanterie- und Panzer-Division* (self-published, Düsseldorf, 1988)

Hinze, R., *To the Bitter End: The Final Battles of Army Groups North Ukraine, A, and Centre, Eastern Front 1944–1945* (Casemate, Philadelphia, 2010)

Irving, D., *Hitler's War* (Focal Point, London, 1991)

Isayenko, N., *Vizyu Protivnika!* (Politizdat, Kiev, 1981)

Jackobsen, H.-A., *1939–1945, Der Zweite Weltkrieg in Chronik und Dokumenten* (Wehr und Wissen, Darmstadt, 1959)

Jentz, T., *Germany's Panther Tank* (Schiffer, Altglen, PA, 1995)

Katukov, M., *Na Ostrya Glavnogo Udara* (Voenizdat, Moscow, 1974)

Kay, A., *Exploitation, Resettlement, Mass Murder: Political and Economic Planning for German Occupation Policy in the Soviet Union 1940–41* (Berghahn, New York, 2006)

Kazakov, K., *Vsegda s Pekhotoi Vsegda s Tankami* (Voenizdat, Moscow, 1969)

Keegan, J., *The Second World War* (Pimlico, London, 1997)

Kershaw, I., *Hitler 1936–1945: Nemesis* (Penguin, Harmondsworth, 2001)

Klapdor, E., *Viking Panzers: The German 5th SS Tank Regiment in the East in World War II* (Stackpole, Mechanicsburg, PA, 2011)

Knobelsdorff, O. von, *Geschichte der Niedersäachsischen 19. Panzer-Division: Bis 31.10.1940 19. Infanterie-Division* (Podzun-Pallas, Friedberg, 1985)

Kobylyanskiy, I., *From Stalingrad to Pillau: A Red Army Artillery Officer Remembers the Great Patriotic War* (University Press of Kansas, Lawrence, KS, 2008)

Kolomiyets, M., *Trofenyye Tanki Krasnoye Armii* (Eksmo, Moscow, 2010)

Koltunov, G., and Soloviev, B., *Kurskaya Bitva* (Voenizdat, Moscow, 1970)

Konev, I., *Zapiski Komanduyushchego Frontom* (Nauka, Moscow, 1972)

Krull, A., *Das Hannoversche Regiment 73. Geschichte des Panzer-Grenadier-Regiments 73 (vormals Infanterie Regiment 73). 1939–1945* (Regimentskameradschaft 73, Hannover, 1967)

Krylova, A., *Soviet Women in Combat: A History of Violence on the Eastern Front* (Cambridge University Press, Cambridge, 2010)

Lehmann, R., *Die Leibstandarte* (Munin, Osnabrück, 1982), nine volumes

Lelyushenko, D., *Moskva – Stalingrad – Berlin – Praga* (Nauka, Moscow, 1987)

Libardi, M., and Orlandi, F., *Mitteleuropa: Mito, Letteratura, Filosofia* (Sylvi Edizioni, Turin, 2011)

Lisov, I., *Desantniki* (Voenizdat, Moscow, 1968)

Lower, W., *Nazi Empire-Building and the Holocaust in Ukraine* (University of North Carolina Press, Chapel Hill, NC, 2005)

Lubs, G., *IR 5: Aus der Geschichte eines Pommerschen Regiments 1920–1945* (self-published, Bochum, 1955)

Maizière, U. de, *In der Pflicht: Lebensbericht eines Deutsches Soldaten im 20. Jahrhundert* (Mittler, Hamburg, 1997)

Manstein, E. von, and Powell, A. (trans.), *Lost Victories: The War Memoirs of Hitler's Most Brilliant General* (Presidio, Novato, CA, 1994)

Manteuffel, H. von, *Die 7. Panzer-Division im Zweiten Weltkrieg* (Traditionsverband Ehemaliger 7. Panzer-Division-Kameradenhilfe, Krefeld, 1965)

Marrus, M. (ed.), *The Final Solution: The Implementation of Mass Murder* (Meckler, Westport, CT, 1989)

Meindl, R., *Ostpreussens Gauleiter: Erich Koch – eine Politische Biographie* (Fibre, Osnabrück, 2007)

Mellenthin, F. von, *Panzer Battles* (University of Oklahoma Press, Danvers, MA, 1956)

Melnikov, S., *Marshal Rybalko: Vospominaniia Byvshego Chlena Voennogo Soveta 3-I Gvardeiskoi Tankovoi Armii* (Politizdat Ukrainy, Kiev, 1980)

Melvin, M., *Manstein: Hitler's Greatest General* (Orion, London, 2011)

Memminger, F., *Die Kriegsgeschichte der Windhund-Division: 16. Infanterie-Division (mot.) 1.7.40-1.10.41; 16. Panzer-Grenadier-Division 2.10.41-30.3.44; 116. Panzer-Division 30.3.44-18.3.45* (Pöppinghaus, Bochum, 1962), three volumes

Milanetti, G., *Gli Angeli Sterminatori: L'incredibile Storia delle Cecchine Sovietiche nell Seconda Guerra Mondiale* (IBN, Rome, 2017)

Militärgeschichtliches Forschungsamt, *Das Deutsche Reich und der Zweite Weltkrieg* (Deutsche Verlags-Anstalt, Stuttgart, 1979–2008), ten volumes

Mitcham, S., *The Rise of the Wehrmacht: The German Armed Forces in World War II* (Praeger Security International, Westport, CT, 2008), two volumes

Moorhouse, R., *Killing Hitler: The Plots, the Assassins, and the Dictator who Cheated Death* (Bantam, New York, 2006)

Moses, D. (ed.), *Empire, Colony, Genocide: Conquest, Occupation and Subaltern Resistance in World History* (Berghahn, New York, 2008)

Moskalenko, K., *Na Yugo-Zapadnom Napravlenii* (Nauka, Moscow, 1973), two volumes

Münsch, K., *Combat History of Schwere Panzerjäger Abteilung 653* (Fedorowicz, Winnipeg, 1997)

Naumann, F., *Mitteleuropa* (Reimer, Berlin, 1915)

Newell, W., *Tyrants: A History of Power, Injustice and Terror* (Cambridge University Press, Cambridge, 2016)

Nietzel, S. (ed.), *Tapping Hitler's Generals: Transcripts of Secret Conversations, 1942–1945* (Frontline, London, 2007)

Olusoga, D., and Erichsen, C., *The Kaiser's Holocaust: Germany's Forgotten Genocide and the Colonial Roots of Nazism* (Faber & Faber, London, 2010)

Paul, W., *Brennpunkte: Die Geschichte der 6. Panzerdivision 1937–1945* (Biblio, Osnaück, 1993)

Pipes, R., *Russia Under the Bolshevik Regime* (Vintage, New York, 1995)

Pivovar, E. (ed.), *Gorod I Voyna Khar'kov v Gody Velikoy Oteuyestvennoy Voyiy* (Aleteya, St Petersburg, 2013)

Raus, E., and Newton, S. (trans.), *Panzer Operations: The Eastern Front Memoir of General Raus, 1941–1945* (Da Capo, Cambridge, MA, 2003)

Röll, H., *Generalleutnant der Reserve Hyacinth Graf Strachwitz von Groß-Zauche und Camminetz: Vom Kavallerieoffizier zum Führer gepanzerter Verbände* (Flechsig, Würzburg, 2011)

Rossino, A., *Hitler Strikes Poland: Blitzkrieg, Ideology and Atrocity* (University Press of Kansas, Lawrence, KS, 2005)

Rotmistrov, P., *Tankovoe Srazhenie Pod Prokhorovkoĭ* (Voenizdat, Moscow, 1960)

Rotmistrov, P., *Stal'naia Gvardiia* (Voenizdat, Moscow, 1984)

Saft, U., *Krieg im Osten* (Militärbuchverlag, Walsrode, 2002)

Sawodny, W., *German Armored Trains in World War II* (Schiffer, Atglen, PA, 1990), two volumes

Scheurig, B. von, *Henning von Tresckow: Eine Biographie* (Ullstein, Frankfurt, 1980)

Schirer, W., *Aufstieg und Fall des Dritten Reiches* (Pawlak, Herrsching, 1977)

Schlaug, G., *Die Deutschen Lastensegler-Verbände* (Motor-Buch Verlag, Stuttgart, 1985)

Schmider, K., *Partisanenkrieg in Jugoslawien 1941–1944* (Mittler, Hamburg, 2002)

Schmidt, A., *Geschichte der 10. Division: 10. Infanterie-Division (Mot.); 10. Panzer-Grenadier-Division* (Fischer, Regensburg, 1984)

Schramm, P. (ed.), *Kriegstagebuch des Oberkommandos der Wehrmacht* (Bernhard & Graefer, Munich, 1982), eight volumes

Schreiber, G., *Deutsche Kriegsverbrechen in Italian: Täter, Opfer, Strafvervolgung* (Beck, Munich, 1996)

Schrodek, G., *Ihr Glaube Galt dem Vaterland: Geschichte des Panzer-Regiments 15 (11. Panzer-Division)* (Schild, Munich, 1976)

Sebag Montefiore, S., *Stalin: The Court of the Red Tsar* (Phoenix, London, 2003)

Senger und Etterlin, F. von, *Die 24. Panzer-Division 1939–1945* (Dörffler, Eggolsheim, 2004)

Service, R., *A History of Modern Russia: From Nicholas II to Vladimir Putin* (Harvard University Press, Cambridge, MA, 2005)

Shtemenko, S., and Daglish, R. (trans.), *The Soviet General Staff at War 1941–1945* (Progress, Moscow, 1970)

Skoroboatov, A., *Harkiv u Casi Nimeckoi Okupacii 1941–1943* (Prapor, Kharkov, 2004)

Sofronov, G., *Vosdushye Desanti vo Vtoroi Mirovoi Voine: Kratkii Voenno-Istoricheskii Ocherk* (Voenizdat, Moscow, 1962)

Sovetskaia Voennaia Entsiklopediia (Voenizdat, Moscow, 1977)

Spaeter, H., *History of the Panzerkorps Grossdeutschland* (Fedorowicz, Winnipeg, 1995), three volumes

Speer, A., *Inside the Third Reich: Memoirs of Alfred Speer* (Macmillan, London, 1970)

Stackelberg, R., *Hitler's Germany: Origins, Interpretations, Legacies* (Taylor & Francis, London, 2002)

Stoves, R., *Die 1. Panzer-Division* (Podzun, Bad Neuheim, 1961)

Sukhorukov, S., *Sovetskie Vozdushnye Dessantnye: Voenno-Istoricheskii Ocherk* (Voenizdat, Moscow, 1986)

Suvorov, V., *The Chief Culprit: Stalin's Grand Design to Start World War II* (Naval Institute Press, Annapolis, MD, 2008)

The Public Papers of F. D. Roosevelt (University of Michigan, Ann Arbor, MI, 2005), thirteen volumes

Thompson, W., *In the Eye of the Storm: Kurt Riezler and the Crises of Modern Germany* (University of Iowa Press, Iowa City, 1980)

Tippelskirch, K. von, *Geschichte des Zweiten Weltkrieges* (Athenäum, Bonn, 1951)

Traditionsverband der Ehemaligen Dritten Panzer-Division, *Armored Bears: The German 3rd Panzer Division in World War II* (Stackpole, Mechanicsburg, PA, 2013)

Vasilevsky, A., and Riordan, J. (trans.), *A Lifelong Cause* (Progress, Moscow, 1981)

Vopersal, W., *Soldaten, Kämpfer, Kameraden: Marsch und Kämpfe der SS-Totenkopfdivision* (Biblio, Osnabrück, 1987), five volumes

Vorontsov, N., Biryukov, A., and Smekalov, A., *Ot Volzhshikh Stepei do Avstriiskikh Alp: Boevoi Put 4-i Gvardeiskoi Armii* (Voenizdat, Moscow, 1971)

Vyatrovych, V., Hrytskiv, R., Derevyanyy, I., Zabilyy, R., Sova, A., and Sodol, P., *Ukrayins'ka Povstans'ka Armiya: Istoriya Neskorenykh* (Chtyvo, Lviv, 2007)

Weidinger, O., *Division Das Reich* (Munin, Osnabrück, 1979), five volumes

Weiss, J., *Lemberg Mosaic* (Alderbrook, New York, 2011)

West, N., *Historical Dictionary of World War II Intelligence* (Scarecrow, Lanham, MD, 2008)

Wray, T., *Standing Fast: German Defensive Doctrine on the Russian Front During the Second World War* (US Army Command and General Staff College, Fort Leavenworth, KS, 1983)

Zaloga, S., *T-34/76 Medium Tank 1941–45* (Osprey, Oxford, 1994)

Zaloga, S., and Ness, L., *Red Army Handbook 1939–45* (Sutton, Stroud, 1998)

Zamulin, V., and Britton, S. (trans.), *Demolishing the Myth. The Tank Battle at Prokhorovka, Kursk, July 1943: An Operational Narrative* (Helion, Solihull, 2011)

Zhadov, A., *Chetyre Goda Voyne* (Voenizdat, Moscow, 1978)

Zhukov, G., *Vospomimaniya I Razmyshleniya* (Olma, Moscow, 2002), two volumes

Ziemke, E., and Carruthers, B., *Stalingrad to Berlin* (Pen & Sword, Barnsley, 2014)

INDEX

Page numbers in **bold** refer to maps.